REDONDO BEACH
CALIFORNIA • 90277

LAW IN PUBLIC HEALTH PRACTICE

LAW IN PUBLIC HEALTH PRACTICE
Second Edition

Richard A. Goodman, Editor-in-Chief

Editors
Richard E. Hoffman
Wilfredo Lopez
Gene W. Matthews
Mark A. Rothstein
Karen L. Foster

OXFORD
UNIVERSITY PRESS

2007

OXFORD
UNIVERSITY PRESS

Oxford University Press, Inc., publishes works that further
Oxford University's objective of excellence
in research, scholarship, and education.

Oxford   New York
Auckland   Cape Town   Dar es Salaam   Hong Kong   Karachi
Kuala Lumpur   Madrid   Melbourne   Mexico City   Nairobi
New Delhi   Shanghai   Taipei   Toronto

With offices in
Argentina   Austria   Brazil   Chile   Czech Republic   France   Greece
Guatemala   Hungary   Italy   Japan   Poland   Portugal   Singapore
South Korea   Switzerland   Thailand   Turkey   Ukraine   Vietnam

Published by Oxford University Press, Inc.
198 Madison Avenue, New York, New York 10016

www.oup.com

Oxford is a registered trademark of Oxford University Press

Library of Congress Cataloging-in-Publication Data
Law in public health practice / edited by Richard A. Goodman . . . [et al.].
—2nd ed.
p. ; cm.
Includes bibliographical references and index.
ISBN-13 978-0-19-530148-9
ISBN 0-19-530148-X
1. Public health laws—United States.   2. Public health
personnel—Legal status, laws, etc.—United States.   3. Public
health—United States.   I. Goodman, Richard A. (Richard Alan), 1949–
KF3775.L384 2006
344.73'04—dc22   2006009743

9 8 7 6 5 4 3 2 1

Printed in the United States of America
on acid-free paper

PREFACE

As the first edition of this book neared completion in fall 2001, the United States suffered terrorist attacks on the World Trade Center and the Pentagon, and was responding to the deliberate release of *Bacillus anthracis* spores through the U.S. postal system. These events raised concerns about our nation's public health infrastructure, including our legal preparedness for public health emergencies at the local, state, and federal levels. Four years later, in fall 2005, as work on this second edition of *Law in Public Health Practice* concluded, the country was coping with the public health implications of an unprecedented outbreak of devastating hurricanes, while intensifying efforts to ensure preparedness for the threat of pandemic avian influenza. Beyond these and other acute public health developments during 2005—and by sheer coincidence—scholars and practitioners alike had been contemplating the evolving field of public health law on the occasion of the centennial anniversary of the Supreme Court's 1905 decision in the landmark case of *Jacobson v. Massachusetts*.

Many chapters in this second edition reflect the nation's continuing experience with public health emergencies and heightened recognition of the paramount role of legal preparedness. In addition to the impact of public health emergencies, however, the years since the first edition have been marked by other major overlapping developments in both public health practice and in the law of public health. We have labored to reflect these changes, too. This edition, therefore, contains four new chapters, complete or near-total revisions of five chapters from the first edition, and numerous key updates and modifications to parts of most of the other chapters.

A new contribution to the book's introductory section presents a perspective on the indispensable roles played by law in great public health achievements of the 20th century, as identified by the Centers for Disease Control and Prevention (CDC). A new chapter on the legal structure of U.S. public health practice extends our efforts in the first edition to provide a comprehensive picture of the foundational roles of law in public health. Other major additions are a new chapter on the role of the judiciary in public health practice and, in parallel with the rapidly growing recognition of the role of law as a tool for preventing chronic diseases, a new chapter covering law in chronic disease prevention.

This second edition of *Law in Public Health Practice* retains the same three-part organizational framework of the first edition, progressing from fundamental principles and foundational concepts in the first section to multidisciplinary core public health functional domains in the second section, to, in the third section, a series of chapters on law in key, selected topical and programmatic areas of public health practice.

To the book's first section have been added, as noted above, the new chapters on the structure of law in public health systems and practice and on the judiciary in public health practice. The new chapter on the structure of law in public health examines the statutory bases of both the federal and state infrastructure of the public health system, including creation of federal agencies that have public health–related responsibilities and powers under the U.S. Constitution. Recognition of the relation between the judiciary and public health, and the need to characterize the varied facets of this relation, are themselves relatively new aspects of the development of the field of public health law and were at the core of a three-year effort by a CDC-supported Collaborating Center on Public Health Law. This new chapter highlights the judiciary's role in ensuring that public health decisions are grounded in law and respectful of individual rights, and the emerging issue of the role of judges and the courts during public health emergencies.

Other major changes in the first section include a radically revised chapter on ethics, law, and public health, which provides an analytic tool for considering ethics as part of public health decision making. In addition to being updated, the chapter on criminal law in public health now covers the evolving concept of forensic epidemiology, which encompasses legal and operational aspects of joint public health and law enforcement investigations of public health events resulting from possible criminal activity. Finally, the chapter on international considerations is substantially updated to address the increased importance of global health issues, the adoption of the new International Health Regulations by the World Health Organization (WHO) in May 2005, the continuing rise of public health threats from terrorism, and the adoption of the WHO Framework Convention on Tobacco Control in 2003.

Within the book's second section, the chapter on legal counsel to public health practitioners expands the overview of boards of health in relation to their rule-making powers and now discusses the relation between institutional review board functions and the legal counsel's office for the health department. Within the chapter on frontline public health, which covers surveillance and field epidemiology, portions of the text addressing emerging developments have been modified to accentuate the law and newer public health surveillance concepts, as well as bioterrorism-related surveillance. The chapter on identifiable health information and the public's health is a total revision of the related chapter in the first edition, with strengthened emphasis on fundamental uses and disclosures of identifiable health data in public health, the legal structures and challenges that underlie public health data uses and disclosures, a core analysis of the public health implications of the Health Insurance Portability and Accountability Act of 1996 Privacy Rule, and distinctions between public health practice and research.

As a result of the myriad developments in law and public health practice after the 2001 terrorism events, as well as the challenges of other interim problems (e.g., the 2003 SARS outbreak and the evolving threat of avian influenza), the second section's chapter on public health emergency law also has been radically revised from its forerunner in the first edition. Major revisions to this chapter include coverage of the role of emergency-management agencies, basic elements of the U.S. emergency-management system, the legal bases for and ramifications of declaring emergencies, the conceptual legal structure of mutual aid agreements, and the role of the military in emergencies. Finally, the chapter on considerations for special populations includes a new case study on the law and health disparities, as explored through issues related to the detection and management of lead poisoning in children.

The book's third section on selected topical areas of law in public health practice has been substantially strengthened with a new chapter on law in the prevention and control of chronic diseases. Two other chapters in this section are near-total revisions of the related chapters in the first edition. These chapters, revised to reflect different conceptual approaches and the relations between law and their respective domains, are the chapters on integrating genetics into public health policy and practice and on injury prevention. Whereas all the other chapters in the third section have been revised, where possible, to include updated citations and other key information, major changes also have been made to parts of the chapters addressing foodborne-disease control, tobacco-use prevention, and reproductive health.

For the second edition of *Law in Public Health Practice*, we sought to preserve and, wherever possible, strengthen the book's emphasis on the essential interdisciplinary nature of the field of public health law. In addition to the authors who contributed to the first edition, we are indebted to the authors—including 61 lawyers, physicians, and other public health practice professionals—who generously contributed their time to this edition. We also thank Carrie Pedersen of Oxford University Press for her critically important input to the contents of the second edition; Deborah Holtzman, Ph.D., of CDC, for her review of many of the chapters; and David Benor, J.D., of the U.S. Department of Health and Human Services, for his careful review of and suggestions regarding many of the book's chapters. We hope this book provides readers in all settings—including public health departments, other public-sector organizations, and academic public health and law—with a clearer understanding of the indispensable role of law in public health practice in the United States.

Atlanta, Georgia   R.A.G.
Denver, Colorado   R.E.H.
New York, New York   W.L.
Chapel Hill, North Carolina   G.W.M.
Louisville, Kentucky   M.A.R.
Decatur, Georgia   K.L.F.

PREFACE TO THE FIRST EDITION

> While the modern health officer must be an educator and a statesman, rather than merely a police officer, many of his duties are still necessarily concerned with law enforcement. . . . Health officers must be familiar not only with the extent of their powers and duties, but also with the limitations imposed upon them by law. With such knowledge available and widely applied by health authorities, public health will not remain static, but will progress.
>
> James A. Tobey (*Public Health Law*, New York:
> The Commonwealth Fund, 1947)

In his classic text on public health law in 1947, James Tobey offered the above perspective on the relevance of law to public health practice. Tobey's notion of more than 50 years ago may be even more pertinent now as public health enters the twenty-first century. Even before the events of September 11, 2001, forced an intensified review of legal authorities for ensuring public health preparedness for emergencies, health departments and public health practitioners had begun increasing their efforts to use law more effectively as a tool for improving the public's health. Examples of such efforts include litigation and other approaches to curbing the effects of the epidemic of tobacco use; the role of environmental law to address myriad environmental hazards; and the complementary roles of science, regulatory authorities, and laws in improving food safety and preventing food-borne infectious diseases, as well as addressing newly emergent infectious disease threats such as the West Nile virus.

The legal basis of public health practice in the United States substantially antedates key public health developments during the last century and even the landmark

1905 U.S. Supreme Court case of *Jacobson v. Massachusetts*. For example, one of the amazing ironies in U.S. public health history is the past and continuing influence of smallpox on law in relation to public health. As public health scholar Dr. Donald Hopkins made clear in *Princes & Peasants*, his treatise on smallpox in history, the legal and epidemiologic strategy of local quarantine to prevent the spread of smallpox was employed on Long Island as early as 1662. In 1731, the Massachusetts Bay Colony passed "An Act to Prevent Persons from Concealing the Small Pox." Moreover, smallpox was at the root of the *Jacobson* case itself—a decision in which the Supreme Court upheld Massachusetts' statutory requirement for smallpox vaccination as a valid application of the state's police power. Now, more than two decades after the eradication of smallpox from natural circulation on the planet, we are confronted with the need to examine legal authorities necessary for countering the potential deliberate use of smallpox and other infectious disease pathogens as weapons of mass destruction.

But infectious diseases are not the sole focus of law in public health practice. The law also has evolved in response to and frames virtually every other problem on the continuum of public health. For example, the law has provided mandates and served as a pivotal public health tool for addressing myriad environmental problems, including lead contamination in paint and the resulting hazards for children; the use of lead as a gasoline additive and its consequent potentiation of air pollution; and the invidious scourge of toxic waste sites. The increasing importance of law as a tool for addressing other noninfectious concerns—such as lung disease, certain cancers, and cardiovascular conditions—is suggested by the roles law and litigation have played in combating the impact of tobacco use on U.S. and global public health.

During workshops on public health law sponsored by the Centers for Disease Control and Prevention (CDC) in 1999 and 2000, major public health stakeholders—groups including health officers, epidemiologists, public health lawyers, educators, and legislators—recognized the need to strengthen the legal foundation for public health practice. The set of tools available to public health practitioners has grown steadily during the past decade and now reflects an expanding array of disciplines, including economics and prevention effectiveness, health communications, and informatics. Public health stakeholders recognized that the field can benefit from adding legal skills, knowledge, and resources to practitioners' tool kits.

Responding to the call of public health stakeholders and others, this book aims to emphasize the law in relation to the practice of public health at local, state, and federal levels. The book is intended especially for practitioners and students of public health practice. Public health practitioners are those whose work is directed toward improvement of the public's health. Among their ranks are public health nurses, sanitarians, health educators, industrial hygienists, epidemiologists, physicians, veterinarians, dentists, administrators, managers, and lawyers.

This book has twin aims. First, because law is a primary determinant for public health and public health practice in the United States, we have tried to identify, define, and clarify the complex principles of law as they bear on the practice of public health. Second, by enhancing the understanding of the legal principles underlying U.S. public health practice, we hope to show how the law may be applied with greater effectiveness and prudence as a tool to improve the public's health.

A word about the development of this book. For obvious reasons multiple authorship poses challenges to the task of organizing and completing any volume, but the nature of our aims demanded a multiauthored approach. Perhaps because of the challenges it posed, the book does not have a true precedent in the field of public health. We have attempted to produce an interdisciplinary volume that bridges two disparate worlds: the realm of law and lawyers, and the realm of public health practice and technicians. The co-editors themselves are a reflection of these different perspectives and disciplines. Two are physicians whose professional experiences have encompassed work at the state and federal levels and involvement with local health departments, community organizations, the legislature, and public health and medical academia. Three are lawyers whose experiences run the gamut from providing legal counsel to health agencies at the federal and municipal levels, to applied legal and policy research, training of students of health and public health practice, and interacting with legislators and public health policy makers. And Karen Foster, the managing editor, has over two decades' experience in editing and producing public health publications, including the CDC's *Morbidity and Mortality Weekly Report.*

This book is divided into three sections that progress from fundamental principles to specific areas of public health practice. The first section provides a foundation in the basic principles and concepts underlying the relation between law and public health practice. It covers such topics as constitutional and statutory bases for public health practice, administrative and regulatory law, and criminal law—as well as the overarching areas of bioethics and international law. The second section covers the law in relation to core functions of public health practice that are multidisciplinary. It deals with the interaction between practitioners and legal counsel, law underlying public health surveillance, outbreak investigations, public health research, confidentiality and privacy, managed care in public health, interventions in emergency response, and special populations. The third section offers a detailed examination of the law in nine prominent areas of public health: genetics, vaccinations, food-borne diseases, blood-borne and sexually transmitted infections, tobacco use, reproductive health, environmental hazards, injuries, and the workplace. To ensure a consistent approach to the law in relation to each of these practice areas, each chapter in this section has a uniform format that includes background to the subject, key legal authorities, legal issues and controversies, practice considerations, and emerging issues.

The contributing authors represent the ranks of the legal and public health practitioners for whom this book is intended and the editors want to thank them sincerely for their efforts. They worked under a tight time line, which, for many, was complicated by the events of September 2001. People within the CDC who have been key in their support of this project include Martha Katz, Kathy Cahill, Bill Gimson, Howard Green, Dr. Ed Baker, Debbie Jones, Patti Seikus, and Dr. Tony Moulton. Drs. Michelle Leverett and Tony Moulton also reviewed material at the editors' request. We appreciate the extremely useful suggestions of Dr. Barry Levy, which helped give early shape to the book. Finally, we are especially grateful to Jeff House of Oxford University Press for his sustained encouragement, ideas, and numerous constructive suggestions at all stages of the book's development.

Atlanta, Georgia   R.A.G.
Louisville, Kentucky   M.A.R.
Denver, Colorado   R.E.H.
New York, New York   W.L.
Atlanta, Georgia   G.W.M.
Atlanta, Georgia   K.L.F.

CONTENTS

Contributors   xvii

Legal Glossary for Public Health Practitioners   xxiii

Introduction: The Interdependency of Law and Public Health   xxvii
Wendy E. Parmet

Perspective: Law and Great Public Health Achievements   3
Anthony D. Moulton, Richard A. Goodman, and Wendy E. Parmet

Section I. Legal Basis for Public Health Practice

1. The Law and the Public's Health: The Foundations   25
Lawrence O. Gostin, F. Ed Thompson, and Frank P. Grad

2. The Structure of Law in Public Health Systems and Practice   45
*Richard A. Goodman, Paula L. Kocher, Daniel J. O'Brien,
and Frank S. Alexander*

3. Regulating Public Health: Principles and Application
of Administrative Law   69
Peter D. Jacobson, Richard E. Hoffman, and Wilfredo Lopez

4. Public Health and the Judiciary   89
Daniel D. Stier and Diane M. Nicks

5. Ethics and the Practice of Public Health   110
Ruth Gaare Bernheim, Phillip Nieburg, and Richard J. Bonnie

6. Criminal Law and Public Health Practice   136
Zita Lazzarini, Richard A. Goodman, and Kim S. Dammers

7. International Considerations   168
David P. Fidler and Martin S. Cetron

Section II. The Law and Core Public Health Applications

8. Legal Counsel to Public Health Practitioners   199
Wilfredo Lopez and Thomas R. Frieden

9. Frontline Public Health: Surveillance and Field Epidemiology   222
Verla S. Neslund, Richard A. Goodman, and James L. Hadler

10. Identifiable Health Information and the Public's Health:
Practice, Research, and Policy   238
*James G. Hodge, Jr., Richard E. Hoffman, Deborah W. Tress,
and Verla S. Neslund*

11. Legal Authorities for Interventions in Public Health Emergencies   262
*Gene W. Matthews, Ernest B. Abbott, Richard E. Hoffman,
and Martin S. Cetron*

12. Considerations for Special Populations   284
*T. Howard Stone, Heather H. Horton, Robert M. Pestronk,
and Montrece M. Ransom*

Section III. The Law in Controlling and Preventing Diseases,
Injuries, and Disabilities

13. Integrating Genetics into Public Health Policy and Practice   323
Ellen Wright Clayton and Mark A. Rothstein

14. Vaccination Mandates: The Public Health Imperative
and Individual Rights   338
Kevin M. Malone and Alan R. Hinman

15. Control of Foodborne Diseases   361
Leslie Kux, Jeremy Sobel, and Kevin M. Fain

16. Bloodborne and Sexually Transmitted Infections   385
Edward P. Richards III and Guthrie S. Birkhead

17. Prevention and Control of Chronic Disease   402
Angela K. McGowan, Ross C. Brownson, Lynne S. Wilcox, and George A. Mensah

18. Prevention and Control of Diseases Associated with Tobacco Use through
Law and Policy   427
*Richard A. Daynard, Mark A. Gottlieb, Edward L. Sweda, Jr., Lissy C. Friedman,
and Michael P. Eriksen*

19. Reproductive Health   452
Bebe J. Anderson, Maurizio Macaluso, and Lynne S. Wilcox

20. Environmental Health and Protection   478
Paul A. Locke, Henry Falk, Christopher S. Kochtitzky, and Christine P. Bump

21. Injury Prevention   506
Daniel D. Stier, James A. Mercy, and Melvin Kohn

22. Occupational Safety and Health Law   528
Gary Rischitelli and Michael A. Silverstein

Index   551

CONTRIBUTORS

Ernest B. Abbott, J.D., M.P.P.
FEMA Law Associates, PLLC
Washington, D.C.

Frank S. Alexander, J.D., M.T.S.
Interim Dean and Professor of Law
Emory University School of Law
Atlanta, Georgia

Bebe J. Anderson, J.D.
Staff Attorney
Domestic Legal Program
Center for Reproductive Rights
New York, New York

Ruth Gaare Bernheim, J.D., M.P.H.
Associate Professor and Director
Division of Public Health Policy
    and Practice
Department of Public Health Sciences
Associate Director
Institute for Practical Ethics and Public
    Life

University of Virginia School of
    Medicine
Charlottesville, Virginia

Guthrie S. (Gus) Birkhead, M.D.,
    M.P.H.
Director
AIDS Institute
Director
Center for Community Health
New York State Department
    of Health
Albany, New York

Richard J. Bonnie, LL.B.
John S. Battle Professor of Law
Professor of Psychiatric Medicine
Director
Institute of Law, Psychiatry, and Public
    Policy
University of Virginia
Charlottesville, Virginia

Ross C. Brownson, Ph.D.
Professor of Epidemiology
Director
Prevention Research Center
Saint Louis University School of Public
   Health
St. Louis, Missouri

Christine P. Bump, J.D., M.P.H.
Associate Attorney
Hyman, Phelps & McNamara, P.C.
Washington, D.C.

Martin S. Cetron, M.D.
Director
Division of Global Migration and
   Quarantine
National Center for Preparedness,
   Detection, and Control of Infectious
   Diseases
Centers for Disease Control and
   Prevention
Atlanta, Georgia

Ellen Wright Clayton, M.D., J.D.
Rosalind E. Franklin Professor of
   Genetics and Health Policy
Professor of Pediatrics
Professor of Law
Co-Director
Center for Biomedical Ethics and Society
Vanderbilt University
Nashville, Tennessee

Kim S. Dammers, J.D.
Assistant U.S. Attorney
U.S. Attorney's Office
Northern District of Georgia
Atlanta, Georgia

Richard A. Daynard, J.D., Ph.D.
Professor of Law
Northeastern University School
   of Law
President

Tobacco Control Resource Center
Boston, Massachusetts

Michael P. Eriksen, Sc.D.
Professor and Director
Institute of Public Health
Georgia State University
Atlanta, Georgia

Kevin M. Fain, J.D.
Associate Chief Counsel
Office of the Chief Counsel
Food and Drug Administration
U.S. Department of Health and Human
   Services
Rockville, Maryland

Henry Falk, M.D., M.P.H.
Director
Coordinating Center for Environmental
   Health and Injury Prevention
Centers for Disease Control and
   Prevention
Atlanta, Georgia

David P. Fidler, J.D.
Professor of Law
School of Law
Indiana University
Bloomington, Indiana

Karen L. Foster, M.A.
Public Health Editor
Decatur, Georgia

Thomas R. Frieden, M.D., M.P.H.
Commissioner
New York City Department of Health
   and Mental Hygiene
New York, New York

Lissy C. Friedman, J.D.
Senior Staff Attorney
Tobacco Control Resource Center
Boston, Massachusetts

Richard A. Goodman, M.D., J.D.,
M.P.H.
Co-Director
Public Health Law Program
Centers for Disease Control and
Prevention
Atlanta, Georgia

Lawrence O. Gostin, J.D., LL.D.
(Hon.)
Associate Dean and Professor
of Law
Georgetown University
Professor of Public Health
Johns Hopkins University
Director
Center for Law and the Public's
Health
Washington, D.C.

Mark A. Gottlieb, J.D.
Executive Director
Tobacco Control Resource Center
Boston, Massachusetts

Frank P. Grad, LL.B.
Joseph P. Chamberlain Professor
Emeritus of Legislation
Columbia Law School
New York, New York

James L. Hadler, M.D., M.P.H.
State Epidemiologist and Director
Infectious Diseases Division
Connecticut Department of Public
Health
Hartford, Connecticut

Alan R. Hinman, M.D., M.P.H.
Senior Public Health Scientist
Public Health Informatics Institute
Task Force for Child Survival and
Development
Decatur, Georgia

James G. Hodge, Jr., J.D., LL.M.
Executive Director
Center for Law and the Public's
Health
Associate Professor
Bloomberg School of Public Health
Johns Hopkins University
Baltimore, Maryland

Richard E. Hoffman, M.D., M.P.H.
Adjunct Associate Professor
Department of Preventive Medicine
and Biometrics
University of Colorado Health Sciences
Center
Denver, Colorado

Heather H. Horton, J.D., M.H.A.
Senior Attorney
Office of the General Counsel
Centers for Disease Control and
Prevention
U.S. Department of Health and Human
Services
Atlanta, Georgia

Peter D. Jacobson, J.D., M.P.H.
Professor of Health Law and Policy
Director
Center for Law, Ethics, and Health
University of Michigan School of
Public Health
Ann Arbor, Michigan

Paula L. Kocher, J.D.
Deputy Associate General Counsel
Office of the General Counsel
Centers for Disease Control and
Prevention
U.S. Department of Health and Human
Services
Atlanta, Georgia

Christopher S. Kochtitzky, M.S.P.
Deputy Director

Division of Human Development and
   Disability
National Center on Birth Defects and
   Developmental Disabilities
Centers for Disease Control and
   Prevention
Atlanta, Georgia

Melvin Kohn, M.D., M.P.H.
State Epidemiologist
Office of Disease Prevention and
   Epidemiology
Oregon Department of Human
   Services
Portland, Oregon

Leslie Kux, J.D.
Food and Drug Administration
Rockville, Maryland

Zita Lazzarini, J.D., M.P.H.
Associate Professor of Community
   Medicine
Director
Division of Medical Humanities,
   Health Law, and Ethics
University of Connecticut Health
   Center
Farmington, Connecticut

Paul A. Locke, J.D., Dr.P.H.
Associate Professor
Department of Environmental Health
   Sciences
Bloomberg School of Public Health
Johns Hopkins University
Baltimore, Maryland

Wilfredo Lopez, J.D.
General Counsel for Health
New York City Department of Health
   and Mental Hygiene
New York, New York

Maurizio Macaluso, M.D., Dr.P.H.
Division of Reproductive Health

National Center for Chronic Disease
   Prevention and Health Promotion
Centers for Disease Control and
   Prevention
Atlanta, Georgia

Kevin M. Malone, J.D., M.H.S.A.
Senior Attorney
Office of the General Counsel
Centers for Disease Control and
   Prevention
U.S. Department of Health and Human
   Services
Atlanta, Georgia

Gene W. Matthews, J.D.
Senior Fellow
North Carolina Institute for Public
   Health
UNC School of Public Health
Chapel Hill, North Carolina

Angela K. McGowan, J.D., M.P.H.
Office of Planning, Evaluation, and
   Legislation
Office of the Director
National Center for Chronic Disease
   Prevention and Health Promotion
Centers for Disease Control and
   Prevention
Atlanta, Georgia

George A. Mensah, M.D.
Chief Medical Officer
Associate Director for Medical Affairs
National Center for Chronic Disease
   Prevention and Health Promotion
Centers for Disease Control and
   Prevention
Atlanta, Georgia

James A. Mercy, Ph.D.
Associate Director for Science
Division of Violence Prevention
National Center for Injury Prevention
   and Control

Centers for Disease Control and
    Prevention
Atlanta, Georgia

Anthony D. Moulton, Ph.D.
Co-Director
Public Health Law Program
Centers for Disease Control and
    Prevention
Atlanta, Georgia

Verla S. Neslund, J.D.
Vice President for Programs
CDC Foundation
Office of the Director
Centers for Disease Control and
    Prevention
Atlanta, Georgia

Diane M. Nicks, J.D.
Circuit Court Judge
Dane County Circuit Court
Madison, Wisconsin

Phillip Nieburg, M.D., M.P.H.
Associate Professor
Division of Public Health Policy and
    Practice
Department of Public Health Sciences
School of Medicine
University of Virginia
Charlottesville, Virginia

Daniel J. O'Brien, J.D.
Principal Counsel
Maryland Department of Health and
    Mental Hygiene
Office of the Attorney General
Baltimore, Maryland

Wendy E. Parmet, J.D.
Matthews Distinguished University
    Professor of Law
Northeastern University School
    of Law
Boston, Massachusetts

Robert M. Pestronk, M.P.H.
Health Officer
Genesee County Health Department
Flint, Michigan

Montrece M. Ransom, J.D.
Public Health Law Program
Centers for Disease Control and
    Prevention
Atlanta, Georgia

Edward P. Richards III, J.D., M.P.H.
Harvey A. Peltier Professor
Director
Program in Law, Science, and Public
    Health
Paul M. Hebert Law Center
Louisiana State University
Baton Rouge, Louisiana

Gary Rischitelli, M.D., J.D., M.P.H.
Assistant Scientist
Center for Research on Occupational
    and Environmental Toxicology
Associate Professor
Public Health and Preventive
    Medicine
Oregon Health and Science University
Portland, Oregon

Mark A. Rothstein, J.D.
Herbert F. Boehl Chair of Law and
    Medicine
Director
Institute for Bioethics, Health Policy,
    and Law
University of Louisville School of
    Medicine
Louisville, Kentucky

Michael A. Silverstein, M.D., M.P.H.
Assistant Director for Industrial Safety
    and Health
Washington State Department of Labor
    and Industries
Olympia, Washington

Jeremy Sobel, M.D., M.P.H.
Foodborne and Diarrheal Diseases
   Branch
Division of Bacterial and Mycotic
   Diseases
National Center for Infectious Diseases
Centers for Disease Control and
   Prevention
Atlanta, Georgia

Daniel D. Stier, J.D.
Public Health Law Program
Centers for Disease Control and
   Prevention
Atlanta, Georgia

T. Howard Stone, J.D., LL.M.
Associate Professor of Bioethics
Department of Bioethics
University of Texas Health Center
Tyler, Texas

Edward L. Sweda, Jr., J.D.
Senior Staff Attorney
Tobacco Control Resource Center
Boston, Massachusetts

F. Ed Thompson, Jr., M.D., M.P.H.
Professor of Medicine

University of Mississippi School of
   Medicine
Jackson, Mississippi
Chief (former)
Office of Public Health Practice
Centers for Disease Control and
   Prevention
Atlanta, Georgia

Deborah W. Tress, J.D.
Principal Senior Attorney
Office of the General Counsel
Centers for Disease Control and
   Prevention
U.S. Department of Health and
   Human Services
Atlanta, Georgia

Lynne S. Wilcox, M.D., M.P.H.
Editor-in-Chief
Preventing Chronic Disease
Office of the Director
National Center for Chronic
   Disease Prevention and Health
   Promotion
Centers for Disease Control and
   Prevention
Atlanta, Georgia

LEGAL GLOSSARY FOR PUBLIC HEALTH PRACTITIONERS

administrative law the body of law created by administrative agencies through rules, regulations, orders, and procedures designed to further legislatively enacted policy goals.

administrative orders (also known as **health hold orders**) orders issued by a health department to a third party to remedy a condition that threatens public health. Depending on state law, the orders can be issued under the health department's police power without specific legislation, under a specific law granting the power to issue general orders, or under specific administrative regulations.

burden of proof the allocation of responsibility to demonstrate that a matter alleged in a court is factually true and to the level of confidence in the allegation required in that particular setting. The level of confidence may be called the "standard of proof" (includes "preponderance of evidence," "clear and convincing evidence," and "beyond a reasonable doubt").

case law court-produced bodies of legal opinions that guide the application of the law.

chain of custody of evidence a legal requirement to ensure the identity and integrity of evidence obtained during an investigation to be admissible in court.

civil commitment a statutorily structured process by which persons with qualifying conditions are legally confined within a designated facility either because they pose a danger to themselves or to protect the safety of others.

Code of Federal Regulations (C.F.R.) official source for federal regulations implementing U.S. congressional statutes.

common law judge-made law that is modified case by case over generations.

contract an agreement between two or more parties creating obligations that are enforceable or otherwise recognizable at law.*

crime an act performed in violation of a specific law passed by the legislature that provides for punishment for violating a duty that an individual owes a community.

customary international law unwritten rules of international law that develop through general and consistent state practice supported by the sense that following the practice is legally required.

defendant a person sued in a civil proceeding or accused in a criminal proceeding.*

dicta discussion in a court decision that addresses an issue outside the direct facts presented by the case and therefore outside the court's holding, and thus is of no precedential value in directing future court decisions.

due process, procedural fundamental protection provided by the Due Process Clause of the U.S. Constitution, or comparable clause in a state constitution, that requires government officials and their agents to follow fair and even-handed procedures when enforcing laws. Basic elements of due process are determined by the nature of the rights and can include notice to the person involved, opportunity for a hearing or similar proceeding, and the right to representation by counsel.

due process, substantive fundamental protection provided by the Due Process Clause of the U.S. Constitution that ensures that a law's overall effect on an individual's fundamental rights, such as the right to procreate and the right to marry, is justified or justifiable.

ex parte communication discussion of the merits of a case between the judge and a party to the case outside the presence of other parties.

federalism the system of government in the United States that is based on the concept of dual sovereignty between the states and the federal government.

felony a crime punishable by high fines and a prison term of 1 year or longer.

habeas corpus a writ employed to bring a person before a court, most frequently to ensure that the party's imprisonment is not illegal.*

home rule a state legislative provision or action allocating a measure of autonomy to a local government, conditional on its acceptance of terms.*

immunity, qualified doctrine that provides that government officials who are performing discretionary functions are immune from civil liability if their actions do not violate clearly established statutory or constitutional rights of which a reasonable person would be aware.

immunity, sovereign a government's immunity from being sued in its own courts without its consent.*

injunction a court order requiring an actor to stop a defined activity that may be prohibited by law or to follow certain prescribed actions to comply with applicable law.

international law the rules that regulate the relationships among sovereign states and other actors, such as international organizations and individuals, in the international system.

---

* Reprinted from *Black's Law Dictionary*, Pocket Edition (BA Garner, Editor-in-Chief), ©1996, with permission of The West Group.

inter alia   among other things.

law   rules that are subject to the enforcement power of a government entity. Law includes the structures, norms, and rules that a society uses to resolve disputes, govern itself, and order relations between members of the society.

litigation   the process of carrying on a lawsuit or the lawsuit itself.*

least restrictive alternative   a view that an intrusion by a regulatory authority into an individual liberty should be limited and reasonable.

memorandum of understanding   an agreement or consensus among parties that does not create an enforceable promise nor specify legal remedies if one party violates the requirements of the agreement.

misdemeanor   a crime punishable by a fine of up to $500, imprisonment for up to 1 year in the county jail, or both.

negligence   the failure to do something that a reasonable person, guided by the considerations that normally regulate human affairs, would do, or the doing of something that a reasonable person would not do.

nuisance, public   an activity that unreasonably interferes with the public's use and enjoyment of a public place or that harms the health, safety, and welfare of the community.

parens patriae   doctrine under which the state asserts authority over a child's welfare.

police power   the residual power held by the states to enact legislation and regulations to protect the public health, welfare, and morals and to promote the common good.

preemption   the legal effect that results when a superior governmental unit blocks an inferior governmental unit from regulating a particular area. The rationale of preemption is to provide national uniformity in certain areas.

prima facie case   the plaintiff's production of enough evidence to allow the fact-trier to infer the fact at issue and rule in the plaintiff's favor.*

prosecutor   public official who represents the government in a criminal case.

stare decisis   a legal doctrine requiring that past judicial decisions generally guide courts in deciding identical, similar, or analogous issues.

strict liability   legal doctrine under which parties are responsible, without proof or fault on their part, for injuries caused by abnormally dangerous activities under their control or products they have manufactured, distributed, or sold.

strict scrutiny   in constitutional law, the standard applied to fundamental rights (such as voting rights) in due process analysis and to suspect classifications (such as race) and classifications based on exercise of a fundamental right in equal protection analysis. Under strict scrutiny, the state must establish that it has a compelling interest that justifies and necessitates the law in question.

subpoena   a court order commanding the appearance of a witness, subject to penalty for noncompliance.*

taking   in constitutional law, the government's actual or effective acquisition of private property either by ousting the owner and claiming title or by destroying the property or severely impairing its utility.*

tort   a civil wrong in which the victim suffers injury to his or her person or damage to his or her property as a result of intentional, negligent, or abnormally dangerous conduct of the injuring party.

treaty   a written agreement between countries, the obligations of which are binding under international law.

United States Code (U.S.C.)   official source for statutory law passed by the U.S. Congress.

warrant requirement   the necessity, based on the Fourth Amendment of the U.S. Constitution, for law enforcement officials to obtain a warrant to search private property.

INTRODUCTION: THE INTERDEPENDENCY OF LAW AND PUBLIC HEALTH

Wendy E. Parmet

Increasingly, public health practitioners in all areas of the profession have recognized law's critical role in public health protection. Whether the public health problem at hand is an emerging infectious agent, such as severe acute respiratory syndrome (SARS); a well-known lethal product, such as tobacco; or a socially complex problem, such as racial disparities, public health professionals have come to appreciate that law must play an important role in any solution. Hence, public health professionals accept the need to have some understanding of the law and an ability to work with legal professionals.

Unfortunately, relatively few lawyers share public health professionals' enthusiasm for interdisciplinary collaboration. Although attitudes have begun to change, most lawyers do not appreciate law's important role in public health protection. Nor are many lawyers aware of the history, perspectives, or skills of public health professionals. Fewer still are aware of the vital role public health has played in the development of their own field.

In fact, law and public health are interdependent fields. They share a history that is far richer and more intimate than many appreciate. More importantly, their futures are interconnected: the success of each field may well depend on its ability to work with the other.

The chapters that follow demonstrate the importance of law to public health, surveying and critiquing the role of law with respect to our most pressing public health concerns. These chapters introduce to members of each profession the key concepts and teachings of the other, as well as the pressing need for interdisciplinary collaboration.

In this brief introduction, I will paint with a broader brush, forsaking an in-depth discussion of any particular public health issue or area of the law for a more general examination of the relation between law and public health. I begin by describing the nature of both fields, pointing out both some of their similarities and some of their sharp differences. I then consider how the two fields have influenced each other and some of the reasons that we should seek further collaboration between the fields. Finally, I discuss some of the steps that have been taken in recent years—especially since the publication of the first edition of this volume—to advance interdisciplinary cooperation, as well as some of the steps that remain if the inevitable interactions between law and public health are to succeed.

Defining Law and Public Health

An understanding of the meanings of the terms "law" and "public health" is useful to any discussion of the relation between them. Both law and public health are complex terms with myriad and contested meanings. Both terms denote a discipline or profession. Yet, each also refers to a complex social phenomenon that exists apart from the activities of the profession that engages with it.

The question of the meaning of the term "law" has fascinated philosophers and students of jurisprudence for millennia. A full discussion is obviously beyond the scope of this introduction. Nevertheless, a few observations are especially pertinent.

Most narrowly, but perhaps most essentially, law can be understood as by the positivists as consisting of the rules or commands enforceable by the positive power of the state.[1] So defined, law includes the statutes, ordinances, regulations, and court rulings that are backed up by the government. This relatively narrow, but important, use of the term "law" occurs commonly in discussions of public health law, for example, when a public health official asks a general counsel whether "the law" permits a public health department to isolate a person suspected of having tuberculosis. When the official asks that question, he or she is asking whether the state gives the department the authority to isolate the person and whether the state will use its power to enforce the department's order. Likewise, when we speak about tobacco-control laws, we are referring to the ordinances, statutes, and regulations that governments use to control the sale or use of tobacco. These laws are laws because governments enforce them.

But the term "law" certainly implies more than the commands imposed by governments and enforceable by courts. Law can be, and is, used to refer to the structures, processes, and norms that a society uses to resolve disputes, govern itself, and construct the relations between its members.[2] In this sense, the statement "The law defers to public health" need not refer to any particular rule or regulation, but to something much larger and less concrete; the system and norms that a society uses to allocate authority and resolve particular questions. Likewise, the statement "The law should value public health" is not so much an opinion about any specific rule as it is a more general point about the value that should be given to public health across the procedures and norms applicable in a society.

The law is also, of course, a profession. When we say someone has "entered the law" or can "think like a lawyer" (the goal of most first-year law school programs), we are not suggesting simply that the person has learned the positive rules that apply in a particular jurisdiction or has mastered a set of skills relating to the structures, norms, and rules by which society orders itself. Rather, we are claiming that the person has joined a profession or calling and shares with others in that field not only experiences and undertakings but also skills and norms.[3] Although the nature and content of these skills and values frequently are debated, they certainly include appreciation for the importance of precedent and process; comfort with complex, deductive, and analogic reasoning; and appreciation of individually based client goals. Lawyers, after all, are supposed to be zealous advocates who help achieve their clients' own goals.[4]

Public health is also an enormously complex phenomenon. A common definition provided by the Institute of Medicine begins by saying that "[p]ublic health is what we, as a society, do collectively to assure the conditions for people to be healthy."[5] That definition emphasizes both the activist and the social nature of public health. It views public health as an endeavor undertaken by people, governments, or organizations. It also implies what many have seen as the key characteristic of public health: its focus on populations.[6] Thus, the Institute envisions public health not simply as an undertaking to make a person healthy, as medicine attempts, but rather as one that aims to provide for the health of a wider grouping, a population, or, as the Institute states, "people."

The term "public health," however, does not refer only to such activities. The term also is used, especially by laypersons, to denote the health status of a group or a population. Thus the statement "Tobacco is a threat to the public health" refers not to an activity but simply to the fact that tobacco jeopardizes the health of a group of people. Likewise, the statement "Alcohol use is a public health issue" conveys the point that alcohol use will impact the health of a population. Importantly, such uses of the term concur with the emphasis, placed by the Institute's definition, on populations rather than on individuals.

The term "public health" has at least one other critical meaning. Like "law," the phrase "public health" refers to a profession or discipline. In 1997, the Acheson Report invoked this understanding when it defined public health as the "art and science of preventing disease, promoting health, and prolonging life through organized efforts of society."[7] Public health is the discipline that carries out this art and science.

As a profession, public health follows law in having its own set of skills and its own ways of seeing and describing the world. Given public health's focus on the health of populations, its world view focuses on or concerns itself with populations.[6] This contrasts significantly with lawyers' special regard for the interests of particular clients. Moreover, public health seeks to pursue a relatively objective goal—maintaining or improving the health of populations. Of course, many disputes exist about what that goal means or requires; nevertheless, lawyers pursue a more subjective end, even if we concede that a more objective, abstract goal—justice—can emerge through an adversarial system that directly represents individual goals.

Several additional distinctions between the ways of lawyers and the ways of public health professionals warrant notice. One pertains to how each comes to "know" something. In the first year of law school, students are immersed in an intense "Socratic" experience in which they are taught to question everything. In the place of common-sense reasoning, students develop (we hope) a strong capacity to question and engage in analogic reasoning, careful textual interpretation, deduction, and persuasive rhetoric. Language is central to their enterprise.

Public health professionals also are taught to question. However, instead of deduction and textual interpretation, they are weaned on the scientific method, which relies on experimentation and empirical verification. In addition, because they rely heavily on biostatistics to analyze and describe the world, public health professionals are far more apt than lawyers to reason quantitatively.[8]

More prosaically, lawyers and public health professionals differ in the nature of their employment, not to mention the remuneration they receive. For the most part, lawyers work in the private sector and represent private sector clients.[9] As a result, they often are likely to perceive their role as being adversarial to "the government." Public health professionals, in contrast, are more apt to work for governments or voluntary organizations.[10] Not surprisingly, they may have a different attitude toward government regulation than do lawyers, who generally represent private interests.

Given these distinctive perspectives and placements, we should not be surprised if lawyers and public health professionals approach matters differently. They may identify different goals, rely on different modes of reasoning, and apply different strategies, making communication and collaboration difficult but not less necessary. Despite their differences, public health and law are closely connected, perhaps even codependent, professions. It is time they become acquainted.

The Impact of Law on Public Health

Public health's dependency on law is more readily apparent than is law's need for public health. Public health's dependence on law is both pragmatic and elemental. The pragmatic need stems from the fact that many public health professionals work in the public sector. There, they attempt to protect and promote the health of populations. Often their jobs require them to enforce or help craft regulations, from local public health codes to federal environmental standards. In drafting and enforcing these regulations, public health professionals, of course, work with positive laws. To do so effectively, they need to know something about how laws are read and applied. They also need to understand the broader legal context in which particular laws lie. Thus, a city public health practitioner needs to know not only her health code but also, ideally, the state and federal laws (including constitutional provisions) that may limit or interact with that code. She also should be able to anticipate, at least broadly, when her actions may be challenged and when she needs advice of counsel.

Sometimes the pragmatic reasons are more dramatic. Since 2001, a series of high-profile public health threats, from SARS to the anthrax attacks on the U.S. mail, have underscored the law's critical role in public health emergencies. In these situations, law can give public health professionals the power and tools they need to accomplish their goals.[11] Laws, however, also can impose hurdles on certain public health interventions. Although these roadblocks, such as the need to provide due process when imposing a quarantine order, at first glance may appear troublesome to some public health professionals, these legal constraints also may help reconcile public health's values with other values, such as autonomy and equality, which are widely held in our society. Interestingly, these values may themselves support public health.[6] Hence, fidelity to law can at times promote public health, even when it seems to create burdens on the public health system.

But the relation between law and public health is not simply pragmatic, existing because public health professionals need to know the legal system to overcome legal obstructions to do their job. The relation is also more elemental. Precisely because public health also is a collective undertaking that aims to achieve population-wide goals and law provides the social structures and norms for achieving those goals, public health needs law to achieve its ends and build a foundation for its support.

Consider first the proposition that public health requires law to improve a population's health. Few would dispute this is so in an emergency, such as a bioterrorist incident when "the law" is represented by law enforcement. But this also is true, day in and day out, as public health confronts the less-salient but far-more-constant causes of human disease and death. As Stephen L. Isaacs and Steven A. Schroeder have demonstrated, law has played a critical role in many of the major public health victories of the last century, including removal of lead from gasoline and reduction of the rates of motor vehicular deaths and smoking.[12] In these cases and many more, law has provided the tools for implementing public health's recommendations.

The recognition that public health relies on law is not new. The history of public health shows us that the earliest known civilizations engaged in public health activities—enforcing sanitation codes, regulating the food supply, and providing care for the sick.[13] These activities, many of which affected the well-being of the communities at issue, were more apt to be founded on religious beliefs than scientific understanding (though a rough empiricism undoubtedly informed many practices). For these early public health practitioners, the chief tool of public health was law. In the ancient world, the practice of public health depended first and foremost on the establishment of a legal system that could ensure the organization and use of civil authority to proscribe practices thought to threaten health and prescribe practices thought to complement it.[13] Then, as now, knowledge of what harms public health was helpful when it was joined with the mechanisms, provided by law, for reducing those threats.

Public health's dependence on law was especially apparent in times of crisis. When plague threatened, law was the chief mechanism to support public health. Whether they relied on enforcement of maritime quarantines or establishment of pest houses, people have invariably depended on law's ability to structure responses and enforce norms in response to public health threats.[14] Indeed, in times of crisis, the most potent variable distinguishing the community that survives a plague from that which does not is not a community's degree of scientific knowledge but rather its legal system's responsiveness and stability. Thus, in the late 19th century, cities in the United States that had established well-organized boards of health and had granted them the requisite legal authority were far better able to endure the threats of cholera and other epidemics than were communities that lacked the legal structure to respond.[15]

Today, the success of public health boards and practitioners remains dependent on the laws that establish their offices, grant their authority, and appropriate their funds. As creatures of the state, public health offices depend absolutely on state laws for existence, financial support, and authority. Law determines whether they may inspect restaurants, kill mosquitoes, or quarantine people for communicable diseases.

Laws also help provide the information that health boards and researchers need to determine their public health priorities and policies. For many years, our epidemiologic understanding depended absolutely on laws mandating the keeping of vital statistics and the reporting of diseases. Even today, when researchers frequently rely on other sources of information, public health professionals count on public health surveillance laws, as well as vital statistics laws, to provide the sentinel of new and emerging health threats.

But it is too easy to believe that law's role in facilitating public health is limited to enactment of so-called public health laws, those relating to the creation and authorization of health offices, tracking of health information, and direct regulation of dangerous activities. Although laws that relate to public health's so-called core functions are critically important, they are just the tip of the legal iceberg relating to public health.

As noted above, law consists most fundamentally of the publicly sanctioned norms and structures that organize human interactions. Thus, law derives from and helps constitute societies, providing them with the tools to order relationships, respond to events, and resolve disputes. In this most fundamental way, law is absolutely essential to public health. Without law in some form, social chaos would ensue. And when social chaos exists, public health is imperiled, not only because of violence but also because of the lack of clean water, wholesome food, and social security necessary for the healthy rearing of children. Instead, stress, uncertainty, and environmental degradation result, each of which threatens the well-being of individuals and their communities. Thus, we should not be surprised that as law breaks down, as it did in the former republics of the Soviet Union in the early 1990s, public health declines.[16]

Even closer to home, in less extreme ways, law as a tool of social ordering is a sine qua non of public health. Consider, for example, Healthy People 2010's goal of eliminating disparities in health.[17] Is this a challenge for science or for law? Even though scientific research may be essential for pinpointing specific factors responsible for disparities, science alone cannot resolve them. No magic pill can be developed to end racial discrepancies in health. Nor can public health officials, acting alone, use their public health skills to solve the problem. Instead, if any meaningful approach to eliminating racial disparities is to exist, it will necessarily emerge from an assortment of social responses that will be informed by public health research but will rely on or be thwarted by law. Thus, even though public health studies and professionals will teach us where some of the problems lie and what needs to be done, we will need to turn to laws to address some of those problems. Perhaps some of those laws will involve core public health functions (such as laws providing for public health clinics in certain neighborhoods), but more remote laws may be needed, too. Perhaps laws relating to affordable housing, zoning, workplace discrimination, income taxation, or drug possession will play a role in abetting or retarding racial disparities. These and many other issues and responses in the domain of law may have to be addressed if the goal of Healthy People 2010 can be even partially realized.

Major public health initiatives, therefore, invariably implicate law. And many times, law—understood both as a discipline and as a set of social tools—can provide a powerful mechanism for dramatically changing the course of public health. The impact that litigation has had on the marketing, regulation, and understanding of cigarettes in the United States demonstrates the potential potency of one legal tool for addressing public health problems.[18]

On the other hand, law has not always been a friend to public health. Law also can defend the interests of industries that threaten the public health, preserve the status quo, and place economic interests above public health. For example, early in the 20th century, U.S. constitutional law was interpreted and applied in such a way as to impose major restrictions on the ability of states to regulate hazardous conditions in the workplace.[19] Today, the First Amendment may present a formidable obstacle to the strict (and perhaps effective) regulation of tobacco advertising.[20] Law is thus always an influence on public health but not necessarily an ally.

The barriers that law may create for public health result from more than happenstance. They emerge, in part, from the very different world views cherished by each discipline. Thus, the legal profession's focus on subjective goals can emphasize individual rights, including rights of property, provision of fair procedures, and imposition of limitations on governmental overreaching. These individual protections may in the long run plant the seeds for a healthy society but, in the short run, may interfere with and block important public health initiatives. Public health officials, therefore, might be forgiven for assuming that law simply throws a hurdle in their way.

That law also can be used positively to enhance a community's well-being—and how that can be done—has been less often appreciated by either lawyers or public health practitioners. However, developments, such as the use of litigation to challenge the tobacco industry and the work of lawyers to address environmental hazards, should in fact remind us that not only does law create the background environment necessary for public health, it can also affirmatively support specific public health goals.[12]

The Impact of Public Health on the Law

So how does public health affect law? Law's dependence on public health, I suspect, is far less salient than public health's dependence on law. However, it is nonetheless critical.

Without question, a minimal degree of public health is necessary for law to function well. Just as public health is imperiled when lawlessness exists, law is threatened when public health is in jeopardy. During the yellow fever epidemic of 1793, for example, civil authority broke down in Philadelphia, threatening not only local law but also the fledgling Constitution, because that city then was the U.S. capitol.[14] In a sense, law is a luxury that is made possible only when a modest degree of public health is achieved. If that is true, then the establishment and maintenance of public health may be the first essential and necessary undertaking for law. Hence, the common law maxim *salus populi suprema lex* represents an understanding that not only must the law serve public health but also that public health is before law.

Law's dependence on public health, however, is not limited to preventing the anarchy that can accompany epidemics. Public health has served law and relates to law in many other subtle ways. For example, one of the continuing challenges in U.S. constitutional law has been to find widely agreed-on arbiters or principles that can be used to help demarcate the boundaries between federal authority and state authority and between the public sphere and individual autonomy. Throughout the 19th and early 20th centuries, courts frequently used the idea of the health of the public as a defining component of the police power to help distinguish federal from state powers and public from individual rights.[21] In a world of contested values and conflicting moral judgments, public health has proven to be one of the most widely accepted rationales for communal action. In that role, public health played a critical, although often unrecognized, role in the development of U.S. constitutional law. Thus, doctrines as diverse as those relating to the Commerce Clause,[22] the right to privacy,[23] and the Fourth Amendment[24] all have been built on and enriched by considerations of public health. Constitutional law, therefore, owes a debt to public health that has yet to be acknowledged.

The discipline and expertise of public health have also proven critical to the development of bureaucratic organizations and administrative law. Indeed, public health boards and agencies are among the most ancient of all administrative agencies. In many places, the medical police long predated and formed the model for what we have come to know as the police.[13] Thus, the tools government uses for enforcing law, and the tools that courts use for reviewing and limiting that enforcement, have developed in the nursery of public health and have been founded in untold ways on understandings gleaned from the struggle to improve communal health.

The Evolving Relationship between Law and Public Health

What do we take from this tale of interdependency? First, that law and public health have developed together and are interconnected in seldom-appreciated ways. Unfortunately, neither the inevitability nor the depth of the relationship can ensure its success. Although neither law nor public health can function without the other, they need not serve each other well. Indeed, history is rife with examples of legal rules and doctrines—from the enforcement of Jim Crow to the doctrine of substantive due process—that have undermined health.

In our own time, the question of whether law will help or hinder the reduction in racial health disparities, the emerging obesity epidemic, or the challenges of emerging infections and bioterrorism remains unanswered. If law is to facilitate public health in each of these areas, and in many others, the connections between law and public health need to be more transparent and better understood. A hundred years ago, the relationship between the two fields was readily apparent. Legal opinions were filled with discussion of public health, and public health officials clearly understood that law was one of their chief tools.

Today, although the relationship is no less critical, it is less salient. The discipline of public health has grown far from its roots in social organization. Increasingly connected to the sciences, both medical and social, public health is in danger of overlooking the critical legal tools necessary for actually implementing and achieving the lessons learned in the laboratory. As public health scholars and practitioners increasingly rely on the tools of quantification and empirical analysis, legal insights, not easily subject to empirical verification, could be lost. Yet public health policy often will succeed only if legal obstacles are overcome and legal tools are used effectively.

The field of law, however, has been even more neglectful than public health has been in recognizing the need for partnership. In the last half-century, law has forsaken its traditional appreciation of public health. Whereas judges once wrote eloquently about public health, they seldom note it in today's opinions. When courts use the phrase "public health," they give it little weight. Contemporary jurists rarely note that public health is both a discipline and a human good.

Law's neglect of public health also is evident in the academy.[10] Although data are incomplete, few lawyers are likely to take a course in public health law or, even more aptly, the law's impact on public health.[25] The common law school course that generally approaches public health law most closely is the course on health law; but that, not surprisingly, has followed the market and focuses for the most part on the regulation and provision of medical services. Few textbooks in the field devote significant attention to public health. Moreover, the "mainstream" courses on torts, constitutional, criminal, and administrative law seldom recognize the public health issues latent in their curriculum.[26] Instead, they emphasize individual rights and the perspectives that economic analysis bear on decision making. That those decisions may affect dramatically the health of populations, and a discipline exists that sheds light on the nature and degree of those effects, is barely ever noted.

Fortunately, the relationship between public health and the law appears to be undergoing a renaissance. The second publication of this volume is one important testament to its arrival. There are many others. For example, since June 2002, the Centers for Disease Control and Prevention and the American Society of Law, Medicine, and Ethics have co-sponsored an annual conference, *The Public's Health and the Law in the 21st Century*, which has been widely attended and has helped to spur analysis and discussion of the many interactions between law and public health. The conference's success suggests that lawyers and public health professionals have found meeting worthwhile. The conference also helped to give birth to the Public Health Law Association, the first professional organization dedicated to promoting "healthy people in healthy communities through dialogue, partnerships, education, and research in public health law."[27]

We also see signs that the academy is beginning to recognize law's importance to public health. The Association of Schools of Public Health lists the ability to "enforce laws and regulations" as one of the ten essential public health services,[28] suggesting that familiarity with the law is understood as an essential part of a public health education. Moreover, public health schools and programs are increasingly partnering with law schools to provide students with an interdisciplinary education. As of 2005, a remarkable 34 schools offer some type of joint JD/MPH program allowing students to study both law and public health.[29]

Slowly, but surely, public health is migrating from the periphery to the mainstream of legal education. In January 2006, for example, the Annual Meeting of the American Association of Law Schools included a program cosponsored by several sections dedicated to discussing how law professors can teach public health issues in the context of traditional doctrinal courses, such as torts or administrative law. This type of discussion is critical because public health and law do not relate only in the narrow confines of a public health law practice. Only by teaching *all* law students about the multiple ways that law influences a people's health, as well as how public health professionals analyze matters, will the many lawyers who do not call themselves public health lawyers be able to respond to the public health issues that will inevitably arise in their practices.

Far more remains to be done. Despite all the exciting conferences, all the enriching scholarship, and all the practice interactions, lawyers and public health workers often remain foreign to each other. Most are not well trained in the other's approaches, and they do not know how best to collaborate. To help them, we need to provide many more opportunities for the average practicing lawyer and the typical public health worker to partner. We also need to use their relationships to enrich and enhance each field. Each profession's perspectives and values have merit. Each can complement the other. When they do, the law will help ensure the conditions necessary for healthy communities, and public health will help foster the law's values of justice, equality, and liberty.

These are ambitious goals. They will not be reached effortlessly. We have no magic bullet. But this book and the concerted efforts that have been and are being taken by many professionals in both fields can help lead us toward a reinvigorated partnership between law and public health.

References

1. Hart HLA. *The Concept of Law*. Oxford, UK: Clarendon Press, 1961.
2. Sarat A, Kearns TR. *Beyond the Great Divide: Forms of Legal Scholarship and Everyday Life*. Ann Arbor: University of Michigan Press, 1993.
3. Terrell TP, Wildman JH. Rethinking professionalism. *Emory Law J* 1992;41:403–32.
4. Zacharias FC. Reconciling professionalism and client interests. *William and Mary Law Rev* 1995;36:1303–74.
5. Institute of Medicine, Committee for the Study of Future Health. *The Future of Public Health*. Washington, DC: National Academy Press, 1988.
6. Mann J. Medicine and public health, ethics, and human rights. *Hastings Cent Rep* 1997;3: 6–13.
7. Begalehole R, Bonita R. *Public Health at the Crossroads: Achievements and Prospects*. Cambridge, UK: Cambridge University Press, 1997:146.
8. Parmet WE, Robbins A. Public health literacy for lawyers. *J Law Med Ethics* 2003;31:701–13.
9. Clark GJ. American lawyers in the year 2000. *Suffolk Law Rev* 2000;33:293–315.
10. Public Health Service, US Department of Health and Human Services. *The Public Health Workforce: An Agenda for the 21st Century*. Rockville, MD: Office of Disease Prevention and Health Promotion, US Department of Health and Human Services, [no date]:4–5. Available at http://www.health.gov/phfunctions/pubhlth.pdf. Accessed September 19, 2005.
11. Gostin LO. The model state emergency health powers act: public health and civil liberties in a time of terrorism. *Health Matrix* 2003;13:3–32.

12. Isaacs SL, Schroeder SA. Where the public good prevailed. *American Prospect* 2001;12: 26–30.
13. Porter D. *Health Civilization and the State: A History of Public Health from Ancient to Modern Times.* London: Routledge, 1999.
14. Parmet WE. Health care and the constitution: public health and the role of the state in the framing era. *Hastings Constitutional Law Q* 1993;20:267–335.
15. Leavitt JW. *The Healthiest City: Milwaukee, and the Politics of Health Reform.* Princeton, NJ: Princeton University Press, 1982.
16. Garrett L. *Betrayal of Trust: The Collapse of Global Public Health.* New York: Hyperion, 2000.
17. Office of Disease Prevention and Health Promotion, US Department of Health and Human Services. *Healthy People 2010. . What Are Its Goals?* Rockville, MD: US Department of Health and Human Services, Office of Disease Prevention and Health Promotion, 2000. Available at http://www.healthypeople.gov/About/goals.htm. Accessed September 19, 2005.
18. Parmet WE, Daynard RA. The new public health litigation. *Ann Rev Public Health* 2000;21:437–54.
19. *Lochner v New York*, 198 US 45 (1905).
20. *Lorillard Tobacco Co v Reilly*, 533 US 525 (2001).
21. Parmet WE. From slaughter-house to Lochner: the rise and fall of the constitutionalization of public health. *Am J Legal History* 1996;40:476–505.
22. *Gibbons v Ogden*, 22 US (9 Wheat) 1, 303 (1824).
23. *Roe v Wade*, 410 US 113 (1973).
24. *Camara v Municipal Court*, 387 US 583 (1967).
25. Goodman RA, Lazzarini Z, Moulton AD, et al. Other branches of science are necessary to form a lawyer: teaching public health in law school. *J Law Med Ethics* 2002;30:298–301.
26. Parmet WE. The neglect of public health in legal education: a review of constitutional law casebooks. Available at http://www.phaionline.org/downloads/ParmetNeglectPublicHealth LegalEducation.pdf. Accessed March 7, 2005.
27. Pestronk RM, Honssinger C, Ransom M. The public health law association: a new partnership in public health practice. *J Law Med Ethics* 2003;31:714–5.
28. Association of Schools of Public Health. What is public health? Available at http://www.asph.org/document.cfm?page=300. Accessed March 7, 2005.
29. Centers for Disease Control and Prevention. Public health law academic programs. Available at www.phppo.cdc.gov/od/phlp/docs/Phlawacademics.doc. Accessed March 7, 2005.

LAW IN PUBLIC HEALTH PRACTICE

PERSPECTIVE: LAW AND GREAT PUBLIC HEALTH ACHIEVEMENTS

Anthony D. Moulton,* Richard A. Goodman,* and Wendy E. Parmet

The iconic work of Dr. John Snow, an acknowledged pioneer in applied epidemiology, illustrates the historical centrality of law to public health. During a protracted outbreak of cholera in London in the 1850s, Dr. Snow's investigation correlated risk for illness with exposure to drinking water from one commercial supplier, including water obtained from the infamous pump on Broad Street. He could not implement his proposed intervention, however, until he appealed to the Board of Governors of St. James Parish and, after extended debate, secured its permission to simply, and dramatically, have the pump handle removed in 1855, thereby contributing to ending the local outbreak.[1]

Law has become more deeply woven in and critical to public health practice and policy since Dr. Snow's day. This perspective will (1) illuminate the central role of law in contemporary public health; (2) distill important themes from the practice of public health law; and (3) project the heightened role law is likely to play in public health practice in the coming decades. The perspective begins with an overview of the contributions of law to selected public health advances in the United States during the 20th century by examining three of ten such achievements identified by the Centers for Disease Control and Prevention (CDC).[2] We then comment on foundational powers and five themes in law and public health that emerge from that history and conclude with an examination of factors that could strengthen the role of law as a tool for improving the health of the public during the 21st century.

*The findings and conclusions in this chapter are those of the author(s) and do not necessarily represent the views of the U.S. Department of Health and Human Services or the Centers for Disease Control and Prevention.

3

We define "public health laws" in practical terms as any laws that have significant consequences for the health of defined populations. The types of law treated are broad and include the federal and state constitutions; congressional and state legislative statutes; rules and regulations adopted by federal, state, and municipal agencies; ordinances; policies of public bodies; and judicial rulings and case law. Consistent with the framework for this chapter, whenever possible we have restricted dates to the 20th century to signify the advances made during that period. Table P-1 gives examples of federal, state and local laws and legal tools supportive of each of the ten great public health achievements.

Law and Public Health Achievements of the 20th Century

In 1999, CDC published a retrospective series of articles on ten "great public health achievements" of the 20th-century United States. The achievements were selected from among many and varied public health accomplishments on the basis of "the opportunity for prevention and the impact on death, illness, and disability" associated with each.[2]

This perspective examines the role law played in three of these achievements, chosen because they are not the principal focus of other chapters in this volume and because they illustrate the indispensable role of law in three different public health domains: control of infectious diseases, motor vehicle safety, and fluoridation of drinking water. Law authorized fundamental public health functions common to all three and, indeed, to virtually all fields of public health practice.

For each of the three achievements, we briefly describe the challenge and nature of the achievement; identify and comment on selected laws that contributed to it; and review some of the implicated legal mechanisms, jurisdictions, and parties. Because laws that contributed to these three achievements are far too numerous to capture here comprehensively, we highlight laws that made especially important contributions and that portray some of the range of legal tools available to public health policymakers, practitioners, and proponents.

Control of Infectious Diseases

The Challenge

Early in U.S. history, infectious diseases were an enduring scourge of the indigenous population and the European colonists alike. Smallpox endemics were frequent, and yellow fever was commonplace, even to the extent of threatening to disrupt the Constitutional Convention.[3] Malaria was endemic as far north as the Ohio River Valley well into the 19th century and was one of many threats encountered by the Lewis and Clark expedition of 1803–1806.[4]

In the United States in 1900, three infectious diseases were the leading causes of death—pneumonia, tuberculosis (TB), and diarrhea/enteritis; together with diphtheria, they accounted for more than one third of all deaths.[5] In that same year, the crude death rate for infectious diseases was 800 deaths per 100,000 persons.[6] Measles, diph-

TABLE P-1 Ten Great Public Health Achievements and Selected Supportive Laws and Legal Tools—United States, 1900–1999

Public Health Achievement	Selected Supportive Laws and Legal Tools
Control of Infectious Diseases	*Local laws*: Sanitary codes and drinking water standards; quarantine and isolation powers; zoning ordinances and building codes; mosquito- and rodent-control program; inspection of food establishments *State laws*: Authority to conduct disease surveillance, require disease reports, investigate outbreaks; regulation of drinking water and waste disposal; regulation of food supplies; licensure of health professionals *Federal laws*: Public Health Service Act of 1944; Safe Drinking Water Act of 1974; National Environmental Protection Act of 1976
Motor Vehicle Safety	*Local laws*: Speed limits; limitation on liquor store hours; penalties for serving inebriated bar patrons; bicycle helmet ordinances *State laws*: Seat-belt, child-safety-seat, and motorcycle-helmet laws; vehicle inspection; driver licensing and graduated drivers license systems; authorization to conduct sobriety checkpoints; zero tolerance for alcohol among drivers under age 21 years; prohibition on alcohol sales to minors; 0.08% blood alcohol content per se laws; speed limits *Federal laws*: Performance and crash standards for motor vehicles; standards for road and highway construction; safety-belt use in some commercial vehicles; financial assistance to states to promote and enforce highway safety initiatives; airbag warning labels; creation of state offices of highway safety; federal court ruling upholding motorcycle-helmet use
Fluoridation of Drinking Water	*Local laws*: Ordinances authorizing fluoridation; referenda and initiatives authorizing fluoridation *State laws*: Legislation authorizing fluoridation; court rulings upholding fluoridation *Federal laws*: Federal court rulings upholding fluoridation of public drinking water supplies; Environmental Protection Agency caps on fluoridation levels
Recognition of Tobacco Use as a Health Hazard	*Local laws*: Excise tax; restrictions on retail sale to minors; clean indoor air laws *State laws*: Excise tax; restrictions on retail sale practices; clean indoor air laws; funding for public education; lawsuits leading to the Master Settlement Agreement of 1998 *Federal laws*: Excise tax; mandated warning labels; prohibition of advertising on radio and television; penalties on states not outlawing sale to persons under age 18 years; financial assistance to state and local tobacco-control programs; Department of Justice lawsuit to recover health-care costs
Vaccination	*Local laws*: School board enforcement of school vaccination requirements *State laws*: Court rulings supporting mandatory vaccination; school admission laws

continued

TABLE P-1   *continued*

Public Health Achievement	Selected Supportive Laws and Legal Tools
	Federal laws: Court rulings supporting mandatory vaccination; licensure of vaccines; financial aid to state vaccination programs
Decline in Deaths from Coronary Heart Disease and Stroke	*Local laws*: Education and information programs *State laws*: Tobacco-control laws; education and information programs *Federal laws*: Food-labeling laws; Department of Transportation funding for bikeways and walking paths; National High Blood Pressure Education Program (1972)
Safer and Healthier Foods	*Local laws*: Standards and inspection of retail food establishments *State laws*: Mandated niacin enrichment of bread and flour; standards and inspection of foods at the producer level; limits on chemical contamination of crops *Federal laws*: Pure Food and Drug Act of 1906 and later enactments to regulate foods and prescription drugs; mandated folic acid fortification of cereal grain products; limits on chemical contamination of crops; food stamps, the Women, Infants, and Children program, and school meals
Healthier Mothers and Babies	*Local laws*: Sewage and refuse ordinances; drinking water codes; milk pasteurization (first mandated by Chicago in 1908) *State laws*: Establishment of maternal and child health clinics; licensure of obstetrics health-care professionals; mandated milk pasteurization; funding for Medicaid services *Federal laws*: Drinking water quality standards; creation of the Children's Bureau (1912) with education and service programs; licensure of sulfa drugs and antibiotics; creation of the Medicaid program
Family Planning	*Local laws*: Funding for family planning clinics *State laws*: Authorization to provide birth control services (North Carolina in 1937); authority to provide prenatal and postnatal care to indigent mothers *Federal laws*: Family Planning Services and Population Research Act; Supreme Court rulings on contraceptive use and abortion
Safer Workplaces	*Local laws*: Authority to inspect for unsafe conditions; building and fire safety codes *State laws*: 1877 and later laws to inspect and regulate workplace safety practices, including toxic exposures; criminal penalties for grossly negligent worker injury or death *Federal laws*: 1936 minimum safety standards for federal contractors; inspection and regulation of mine safety; mandates on states to adopt minimum workplace safety standards

theria, pertussis, smallpox, and other infectious diseases were a scourge of children and, joined by poliomyelitis and other infectious diseases, remained a constant source of dread for parents. And for good reason: measles and diphtheria in 1920, taken together with pertussis in 1922, accounted for more than 725,000 cases and caused 25,000 deaths among children and adults.[7]

The Achievement

The U.S. death rate for infectious diseases fell substantially during the first half of the 20th century. One major exception was the impact of the influenza pandemic of 1918–1919, when deaths from infectious diseases neared 1000 for every 100,000 persons. The period from 1938 to 1952 witnessed an especially rapid decline in the infectious disease death rate and by the mid-1950s, it had dropped below 75 deaths per 100,000 persons with further but more gradual decreases into the early 1980s.[6] The HIV/AIDS epidemic reversed the trend for several years, but the infectious disease rate continued to decline later in the century. This historic gain in the health of the general public was mirrored in the health and survival of children. In 1900, 30.4% of all U.S. deaths occurred among children under age 5 years; by 1997, deaths among children accounted for only 1.4% of all deaths.[5]

In addition to these dramatic advances were important successes against specific infectious diseases. For example, smallpox was eradicated from the globe during the 20th century. Measles, paralytic polio, and diphtheria were nearly eliminated from the United States, and the prevalence of pertussis, mumps, rubella, and *Haemophilus influenzae* type B fell by more than 95%. Pneumonia, TB, and diarrhea/enteritis also declined sharply.[7] Reflecting these successes, chronic diseases eclipsed infectious diseases as a cause of death by the latter decades of the 20th century: by 1997, heart disease and cancer were the proximate causes of more than half of all deaths in the United States.[5]

A wide range of technical and scientific advances contributed to this 20th-century public health achievement, including improved epidemiologic practice, sanitation and housing, medical and laboratory science, and health education. Law, however, was indispensable to the translation of these advances into effective public health interventions.

The Role of Law

Some of the earliest public health interventions in colonial America directed at infectious diseases were based in law. Perhaps most prominent were local quarantine laws to interrupt smallpox transmission. Basic sanitary improvements contributed greatly in the fight against infectious diseases. The "sanitary movement" began in the mid-19th century and was given powerful voice in a famous report commissioned by the Massachusetts legislature and written by Lemuel Shattuck in 1850.[8]

Practical implementation of the movement's reforms took shape at the city, county, and state levels. Local governments established drinking water treatment and sewage facilities by ordinance; created a regime of inspection and regulation of food producers, wholesalers, and retailers to prevent outbreaks of foodborne infectious diseases; organized rodent-control programs; and adopted zoning and building codes to reduce urban crowding and exposure to industrial and commercial hazards. By the latter half of the 20th century, the federal and state governments had enacted safe drinking water and environmental protection legislation that instituted comprehensive regimes of inspection and financial aid for construction of drinking water, sewer, and storm water facilities. Local mosquito-control districts (political subdivisions of states), along with state and federal government programs, effectively eliminated malaria from the United States.

More coercive interventions, such as resorting to quarantine and isolation during plague outbreaks in California at the turn of the 19th into the 20th century, involved the state and local governments' traditional police powers to protect the community from infectious diseases and other threats to the public's health, although their use there has been questioned. Four decades into the century, enactment of the Public Health Service Act in 1944 gave the federal government codified authority to combat infectious diseases, including broad, discretionary powers to "prevent the introduction . . . or spread of communicable diseases . . . into the states."[9]

The science of vaccination advanced rapidly during the 19th century and was complemented by advances in public health law. During the 1850s, Massachusetts became the first state to require vaccination (for smallpox) as a condition of school admission.[10] By the end of the century, all states had adopted laws requiring vaccination of children for admission to school, with exemption where a child's medical condition made vaccination unwise or where the family's religious or philosophic beliefs would be violated.[11]

Concerns about safety and effectiveness, as well as resistance to government compulsion, at times have threatened attempts to prevent disease outbreaks. Here, law played a pivotal role, most importantly in the landmark 1905 U.S. Supreme Court *Jacobson v. Massachusetts* ruling that upheld state-mandated vaccination for smallpox on the grounds that allowing a personal-choice exemption would "practically strip the legislative department of its function to . . . care for the public health . . . when endangered by epidemics of disease" and, more generally, that "[t]here are manifold restraints to which every person is necessarily subject for the common good."[12] *Jacobson* deserves recognition also for setting forth the rationale for what a leading public health legal scholar terms the "legitimate exercise of the police powers for public health purposes": necessity, reasonable means, proportionality, and harm avoidance.[13]

In the early- and mid-20th century, states and localities adopted laws requiring isolation and mandating treatment for persons with TB. Laws were enacted also to trace the contacts of persons with sexually transmitted diseases and later HIV and to require notification of their at-risk partners. Primarily in the latter half of the 20th century, the states and the federal government adopted a host of legal tools to authorize and operate vaccination programs for children, elders, and others. A prominent federal example was congressional appropriation of funds for polio vaccination in 1955 (69 Stat. 704). Subsequent actions included authorization for vaccination in the Medicaid and Medicare programs; congressional creation of the National Vaccine Injury Compensation Program[14] in 1988 and the Vaccine for Children Program in 1994 (Section 1928 of the Social Security Act);[15] state laws mandating childhood vaccination as a condition of school admission; and laws and agency regulations requiring that elders in institutional settings be offered vaccination for influenza and pneumococcal disease.

The development of antibiotics presented public health with a powerful technical tool against infectious diseases that displays another dimension of law in service to public health. As with vaccines, antibiotics may be sold in the United States only after successful completion of safety and efficacy tests and with formal approval by the Food and Drug Administration (FDA). With its legal origins in the landmark Food and Drugs Act of 1906[16] and the Food, Drug, and Cosmetic Act of 1938,[17] FDA licensed vaccine (for influenza) for the first time in 1945. FDA contemporaneously began approving antibiotics to treat and prevent the spread of enteric pathogens, bacterial pneumonias, TB, and other infectious diseases. Also important was congressional creation of, and funding for, infectious disease programs at CDC and for that agency's ongoing public health research efforts and its technical assistance to state and local public health agencies.

Motor Vehicle Safety

The Challenge

Among the vast transformations of U.S. society in the 20th century was the nation's embrace of automobiles, trucks, and other motor vehicles. From 1925 through 1997, the number of drivers increased sixfold and the number of motor vehicles elevenfold. The number of miles traveled in motor vehicles annually increased tenfold to more than 2.5 trillion.[18] The number of registered automobiles in the United States multiplied from 8000 in 1900 to 239 million in 2003, and the number of licensed drivers grew to nearly 197 million.[19]

These trends brought a new and often deadly set of risks for drivers, passengers, cyclists, and pedestrians. During the past 100 years, more than 2.8 million persons have died, and nearly 100 million persons have been injured, on U.S. roads and highways.[19] By the early 21st century, motor vehicles accounted for more than 90% of all transportation-related deaths in the United States.[20]

The Achievement

The public health achievement related to the 20th-century "motorization" of the United States was a dramatic, long-term decline in the motor vehicle–related death rate. One of the broadest measures, the number of deaths for every 100 million vehicle miles traveled (VMT), fell by 90% from 1925 (17 per 100 million VMT) to 1997 (1.7 per 100 million VMT). From 1912 through 2001, motor vehicle–related deaths per 10,000 registered vehicles declined by 94% (from 33 to fewer than 2). In 1912, when the number of registered vehicles totaled only 950,000, 3100 motor vehicle–related fatalities occurred. By dramatic comparison, in 2001, when registrations had increased to 231 million, 42,900 people died. More recently, the rate of motor vehicle–related deaths caused by specific risk factors has decreased significantly. For example, National Highway Traffic Safety Administration (NHTSA) data indicate that fatalities in alcohol-related crashes declined by 36% from 1982 to 2004. The fatality rate per 100,000 population for motor vehicle occupants declined by 43% from 1966 to 2004.[21]

Despite these remarkable achievements, motor vehicle crashes continue to account for an estimated 43,000 deaths annually. In 2002, motor vehicle–related injuries were the leading cause of death for all persons aged 1–34 years,[22,23] and an estimated 4.5 million people sought medical care in a hospital emergency department for nonfatal motor vehicle–related injuries at an aggregate cost exceeding $200 billion.[19]

The Role of Law

The causes of the decline in the rate of motor vehicle–related deaths during the first part of the 20th century can be attributed to multiple factors, including changes in vehicles, drivers, and roads. The specific contribution made by each factor, however, is unclear. Vehicle-safety laws were adopted as early as the 1930s (for example, Maryland's 1932 statute mandating car-safety inspections, the first such requirement in the nation), but their contributions have not been systematically evaluated.[24]

After a long, albeit irregular, decline from 1925 to the early 1960s, the motor vehicle–related death rate reversed direction and climbed for five successive years.[18] Congress passed and President Lyndon B. Johnson signed the National Highway Traffic and Motor Vehicle Safety Act[25] and the Highway Safety Act[26] in 1966. These paved the way for an intensified effort by the federal government to set standards for motor vehicles and highways to improve safety. The National Highway Traffic and Motor Vehicle Safety Act created the National Highway Safety Bureau (NHSB), NHTSA's predecessor, and authorized it to set safety standards for highways and new cars, beginning with the 1968 models, focusing on accident avoidance, crash protection, and post-crash survivability; and addressing such vehicular systems as braking, tires, windshields, lights, door strength, fuel systems, and transmission safety controls.[24] Automobile manufacturers initially were not required to develop new systems but eventually did so to comply with the standards.

These federal laws sparked additional law-based interventions at the federal and state levels. The federal Department of Transportation (DOT) promulgated highway design and construction standards for states receiving federal highway financial support. In 1968, DOT required all new cars sold in the United States to be equipped with seat belts, and requirements followed for head rests, air bags, and other mandatory built-in safety features.[24] In the Intermodal Surface Transportation Efficiency Act of 1991,[27] Congress combined funding incentives and penalties to encourage states to enact and enforce seat-belt laws.

Focusing on driver behavior as a risk factor, state governments imposed speed limits and mandated driver testing and licensing; licensing of commercial drivers; and, more recently, graduated licensing for young drivers and restrictions on driving by the elderly. Threatened with federal financial penalties posed by the National Minimum Drinking Age Act of 1984,[28] all states raised the age for purchase and public possession of alcoholic beverages to 21 years. Congress used a similar financial threat to encourage states to adopt laws making it a per se offense to drive with a blood alcohol concentration of 0.08% or higher. On their own initiative, states and municipalities regulated the sale of alcoholic beverages to minors and set limits on the hours of bars.

The states also employed law-based measures—such as the mandated use of occupant restraints and protective devices—to mitigate the consequences of motor vehicle crashes. For example, in 1978, Tennessee was among the world's first jurisdictions to adopt legislation requiring infants and small children to be properly restrained during transport in motor vehicles,[29] and, in 1984, New York enacted the first U.S. seat-belt law.[24] By 1988, 31 states had enacted seat-belt laws, and by the end of the century, 49 states had adopted seat-belt laws for adults, and all had adopted child safety–restraint laws, albeit with great diversity in their provisions, implementation, and enforcement.[30,31]

All these laws contributed to the reduction of motor vehicle–related deaths and morbidity in the latter part of the 20th century. Two key indicators show the magnitude of this public health achievement. During 1966–2000, the motor vehicle–related fatality rate per 100,000 population fell by 42.5% (from 25.89 to 14.86 deaths per 100,000 population). During the same period, the fatality rate per 100 million VMT fell by 72.2% (from 5.50 to 1.53 fatalities per 100 VMT).[21] These declines were associated with such law-based measures as the Motor Vehicle Safety Act of 1966, the federal 55-mile-per-hour speed limit on interstate highways, federal and state laws intended to reduce drunk driving, and seat-belt and other occupant-restraint laws. Although the causal contributions of such laws have not been incontrovertibly established, in part because of the many confounding environmental and other factors, strong evidence nonetheless associates many of them with enhanced motor vehicle safety.

Fluoridation of Drinking Water to Prevent Dental Caries

The Challenge

CDC reported that "[a]t the beginning of the 20th century, extensive dental caries [tooth decay] was common in the United States and in most developed countries" and that "[n]o effective measures existed for preventing [the] disease. . . ."[32] Effective preventive interventions did not emerge until the 1950s, when epidemiologic studies demonstrated the benefits of adjusting the level of fluoride in drinking water to an optimal level for reducing tooth decay.

The Achievement

Fluoridation is a focused public health intervention comprising a single technical tool, "the deliberate addition of the natural trace element fluorine . . . into drinking water in accordance with scientific and dental guidelines."[33] In this form, fluoride increases the resistance of the tooth surface to acids produced by bacteria and inhibits the action of bacteria resident in dental plaque. Fluoridation exemplifies the type of intervention that modifies the environment of the targeted beneficiaries, distinct from interventions that seek to modify behavior per se.

Fluoridation was a public health achievement of the second half of the 20th century. In 1945, Grand Rapids, Michigan, became the first U.S. city to fluoridate its drinking water when the city council approved participation in a study conducted by the Public Health Service (PHS). More cities followed rapidly, and, by 2002, some four decades after PHS officially recommended addition of fluoride to public drinking water supplies, 170 million Americans (67% of the population) were served by fluoridated water supplies, primarily serving medium-size and larger urban centers.[34]

According to standard indicators, from 1966–1970 to 1988–1994, the incidence of dental caries declined by 68% among children under age 13 years. Adults also benefited. In 1960–1962, 20% of all adults aged 45–54 years had lost all their permanent teeth; by 1988–1994, that proportion had declined by more than half, to 9.1%.[32]

Adoption of fluoridation, however, is not universal. In 2002, the proportion of people served by fluoridated public water systems ranged from 100% in the District of Columbia to 2% in Utah.[35] In only 24 states did 75% or more of persons served by community water systems receive fluoridated water. Nonetheless, it is remarkable that in the span of just half a century a new public health intervention had been introduced, adopted widely, and proven by science to yield remarkable health benefits for most Americans.

The Role of Law

Fluoridation is manifestly a law-based intervention given that fluoride is added to public drinking water supplies and to school water supplies only when a government body so authorizes. Despite its technical simplicity, fluoridation's reliance on law illustrates the intricate interplay of law with public health and the great heterogeneity evident in the provisions of public health laws and in their mechanisms of operation and implementation, especially at the state and local levels.

The law of fluoridation of public drinking water varies considerably from state to state. Massachusetts state law, for example, empowers the state's more than 400 local boards of health to mandate fluoridation in their jurisdictions at their option,[36] whereas in Ohio, the state legislature enacted a law in 1969 mandating fluoridation of all water supplies serving more than 5000 people.[37] California passed a law in 1995 requiring fluoridation of all public water systems having 10,000 or more service connections (Cal. Health & Safety Code §116410).[38] In 1999, Nevada enacted a law requiring fluoridation of water supplies only in counties with populations greater than 400,000 persons (i.e., Clark County, home of Las Vegas).[39] As with many public health functions, implementation of fluoridation, once authorized, is overseen by a state or local authority. In most states the environmental protection or natural resources agency oversees the quality of public drinking water supplies, inspecting them for fluoride content and other substances, and for operational effectiveness.

In addition to states' enactments, federal agencies play a significant role in fluoridation pursuant to congressional authorization and funding. The U.S. Environmental Protection Agency (EPA) regulates public drinking water supplies under the Safe Drinking Water Act of 1974, as amended.[40] Fluoride can occur naturally in water at levels much higher than at levels recommended by PHS to prevent tooth decay. EPA caps fluoride levels in drinking water of four parts per million to reduce the risk for rare adverse health effects. In addition to this overtly regulatory approach, CDC relies on its general powers under the Public Health Service Act to develop, publish, and periodically update recommendations for the operation of fluoridated water systems, which it first did in 1979.[33]

People concerned that fluoride may have adverse health effects often vigorously oppose fluoridation. Such opposition has influenced decision making, even though numerous, rigorous scientific studies have found fluoridation to pose no health risks. Opponents have employed a variety of strategies, including initiative petitions to overturn fluoridation laws, and have challenged fluoridation in state and federal courts, alleging violation of religious freedom and other rights guaranteed by the U.S. and state constitutions. State and local governments have responded in different ways: some require a local referendum on fluoridation; others authorize local boards of health or other bodies to make the decision. The judicial branch of state and federal government played a central role in the 20th-century success of fluoridation. The courts upheld fluoridation consistently, including rulings by "[t]he highest courts of more than a dozen states. . . ."[41] Moreover, the U.S. Supreme Court denied "review of fluoridation cases thirteen times, citing that no substantial federal or constitutional questions were involved."[42]

Foundational Powers and Emergent Themes

This perspective has highlighted the operation of legal powers foundational to public health as well as five themes important to an understanding of the evolving role law plays in public health. Among the most fundamental powers authorizing government action for the well-being of the community are the police powers reserved to the states by the Tenth Amendment to the U.S. Constitution. One suggested definition for the police powers is: "The inherent authority of the state . . . to enact laws and promulgate regulations to protect, preserve, and promote the health, safety, morals, and general welfare of the people."[43] Long recognized in British law and cited by the U.S. Supreme Court as early as its 1824 *Gibbons v. Ogden* ruling (22 U.S. 1 [1824]), the police power is the ground for the state laws reviewed above. The states' public health police powers also are reflected in legislatures' authorization for public health agencies to designate certain diseases as reportable by health-care providers, to conduct surveillance for those and related conditions, to develop and implement preventive programs, and to adopt regulations to implement those laws. The police powers thus encompass such specific, law-based interventions as school vaccination laws, the 0.08% blood alcohol level standard, and fluoridation of drinking water. This underlying principle of U.S. jurisprudence—that the states have deep-rooted authority to act to protect the general well-being—is both foundational and enduring.

The first and most important of the five emergent themes this review brings forward is the indispensable contribution of law to public health achievements. Important qualifications are, however, that law clearly was not a sufficient condition for any single achievement and that the scope of the law's contribution varied across the individual achievements in many important ways. In addition to law, public health successes require coordinated and complementary applications of epidemiology, laboratory science, health education, and many other disciplines. For example, development of modern bacteriology contributed to formulation of "sanitary movement" interventions and, in turn, to calls for laws as vehicles for their implementation. In the same era, separate laws created the state and local health departments that would devise new interventions and apply rapidly evolving scientific knowledge to public health policy and practice.

Second, even though explicit public health legal powers have been vested in local and state governments and in the federal government, authority also is distributed widely throughout the polity. This diffusion of authority, evident also in public education, among other fields, reflects both federalism and the structure of U.S. democratic institutions. Among the many government bodies that shape public health laws are the Congress; the President and agencies of the federal Executive Branch; state, county, and city counterparts; the federal, state, and local courts; and a host of special-purpose entities, such as school districts, water-supply and sanitary districts, local and state boards of health, housing authorities, and highway and transportation agencies.

Also important to the 20th century public health achievements were actions exerted by such private actors as scientific and civic associations, nonprofit organizations of many different types, and interest groups. Their actions included campaigns to influence elected officials, voter ballot initiatives, and commentary on proposed regulations, among others. Civic groups pushed for food-safety reforms following publication of Upton Sinclair's 1906 exposé *The Jungle*, Mothers Against Drunk Driving advocated for safe-driving laws, and the American Dental Association called for fluoridation of drinking water. Private parties also used litigation—a form of common law regulation—for such measures as regulations to reduce pollution of drinking water, statutes requiring childhood vaccination, and laws mandating standards for motor vehicle safety. As one example, a federal court ruled in 1968 in favor of a person injured in a motor vehicle crash, holding that General Motors in the specific case and automobile manufacturers more generally had a responsibility to foresee the possibility of human damage associated with the use of their products and to take reasonable steps to prevent that damage.[44] For their part, automobile and other manufacturers sought to reduce the economic burden of government regulation, variously opposing adoption of new regulations, advocating for uniform federal law over heterogeneous state laws, promoting voluntary standards, and pursuing still other strategies.

Third, the legal tools used in support of the 20th-century public health achievements were many in number, diverse in their mechanisms of operation, and located at many different points on a gradient ranging from a high degree of voluntarism to a high degree of coercion. At one end, for example, was the legally authorized government provision of information and education about the benefits of proper food preparation and waste disposal. At the other was punitive action, such as EPA financial penalties, on municipalities out of compliance with federal drinking water standards. In the broad middle ground were such tools as incentives (e.g., provision of free vaccination for low-income children through the Vaccines for Children program), use of common-law legal liability (e.g., to challenge unsafe automobile designs), statutory creation of citizens' rights to bring litigation against alleged violators of drinking water regulations, regulation of individuals (e.g., mandatory childhood vaccination and use of seat belts), regulation of businesses and professionals (e.g., licensing of pharmaceutical products and health-care providers, and inspection of food and drug producers and retailers), and federal regulation of lower governments (e.g., incentives for states to lower the legal standard for drunk driving).

Fourth, the effectiveness of law as a public health tool was powerfully mediated by factors of enforcement and compliance. For example, fluoridation laws are among the closest to self-implementing in that, once the legal basis is in place, proficient management of a drinking water supply plant essentially effects the intervention. Most public health laws, however, rely more on active government education and enforcement for successful implementation. For example, the failure of medical providers and parents to observe recommended vaccination schedules can compromise childhood vaccination. Legally authorized programs of vaccination education for healthcare providers encourage observation of vaccination laws. Government-mandated food labeling and standards for motor vehicle safety require ongoing oversight. Sustained education and enforcement efforts directed toward drivers are needed if motor vehicle seat-belt and child safety–restraint laws are to be effective.

Fifth, law-based interventions may be controversial, often in ways that implicate the most fundamental laws of the country, as well as sensitive social and cultural issues. The use of public health law in the 20th century United States stimulated controversy on many points, none more fundamental in our constitutional scheme than the protection of civil rights. For example, to interrupt the spread of bubonic plague in the late 1890s, area quarantine (or cordon sanitaire) was imposed differentially by the San Francisco health department. Rather than target quarantine according to identified cases, city health officials sealed off a 12–block area specifically because it was inhabited predominantly by ethnic Chinese who were believed, erroneously, to be the principal vector of infection. This violation of civil liberties ultimately led to a 1900 federal appeals court ruling that the quarantine was "unreasonable, unjust, and oppressive, and therefore contrary to the laws limiting the police powers of the state and that it is discriminating in its character and contrary to the provisions of the Fourteenth Amendment of the U.S. Constitution."[45] Echoes of that case surfaced a century later when a California county health department incarcerated a non-English-speaking Laotian immigrant for allegedly refusing to complete prescribed TB therapy. A federal court and a state court found the government at fault, ordering an award to the plaintiff of $1.2 million and prohibiting future use of the county jail to detain noncompliant TB patients.[46]

A different example, from the field of motor vehicle injury, illustrates the role advocacy groups and elected officials can play in using law to protect the public's health. A DOT standard issued under the Highway Safety Act of 1966[47] required all states to adopt universal helmet-use laws to protect motorcycle riders or to forfeit part of their federal highway funding. By 1975, 47 states and the District of Columbia had complied. Opposition flourished, however, and led Congress to amend the 1966 act to remove the sanctions.[48] Despite the clear benefits in the form of lives saved and injuries and disabilities prevented, many state legislatures were reluctant to mandate helmet use, and some began to repeal helmet laws. A later federal financial incentive had little effect, with the result that, as of July 2005, only 20 states had universal helmet laws on their books, 26 states had "partial laws," requiring some riders to wear helmets, and four were completely without motorcycle helmet laws.[49]

These five themes permeated U.S. public health and public health law in the 20th century. They remain at work today and will be among the most important factors shaping public health practice in the coming decades.

Law and Public Health Challenges of the Early 21st Century

Evolution in health threats and continuing development of innovative responses by public health policymakers and practitioners shaped the 20th-century role of law. At least three dynamics will give further shape to that role in the new century: change in the nature of threats to the health of the public, change in jurisprudential patterns, and innovation in the armamentarium of public health interventions.

Change in the Nature of Public Health Threats

During the 20th century, chronic diseases overtook infectious diseases as the leading cause of U.S. mortality and morbidity. Of the ten most important causes of death in 2000, the top four, the sixth, and the eighth were chronic diseases: heart disease, malignant neoplasm (cancer), cerebrovascular disease, chronic lower respiratory tract disease, diabetes mellitus, and Alzheimer disease. Heart disease and cancer together accounted for half of all deaths. Of the nine most important underlying or "actual" causes of death, all but two were associated with individual behavior: tobacco use, poor diet and physical inactivity, alcohol consumption, motor vehicle injury, firearms, sexual behavior (including HIV/AIDS), and illicit drug use.[50] In 1996, the top twenty causes of disability-adjusted life years reflected a similar preponderance of chronic and behavior-related mortality and morbidity.[51]

The 21st century may bring new or intensified health threats such as pandemic influenza, bioterrorist attacks, and dangers resulting from natural disasters. Barring an extraordinary catastrophe, however, chronic diseases most likely will predominate in the foreseeable future, especially given the aging of the U.S. population, the time involved in achieving broad behavioral change, and the probability that pharmaceutical and other technologic progress will continue to create tools to combat infectious diseases.

Change in Jurisprudential Patterns

Evolution in patterns of court rulings bears directly on the future role of law in public health. In their decisions, courts can shape permissible public health interventions, modify the locus of authority among jurisdictions and agencies, and influence legal doctrines. For example, federal appeals court rulings on First Amendment protection of commercial speech have varied over the years with important implications for advertising for tobacco, alcohol, and other products determinative of public health.[43] The deference the Rehnquist Court gave to the states—for example, in striking down a congressional law prohibiting firearms within a specified radius of schools—also illustrates how shifts in judge-made law can shape the jurisprudential context of public health law.

Evolution in academic law could have similar effects, albeit over an extended period. For instance, development in the "law and economics" field—which promotes market-based approaches over government regulation of the private sector—might question traditional reliance on government mechanisms to advance the health of the public. This and other possible developments in prevailing legal doctrine could have important shaping influences on public health law.

Innovations in Public Health Interventions

The 1990s and the opening years of the 21st century brought heightened innovations to public health interventions and law with three notable focal points: chronic disease prevention, preparedness for terrorism and other public health emergencies, and the overarching legal powers of state health departments. In the area of chronic disease prevention, conceptual frameworks were encouraged for use of law in supporting interventions directed at cardiovascular disease and physical inactivity.[52] A compendium was published of a wide array of legal and policy interventions to shape the physical environment—built structures and natural areas alike—to foster healthy behavior.[53] Zoning and other land use policies were explored as tools to control location of fast-food retailers and to limit access to retail tobacco outlets.[54,55] National education organizations issued model laws and policies that school boards may adopt to improve the nutritional value of school meals and to encourage physical activity. In the 1990s and the first years of the new century, state governors, legislators, and other elected officials sponsored novel legislative and regulatory approaches to address youth obesity,[56] access to cancer screening and counseling,[57] and children's oral health.

Stimulated in part by the autumn 2001 terrorist and anthrax attacks, public health law specialists prepared a draft model law to help states assess their legal preparedness for public health emergencies;[58] developed and disseminated related training courses for state and local public health, law enforcement, and emergency management professionals; issued public health law bench books for state judges;[59] and trained state attorney generals' lawyers, as well as healthcare providers' legal counsel, in the legal framework that governs their clients during public health emergencies.

In 2004, the Turning Point initiative published the first-ever model state public health law for interested states to use in shaping general powers for their public health agencies consistent with the public health system reforms sparked by the landmark 1988 Institute of Medicine (IOM) report *The Future of Public Health* and reinvigorated by the 2003 IOM report *The Future of the Public's Health in the 21st Century*.[60] The Turning Point's vision was reflected in Alaska's enactment of 2005 legislation making sweeping changes in the general legal authorities of the state's public health agency.[61]

The creativity represented in these and other innovations suggests that law will gain potency as a public health tool in the early decades of the 21st century. That prospect is heightened by the rapid growth in research that makes the scientific case for law as an effective public health tool. In the late 1990s and early 2000s, major peer-reviewed biomedical and public health journals increasingly contained articles reporting on the findings of empirical research on the impact of law on the health of the public. This literature contains the work of the Task Force for Community Preventive Services[62] and of the Cochrane Collaboration,[63] independent organizations that conduct systematic reviews (or meta-analyses) of published peer-reviewed research on public health interventions.

The Task Force began its work in 1996, the Cochrane Collaboration in 1993. By March 2005, the two organizations had issued recommendations for a broad spectrum of public health interventions, including vaccination requirements for child care and for school and college attendance; standing orders for adult vaccination; 0.08% blood alcohol concentration laws (and lower levels for young or inexperienced drivers); sobriety checkpoints; child-safety-seat laws; primary (versus secondary) enforcement of safety-belt laws; and community water fluoridation.

The Task Force and Cochrane findings gave important scientific support to the role of laws as a type of public health intervention, a type of credibility unimagined at the dawning of the 20th century. This new support, combined with the energetic spirit of innovation evident in public health law in recent years, are powerful signs that law will make at least as great a contribution to the public's health in the 21st century as it did in the century just ended.

Conclusion

This perspective testifies to the powerful contribution law can make to the public's health and to the dynamic nature of law as a public health tool. As a tool, law evolved throughout the 20th century in tandem with evolution in the threats posed to the public's health and along with rapid developments in the science and practice of public health. In addition, evidence clearly exists of the contribution public health has made to law. Perhaps the best example is the 1905 *Jacobson v. Massachusetts* ruling that addressed, in part, the legal boundaries of individual autonomy. Public health and law, to put it differently, are sibling fields that develop in close interrelation with each other.

A current thrust in public health and medicine is toward "evidence-based" practice. This perspective, taken together with the other chapters in this volume, evidences a rich and growing empirical basis for designing and applying laws and legal tools to address specific goals in public-health practice. Law-based interventions, like other policy-based or "structural" interventions, have great potential to improve the public's health because, for the most part, they apply to broad populations and can be designed to restrict individual behavior minimally by shaping the environment in which each of us makes key decisions affecting our health and that of our families and communities.

The opening decades of the 21st century are virtually certain to be a golden age in public health law. The confluence of rapidly unfolding public health threats (for example, the potential for pandemic influenza and the accelerating toll of chronic diseases), equally rapid gains in scientific knowledge, and developments in U.S. jurisprudence, collectively create new opportunities and demands for public health interventions that can benefit broad populations in ways that are effective, cost-effective, and respectful of the individual rights enshrined in the Constitution—the last perhaps being the highest standard against which to judge applications of law to public health practice needs and priorities.

We thank William Bailey, D.D.S., M.P.H.; William Maas, D.D.S., M.P.H.; Scott Presson, D.D.S., M.P.H.; and Karen Sicard, M.P.H., R.D.H., all with CDC's National Center for Chronic Disease Prevention and Health Promotion; Ann Dellinger, Ph.D.,

M.P.H., and David Sleet, Ph.D., F.A.A.H.B., both with CDC's National Center for Injury Prevention and Control, and Julie Ross, M.P.H., with the National Highway Traffic Safety Administration, for their important contributions to this perspective. We also thank Kim McWhorter, Emory University Rollins School of Public Health and School of Law, for her valuable research and editorial assistance.

References

1. Summers J. *Soho—A History of London's Most Colourful Neighborhood.* Bloomsbury. London: Bloomsbury Publishing Ltd, 1989:113–7.
2. CDC. Ten great public health achievements—United States, 1900–1999. *MMWR* 1999;48: 241–3. Available at http://www.cdc.gov/mmwr/preview/mmwrhtml/00056796.htm. Accessed April 2, 2006.
3. Powell JH. *Bring Out Your Dead: The Great Plague of Yellow Fever in Philadelphia in 1793.* Philadelphia: University of Pennsylvania Press, 1993.
4. Ambrose SE. *Undaunted Courage.* New York: Simon & Schuster, 1997.
5. CDC. Achievements in public health, 1900–1999: control of infectious diseases. *MMWR* 1999;48:621–9. Available at http://www.cdc.gov/mmwr/preview/mmwrhtml/mm4829a1 .htm.Accessed April 2, 2006.
6. Armstrong GL, Conn LA, Pinner, RW. Trends in infectious disease mortality in the United States during the 20th century. *JAMA* 1999;281:61–6.
7. CDC. Achievements in public health: impact of vaccines universally recommended for children—United States, 1900–1998. *MMWR* 1999;48:243–8. Available at http://www .cdc.gov/mmwr/preview/mmwrhtml/00056803.htm. Accessed April 2, 2006. CDC. Achievements in public health, 1900–1999: control of infectious diseases. *MMWR* 1999; 48:621–629. Available at http://www.cdc.gov/mmwr/preview/mmwrhtml/mm4829a1 .htm. Accessed April 2, 2006.
8. Shattuck L. *Report of the Massachusetts Sanitary Committee, 1850.* Available at http: //biotech.law.lsu.edu/cphl/history/books/index.htm. Accessed March 23, 2006.
9. Pub L 410 (1944).
10. Malone KM, Hinman AR. Vaccination mandates: the public health imperative and individual rights. In: Goodman RA, Rothstein MA, Hoffman RE, Lopez W, Matthews GW, Foster KL, eds. *Law in Public Health Practice.* 1st ed. New York: Oxford University Press, 2003:262–84 (citing Duffy J. *J Hist Med Allied Sci*).
11. Hodge JG Jr, Gostin LO. School *Vaccination Requirements: Historical, Social, and Legal Perspectives.* Baltimore: Center for Law and the Public's Health, 2000. Available at http: //www.publichealthlaw.net/Research/PDF/vaccine.pdf. Accessed March 27, 2006.
12. *Jacobson v Massachusetts*, 197 US 11, 25 S Ct 358 (1905).
13. Parmet WE, Scott C, Hodge JG Jr, Nahmias DE, DeMaria A Jr, Rees CM. Plenary program: *Jacobson v. Massachusetts. J Law Med Ethics*, 2005;33(Suppl):24–7.
14. 42 USC §§300aa–300aa9 (2006).
15. 42 USC §1396s (2006).
16. Pub L 59-384, 34 Stat 768 (1906).
17. 21 USC §§301–399 (2006).
18. CDC. Achievements in public health, 1900–1999: motor vehicle safety—a 20th century public health achievement. *MMWR* 1999:48:369–74. Available at http://www.cdc.gov/ mmwr/preview/mmwrhtml/mm4818a1.htm. Accessed April 2, 2006.
19. National Safety Council. *Injury Facts.* Itasca, IL: National Safety Council Press, 2004.

20. Evans L. *Traffic Safety*. Bloomfield Hills, MI: Science Serving Society, 2004.

21. NHTSA. Table 13. Persons killed, by highest blood alcohol concentration (BAC) in the crash, 1982–2004. *Traffic Safety Facts 2004: A Compilation of Motor Vehicle Crash Data from the Fatality Analysis Reporting System and the General Estimates System*. Washington, DC: NHTSA, 2004:32 (DOT-HS-809–919). Available at http://www-nrd.nhtsa .dot.gov/pdf/nrd-30/NCSA/TSFAnn/TSF2004.pdf. Accessed April 7, 2006.

22. CDC. *10 Leading Causes of Death, United States (2002)*. Available at http://webapp .cdc.gov/cgi-bin/broker.exe. Accessed November 22, 2005.

23. CDC. *10 Leading Causes of Unintentional Injury Deaths, United States (2002)*. Available at http://webapp.cdc.gov/cgi-bin/broker.exe. Accessed November 22, 2005.

24. Institute of Medicine. *Reducing the Burden of Injury: Advancing Prevention and Treatment*. Washington, DC: National Academy Press, 1999.

25. Pub L 89-563, 80 Stat 718 (1966).

26. 23 USC §§402–412 (2006).

27. Pub L 102-240, 105 Stat 1914 (1991).

28. 23 USC §158 (2006).

29. Waller PF. Public health's contribution to motor vehicle injury prevention. *Am J Prev Med* 2001:21:3–4.

30. NHTSA. Overview. *Traffic Safety Facts, 2003 Data*. Washington, DC: NHTSA, 2005 (DOT HS 809 767). Available at http://www-nrd.nhtsa.dot.gov/pdf/nrd-30/NCSA/TSF2003/ 809767.pdf. Accessed April 10, 2006.

31. NHTSA. Laws: strengthening child passenger safety laws. *Traffic Safety Facts*. Washington, DC: NHTSA, 2003. Available at http://www.nhtsa.dot.gov/people/injury/Newfact-sheet03/fact-sheets04/Laws-CPS.pdf#search='Strengthening%20Child%20 Passenger%20Safety%20Laws'. Accessed April 10, 2006.

32. CDC. Achievements in public health, 1900–1999: fluoridation of drinking water to prevent dental caries. *MMWR* 1999:48:933–40. Available at http://www.cdc.gov/mmwr/preview/mmwrhtml/mm4841a1.htm. Accessed April 2, 2006.

33. CDC. Engineering and administrative recommendations for water fluoridation, 1995. *MMWR* 1995:44(RR-13). Available at http://www.cdc.gov/mmwr/preview/mmwrhtml/ 00039178.htm. Accessed April 2, 2006.

34. CDC. Recommendations for using fluoride to prevent and control dental caries in the United States. *MMWR* 2001;50(RR-14). Available at http://www.cdc.gov/mmwr/preview/ mmwrhtml/rr5014a1.htm. Accessed April 2, 2006.

35. CDC. Oral Health Resources. *Fluoridation Statistics 2000: Status of Water Fluoridation by State*. Available at http://www.cdc.gov/OralHealth/factsheets/fl-stats-states2000 .htm. Accessed June 27, 2005.

36. Mass Gen Laws, Ch 111 §8C (2005).

37. Ohio Rev Code Ann §6109.20 (2006).

38. Association of State and Territorial Dental Directors. *Best Practice Approaches for State and Community Oral Health Programs*. Jefferson City, MO: Association of State and Territorial Dental Directors, 2003.

39. Nev Rev Stat Ann §445A.055 (2005).

40. 42 USC §300f–300j-26 (2006).

41. American Dental Association. *Fluoridation Facts*. Available at http://www.ada.org/public/topics/fluoride/facts/fluoridation_facts.pdf. Accessed June 27, 2005.

42. Block LE. Antifluoridationists persist: the constitutional basis for fluoridation, *J Public Health Dent* 1896;46:188–9 (cited in American Dental Association Fluoridation Facts). Available at http://www.ada.org/public/topics/fluoride/facts/fluoridation_facts.pdf. Accessed June 27, 2005.

43. Gostin LO. *Public Health Law*. Berkeley: University of California Press, 2000.
44. *Larsen v General Motors Corp*, 391 F 2d 495 (1968).
45. *Jew Ho v. Williamson et al.*, 103 F. 10 (U.S. Court of Appeals 1900).
46. *Souvannarath v Hadden*, 95 Cal App 4th 1115 (2002).
47. 23 USC 402–412 (2006).
48. National Highway Traffic Safety Administration. *Evaluation of the Repeal of Motorcycle Helmet Laws in Kentucky and Louisiana*. Available at http://www.nhtsa.dot.gov/people/injury/pedbimot/motorcycle/kentuky-la03/. Accessed November 25, 2005.
49. Insurance Institute for Highway Safety/Highway Loss Data Institute. *Helmet Use Laws*. Available at http://www.hwysafety.org/laws/state_laws/helmet_use.html. Accessed November 30, 2005.
50. Mokdad AH, Marks JS, Stroup DF, Gerberding JL. Actual causes of death in the United States, 2000, as corrected. *JAMA* 2004:291:1238–45 [corrected in *JAMA* 2005:293:293–4].
51. McKenna MT, Michaud CM, Murray CJ, Marks JS. Assessing the burden of disease in the United States using disability-adjusted life years. *Am J Prev Med* 2005:28:415–23.
52. Mensah GA, Goodman RA, Zaza S, et al. Law as a tool for preventing chronic diseases: expanding the range of effective public health strategies. *Prev Chronic Dis* 2004;1:1–8.
53. Lamson E, Colman V. *Nutrition and Physical Activity: A Policy Resource Guide*. Olympia, WA: Washington State Department of Health, 2004. Available at http://www.doh.wa.gov/cfh/steps/publications/nutrition_activity_policy_guide_final.pdf. Accessed April 2, 2006.
54. Mair JS, Pierce MW, Teret SP. *The Use of Zoning to Restrict Fast Food Outlets: A Potential Strategy to Combat Obesity*. October 2005. Available at http://www.publichealth law.net/Zoning%20Fast%20Food%20Outlets.pdf#search='The%20Use%20of%20 Zoning%20to%20Restrict%20Fast%20 Food%20Outlets'. Accessed April 2, 2006.
55. Ashe M, Jernigan D, Kline R, Galaz R. Land use planning and the control of alcohol tobacco, firearms, and fast food restaurants. *Am J Public Health* 2003;93:1404–8.
56. CDC. *CDC State Legislative Information: Search for Bills*. Available at http://apps. nccd.cdc.gov/DNPALeg/. Accessed November 25, 2005.
57. Ala Code §27-50-4 (2005).
58. Center for Law and the Public's Health. *Model State Public Health Laws*. Available at http://www.publichealthlaw.net/Resources/Modellaws.htm#MSEHPA. Accessed November 25, 2005.
59. Schofield AR, Chezem LL. *Public Health Law Bench Book for Indiana Courts*. Available at http://www.publichealthlaw.info/INBenchBook.pdf. Accessed November 25, 2005.
60. Public Health Statute Modernization National Excellence Collaborative. *Turning Point: Model State Public Health Act*. Available at http://www.hss.state.ak.us/dph/improving/turningpoint/PDFs/MSPHAweb.pdf, Accessed November 25, 2005.
61. Alaska Stat §§18.15.390–18.15.395 (2005).
62. The Community Guide. Available at http://www.thecommunityguide.org. Accessed September 25, 2006.
63. The Cochrane Collaboration. Available at http://www.cochrane.org. Accessed September 25, 2006.

Section I

Legal Basis for Public Health Practice

Chapter 1

THE LAW AND THE PUBLIC'S HEALTH: THE FOUNDATIONS

Lawrence O. Gostin, F. Ed Thompson,* and Frank P. Grad

The law has played a vital role in public health since the founding of the Republic when the principal threats to health and safety were epidemic diseases. Law creates public health agencies, designates their mission, provides their authority, and limits their actions to preserve a sphere of freedom protected by the Constitution. The law, therefore, always has been vital to public health. The importance of the field of public health law, however, never has been more apparent than now, after the dramatic public health events in the beginning of the 21st century: the anthrax attacks through the U.S. Postal Service in 2001 and the looming threat of bioterrorism they underscored; the spread of West Nile virus in the Western Hemisphere; the smallpox vaccination efforts of 2003; the appearance of severe acute respiratory syndrome during 2002–2003; the growing epidemic of obesity and its consequences in relation to other chronic disease problems, such as diabetes, hypertension, and heart disease; the continued emergence of new environmental hazards; the gathering shadow of pandemic influenza; and natural disasters, such as Hurricane Katrina in August 2005.

In each of these 21st-century "shadows on the land," legal issues figured prominently in—and sometimes complicated—protection of the public's health. These threats, old and new, teach us about the importance of a strong public health infrastructure, and they remind us of the need for appropriate public health powers.

*The findings and conclusions in this chapter are those of the author(s) and do not necessarily represent the views of the U.S. Department of Health and Human Services or the Centers for Disease Control and Prevention.

The acute events and emergent threats of the early 21st century forcefully reminded us that—unlike with lifestyle-related health problems, such as heart disease, lung cancer, and stroke—individuals often can do little or nothing to protect themselves against these health threats and must depend on the actions of society, and of government in particular, to protect their health. With this increased recognition of the need for appropriate public health powers comes increased need for balance. Public health laws, of course, are about not only power but also restraint. To be effective, public health officials need to act with strong scientific evidence and with fairness and toleration.

In this chapter, we present the foundations of the integral relations between law and public health practice, including definition, infrastructure, constitutional underpinnings, and powers. For more in-depth examinations of selected foundational topics, we refer readers to additional texts and resources.[1–4] Before turning to a careful exploration of the legal basis of public health, we examine fundamental aspects of the field of public health.

The Population Basis for Public Health

Defining Public Health

The effort to capture the entire spectrum of public health activity in one definition is complex and challenging. The field of public health is broad, and the mix of disciplines makes justice difficult to bestow on all of them. The definition of public health in the 1988 report *The Future of Public Health* from the Institute of Medicine (IOM) has gained wide acceptance: "Public Health is what we, as a society, do collectively to assure conditions in which people can be healthy." The IOM then identifies public health's mission as "fulfilling society's interest in assuring conditions in which people can be healthy."[5]

Several important and distinctive concepts are packed into the mission phrase: public health's collective action on society's behalf ("fulfill *society's interest*" and "*assuring* the conditions"), a broad view of the determinants of health ("the *conditions in which* people can be healthy"), and an emphasis on populations rather than individuals ("in which *people* can be healthy"). In addition to these characteristics, public health is unique among health-related fields for the value and emphasis it places on prevention, protection, community health, education, and partnerships with varied organizations.

The mandate to "fulfill society's interests" and "assure" healthy conditions and quality services places public health in frequent and compelling contact with the legal system. Likewise, "the conditions in which people can be healthy" recognizes the salience of the root causes or determinants of health—particularly those that may not be obvious, immediate, or perceived to be within the purview of other parts of the health system. In practice, this requires attention to the prevention of disease (not just its detection and treatment) and to a view of disease that acknowledges the health implications of income, education, employment, and community.

Although the public health system often works in close partnership with the medical-care system to protect the public's health, many aspects of public health are not only essential but also unique. Different approaches to tobacco are a good example of these complementary approaches. Tobacco, the underlying cause of one of every five deaths in the United States, is a serious public health threat and causes a variety of diseases in smokers and in others exposed to tobacco. The medical-care system focuses on treating the emphysema, lung cancer, and heart disease that result from tobacco use and provides individual counseling and perhaps assistance with smoking cessation (e.g., prescribing a nicotine patch for a smoker who wants to quit). The public health approach, on the other hand, seeks to change social norms about smoking and aims to prevent tobacco addiction in the first place, especially among children.

Both approaches are needed, but they emphasize different points on the disease continuum (from prevention to treatment), and thus the two parts of the system employ different tools. In the medical-care system, health-care providers focus on diagnosing and treating an individual patient. In the public health system, the "patient" is the community or an entire population. Diagnosis focuses on identifying risk factors and preventing disease or its consequences, and treatment might involve policy changes, media campaigns, environmental changes, or enforcement of regulations. Medical care usually is offered according to a medical model in selected settings, such as physicians' offices, hospitals, and clinics, whereas public health involves numerous disciplines (e.g., medicine, epidemiology, economics, law, political science, sociology, psychology, and anthropology), settings (e.g., schools and workplaces), and tools (e.g., the news media; regulatory authority; and changes to policies, the environment, and individual behavior).

Public health also is unique in its status as a common good.[6] National disease surveillance systems that track the health status of populations, laboratory tests and techniques that track strains of disease, and teams of epidemiologists and other scientists that can be deployed when outbreaks occur illustrate functions that no single private or nonprofit entity could support and for which few, if any, market-based financial incentives exist. In this sense, the results of public health activities are truly common goods that benefit all of us, whether we are wealthy or poor, insured or uninsured, urban or rural, healthy or sick.

Public Health's Infrastructure

The 1988 and 2003 IOM reports found disarray in the public health system and suggested three core functions for public health as a new framework to return public health to its roots: assessment, policy development, and assurance.[5,7] The law is important in establishing each of these three vital roles within public health agencies. These three overlapping functions encompass the entire spectrum of public health activity, from surveillance functions that detect and monitor disease and injury patterns, to developing policies that promote health and prevent disease and disability, to ensuring that data-driven interventions address the health issues identified through assessment activities. The cycle is renewed continuously as assessment activities detect whether progress has been made, leading to a subsequent set of policy actions, interventions, and reassessment (Figure 1-1).

These core functions, in turn, were further delineated into more specific "essential services" of public health,[8] which since have formed the basis for planning docu-

Figure 1.1. The Core Functions of Public Health
Source: Adapted from the Washington State Public Health Improvement Plan

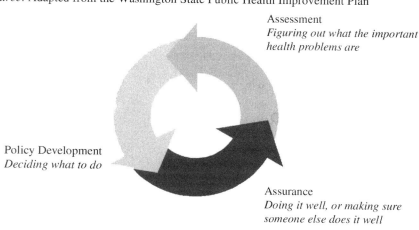

Assessment
Figuring out what the important health problems are

Policy Development
Deciding what to do

Assurance
Doing it well, or making sure someone else does it well

ments (such as *Healthy People 2010*[9]) and ongoing research on the status of public health practice. The "public health system" responsible for these core functions and essential services includes a wide array of public and private entities, directly health-related and otherwise. Its core is the government public health system. Legally and functionally, this core has three equal and interdependent components: local, state, and federal public health agencies. Often characterized as the "three-legged stool" of public health, the government public health system's effectiveness depends on the strength of all three "legs" and on recognition by each of the distinct and critical roles of the others.

Beyond the government public health system, clinical-care providers, health-care organizations, pharmaceutical and medical device companies, charitable foundations, academic institutions, health-care payers, and others not even directly involved in health care constitute the larger public health system, as described by the IOM in its 2003 report, *The Future of the Public's Health in the 21st Century*.[9]

Although the public health system indeed has been underfunded for decades, its contributions have been impressive. As British physician Geoffrey Rose[10] observed:

> Measures to improve public health, relating as they do to such obvious and mundane matters as housing, smoking, and food, may lack the glamour of high-technology medicine, but what they lack in excitement they gain in their potential impact on health, precisely because they deal with the major causes of common disease and disabilities.

Public health's most dramatic accomplishment is the extension of the average life span, from 45 years at the turn of the 20th century to nearly 80 years today. Of these 35 years of "extra" longevity, only 5 or so can be attributed solely to advances in clinical medicine. Public health can take a large part of the credit for the other 30 years, thanks to improvements in sanitation, health education, development of effective vaccines, and other advances (Box 1-1).[11] Current U.S. Census forms include three digits for recording a respondent's age—a tribute to the growing number of centenarians among us, now estimated to be approximately 70,000 Americans. For most of these achievements, law has played a vital role in relation to, for example, compulsory vaccinations, food and drug safety, regulation of the water supply, personal-control measures for contagious diseases, tobacco regulation (taxation, labeling and advertising, and tort actions), and regulation of car design and seatbelt use. Overall, these achievements highlight public health's protective role—the constant struggle to identify and minimize risk, whether emanating from our own behaviors or from behaviors of others; the environments in which we live and work; our genetic legacy; or, as is often the case, some interplay among these.

Future Challenges

Of course, "fulfilling society's interest" is a task as immense as protecting the public's health (not only in the United States but also around the globe), and much remains undone. In the decades ahead, we are bound to face both known and unanticipated challenges. Known challenges[12] include the following:

- Achieving meaningful *changes in health-care systems*, including instituting a rational health-care system that balances equity, cost, and quality; and eliminating health disparities among racial and ethnic groups.
- Focusing on the chronologic milestones of *childhood and old age* by investing in children's emotional and intellectual development and working to achieve not only a longer life span but also a longer "health span" that offers a better quality of life, mobility, and independence for the growing population of seniors.
- Addressing the *risks posed by our lifestyles and the environment*, such as incorporating healthy eating and physical activity into daily life (to combat the twin epidemics of obesity and diabetes, among many other adverse health outcomes); responding to emerging infectious diseases (including new pathogens spread by travel, migration, and commerce, as well as microbial adaptation sped along by inappropriate use of antibiotics); and balancing economic growth with protection of our environment.
- Applying current knowledge and unlocking persistent mysteries about *the brain and human behavior* by recognizing and addressing the contributions of mental health to overall health and well-being and reducing the toll of violence (including homicide, suicide, and other types of violence) in society.
- Exploring *new scientific frontiers* and applying *new scientific knowledge* (e.g., the mapping of the human genome) equitably, ethically, and responsibly. In many of these areas—including child development, mental health, obesity and physical activity, the environment, bioterrorism, and aging—promising, science-based interventions are available and deserve support and broader implementation. In other areas—particularly the needs to delineate a rational health-care system, eliminate health disparities, curb violence, and manage new genetic knowledge—the course of action is less clear or even potentially divisive.

BOX 1-1. A Century of Public Health Accomplishment—United States, 1900–1999

Thirty years of increased longevity
Vaccinations
Healthier mothers and babies
Family planning
Safer and healthier foods
Fluoridation of drinking water
Control of infectious diseases
Decline in deaths from heart disease and stroke
Recognition of tobacco use as a health hazard
Motor vehicle safety
Safer workplaces

Source: CDC. Ten great public health achievements—United States, 1900–1999. *MMWR* 1999;48:241–3.

As with past public health achievements, these future challenges will demand a blend of scientific innovation, technical and managerial expertise (especially regarding implementing community-level health programs), persuasion, courage, and the skillful application of legal principles and tools. Public health's unique perspective can alter how these policy debates are framed and interpreted. By understanding and applying legal tools and principles that already have helped secure public health's achievements in the past century, the public health field can accelerate improvements in the public's health for decades to come.

Conceptual Foundations for Relating Law to Public Health Practice

Public health law plays a unique role in ensuring the population's health. To demonstrate its importance, defining public health law and the public health law infrastructure are helpful.

Defining Public Health Law

Public health practice is framed by and draws on a broad spectrum of laws from all sources, including constitutions, legislative enactments, promulgated regulations, common law, and even treaties. These laws also represent foundational fields and legal disciplines, such as constitutional, property, criminal, and tort law, as well as specialty areas, such as environmental, food and drug, and occupational health law.

Some laws, such as those creating public health agencies and/or powers expressly delegated to those agencies (e.g., the power to quarantine or isolate individuals or to require disease reporting for public health surveillance) even might be considered primarily public health laws. One paradigm for viewing the relation between law and public health practice has been gaining acceptance and momentum over the past decade. This paradigm, which is itself referred to as "public health law," has framed this field primarily from a perspective of scholarship:

> Public health law is the study of the legal powers and duties of the state, in collaboration with its partners, to assure the conditions for people to be healthy (e.g., to identify, prevent, and ameliorate risks to health in the population) and the limitations on the power of the state to constrain the autonomy, privacy, liberty, proprietary, or other legally protected interests of individuals for the common good. The prime objective of public health law is to pursue the highest possible level of physical and mental health in the population, consistent with the values of social justice.[1] (p. 4)

This definition suggests seven essential determinants for the nexus of law and public health practice, which correspond with the characteristics of public health itself described in the previous section:

- *Government*: Public health activities are the primary (but not exclusive) responsibility of government. Government creates policy and enacts laws and regulations designed to safeguard community health.
- *Coercion and the limits on power*: Public health officials possess the power to coerce individuals and businesses to protect the community, rather than relying on a near universal ethic of voluntarism. However, constitutional safeguards of liberty limit these powers.
- *The public health system*: Public health agencies are at the center of a multisectoral public health system. Public health agencies can act as a catalyst for action by other government departments and stimulate, coordinate, and regulate nongovernment actors. The IOM focuses on five actors: health-care institutions, the community, businesses, the media, and academe.
- *Populations*: Public health focuses on the health of populations. Certainly, public health officials are concerned with access and quality in medical care, but their principal concern is to create the conditions in which communities can be healthy.
- *Communities*: Local entities such as churches, civic organizations, and health advocacy groups can contribute to their neighbors' health. Community involvement can effectively promote healthy activities.
- *Prevention*: The field of public health emphasizes prevention of injury and disease, as differentiated from their amelioration or cure. Many of public health's most potent activities are oriented toward prevention such as vaccination, health education, and seat belt regulation.
- *Social justice*: Social justice is central to the mission of public health. "Justice" requires the fair and proper administration of laws and has three important attributes of special relevance to public health law: nondiscrimination, fair procedures, and fair allocation of benefits and burdens.

The Public Health Infrastructure and the Law

The public health infrastructure includes public health laws (statutes principally at the state level that establish the mission, functions, powers, and structure of public health agencies) and laws about the public's health (laws and regulations that offer a variety of tools to prevent injury and disease and promote the public's health). Laws concerning public health practices are scattered across countless statutes and regulations at the state and local levels. Problems of antiquity, inconsistency, redundancy, and ambiguity often render these laws ineffective, or even counterproductive, in advancing the population's health. In particular, health codes frequently are outdated, constructed in layers over different periods of time, and highly fragmented among the 50 states and the territories.[13]

The Model State Emergency Health Powers Act (MSEHPA) was developed in late 2001 as a tool for lawmakers, policymakers, and public health officials to assess the adequacy of their legal authorities in relation to emergency preparedness and response needs. Additionally, the Turning Point Model State Public Health Act (TPMSPHA) was developed to help overcome the problems caused by the existing public health infrastructure and to move to a more modern system of public health regulation.

Model State Emergency Health Powers Act

In the aftermath of the events of September 11, 2001, the President and the Congress began to enhance the nation's emergency preparedness and response capacities and included strengthening of key aspects of the public health infrastructure. The Center for Law and the Public's Health at Georgetown University and Johns Hopkins University drafted the MSEHPA at the request of the Centers for Disease Control and Prevention and with review by members of national organizations representing governors, legislators, attorneys general, and health commissioners.[14] Because the power to act to preserve the public's health is constitutionally reserved primarily to the states as an exercise of their police powers, the MSEHPA is designed for state, not federal, legislative consideration. It provides the responsible state actors with a framework menu of the powers they need to detect and contain a potentially catastrophic disease outbreak while protecting individual rights and freedoms. The MSEHPA was introduced in whole or part through bills or resolutions in at least 44 states and the District of Columbia. At least 33 states have passed bills or resolutions that include provisions from or closely related to the act.[15]

A major purpose of the MSEHPA was to provide a framework allowing for the facilitation of the detection, management, and containment of public health emergencies while appropriately safeguarding personal and proprietary interests. The MSEHPA contains provisions giving rise to two kinds of public health powers and duties: those that exist in the pre-emergency environment (pre-declaration powers, including planning and surveillance) and a separate group of powers and duties that come into effect only after a state's governor declares a public health emergency (post-declaration powers, including management of property and protection of persons). Despite its relatively wide use across the country, the MSEHPA was controversial because it contains provisions authorizing the use of compulsory powers such as vaccination, isolation, and quarantine.[16]

The Turning Point Model State Public Health Act

The Turning Point Model State Public Health Act,[15] drafted by a consortium of state and federal partners, adopts contemporary reform principles to modernize public health law. These reforms aim to define the mission and functions of public health agencies, afford a full range of powers to those agencies, and impose limits on those powers to safeguard personal liberties.

Define the mission and functions. Broad and well-considered statements of mission and functions are important for organizational, political, and legal reasons. From an organizational perspective, these statements establish the purposes or goals of public health agencies, thereby informing and influencing the activities of government. From a political perspective, they provide a measure of the kinds of activities that are politically sanctioned. From a legal perspective, courts defer to statements of legislative intent, and may permit a broad range of activities consistent with the statutory language.

Provide a full range of powers. Although voluntary cooperation is vital to public health officials, they need a full range of powers to ensure compliance with health and safety standards. Officials in many states can choose either exercising draconian authority, such as deprivation of liberty, or refraining from coercion at all. Public health officials need a more flexible set of tools, ranging from incentives and minimally coercive interventions to personally restrictive measures.

Impose limits on powers. Public health statutes should carefully balance power exercised for the common good with restraints on power to protect personal freedom. Restraint on power has both substantive and procedural aspects. Substantively, state statutes should articulate clear criteria for the exercise of public health powers based on objective risk assessments. Procedurally, public health statutes should require fair processes whenever deprivation exists of a personal, proprietary, or other legally protected interest.

Law reform, of course, cannot guarantee better public health. However, by crafting a consistent and uniform approach, carefully delineating the mission and functions of public health agencies, designating a range of flexible powers, and specifying the criteria and procedures for using those powers, the law can become a catalyst, rather than an impediment, to reinvigorating the public health system.

Law as a Tool to Safeguard the Public's Health

Laws regarding public health practice constitute the foundations for public health practice while providing tools for public health officials. At least seven models exist for legal intervention designed to prevent injury and disease and promote the public's health. Although legal interventions can be effective, they often raise social, ethical, or constitutional concerns that warrant careful study.

Model 1 is the power to tax and spend. This power, found in federal and state constitutions, provides government with an important regulatory technique. The power to spend enables government to set conditions for the receipt of public funds. For example, the federal government grants highway funds to states on condition they set the drinking age at 21 years.[17] Similarly, federal spending for water treatment works imposes standards for maintenance and safety. The power to tax provides strong inducements to engage in beneficial behavior or refrain from risk behavior. For example, taxes on cigarettes significantly reduce smoking, particularly among young people.

Model 2 is the power to alter the informational environment. Government can add its voice to the marketplace of ideas through health promotion activities such as health communication campaigns; by providing relevant consumer information through labeling requirements; and by limiting harmful or misleading information through regulation of commercial advertising of unsafe products (e.g., cigarettes and alcoholic beverages).

Model 3 is the power to alter the built environment. The design of the built or physical environment can hold great potential for addressing the major health threats facing the community (e.g., planning, zoning, and other land use standards). Environments can be designed to promote livable cities and facilitate health-affirming behavior by, for example, encouraging more active lifestyles, improving nutrition, reducing violence, and increasing social interactions.[18]

Model 4 is the power to reduce socioeconomic disparities. A strong and consistent finding of epidemiologic research is that socioeconomic status is correlated with morbidity, mortality, and functioning. These empirical findings have persisted across time and cultures and remain viable.[19]

Model 5 is direct regulation of individuals (e.g., seatbelt and motorcycle helmet laws), professionals (e.g., licenses), or businesses (e.g., inspections, certifications, and occupational safety standards). Public health officials regulate pervasively to reduce risks to the population.

Model 6 is indirect regulation through the tort system. Tort litigation can provide strong incentives for businesses to engage in less risky activities. Litigation has been used as a tool of public health to influence manufacturers of automobiles, cigarettes, and firearms. Litigation resulted in safer automobiles; reduced advertising and promotion of cigarettes to young people; and encouraged at least one manufacturer (Smith & Wesson) to develop safer firearms.

Model 7 is deregulation. The impact of laws sometimes may be detrimental to public health and may impede effective action. For example, criminal laws proscribe the possession and distribution of sterile syringes and needles. These laws, therefore, make engagement in HIV-prevention activities more difficult for public health officials.

The government, then, can apply many legal "levers" to prevent injury and disease and promote the public's health. Legal interventions can be highly effective and need to be part of the public health officer's arsenal. At the same time, legal interventions can be controversial, raising important ethical, social, constitutional, and political issues. These conflicts are complex, important, and fascinating for students of public health.

The Constitutional Underpinnings for Uses of Law in Public Health Practice

No inquiry is more important to public health than understanding the role of government in the constitutional design. If, as we have suggested, laws in public health practice principally address government's assurance of the conditions for the population's health, then what activities must government undertake? The question is complex, requiring an assessment of duty (what government must do), authority (what government is empowered but not obligated to do), and limits (what government is prohibited from doing). In addition, this query raises a corollary question: Which government is to act? Some of the most divisive disputes in public health are among the federal government, the states, and the localities about which government has the power to intervene.

Government Duties to Ensure the Public's Health

Given the importance of government in maintaining public health (and many other communal benefits), one might expect the U.S. Constitution to create affirmative obligations for government to act. Yet, by standard accounts, the Constitution is cast purely in negative terms and generally has not been interpreted as granting, mandating, or otherwise conferring affirmative duties on government to act to improve public health. The Supreme Court remains faithful to this negative conception of the Constitution, even in the face of dire personal consequences. In *DeShaney v. Winnebago County Department of Social Services*, the Supreme Court held that government has no affirmative duty to protect citizens.[20] In that case, a 1-year-old child, Joshua DeShaney, was beaten so badly by his father that he was left profoundly retarded and had to be institutionalized. The social services department was aware of the abuse but took no steps to prevent further injuries to Joshua. This negative theory of constitutional design, although well accepted, is highly simplified and, in the words of Justice Blackmun, represents "a sad commentary upon American life and constitutional principles."

The Supreme Court recently applied this reasoning in the heart-wrenching case of *Castle Rock v. Gonzalez*, where the Court held that an individual who has obtained a restraining order does not have a constitutionally protected property interest in having the police enforce the restraining order when they have probable cause to believe it has been violated.[21] Rebecca Gonzalez obtained a restraining order against her husband, but the police ignored her repeated requests to enforce the order after he abducted their three children. The husband ultimately murdered the three children and committed suicide. The Court found that the state has no affirmative duty to protect citizens, even if the statute states that police must enforce restraining orders.

Federal Powers to Ensure the Conditions for Public Health

In theory, but not reality, the United States is a government of limited powers. The federal government possesses considerable authority to act and exerts extensive control in the realm of public health and safety. The Supreme Court, through an expansive interpretation of Congress's enumerated powers, has enabled the federal government to maintain a vast presence in public health—in matters ranging from biomedical research and provision of health care to control of infectious diseases, occupational health and safety, pure food and drugs, and environmental protection. The main constitutional powers for federal action in the realm of public health are the powers to tax and spend and to regulate interstate commerce.

At face value, the power to tax and spend has one overriding purpose: to raise revenue to provide for the good of the community. Without the ability to generate sufficient revenue, the legislature could not provide services such as transportation, education, medical services to the poor, sanitation, and environmental protection. The power to tax is also the power to regulate risk behavior and influence health-promoting activities. Broadly speaking, the tax code influences health-related behavior through tax relief and tax burdens. Tax relief encourages private health-promoting activity, and tax burdens discourage risk behavior.

Through various forms of tax relief, government provides incentives for private activities that it views as advantageous to community health. The tax code influences private health-related spending in many other ways: encouraging child care to enable parents to enter the work force; inducing investment in low-income housing; and stimulating charitable spending for research and care.

Taxation also regulates private behavior by economically penalizing risk-taking activities. Tax policy discourages a number of activities that government regards as unhealthy or dangerous. Consider excise or manufacturing taxes on tobacco, alcoholic beverages, or firearms. A public health threat caused by human behavior or business activity that cannot be influenced by the taxing power is difficult to imagine. Similarly, the spending power does not simply grant Congress the authority to allocate resources; it is also an indirect regulatory device. Congress may prescribe the terms on which it disburses federal money to the states.

More than any other enumerated power, the Commerce Clause affords Congress potent regulatory authority. The Commerce Clause gives Congress the power to regulate commerce "with foreign Nations, and among the several States, and with the Indian Tribes."[22] At face value, the Commerce Clause is limited to controlling the flow of goods and services across state lines. Yet, as interstate commerce has become ubiquitous, activities once considered purely local have come to have national effects and have accordingly come within Congress's commerce power. The Supreme Court's broad interpretation of the Commerce Clause has enabled national authorities to reach deeply into traditional realms of state public health power.

The Rehnquist Court, however, recast the Commerce Clause with an effect of gradually returning power from the federal government to the states. In the process, the Court held that Congress lacks the power to engage in social and public health regulation primarily affecting intrastate activities. For example, the Court has held that Congress lacks the power to regulate firearms near schools[23] and to provide a remedy for victims of sexual violence.[24]

However, the ultimate course and reach of the Rehnquist Court's federalism revolution is uncertain. For example, in *Gonzalez v. Raich*, the Court held that Congress' Commerce Clause authority includes the power to prohibit the local cultivation and use of marijuana for medical purposes in compliance with California law.[25] However, barely a week after *Raich* was decided, the Court declined to hear federalism cases involving such key public health issues as federal authority over endangered species and homemade machine guns, suggesting perhaps that the Rehnquist Court's federalism revolution is on the wane.

Police Powers: State Power to Regulate
for the Public's Health and Safety

The "police power" is the most famous expression of the natural authority of sovereign governments to regulate private interests for the public good. One definition of the police power is:

> The inherent authority of the state (and, through delegation, local government) to enact laws and promulgate regulations to protect, preserve and promote the health, safety, morals, and general welfare of the people. To achieve these communal benefits, the state retains the power to restrict, within federal and state constitutional limits, private interests—personal interests in autonomy, privacy, association, and liberty as well as economic interests in freedom to contract and uses of property.[1] (pp. 47–48)

The linguistic and historical origins of the concept of "police" demonstrate a close association between government and civilization: *politia* (the state), *polis* (city), and *politeia* (citizenship).[26] "Police" was meant to describe powers that permitted sovereign government to control its citizens, particularly for promoting the general comfort, health, morals, safety, or prosperity of the public. The word had a secondary use as well: "the cleansing or keeping clean." This use resonates with early-20th-century public health connotations of hygiene and sanitation.

States exercise police powers to ensure that communities live in safety and security, in conditions conducive to good health, with moral standards, and, generally speaking, without unreasonable interference with human well-being. Police powers legitimize state action to protect and promote broadly defined social goods.

To achieve common goods, government is empowered to enact legislation, regulate, and adjudicate in ways that necessarily limit private interests, provided its actions are consistent with constitutional protections of life, liberty, and property. Thus, government has inherent power to interfere with personal interests in autonomy, privacy, association, and liberty as well as economic interests in ownership, uses of private property, and freedom to contract. State power to restrict private rights is embodied in the common law maxim *Sic utere tuo ut alienum non laedas* ("Use your own property in such a manner as not to injure that of another"). The maxim supports the police power, giving government authority to determine safe uses of private property to diminish risks of injury and ill-health to others.[27] More generally, the police power affords government the authority to keep society free from noxious exercises of private rights. The state retains discretion to determine what is considered injurious or unhealthful and the manner in which to regulate, consistent with constitutional protections of personal interests.

The police powers have enabled states and their subsidiary municipal and other local corporations to promote and preserve the public health in areas ranging from injury and disease prevention to sanitation, waste disposal, and water and air protections. Police powers exercised by the states include vaccination, isolation, and quarantine; inspection of commercial and residential premises; abatement of unsanitary conditions or other health nuisances; regulation of air and surface water contaminants; restriction on the public's access to polluted areas; promulgation of standards for pure food and drinking water; extermination of vermin; fluoridation of municipal water supplies; and licensure of physicians and other health-care professionals. These are the kinds of powers exercised daily by state and local public health agencies, as the following discussion demonstrates.

Public Health Powers: Regulation of Persons, Professionals, and Businesses

The powers available to public health officials in state statutes are pervasive, as the previous discussion of police powers illustrates. Although systematically examining the full scope and complexity of the public health powers is not possible, in this section we briefly outline selected principal authorities, many of which are detailed in subsequent chapters. These authorities group into the categories of the power to regulate persons, professionals, and businesses to safeguard the common good.

Regulation of Persons to Prevent Transmission of Communicable Disease: Autonomy, Privacy, and Liberty

Public health officials traditionally have had a variety of powers to control personal behavior for preventing transmission of a communicable disease. These powers are essential to ensure effective surveillance and response to epidemics. The exercise of compulsory powers, however, also can interfere with autonomy, privacy, and liberty. As a society, we face hard trade-offs between the common good and the rights of individuals to a sphere of freedom. This section illustrates three communicable disease powers: medical examination and testing, vaccination, and isolation and quarantine. In each case, although government has the authority to act, it must do so in accordance with procedures and standards set in federal and state constitutions.

Medical Examination and Testing

State laws empower public health officials to compel individuals to submit to testing or medical examination. Generally, testing and clinical examinations are not regarded as harsh legal requirements when the person may benefit. Some states require testing or examinations for sexually transmitted disease before marriage on the assumption that such testing can help prevent the spread of infection. Persons who engage in certain occupations, such as food handling, nursing, and teaching, are required to submit to testing and examinations to be permitted to practice their occupation. Again, the rationale is that these examinations are useful in preventing disease (e.g., food handlers tested for typhoid or salmonellosis).

Compelling a person to undergo testing or examination is an invasion of autonomy and privacy and, therefore, requires clear justification. Consider a Supreme Court decision that found compulsory drug testing of pregnant women to violate the Fourth Amendment's proscription against unreasonable searches and seizures. Because the test information was shared with the police, the Court found that testing lacked sufficient justification.[28] By analogy, a public health officer could not order a woman to undergo an examination for a sexually transmitted disease when no reason existed to believe she was infected.[29]

Compulsory Vaccination

Compulsory vaccination has become a major tool of public health practice, even though its constitutionality was not upheld by the U.S. Supreme Court until the seminal case of *Jacobson v. Massachusetts* in 1905.[30] The 100th anniversary of the Jacobson decision in 2005 resulted in intriguing scholarly debate.[31,32] The principle established in upholding required smallpox vaccination has been applied in other compulsory vaccination requirements, with particular applicability to childhood diseases such as measles, rubella, and mumps.

Virtually all states permit religious exemptions from compulsory vaccination. State Supreme Courts (with the exception of Mississippi[33]) have permitted legislatures to create exemptions for religious beliefs.[34] Even so, courts sometimes strictly construe religious exemptions, insisting that the belief against compulsory vaccination must be "genuine," "sincere," and an integral part of the religious doctrine.[35] A minority of states also permit exemptions based on conscientious objections.

Isolation and Quarantine

Public health officials have the power to isolate or quarantine persons who are infected or have been exposed and who pose a danger to the public's health. These are drastic remedies to prevent the spread of disease and are not used with any frequency today.

Still, the modern courts have required rigorous procedural due process before individuals can be isolated or quarantined. In *Greene v. Edwards*, the West Virginia Supreme Court reasoned that little difference exists between loss of liberty for mental health reasons and the loss of liberty for public health rationales.[36] Persons with an infectious disease, therefore, are entitled to similar procedural protections as persons with mental illness facing civil commitment. These procedural safeguards include the right to counsel, a hearing, and an appeal. Such rigorous procedural protections are justified by the fundamental invasion of liberty occasioned by long-term detention; the serious implications of erroneously finding a person dangerous; and the value of procedures in accurately determining the complex facts, which are important to predicting future dangerous behavior.

Regulation of Professions, Businesses, and Nuisances: Economic Liberty

Public health officials have powers to regulate professions and businesses to safeguard the public's health and safety. These powers are important to ensure that professionals and businesses act in reasonably competent and safe ways. Professionals and businesses, however, also sometimes contest the validity of these powers because they interfere with economic freedoms to use property, enter into contracts, and pursue a profession. This section discusses several important regulatory powers: licensure, inspections, and nuisance abatement.

Licensure as a Tool of Public Health

When a person is born, his or her birth certificate is likely to be signed by a licensed physician. When he or she dies, a mortician, also licensed by a state agency, buries him or her. Between birth and death, many other agencies with health responsibilities are regulated through the device of professional, occupational, or institutional licensure. A discussion of licensure therefore follows logically the subject of restrictions of the person because licensure is a restriction, an imposition of conditions limiting the person's freedom to carry on an activity, profession, occupation, or business of choice. The license requirement thus limits both the person's liberty and the use of the person's property. The imposition of such a restraint is justified because it protects the public health, safety, and welfare.[37] Public health law, as an early field of administrative law, has used licensure effectively for many generations. The occupations and callings in the general area of public health are among the earliest of licensed occupations.

Licensure, like other police powers, is an authority delegated by the legislature. It authorizes a licensing agency, either a board of health, a board of regents, or a special professional or occupational board, to promulgate rules relating to license applications and to control the licensed activity. The licensing law that delegates powers to the licensing agency may prescribe narrow or broad powers, granting it limited ministerial scope, such as collection of fees, or it may delegate broad regulatory powers to set rules for the exercise of the activity and giving the agency broad regulatory powers. The task does not end with granting licenses. The licensing agency generally has the continuing obligation to supervise the particular licensed activity. The obligation includes both the formulation of policy and the setting of standards in the light of what may be rapidly changing technology in the field and what may be changing needs of the people for protection.

Three major uses of licensure exist in areas related to public health. The first two are primarily matters of public health control or regulation. The first involves the licensing of people engaged in public health professions or occupations, such as physicians, dentists, nurses, physiotherapists, occupational therapists, psychologists, x-ray technologists, nutritionists, and other allied health professionals. The second category is institutional licensure, such as state licensure of hospitals, intermediate-care facilities, nursing homes, clinics and ambulatory-care centers, and other places where patient health services are delivered, such as clinical and x-ray laboratories, including pharmacies and other businesses directly involved in rendering services. The third category is business that is not directly involved in providing health care and goods related to health care, such as milk pasteurizing, food, energy, and public waste treatment.

Because licenses limit a person's freedom to engage in particular activities, and because licensure grants a particular group of persons and businesses something of a monopoly, broad licensing powers can be justified only to protect the public health, safety, and welfare. Thus, all of the constitutional limitations that apply to the police power clearly apply in general to the grant of licenses and to the scope and fairness of licensing regulations. Licensure, in particular, should not be used as a device for economic control to restrict access to the field.

Licenses are now generally regarded as protected property rights. A license to carry on a business or engage in an occupation or profession has great value to the person or business that holds it. The question of whether the government can revoke a license at any time, because it was once considered a mere privilege, no longer is valid.

A license, particularly in the field of institutional and occupational license in public health, incorporates valuable rights. Such a license is protected by due process and cannot be revoked or suspended without proper notice and hearing.

Searches and Inspections

Inspections are a common tool in public health designed to protect the population's health and safety. They are used to determine whether conditions exist that are deleterious to health and that violate public health standards or rules designed to bring about proper healthful performance of particular businesses, trades, and industries. Administrative inspections, unlike criminal law searches, are not intended primarily to uncover evidence to be used in the prosecution of a crime.

Although the emphasis of searches and inspections differs, for constitutional purposes courts generally have regarded inspections as a lesser species of searches that must be conducted with constitutional safeguards. Inspections may uncover violations of health standards, for which violators may be prosecuted and penalties imposed. Inspections span the entire field of public health–related law. Inspections may be conducted to ensure health and safety in health care (e.g., hospitals and pharmacies), agriculture, nuclear power, food and drugs, workplaces, restaurants, housing, plumbing, and child care.

Sometimes inspections are referred to as administrative searches, but this term may be confusing in light of the use of the term "search," which usually applies to criminal prosecutions. However, both searches and inspections are subject to review under the Fourth Amendment, which proscribes "unreasonable" searches and seizures. Before 1967, health and housing inspections generally were treated as reasonable searches, causing few constitutional problems. In *Camara v. Municipal Court of San Francisco* (1967), the U.S. Supreme Court held that the Fourth Amendment also applied to administrative searches and inspections.[38] Mr. Justice White, writing for the Court, held that a housing inspection was an intrusion on the privacy and security of individuals protected by the Fourth Amendment. Consequently, the public health authority usually must obtain a judicial warrant for an inspection. Inspection warrants, however, normally would be granted if the inspection is based either on the knowledge of an existing violation or on a clear standard for routine inspections.[39]

Although the Supreme Court has significantly changed the law of inspections, most inspections, both before and after the decision in 1967, were carried out without a warrant because owners or occupants of premises generally will consent to inspections. Moreover, some exceptions exist to the inspection warrant requirement. For example, an exception exists for "pervasively regulated" businesses (e.g., businesses selling firearms or alcoholic beverages). Pervasively regulated businesses have been regulated so thoroughly and for so long that persons who engage in the businesses have given up any "justifiable expectation of privacy."[40]

The Control of Nuisances and Dangerous Conditions

The vast field of tort law includes intentional or negligent injuries to persons and harm to property. It includes, for instance, medical malpractice and products liability affecting the manufacture of drugs and vaccines. Because the vastness and complexity of the broad area of torts prevents its general inclusion in this section, this section instead focuses predominantly on public, rather than private, remedies to nuisances.

The term "nuisance" covers both public and private nuisances. In the public health context, the primary concern is with public nuisances, a term that covers a variety of conditions that violate requirements of health and safety. A nuisance is a condition that constitutes an interference with the public right to pursue the normal conduct of life without the threat to health, comfort, and repose, ranging variously from matters of significant annoyance to conditions that impose significant risks to health and safety, such as excessive noise, stenches, filth that attracts insects or rodents, and chemical wastes that contaminate the water supply. Facilities that generate smoke, soot, chemical odors, or other substances regarded as air pollutants also may be public nuisances. All these examples represent potential interference with the rights of the public, and all are prohibited by law. Although any number of these examples would be treated in earlier days as common law nuisances, public nuisances are today defined by statute or ordinance and are considered public offenses subject to criminal prosecution.[41,42] Depending on the specific legislation, nuisances also may result in injunctive relief requiring "abatement."

The abatement of a public nuisance often involves the invasion of private property, so it must be clearly justified. If a health officer abates a nondangerous condition or acts excessively in light of the danger posed, then the purported abatement may constitute a "taking" or damaging of private property without due process of law, in violation of the Fourteenth Amendment. In such cases, the property owner may recover appropriate damages for the loss.[43]

The Future of Public Health Law

Public health law is experiencing a period of renaissance in the United States. The events of September 11, 2001, provoked a national debate about the adequacy of the public health law infrastructure, and both federal and state governments began to examine the need for emergency health powers legislation. More than this, spurred on by public debate and academic research, national and state authorities are awakening to the possibilities of law reform to improve the public's health.

However, because the interest in public health law is due at least partly to fear of a terrorist attack, a risk exists that civil liberties will be inappropriately sacrificed in the name of national security. Although control over persons or property is necessary to promote the common good in a well-regulated society, such actions have negative implications. Coercive measures infringe individual rights—autonomy, privacy, liberty, and property. Laws in public health practice, especially during a time when society is at heightened risk, require careful examination of the trade-offs between collective goods and personal freedoms. Policymakers are realizing that effective laws relating to public health must be clear and consistent and afford strong and effective powers to public health officials. At the same time, a high-quality law must respect personal freedoms and treat groups with fairness and tolerance.

Thus, law is a means to achieving better health in a society, while simultaneously limiting the extent to which individual rights are sacrificed for the common good. The law, of course, cannot guarantee better public health. However, by crafting a consistent and uniform approach, carefully delineating the mission and functions of public health agencies, designating a range of flexible powers, specifying the criteria and procedures for using those powers, and protecting against discrimination and invasion of privacy, the law can become a catalyst, rather than an impediment, to reinvigorating the public health system.

References

1. Gostin LO. *Public Health Law: Power, Duty, Restraint.* 2nd ed. Berkeley and New York: University of California Press and Milbank Memorial Fund. In press, 2007.
2. Gostin LO. *Public Health Law and Ethics: A Reader.* Berkeley: University of California Press, 2002.
3. Grad FP. *Public Health Law Manual.* 3rd ed. Washington, DC: American Public Health Association, 2005.
4. Tobey JA. *Public Health Law: A Manual of Law for Sanitarians.* Baltimore: Williams & Wilkins, 1926.
5. Institute of Medicine. *The Future of Public Health.* Washington, DC: National Academy Press, 1988.
6. Gostin LO. Health of the people: the highest law? *J Law Med Ethics* 2004;32:509–15.
7. Institute of Medicine. *The Future of the Public's Health in the 21st Century.* Washington, DC: National Academy Press, 2003.
8. Baker EL, Melton RJ, Stange PV, et al. Health reform and the health of the public. *JAMA* 1994;272:1276–82.
9. Office of Disease Prevention and Health Promotion, US Department of Health and Human Services. *Healthy People 2010.* Available at http://www.healthypeople.gov. Accessed October 12, 2005.
10. Rose G. *The Strategy of Preventive Medicine.* Oxford: Oxford University Press, 1992:95–106.
11. CDC. Ten great public health achievements—United States, 1900–1999. *MMWR* 1999; 48:241–3.
12. Koplan JP, Fleming DW. Current and future public health challenges. *JAMA* 2000;284: 1696–8.
13. Gostin LO. Public health law reform. *Am J Public Health* 2001;91:1365–8.
14. Gostin LO, Sapsin JW, Teret SP, et al. The Model State Emergency Health Powers Act: planning and response to bioterrorism and naturally occurring infectious diseases. *JAMA* 2002; 288:622–8.
15. The Center for Law and the Public's Health. *Model State Public Health Laws: The Turning Point Model State Public Health Act.* Available at http://www.publichealthlaw.net/Resources/Modellaws.htm. Accessed October 12, 2005.
16. Gostin LO. Public health law in an age of terrorism: rethinking individual rights and common goods. *Health Aff* 2002;21:79–93.
17. *South Dakota v Dole,* 483 US 203 (1987).
18. Perdue WC, Stone LA, Gostin LO. The built environment and its relationship to the public's health: the legal framework. *Am J Public Health* 2003;93:1390–4.

19. Syme LS. Social and economic disparities in health: thoughts about intervention. *Milbank Q* 1998;76:493–505.
20. *DeShaney v Winnebago County Department of Social Services*, 489 US 189, 213 (1989).
21. *Castle Rock v Gonzalez*, 125 S Ct 2796 (2005).
22. US Constitution, Article I, §8.
23. *United States v Lopez*, 115 S Ct 1624 (1995).
24. *United States v Morrison*, 120 S Ct 1740 (2000).
25. *Gonzalez v Raich*, 125 S Ct 2195 (2005).
26. *Webster's Third New International Dictionary*, Unabridged. Springfield, MA: Merriam-Webster, 1986:1753.
27. *Commonwealth v Alger*, 7 Cush 53, 96 (Mass, 1851).
28. *Ferguson v City of Charleston*, 121 S Ct 1281 (2001).
29. *Irwin v Arrendale*, 17 Ga App 1, 5–6, 159 SE 2d 719, 724 (1967).
30. *Jacobson v Massachusetts*, 197 US 11 (1905).
31. Parmet WE, Goodman RA, Farber A. Individual rights versus the public's health—100 years. *N Engl J Med* 2005;352:652–4.
32. Gostin LO. *Jacobson v. Massachusetts* at 100 years: police power and civil liberties in tension. *Am J Public Health* 2005;95:576–81.
33. *Brown v Stone*, 378 So 2d 218, 223 (Miss 1979).
34. *Mason v General Brown Cent School Dist*, 851 F 2d 47 (2d Cir 1988).
35. *Berg v Glen Cove City School Dist*, 853 F Supp 651 (EDNY 1994).
36. *Greene v Edwards*, 263 SE 2d 661, 663 (1980).
37. Johnston PA. *Administrative Procedure: Occupational Licensing Boards 1*. Chapel Hill: University of North Carolina Press, 1953.
38. *Camara v Municipal Court of San Francisco*, 381 US 523 (1967).
39. *Marshall v Barlow's, Inc*, 436 US 307 (1978).
40. *Colonnade Catering v United States*, 397 US 72 (1970).
41. *Lawton v Steele*, 152 US 133 (1894).
42. State ex rel *Haas v Dionne*, 42 Or App 851, 601 P 2d 894 (1979).
43. *Peters v Township of Hopewell*, 534 F Supp 1324 (1982).

Chapter 2

THE STRUCTURE OF LAW IN PUBLIC HEALTH SYSTEMS AND PRACTICE

Richard A. Goodman,* Paula L. Kocher,*
Daniel J. O'Brien, and Frank S. Alexander

Public health practice in the United States is carried out by an estimated workforce of 448,000 persons who serve in government agencies at federal, state, and local levels.[1] At the federal level, examples of agencies with primary public health missions or some public health–related roles are the Centers for Disease Control and Prevention (CDC), the Food and Drug Administration (FDA), and the Environmental Protection Agency (EPA). Federal agencies have explicit, statutorily created regulatory powers passed by Congress; implemented by the Executive Branch; and interpreted by the federal judiciary to ensure compliance with the U.S. Constitution. Some of these agencies function as regulatory bodies; others do not. At the state and local levels, legislative bodies—including state legislatures—act under state constitutions to pass statutes creating state and local public health agencies and boards of health, articulating powers to ensure the public's health, and delegating public health–related powers to government subdivisions and an estimated 2912 local public health agencies.[2]

This chapter examines the structure of law underlying U.S. public health practice by focusing on the statutory basis of the federal and state/local infrastructure of the U.S. public health system, including creation of federal agencies having public health or related responsibilities and powers under the U.S. Constitution and, similarly, state and local agencies with public health roles, responsibilities, and powers. The chap-

* The findings and conclusions in this chapter are those of the author(s) and do not necessarily represent the views of the U.S. Department of Health and Human Services or the Centers for Disease Control and Prevention.

45

ter describes the structure of law and statutory basis of public health systems and practice in two main sections. The first section examines the statutory basis of public health practice at the federal level, and the second section explores this for state-level public health systems and practice. These sections also implicate certain key foundational legal concepts, including federalism and preemption, that are highly relevant to understanding the interplay between legislative enactments and public health practice at all levels.

Statutory Basis of Federal Public Health Practice

The federal government's statutorily created roles in public health practice date at least to 1796 when, on May 27 of that year, Congress passed the first National Quarantine Act, which addressed federal quarantine activities in relation to the states' enforcement of their own quarantine laws.[3] In the more than two centuries since then, Congress has acted under a core set of Constitutional provisions to pass numerous statutes providing for a broad spectrum of federal roles in U.S. public health practice. These statutes have provided for public health systems and the federal government's involvement in public health practice in at least three ways: (1) creation of a federal infrastructure in public health through, for example, the strategic and administrative framework of the U.S. Public Health Service (PHS), and the explication of authorities and powers for carrying out key public health functions (e.g., quarantine) under certain circumstances; (2) establishment of federal public health agencies with explicit regulatory authorities and functions (e.g., FDA and the Occupational Safety and Health Administration), public health nonregulatory agencies (e.g., CDC), and several other federal agencies that have major public health–related powers and duties (e.g., EPA and the National Highway Traffic Safety Administration); and (3) appropriation of funds to directly support federal agencies' work in public health or for federal agencies to disburse to the states for public health activities.

This section begins by providing a historical context for understanding the statutory basis for public health systems and practice at the level of the federal government. This historical context reviews selected milestones in Congressional legislation relating to public health. Following the historical context, the section briefly reviews the concepts of federalism and preemption, both of which are major determinants framing and modulating the relation between federal and state laws involving public health. The section then examines organizational schemes for, and provides examples of, more contemporary, federally enacted public health and related programs, mandates, powers, and practice activities.

Historic Milestones in Federal Public Health Legislation

In 1939, after Congress' creation of the Federal Security Agency and the transfer of PHS from its longstanding home in the Treasury Department to that new agency, then–Surgeon General Thomas Parran observed: "The past 141 years have witnessed the evolution of the Service from a small organization, devoted solely to the medical care of American merchant seamen, to a national health agency, broad in scope and manifold in its functions which affect directly or indirectly the health of the people."[3] Surgeon General Parran's perspective emphasized the historic scope and scale of federally legislated changes affecting public health in the United States dating from PHS's origins in 1798 and, as noted above, even earlier to at least 1796, when Congress passed the first national act on quarantine.

Milestone federal legislation involving public health included creation of federal public health infrastructure, establishment of federal public health agencies, appropriation of funds supporting federal and state public health activities, and explication of public health legal authorities and powers. From the nation's origins until nearly the middle of the 20th century, when the Public Health Service Act of 1944 (PHSA) was passed, these federal statutes constituted a broad range of public health interests. These interests included the federal government's uses of quarantine authorities, a federal role in a system of prepaid medical care for merchant seamen that ultimately evolved into part of PHS, promotion of smallpox vaccination, creation of a National Board of Health, health inspection of immigrants, regulation of biologics, fostering of cooperation with state and local public health agencies, response to the influenza pandemic of 1918–1919, creation of the National Institutes of Health (NIH), and addressing the nursing shortage during World War II (Table 2-1). One of these milestones, the early and subsequent enactment of federal quarantine authorities, illustrates clearly the formative and enduring influence of federal law on U.S. public health practice.

The first National Quarantine Act, an early piece of federal legislation involving public health, also implicated states' rights concerns.[3] This Act, passed by Congress on May 27, 1796, limited federal quarantine activities to any cooperation first requested by the states in enforcing their own quarantine laws. Enactment of this law followed debate within Congress focusing on states' rights and the issue of whether quarantine should be a function of the federal government or of the states. The first act was superseded by a second quarantine act in 1799 with language that strengthened the requirement for federal personnel to assist in enforcing state and local health laws.

On April 29, 1878, Congress passed a new National Quarantine Act, which created a "disease-intelligence system" managed at the federal level. The Act authorized the Supervising Surgeon General of the Marine Hospital Service to make rules and regulations for detaining ships either having cases of contagious diseases onboard or coming from foreign ports in which contagious diseases were present.[3] Consular officers in foreign ports were to report to the Surgeon General the existence of contagious diseases in those ports and the departure of ships from those ports bound for the United States. They also were to make weekly reports about sanitary conditions in those ports. The Surgeon General, in turn, was required to notify U.S. ports of entry about ships inbound from such originating ports. In addition, the Surgeon General was to make reports on a weekly basis to medical officers of the Marine Hospital Service and to state and local public health authorities regarding information received from the consular officers. The first report, issued July 13, 1878, was entitled "Bulletin of the Public Health" and has been cited as the forerunner to today's public health bulletin, the *Morbidity and Mortality Weekly Report*, published by CDC.[8] Even though this 1878 legislation resulted in federal-level public health authority,

TABLE 2-1   Selected Milestones in the Early Evolution of Federally Legislated Policy Relating to Public Health, 1796–1944

Date	Law and Significance
1796	*National Quarantine Act*: Passed by Congress on May 27, this Act limited federal quarantine activities to any cooperation first requested by the states in enforcing their own quarantine laws.[4] The enactment followed Congressional debate about states' rights and whether quarantine should be a federal or state function. (This Act was superseded in 1799 by a second quarantine Act with language that strengthened the requirement for federal personnel to assist in enforcing state and local health laws.[4])
1798	*Act for the Relief of Sick and Disabled Seamen*: Effective on July 16 and signed into law by President John Adams, this Act compelled prepayment of medical care for merchant seaman and helped lay groundwork for the eventual U.S. Public Health Service.[5]
1813	*Act to Encourage Vaccination*: Signed by President James Madison on February 27, this Act authorized the President to appoint an agent to promote smallpox vaccination and also provided for letters and packages containing vaccine matter to be sent through U.S. mail free of postage.[6] It was repealed effective May 4, 1822, at the recommendation of a Congressional committee investigating a cluster of deaths in persons who inadvertently had been vaccinated with real smallpox scabs
1878	*National Quarantine Act*: Passed by Congress on April 29, this Act created a "disease-intelligence system" managed at the federal level, providing authority for the Supervising Surgeon General of the Marine Hospital Service (MHS) to make rules and regulations for the detention of ships either having cases of contagious diseases on board or coming from foreign ports in which contagious diseases were present.[7] The Surgeon General was to report weekly to MHS medical officers and to state and local public health authorities regarding information received from the consular officers. The first report, issued July 13, 1878, was entitled "Bulletin of the Public Health" and has been cited as the forerunner to the *Morbidity and Mortality Weekly Report*.[8]
1879	*National Board of Health*: On March 3, Congress enacted legislation creating a National Board of Health and a supporting appropriation of $50,000.[9] The Board's roles were to include framing rules and regulations for preventing the introduction of contagious diseases into the United States; making special investigations any place in the United States or at foreign ports; obtaining information about matters affecting public health and responding to relevant questions from government departments and the states; and reporting to the next session of Congress on a plan for a national public health organization, "special attention being given to the subject of quarantine, both maritime and inland, especially as to regulations which should be established between State or local systems of quarantine and a national quarantine system."
1891	*Immigration law and health inspections*: An immigration act passed on March 13 contributed to the expansion of federal quarantine stations during the early 1890s and required the health inspection of immigrants by physicians of the MHS.[10] The law mandated the exclusion of "all idiots, insane persons, paupers or persons likely to become public charges, persons suffering from a loathsome or dangerous contagious disease" and criminals.
1893	*New national quarantine act*: During the international cholera epidemic, President Benjamin Harrison signed a new national quarantine act into law that had been enacted on February 15 with provisions including the requirement that ships departing foreign ports for the United States must have a bill of health signed by a

TABLE 2-1 (continued)

Date	Law and Significance
	U.S. consul; authorization for the President to detail MHS physicians to foreign ports to serve in consuls' offices and inspect vessels; the requirement that ships arriving in the United States must obtain a certificate of rules compliance from the federal quarantine officer before passengers were discharged; expansion of the number of federal quarantine stations; and provisions mandating the Surgeon General to examine all state and municipal quarantine regulations.[11] In the case of any regulations deemed inadequate, the Secretary of the Treasury was empowered to make additional rules.
1902	*An Act to increase the efficiency and change the name of the United States Marine Hospital Service*: On July 1, the term "public health" was formally institutionalized within the federal government when President Theodore Roosevelt signed this act into law, changing the Hospital Service's name to "Public Health and Marine Hospital Service of the United States."[12] This act also legalized the federal government's role in public health by establishing key administrative divisions (e.g., domestic quarantine, foreign and insular quarantine, sanitary reports and statistics, and scientific research); providing for an annual meeting of state and territorial health authorities with the Surgeon General; and empowering the Surgeon General to prepare and distribute to state and territorial health authorities forms for the compilation and collection of statistics on morbidity, mortality, and other vital statistics data.
1902	*An act regulating biologics*: On July 1, the President also signed "An Act to regulate the sale of viruses, serums, toxins and analogous products in the District of Columbia, to regulate interstate traffic in such articles, and for other purposes."[13] This act—which was attributed to concern some physicians had about the adulteration of smallpox vaccine and diphtheria antitoxin—established a national system of biologics standards.
1912	*Act changing name of the Service*: On August 14, the President signed into law yet another new name, the Public Health Service.[14] The act mandating this name change covered other provisions, including authorizations for additional federal powers and functions in public health, such as authority for the Public Health Service "to study and investigate the diseases of man and propagation and spread thereof, including sanitation and sewage and the pollution either directly or indirectly of the navigable streams and lakes of the United States."
1913	*Sundry Civil Appropriations Act*: This act, signed by the President on June 23, provided funds to support the new Public Health Service law of 1912.[15] These funds included $200,000 for field investigations; $47,000 and $25,000 earmarked for addressing pellagra and trachoma, respectively; and $20,000 more allocated to the Hygienic Laboratory.
1918	*Act appropriating monies for cooperation with state agencies*: On July 1, Congress appropriated $1,000,000 "[f]or cooperation with state and municipal health authorities in the prevention of the spread of contagious and infectious diseases in interstate traffic, including the sanitation of areas adjoining military and naval reservations and Government industrial plants, in order to properly to safeguard the health of the military forces and Government employees."[16]
1918	*Authorizations for combating venereal diseases*: On July 9, Congress passed legislation authorizing the establishment of a Division of Venereal Disease in the Public Health Service and broadening the scope of control activities to a joint effort by state health departments and the Public Health Service.[17]

(continued)

TABLE 2-1   (continued)

Date	Law and Significance
1918	*Appropriations to counter the Spanish influenza pandemic*: On October 1, Congress appropriated $1,000,000 for response efforts to the "Spanish influenza" pandemic.[18] The Public Health Service's Director of Interstate Quarantine was made responsible for managing these funds.
1921	*Sheppard-Towner Act providing for grants-in-aid to states*: On November 19, President Harding signed this act which expired on June 30, 1929.[19] On the basis of a grants-in-aid model used to promote road building, this act provided federal grants to establish state centers for teaching mothers about prenatal and infant care and created a Federal Board of Maternity and Infant Hygiene with authority to approve states' plans for use of the funds.
1929	*Act establishing the Narcotics Division*: On January 19, President Coolidge signed into law an act establishing the Narcotics Division of the Public Health Service which specified the creation of two hospitals for confining and treating federal prisoners addicted to certain drugs and addicts who voluntary presented for treatment.[20] The unit's name eventually was changed to the Division of Mental Hygiene.
1930	*Ransdell Act creating the National Institutes of Health*: On May 26, President Hoover signed into law the Ransdell Act passed in order "To establish and operate a National Institute of Health, to create a system of fellowships in said institute, and to authorize the Government to accept donations for use in ascertaining the cause, prevention, and cure of disease. . . ."[21]
1935	*Title VI of the Social Security Law*: The Public Health Title (Title VI) of the Social Security Law of 1935 authorized annual expenditures of up to $2,000,000 for "the investigation of disease and the problems of sanitation."[22] In October 1936, Surgeon General Parran reported that "[u]nder the provisions of the Social Security Act, a national health program has been made possible for the first time in the history of the Public Health Service" and that this program, implemented with the advice and assistance of the state health officers, included grants-in-aid to the states which especially addressed venereal disease control.
1939	*Impact of the Reorganization Act*: As a result of the Reorganization Act—which combined federal health, education, and welfare agencies—at the close of the fiscal year on June 30, 1939, the Public Health Service was transferred from the Treasury Department to the Federal Security Agency.[23] Other organizations included in the Federal Security Agency were the Children's Bureau, with programs in maternal and child health services, and the Food and Drug Administration, formerly of the Department of Agriculture.
1943	*Law creating Nurse Corps*: The United States Nurse Corps bill, aimed at solving the nursing shortage of WWII by providing financial support for nurse education, was signed into law by President Roosevelt in June 1943.[24] This legislation was to be administered by the Public Health Service.
1944	*Public Health Service Act*: Enacted on July 1, The Public Health Service Act of 1944 (Public Health Law 410) recodified Public Health Service laws, consolidating and revising existing legislation.[25] One provision empowered the Surgeon General to "make grants in aid to universities, hospitals, laboratories, and other public or private institutions and individuals," providing a legislative basis for grant support for expanding research beyond cancer. This law also created a new Division of Tuberculosis Control.

Source: Unless otherwise indicated, adapted from Furman.[3]

language inserted within the Act reflected ongoing debate about state and local roles in public health, including a stipulation that such rules and regulations must not "conflict with or impair any sanitary or quarantine laws or regulations of any State or municipal authorities."[3]

Contemporary federal quarantine authority resides in Section 361 of the PHSA.[26] Under circumstances described in this statute, the U.S. government has the authority to make and enforce regulations necessary to prevent introduction, transmission, and spread of communicable diseases from foreign countries into the United States and from one state or possession to another.[27] Such regulations are found at 42 C.F.R., Parts 70 and 71, and address both interstate and foreign quarantine. By Executive Order, the communicable diseases are specified for which individuals are subject to apprehension, detention, and conditional release (see Executive Order 13295 of April 4, 2003, as amended by Executive Order 13375 of April 1, 2005). The following communicable diseases are listed in the executive order: cholera; diphtheria; infectious tuberculosis; plague; smallpox; yellow fever; viral hemorrhagic fevers (Lassa, Marburg, Congo-Crimean, South American, and others not yet isolated or named); severe acute respiratory syndrome; and influenza caused by novel or reemergent influenza viruses causing, or having the potential to cause, a pandemic.

Federalism and Preemption

The concepts of both federalism and preemption are important determinants affecting the interplay between federal and state laws involving public health. These concepts, defined more fully elsewhere in this book (see Chapter 3), are briefly reviewed here because of their critical relevance to understanding the operation of legislatively enacted laws in relation to public health practice at the federal, state, and local levels.

As is the case for many services provided and some areas regulated by government, public health practice in the United States is carried out within a dual government and legal system of federalism. Federalism is the relationship and distribution of power between the individual states and the national government.[28] In this system, and under the U.S. Constitution, each of the 50 states possesses substantial independent legal authority but also is subject to the federal government's legal authorities, which overlap those of the states.[29] The federal government, under the U.S. Constitution, is a government of limited powers, possessing authority only when expressly or impliedly grounded in the U.S. Constitution. All other powers are reserved to the states or to the people.[30] The 18 express powers begin with the essential General Welfare Clause, include the Commerce Clause, and conclude with the Necessary and Proper authority to enact all laws appropriate to its powers.[31] Public health in the U.S system of federalism comprises laws, agencies, authorities, and exercise of powers at local, state, and federal levels of government.

Preemption refers to the power of the federal government to prevent or preclude state efforts to regulate a particular area or, similarly, for state government to prevent local efforts to regulate. More specifically, under the Supremacy Clause of Article VI of the Constitution, when direct conflict exists between a federal statute (that has independent constitutional grounding) and state statute, then the state law must yield to the federal law (i.e., the federal law preempts the state law), and the state statute cannot be enforced to the extent of the conflict. The Supreme Court recently underscored this when it stated, "The Supremacy Clause unambiguously provides that if there is a conflict between federal and state law, federal law shall prevail."[32]

Some intricacies of the preemption principle are illustrated in the potential operation of federal and state quarantine authorities. Although preemption may be found without express statutory language indicating that it applies, in the quarantine statute, it specifically states that neither Section 361 nor regulations promulgated under its authority shall supersede any provision in state law, unless it conflicts with the exercise of federal authority (see 42 U.S.C. §264[e], added in 2002 by Public Law 107–188). A state's exercise of its quarantine authority, even if the Department of Health and Human Services (DHHS) believed this authority to be wrongly asserted, probably would not conflict with an exercise of federal authority. Thus, although regulations implementing the quarantine statute provide for the assertion of federal authority when it is determined that "inadequate local control" exists, this is not likely to authorize federal preemption of state authority when it believes a state has wrongly imposed quarantine.

In addition to the preemption principle applying in the situation of a federal-state conflict, preemption may be found under other conditions, including when Congress acts to cover or "occupy the field" (e.g., in the field of nuclear regulation), when uniform national standards are needed, and when interests of the federal government are at stake. Similarly, a state legislature may "preempt" the exercise of local power by a subdivision or inferior government unit by adopting legislation that covers an area of concern also covered by a local ordinance. Therefore, even though a municipality may have the power to adopt a regulatory ordinance or to impose a tax, state legislation may preempt the municipal power or the local ordinance may be held to conflict with the state statute. For example, in relation to efforts to establish tobacco smoke–free indoor environments, preemptive state legislation in some states may prohibit communities from enacting laws that are more stringent than state law. As of December 31, 2004, a total of 19 states had at least one type of preemptive provision for smoke-free indoor air legislation.[33]

Federally Legislated Public Health: Mandates, Powers, and Programs

The basis for Congress to enact legislation involving the federal government in public health derives from grants of power enumerated by the Constitution. These powers reside especially within Article I, Section 8, and include the Commerce Clause —which permits Congress to address health through regulation of interstate and foreign commerce—and the Tax and Spend Clause, which enables Congressional legislation to cover health through revenue generation and spending in support of the general welfare and public good, tax burdens that deter health-risk behaviors, and tax relief that creates incentives for health-enhancing activities (see also Chapter 1).[34,35,a] Constitutional delegations of authority also could allow Congress to enact statutes related to the public's health by way of plenary authority over immigration matters, and regulation of the mails through empowerment to establish post offices.[34] Another Article I provision implicated in Congress' ability to enact laws directly and indirectly affecting public health is the Necessary and Proper Clause (Article I, §8, Cl. 18), which permits Congress to legislate on a spectrum of matters not specifically touched on in the Constitution.

The remainder of this section is divided into three subsections outlining three broad categories of federal statutes involving public health. These categories include statutes that (1) create federal public health infrastructure; (2) establish federal public health agencies, programs, and services; and (3) appropriate funds supporting federal and state public health activities.

Statutes Creating Federal Public Health Infrastructure

Federal statutes creating federal public health infrastructure include laws that establish personnel frameworks, such as PHS itself, and laws explicating authorities and powers, such as federal quarantine authority. The category of statutorily created infrastructure also includes laws that, while not creating agencies, might otherwise affect both regulatory and nonregulatory agencies. Examples of this category are laws governing the management and safekeeping of or access to information maintained by public health agencies, such as the federal Freedom of Information Act, the Health Insurance Portability and Accountability Act, and the federal Privacy Act (see also Chapter 10), as well as laws such as the federal Administrative Procedure Act, the Federal Advisory Committee Act, and the Paperwork Reduction Act, which establish operating principles and rules for certain activities carried out by federal agencies.

Legislation authorizing federal public health powers is found in the PHSA, which was first passed by Congress in 1944 and codified to Title 42 of the United States Code. At the outset, those authorities set forth the organizational structure for federal agencies authorized to carry out public health functions for the Executive Branch; gave broad authorities for carrying out certain public health functions; and established relationships with other entities (e.g., foreign, state, and local governments; institutions of higher education; and other private nonprofit institutions, for-profit organizations, and individuals concerned with public health). PHS was established in what now is DHHS, and its power was delineated in numerous sections of the PHSA.

The Secretary of Health and Human Services carries out the power of PHS under Section 301 to "conduct in the Service, and encourage, cooperate with, and render assistance to other appropriate public authorities, scientific institutions, and scientists in the conduct of, and promote the coordination of, research, investigations, experiments, demonstrations, and studies relating to the causes, diagnosis, treatment, control, and prevention of physical and mental diseases and impairments of man. . . ."[36] This section provides these sweeping powers in the context of a spectrum of activities, including making grants to universities, hospitals, laboratories, and other public or private institutions, and to individuals; allowing the sharing of PHS facilities with appropriate public authorities, health officials, and scientists engaged in special study; providing for treatment of persons at PHS institutions, hospitals, and stations as part of a study; making available technical advice and assistance on relevant statistical methods, as well as the practical application of public health research; and supplying to individuals and entities, for research purposes, substances and living organisms.

The passage of other provisions within the PHSA is responsible for the strong and enduring relations between federal and state public health authorities. For example, Section 311, entitled Federal-State Cooperation, authorizes four important powers. First, this section explicitly addresses the imposition of quarantine and response by public health authorities at both the federal and state levels. Specifically, it allows the Secretary to accept from state and local authorities "any assistance in the enforcement of quarantine regulations made pursuant to this Act." The Secretary is required to assist state and local authorities in enforcing "their quarantine and other health regulations" and is expected to help those authorities in preventing and suppressing communicable disease and in other public health matters, and to advise on matters relating to the preservation and improvement of public health in those jurisdictions. A second power given to the Secretary is to encourage cooperative activities between the states in planning for their current and future public health needs and establishing and maintaining adequate public health services and other public health activities. For example, CDC developed a "best practices" guide for states, based on the demographics and unique needs of each state, that can be used to custom design and implement tobacco-control programs that effectively prevent and reduce tobacco use. Elements of such a program could include initiatives aimed at cessation and counter-marketing, and enforcement of ordinances and laws prohibiting smoking in public places or sales of tobacco products to minors. Surveillance and evaluation also are key contributors to implementing a successful tobacco-control program. The "best practices" guide is particularly useful because it includes estimated costs for these programs.

A third power described in Section 311 authorizes the Secretary of Health and Human Services to "deploy" personnel, equipment, medical supplies, and "other resources of the Service and other agencies under the jurisdiction of the Secretary" to control epidemics of any disease or condition and to respond to other health emergencies or problems. To cooperatively plan for emergencies and other public health problems, this provision also allows for the Secretary to enter into agreements between PHS and public and private community health programs and agencies. Finally, under the federal-state cooperation authorities, the Secretary is granted broad authority to temporarily lend aid and assistance to state and local authorities who request it in responding to health emergencies; the Secretary may seek reimbursement of such aid if it is determined to be reasonable.

Statutes Establishing Federal Public Health Agencies, Programs, and Services

Through statutory enactments, Congress has created federal agencies that have a broad spectrum of responsibilities for programs, services, and other activities affecting the public's health. These agencies may be fundamentally regulatory or nonregulatory. Examples of fundamentally regulatory agencies are FDA and the Occupational Safety and Health Administration, both of which possess congressionally delegated powers for policy development, rulemaking, and adjudication (see also Chapters 15 and 22).

An example of a fundamentally nonregulatory agency is CDC, which (with several exceptions) has not been given rulemaking or other such congressionally delegated powers. In addition to their rulemaking powers and roles, regulatory agencies may be responsible for enforcing certain statutes. For example, EPA enforces provisions of the Clean Air Act and the Federal Insecticide, Fungicide, and Rodenticide Act, as well as numerous other environmental statutes (see also Chapter 20).

Although the broad authorities of sections 301 and 311 of the PHSA might appear to sufficiently enable PHS to address public health matters on the federal level, the PHSA and other statutes in fact provide PHS with many additional statutory authorities that are disease-, condition-, or population-specific. These authorities cover a wide range of public health matters and enable a variety of public health responses. Such authorities include programs and funding to address mental health and substance-abuse disorders conducted by the Substance Abuse and Mental Health Services Administration, whose grants to states, territories, federally recognized tribes or tribal organizations, and private nonprofit community-based organizations, among others, provide for comprehensive substance-abuse and mental health clinical treatment and recovery support. An important responsibility of the Substance Abuse and Mental Health Services Administration's Center for Substance Abuse Prevention is its compliance oversight of the Synar Amendment, a law found at 42 U.S.C. 300x-26, requiring that, as a condition of receiving federal funding, states have laws prohibiting the sale and distribution of tobacco products to any person younger than age 18 years (see also Chapter 18). Additionally, the Health Resources and Services Administration (HRSA), another PHS agency, provides for a wide range of health-care services, including programs for delivery of HIV/AIDS services, primary health care, maternal and child health, health professions, health-care systems, and rural health policy. Through such funding mechanisms as grants, contracts, and loans, HRSA carries out its mission to lead and direct programs and activities that will improve the health services for all people of the United States.

In addition to authorizing public health services and activities, federal statutes create the organizational infrastructure to conduct those activities. For example, the numerous institutes of NIH are authorized explicitly in the PHSA. By comparison, HRSA and CDC were not created by statute, although (as noted above) they have specific authorities throughout the PHSA. HRSA, as it is known and organized today, formally was established through a reorganization published in the *Federal Register* in September 1982 (47 FR 38409). With Congressional approval, CDC was established in 1946 as the Communicable Disease Center (formerly the Malaria Control in Wartime Areas).[37] Whether by administrative action or statutory design, agencies of PHS are legally authorized to carry out a remarkable number of programs and activities that are funded in the billions of dollars.

Statutes Appropriating Funds Supporting Public Health Activities

Although Section 311 does not provide for awards of grants to states and their political subdivisions, the Secretary of Health and Human Services is authorized to make grants to such entities in numerous other sections of the PHSA, including the aforementioned Section 301. Provisions throughout the PHSA generally provide for a ceiling of financial support for states; Congressional appropriations committees determine whether such authorized appropriations will be funded and at what levels.

The appropriations law that Congress passes every fiscal year for the operation and activities of DHHS serves more than the legal authority for funding the department; it also provides substantive law. For example, it authorizes the receipt of user fees into the CDC account when the agency is legally authorized to charge user fees, such as for preparation of biologic products for use in the laboratories of private entities. CDC may not, however, use funds available for injury prevention and control to advocate or promote gun control.

Just as the federal government uses the authorities in the PHSA and DHHS appropriations to build and maintain critical relationships with state and local public health authorities, Section 307 of the PHSA (42 U.S.C. 242l) allows collaboration and consultation by DHHS with other countries in endeavors in biomedical research, health-care technology, and health services research and statistical activities. While permitting a variety of collaborative activities and authorizing the expenditure of federal funds and use of resources from foreign countries, this section requires a showing that the activity undertaken, or funding spent, was to advance or improve the health status of the American people.

Statutory authorities also have provided for establishment of private nonprofit foundations to support the work—both financially and through the provision of voluntary services—to two PHS agencies, CDC and NIH. In this and other ways, CDC and NIH can accept gifts that support the agencies' respective missions. In recent years, the foundations have raised several million dollars and helped facilitate opportunities for scientists and other health experts to support the work of CDC and NIH, including at their facilities, often in areas that otherwise would not be funded through Congressional appropriations. Additionally, the foundations have worked to promote development of public-private partnerships that serve the agencies' public health and biomedical research missions.[38,39]

State and Local Public Health Systems and Practice

The Nature of State Law

At the level of state and local governments, both law and legal authority differ markedly from national-level law and authority. The fact that state law differs from federal law is only the beginning of the complexity in this area, for no two states have identical constitutions, and within each state exist a wide range of public health law and authority among the variety of local governments.[40] Public health law at the level of state and local governments is grounded in their unique legal status in our constitutional system.

In contrast to the federal government structure, the nature of fundamental legal authority of state governments is that plenary authority exists in the state as expressed through the state legislature. The state legislature has all authority except and unless limited by the state constitution. State constitutions generally exist as limits on the inherent power of the state, not as grants of authority to the state government. Both state and local governments are constrained by the federal Constitution—although the U.S. Supreme Court has resurrected in the last decade conceptions of states' rights as against the federal government in ways not seen since immediately before the Civil War.[41–44] With this different paradigm for the allocation of power and authority at the state level, state constitutions still retain many provisions that parallel the federal Constitution, such as fundamental rights (due process and equal protection) and liberties (free speech and religion).

State constitutions tend to be relatively silent on the topic of public health. Possible explanations for this include the relatively recent history of diversification of program roles and responsibilities that state and local government agencies have for public health, the plenary legislative authority of state governments, and the fact that when many states' constitutions were written, public health services were assumed to be within the power of the government. Regardless of the reasons, few express references to public health exist in state constitutions today. New York and Washington are two of the few exceptions, and even these tend to confirm the inherent authority—but not the obligation—of the state to legislate in the field of public health.[45,46] The Kansas constitution is one of the few that impose an affirmative obligation on the state to meet public health needs, and this is in the context of "institutions for the benefit of mentally or physically incapacitated or handicapped persons."[47]

No two states possess identical legal frameworks for public health. This heterogeneity of law and public health is compounded by the complex allocation of authority between state governments and the multitude of local governments that exist in each state (counties, cities, townships, villages). As a threshold proposition, local governments in the United States have no special standing or rights under the federal Constitution.[48] The rights, powers and authority of local governments are either delegated by the state legislature or derived directly as a grant of authority from the state constitution. The extent of local government authority and autonomy to legislate and to regulate is loosely referred to as local government "home rule."

Many states, particularly those in the Midwest, follow a doctrine known as "Dillon's Rule."[49] Developed largely in the 19th century, this doctrine provides that local governments have only such authority and power as is expressly granted to them by the legislature. In the face of legislative silence on an issue—such as local regulation of handguns or of smoking in public facilities—or ambiguity in the interpretation of a statute, Dillon's Rule is commonly invoked to deny the legal authority of a local government to act.

The strongest form of local government home rule powers is found in states where the state constitution explicitly grants legal authority to local governments. This "constitutional home rule" typically provides that counties or municipalities (or both) may exercise certain powers on behalf of the inhabitants and property within their jurisdictional boundaries. When the constitutional provision directly authorizes a local government to exercise "police powers" or to act in pursuit of "the general welfare," the local government will have broad authority to act in the field of public health unless and until the state legislature limits such authority. An example of a strong constitutional home rule provision for public health is the grant in the Illinois constitution of "the power to regulate for the protection of the public health."[50] Georgia's constitution has a parallel provision authorizing counties and municipalities to provide "public health facilities and services, including hospitals, ambulances and emergency rescue services, and animal control."[51] However, even when a constitutional provision addresses public health powers of local governments, such authority is likely to be subject to being overridden by a "general law" in which the state legislature specifically addresses the subject matter.[b]

When a state constitution does not address home rule powers of local governments, the most common approach is for the state to enact general legislation that summarizes, or lists, the powers of local governments. Known collectively as "legislative home rule," such statutes are the primary source of powers of the local governments. As with constitutional provisions, if a state's general statute on municipalities, counties, or other local governments contains a broad grant of or provision for "general welfare" or "police power," then such a provision will provide sufficient authority for at least the basic range of public health regulation and licensing. Some states have yet another variation on this allocation of power: state grant to a specific city of a "charter." These charter cities most commonly have a much broader and stronger range of home rule powers.[c]

When a local government has apparent authority to act in the field of public health, it will in most instances still be subject to the possibility of state legislative action that limits, restricts, or contradicts local action. This "preemption" of local actions by state law directly parallels federal preemption of state law as noted above (also see Chapter 3). As creatures of the state that depend primarily on delegated authority, local governments may find that state law preempts ordinances addressing public health issues. Such preemption can occur even when the state chooses not to regulate the subject matter but simply to deny authority to local governments to regulate in that field.[33]

Sources and Definitions of Public Health Authority

The sources of public health law at the level of state and local governments are as broad as the range of topics that fall within the meaning of public health. One commentator has suggested four basic categories of public health exist in the context of law and policy: health promotion and disease prevention; assessment, data collection, and data analysis; medical services; and leadership and policy development.[52] Given this broad range of activities that may exist at the state and local levels, one is not likely to find a single statute, a single ordinance, or even a single administrative agency that encompasses the entire scope of law and public health. For example, in a given state, the operation of mental health facilities may rest in an express constitutional provision, while at the same time no express constitutional or statutory authority may exist for compulsory vaccinations—leaving such authority to be grounded in the state's "inherent" police power.

State and Local Public Health Systems

Under the constitutional doctrine of reserved powers, the 50 states retain enormous authority to protect the public's health. The states shoulder their broad public health responsibilities through work carried out by both state and local health agencies. Traditionally, state health departments exercise "border-to-border" regulatory authority, whereas local health agencies act within a smaller region, such as a county or city.

Although state and local health agencies are the backbone of the nation's public health system, even at the state level, public health responsibilities extend well beyond the "health department." Many other public-sector, as well as private-sector, organizations also play key roles in public health. For example, school boards help enforce mandatory vaccination requirements; sanitation and water supply authorities manage waste and protect drinking supplies; and local hospitals and private health insurers may support local clinics and related outreach programs. In recent years, state labor departments have supported workplace smoking restrictions in an effort to protect employees from health hazards associated with exposure to environmental tobacco smoke.

The relationship between state and local health agencies can be structured in different ways. As discussed previously, certain municipalities and counties may have "home rule" authority that grants the local jurisdiction preeminent responsibility for establishing and enforcing health standards. New York City and Baltimore operate in this manner. Not all localities, however, are afforded this type of independent authority. Many local health agencies exercise powers delegated to them by the state health department. In addition, a state legislature may pass a statute imposing direct responsibilities on the local department. Regardless of the source of local health powers, state law will generally vest responsibility for exercising these responsibilities in a policy-setting body such as a city council, board of county commissioners, or board of health. The local health officer typically functions as an agency's chief executive officer and supervises the staff, who implement the programs on a daily basis.

On a broader level, states often consolidate core public health functions into some form of "state health department." No single model best describes the "typical" state department. In recent decades, however, as health expenditures have absorbed larger portions of states' budgets, a trend has existed toward the creation of omnibus agencies responsible for an array of health-care delivery and financing functions. These organizations may combine traditional public health activities with environmental programs or with other human service agencies. These organizational arrangements are not necessarily static and evolve over time as a function of new initiatives and funding mandates.

This movement toward consolidation of health functions into a single cabinet-level agency is illustrated by the statutes creating the Maryland Department of Health and Mental Hygiene (DHMH) and its related county health departments.[d] This comprehensive health agency was not created from whole cloth. Instead, DHMH, like other comparable agencies, evolved as community health priorities changed and scientific capabilities evolved. For example, Maryland's first psychiatric hospital was chartered by the legislature in the mid-18th century. The state's current mental health code, which DHMH administers, descended directly from this initial statutory act. A similar evolutionary process began in 1933 when Maryland's Commissioner of Health invited the Rockefeller Commission to study the state's antiquated "bedding and hygiene" laws. The resulting recommendations formed the basis for Maryland's modern public health code. The Maryland DHMH was formed in 1969 to administer these provisions.[53]

In its modern form, DHMH is directed by statute to "adopt general policy for, and adopt standards to promote and guide the development of, the physical and mental hygiene services of the [state] and its subdivisions."[54] Maryland's Secretary of Health and Mental Hygiene acts as the agency's chief executive officer and is "responsible for the health interests of the people of [Maryland] and shall supervise generally the administration of the health laws of this State and its subdivisions."[55] As a part of this mandate, the agency exercises each of the traditional public health functions. In particular, DHMH plays a leading role in statewide disease prevention efforts (see Health-General Title 18), health statistics recordkeeping (see Health-General Title 4), provision of medical services (see Health-General Titles 7, 8, and 10), and overall policy development (see Health-General Title 19 and §2–105[c]) (requiring, respectively, development of both a "State health plan" and a more specific "State health improvement plan").

Also, like other omnibus agencies, the scope of DHMH's statutory responsibilities has changed over time. For example, environmental and juvenile service programs have been reorganized into their own cabinet-level departments, and in recent decades, health-care financing responsibilities have grown substantially. DHMH administers the Medicaid Program (see Health-General Article Title 15) and funds an elaborate system of care for persons with mental and developmental disabilities (see Health-General Article Titles 7 and 10). Moreover, the agency licenses all health-care professionals, sets hospital payment rates, and controls health-care facility expansion through a certificate-of-need program.

Regardless of the organizational design of the state agency, several key powers and responsibilities are essential to the operation of a public health system. First, some entity typically is given overall responsibility for protecting the health of all residents of a particular jurisdiction. As already noted, in Maryland, the Secretary of Health and Mental Hygiene is "responsible for the health interests of the State" and is given explicit authority to "carry out and enforce the provisions of [the health] article . . ." (see Health-General Article §2-104[m]). In the absence of more specific language, this plenary grant of authority is the basis for many public health measures. Second, the agency often is afforded "rulemaking" power, which permits executive branch officials to propose regulations needed to implement public health programs. In Maryland, the Secretary "may adopt rules and regulations to carry out the provisions of law that are within the jurisdiction of the Secretary" (see Health-General Article §2-104[b]). Finally, the public health agency must have implicit or explicit authority to conduct the business of health care. In particular, agencies need the legal authority to receive funds, collect fees, make grants, issue contracts, and enter into cooperative arrangements with public and private entities (see Health-General Article Titles 2, 11, 15, 16, and 18).

In addition to these generic responsibilities, state health codes authorize state and local officials to engage in a range of more specific public health functions. Some of these responsibilities and functions predate the formation of the nation. Many other measures intended to enhance health status have grown incrementally over the last two centuries. Part of this growth may be attributable to the inclusion of constitutional protections in otherwise traditional public health–related statutes. One modern version of illustrative public health functions is found in the Turning Point Model Public Health Act (Table 2-2).[56] In comparison, the state law often will be more detailed than its Model Act counterpart. Today, state licensing statutes—regardless of whether they regulate restaurants, doctors, or hospitals—are unlikely to be adopted without some enunciation of legislative intent. State officials and legislators involved in framing new public health measures typically join with interest groups to define the scope of the legislative grant of authority and to specify the parameters of the new regulatory program.

In Maryland, although the state health code addresses each of the public health functions shown in Table 2-2, implementation of these programs is not solely the responsibility of a state health department. To the contrary, citizens expect their local officials to respond to needs and complaints related to public health. For example, they may contact the local clinic to obtain vaccination schedules, the sanitation department to report rodent infestations, and the county health department to complain about possible foodborne diseases or outbreaks. Knowing this, state legislators can choose to delegate primary oversight of these functions to a local board of health. In Maryland, each county has a local board—comprising the county commissioners or members of the county council—which appoints the local health officer with the approval of the state's Secretary of Health (see Health-General Article §3-202). In conjunction with the county health officer, the board of health implements state and local health laws. Except for areas where a county exercises independent home rule authority, Maryland's Secretary of Health and Mental Hygiene and the local health officer work together to implement the state's public health programs.

TABLE 2-2   Core Public Health Functions and Comparison of Selected Provisions from the Model Public Health Act and Maryland's Health-General (HG) Statutes

Core Public Health Function	Model Act Provision*	Maryland Statutory Provision
Disease surveillance activities	Agency may collect information needed to "further the mission or goals of public health" (§5-102)	Agency may investigate and obtain reports about contagious and infectious diseases (HG §18-102)
Disease control activities	Agency may use powers to "prevent [and] control" public health threats (§5-101)	Local health officer shall "act immediately" to halt the spread of infectious or contagious disease (HG §18-208)
Authority to abate nuisances	Agency may order owner to "avoid, correct, or remove" nuisance (§5-111)	County board of health may "adopt and enforce" rules on "any nuisance or cause of disease" (HG §3-202)
Authority to adopt licensing standards	Agency shall license business or activity "that may be detrimental to" public health—includes food service, health-care facilities and practitioners (§5-110)	Over 500 pages of statutes governing facility and practitioner licensing requirements (Health Occupations and Health-General Articles)

* Adapted from the Turning Point Collaborative Model Act (www.turningpointprogram.org).[53]

Most regulatory bodies, including state and local health departments, can choose to enforce their public health objectives by either (1) adjudicating individual cases or (2) adopting broader rules or regulations that will govern resolution of the problem for all affected members of the public. The calculus for choosing the appropriate enforcement mechanism can be complex. However, once an enforcement action is under way or a regulatory standard is challenged in litigation, a degree of judicial deference often is afforded the agency's expert policy judgments. The state's Administrative Procedure Act may establish deferential standards for judicial review of an agency's scientific or regulatory decisions.[e]

To achieve a particular public health objective, mere statutory authority of a health department to take certain actions may not alone be sufficient. Rather, the regulatory body should be able to persuasively convey to citizens why certain actions are in their self-interest. When these persuasive measures fail to achieve the needed outcome, the state or local health department then may use defined legal strategies and mechanisms to achieve these ends (Table 2-3 and Table 2-4).

A limited number of legal mechanisms (e.g., regulations and injunctions) allow state and local agencies to implement public health policies. Depending on the circumstances, some mechanisms more effectively protect the public health than others. Regulations are broad-based but difficult to adopt and expensive to enforce. Injunctive actions seeking abatement of a specific nuisance can be crafted to quickly address particular conditions or threats. However, injunctions have limited utility where the threat is posed by numerous individuals, each of whom has "a different story to tell." The following example illustrates how, when confronted with an emerging threat, public health authorities might consider the relative merits of several legal interventions (Box 2-1). This process of considering interventions raises two fundamental questions. First, does the state or local official have the legal authority to respond to the problem? Second, given the interplay of federal, state, and local laws, what is the most effective means of responding to the threat? This complex interaction between powers and practical constraints, and between mandated standards and voluntary compliance, can make the practice of public health law as much an art as a science.

Summary

In this chapter, we aimed to examine the structure of law under the U.S. Constitution, which frames and specifies public health practice. In particular, we focused on the statutory basis of the federal and state public health systems. The basis for Congress to enact legislation involving the federal government in public health derives from grants of power enumerated by the Constitution, including the general welfare clause, the Commerce Clause, the Tax and Spend Clause, and the Necessary and Proper Clause. The federal government's statutorily created roles in public health practice date to the late 18th century. Since then, Congress has assigned the federal government a spectrum of roles in public health practice by passing laws that create federal public health infrastructure; establish federal pub-

TABLE 2-3   Selected Legal Strategies and Mechanisms for Implementing Public Health Objectives and Related Limitations

Legal Strategies for Achieving Public Health Objectives	Limitations on the Use of This Legal Strategy
State legislature enacts public health statute	Adoption of legislation may require several months or years.
	Legislative amendments may modify meaning and scope of original legislative proposal.
	Difficult to revise statute in subsequent years.
	Subject to constitutional limitations such as federal preemption doctrine and due process requirements.
Public health agency proposes and adopts regulations	Public health agency must have general authority to adopt regulations.
	Public health regulation must be no broader than and consistent with the agency's existing statutory authority.
	Regulation subject to legislative override through passage of subsequent legislation.
Public health agency initiates enforcement action in court or through administrative proceeding	Public health agency must have statutory or regulatory enforcement authority.
	Strict rules apply to judicial proceedings while more flexible rules may govern administrative cases.
	Resolution of particular enforcement action governs only the rights of the parties to the proceeding.
Declaratory judgment action	Restricts applicability of specific statute to specific set of facts.
	Is not "self-executing" and may require agency to initiate subsequent enforcement action.
Public health agency grants and contracts	Give agency limited capacity to specify goals and "deliverables."
	Permit funding of only selected vendors or grantees.
	More useful as "carrot" to encourage desired behavior; less useful as "stick" to prohibit adverse behavior.
Public health agency issues informal directive	Vehicle for providing only advisory health information and recommendations for protective measures.
	If voluntary compliance not forthcoming, then formal enforcement action required.

lic health agencies, programs, and services; and appropriate funds supporting federal and state public health activities.

Under the constitutional doctrine of reserved powers, the 50 states retain enormous authority to protect the public's health. At the state and local levels, state legislatures and other legislative bodies act under state constitutions to pass statutes creating state and local public health agencies and boards of health, articulating powers to assure the public's health, and delegating public health–related powers to government subdivisions. In contrast to the federal government structure, the nature of fundamental

TABLE 2-4   Illustrative Public Health Objectives and Applications of Legal Interventions

Public Health Objective	Statute	Regulation	Enforcement Action	Grant or Contract
Reducing West Nile virus threats through commu-nity-wide abatement of standing water pools.	Applies broadly to entire community. Slow legislative process.	Requires statutory authority. Flexible standards allow varied enforcement approaches.	Case specific. Demonstrates serious-ness of agency intent.	Allows agency to select vendors with needed abatement expertise. Expenses may be charged to violators.
Patient with antibiotic-resistant TB receives needed inpatient treatment.	Provides needed basis for coercive treatment. Specifies due process protections.	Same as above.	Same as above.	Payment of living expenses to patient may encourage voluntary compliance.
Restaurant adopts new food-handling protocols reducing threat of bacterial contamination.	Applies broadly to entire regulated community. Legislative exceptions may limit breadth of enforcement.	Same as above.	Same as above.	Grants may cover imple-mentation expenses. Speeds compliance.

BOX 2-1. Case Study: *Pfiesteria* in Tidal Rivers

Background/Problem

Beginning in 1997, watermen on Maryland's Eastern Shore began reporting mysterious fish-kill outbreaks on several tidal rivers. Thousands of menhaden and other fish species would suddenly exhibit lesions and abnormal patterns of movement just before dying. Also, a local internist was quoted in the paper stating that he had treated several watermen and recreational fishermen for rashes, lethargia, and unexplained loss of memory.

State and local health department officials began assembling case studies. Patients consented to release of their medical records to a group of medical-school professors and other experts who confirmed the clinical findings. At the same time, state environmental scientists examined the relation between certain types of algae blooms, the menhaden lesions, and environmental exposures to local fishermen, and preliminarily concluded this problem may have been associated with exposures to blooms of the marine microorganism *pfiesteria piscicida*.

On the basis of these clinical findings, state and local health officials issued a series of public health declarations restricting recreational and commercial activities on certain rivers. The Secretary of Health issued an "open letter" to consumers explaining the research findings. Within the next several years, groundbreaking legislation aimed at regulating agricultural use of fertilizers and requiring waste-management plans passed the Maryland General Assembly.

Comment

State health departments may exercise a broad array of powers to protect the public health. As the *Pfsteria* example illustrates, however, regulatory and "coercive" powers are not necessarily the most effective tool available to public health officials. The ability to focus specialized clinical resources on a particular health threat through cooperative agreements and funding arrangements with professional societies and academic institutions can be of enormous use in persuading members of the public to take certain actions. Once empirical support for a public health intervention is established, public health officials are better able to motivate voluntary compliance by members of the public. Boating and fishing on the Pocomoke River ceased during *Pfsteria* blooms not because a regulation was adopted. Instead, voluntary compliance occurred largely because credible scientific evidence indicated that fisherman could suffer serious health consequences. Toronto health officials reported much the same behavior during the SARS outbreak. With relatively few exceptions, when court orders were required, citizens voluntarily complied with quarantine directives issued by city health workers.

legal authority of state governments is that plenary authority exists in the state as expressed through the state legislature—the state legislature has all authority except and unless limited by the state constitution. Partly because state constitutions tend to be relatively silent on the topic of public health and because no two states have identical constitutions, no two states possess identical legal frameworks for public health. This heterogeneity of law and public health is compounded by the complex allocation of authority between state governments and the multitude of local governments within each state.

The states shoulder their broad public health responsibilities through work carried out by both state and local health agencies. States often consolidate core public health functions into some form of "state health department." No single model best describes the "typical" state department. In recent decades, a trend has existed toward creation of omnibus agencies responsible for an array of health-care delivery and financing functions. These organizations may combine traditional public health activities with environmental programs or with other human service agencies. Regardless of the state agency's organizational design, several key powers and responsibilities are essential to the operation of the public health system, including overall responsibility for protecting the health of all residents of a particular jurisdiction; "rulemaking" power that permits executive branch officials to propose regulations needed to implement public health programs; and implicit or explicit authority to conduct the business of health care (e.g., legal authority to receive funds, collect fees, make grants, issue contracts, and enter into cooperative arrangements with public and private entities). In addition to these generic responsibilities, state health codes authorize state and local officials to engage in a range of more specific public health activities.

We gratefully acknowledge the assistance provided by Michael Smith and by Karen McKie, J.D., in research related to the development of this chapter, and the suggestions provided by David E. Benor, J.D.

Notes

a. For example, see *South Dakota v. Dole*, 483 U.S. 203 (1987) (holding for constitutionality of making receipt of funds for federal highways contingent on a state's increasing its drinking age).

b. Georgia Constitution, Article IX, §2, ¶ I ("for which no provision has been made by general law"); New Mexico Constitution, Article X, §6 (municipality may "exercise all legislative powers and perform all functions not expressly denied by general law").

c. The City of Baltimore has express home rule authority in the Maryland constitution to borrow funds for emergencies for "preserving the health" of the City (Maryland Constitution, Article XI, §7).

d. Examples of the statutory basis of state public health practice included in this section especially are drawn from Maryland because of the expertise of one of the authors (DO).

e. See *Spencer v. Maryland State Board of Pharmacy*, 380 Md. 515, 846 A.2d 341 (2004). See also State Government Article §10–213(i) (under Maryland's APA, "[t]he agency . . .

may use its expertise, technical competence, and specialized knowledge in the evaluation of evidence").

References

1. Bureau of Health Professions, National Center for Health Workforce Information and Analysis, Health Research and Services Administration. The public health work force, enumeration 2000. Available at http://www.cumc.columbia.edu/dept/nursing/institutes-centers/chphsr/enum2000.pdf. Accessed December 20, 2005.
2. Hajat A, Brown CK, Fraser MR. *Local Public Health Agency Infrastructure: A Chartbook.* Washington, DC: National Association of County and City Health Officials, 2001.
3. Furman B, Williams RC. *A Profile of the United States Public Health Service 1798–1948.* Bethesda, MD: US Department of Health, Education, and Welfare, National Institutes of Health, 1973 (DHEW publication no [NIH] 73-369).
4. Act of May 27, 1796, Ch 31, 1 Stat 474, *repealed by* Act of February 25, 1799, Ch 12, 1 Stat 619.
5. Act of July 16, 1798, Ch 77, 1 Stat 605.
6. Act of February 27, 1813, Ch 37, 2 Stat 806, *repealed by* Act of May 4, 1822, Ch 50, 3 Stat 677.
7. Act of April 29, 1878, Ch 66, 20 Stat 37.
8. CDC. Preface. In: Goodman RA, Foster KL, Gregg MB, eds. *Highlights in Public Health.* Atlanta: US Department of Health and Human Services, CDC, [no date]:v–vi.
9. Act of March 3, 1879, Ch 202, 20 Stat 484.
10. Act of March 3, 1891, Ch 551, 26 Stat 1084.
11. Act of February 15, 1893, Ch 114, 27 Stat 449, *amended by* Act of June 19, 1906, Ch 3433, 34 Stat 299.
12. Public Health and Marine-Hospital Service Act, Pub L 57-236, 32 Stat 712 (1902).
13. Act of July 1, 1902, Pub L 57-244, 32 Stat 728.
14. Act of August 14, 1912, Pub L 62-265, 37 Stat 309.
15. Act of June 23, 1913, Pub L 63-3, 38 Stat 4.
16. Act of July 1, 1918, Pub L 65-181, 40 Stat 634, 644–45.
17. Act of July 9, 1918, Pub L 65-193, §§3–6, 40 Stat 845, 886–87, *amended by* La Follette-Bulwinkle Act, Pub L 75-540 (1938).
18. HJ Res 333, 65th Cong, 40 Stat 1008 (1918).
19. Sheppard-Towner (Maternity) Act, Pub L 67-97, 42 Stat 224 (1921).
20. Act of January 19, 1929, Pub L 70-672, 45 Stat 1085.
21. Ransdell Act, Pub L 71-251, 46 Stat 379 (1930).
22. Social Security Act of 1935, Pub L 74-271, §§601–03, 49 Stat 620, 634–35.
23. Reorganization Act of 1939, Pub L 76-19, §§201, 205, 53 Stat 561, 1423–24.
24. Nurses Training Act, Pub L78-74, 57 Stat 153 (1943).
25. Public Health Service Act of 1944, Pub L 78-410, 58 Stat 682.
26. 42 USC §264.
27. Misrahi JJ, Foster JA, Shaw FE, Cetron MS. HHS/CDC legal response to SARS outbreak. Emerg Infect Dis 2004;10:353–5.
28. *Black's Law Dictionary.* Abridged 6th ed. St. Paul, MN: West Publishing Co, 1991.
29. Sager S. The sources and limits of legal authority. In: Morrison AB, ed. *Fundamentals of American Law.* New York: Oxford University Press, 1997:27–56.
30. US Constitution, Amendment X.

31. US Constitution, Article I, §8.

32. *Gonzales v Raich*, 545 US 1 (2005).

33. CDC. Preemptive state smoke-free indoor air laws—United States, 1999–2004. *MMWR* 2005;54:250–3.

34. Tobey JA. *Public Health Law*. 3rd ed. New York: The Commonwealth Fund; 1947.

35. Gostin LO. *Public Health Law: Power, Duty, Restraint*. Berkeley: University of California Press, 2000.

36. 42 USC 241.

37. Etheridge EW. *Sentinel for Health: A History of the Centers for Disease Control*. Berkeley: University of California Press, 1992.

38. 42 USC 280e-11.

39. 42 USC 290b.

40. CDC. *Profile of State and Territorial Public Health Systems: United States, 1991*. Available at http://wonder.cdc.gov/wonder/sci_data/misc/type_txt/stprof91.asp. Accessed December 20, 2005.

41. *Board of Trustees v Garrett*, 531 US 356 (2001).

42. *United States v Morrison*, 529 US 598 (2000).

43. *Kimel v Florida Board of Regents*, 528 US 62 (2000).

44. *Alden v Maine*, 527 US 706 (1999).

45. NY Constitution, Article XVII, §3 ("the protection and promotion of the health of the inhabitants of the state are matters of public concern").

46. Wash Constitution, Article XX, §1, 2 (provides for the creation of a state board of health).

47. Kan Constitution. Article XV, §3.

48. *Hunter v City of Pittsburgh*, 207 US 161 (1907).

49. Frug GE. The city as a legal concept. *Harvard Law Rev* 1980;93:1057–154.

50. Ill Constitution, Article VII, §6.

51. Ga Constitution, Article IX, §3, ¶ III(a)(3).

52. Gostin LO. Burris S, Lazzarini Z. The law and the public's health: a study of infectious disease law in the United States. *Columbia Law Rev* 1999;99:59–128.

53. 1969 Md Chap Laws, §77.

54. Md Code Ann, Health-Gen §2-105(a) (2006).

55. Md Code Ann Health-Gen §2-105(b) (2006).

56. Turning Point. Available at www.turningpointprogram.org. Accessed December 20, 2005.

Chapter 3

REGULATING PUBLIC HEALTH: PRINCIPLES AND APPLICATION OF ADMINISTRATIVE LAW

Peter D. Jacobson, Richard E. Hoffman, and Wilfredo Lopez

Public health practice frequently involves regulatory endeavors shaped by and grounded in administrative law. The core functions of public health practice are authorized, developed, and implemented through the administrative law's regulatory processes. Most public health actions, whether developing sanitation codes, responding to a disease outbreak, or enforcing environmental regulations, are subject to administrative law requirements. In this sense, public health practice can be viewed as a branch of administrative law. Proper use of the administrative process is therefore an essential aspect of successful public health practice and management.

In this chapter, we examine the key aspects and requirements of public health regulation. We will focus on how state and local public health practitioners can translate legal authority into effective public health practice and management. Our goals are twofold: first, to set forth the mechanics of the administrative process; and second, to provide a practical context for using the administrative process to the practitioner's advantage. Understanding and effectively using the administrative process will both facilitate public health practice and invite public support for public health policies.

Background

Administrative law is simply the body of law created by regulatory agencies through rules, regulations, orders, and procedures designed to further legislatively enacted policy goals.[1] All regulatory agencies, including public health departments, are responsible for implementing and enforcing legislation. By issuing and enforcing regulations, they create a body of administrative law. Administrative agencies must adhere to specific procedural requirements, set forth by the legislative branch, before taking any action. In conducting their business, administrative agencies operate on two levels: they issue rules and they adjudicate challenges on enforcement of the rules.

Public health regulation dates to the early days of the new American republic. The first federal health-related provision passed on July 31, 1789, the first year Congress met under the new Constitution. The provision provided funding for quarantine inspections by charging all ships entering U.S. ports a 20-cent bill-of-health fee.[2] During the mid-19th century, cities and then states established boards of health to oversee sanitation and quarantine requirements. In 1856, Louisiana created a statewide board of health. By 1873, Massachusetts, California, and Michigan also had formed state boards of health, and 19 additional states followed that model by 1879. States were concerned primarily with controlling infectious diseases, such as smallpox and yellow fever, and with improving sanitation. For example, early state regulations to combat smallpox and yellow fever involved quarantines and smallpox inoculations, actions that were highly controversial.[a]

After the Civil War, the states became more active in regulating public health, especially in establishing a systematic public health infrastructure and creating mental health hospitals. A national health board was formed in 1879 and, for four years, attempted to establish itself by aiding the states in their quarantine regulations. But years of sparring with the state health departments and interdepartmental wars with the Marine Hospital Service were too much for this fledgling agency. By 1883, the National Health Board had disintegrated.[3]

National quarantine regulation was placed under the purview of the Marine Hospital Service in 1890. That agency oversaw marine quarantines but was limited to control of plague, cholera, typhus fever, yellow fever, smallpox, anthrax, and leprosy. In 1902, Congress passed an act reorganizing health care into the United States Public Health and Marine Hospital Service. The United States Public Health Service was named as such in 1912, but public health policy remained largely a state- and local-based effort.

Much public health activity during the 20th century and into the 21st century occurred at the state level. From designing and enforcing sanitation codes and maintaining responsibility for water and sewage inspections to designing disease-control strategies, state and local health departments have been the leading public health practitioners.

Until recently, public health has been exclusively the domain of government agencies. With the shift of health care to an increasingly market-based system and the rising distrust of government, the public health system has come under increasing pressure to involve the private sector in providing public health services. Although the bulk of traditional public health services remain a government responsibility, many public health agencies rely on partnerships with the private sector to achieve their public health goals. Public-private partnerships include programs such as Medicaid managed care and the formation of state public health institutes that are not attached to a government unit.[b]

Regulating Public Health

We use the term "regulation" to encompass both legislative and regulatory oversight of the public health system. As a government responsibility, the public health system depends on legislative authority for its practices and funding. Inherent in state sovereignty is the police power to protect the public's health and welfare. That has translated into a broad grant of authority from state legislatures to state and local health departments to prevent the spread of disease.

Regulatory agencies (both state and federal) are part of the executive branch and are created by legislatures, and exist largely to implement policy enacted by the legislative branch. Congress and state legislatures usually enact broad policy statements, delegating the details to the appropriate regulatory agency. Even though regulatory agencies are part of the executive branch, the nature and scope of specific legislation and the presence or absence of funding to implement legislative policies generally determine the agenda of a given regulatory agency. For instance, Congress enacted broad language to protect patient privacy under the Health Insurance Portability and Accountability Act (HIPAA) but did not specify how the goals of the Act should be accomplished. The details of developing regulatory guidance for and implementation of HIPAA were delegated to the Department of Health and Human Services.

At the federal level, many of the administrative agencies, such as the Consumer Product Safety Commission and the Federal Trade Commission, are independent of the executive branch, even though the executive branch exerts substantial control over regulatory policy through political appointments. Regulatory agencies at the state and local levels usually are not independent of the executive branch. In fact, the executive branch often sets state public health policy, although local agencies may have either congruent or independent authority subject only to local boards of health.

The justification for public health regulation has been the need for the state to exercise its police powers to act in the public's health to: prevent the spread of infectious diseases; prevent injuries; protect against environmental harms; destroy contaminated products; and in some instances, provide safety net services of last resort. The range of public health responsibilities at the beginning of the 21st century is remarkably expansive. As noted above, government has always assumed responsibility for protecting the public's health.

In contrast, the general justification for regulating private health care is to redress market failure,[4] that is, where market competition is not working or where barriers exist to competition that can be eliminated only by government or other non-market institutions.[5] In the private sector, self-regulatory entities have emerged to oversee how health care is delivered. During the 1950s, the Joint Commission on Accreditation of Hospitals (now known as the Joint Commission on Accreditation of Healthcare Organizations) was formed as a voluntary entity to establish quality-of-care standards for hospitals and to accredit facilities adhering to the standards. During the 1980s, the National Commission on Quality Assurance was formed to accredit managed-care organizations.

No similar self-regulatory structures have gained equal prominence in public health regulation. For the most part, elected officials and legislative committees play that oversight role. In Michigan, for instance, the public health officer needs approval from the local board of health (politically elected) to take regulatory actions. Several organizations have emerged to monitor certain aspects of public health practice. These organizations might stimulate changes in public health practice and management that will influence regulatory policy. For example, the National Association of City and County Health Officers conducts surveys and offers a forum for public health officials. The National Association of Local Boards of Health provides similar functions for officials with public health oversight responsibilities.

Although based on a regulatory model, the public health system has been slower than the private health-care system to adopt performance assessment systems. In recent years, however, the National Association of Local Boards of Health has developed a National Public Health Performance Standards Program on the basis of a self-assessment instrument.[6] The instrument measures compliance with standards established for ten essential public health services, including workforce development and identification of health hazards in the community. Meeting these standards will implicate regulatory policies.

One of the most important and unique functions of public health agencies is assessment of the status of a community's health to control outbreaks and prevent the spread of disease. This assessment is commonly achieved through population-based surveillance. No academic institution or other government agency is positioned or authorized to conduct population-based disease surveillance. Generally, the concept of disease surveillance is authorized by state legislatures, and the details of determining what diseases are assessed and how they are assessed are determined through regulation. For reportable or notifiable diseases in which a public health response exists to each reported case, such as tuberculosis, every case must be counted. Until the 1980s, reporting in most states was based exclusively on a physician's diagnosis. Redundant, overlapping reporting systems were developed in the 1980s to overcome delays and/or absence of reporting by physicians. These systems required reports from not only physicians but also hospitals and laboratories. For example, 1985 Colorado Board of Health regulations required physicians and hospitals to report cases of AIDS, and laboratories to report persons with positive serologic tests for HIV. Sometimes, prevalent cases are required to be reported (as with infections caused by HIV or hepatitis C) because such infections, even in asymptomatic people, are contagious. Reporting also may involve secondary data sources, such as a hospital discharge data set, as with severe traumatic brain injuries in Colorado. Hospital discharge data may be transmitted to an intermediate agency, such as a hospital association, that uses the data for proprietary purposes in addition to the facilitating reporting by hospitals. This private, intermediary role may be modified by new federal HIPAA regulations, especially if named data are collected.

Authority

Debates over the role of government in the private economy date to the emergence of the U.S. market economy in the early 19th century. At that time, the Federalists, led by Alexander Hamilton, argued that a government presence was needed to guarantee property, enforce contracts, and encourage the nascent entrepreneurial ethos.[7]

In contrast, the Jeffersonians argued against intrusive government and in favor of self-reliance. That dynamic continues today over the proper regulatory oversight of health-care delivery and public health.

Federalism

Our system of government is based on the concept of dual sovereignty between the states and the federal government, known generally by the term "federalism." In a federalist system, states and the federal government share sovereignty over domestic policy.[c] One of the enduring tensions in U.S. political history is the shift between the two for control over policy. Before the New Deal era of the 1930s, states' rights dominated public policy, whereas during the 1930s–1970s, the federal government was in control. Now the trend has shifted again, with states dominating the policy arena, although the availability of federal funds continually supports state and local public health activities.

Under the Constitution, certain rights and responsibilities, such as preparing for the common defense and conducting international affairs, are reserved to the federal government. Before the 20th century, this grant of authority was interpreted narrowly, greatly limiting the federal government's involvement in health-related legislation. Indeed, the Tenth Amendment reads: "The powers not delegated to the United States by the Constitution, nor prohibited by it to the states, are reserved to the states respectively, or to the people." This was intended to ensure that the federal government would not encroach too heavily on the autonomy of the state governments and maintain a federalist structure of government, which is to say a government comprising different autonomous levels. Even though the Tenth Amendment expressly limits federal power, it still allows the federal government to control different areas of law without dependence on the states.

Thus, public health activities are traditionally within the states' authority. Before the enactment of Medicare and Medicaid in 1965, health-care regulation was an area left almost exclusively to the states.[d] Using the police powers, that is, the inherent right of a sovereign government to protect the health and welfare of the state's citizens, states have taken lead responsibility for regulating how public health services should be defined, organized, and delivered; how they should be monitored; and the relationship between the public and private sectors regarding public health services.

Preemption

An important aspect of the balance between federal and state authority and between state and local primacy is the concept of preemption. Preemption means that the superior government unit can block the inferior government entity from regulating a particular area. The rationale is to provide national uniformity in certain areas. When Congress legislates in an area and reserves power to the federal government, states may not regulate. For example, the federal government has exclusive authority for regulating nuclear power. That precludes, or preempts, any state or local attempts to regulate this field. At the state and local levels, preemption laws prevent local authorities from enacting restrictions that are more stringent than, or at variance with, the state laws. In tobacco control, for instance, many state laws state specifically that local ordinances may not be stronger than the statewide law.[e] Preemption is an important strategy used by various industries to avoid more stringent local regulation.

Many preemptive laws actually have diminished the level of protections previously afforded by local regulation where the local laws were more stringent than state measures. Beyond preventing localities from enacting ordinances that address community-specific needs, preemption reduces the amount of debate over local policies. A local debate helps to educate the community about the potential dangers of a particular public health problem (such as a debate with a city council about exposure of workers to customers' tobacco smoke in restaurants and other public places). Thus, communities lacking the ability to participate in local debates over public health decisions may pay less attention to the dangers involved and may be less aware of ways to address the problem.

Regulatory Authority

Because regulatory agencies derive their authority as delegated by the legislature, agencies must act within the bounds set by the legislature. At the federal level, affected industries have challenged regulations on the basis that Congress has unconstitutionally delegated authority to the regulatory agencies. The industries argue that Congress has not provided adequate guidance to the agencies but has instead transferred its legislative authority to the agencies. Although a few such cases have succeeded, courts have not been overly receptive to unlawful delegation challenges.

At the state level, the delegation doctrine has not raised any problems. In most states, public health legislation amounts to a broad grant of authority to enact regulations and policies to protect the public's health. Within that broad delegation of authority, agencies are expected to exercise discretion on the basis of their technical knowledge and expertise. For the most part, agency exercise of discretion will be uncontroversial, but remains a source of potential challenge. In *Boreali v. Axelrod*, for example, the court ruled that the state health department went beyond its authority to create a separate council to issue tobacco-control regulations.[8] The court held that, because these issues were stalled in the legislature and because the council decided economic and social policy issues that are usually within the legislative sphere, the agency exceeded its scope of authority. Likewise, in 2000, the Supreme Court refused to uphold the authority of the Food and Drug Administration to promulgate tobacco-control regulations, arguing that Congress had never clearly delegated such authority to the agency.[9]

Constraints on Authority: Personal Liberties

An important constraint on regulatory authority is that the intrusion into individual liberties must be limited and reasonable. The phrase "least restrictive alternative" captures this sentiment. Many public health actions, ranging from tobacco control to vaccination requirements, restrict an individual's Fourteenth Amendment liberty interests. In determining whether the regulation intrudes too much into personal freedoms, courts will attempt to balance the agency's legitimate need to protect the public's health with the individual's right to freedom from excessive government interference in personal lifestyle choices. Agencies must therefore weigh the nature of the public health benefits against the nature and extent of the abridgement into individual liberties. As an example of how a public health agency might think about balancing these competing interests, see the Public Health Intervention Matrix (Table 3-1).

For example, suppose a public health agency determines a person with cavitary pulmonary tuberculosis is not compliant with directly observed therapy being administered in the agency's tuberculosis clinic. In considering how to address the state's legitimate interest in preventing transmission of *Mycobacterium tuberculosis*, the agency needs to consider a number of potential actions. The agency's response might depend on whether the bacterium is multidrug resistant, the risk that the infection is now contagious, the reasons that the patient has been noncompliant with therapy, and the options available under existing state law. The agency could issue an administrative isolation order confining the patient to home until he or she is no longer contagious, seek a court order confining the patient to a locked hospital ward until he or she is no longer contagious, or seek a court or administrative order requiring the patient to complete a full course of therapy. The risk to the public is greatest if the bacterium is multidrug resistant because of the difficulty and cost in treating active or latent infection in that instance.

The tension between protecting the public's health without unduly infringing on individual liberties animates some of the most difficult public health policy challenges. In particular, agencies must protect the public's health without invading personal privacy, which is not always an easy task. For instance, agencies want individually available data on HIV/AIDS to trace contacts, but some assert that doing so may discourage the very reporting needed to identify infected persons and to understand prevalence trends.

Rulemaking Authority

One of a public health agency's most important functions is to issue regulations and then enforce them.[f] Those opposing the department's regulations or regulatory authority have two opportunities to challenge any regulations—immediately after the promulgated regulations appear in the *Federal Register* and then when they are applied against a particular entity.

Issuing Regulations

Gathering Information

In preparation for considering what regulations to adopt, public health agencies need to gather appropriate information to assess the scope and content of the regulations. Agencies generally have authority to gather needed information. Agencies also may choose to conduct a public hearing solely to explore specific problems and getting input from the public. Another way is to gather data through routine inspections and investigations.[g] More often, agencies will conduct a hearing after issuing a proposed regulation.

TABLE 3-1   Public Health Intervention Matrix

Balancing Framework	Activity	Public Health Justification	Public Health Strategy/Intervention	Legal Issues	Political Feasibility
1) Nature of abridgement	Tobacco				
2) Extent of abridgement	Motorcycle/Bicycle Helmets				
3) Nature of the public health benefits					
a) Is the state's interest compelling?	Cellular Phones				
b) Reasonable relationship	Seatbelts				
4) Cost of the public health intervention	Obesity				
5) Alternatives to the intervention (least intrusive means)	Guns				
6) Extent of harm to third parties if no intervention	Drunk Driving				
7) Voluntary versus involuntary risk	Domestic Violence				

The data gathering process is essential for successful regulatory activity because it forces the agency to examine the justification for the regulation and the availability of supporting documentation. It also forces the agency to assess alternatives to the regulation, objections that should be anticipated, and exposes the need for additional data collection.

Once the authority to act is clear, the important considerations are to determine whether and why to regulate. The health officer must "sell" the need for regulation to the politicians with authority to act and to the public. To do so, the agency needs to fully investigate the nature of the problems that the regulation will address and how the proposed regulations will improve the public's health. Any supporting documentation, along with the rationale (justification) for the rule, should be presented at the public hearing. To minimize challenges to or lack of compliance with the rule, a compelling rationale is important for why the regulation is needed and how it will address a serious public health problem.

The Process

The administrative process is rooted in notions of due process and fairness, that the public has an opportunity to review and comment on the regulations. If statutorily mandated procedures are not strictly followed, courts will rule that the regulation has not been appropriately issued. The procedures are set forth in administrative procedures acts, which set forth the "rules of the game" for agency actions.

The key process requirements are provision of notice to the public and solicitation of public input. These notice requirements sometimes can be suspended to respond to an emergency, but the ordinary process will include notice and an opportunity to be heard. Most state codes will be very specific about the requirements regarding time and place of a hearing and the specific subject matter. For instance, Michigan permits both the state and local public health agencies to promulgate rules "necessary or appropriate to implement" the department's functions.[10] Before adopting such rules, the department must hold a public hearing to allow any person to present data and arguments for or against the regulation. A notice of the hearing must be published "not less than 10 days before the public hearing and not less than 20 days before adoption of the regulation."[11]

At the federal level, the Administrative Procedures Act determines the process of promulgating regulations. With exceptions only for emergency situations, all regulations must first be issued as a Notice of Proposed Rulemaking and published in the *Federal Register*. As part of the process, interested citizens are given a certain period for submitting comments. The agency then reviews the comments. When the final regulation is published in the *Federal Register*, the agency's response to the comments is included. Then the final regulation is incorporated into the Code of Federal Regulations. At the state level, either the public health code or the state's administrative procedures act specifies the requirements an agency must meet before a valid regulation is put in place. Each state differs in regard to when and how the proposed regulations must be made available, but few states make agency regulations as accessible as the Code of Federal Regulations.

At the federal level, each agency promulgating a regulation must submit a regulatory impact analysis to the Office of Management and Budget. In addition, the concept of a negotiated regulation between industry and government has become increasingly popular. In the negotiated regulation process, the regulatory agency meets with the affected industry to develop a regulatory approach that is acceptable to each side to avoid contentious and time-consuming litigation.[h] Some states have a similar requirement or process. In Colorado, a regulatory analysis is required with any proposed regulations.[12] Agencies must engage as many potential stakeholders as possible in discussing the proposed rule before holding the public hearing.

Industry groups opposed to the regulation often will challenge it as being beyond the agency's scope of authority. In tobacco-control regulations, for example, affected industry groups (including the tobacco industry and retail merchants) may argue that a local regulation is invalid because it is preempted by state law or because the legislature has not granted or delegated sufficiently broad regulatory authority to the local agency. Although most of these challenges lose, some have succeeded[13,14] and may effectively delay the regulation's start date. Thus, public health practitioners need to work with their agencies' attorneys to clarify the nature of their regulatory authority before proposing a regulation.

Public health practitioners should view the public hearing as an opportunity to diffuse opposition and to engage the public and generate public support for the regulation. Coalitions of supporters may form in ways not previously anticipated because the hearing offers them an opportunity to participate. Such public support is important in an era of general distrust of government and for moving aggressively into controversial areas.

Challenging Regulations

Once the regulations go into effect, additional opportunities exist to challenge their application. Just as state public health codes specify what must be done to enact regulations, the codes also specify actions to be taken to enforce them. Again, the key is maintaining due process notions.

Suppose, for instance, that a local health department enacts a regulation regarding restaurant inspections for compliance with food and sanitation laws. During a routine inspection (or in response to a formal complaint), the investigator uncovers evidence that the proprietor violated the regulation. The investigator may issue a summons for a fine of $50 for a first offense. At that point, the proprietor can either pay the fine or contest it. If the owner contests, he or she is entitled to a fair hearing before an impartial administrative law judge.

Before a particular case can proceed, the defendant must be informed of the charges so he or she can prepare an adequate defense. Although the rules of evidence are not as strict as for a judicial proceeding, the violator is entitled to a full and fair hearing. Due process protections permit the defendant to be represented by an attorney (if desired—the defendant certainly is allowed to represent himself or herself), to present witnesses and evidence, and to cross-examine the government's witnesses. The entire hearing will be recorded, with the full record being available on appeal.

At the conclusion of the hearing, the administrative law judge must write a formal opinion. The opinion must set forth the judge's finding of facts and reasoning for reaching the decision. In Michigan, the health department reviews the opinion and can affirm, dismiss, or modify the decision. If a fine or other sanction is imposed, the violator can request the local board of health review the decision. If still dissatisfied with the decision, the violator can appeal to the local courts. Before the violator can seek judicial review, he or she must exhaust all available administrative remedies. This may include appealing first to the chief health officer and then to the local board of health. The full range of appropriate administrative remedies will be set forth in the public health code.

Judicial Standards of Review

An important aspect of public health practice is the interplay between legislation and regulation. As noted, regulatory authority is delegated by the legislature. Once regulations are enacted or applied, courts may be asked to rule on their validity. In one sense, judicial standards of review are fairly easy to describe. In reality, however, they are notoriously difficult to apply. Two general principles of the judicial standard of review are important to public health practitioners.

First, courts generally should defer to the regulatory agency's expertise in reviewing the regulations. Under the Supreme Court's Chevron doctrine,[15] as long as the regulatory record, when viewed as a whole, supports the agency's determination, courts should not intervene, even if a court might have reached a different decision on the basis of the same facts. Because the expertise, the ability to collect and analyze data, and the ability to conduct further studies all rest with the agency, courts are reluctant to overturn a regulation.

Second, courts defer to the agency's findings on the basis of the agency's factual review of all pertinent aspects of the regulation. As with appellate review of a jury verdict in a civil case, the appellate courts depend on the written record and justification provided by the agency. The agency's findings should be overturned only if they are arbitrary and capricious (i.e., not based on facts in the record), when the authority to act is not clear, or when the agency omits analyses required by the legislature.

Courts generally are less deferential when reviewing the agency's interpretations of its regulations, which agencies often do through subsequent policy statements. In part because the policy statements are not issued on the basis of public comment and review, courts tend to be considerably less deferential when reviewing an agency's policy interpretation of its regulations. This is important for enforcement. If the violation is clear from the regulations, courts usually will side with the agency. But if the public health agency relies on a policy statement to find a violation, courts may not necessarily uphold the agency, particularly if the agency has not disseminated the policy statements to potential violators.

Administrative Strategies and Remedies

Much of the art of public health practice is deciding what actions to take in response to a public health code violation. A public health agency can use a broad range of remedies to enforce its regulations. Should states with referral authority for criminal activities seek a criminal punishment or is a civil fine sufficient? Should the agency seek fines or try to enjoin the activity? Deciding which remedy to pursue requires knowledge both of the range of potential sanctions and the trade-offs involved. Each state's public health code is likely to specify the range of permissible sanctions and remedies.

Civil Strategies and Remedies

Civil Sanctions

Civil sanctions involve a range of options, from monetary penalties to injunctions. The purpose of civil fines is simply to provide an inducement to comply with the regulations. Failure to comply can be costly.

Most public health codes specify the amount of money a violator will pay. A civil fine usually is graduated on the basis of the number of violations, with repeat violators paying successively higher amounts. For example, a statute regulating noise levels may specify a $50 fine for the first offense, $100 for a second, and $500 for a third.

Another civil remedy is use of the licensure authority to ensure compliance and deter violations. Many activities affecting public health require a license from the state or from the local authorities. For example, tobacco and alcohol vendors are licensed. If they sell tobacco or alcohol to minors, their vendor's license can be suspended after an appropriate hearing. License suspension is a particularly valuable remedy for enforcing restrictions on the sale of tobacco and alcohol to minors. Although the investment in enforcing these laws is not trivial, a vendor may respond more positively to losing his or her license than to a simple fine (which the vendor may treat as just the cost of doing business). From a practical standpoint, licensing fees (along with fines paid for violations) may well sustain an aggressive enforcement effort.[16]

A related use of licensing authority deals with state oversight of health-care facilities. All states license both health-care facilities and providers. State and local authorities can use the licensure process to ensure these facilities comply with local health and safety codes.

One strategy to consider is use of the taxing authority. Almost all states, for instance, tax cigarettes and alcohol. Some states authorize taxing at the local level as well. In an era of anti-tax fervor, generating public support for new taxes is difficult. But the public generally supports the concept of taxing alcohol and cigarettes, even if disagreement is considerable about the optimal taxing levels.

Injunctions

Injunctions are an important component of local public health practice. An injunction is a court order requiring an actor to stop a defined activity prohibited by law. For example, if a firm or individual violates noise pollution ordinances, the public health department can either cite the violator for civil penalties or ask a court to enjoin the activity. Injunctions are issued when a violation of the law is ongoing, such as when exposure of the public to a disease risk is ongoing, monetary damages are not available, and harm would be irreparable if the injunction were denied. For example, an injunction might be used to close a restaurant until the cause of an outbreak of salmonellosis has been identified and eliminated. Courts must balance the equities between the need to continue the activity and the public's health.

A controversial use of injunctions has been to enjoin HIV-infected persons who, despite counseling, continue to expose other people to the virus. The purpose of the injunction is to stop the risky behavior, but because of the manner in which HIV usually is transmitted, i.e., by unsafe or unprotected sexual activity and by sharing contaminated needles, compliance with the injunction is difficult to monitor. Degrees exist of evidence of noncompliance; diagnosis in a sex partner of the index patient of an acute sexually transmitted disease, such as gonorrhea, is stronger evidence of unsafe behavior than assertion of a sex partner that he or she was not informed of the HIV infection in the index patient and so had unprotected sex. HIV is a lifelong infection, and even if HIV is not detectable in the serum, the infected person still may transmit the virus. Therefore, an injunction could be enforced indefinitely or until a treatment is found for HIV that renders it noncontagious. Furthermore, controversy exists about whether unsafe sex between two consenting adults, of whom one or both are HIV-infected, represents a public health threat. The injunction could be viewed as one of several types of therapeutic intervention designed to protect the public health. Its value in comparison to repeated, intensive behavior counseling and social therapy must be individually evaluated. Little long-term experience exists to guide the agency or the courts in this area of public health practice.

Litigation

A related civil strategy is litigation. This controversial approach has met with limited success in high-visibility areas. States successfully have used litigation to compel a settlement with the tobacco industry over the costs of tobacco-related disease to state Medicaid programs. Localities have tried a similar strategy against gun manufacturers for failing to monitor the distribution of their products. So far, these suits have been limited or thrown out altogether in the appellate courts, despite some initial success among jurors. In addition, some states have responded to local agency lawsuits by enacting laws that allow only the state to sue, thereby preempting such litigation.

One advantage of litigation is that it may result in settlement negotiations that an industry might not otherwise be willing to join. But a disadvantage is the cost of litigation and the potential for the state legislature to enact laws preempting such litigation.

Criminal Strategies and Remedies

Many public health statutes provide for both civil and criminal fines. Because agencies and courts generally are reluctant to characterize a public health violation as a criminal matter, most fines sought are civil in nature. For instance, most statutes for code violations, such as for nuisance or pollution, are defined as misdemeanors (minor crimes) subject to a criminal or civil fine. Most of the time, the agency ignores the criminal aspect and simply seeks a civil fine.

In some instances, however, a violation is so severe as to warrant a criminal sanction. The most obvious case is when a firm dumps toxic and hazardous wastes into the environment and ignores an agency's or court's order to cease the activity. At that point, a civil fine may be considered an insufficient penalty, and the violation may justify a criminal indictment. For both political and legal reasons, the evidence must be very strong, and the activity must be egregious to support a criminal trial. Unlike a civil action, the state in a criminal trial must show beyond a reasonable doubt that the defendant intended to violate the laws. This is a high standard and support for criminal investigations has been slow in coming.

Traditional Public Health Strategies and Remedies

Some of the most difficult decisions a public health agency must make regard when to exercise traditional public health remedies to halt the spread of disease. Agencies usually attempt to impose the least restrictive method to outbreak control. For example, in the past when measles occurred in a child attending school, public health agencies often issued a school exclusion order rather than requiring all under-vaccinated children to be vaccinated. The exclusion order meant that nonvaccinated or undervaccinated children were sent home and could not be readmitted to school until the outbreak was over, generally two to four weeks after onset of illness in the last reported case. However, the excluded children were not required to be vaccinated. The effect on disease control of such an order was to remove potentially susceptible children from contact with children who were infectious or incubating measles, thereby, preventing a subsequent generation of disease. At a time in the United States when fear and distrust of vaccinations by the population is increasing, a public health remedy is useful that does not require vaccination but effectively stops disease transmission. Measles, however, is now rare in the United States, and this remedy may not be as effective with other communicable diseases, such as varicella, or in non-school settings, such as child-care centers and adult workplaces.

Two areas that seem receptive to the use of traditional public health strategies but raise surprising complications are distribution of needles to users of illicit drugs who have HIV or AIDS and disease reporting requirements. In the former situation, many states have criminal statutes preventing the exchange of clean needles. How can a public health agency develop and implement a needle-exchange program without violating the laws against distribution? In the latter case, agencies need to collect a wide range of data to monitor disease prevalence trends, but increasing concern for individual privacy and confidentiality enhances the risk that individually identifiable data could be disclosed.

Public health agencies also have the power to conduct screening examinations for various diseases. These are useful for monitoring disease prevalence trends. For instance, several states track reports of prenatal substance exposure and HIV exposure to monitor disease trends.[17] The controversial aspect of these prevalence tracking efforts is whether to identify individuals for contact tracing in the case of HIV and for referral to child welfare authorities in the case of prenatal substance exposure. Some states mandate screening for certain populations or diseases. Colorado permits HIV screening of prisoners without their knowledge and consent.[18] Other states, including Wisconsin, mandate screening and reporting to detect prenatal substance exposure.

Education is another traditional public health strategy that must be viewed as complementary, but integral, to the regulatory process. Education has had some stunning successes, particularly in conjunction with regulatory activity. For example, the designated-driver advertising campaign has dramatically reduced deaths caused by drunken driving. Although less dramatic (and somewhat more contentious), the accumulated information from education campaigns about the dangers of tobacco use has contributed to reduced adult and teen smoking rates over time.

Trade-Offs in Selecting Remedies

As the above discussion suggests, public health agencies often must make trade-offs in deciding which remedies to pursue. Regulations generally must be written to protect the community without unduly burdening the individual freedoms the law preserves. More specifically, agencies always must be concerned about how their scarce resources will be allocated. Retaining public support is critical in securing this balance.

Some of the inherent trade-offs are obvious. For instance, speed of securing a fine, rather than the heightened administrative burden of seeking an injunction or a criminal sanction, is one such consideration. Another is concern with political feasibility. In many instances, the public health code will require a final decision from an elected official (such as a local board of health) before the public health action can be undertaken.

As a general proposition, public health agencies need to consider: the targets of the proposed regulation; data available to support the regulation; anticipated interest group opposition; the cost of the chosen strategy; its potential effectiveness (both in terms of achieving the desired goal and in reaching a large number of people); and the equities involved in pursuing the regulation. Another factor to consider, similar to what physicians face in the private health system, is that public health officials no longer control the flow of information as they once did. The availability of information over the Internet and the speed with which information and rumors (such as the alleged relation between autism and the measles-mumps-rubella vaccine) can spread through the body politic clearly complicates the process of promulgating and enforcing public health regulations.

Burden of Proof

In selecting a remedy, one practical consideration is which party will have the burden of proof if the local public health agency's decision is challenged. For example, suppose an entity's activities arguably violate an ordinance's noise levels. The agency can seek an injunction, issue a cease-and-desist order, or seek damages. The advantage of a cease-and-desist order is that if the entity challenges the order or fails to comply with it, the entity would have the burden of proving the agency exceeded its authority or is arbitrarily and capriciously executing its regulatory authority. If, on the other hand, the agency seeks an injunction, it would have the burden of proving the noise is detrimental to public health and is acting within the scope of its authority.

Warrantless Searches

Another tactical decision a local public health agency needs to make is whether to obtain a warrant before inspecting premises to determine compliance with local ordinances or state laws. A fundamental way in which states and localities exercise their inherent police power is by conducting inspections. Statutes usually give the health officer broad authority to inspect "pursuant to a search warrant when required by law, without fee or hindrance" any premises, matter or thing within its jurisdiction, particularly with regard to places where services are provided for children.[19] Without consent for a search, the Fourth Amendment generally prohibits unreasonable searches and seizures without a judicially obtained warrant based on probable cause to believe public health codes have been violated.

As an exception to the warrant requirement, courts have upheld warrantless searches in emergency situations and in pervasively regulated businesses. Frank Grad notes that this exception "applies to enterprises that are so thoroughly regulated, and which in some instances have been regulated for a long time, so that any person who engages in the business gives up any 'justifiable expectation of privacy.'"[20] A warrantless inspection will be upheld as long as it is an essential aspect of the regulatory mechanism, a substantial public interest exists in the effectiveness of the regulation and is limited in time, scope, and duration.

Yet, what constitutes a pervasively regulated business or when a warrantless search would be appropriate is not always clear. A person operating a licensed group family day care in the home cannot refuse an inspector access to any part of the home, even though demanding access to a bedroom might appear to be an invasion of a legitimate expectation of privacy. Such enterprises are pervasively regulated, with only limited numbers of children allowed and with required numbers of adults providing supervision. An inspector must be able to verify that children are not being hidden from sight in the bedroom or the basement. Conversely, suppose that a restaurateur has an office above the restaurant and the local public health department receives complaints about smoking in the office in violation of the local nonsmoking ordinance. Without consent, would a warrantless search to seize ashtrays as evidence be appropriate? Just because the restaurant itself is pervasively regulated does not mean the office is as well. Therefore, obtaining a search warrant would be advisable.

Future Challenges

In terms of the public health regulatory environment, state and local public health policymakers should be prepared to address several challenges. These challenges range from technical concerns (e.g., cost-benefit analysis) to conceptual concerns (e.g., public health as a collective enterprise).

Cost-Benefit Analysis

Two factors strongly suggest that some form of cost-benefit analysis (i.e., cost-effectiveness analysis, risk-utility analysis) will become standard practice for issuing state and local public health regulations. First, the federal government is increasingly using some form of cost-benefit analysis in issuing its regulations. Sooner or later that will lead to expectations that state and local regulations will also incorporate this analysis. Second, public pressure for more efficient government will force state and local officials to justify the cost of each and every regulation in terms of benefits to the community.

The problem at the local level will be that gathering and analyzing cost-benefit data can be time-consuming, especially if staff have not been trained to gather or analyze data. Defining the intangible benefits always is difficult. On the negative side, this will slow the regulatory process and force agencies to choose between competing regulations. More positively, regulations issued with a solid cost-benefit analysis will be easier to justify to the public.

Regulatory Takings

Under the Fifth Amendment, the government cannot confiscate private property without paying just compensation. For example, when a local government condemns a property to construct a road under eminent domain, the government must pay the owner the property's fair market value. Until the mid-1980s, the takings doctrine only applied to an actual condemnation of the property. Regulations generally were exempt from this doctrine. Starting in the early 1990s, the Supreme Court expanded the meaning of the Takings Clause to include partial regulatory takings.[21] If, for instance, the Environmental Protection Agency declares part of one's property a protected wetland, diminishing the value of the entire parcel but only regulating a portion, the owner could request compensation under the Fifth Amendment.

The implications of this doctrinal shift for public health regulation are profound. Although the takings doctrine has not yet interfered with the government's ability to enact zoning, rent control, or environmental regulations, the takings doctrine acts as a limitation on the range of regulatory strategies the government can pursue. At a minimum, public health agencies may need to think twice about taking certain actions. For instance, regulatory takings issues may be raised for ordering herds of deer and elk to be killed if they are in a region with chronic wasting disease (a transmissible spongiform encephalopathy). Likewise, ordering sheep to be killed if they originate from a farm where scrapie (another transmissible spongiform encephalopathy) has been detected may result in a takings challenge.

[handwritten margin note: CWD + scrapie]

As a general proposition, however, public health officials can confiscate, embargo, and destroy contaminated goods without paying just compensation. Many public health laws and regulations authorize the health agency to seize, embargo, and even destroy food, drugs, articles, or other goods that are in violation of law, adulterated, misbranded, unfit for consumption or use, or constitute a danger to the public's health.[22] Government must ascertain whether any part of the seized material is salvageable because it is not in violation or not dangerous and return such portion of the embargoed material. Similarly, government can seize and humanely euthanize dangerous or vicious animals.[23] Due process opportunities to be heard or even hearings may need to be provided; but it is axiomatic that government can embargo inherently dangerous products or things and destroy them without having to pay compensation. If seizing and destroying property is essential to protect the public's health, this property is not being taken for the government's benefit. Therefore, no compensation or damages will be paid.

Public-Private Partnerships

Public health practice at the beginning of the 21st century must take into account certain fundamental policy shifts. In particular, the health-care system is increasingly competitive, based on market principles, and the public seems less willing to support investments in public health. As a result, public health agencies must develop alternative strategies to regulation that involve public-private partnerships. Most state codes permit public health agencies to contract with the private sector for goods or services. Perhaps the most dramatic of these public-private arrangements is Medicaid managed care. State Medicaid agencies use their contracting authority to solicit bids from the private sector to provide Medicaid services.

The use of public-private partnerships to provide public health services presents both opportunities and challenges. The opportunities are to use such partnerships to achieve public health goals without issuing regulations or going through contentious litigation challenging the regulations. By using the contracting mechanism, public health agencies can specify the terms of engagement and set the expectations for how the programs will be monitored. But serious challenges need to be confronted. One is that the resources to monitor adequately the contracts may not be available. Another challenge is to negotiate contractual terms that reflect public health goals. A more serious concern is that shifting public health services to the private sector will call into question the need for the public health system altogether.

New Public Health Concerns

The public health regulatory model is based on controlling communicable diseases. For many future activities, that model still will be appropriate and effective, but the potential use of large-scale quarantine to control outbreaks of SARS or diseases resulting from a bioterrorist attack may present challenges never seen before. Furthermore, public health concerns are not limited to communicable diseases, and a different regulatory strategy may be needed for issues not falling within that approach. Take, for example, questions regarding obesity and genetics technologies. Are these public health issues? Is there legal authority for public health department attempts to regulate in these areas? If so, what types of regulatory strategies might be considered?

Even the old verities will arise in different ways. When *Jacobson v. Massachusetts* was decided, few people refused the smallpox vaccination. Now, every state has a statute exempting individuals from vaccination on the basis of religious or medical criteria, and a number of states allow for an exemption based on personal or philosophic objections to vaccination. Add to this the concerns about neurologic effects of pertussis vaccination, fears about measles-mumps-rubella vaccine causing autism and hepatitis B vaccine causing multiple sclerosis, and the real association of the original rotavirus vaccination and intussusception. A health department is thus likely to confront a growing number of parents who choose to leave their children unvaccinated. The parents may make their decisions on the basis of personal concerns about the risks for vaccination and do not understand the cumulative effect of many such personal decisions is to increase each unvaccinated child's risk of acquiring a particular communicable disease.

At a time of general public distrust for government and a declining investment in public health resources, public health agencies need to be cognizant of alternative strategies to achieve public health objectives. One approach is to rely on moral suasion to convince the public that certain actions need to be taken. One might view this as similar to an education strategy, but it needs to be thought of in broader terms than simply an attempt to educate the public. Instead, it means using local media and the Internet to make the case for public health and using the moral high ground to advocate for public health strategies.

Public Health as a Collective Enterprise

Public health regulations are based on population data and science and designed to achieve the greatest good for the greatest number. However, that collective goal conflicts with the ethos of individualism now dominating social policy. Public health agencies must balance their mandate to protect communities from the spread of contagious diseases with their responsibility to not unduly burden individuals who do not want to be protected (i.e., vaccinated). Although uninfected people have an individual right to remain uninfected and take advantage of the vaccination exemption, this is never just an individual decision because serious public health implications exist for society if the individual contracts and transmits the disease. Therefore, representing both interests simultaneously is challenging.

Notes

a. See, for example, *Jacobson v Massachusetts*, 197 U.S. 11 (1904), rejecting an individual's challenge to a Cambridge, Massachusetts, law mandating smallpox inoculations.

b. For a critique of these arrangements, see Jacobson PD. Form versus function in public health, *J Public Health Manage Pract* 2002;8:92–4.

c. The Tenth Aamendment reads: "The powers not delegated to the United States by the Constitution, nor prohibited by it to the states, are reserved to the states respectively, or to the people." This was intended to ensure the federal government would not encroach too heavily on the autonomy of the state governments and to maintain a federalist structure of government.

d. See, for example, *Dukes v. U.S. Healthcare, Inc.*, 57 F.3d 350, 357 (3d Cir. 1995). Article 1, Section 8, of the Constitution provides federal jurisdiction over health matters to promote the general welfare.

e. Not all preemption provisions are alike. Massachusetts' preemption applies only to the sale of cigarette rolling paper, whereas other states preempt local jurisdictions from enacting any clean indoor air restrictions (i.e., Florida).

f. In rare circumstances, an agency with public health functions may not be a regulatory agency. For example, the Centers for Disease Control and Prevention has enormous public health responsibility but does not issue or enforce regulations.

g. For a thorough summary of information-gathering techniques, see Grad FP. *The Public Health Law Manual*. 3rd ed. Washington, DC: American Public Health Association, 2004.

h. To think that affected industries were ignored in regulatory policy before reg-neg would be naive, but the explicit inclusion of the industry in the regulatory process is substantially different.

References

1. *Black's Law Dictionary*. Abridged 6th ed. St. Paul, MN: West Publishing Co., 1991.
2. Federal Statutes at Large, Vol. 1, p. 44.
3. Smillie WG. *Public Health: Its Promise for the Future*. New York: Arno Press, 1976.
4. Jost TS. Oversight of quality medical care: regulation, management or the market? *Arizona Law Rev* 1995;37;825–68.
5. Arrow KJ. Uncertainty and the welfare economics of medical care. *Am Economic Rev* 1963;53:941–73.
6. Centers for Disease Control and Prevention. National Public Health Performance Standards Program. Available at http://www.cdc.gov/od/ocphp/nphpsp/index.htm. Accessed August 4, 2005.
7. Sellers C. *The Market Revolution: Jacksonian America, 1815–1846*. New York: Oxford University Press, 1991.
8. 517 NE 2d 1350 (NY 1987).
9. *Food and Drug Administration v Brown & Williamson Tobacco Corp*, 529 US 120 (2000).
10. Mich Comp Laws Ann, Part 333, §§2233 and 2441.
11. Mich Comp Laws Ann, Part 333, §2442.
12. Colo Rev Stat, Title 24, Article 4, §103 (2.5)(a).
13. *Boreali v Axelrod*, 517 NE 2d 1350 (NY 1987)
14. *Brewery, Inc v Delaware City-County Board of Health*, No 98CVH-12-413 (CP Delaware County, Ohio, July 22, 1999).
15. *Chevron USA, Inc v Natural Resources Defense Council, Inc*, 467 US 837 (1984).
16. Jacobson PD, Wasserman J. Tobacco control laws: implementation and enforcement. *J Health Politics, Policy Law* 1999;24:567–98.
17. Zellman GL, Jacobson PD, Bell RM. Influencing physician response to prenatal substance exposure through state legislation and workplace policies. *Addiction* 1997;92:1123–31.
18. Colo Rev Stat, Title 25, Article 4, §1405(8)(a)(IV).
19. New York City Charter, §566; and New York City Health Code, §§3.01 and 3.05, 24 RCNY 3.01 and 3.05.
20. Grad FP. *The Public Health Law Manual*. 3rd ed. Washington, DC: American Public Health Association, 2004.
21. *Lucas v South Carolina Coastal Council*, 505 US 1003 (1992).
22. New York City Health Code, §§3.03 and 71.11, 24 RCNY 3.03 and 71.11.
23. New York City Health Code, §161.07, 24 RCNY 161.07.

Chapter 4

PUBLIC HEALTH AND THE JUDICIARY

Daniel D. Stier* and Diane M. Nicks

> We are under a Constitution, but the Constitution is what the judges say
> it is, and the judiciary is the safeguard of our liberty and our property under
> the Constitution.
> >   Charles Evans Hughes, American Jurist and Statesman, 1862–1948

> The prophecies of what the courts will do in fact, and nothing more pre-
> tentious, are what I mean by the law.
> >   Oliver Wendell Holmes, Jr.[1]

As in other types of disputes, disputes involving public health ultimately may proceed to the courts. When they do, they present issues of public welfare that demand
efficient, yet careful and correct, resolution. The parties to these cases face special
challenges, including the need for public health officials and other parties to disputes
or involved in actions to understand the workings of the court system, or the need
for judges to understand certain technical issues about public health or to make relevant evidentiary determinations.

Public health officials ordinarily spend little time in court. Consequently, they
frequently lack a working knowledge of the system in which their public health

* The findings and conclusions in this chapter are those of the author(s) and do not necessarily represent the views of the U.S. Department of Health and Human Services or the Centers for Disease Control
and Prevention.

actions will be tested. Judges, on the other hand, rise to the bench from various types of law practice: many were criminal prosecutors and therefore possess criminal law expertise; others were civil trial lawyers and have expertise in areas such as tort law. However, judges generally lack background and expertise in many specialized areas of law, including public health. Therefore, when a legal issue involving public health needs judicial resolution, judges must be "educated" about both the relevant law and public health considerations. Depending on the type of case, they, or the juries sitting in their courtrooms, also may need to be fully informed about technical or scientific facts, epidemiologic or otherwise, to make appropriate factual findings.

Just as the judiciary periodically may require enhanced understanding about a public health issue, public health officials must be thoroughly familiar with judicial rules and procedures and ready to inform the presiding jurist about the law and facts. Put simply, public health officials and attorneys must know their way around the courthouse.

In this chapter, we explore the relations between public health and the judiciary, defined broadly as the U.S. court system, essential functions of the court system, essential people within the court system (e.g., judges and juries; however, we make only passing references to the role of juries), and procedural rules and customs under which the courts resolve disputes and operate. We briefly introduce the structure and function of federal and state courts and describe how federalism requires state and federal courts to share power. Next, we discuss several public health law–related cases decided by courts. While showing that courts generally grant broad deference to officials endeavoring to protect the public's health, the cases also illustrate (1) judicial insistence on the existence of underlying legal authority; (2) attention paid by courts to the facts on which public health actions are based; (3) judicial balancing of protection of public health and individual rights; (4) impact of federalism on judicial decisions; and (5) potential for judicial interpretation to change over time. Finally, we address the emerging issue of the courts' roles in and preparedness needs for public health emergencies.

Structure and Function of the Judicial System

In general, the role of the judiciary is to resolve disputes. At the federal level, the role is founded in Article III of the U.S. Constitution, establishing the federal judiciary to resolve "cases and controversies" involving federal law or certain parties. State judicial systems similarly are established by state constitutions for resolving cases and controversies generally involving state and local laws. The U.S. Congress and state legislatures establish the structures of the federal and state court systems, respectively. In the public health context, court actions can take several forms, including affirming and enforcing an order of a public health official as a proper exercise of discretion; overturning an order of a public health official for lack of statutory authority; or striking down a public health law or order for interfering with an individual's constitutional right to liberty (Box 4-1).

Box 4-1. Possible Court Measures in Public Health and Other Cases

- Authorize, affirm, reverse, or modify agency decisions
- Monitor or oversee agency action to ensure compliance with court orders
- Issue injunctions or restraining orders, temporarily or permanently prohibiting or requiring agency action
- Compel compliance with court orders through use of contempt powers involving imposition of sanctions, including confinement or financial penalties
- Require or authorize production or evidentiary submission of information, including otherwise confidential information
- Compel, prohibit, or impose conditions on deposition or courtroom testimony of agency officials or employees
- Order redaction or *in camera* review (by the judge in his or her chambers) of confidential information

---

Federal Courts

The Supreme Court is the only court directed to be established by Article III, Section 1, of the Constitution. It is the United States' court of last resort. In a small number of cases, the Court has original jurisdiction.[2] Otherwise, the Court generally has discretion over whether to take an appeal. Appeals usually are initiated with the filing of a writ of certiorari from either a U.S. court of appeals or a state supreme court.[3]

Congress creates "inferior courts" under the discretion granted by Article III, Section 1. There are 94 federal trial courts, called district courts.[4] District courts hear civil and criminal cases. Public health cases can arise in a criminal context but generally are civil. Most civil cases arise under either the courts' "federal question" jurisdiction or "diversity" jurisdiction.[5] Federal questions are simply those arising under the Constitution, laws, or treaties of the United States. Diversity jurisdiction most commonly exists where the controversy is between citizens of different states or citizens of a state and citizens or subjects of a foreign state. The disputed amount in a diversity case must exceed $75,000.

The district courts are organized into 12 regional circuits, each with a court of appeals.[4] A court of appeals hears appeals of decisions arising from the district courts within its circuit.[6] Appeals are heard and decided on the basis of the record made before the district court.

State Courts

The caseload of the state courts vastly exceeds that of the federal courts for both civil and criminal cases.[7] State courts handle virtually all cases involving divorce and child custody, probate and inheritance, real estate, and juvenile issues, and most cases involving criminal prosecution, contract disputes, traffic violations, and personal injury.[4] Most public health cases are decided in state courts.

Each state, as well as the District of Columbia and Puerto Rico, has its own court system. The state systems have structural characteristics that are generally similar to those of the federal judicial system. All include a court of last resort, typically called the supreme court. Most states have an intermediate court of appeals. All have courts of general jurisdiction, and most have courts of limited jurisdiction. Even though they share general characteristics, the structural details of state court systems vary widely. For example, Georgia's court system includes courts of general jurisdiction, called superior courts; eight additional types of limited jurisdiction courts; and two levels of appellate courts. On the other hand, the entire court structure in North Dakota comprises a unified trial court and a single appellate court of last resort.[8]

Quasi-Judicial Decision-Makers

Administrative law judges/hearings officers (ALJs) are located not in the judicial branch of state and federal government but in the executive branch. Nonetheless, they merit mention because administrative procedure acts and other laws frequently require that disputes involving government agencies—including public health agencies —initially be heard and decided by ALJs. In contrast with courts, ALJs generally work in specialized areas of law within their agencies and therefore have technical background and expertise in those areas. They generally are authorized to find the facts, draw legal conclusions, and issue decisions in the cases before them. They are not, however, authorized to decide constitutional questions; that function is reserved to the courts. Decisions of ALJs sometimes are subject to finalization by the administrative agency and always are subject to judicial review. Although the rules of practice and procedure before ALJs generally are less rigorous than court rules, proceedings before them resemble those before courts, and ALJs are of course required to adhere to constitutional principles.

Federalism: Sharing of Powers between State and Federal Courts

The U.S. system of government is based on federalism—a sharing of powers between the federal and state governments. The U.S. Constitution in Article I, Section 8, and the Tenth Amendment frame the system. Article I, Section 8, authorizes the federal government to make the laws "necessary and proper" to execute the powers listed in the article. Included among the listed powers are the authority to tax and spend for the general welfare, to regulate commerce, and to establish "inferior" courts, post offices, a monetary system, uniform systems of naturalization and bankruptcy, and an army and navy. Chief among those powers with respect to most issues, including public health, are the power to tax and spend and the power to regulate commerce. The Tenth Amendment reserves to the states all powers not listed in Article I, Section 8. Thus, to the extent that the listed federal powers are given an expansive interpretation, the reserved power of the states is diminished. Conversely, limiting interpretations of federal power increase the relative power of the states.

Since the earliest days of the Constitution, interpretation of the relative powers of state and federal governments has been a matter of intense debate in Congress, in the states, and—most importantly for our purposes—in the courts. Since *McCullough v. Maryland*, 17 U.S. 316 (1819)—where the Supreme Court held that Congress, under the "necessary and proper" clause and the Court's doctrine of "implied powers," had the power to establish a national bank even though that power was not expressly listed in Article I, Section 8—the courts have regularly interpreted and established the constitutional boundaries between enumerated federal powers and reserved state powers. A modern-day example is *United States v. Lopez*, a 1995 Supreme Court decision holding that the power to regulate commerce did not authorize Congress to make possession of a gun within 1000 feet of a school a federal crime, as it attempted to do in the Drug Free School Zone Act of 1990.[9]

The U.S. court system itself is based on the principle of federalism. The court systems of the states were developed simultaneously with establishment of the federal judicial system. That fact, coupled with retention by the states of their autonomy, led to complexity and overlap in federal and state court jurisdiction.[7] Although resolution of constitutional issues, for example, generally is considered a federal court activity, state courts hear and decide cases arising under both the U.S. Constitution and federal law, unless prohibited by federal law from doing so. Also, not uncommonly, a federal court has jurisdiction over prosecution of behavior alleged to constitute a crime under federal law, whereas a state court has jurisdiction over prosecution of the same behavior alleged to constitute a violation of state law. Likewise, civil litigation may be filed in either state or federal court.

Demonstrating the continuing vitality of this jurisdictional complexity—and the ability of Congress to pass laws affecting court jurisdiction—is the existence of the Judicial Conference Committee on Federal-State Jurisdiction.[10] Composed of federal and state judges from trial and appellate levels, the committee advises the Judicial Conference on federal and state court jurisdictional issues. Acknowledging the doctrine of federalism and the limited jurisdiction of federal courts, the committee proceeds from a belief that the role of federal courts is to complement the essential role played by state courts in handling both state and federal law issues.

As with other types of cases, federal courts have jurisdiction over cases involving public health issues only if a "federal question" is presented or if "diversity of citizenship" exists. For example, "federal question" jurisdiction would exist with regard to a constitutional due process challenge to either federal or state government efforts to detain or quarantine an individual suspected of having an infectious disease. "Diversity" jurisdiction would exist if a citizen of one state suspected of having an infectious disease challenged efforts of another state to prevent entry into the state and if the individual could reasonably allege suffering monetary damages in excess of $75,000. In the likely event that an individual in that circumstance alleged a constitutional deprivation, such as the loss of liberty resulting from a quarantine order, the court would of course also have federal question jurisdiction over the constitutional claim.

State courts retain all powers not granted to the federal courts by the Constitution. They have jurisdiction over claims arising out of state constitutions and laws, and, unless prohibited by federal law, also may be able to hear and decide issues involving the U.S. Constitution and federal laws. In a public health context, legal issues generally involve the exercise of the police power by public health agencies. Although not expressly referenced in the Constitution, the courts universally recognize the existence of the police power as the power reserved to the states for creation and implementation of laws to protect the public's health, safety, and welfare. Consistent with this broad reserved power, most public health laws and regulations reside at the state (and local) level. State courts have jurisdiction over issues arising out of those state laws and regulations. Not surprisingly, therefore, cases involving public health legal issues most commonly are filed and resolved in state courts.

Public Health Law Cases in Court

This section discusses the relation between the judiciary and public health through an examination of selected cases involving disputes resolved by the courts (Table 4-1). However, understanding that disputes involving every type of public health issue may wend their way to court is important. As demonstrated in other chapters in this book, those issues arise from public health areas as diverse as environmental protection, injury prevention, eradication of nuisances, reproductive health, and infectious disease control. This review of selected cases demonstrates six themes and principles characterizing the judiciary's involvement with public health, beginning with the courts' general position of granting broad deference to public health authority.

Deference to Public Health Authority

Recognizing the critical importance of protecting public health, courts often defer to discretion exercised by public health officials pursuant to the police power and broad legislative grants of authority. In the landmark, over-100-year-old decision in *Jacobson v. Massachusetts*, 197 U.S. 11 (1905), the U.S. Supreme Court established the boundaries of discretion granted to agencies to protect the public health. In response to an outbreak of smallpox in the early 1900s, the Cambridge Board of Health used its state statutory authority to require vaccination of residents who had not been vaccinated within the past five years. The defendant, Henning Jacobson, refused to comply with the vaccination requirement, was convicted and fined, and appealed his conviction through the Massachusetts courts to the U.S. Supreme Court. Writing for the court, Justice Harlan pronounced that, under settled principles, "the police power of a state must be held to embrace, at least, such reasonable regulations established directly by legislative enactment as will protect the public health and the public safety."[11] Furthermore, while discussing the limits imposed on exercise of the police power, Justice Harlan nonetheless spoke in terms of the community's *right* to protect itself: "Upon the principle of self-defense, of paramount necessity, a community has the right to protect itself against an epidemic of disease which threatens the safety of its members" (emphasis added).[12]

Deference to agency expertise is a judicial principle generally applicable to all government regulatory agencies. The leading case on the principle of deference,

TABLE 4-1 Selected Court Decisions Relevant to Public Health Practice

Name	Court	Issue	Comments
McCullough v. Maryland, 17 U.S. 316 (1819)	U.S. Supreme Court	Was Congress constitutionally empowered to establish a national bank?	Early example of judicial interpretation and establishment of boundaries between federal and state powers.
United States v. Lopez, 514 U.S. 549 (1995)	U.S. Supreme Court	Was Congress constitutionally empowered to criminalize handgun possession near schools?	Recent example of judicial interpretation and establishment of boundaries between federal and state powers.
Jacobson v. Massachusetts, 197 U.S. 11 (1905)	U.S. Supreme Court	Was the state constitutionally permitted to require vaccination?	Landmark decision establishing judicial role in balancing the exercise of police power against protection of individual rights.
Chevron, U.S.A., Inc., v. Natural Resources Defense Council, Inc., 467 U.S. 837 (1984)	U.S. Supreme Court	To what extent will the court defer to agency action?	Leading case on the issue, holding that court will not substitute its judgment for that of the agency in the absence of Congressional direction to the contrary.
City of New York v. New St. Mark's Baths, 130 Misc. 2d 911, 497 N.Y.S.2d 979 (1986)	Supreme Court of New York, Special Term, New York County	Did public health officials have discretion to close a gay bathhouse in an effort to stop spread of HIV infection?	Court broadly deferred to officials' "scientific view" in the absence of evidence that motive for closure was not an "illusory pretense."
Continental Seafoods, Inc. v. Schweiker, 674 F.2d 38 (D.C. Cir. 1982)	U.S. Court of Appeals, Washington, D.C.	Was food safety official authorized to remove product from the food supply?	Agency had discretion to remove food product even if proper handling/cooking would ensure safety.
United States v. 1200 Cans . . . Pasteurized Whole Eggs, 339 F. Supp. 131 (N.D. Ga. 1972)	U.S. District Court, Northern District of Georgia	Was food safety official authorized to remove product from the food supply?	Agency had discretion to remove food product even if it could not show illness caused by product consumption.

(*continued*)

TABLE 4-1 (continued)

Name	Court	Issue	Comments
American Textile Manufacturers Institute, Inc. v. Donovan, 452 U.S. 490 (1981)	U.S. Supreme Court	Was labor official required to perform cost/benefit analysis before promulgating a worker safety regulation?	Court held that Congress had determined that worker safety was of paramount concern to the extent it could be achieved.
American Brass Company and another v. State Board of Health and another, 245 Wis. 440, 15 N.W.2d 27 (1944)	Wisconsin Supreme Court	Could state health and pollution control agencies issue a joint order to halt water pollution?	Despite laudable goal, court refused to permit a joint order in the absence of relevant statutory authority.
Boreali v. Axelrod, 71 N.Y.2d 1, 517 N.E.2d 1350 (1987)	Court of Appeals of New York	Did local health agency have authority to impose smoking restrictions in public places?	Despite the dangers of second-hand smoke, court found no legal authority for the proposed restrictions.
Vinson et al. v. Home Builders Association of Atlanta et al., 233 Ga. 948, 213 S.E.2d 890 (1975)	Supreme Court of Georgia	Could public health statute be used to impose swimming pool safety regulations?	Court viewed pool regulations as public safety measures, and was unwilling to conclude that they were authorized by the public health statute.
Lucas v. South Carolina Coastal Council, 505 U.S. 1003 (1992)	U.S. Supreme Court	Was state agency authorized to ban island residential construction?	Regardless of the public interest in protecting the environment, the court warned that environmental protection activities must be based on proper legal authority.
Daubert v. Merrell Dow Pharmaceuticals, 509 U.S. 579 (1993)	U.S. Supreme Court	What is the court's role in admitting scientific evidence?	In contrast with the role of some state courts, federal courts must monitor the reliability of scientific evidence.
Ferguson v. City of Charleston, 532 U.S. 67 (2001)	U.S. Supreme Court	Did nonconsensual drug testing of pregnant women constitute unlawful search and seizure under the Fourth Amendment?	Sharing of the test results with law enforcement stripped the testing of otherwise legitimate public health purpose, and rendered the testing unconstitutional.

Case	Court	Question	Holding
Greene v. Edwards, 263 S.E.2d 661 (1980)	Supreme Court of Appeals of West Virginia	Did circumstances surrounding detention of tuberculosis patient violate due process requirements?	Despite due process violation, court permitted further detention to permit public health officials to implement appropriate due process safeguards.
The City of Newark v. J. S., 652 A.2d 265 (1993)	Superior Court of New Jersey, Law Division, Essex County	Did circumstances surrounding detention of tuberculosis patient violate due process requirements?	Court salvaged a constitutionally defective public health statute by grafting onto it the due process protections of the mental illness commitment statute.
People v. Chicago Wire Magnet Corp., 126 Ill.2d 356 (1989)	Illinois Supreme Court	Was a state criminal prosecution of an employer for worker exposure to harmful substances preempted by the Occupational Safety and Health Act of 1970 (OSHAct)?	The court allowed the prosecution to proceed because (1) Congress had neither expressly nor implicitly preempted it, (2) criminal prosecution and health and safety regulation are areas of traditional state concern, and (3) prosecution would further OSHAct's worker protection goal.
Geier v. American Honda Motor Co., 529 U.S. 861 (2000)	U.S. Supreme Court	Was a state tort lawsuit arising from injuries suffered in an auto crash preempted by federal auto safety regulations?	The state law claim of negligence for failure to install airbags interfered with the federal regulatory scheme, and was therefore preempted.
U.S. Oil v. City of Fond du Lac, 199 Wis.2d 333 (1996)	Wisconsin Supreme Court	Was a local ordinance restricting tobacco sales preempted by state law?	While questioning the wisdom of interfering with tobacco sale restrictions, the court held that the state legislature had preempted the ordinance through its enactment of a complex tobacco tax and distribution system, coupled with insistence on strict local conformance to state law.

(continued)

97

TABLE 4-1 (continued)

Name	Court	Issue	Comments
In re Halko, 246 Cal. App.2d 553 (1966)	Court of Appeal of California	Did circumstances surrounding detention of tuberculosis patient violate due process requirements?	In contrast with more recent due process decisions, this 1966 decision permitted lengthy detention of a tuberculosis patient because "reasonable ground exists to support the belief" that the detainee had tuberculosis.
United States v. Morrison, 529 U.S. 598 (2000)	U.S. Supreme Court	Is Congress constitutionally empowered to create a civil remedy for sexual violence victims?	The Court held that the commerce clause did not bestow upon Congress a "general police power of the sort retained by the States."
Gonzales v. Raich, 125 S.Ct. 2195 (2004)	U.S. Supreme Court	Is Congress constitutionally empowered to prohibit local cultivation and use of marijuana?	The Court's approval of Congressional authority negated the California law authorizing limited marijuana use for medical purposes.

Chevron USA, Inc. v. Natural Resources Defense Council, Inc., 467 U.S. 837 (1984), holds that if Congress has not directly spoken on an issue pending before a court, the court will not substitute its judgment for a permissible interpretation by the agency.

State courts generally provide similar deference to state agencies. Great deference is likely to be accorded to public health officials when they act to protect the public from a serious health threat. For example, in *City of New York v. New St. Mark's Baths*, 130 Misc.2d 911, 917, 497 N.Y.S.2d 979 (1986), where public health officials ordered the closing of a gay bathhouse in New York City in an effort to stop the spread of HIV infection, the court upheld a closure order over the bathhouse owner's contentions that the closure decision lacked sound scientific support. The court clearly articulated its deferential standard on such issues: "It is not for the courts to determine which scientific view is correct in ruling upon whether the police power has been properly exercised. The judicial function is exhausted with the discovery that the relation between means and end is not wholly vain and fanciful, an illusory pretense."

Courts also have shown deference to public health officials' efforts to ensure food safety. For example, in *Continental Seafoods, Inc. v. Schweiker*, 674 F.2d 38 (D.C. Cir. 1982), a federal court of appeals found that the mere existence of a pathogen in a food product was an adequate basis for removing a product from the food supply as "injurious to health" even though the product would be safe if properly cooked and handled. Similarly, in *United States v. 1200 Cans . . . Pasteurized Whole Eggs*, 339 F. Supp. 131 (N.D. Ga. 1972), a federal court in Georgia ruled that the agency seeking removal of the product is not obligated to demonstrate that anyone has become ill from consuming the product.

Finally, the Supreme Court articulated judicial deference with regard to the Secretary of Labor's exercise of powers to protect worker health under the Occupational Safety and Health Act of 1970 (OSHAct) in *American Textile Manufacturers Institute, Inc. v. Donovan*, 452 U.S. 490, 509 (1981). In rejecting the cotton industry's challenge to a standard regulating exposure to cotton dust, the Court disposed of the industry's argument that the Secretary was required to perform a cost-benefit analysis before establishing the new standard by explaining that Congress directed the Secretary

> to issue the standard that "most adequately assures . . . that no employee will suffer material impairment of health," limited only by the extent to which this is "capable of being done." In effect then, as the Court of Appeals held, Congress itself defined the basic relationship between costs and benefits, by placing the "benefit" of worker health above all other considerations save those making attainment of this "benefit" unachievable. Any standard based on a balancing of costs and benefits by the Secretary that strikes a different balance than that struck by Congress would be inconsistent with the command set forth [by Congress]. Thus, cost-benefit analysis by OSHA [the Occupational Safety and Health Administration] is not required by the statute.

Review of the Legal Authority Underlying Challenged Public Health Measures

Courts will not defer to public health agencies where their actions are not supported by adequate legal authority. As exemplified by three state appellate court decisions from around the country spanning several decades, courts will not permit public health officials to confront even serious public health threats—such as water pollution, smoking, and unfenced swimming pools—if they lack appropriate authority under statute or regulation.

A 60-year-old Wisconsin Supreme Court case, *American Brass Company and another v. State Board of Health and another*, 245 Wis. 440, 451–52, 15 N.W.2d 27 (1944), shows that, despite judicial recognition of the potential desirability and effectiveness of a particular administrative action, the court will not uphold that action unless it finds that the legislature authorized it. The State Board of Health had broad power to protect public health, and another state agency—the Committee on Water Pollution—had similar authority to address pollution issues. Faced with improper discharge of water pollutants, the agencies issued a joint order requiring the American Brass Company to undertake certain waste-disposal improvement measures; American Brass challenged the order. The court acknowledged increasing judicial deference to the broad authority granted to administrative agencies by the legislature and recognized that a joint order might be an efficient means of addressing water pollution issues. Nonetheless, it overturned the joint order, concluding the legislature did not intend to authorize the joint exercise of powers. No provision explicitly authorized the promulgation of joint orders and the separate and distinct appeal mechanisms for each agency further evinced a lack of legislative intent to create such authority. The court concluded, "It may be a great convenience to the State Board of Health and the Committee on Water Pollution to operate together inasmuch as they exercise complementary powers. If that is true, then the statutes should so provide."

In New York, the Court of Appeals likewise was unable to ascertain a legislative intent to authorize the agency action challenged in *Boreali v. Axelrod*, 71 N.Y.2d 1, 517 N.E.2d 1350 (1987). In February 1987, the Public Health Council, acting under broad statutory authority, promulgated comprehensive regulations restricting smoking in public places. The court acknowledged the harmful effects of smoking on the public's health, particularly noting that mounting evidence of harm caused to nonsmokers by exposure to tobacco smoke had become a serious concern of public health professionals ("[W]e stress that this case presents no question concerning the wisdom of the challenged regulations, the propriety of the procedures by which they were adopted or the right of government in general to promulgate restrictions on the use of tobacco in public places"[13]). In addition, like the Wisconsin court in the preceding case discussion, the New York court recognized how commonly courts deferred to the discretion of administrative agencies under broadly worded statutes. Consideration of four factors, however, persuaded the court that the Public Health Council lacked authority to promulgate the regulations: (1) the regulations contained exceptions based on economic and social (rather than public health) considerations; (2) the regulations were written on a "clean slate" without benefit of legislative guidance; (3) the legislature had failed to expand restrictions on smoking in public places, as evidenced by non-passage of over 40 bills attempting to expand restrictions; and (4) no public health expertise was involved in construction of the regulations. Even then, perhaps signaling the extent of its willingness to defer to agency discretion, the court explained that each factor standing alone would not have been sufficient to doom the regulation but, instead, that the result solely reflected the coalescence of all four factors.

A similar result was reached in *Vinson et al. v. Home Builders Association of Atlanta et al.*, 233 Ga. 948, 213 S.E.2d 890 (1975). Relying on its statutory authority to "prevent and suppress disease and conditions deleterious to health," the DeKalb County (Georgia) Board of Health attempted to require lifeguards, safety equipment, gates, and fences at swimming pools of apartments, condominiums, and subdivisions. Although the Supreme Court of Georgia labeled "axiomatic" the authority of state, county, and municipal agencies under the police power to enact regulations to protect public health and safety, it was unwilling to extend the scope of the pubic *health* statute to include authorization to undertake the sort of public *safety* measures proposed by the Board. In addition, even though many public health officials undoubtedly disagree with the proposition that public health does not encompass injury prevention, the point is that courts can and do make such determinations in the absence of specific legislative underpinnings.

Because failure to carefully assess legal authority can result in ineffective or inefficient public health actions, public health officials should be cognizant of the Supreme Court's decision in *Lucas v. South Carolina Coastal Council*, 505 U.S. 1003, 1031 (1992). Although not a public health case—the issue was whether the state's zoning prohibition against residential construction on a barrier island constituted a "taking" for which just compensation must be paid—the Court's cautionary comments to the state as it remanded the case to the lower court are highly instructive: "[T]o win its case South Carolina must do more than proffer the legislature's declaration that the uses Lucas desires are inconsistent with the public interest, or the conclusory assertion that they violate a common-law maxim. . . ." Despite the laudable purpose and effect of protecting the public interest, the Court made clear its intent to require the state to articulate the legal authority underlying its actions.

Review of the Facts on Which Legal Authority Is Exercised

Public health officials frequently ask their legal counsel whether they have legal authority to act. The ensuing discussion always should include thorough exploration of the facts on which action is contemplated. Courts decide cases by applying relevant law to a set of facts. In technical terms, they make findings of fact and conclusions of law, and base their decisions on those findings and conclusions. In anticipation of judicial scrutiny, public health officials and their attorneys should devote careful attention to the facts on which they intend to base their decisions. In cases involving particularly complex or conflicting medical or epidemiologic facts, testing the credibility of evidence before its submission against the "devil's advocacy" of outside experts even may be advisable.

The factual basis for a public health action is as important as the legal basis. Suppose, for example, a public health official directs the quarantine of a person suspected of exposure to a vaccine-preventable communicable disease under a statute expressly authorizing such action. In a judicial challenge to the quarantine decision, the court certainly will review the statute to determine the existence of legal quarantine authority. However, the court will be equally concerned with whether facts support the quarantine decision. Evidentiary issues include the disease itself and its incubation period, date(s) of the person's exposure to the disease, whether the person has been vaccinated against the disease, and whether a less-restrictive means of protecting public health is available. A court may tolerate some factual weakness in the case (e.g., evidence of the precise date of exposure to the disease may not be required if exposure within a critical time period can be conclusively established). However, approval of the quarantine decision will ultimately depend on the degree to which the public health official introduces credible evidence in support of the decision.

Public health officials should understand the basis by which courts determine whether scientific testimony or documents meet the standards necessary to permit their introduction into evidence. Standards vary among jurisdictions. In some states, the role of the court is limited to determining whether the witness qualifies as an expert and whether the offered evidence is relevant. If the judge permits its introduction, the jury is left to weigh the evidence's reliability. In the federal system, on the other hand, courts are responsible for ensuring that unreliable scientific testimony or documentation is not admitted as evidence. *Daubert v. Merrell Dow Pharmaceuticals*, 509 U.S. 579 (1993), requires federal courts to determine evidentiary reliability on the basis of scientific principles and methodology, considering whether, for example, the "evidence" has been tested or subjected to peer review, or has a known error rate.

Of critical judicial importance is whether the actions of a public health official in fact have a public health purpose. *Ferguson v. City of Charleston*, 532 U.S. 67 (2001), involved the city hospital's practice of testing (without consent) pregnant patients for drug use, reflecting a policy developed in response to an apparent increase in cocaine use by some patients. Under the policy, positive findings were shared with law enforcement with results including criminal arrest and prosecution. The hospital maintained that the policy had a public health rationale, in other words, threat of arrest would dissuade patients from drug use. Patients arrested under the policy challenged it on the ground that the nonconsensual drug tests constituted illegal searches under the Fourth Amendment. The Court of Appeals disagreed and held for the hospital. The U.S. Supreme Court, however, reversed: the fact that the test results were shared with law enforcement led the Court to conclude that the nonconsensual drug tests violated the Fourth Amendment. The Court rejected the hospital's claim of a public health rationale, concluding that the "stark and unique fact that characterizes this case is that [the policy] was designed to obtain evidence of criminal conduct by the tested patients that would be turned over to the police and that could be admissible in subsequent criminal prosecutions."[14]

Balancing Public Health and Protection of Individual Rights

Jacobson established that public health officials may not unduly interfere with the fundamental rights of individuals. Though certainly not exclusive, the rights most typically implicated include due process and equal protection under the Fifth and Fourteenth amendments and freedom of religion and association under the First Amendment. Since *Jacobson*, those rights generally have evolved to a point of fairly precise judicial articulation. The following two cases involved procedural due process and are discussed here to illustrate the dynamic nature of the court's balancing role.

In the case of *Greene v. Edwards*, 263 S.E.2d 661 (1980)—which involved a challenge by a patient with active tuberculosis (TB) who involuntarily was confined to a hospital—the court articulated the requisite procedural due process elements as including (1) adequate written notice of grounds for the proposed action and underlying facts; (2) access to legal counsel; (3) right to be present at the hearing, to cross-examine, and to confront and present witnesses; (4) a standard of proof requiring clear, cogent, and convincing evidence; and (5) access to a transcript for appeal. The statute used by public health officials in that case did not afford those essential elements to the petitioning patient who was believed to have active communicable TB. Although the court therefore ruled in favor of the patient, it neither struck down the statute nor granted the patient's request for release into the community. Rather, the court ordered the patient held for 30 days, while allowing that time for public health officials to provide the requisite due process in a new proceeding. Acknowledging that public health officials had failed to meet due process requirements, the court nonetheless was unwilling to order the release sought by the patient in view of the threat that release would pose to public health.

The second case, *The City of Newark v. J. S.*, 652 A.2d 265, 277 (1993), also involved creative judicial balancing of due process rights against the need to protect public health. Again, the case involved a due process challenge to a public health statute used to detain a TB patient. The court noted a decided lack of due process in the antiquated 1912 state statute. Rather than striking it down, though, the court grafted the due process protections built into New Jersey's mental illness involuntary commitment statute onto the public health statute. In its decision, the court stated:

> It must be remembered that this statute was first enacted in 1912, yet it had provisions requiring notice and a judicial hearing. The statute required proof that the person be "an actual menace to the community or to members of his household." The Legislature intended to permit the confinement of someone with TB but only under circumstances consistent with due process. Many of the rights we now recognize were unheard of in 1912. The ADA [Americans with Disabilities Act] did not exist. Declaring the statute unconstitutional and leaving citizens of New Jersey with no shield against the rare person with TB who poses a true significant risk to others would be the true frustration of legislative intent. Therefore I construe [the TB control statute] so as to include those rights necessitated by contemporary standards of due process and by the ADA. Such a construction effectuates the legislative intent.

Although many states have modernized their statutes to include full due process protections, obviating the need for the sort of "legislating from the bench" that occurred in these decisions, the two cases demonstrate judicial capacity to appropriately defer to constitutional principles while protecting public health.

Federalism/Preemption Concerns

Generally, if the federal government has fully covered an issue by federal legislation or regulation or if Congress has declared that states should not pass laws on a particular subject on which Congress has acted, then the states are barred from legislating in this area (see Chapter 2). States have somewhat similar preemption authority with regard to their relationship with local governments. Thus, whereas actions taken by a state public health official may have ample support in state law, those actions will be struck down if a court determines federal law preempts them. Similarly, local public health actions may be preempted by state law.

In *People v. Chicago Wire Magnet Corp.*, 126 Ill.2d 356 (1989), the Illinois Supreme Court engaged in classic preemption analysis before concluding that the state action was not preempted by federal regulation. In this case, the State of Illinois charged the defendant manufacturer and its officers with criminally exposing 42 employees to harmful substances during manufacturing processes. The Occupational and Safety Health Act of 1970 regulated the handling, use, and storage of those substances. Citing the comprehensive nature of the Act's regulation, the employer defendants argued that OSHA preempted the state criminal prosecution. In particular, it relied on the OSHAct provision providing that states could implement only their own occupational health and safety plans on receiving federal approval. The court rejected this preemption claim, quoting the rule announced by the U.S. Supreme Court in *Jones v. Rath Packing Co.*, 430 U.S. 519, 525 (1977): "Where . . . the field which Congress is said to have pre-empted has been traditionally occupied by the States, . . . 'we start with the assumption that the historic police powers of the States were not to be superseded by the Federal Act unless that was the clear and manifest purpose of Congress.'"[15] The court did not find a "clear and manifest purpose of Congress" because Congress had not expressly preempted state prosecutions and the regulation itself was not the sort of comprehensive regulatory scheme that implicitly preempted action under state law. In addition, the Court's finding that criminal prosecution and health and safety regulation were areas of traditional state concern weighed against the preemption claim. Finally, the state action did not conflict with the OSHAct regulation. Indeed, the court found that state criminal prosecutions would further the OSHAct's goal of "assur[ing] so far as possible every working man and woman in the Nation safe and healthful working conditions."[16]

The opposite conclusion was reached in *Geier v. American Honda Motor Co.*, 529 U.S. 861 (2000), where the Supreme Court found that the state lawsuit at issue conflicted with a comprehensive federal regulatory plan and, therefore, was barred by preemption principles. Plaintiff Geier and her parents sued an auto manufacturer, alleging that her serious injuries suffered in an auto accident were due to the auto manufacturer's negligent failure to install a driver-side airbag. The manufacturer asserted that the National Traffic and Motor Vehicle Safety Act of 1966 and regulations subsequently promulgated by the U.S. Department of Transportation (DOT) preempted state law tort litigation. Although neither the Act nor the regulations expressly preempted the litigation, the Court determined that the plaintiffs' tort claim conflicted with the federal regulatory plan governing passive restraint devices. At the outset, the Court found that DOT's historical regulatory approach was to provide options to manufacturers while gradually mandating use of passive restraint devices, including airbags. The Court also was persuaded that DOT's approach reasonably balanced considerations of cost, technical safety, technologic development, and consumer acceptance of the devices. The Court therefore held that the litigation based on state law was preempted by the federal regulation.

Similarly, a court may determine that state law preempts local laws. For example, in 1993, the city of Fond du Lac, Wisconsin, passed an ordinance banning self-service cigarette displays that allowed access to single packs without merchant assistance.

The ordinance was supported by a study showing alarmingly high cigarette use by teens and effective techniques for reducing teen smoking developed by an Illinois community. However, affected convenience stores challenged the ordinance on the basis that state law preempted the city's ordinance. The convenience stores argued that the legislature considered tobacco regulation a matter of statewide concern, by adopting a comprehensive tax and distribution scheme and directing that local governments strictly conform to state law. In its decision, the appellate court agreed with the convenience stores and stated, "Although the legislature's adherence to this policy may be an unwise course considering how it restricts localities, such as Fond du Lac, from taking affirmative steps towards ending illegal teenage tobacco use, the resolution of this problem will have to arise from the political process" (*U.S. Oil v. City of Fond du Lac*, 199 Wis.2d 333, 352 [1996]).

Judicial Interpretation of the Law May Change Over Time

The U.S. system of government is one "of laws and not of men."[17] Consistent with deference to law, judicial decision-making is rooted in the doctrine of stare decisis, which requires that past decisions generally guide courts when they decide identical, similar, or analogous issues.[18] Lower courts are bound by and must follow precedent set by courts above them, and higher courts will follow their prior decisions, unless compelling reasons for change are evident. Nonetheless, judicial philosophies and attitudes change over time. Change may reflect a multitude of factors, including the attitudes and philosophies of those who appoint or elect judges, new economic or societal issues, and a need for government or the private sector to play a greater or lesser role at a given point in time. Regardless of the reason, however, a net effect is that judicial interpretation of the law may shift with time.

Trial courts preside over cases to ensure that the facts are fairly determined on proper evidence—either by a jury or by the court in a "bench" trial—and the law as provided in statutes or case law established by higher courts is appropriately applied to those facts. Judicial interpretation does not change at the trial level. Instead, prior decisions may be modified or overturned in the appellate courts—principally the courts of last resort.

One example of judicial interpretation over time involves the parameters of procedural due process. More than 100 years ago, in *Jacobson*, the U.S. Supreme Court generally acknowledged the need to be attentive to individual rights. As recently as 40 years ago, a state appellate court upheld multiple successive six-month public health orders isolating a TB patient, extending the protection of individual rights no further than requiring compliance with the statute authorizing such orders if "reasonable ground exists to support the belief" that the person had TB (*in re Halko*, 246 Cal. App. 2d 553, 558 [1966]). Since then, of course, courts in cases such as *Greene* and *City of Newark* have articulated clear due process requirements and demanded compliance where public health officials seek to restrict a person's movement.

U.S. Supreme Court decisions during the past decade involving principles of federalism also illustrate change in judicial interpretation. In *Lopez*, the Court rejected the contention that Congress could criminalize handgun possession on school property under its Commerce Clause authority. Underlying the holding was the conclusion that possession of a handgun on school property did not substantially affect inter-state commerce. The Court expressed unwillingness "to convert congressional authority under the Commerce Clause to a general police power of the sort retained by the States," noting that "[s]ome of our prior cases have taken long steps down that road, giving great deference to congressional action."[19] The Court again refused to take "steps down that road" in *United States v. Morrison*, 529 U.S. 598 (2000), where it held that neither the Commerce Clause nor the Due Process Clause authorized Congress to create a civil remedy for victims of sexual violence. However, then Chief Justice Rehnquist, who wrote for the Court in *Lopez* and *Morrison*, dissented in *Gonzales v. Raich*, 125 S. Ct. 2195 (2004). In that case, the Court appeared to return to an approach of "great deference to congressional action" in holding that the Commerce Clause authorized Congress to prohibit the local cultivation and use of marijuana that otherwise would have complied with California's law authorizing limited marijuana use for medical purposes. Because the Court's composition had not changed, however, an alternate explanation may be that the decision is more attributable to the particular facts of the case than to a change in the Court's views on federalism.

An Emerging Issue: The Judicial System in a Public Health Emergency

Until recently, past examples of the potential for public health events to disrupt judicial operations—such as the impact of epidemic smallpox in 1636 and 1659, causing relocations of the General Court of the Massachusetts Bay Colony to sites outside Boston, and in 1702, requiring the New York Supreme Court to convene on Long Island—may have been thought of as interesting but irrelevant historical footnotes.[20] But judicial interest in planning for recovery from disasters, already stimulated by the 2001 World Trade Center and anthrax attacks, was reinforced by the dramatic adverse impact of the 2005 hurricanes on court operations in Louisiana, Mississippi, Alabama, and Florida. In the immediate aftermath of Hurricane Katrina, courts were forced to suspend operations, relocate, or temporarily close. Orders were issued to close court operations, suspend deadlines, and authorize practice by affected lawyers in jurisdictions other than where licensed. Courts around the country were asked to volunteer supplies, equipment, and other resources. The National Center for State Courts responded to the Katrina disaster by adding to its Web site the "Clearinghouse for Courts Affected by Hurricane Katrina," which updated information about court operations affected by hurricanes Katrina and Wilma.[21] In addition, some courts have developed "disaster recovery plans." Those that have not are encouraged to do so.[22]

Beyond planning for recovery from devastation caused by hurricanes or other natural disasters, courts are recognizing the need for an "all hazards" approach to emergency contingency planning for other potentially catastrophic events, such as an influenza pandemic, a bioterrorism event, or a "dirty bomb." Although courts must have plans in place for "picking up the pieces" after a disaster, they also need to develop contingency plans to enhance their ability to continue operations during any type of emergency. Continued functioning of the judicial system is of equally and critically important concern to public health officials: unavailability of the courts means that public health officials and affected citizens would be deprived of the mechanism for resolving disputes that may be triggered by public health emergency actions.

Public health officials and the judiciary are working together to address these and other public health issues of mutual interest. For example, one resource recently developed for and disseminated to the judiciary in Indiana is a public health law "bench book."[23] Judges commonly use bench books as functional practice guides designed to accelerate their understanding of specific areas of the law. The Indiana public health law bench book, which especially emphasizes legal authorities and checks involving acute disease problems and public health emergencies, also is a template for public health law bench books for other states. In addition, law and public health conferences and seminars are beginning to explore the role of the judiciary in public health, and federal and state working groups increasingly recognize the judiciary as an important component of public health readiness. Thus, public health officials may seek new opportunities to cooperate with the judiciary and judicial education agencies in developing resources such as public health law bench books, participating in judicial education seminars, and planning for public health emergencies.

The Michigan Supreme Court has developed the "Business Contingency and Emergency Procedures Plan," which is designed to provide an emergency judicial assignment process.[24] This plan establishes a communication link between the State Court Administrative Office and the Michigan Office of Attorney General; lists statewide primary and backup contacts for the Office of Attorney General; establishes primary and secondary contacts for each of four judicial regions; and provides contact information for the judges responsible for covering each region. The plan also prescribes two sets of processes and procedures, depending on the level of emergency: the procedures relating to Emergency Level 1 (Critical) are designed to ensure immediate access to judicial resources; those relating to Emergency Level 2 (Urgent) are intended to obtain access to judicial resources as soon as practicable. In Indiana, the Division of State Court Administration and the Judicial Conference Court Management Committee are developing a template to be used by trial courts in developing continuity of operations plans, with special emphasis on the public health aspect of disaster recovery.[25]

Whether occurring naturally or as a result of bioterrorism, widespread outbreaks of severe infectious diseases potentially pose unique challenges for the judicial system. Many of the court cases discussed in this chapter involved attempts to isolate or quarantine persons with infectious diseases who posed a threat to public health. As demonstrated by the 2003 outbreak of severe acute respiratory syndrome, some communicable infectious diseases can spread rapidly and may create a need to quarantine thousands. In Toronto, approximately 30,000 people were quarantined, and virtually all of them voluntarily complied.[26] However, because voluntary quarantine compliance cannot always be reasonably presumed, public health agencies need to work with the judicial system to establish practices and procedures for the prompt protection of public health while simultaneously safeguarding the civil rights of those for whom civil confinement, such as isolation or quarantine, or other compulsory measures might be indicated.

During catastrophic infectious disease outbreaks or other public health emergencies, providing timely due process access to the courts for large numbers of persons may create serious logistical difficulties for the judicial system. Such difficulties might be compounded by the threat posed by potentially infectious persons to judges, lawyers, and other court staff. Moreover, courtroom hearings conducted in the usual face-to-face manner would be inadvisable; an alternative would be to employ electronic methods of communication, such as two-way closed-circuit television. If, however, even some of these methods proved insufficient, then courts might determine it necessary to approve curtailment of at least some individual rights through the issuance of blanket orders or other measures that in nonemergency situations would be considered inappropriate.

Even under the direst of circumstances, however, most courts would be reluctant to authorize significant due process "shortcuts." Likewise, courts may be somewhat wary of engaging in planning discussions with public health officials regarding those sorts of measures, particularly because the judiciary values its independence: judges base their decisions on the law and facts of each case, and courts never will permit ex parte communications (discussion of the merits of a case between the judge and a party to the case outside the presence of other parties).[27] Furthermore, public health officials may encounter some judicial reluctance to discuss in the abstract the circumstances, if any, under which judges might consider deviating from normal due process standards.

Public health officials can attempt to identify justices or judges interested in public health emergency preparedness. When approaching those members of the judiciary regarding plans for public health emergencies, public health officials should focus the discussion on strategies and mechanisms that should be available to courts in public health emergencies should courts decide to employ them. The circumstances under which those strategies and mechanisms would be employed should appropriately and respectfully be left for judicial determination.

Conclusion

The judicial system performs the important function of resolving legal disputes relating to public health. Public health agencies must anticipate the need to articulate to courts the legal and factual underpinnings of their actions. Similarly, agencies and their attorneys must develop a thorough understanding of court jurisdiction, practices, and protocols. Particularly in regard to legal issues involving public health emergencies, public health officials should work with courts to develop contingency plans for equitably and efficiently resolving those issues. Although the independence of the judiciary prohibits discussion of the substance of those issues, jointly planning the means and methods of resolving those issues in a public health emergency is not barred. Judges and public health officials can cooperate to ensure that actions to protect public health have a solid legal foundation and respect the rights of individuals affected by those actions.

References

1. The path of the law. 10 *Harvard Law Rev* (1897).
2. 28 USC §1251.
3. 28 USC §§1254, 1257.
4. Administrative Office of the US Courts. *Understanding the Federal Courts*. 2003. Available at http://www.uscourts.gov/understand03/media/UFC03.pdf. Accessed February 2, 2006.
5. 28 USC §§1331, 1332.
6. 28 USC §1294.
7. National Center for State Courts. *Overview*. Available at http://www.ncsconline.org/D_Research/csp/2003_Files/2003_Overview.pdf. Accessed February 2, 2006.
8. National Center for State Courts. State Court Structure Charts. Available at http://www.ncsconline.org/D_Research/Ct_Struct/Index.html. Accessed February 2, 2006.
9. 514 US 549 (1995).
10. Committee Protects Federal Courts, Recognizes Unique Nature of State Courts [interview with Judge Frederick P. Stamp, Jr.]. *The Third Branch: The Newsletter of the Federal Courts*. Available at http://www.uscourts.gov/ttb/oct02ttb/interview.html. Accessed February 2, 2006.
11. 197 US 11, 25.
12. 197 US 11, 27.
13. 517 N E 2d 1350, 1353.
14. 532 US 67, 85–86.
15. 126 Ill 2d 356, 367.
16. 126 Ill 2d 356, 373.
17. Massachusetts Constitution, Part the First, Article XXX (1780).
18. 20 Am Jur 2d Courts §147 (2004).
19. 514 US 549, 567.
20. Hopkins DR. *Princes and Peasants: Smallpox in History*. Chicago: University of Chicago Press, 1983.
21. National Center for State Courts. Available at http://www.ncsconline.org. Accessed February 2, 2006.
22. National Center for State Courts. *News Alert! Do You Have a Disaster Recovery Plan?* Available at http://www.ncsconline.org/What'sNew/NewsAlerts/NewsAlertHaveRecoveryPlan.html. Accessed February 4, 2006.
23. Centers for Disease Control and Prevention. Public Health Law Program. Available at http://www2a.cdc.gov/phlp. Accessed February 2, 2006.
24. Michigan Supreme Court. State Court Administrative Office. *Business Contingency and Emergency Procedures Plan*. Available at http://www.michigan.gov/documents/Attachment_A_97106_7.pdf. Accessed February 2, 2006.
25. O'Brien C. Division of State Court Administration and the Judicial Conference Court Management Committee to begin disaster recovery planning project in 2006. *Indiana Court Times* 2005;14(Fall/Winter):6. Available at http://www.in.gov/judiciary/admin/court-times/news14-3.pdf. Accessed February 2, 2006.
26. Public Health Agency of Canada. SARS in Canada: anatomy of an outbreak. In: *Learning from SARS*. Ottawa, Ontario: Health Canada, 2003. Available at http://www.phac-aspc.gc.ca/publicat/sars-sras/naylor/2_e.html. Accessed February 2, 2006.
27. 56 Am Jur 2d Motions, Rules, and Orders §45 (2004).

Chapter 5

ETHICS AND THE PRACTICE
OF PUBLIC HEALTH

**Ruth Gaare Bernheim, Phillip Nieburg,
and Richard J. Bonnie**

> Throughout human history, the major problems of health that men have
> faced have been concerned with community life. . . .
>
> George Rosen[1]

Public health officials increasingly must address ethical conflicts in day-to-day practice to be effective decision-makers and leaders in the community. Even though the
complex relationship between health and community life has been recognized throughout human history, the vision of "healthy people in healthy communities" now is emphasized as public health's guiding vision, with health explicitly characterized as a social
and political undertaking.[2,3] Public health professionals are expected not only to work
in partnerships and function collaboratively with communities, stakeholder groups, and
citizens—who have widely varying values—but also to confront complex behavioral
and social factors related to health in the community.

Almost any government public health action, therefore, invites two types of challenge, particularly given the central role of individual liberty and property rights
in our legal and political traditions. First, underlying public health decisions in a
particular case are different ethical viewpoints in society about the appropriate *scope*
of legal authority; for example, should government's role be limited to infectious
disease control and collective action problems such as community water fluoridation
or should it be broadened to include chronic diseases and behavioral risk factors
(such as sedentary lifestyle) or even socioeconomic factors that affect the population's health?[4-6] A second related set of background ethical controversies involves
the appropriate *means* of public health intervention; for example, to influence be-

havioral risk factors, should government action be limited to educational efforts to facilitate individual choice or should it extend to shaping social norms through the media, or outlawing risk-taking behavior, such as motorcycle riding without a helmet?[7–9]

Legal and ethical analyses play complementary roles in helping public health officials mediate conflicts and questions about the relationship between the individual's and the community's interests in health, as well as about the appropriate scope and means of public action. Decisions about where to draw the line between private and public spheres are even more complex because the spheres are not static and are influenced over time by varied and often changing values in society.[10] Balancing competing interests and providing justifications for public health policies, therefore, are required continuously in public health practice, as cultural values shift and as the political, economic, legal, and social context evolves.

Public health ethics, as both a field of study and a tool to aid real-world decision-making, is receiving increasing professional and scholarly attention, most recently in response to myriad ethical issues in the context of bioterrorist and emerging infectious disease threats; chronic disease concerns, such as obesity; and the shortage of influenza vaccine. Whereas law is a formal institution with public proceedings and a focus on government authority and limitations on state power, public health ethics is less formal and involves exploring society's values and justifications for collective public health decisions when law is not determinant. To address ethical questions, recent reports point out the need for public health officials to develop competencies in public health ethics,[a] and public health leaders have developed a code of ethics for the profession as a guide for public health practice.[11] In addition, the Centers for Disease Control and Prevention has established a national ethics advisory group[12] and some health department officials at the state and local level encourage training in practical ethics for their organizations.[13]

Our goal in this chapter is to illustrate how ethical analysis can be a helpful tool, along with legal analysis, to support and enrich public health decision making. We will provide (1) an overview of the complementary roles of public health ethics and law; (2) an approach to public health ethics, including a framework to guide ethical reflection, deliberation, and justification in practice; (3) examples of common ethical themes and tensions between individual and collective interests; (4) an understanding of the role of professional ethics, as expressed in the new public health code of ethics; and (5) an outline of ways to integrate ethics into practice within public health organizations.

The Complementary Roles of Ethics and Law in Public Health

Laws influence the public's health in numerous ways—for example, by establishing the foundation for the powers and duties of the state to protect public health, prescribing limitations on the power of the state to constrain individual liberty and other private interests to promote public health, and creating incentives and disincentives for individual and organizational behaviors that affect health.[14] Ethical perspectives provide an implicit foundation and the underlying values for all of these legal influences, and the laws implicated in public health practice, like all laws, are subject to ethical scrutiny and ongoing public oversight and change. At any given time, citizens might ask, "Do particular laws adequately express, embrace, or protect society's values?" For example, the laws protecting the confidentiality of persons with public health reportable diseases were at issue in the early years of the HIV epidemic as named reporting became controversial, and the underlying ethical values were debated.

In addition, laws often are framed broadly, leaving much room for administrative discretion about when to use public health authority and about which intervention is more ethically appropriate when more than one alternative course of action is legally permissible. Furthermore, the need to enact new laws—such as those passed in response to bioterrorist threats—is ongoing, and these revised or new laws often raise ethical concerns and must be justified by some appeal to underlying social values.[15,16]

In public health practice, when law is not determinative or is unsettled, public health officials often are called on to offer explicit *ethical* justifications and reasons for particular public health actions. *Public health ethics*[b] is a relatively new field that involves ongoing professional and public discourse about the balancing of individual and societal interests and about justifying particular public health interventions on the basis of "what is right and good" for health and social welfare.[17–20] It offers a systematic approach to balancing competing moral considerations and making trade-offs, similar to the process officials use in making other public health trade-offs about costs and benefits. Instead of balancing "quantifiable" health gains or losses, however, public health ethics focuses on identifying, weighing, and balancing the ethical values and moral claims at stake in a public health action. The process involves assigning weight or strength to an ethical value and deciding when, in a particular situation, one value "overrides" another competing or conflicting ethical value.

For example, briefly consider the case of a tuberculosis (TB) outbreak. Although a jurisdiction's laws may provide authority to detain individuals who are noncompliant with their TB treatment regimen, officials must decide in a particular case whether and how to use that authority. A public health official must be able to demonstrate that protecting the public's health (a utilitarian value) carries more weight and should override another moral claim at stake in the situation, namely, an individual's liberty interest to both reject treatment and remain in the community.

Ethical analysis and public justification depend on weighing the ethical considerations at stake *in the particular context*: the nature, risk, and potential gravity of harm to the population; an individual's particular circumstances that necessitate restrictions on personal liberty; and other related factors. This simple TB scenario illustrates that in public health, moral analysis is real-time and socially situated.[21] Justification to the public for the action is indispensable, and merely saying that the law permits this action is not sufficient. Accountability to and transparency with the public requires that reasons, explanations, and justifications for practices of quarantine be provided. Justification requires that public health officials state, "We are choosing to impose quarantine because . . ." Justification is required to members of society who are stakeholders—constituting a "collective" patient—because they themselves have a stake in the protection of the values of liberty and privacy that are sometimes overridden for their benefit.[22]

Justification plays a key role in public health ethics because public consent is the source of moral authority and legitimacy for public health decision making in a democratic political order. One political theorist emphasizes the responsibility of public authorities to reflect the moral understanding of the group in whose name any decision is being made and to justify decisions in a way the public will find persuasive by pointing out that moral judgments, unlike scientific judgments, are "everyone's job" in society.[23] In addition, transparency in decision making is crucial because it respects individuals as members of the political community and, therefore, lays the foundation for public involvement, cooperation, and trust. Commentators emphasize that public health action in a liberal democracy must rely on not force but persuasion and public trust grounded in transparency, accountability, and human rights.[24]

Approaches to Public Health Ethics

Public health ethics is an analytic and imaginative process that, through ongoing efforts to specify and assign weights or importance to public values, helps forge professional and public consensus about public health action in the context of particular cases and policies. Thus, public health ethics does not entail a commitment to any particular ethical theory or method, although theories can provide conceptual clarity and guidance—for example, when assessing the options to manage a patient with infectious TB who does not adhere to a treatment regimen, explicating such concepts as harm or coercion is useful.[25] Similarly, when assessing the benefits of a particular allocation strategy—for example, for scarce influenza vaccine—it is necessary to distinguish among the types of benefits, namely, between social utility (which might take into account an individual's social role as an emergency responder) and medical utility (which might lead to further distinctions according to whether the medical benefit should be measured by its effect on the most vulnerable or on those most likely to be exposed and spread the flu across the general population).

Some influential ethical theories include those that focus on the outcomes of actions (e.g., consequentialism) and others that focus on rights, duties, or other intrinsic moral features of actions (e.g., deontology). On the basis of these and other theories, the following major ethical themes or considerations have emerged in contemporary public health discourse: (1) utilitarian, which emphasizes a decision's consequences, in other words, its effect on the sum balance of benefits over harms in the population; (2) justice, which focuses on the fair distribution of benefits and burdens, and ensuring the opportunity to participate in decisions that affect one's interests; and (3) liberty and rights, which emphasize individual interests. These themes and related ethical tensions will be explored further later in this chapter. Other public values of particular importance for government health officials include transparency, trustworthiness, promise-keeping, protection of confidentiality, and protection of vulnerable individuals and communities from undue stigmatization.[11,13,17,18]

Although simple formulas do not guarantee morally sound decisions, frameworks can be useful to guide ethical analysis. The public health ethics framework provided in this chapter (Box 5-1) draws on the major ethical considerations in public health discourse and is designed to provoke rigorous deliberation about decisions in public health agencies or ethics advisory groups.[17,22,26,27] The framework contains three main prongs: (1) analysis of the ethical issues; (2) evaluation of the ethical dimensions of the public health options; and (3) justification for a particular action. The ethics framework provides a series of questions for public health decision-makers. In deliberation about public health cases, often one or more of the questions become the primary focus for the ethical analysis in a particular case. (See boxes 5-2 and 5-3 for brief examples of case analyses that draw on particular questions from the framework.)

1. Analyze the Ethical Issues in the Situation

As a first step, public health officials need to clarify the risks or harms of concern in the situation, as well as the goal of public health action. Although answers to these questions often seem obvious, careful analyses may reveal separable concerns or unclear goals that limit good decision-making and cloud justification. For example, for public health programs promoting sexual abstinence in youth, are the public health goals primarily prevention of sexually transmitted diseases, healthy adolescent development, prevention of teenage pregnancy, or prevention of pregnancies outside of marriage? This question is not posed to challenge any one of these potential goals but rather to clarify the goals to *more clearly* reason about and provide justification for the program.

The framework also poses questions to elucidate the moral claims of the various stakeholders in a particular policy or case, drawing on another approach to ethical analysis called "stakeholder theory." This approach is believed to have particular relevance for public health ethics because it implicitly focuses on the fundamental partnership of public health professionals with individuals and groups in the community as together they assess the value-laden benefits and harms of particular public health actions. Although essentially utilitarian, the stakeholder theory makes explicit the costs and benefits to different groups and recognizes the complex ongoing nature of the human relationships involved.

To clarify society's expectations of and the options available to public health officials, the framework elicits information about relevant laws and regulations, as well as about the statutory basis for public health authority in a particular situation and the guidance provided to public health leaders by professional codes of ethics. In addition, the framework invites consideration of previous cases. An analysis of a new situation's relevant similarities to and differences from paradigm or precedent cases— cases that have gained a relatively settled moral consensus—often provides an important starting point or presumption in deliberation.[17] Because ethical reflection on any public policy issue takes place within a particular community with a unique history and culture, the framework specifically asks that the conflicting ethical tensions be clarified in the political-social context because ethical norms and tensions can vary from community to community. What may be morally acceptable in some communities, for example, needle-exchange programs to prevent HIV transmission, may not be in others.

BOX 5-1. Framework for Analysis and Deliberation about Ethical Issues in Public Health

1. Analyze the Ethical Issues in the Situation

- What are the public *health risks and harms of concern*?
- What are the public health *goals*?
- Who are the *stakeholders*? *What are their moral claims*?
- Is the source or scope of legal *authority* in question?
- Are *precedent cases* or the historical context relevant?
- Do *professional codes of ethics* provide guidance?

2. Evaluate the Ethical Dimensions of the Alternate Courses of Public Health Action

- *Utility*: Does a particular public health action produce a *balance of benefits over harms*?
- *Justice*: Are the benefits and burdens *distributed fairly* (distributive justice)? Do legitimate representatives of affected groups have the *opportunity to participate* in making decision (procedural justice)?
- *Respect for individual interests and social value:* Does the public health action *respect individual* choices and interests (autonomy, liberty, privacy)?
- *Respect for legitimate public institutions*: Does the public health action *respect professional and civic roles* and values, such as transparency, honesty, trustworthiness, consensus-building, promise-keeping, protection of confidentiality, and protection of vulnerable individuals and communities from undue stigmatization?

3. Provide Justification for a Particular Public Health Action

- *Effectiveness*: Is the public health goal likely to be accomplished?
- *Proportionality*: Will the probable benefits of the action outweigh the infringed moral considerations?
- *Necessity*: Is overriding the conflicting ethical claims necessary to achieve the public health goal?
- *Least infringement*: Is the action the least restrictive and least intrusive?
- *Public justification*: Can public health agents offer public justification for the action or policy, on the basis of principles in the Code of Ethics or general public health principles, that citizens—in particular, those most affected—could find acceptable in principle?

---

2. Evaluate the Ethical Dimensions of Public Health Options

To choose from among numerous public health options, it is appropriate initially to identify the moral considerations or ethical principles that have the strongest weights or value in the particular community for any given situation, as expressed and

BOX 5-2. Protecting Individuals: A Noncooperative HIV-Infected Patient

You are legal counsel to the county health department and are confronted with this problem.

A young HIV-infected man has been receiving care from his county health department through a federally funded Ryan White program. He has remained healthy and has not yet reached the immunologic threshold at which antiretroviral drugs are recommended. He has said he is not in a long-term relationship, has provided only a work phone number (although he has asked not to be contacted there), and has declined to provide sexual contact information to the clinic's public health nurse, saying he had become infected while traveling outside the United States and he "always" uses condoms when having sex. He denies injection-drug use.

While providing information to a young married woman (A) who is being seen in the health department's family planning clinic, the same public health nurse is startled to see the name of the HIV-infected man listed in the chart as the woman's husband. The young woman states that one of her reasons for wanting female-controlled contraception is that she has now heard from a mutual friend that her husband is having a sexual relationship with another woman (B). She does not want to become pregnant until the issues in her relationship are resolved. Her husband, however, refuses to use condoms. Woman A adds that she was told that the "other woman" is unaware her husband is married. Woman A is willing to provide the name of Woman B.

The nurse realizes that Woman A is unaware her husband is HIV infected. Even though HIV testing and counseling are now routinely offered during visits to this family planning clinic, and even though she agrees to testing for syphilis, gonorrhea, and chlamydia, the woman refuses HIV testing. Even strong encouragement to be HIV tested does not change her mind.

Later that day, the nurse contacts the HIV-infected man by phone at his work and tells him she is now aware he is married. She asks him to come into the clinic to discuss how to protect his wife from HIV infection, but he refuses. Over the next few days, the nurse repeatedly attempts to contact the husband at work, and he refuses to speak with her.

The nurse urgently calls you, as counsel to the county health department, to discuss the health department's options in this situation. She wants to discuss the law and ethics of two related issues: (1) whether to notify the wife about her husband's HIV infection, and (2) whether to forcefully seek "partner notification" information for Woman B.

What are the ethical and legal issues to be considered?

1. Analyze the Ethical Issues in the Situation

As in most HIV/AIDS situations, the *public health goals* in this situation would appear to be both (1) minimizing subsequent HIV transmission and (2) optimizing care of already-infected people, while doing both in the context of justice.

(continued)

116

In terms of *risks and harms*, both Woman A and Woman B are at risk of becoming infected with HIV—if not already infected. If either or both already are HIV infected, then they are at a *different* risk by virtue of missing opportunities for appropriate HIV care (e.g., opportunistic infection prophylaxis, antiretroviral treatment) because they are unaware of their infection.

This situation has at least four *stakeholders*: the husband, the two women, and the public, which expects the state to protect the women and others from disease transmission.

In terms of *moral claims*, the husband has some expectation of privacy and confidentiality—both standard components of public health practice. However, such claims are not absolute and can be overridden by competing moral claims.

The wife has at least two moral claims, each of which competes with her husband's claim. One is based on an expectation that her husband will protect her from inordinate risks of his activities. A second claim is that society will protect her from *known* risks. In this case, the fact that the husband already is benefiting medically from knowing about his infection also may be a factor to be weighed.

The claims of Woman B are less clear. She, too, may have a claim based on society's obligation to protect her from known risks, in this case, unknowingly engaging in unprotected sexual activity with a person who knows he is infected with HIV and who, in fact, is benefiting from public care.

2. Evaluate the Ethical Dimensions of Public Health Options

Assume the law of the jurisdiction permits, but does not require, the public health nurse to notify the sex partners of an HIV-infected patient of their exposure.

- *Regarding notifying the wife (Woman A) of her husband's HIV infection*: Given the very real risk to the wife of becoming HIV infected and the ultimately fatal nature of HIV/AIDS, the nurse asks if any justification exists for not notifying the wife about her husband's HIV infection (if the husband persists in not telling her himself). What are the justice aspects of this question? How are the benefits and burdens distributed? Does the "need to warn" the wife outweigh respect for the husband's autonomy and his expectation of confidentiality?
- *Regarding notifying Woman B about the man's HIV infection*: The nurse asks whether the health department's obligation to Woman B differs from the obligation to his wife. That is, do the circumstances justify the health department's directly notifying her about her risk for HIV? Does the "need to warn" Woman B outweigh the husband's autonomy and his expectation of confidentiality?

3. Provide Justification for a Particular Public Health Action

The nurse strongly makes the case to you for notifying Woman A, the wife, pointing out that notification of the wife will help accomplish the goal of preventing

(continued)

BOX 5-2. (*continued*)

HIV transmission, or, if the wife already is infected, will help reduce morbidity by optimizing the wife's care. She claims that this benefit far outweighs any infringement of confidentiality and that the husband has forfeited much of his confidentiality claim by knowingly continuing sexual relations with his wife without using a condom.

She makes the case that burdens and benefits of notifying the wife are distributed in a way that at least partially compensates for the uneven distribution of burdens (more to the wife) and benefits (more to the husband). Although the notification indeed is intrusive in terms of privacy and confidentiality, the nurse makes the case that such action meets the justificatory conditions, particularly in that it will be effective in reducing morbidity, and, given the gravity of the potential harm, it is necessary and proportional (i.e., the probable benefits of the action outweigh the infringed confidentiality considerations).

Regarding Woman B, the ethical analysis may be more difficult because of uncertainty about the facts of the situation, including even her identity. The answer to the framework's initial question about risks and harms is not yet clear because the information regarding Woman B's potential exposure was not provided by an actual party to the alleged sexual encounter. Whether and how the nurse should ascertain the validity of Woman A's claim about Woman B's relationship with the HIV-infected man will depend on many factors, such as whether it can be done in a way to protect the privacy of Woman B, given the potential social harm to her that could be caused by information-gathering, as well as in a way to protect the confidentiality of the HIV-infected patient. A key question in this case is, How much investigative work should a public health official do about potential HIV exposure during private sexual behavior on the basis of a third-party claim? Given the gravity of the potential harm to Woman B and her sexual contacts, the urgent need for more direct information from the HIV-infected man himself regarding Woman B's potential exposure could justify a visit to his workplace by a health department official.

---

embodied in the community's laws, policies, and practices, as well as its myths and stories. The historical context and previous cases are particularly helpful in identifying these presumptive values.

Again, using a TB outbreak as an example, to analyze options for public health action if particular patients (for example, poor immigrants) are noncompliant with their treatment regimen, one might consider the options of detaining the patients or alternately including them in a directly observed therapy (DOT) program. For each option, deliberation might focus on the following questions raised in the framework: Does the option of patient detention (or alternately, of enrollment in the DOT program) produce a balance of benefits over harms? Are the benefits and burdens distributed fairly? The answers to these questions would depend in part on the values

BOX 5-3. Controlling Infectious Disease: Retrospective Assessment of an Urban Tuberculosis Outbreak

During a period of increasing morbidity from tuberculosis (TB) during the early 1990s, New York City updated its health code to facilitate use of legal action to ensure treatment compliance of TB patients.[28] Briefly, patients who were considered noncompliant with treatment regimens could be issued legal orders requiring directly observed therapy for TB, or if noncompliant with that intervention, requiring mandatory detention in a locked hospital ward.

Although TB program goals were met, as measured by the reduction both of new TB disease and drug-resistant TB, the program was criticized for two reasons. First, mandatory detention could be invoked for people who might be "expected" by observers to fail to adhere to less restrictive interventions rather than those documented to have already failed to adhere to the intervention. That is, incarceration was based on predicted noncompliance with a TB-treatment regimen rather than on the infectiousness—and thus immediate risk to the public—of TB patients.[29,30] Second, incarceration could continue until the entire treatment course had been completed, even though the period of infectiousness would have ended well before completion of TB treatment.

Whether the public health actions in this case were justified depends on whether they met the justificatory conditions posed in Part 3 of the framework (Box 5-1) and thus satisfied the conditions to override individual liberties (the conflicting values in this case). Given the presumptive value of respecting liberty, some observers believed the possibility of using less restrictive approaches to ensure compliance had not received sufficient attention, particularly because assessments of future compliance with treatment[29] and future risk to the public from TB patients rendered noninfectious by partial treatment are not an exact science.[30] In addition, the policy might be challenged on grounds of "necessity" because, as commentators emphasize, "other things being equal, the persuasion of, or the provision of financial or other incentives to, persons with TB to complete their treatment until cured should have priority over forcibly detaining them in order to ensure their completion of treatment."[22] At some point in an infectious disease outbreak, the disease risk and the gravity of the potential harm to the population's health could be so high that a public health emergency could be declared. In that case, given the strong legal authority and scope of public health to act in an infectious disease emergency, the presumption would shift so that public health action that trumps individual liberties could be justified, as long as appropriate due process procedures were followed.

and relations in the particular context, including the degree of trust and cooperation between the immigrant community and the public health workers.

Some commentators argue that a priority or presumption exists for liberty over coercion in public health measures in the United States. A priority or a presumption for liberty would mean that to justify use of their legal authority to either detain patients with infectious TB in a particular case or to require enrollment in a DOT program, public health officials would have the burden of showing that the public health value of utility in this circumstance (perhaps because the potential public health risk and harm are great) overrides the liberty interest of those detained and the burdens imposed on a particular vulnerable community. Demonstrating that both detaining the patients and enrolling them in a DOT program are ethically defensible options might be possible. The question then becomes, how does one choose and justify one option over another? Part 3 of the framework poses questions to help public health decision-makers justify a particular option.

3. Provide Justification for a Particular Public Health Action

The framework includes six justificatory conditions, listed in the form of questions for deliberation to provide a principled way to determine whether, in a particular situation, choosing one action that promotes one value, such as public health benefit (utilitarian value), warrants overriding other values, such as individual liberty or justice. The conditions require that, to override liberty, for example, the public health action must be effective, necessary, the least restrictive or intrusive means, proportional, impartial, and be publicly justifiable, namely, that public health officials offer moral reasons that in principle citizens could find acceptable.[17]

Lawyers will recognize that many of these conditions are analogous to those that must be satisfied to justify restrictions on certain constitutionally protected liberties, such as freedom of speech. However, legal and ethical analyses have different starting points and functions: legal analysis starts with settled law to address questions of legal authority and limitations on the state's power to infringe individual interests, whereas ethical analysis begins with an exploration of society's values to guide decision making when law is indeterminant and scientific and/or professional uncertainty exists about appropriate action.

In explaining their choices to the public, public health officials should justify actions and policies with rhetorical strategies that build community support and trust. Appeals might be made to principles, rules, rights, virtues, analogies, or paradigm cases. In discussing public health responses to bioterrorism, for instance, commentators highlight the role of civic imagination in public health ethics, which, in contrast to detached moral principles, can build community relationships and provide motivation and emotional energy for good citizenship. Through justification and imaginative engagement with the public, which may include personal narratives and stories from history or literature, public health officials and the community together can imagine various scenarios and the different ways community members may respond to threats. In this way, public health officials can help *create* community bonds and shape collective responses.[22] Another commentator used the example of vaccination policies to emphasize that public health officials must continuously build and strengthen community support for public health interventions, even for programs as well supported as vaccination policies were throughout the 20th century. With some challengers in recent years arguing to extend state vaccination exemptions beyond religious objections to those with beliefs about the safety of vaccination, the onus is on public health to continually demonstrate the safety, efficacy, and importance of mandatory vaccination or to risk state legislatures giving greater weight to individual liberty interests and asserted parental rights than to programs that benefit the population.[10] For numerous public health programs, then, public justification takes place over time and within an ongoing relationship that continuously builds community support for collective public health action.

Common Themes: Balancing Individual Interests and Public Good

Much traditional ethical analysis of public health has focused on the appropriate use of coercive or mandatory government action and typically has been framed as a "balancing" of individual rights or interests against the potential public health harms and risks to identifiable individuals or to the public in general. Analysis usually focuses on the scientific assessment of the severity and type of harm and the degree of risks, as in the claims of individuals for exemption to vaccination requirements or in decisions to quarantine or otherwise detain infectious individuals. Often implicit as well are questions about whether the public health benefits and burdens are distributed fairly. In this section, we explore two variations in public health ethics on the "individual rights versus public good" theme by examining the ethical dimensions of different public health interventions: screening and regulating individual behavior.

Balancing Individual Rights and Public Health Benefits: Screening

The following ethical analysis of public health screening illustrates how the ethical analysis framework (Box 5-1) can guide decision making.[17] The focus is a public health agency's consideration about whether to implement a screening program for HIV infection, TB, another infectious disease, or a genetic condition. Commentators distinguish two features of screening programs: the degree of voluntariness (from voluntary to mandatory) and the extent of screening (universal versus selective). When balancing the competing values (public benefit and individual rights) of a potential public health program, such as a screening program, the justificatory conditions listed in Section 3 of the ethics framework generally prioritize selective programs over universal ones and voluntary programs over mandatory ones. The justificatory conditions require public health officials to consider whether any proposed program is likely to realize the public health goal (effectiveness), whether its probable benefits will outweigh the infringed general moral considerations (proportionality), whether the policy is essential to realize the end (necessity), whether it involves the least infringement possible consistent with realizing the goal (least infringement), and whether it can be publicly justified.

Different screening programs may fail to satisfy one or more of the justificatory conditions. To detect HIV infection, for instance, neither mandatory nor voluntary universal screening can meet these conditions in the society as a whole. Some voluntary and some mandatory selective screening programs for HIV infection can be justified, whereas others cannot. Mandatory screening of donated blood, organs, sperm, and ova is easily justified, and screening of individuals also may be justified in some settings where they can expose others to body fluids and potential victims cannot protect themselves.[17] The question of whether and under what conditions screening of pregnant women for HIV infection should be instituted has been particularly controversial. Even before the advent of effective treatment for HIV infection and the identification of zidovudine (AZT) as effective in reducing the rate of perinatal transmission, there were calls for mandatory screening of pregnant women, especially in "high-risk" communities. Without options for treatment, however, mandatory screening was not justified, given the violations of autonomy, privacy, and justice. The justificatory conditions were not met.[17] Now that HIV-infected pregnant women can be given combination drug therapies that, together with C-sections and avoidance of breast-feeding, can reduce the risk for transmission to babies to as low as 1%, the weight of the arguments has shifted. Focusing on utility and efficiency, federal guidelines now recommend screening of all pregnant women for HIV as part of routine prenatal care.

Balancing Individual Rights and Public Health Benefits: Regulating Individual Behavior

Ethical and legal justification for the state's authority to regulate individual behavior to protect the health of the population is well established. In 1905, the landmark Supreme Court case *Jacobson v. Massachusetts* expressed the philosophic underpinnings for state collective action in terms of the social compact or covenant, citing the "manifold restraints to which every person is necessarily subject for the common good." Public health authorities historically have justified exerting control over individuals by demonstrating that burdens on individual liberties are outweighed by reasonable evidence of harm or risk for harm, usually from infectious disease, to the health of others.[31]

More controversial, however, are public health interventions aimed at individual behaviors that do not directly or immediately threaten the health of third parties. With increasing evidence linking causes of mortality and morbidity in industrialized countries to behavioral factors such as smoking, diet, and risk-taking, some public health interventions, such as motorcycle helmet laws, attempt to promote the population's health by mandating precautionary behavior. Such government regulation often is challenged as paternalistic, in that autonomous individuals' known preferences or actions are restricted or overridden, not because of a threat to the health of others but to benefit the very individuals whose preferences or actions are overridden.

Paternalistic interventions are deeply suspect in liberal democracies that value individual rights and liberty. Philosophic support for the antipaternalism principle is found in John Stuart Mill's argument that society should allow autonomous individuals to live according to their own beliefs, as long as they do not interfere with a like freedom of others or cause significant harm.[32] Public health interventions that benefit people considered unable to decide for themselves, such as children, are universally accepted as a considered justifiable form of paternalism (usually called "weak" or "soft" paternalism). In law, this is an example of *parens patria*. Public health interventions for the benefit of competent adults, however, such as requirements for motorcycle and bicycle helmets, continue to be debated. Some have argued that these laws represent an example of justified paternalism because they demonstrably enhance individual welfare with only a trivial loss of freedom. Others have argued that these requirements are not really paternalistic at all because injured motorcyclists impose costs on others, such as direct medical costs, indirect costs of lost productivity or earnings, or emotional costs (psychologic distress of others witnessing individual harm resulting from particular risk-taking behavior).

Other liberty-restricting interventions that produce both individual and collective health benefits, such as water fluoridation, also have been challenged as paternalistic. Whether these interventions actually restrict "liberty" in any meaningful sense can be questioned; but even if we assume fluoridating the water supply restricts the liberty of a person who does not want to consume the fluoride, we can argue that water fluoridation, because it provides the most practical and cost-effective way to achieve legitimate public goals, justifies the burdens imposed on the minority. Justifications for this and similar public health actions have been framed in terms of cost-sharing, collective action, economy of scale, or efficiency.

Benefits and burdens in public health settings in which paternalism is a concern must be balanced against the values of justice and of the sustenance of trust with members of the community. For example, important considerations sometimes include whether legislation benefits or burdens a vulnerable minority; whether it singles out one risk behavior, such as motorcycling without helmets, and not other similar behaviors, such as bicycling without helmets; whether individuals most affected by the intervention have had sufficient opportunity to express their concerns; and whether unintended consequences and social costs may result from the intervention, such as stigmatization or discrimination.

The Code of Ethics and Public Health Professionals

Professional codes of ethics provide important information for ethical analysis about the context and the complex relationships involved in public health, and thus are the basis of a question in Part 1 of the framework (Box 5-1). Codes help society and professionals address a number of questions: How does the public expect and rely on professionals to act? What are public health professionals' core values?

Codes of ethics generally describe the moral ideals and values of a profession, in part to lay the foundations for trust with those they serve and to establish the profession's particular identity. The relationships between a profession and the public are negotiated over time, and as expressed in a code or the guidelines of professional societies, can serve as a presumption about appropriate professional action in a given situation.[33–37]

Recognizing that the "backgrounds and perspectives of people who identify themselves as public health professionals are as diverse as the multitude of factors affecting the health of the population," public health leaders nonetheless recently have developed a Public Health Code of Ethics for the profession that addresses the relationship between public health institutions and the populations they serve.[38] The Public Health Leadership Society, in consultation with public health practitioners from across the nation, promulgated the "Principles of the Ethical Practice of Public Health" (Code) (Box 5-4), which was adopted formally by the American Public Health Association executive board in 2002 and subsequently has been either adopted or endorsed by at least six other national organizations.[39] The current principles are broad statements that will be updated over time to incorporate evolving values and lessons learned from practitioners. For practitioners and the public, the Code can clarify the values and goals of the public health profession.

Using the Code of Ethics: Disclosing Information to the Public in an Emergency

To demonstrate how the Code can help provide guidance in public health ethics, we present a case used by public health leaders in recent national forums. The hypothetical scenario explores what public health officials should do when an infectious disease outbreak occurs—such as with severe acute respiratory syndrome or avian influenza—if officials are concerned about the public's potential overreaction to news of the outbreak. For instance, when, if ever, is it ethical for public health officials to withhold information from the public, particularly if scientific uncertainty exists about the infectious agent? Practitioners emphasize that they, as public health professionals, have particular obligations to the communities they serve and that the Code can serve as a reference point to explain their obligations in a particular situation, such as an infectious disease outbreak.

For example, drawing on the Code, a county health department director might emphasize one of its central values, which states that the effectiveness of institutions depends heavily on the public's trust and that factors contributing to trust include communication; truth telling; transparency (i.e., not concealing information); accountability; reliability; and reciprocity. Acknowledging that public health officials in an evolving outbreak may have some latitude to decide when and how information should be disclosed to minimize social disruption, a health director would point to other principles from the Code that seem to limit this discretion and suggest that even information about scientific uncertainty should be revealed to the community as soon as possible, accompanied by reassurances of continued information and guidance. Particularly relevant is Principle 7 of the Code: "Public health institutions should act in a timely manner on the information they have within the resources and the mandate given to them by the public."[40] Emphasizing the importance of transparency with the community and public trust, public health officials generally maintain their ethical obligations, as stated in the Code, proscribe withholding information from the public.[c]

One might argue, therefore, that any decision to withhold information from the public because of a perceived high risk for grave harm almost certainly would need to be a political decision made, not by the public health official but rather by a political leader, such as the governor, on the basis of statutory authority to declare an emergency and take emergency actions. In such a situation, public health officials

BOX 5-4. The Principles of the Ethical Practice of Public Health

1. Public health should address principally the fundamental causes of disease and requirements for health, aiming to prevent adverse health outcomes.
2. Public health should achieve community health in a way that respects the rights of individuals in the community.
3. Public health policies, programs, and priorities should be developed and evaluated through processes that ensure an opportunity for input from community members.
4. Public health should advocate for, or work for the empowerment of, disenfranchised community members, ensuring that the basic resources and conditions necessary for health are accessible to all people in the community.
5. Public health should seek the information needed to implement effective policies and programs that protect and promote health.
6. Public health institutions should provide communities with the information they have that is needed for decisions on policies or programs and should obtain the community's consent for their implementation.
7. Public health institutions should act in a timely manner on the information they have within the resources and the mandate given to them by the public.
8. Public health programs and policies should incorporate a variety of approaches that anticipate and respect diverse values, beliefs, and cultures in the community.
9. Public health programs and policies should be implemented in a manner that most enhances the physical and social environment.
10. Public health institutions should protect the confidentiality of information that can bring harm to an individual or community if made public. Exceptions must be justified on the basis of the high likelihood of significant harm to the individual or others.
11. Public health institutions should ensure the professional competence of their employees.
12. Public health institutions and their employees should engage in collaborations and affiliations in ways that build the public's trust and the institution's effectiveness.

From reference 40.

who referred to the Code for guidance would point out the strong ethical values and presumption in public health for transparency and thus trigger an ethical analysis by government leaders based on the understanding that a strong justification is needed to override transparency, even in an emergency (Box 5-5).

BOX 5-5. Case: Public-Private Partnerships and the Code of Ethics

As health director of a local public health district that has significant childhood and adult dental health needs and a high prevalence of obesity, you are approached by a local fast-food restaurant (a national chain franchise). The restaurant manager offers to partner with your health agency to improve the community's dental health by funding a community dental health program. Dental health care is not a mandated or presently funded local public health service. The restaurant wants to donate $100,000 per year toward a community dental health education program that your agency will develop and manage. In return, the restaurant manager wants to have the restaurant's name listed as a project partner on all dental health education material, and he would like to participate in the distribution of the material to the community. Should you partner with the restaurant?

Analysis

In an era of limited resources and significant competing demands, public health officials acknowledge the need to seek partnerships and coalitions aggressively, yet also recognize the potential conflicts and tensions in these relationships.[41] Whether and how to enter into public-private partnerships depends, in part, on the congruence of the partners' missions and goals and whether perceived or real conflicts of interest or conflicts of obligation and accountability exist for the public health agency that would undermine and outweigh the potential positive health benefits of the relationship.[42] A source of guidance for some public health officials are the Principles of the Ethical Practice of Public Health (Code of Ethics), and at least two principles are relevant for this case: Principle 12, which encourages development of collaborations and affiliations in ways that build the public's trust and the institution's effectiveness; and Principle 3, which calls for processes that ensure an opportunity for input from community members. On the basis of these principles, Dr. Jody Hershey, a county health director, believes the public health official should seek information and guidance from community members and the public health agency staff about whether entering into a corporate partnership would in fact affect the agency's ability to regulate the restaurant, and whether the relationship would be perceived by the public as compromising the agency's effectiveness and the public health official's integrity (Dr. Jody Hershey, personal communication, September 23, 2005, Virginia). Given the significant potential community health benefit, the principles suggest that key factors in structuring partnerships with private community organizations would be ensuring the community's involvement in assessing the potential relationship, as well as transparency with community stakeholders about all aspects of the relationship once it is established. Such consultation with community stakeholders will provide important information about intended and possible unintended consequences of the partnership, for

(continued)

126

example, symbolic approval of a particular business or of a product. Community stakeholders must be involved in the decision about whether the partnership produces a net balance of benefits over costs to ensure the community's trust in the public health agency is not jeopardized.

Question for Discussion

Would the decision to partner be different if the restaurant also wanted to maintain a Web site on dental health for the health department that displayed the name of the company?

Public Health Lawyers and Ethics

Public health lawyers can be confronted with professional ethical dilemmas that result from their numerous obligations as employees of a public agency (see also Chapter 8). One key question is, who is the client of the government public health lawyer? Possibilities include the public, the government as a whole, the health department, and the public health official who heads the department. Although their role primarily is to interpret law and regulations and to provide guidance on adherence to legal requirements to the health department, public health lawyers recently have begun discussing broader roles in ethical analysis, based in part on the synergy between the values expressed in the Public Health Code of Ethics and the law. The chief legal counsel for one state health department has suggested that the lawyer should be a key member of the team that addresses a public health ethics issue. She believes it is imperative that counsel know what the current law does and does not permit and appreciate the civil liberties underpinnings of the law—to offer guidance on how the law might be interpreted.[43]

As with other lawyers in government, counsel for public health agencies can differ significantly in their conceptions of their role and of their ethical obligations.[44] For example, counsel occasionally may become aware of a program implemented without explicit legal authority about which the community may be divided. Such a case might be HIV-education funding for a community project that also provides needle exchange to reach injection-drug users. What should be counsel's role in this situation? A decision to act on this information requires complex balancing of the following types of considerations: (1) the lawyer's professional responsibility to ensure that public funds are expended strictly according to explicit directives, and (2) the lawyer's obligation as a public servant and public health official to support policies that enhance the health of the population in general and of a vulnerable subgroup of the population in particular.

Lawyers working in public service have a complex obligation as trusted agents of the community to help the agency efficiently and effectively conduct its public health mission while also ensuring the agency operates within the boundaries of its legal authority. In an office where the instrumental conception prevails, lawyers would be inclined to interpret funding directives liberally to help the agency accomplish its public health goals. On the other hand, in an office where the quasi-judicial or risk-manager role prevails, lawyers would tend toward more conservative interpretations of legal authority and would not be viewed by their clients as partners in strategic planning. Although either conception may be ethically permissible, individual lawyers may be more comfortable in one role or the other. An explicit clarification of the particular role played by the lawyer in any given situation may provide important contextual information for an ethical analysis of a public health intervention or policy.

Human Rights and the Public Health Code of Ethics

The first underlying value of the Code is: "Humans have a right to the resources necessary for health. The Public Health Code of Ethics affirms Article 25 of the Universal Declaration of Human Rights, which states in part, 'Everyone has the right to a standard of living adequate for the health and well-being of himself and his family. . . .'"[40]

The idea of "human rights as a public health value" has been advocated as a way to focus attention on fundamental social and economic inequalities and expand the scope of public health.[10] Commentators continue to debate whether tensions exist between individual rights and public health perspectives.[45,46] Although some conflicts seem inescapable (for example, individuals sometimes must submit to drug testing), human rights and public health are concordant in many important ways. Both human rights and public health are concerned with promoting and protecting human welfare and both increasingly recognize the vital role that social and environmental conditions play in achieving this goal. As pointed out in a recent World Health Organization publication, "A health and human rights approach can strengthen health systems by recognizing inherent differences among groups within populations and providing the most vulnerable with the tools to participate and claim specific rights."[47] Human rights concepts, like other principles espoused in the Code, provide public health practitioners with ideals to draw on when making rhetorical appeals about professional obligations and public health goals.

Integrating Ethical Considerations into Public Health Practice

Ethical reasoning in public health practice can be both a tool to analyze particular cases and an ongoing process within the agency's management structure. As described in the following section, it involves integrating ethics into the daily practices of an organization, such as information collection and policymaking. Consideration of the ethical dimensions of actions (or decisions not to act) by public health practitioners should include an examination of the broad spectrum of potential actions and decisions as they commonly occur in public health practice. Our goal in this section is to increase awareness of—rather than provide answers to—the relevant issues when officials are contemplating, creating, and evaluating public health interventions.

Recognizing the Existence of a Problem

The involvement of public health practitioners in an actual or perceived public health–related problem or event often begins with a concern about a threat to the public. That initial concern may be based on information from a reportable disease surveillance system, from a disease registry or other data source, or from entirely anecdotal reports. An initial practitioner decision may be how to respond to the potential existence of a problem, at least to the extent of acting—or declining to act—to obtain additional data. The threshold for such recognition can be set in a variety of ways (e.g., statistical, intuitive, supervisor's mandate) and therefore may have one or more ethical components. Alternatively, sometimes a decision to obtain additional information before acting or responding could be perceived as contributing to a delay in implementing an effective response, thus contributing to additional morbidity. Obviously, those who make decisions about the need for additional information should not have any personal conflict of interest that could affect their willingness to acknowledge the problem.

Collecting Additional Information

Assuming a decision is made to obtain more information either to confirm a problem's existence or to better characterize it, additional collection efforts can be undertaken using one or more of several partially overlapping methods (e.g., outbreak investigation, community survey, additional active surveillance activity). Decisions about which individuals or groups should be sources for information or specimens and how the information or specimens will be collected can have ethical dimensions (e.g., targeting the information collection effort so it is representative and fair in terms of distributing the information collection burden and so any stigma and dignitary harms caused by that collection effort are minimized). The mechanics of obtaining these additional data can also have ethical dimensions in terms of the amount of attention paid to issues of informed consent and to privacy and confidentiality concerns (e.g., considering informed consent issues in outbreak investigation situations).

Distinguishing Research from Practice

Debate sometimes is heard about whether data-collection aspects of surveillance, outbreak investigations, health services research, program evaluation, or other standardized information-collection activities carried out by local, state, or federal public health authorities represent research or public health practice (see also Chapter 10).[48] Activities considered research fall under the U.S. Code of Federal Regulations (45 C.F.R. 46), which guides research ethics and thus requires involvement of the institutional review board process. Activities considered practice (i.e., nonresearch) do not fall under the extant federal research regulations.

This difference in labeling an activity as research or practice may be less important from an ethical perspective than from an administrative one. Regardless of how an activity is classified, the concern of greatest interest is the nature and extent of external ethical review a government data-collection activity should undergo. The key issue in any context is whether any member of the public is put at significant risk by that activity. At the outset of any such activity, a responsible individual or group explicitly should address the issue of risk. A determination of "no significant risk" should be documented in some accountable way. If risk (e.g., to privacy, confidentiality, dignity) is—or might be—involved, then a more thorough review of risks and benefits should be conducted by a publicly accountable group or individual, even when institutional review board involvement is not formally required. The groups or individuals that conduct the review may become relevant.

Specific Ethical Issues in Legally Sanctioned Disease Surveillance and Outbreak Investigations

The ethical dimensions of surveillance and outbreak investigations require balancing of individual interests in privacy and confidentiality with the public's need for information. Surveillance for diseases for which reporting is mandated by law and investigation by competent government authorities of outbreaks of diseases of public health importance are activities for which individual consent is not explicitly required. However, the nonconsensual nature of these data-collection processes means that attention to privacy and confidentiality concerns should be paramount in the process of collecting and storing the data and specimens. In addition, any invasion of privacy can be minimized—and more easily justified—by collection of only the identifying information clearly needed for subsequent disease-control efforts and by removal of identifying information from data and specimens once maintaining that information is no longer useful.

Privacy and confidentiality, although partially overlapping concepts, are not identical.[27] *Privacy* refers to the individual's interest in limiting access to his or her body (or to specimens) or to personal information. *Confidentiality*, which sometimes is considered a subset of privacy, refers to the legal and ethical obligations to restrict *redisclosure* of private information originally disclosed to others in a confidential (e.g., patient-doctor) relationship.

Outbreak investigations also may be ethically more complicated for other reasons. For example, some public health practitioners consider epidemic illness of uncertain origin in members of the public as sufficient justification for expecting the cooperation of ill people (or the cooperation of family members) in outbreak investigations without having to conduct formal and explicit informed-consent procedures. However, that rationale becomes less helpful when persons not directly affected by disease are involved in outbreak investigations. For example, the justification for not routinely obtaining standard explicit informed consent from persons serving as uninfected controls (e.g., randomly selected, unaffected neighbors or coworkers) in outbreak-related case-control studies is a more complex informed-consent issue.

Analyzing and Presenting Information

Analysis and presentation of the additional collected information may be straightforward but also may have subtle ethical dimensions. For example, how rigidly or loosely a statistical threshold is set for signifying the existence of a problem ($p < 0.05$? $p < 0.001$? $p < 0.10$?) can determine whether a problem's existence is identified or missed. How information in a written or oral report is framed or portrayed can determine whether the report's conclusions about a disease or its risk factors will stigmatize certain individuals or groups. Whether reports are provided in a timely fashion to the representatives of groups contributing information to the data-collection process can affect subsequent levels of trust by affected communities.

Formulating a Response or Intervention

Once the existence of a problem is confirmed or at least strongly suspected, a response is likely to be contemplated. An appropriate public health response can take many forms and have several ethical dimensions. For example, the New York City TB situation involved a decision about whether the response should be the more traditional health promotion role or should involve the government's health protection role—in that case, the use of public health's police powers. Resource allocation decisions provide other potential problems. The principle of justice requires either that intervention programs allocate resources to ensure sufficient coverage of vulnerable populations or, if sufficient resources are not available for complete coverage, that they create and maintain an equitable and transparent system for rationing resources.

Ethical Aspects of Choosing a Policy Instrument

Government public health professionals have many policy instruments available for public health interventions, from education and information management (e.g., health promotion campaigns), to direct regulation (e.g., compulsory screening of newborn infants), to taxation. Public health policy instruments can be sorted into six general categories: (1) regulating or otherwise influencing conditions under which goods or services are available, which encompasses prohibitions as well as various forms of regulated access; (2) regulating the presence of health-enhancing or health-reducing substances or conditions in the physical environment; (3) regulating or otherwise affecting the flow of information and messages relating to health and behavior; (4) prescribing sanctions or loss of privileges to deter undesired behavior and require desired individual behavior; (5) using noncoercive incentives and disincentives for individual behavior, which include taxes and other mechanisms to affect the cost of target behaviors; and (6) influencing social norms (including attitudes and beliefs) about health and behavior.[49]

The relevant ethical considerations differ markedly across the categories. The third category for example, raises substantial questions about the justifications for suppressing the free flow of information, whereas use of sanctions to coerce compliance accentuates concerns about paternalism and the tensions between public health and individual liberty. Three factors, each of which raises its own ethical concerns, are particularly important for deciding which approach to use when individual rights are implicated: (1) whether the intervention is the least restrictive of individual rights, (2) whether efforts have been made to reduce any negative effects of the infringement, and (3) whether the intervention's burdens do not disproportionately affect a minority or vulnerable population. Aside from tensions between liberty and public health, other prominent ethical concerns relate to the proper thresholds for identifying risks as a matter of public concern in environmental health and safety regulation and the proper scope of public health efforts to shape social norms.

Government public health interventions also can include health education and social marketing campaigns designed to encourage individuals to change health behaviors for their own good and at the same time to encourage change in the social norms in the population. Health promotion campaigns have focused on smoking, alcohol abuse, drunk driving, and seatbelt use and led to changing social norms. Although health-education programs communicating factual information about health and behavior usually are purported to enhance individuals' choices to lead healthier lives, some health promotion and social marketing campaigns raise ethical questions about the appropriate role of government in shaping social norms and individual lifestyles. Ruth R. Faden has provided a useful framework for analysis of health promotion campaigns in relation to individuals, distinguishing between persuasion, which includes appeals to reason that enhance the autonomy and decision-making capacity of individuals, and manipulation (both manipulation of information and psychologic manipulation), which undermines an individual's capacity for autonomous behavior.[50]

Although autonomy-enhancing public health programs seem ethically preferable to interventions that restrict individual liberty, a more complex ethical analysis would be warranted to assess the appropriate role of health campaigns designed to change social values over time. Important considerations would be the degree of community involvement in a decision to focus on certain risk behaviors, including involvement of all stakeholders; the types of information or marketing materials used; and whether persons targeted by the campaign were informed of its goals.

Evaluating the Public Health Response

As with other individuals directing the use of public resources, public health practitioners are obligated to ensure through informal or formal evaluation the effective and efficient use of resources.[51] Enough new information about subsequent disease occurrence must be collected after an intervention to document accomplishment of these goals or to indicate how an improved intervention could accomplish them. Information collection may take the same form as the original data-collection process (and involve similar ethical concerns) or, as sometimes happens, a specific program evaluation effort can occur.

Often, these evaluation activities must take place without specific informed consent for each data extraction step. In fact, in many settings such as evaluation of quality of health services, the routine obtaining of informed consent is considered infeasible. Despite the absence of a formal individualized consent process, however, privacy and confidentiality issues still are likely to be of some concern to persons whose information is being used, and evaluation activities should be conducted with such concerns in mind. Such program evaluation activities sometimes offer the possibility of removing identifying information from data files before or as they are extracted for evaluation. In any case, the minimum amount of identifying information should be obtained, and the identifying information obtained should be removed at the earliest possible moment.

Conclusion

Our goal in this chapter is to familiarize public health practitioners and lawyers with approaches to public health ethics so they can better respond to the ethical questions they encounter in their practices. The purpose is to facilitate critical reflection and deliberation about reasons—ethical justifications—for particular decisions and courses of action.

Public health ethics is a new and rapidly evolving field that can offer public health professionals a complementary tool, along with legal analysis, to guide decision making in practice. Heightened awareness of ethical principles, precedent-setting cases, and stakeholder claims will enrich public health practice so that officials address the need for moral, as well as scientific and political, justifications for public health activities.

Notes

a. For an in-depth discussion of competencies and recommendations for education in public health generally, see Institute of Medicine. *Who Will Keep the Public Healthy? Educating Public Health Professionals for the 21st Century.* Washington, DC: National Academy Press, 2003; for a particular discussion of ethics, see pp. 98–105. Another examination of competencies is the MPH Core Competency Development Project of the Association of Schools of Public Health, which lists "Professionalism and Ethics" as one of the six cross-cutting competency domains its Version 1.2 draft posted July 15, 2005, at http://www.asph.org/document .cfm?page=851.

b. Public health ethics generally is distinguished from medical ethics on the basis of public health's focus on the health of the entire population (rather than the health of individual patients); its emphasis on health promotion and prevention; its populationwide collection and use of data; and its community perspective that highlights both the interdependence of individuals and organizations and the complex interactions of many factors—biologic, behavioral, social, and environmental—in health. Public health ethics is understood to be teleologic (end-oriented) and consequentialist—population health is both the end that is sought and the outcome measure. For a philosophic exploration of these issues, see Boylan M, ed. *Public Health Policy and Ethics.* Dordrecht/Boston/London: Kluwer Academic Publishers, 2004.

c. Alan Melnick, Director, Clackamas County Health Department, Oregon; Public Health Leadership Society Executive Board Member. Personal communication, June 14, 2004, Atlanta.

References

1. Rosen G. The origins of public health. In: *A History of Public Health.* Expanded edition. Baltimore: Johns Hopkins University Press, 1993:1–5.
2. Institute of Medicine. *The Future of the Public's Health in the 21st Century.* Washington, DC: National Academy Press, 2003.
3. Institute of Medicine. *Promoting Health: Intervention Strategies from Social and Behavioral Research.* Washington, DC: National Academy Press, 2000.
4. Marmot MG. Understanding social inequalities in health. *Perspect Biol Med* 2003;46(3 suppl):S9–23.

5. Epstein RA. Let the shoemaker stick to his last. *Perspect Biol Med* 2003;46(3 suppl):S138–59.

6. Meyer IH, Schwartz S. Social issues as public health: promise and peril. *Am J Public Health* 2000;90:1189–91.

7. Hall MA. The scope and limits of public health law. *Perspect Biol Med* 2003;46(3 suppl):S199–209.

8. Novak WJ. Private wealth and public health. *Perspect Biol Med* 2003;46(3 suppl):S176–98.

9. Rothstein MA. Are traditional public health strategies consistent with contemporary American values? *Temple Law Rev* 2004;77:175–92.

10. Rothstein MA. Rethinking the meaning of public health. *J Law Med Ethics* 2002;30:144–9.

11. Thomas JC, Sage M, Dillenberg J, Guillory VJ. A code of ethics for public health. *Am J Public Health* 2002;92:1057–9.

12. Couzin J. Ethicists to guide rationing of flu vaccine. *Science* 2004;306:960–1.

13. Bernheim RG. Public health ethics: the voices of practitioners. *J Law Med Ethics* 2003;31:S104–7.

14. Gostin LO. A theory and definition of public health law. In: *Public Health Law: Power, Duty, Restraint*. Berkeley: University of California Press, 2000:1–22.

15. Gostin LO, Sapsin JW, Teret SP, et al. The Model State Emergency Health Powers Act. *JAMA* 2002;288:622–8.

16. Annas GJ. Bioterrorism, public health, and civil liberties. *N Engl J Med* 2002;346:1337–42.

17. Childress JF, Faden RR, Gaare RD, et al. Public health ethics: mapping the terrain. *J Law Med Ethics* 2002;30:170–8.

18. Roberts MJ, Reich MR. Ethical analysis in public health. *Lancet* 2002;359:1055–9.

19. Bayer R, Fairchild AL. The genesis of public health ethics. *Bioethics* 2004;18:473–92.

20. O'Neill O. Public health or clinical ethics: thinking beyond borders. *Ethics Int Aff* 2002;16:35–45.

21. Walker MU. *Moral Contexts*. Lanham, MD: Rowman & Littlefield, 2003.

22. Childress JF, Bernheim RG. Beyond the liberal and communitarian impasse: a framework and vision for public health. *Florida Law Rev* 2003;55:1191–1205.

23. Nagel T. Moral epistemology. In: Bulger RE, Fineberg HV, eds. *Society's Choices: Social and Ethical Decision Making in Biomedicine*. Washington, DC: National Academy Press, 1995:201–14.

24. Annas GJ. Bioterrorism, public health and human rights. *Health Aff* 2002;21:94–7.

25. Benjamin M. Between subway and spaceship: practical ethics at the outset of the twenty-first century. *Hastings Cent Rep* 2001;31(July-August):24–31.

26. Kass NE. An ethics framework for public health. *Am J Public Health* 2001;91:1776–82.

27. Beauchamp TL, Childress JF. *Principles of Biomedical Ethics*. 5th ed. Oxford: Oxford University Press, 2001.

28. Gasner MR, Maw KL, Feldman GE, et al. The use of legal action in New York City to ensure treatment of tuberculosis. *N Engl J Med* 1999;340:359–66.

29. Campion EW. Liberty and the control of tuberculosis. *N Engl J Med* 1999;340:385–6.

30. Coker R. Tuberculosis, non-compliance and detention for the public health. *J Med Ethics* 2000;26:157–9.

31. Colgrove J, Bayer R. Manifold restraints: liberty, public health, and the legacy of *Jacobson v Massachusetts*. *Am J Public Health* 2005;95:571–90.

32. Mill JS. Introductory *and* On individuality, as one of the elements of well-being. In: On liberty. *Collected Works of John Stuart Mill*. Toronto: University of Toronto Press, 1977.

33. Sommer A, Akhter M. It's time we became a profession. *Am J Public Health* 2000;90: 845–6.
34. Callahan D, Jennings B. Ethics and public health: forging a strong relationship. *Am J Public Health* 2002;92:169–76.
35. Olick RS. Codes, principles, laws, and other sources of authority in public health. *J Public Health Manag Pract* 2004;10:88–9.
36. Weed DL, Mink PJ. Roles and responsibilities of epidemiologists. *Ann Epidemiol* 2002;12: 67–72.
37. Weed DL, McKeown RE. Science and social responsibility in public health. *Environ Health Perspect* 2003;111:1804–8.
38. Thomas JC. A code of ethics for public health. *Am J Public Health* 2002;92:1057–9.
39. Thomas JC. Skills for the ethical practice of public health. *J Public Health Manag Pract* 2005;11:260–1.
40. Public Health Leadership Society. *Principles of the Ethical Practice of Public Health.* Available at http://www.phls.org/products.htm. Accessed December 16, 2005.
41. Reich MR, Hershey JH, Hardy GE, Jr, Childress JF, Bernheim RG. Workshop on public health law and ethics I & II: the challenge of public/private partnerships. *J Law Med Ethics* 2003;31(Suppl):90–3.
42. Reich MR. Public-private partnerships for public health. *Nat Med* 2000;6:617–20.
43. Murphy A. Public health ethics in action. In: *The Public's Health and the Law in the 21st Century. Proceedings of the 4th Annual Partnership Conference on Public Health Law, Atlanta, GA, June 13, 2005.* Boston: American Society of Law, Medicine, and Ethics. In press.
44. Hazard GC Jr, Koniak SR, Cramton RC, Cohen GM, Lawyers for the government. In: *The Law and Ethics of Lawyering.* 4th ed. New York: Foundation Press, 2005.
45. Gostin LO. Public health, ethics, and human rights: a tribute to the late Jonathan Mann. *J Law Med Ethics* 2001;29:121–30.
46. International Federation of Red Cross and Red Crescent Societies, Francois-Xavier Bagnoud Center for Health and Human Rights. Human rights: an introduction. In: Mann JM, Gruskin S, Grodin MA, Annas GJ, eds. *Health and Human Rights: A Reader.* New York: Routledge, 1999:21–8.
47. World Health Organization. *A Human Rights Approach to TB: Stop TB Guidelines for Social Mobilization.* Geneva: World Health Organization, 2001.
48. MacQueen KM, Buehler JW. Ethics, practice, and research in public health. *Am J Public Health* 2004;94:928–31.
49. Bonnie RJ. The efficacy of law as a paternalistic instrument. In: Melton GB, ed. *The Law as a Behavioral Instrument.* Lincoln: University of Nebraska Press, 1985:131–211.
50. Faden RR. Ethical issues in government-sponsored public health campaigns. *Health Educ Q* 1987;14:27–37.
51. Institute of Medicine. Summary. In: *The Future of Public Health.* Washington, DC: National Academy Press, 1988:1–18.

Chapter 6

CRIMINAL LAW AND PUBLIC HEALTH PRACTICE

Zita Lazzarini, Richard A. Goodman,*
and Kim S. Dammers

This chapter introduces the unique characteristics of criminal law, provides a broad overview of the many substantive areas in which criminal law and public health law interact, and discusses in some depth the concept of forensic epidemiology and the role of criminal exposure and transmission laws.

Protecting Public Health, Safety, and Welfare

Definitions and Goals

A good legal definition of a crime is "an act performed in violation of duties that an individual owes to the community. It includes both harmful conduct (*actus reus*) and a culpable state of mind (*mens rea*)."[1] Public health can be defined as "what we, as a society, do to create the conditions in which people can be healthy."[2]

Broadly defined, the goal of the public health system is to protect the public health. Specifically, this emphasizes an approach to preventing disease and promoting health for the entire population of a specified area rather than for a single patient, as in traditional medicine. A good public health system includes methods for identifying

---

* The findings and conclusions in this chapter are those of the author(s) and do not necessarily represent the views of the U.S. Department of Health and Human Services or the Centers for Disease Control and Prevention.

patterns and sources of disease, assessing risk for disease, adopting the most appropriate measures to prevent and control disease, promoting healthy behaviors for individual members of society, and educating the public and policymakers about health risks and health benefits.

In comparison, the goals of the criminal justice system are to protect the public safety and welfare through preventing, detecting, investigating, and prosecuting crime. Criminal prosecution and its sanctions aim to punish violators, deter future crime, impose a measure of retribution against the offender on behalf of society that is roughly commensurate with the perceived seriousness of the crime, and reflect and/or influence society's norms of appropriate behavior.

Society, through its lawmakers, has determined that some behavior with public health implications is so dangerous that it merits criminal sanctions. At times, health officials support such sanctions; in other situations, they prefer noncriminal solutions. In terms of pure utility, public health officials sometimes harness aspects of the criminal justice system to achieve public health goals, while law enforcement relies on scientific techniques and specialized knowledge developed in public health investigations. At times, what begins as an investigation of a public health issue may turn into a criminal investigation, and, occasionally, the reverse is true. Although the objectives of public health and criminal justice overlap in significant ways, their mingling may have unintended or contradictory effects, and use of techniques developed for population-level health studies may require special oversight and privacy guarantees when applied in the criminal justice system.

Criminal and Public Health Law: Core Differences and Similarities

Both criminal law and public health provisions derive their authority from related duties of government. Public health authorities must protect the public health and welfare, whereas law enforcement seeks to protect the peace, welfare, and morals of society. The police power—defined as the residual power held by the states to make legislation and regulations to protect the public health, welfare, and morals and to promote the common good (*Jacobson v. Massachusetts*, 197 U.S. 11 [1905])—underpins both public health and criminal provisions. Moreover, enforcement of public health measures and transgressions of the criminal law often involve the same mechanisms and even common sanctions.

The sources of criminal law and public health law can differ. Most public health law is articulated in statutes (adopted by the legislature) and regulations (promulgated by state or federal agencies on the basis of the authority of the executive). Courts review and interpret public health–related legislation and produce "case law"—bodies of legal opinions that guide the application of the law. Criminal law also is codified in statutes and regulations. Criminal law (and to a lesser degree public health law) also owes much of its basic structure to the "common law"—judge-made law that is modified case by case over generations. For example, most jurisdictions now have statutes defining the varying degrees of homicide, assault, battery, and burglary. However, most of these distinctions are tied closely to generations of common law decisions in which judges defined and distinguished the elements of the different crimes and the types of intent required for conviction. In public health, the common law roots are more deeply buried, but familiar public health concepts such as "nuisance" have common law origins.[3]

Finally, although public health law and criminal law begin with the same source of government power and similar duties, their articulated goals diverge in important ways. Both try to protect the public's health and welfare. Criminal law, however, also explicitly seeks to punish and exact retribution for wrongs done to society.[1,4] Public health and criminal law share similar roots of authority, yet criminal law retains distinguishing characteristics with which public health practitioners should be familiar.

Power of the State

In a criminal prosecution, a prosecutor who argues the case on behalf of the people of the state or commonwealth usually represents the government's interest. The prosecutor implements particular criminal laws by seeking sanctions against a defendant accused of violating those laws. The defendant (usually a person, although in some instances, an incorporated entity may be criminally charged) is represented by his or her own attorney. The fact that the government has permanent staff to investigate and prosecute violations of criminal law and has regularly budgeted funds from the taxpayers to carry out these prosecutions highlights an important aspect of criminal law—the potential imbalance of power between the two sides. On one side of the case, the state has substantial resources to pursue a conviction against an individual. On the other side, the defendant, an individual, may lack education, sophistication, understanding, or even the ability to gain a thorough understanding of the issue being litigated and usually cannot match the government's extensive resources.

The public health arena usually lacks the overt drama of the courtroom (except in rare occurrences of epidemic disease), yet the power of public health authorities also extends deeply into individuals' lives through regulation of a wide range of commercial, personal, and daily activities. Although rarely used, the coercive powers of public health can be as drastic as depriving individuals of liberty. Less intrusive actions on behalf of public health still can have weighty consequences. For example, public health authorities can condemn property, regulate access to food and medicines, restrict the import and export of products, and control the flow of intensely sensitive personal information. None of these powers should be taken lightly, and the potential impact of each on individuals can have long-term consequences, as can involvement with the criminal justice system.

Due Process

Offsetting the power of the government against a criminal defendant is a series of important rights that attach to a prosecution. Many of the rights are derived from interpretations of the U.S. Constitution. Both the Fifth and Fourteenth amendments to the U.S. Constitution guarantee due process when an individual is to be deprived of his or her liberty or property. Broadly speaking, the Fifth Amendment protects directly against denial of due process by the federal government, and the Fourteenth Amendment extends this protection to shield individuals from state action. Due process in criminal cases guarantees clear notice of the charges brought against a defendant, the presumption of innocence until guilt is proven beyond a reasonable doubt, a right to a hearing before an impartial decision-maker, the opportunity to present evidence and to cross-examine witnesses at that hearing, the right to appeal the decision on the basis of an accurate written record, and the critical right to the appointment of counsel for defendants who cannot afford one.

In public health, due process rights also apply to any person whose liberty or property rights are threatened by public health actions. Where public health authorities seek to deprive individuals of liberty (e.g., confinement for disease control or civil commitment), due process guarantees protections similar to those in criminal prosecutions. For lesser intrusions on rights (e.g., disease surveillance, mandatory physical examinations, or testing), courts have interpreted the Fifth and Fourteenth amendments as demanding fewer procedural protections. In determining what degree of protections accrue in individual cases of public health action, courts will consider (1) the nature of the interest or liberty subject to limitation, (2) the risk for erroneous decision-making, and (3) the fiscal and administrative burdens of applying additional procedural protections.[5] Overall, courts will impose much more extensive protections where the right or interest involved is important, the risk for erroneous deprivation of the right is real and substantial, and the burdens of providing that protection are not disproportionate to the benefits.

Burden of Proof

"Burden of proof" refers to the allocation of responsibility to demonstrate that a matter alleged in a court is factually true and to the level of confidence in the allegation required in that particular setting (sometimes also called "standard of proof"). Generally, the prosecution (criminal cases) or the plaintiffs (civil cases) bear the burden of proof for all the major elements of a case. For example, to convict a defendant of violating a law against exposure or transmission of HIV infection, the prosecution (under most statutes) would have to prove that (1) the defendant knew he or she was HIV infected, and (2) he or she knowingly exposed another person through sexual intercourse, sharing of injection equipment, or other behavior prohibited in the statute. Without the prosecution's proof, the defendant does *not* have to prove his or her innocence, although he or she would clearly want to refute any prosecution evidence of the key elements. In contrast to civil law (dealt with elsewhere in this book and including torts, contracts, and property law), criminal law demands the highest standard of proof for conviction before punishment can be imposed— proof of guilt of violating the law "beyond a reasonable doubt." In general, public health proceedings require findings be based only on "a preponderance of the evidence," meaning that the evidence presented indicates that an event more likely than not occurred or a fact more likely than not is true. However, when public health authorities seek to confine an individual who poses a danger to the public health (such as to isolate a person with infectious tuberculosis [TB]) or seek to impose other significant burdens on individual liberties (such as court-ordered directly observed therapy [DOT]), due process demands that the findings be based on "clear and convincing evidence"—a higher standard than preponderance of the evidence but somewhat less stringent than "beyond a reasonable doubt."[6,7] Some legal authorities have endeavored to assign numerical values to the different standards of proof with varying degrees of success. The easiest standard to translate into numerical probabilities is "by a pre-ponderance," which is widely agreed to mean a probability of greater than 50% (p>0.5) that the facts, as asserted by the public health authorities, are true. Assigning probabilities to "clear and convincing evidence" and to "beyond a reasonable doubt" is more problematic.[8] In fact, one state supreme court reversed a lower court ruling where the trial court had instructed the jury that "beyond a reasonable doubt" was about "seven and a half" on a scale of one to ten (p>0.75). The Nevada Supreme Court held that "reasonable" is an inherently qualitative concept and should not be reduced to numbers.[9]

Penalties

Violations of the public health code (e.g., specific orders of a commissioner of health or of a local board of health) may be punishable as misdemeanors or other crimes. Traditionally, misdemeanors were punishable by a fine of up to $500, imprisonment for up to one year in the county jail, or both.[10] Violations of public health regulations and public health-related offenses, such as violating environmental regulations or breaching mandated confidentiality, also may be felonies, which traditionally are punishable by a prison term of one year or longer and higher fines. A felony conviction results in more serious and long-term consequences for the defendant.

Administrative Courts and Criminal Law

In more populous jurisdictions, administrative courts or other civil tribunals may adjudicate less serious violations of the local health code or other local public health measures. These courts hear less serious violations that tend to occur frequently and require regular imposition of fines or abatement orders to maintain the public safety or health. The New York City Health Code, for instance, allows closure of buildings that pose a condition dangerous to life or health (New York City Administrative Code, §§17-142–17-159, concerning a public nuisance). The New York Board of Health, an appointed administrative body, hears many of these cases and assesses penalties for nuisances, and can order closure of buildings. Although administrative law courts often are characterized as a lower form of proceeding than ordinary civil courts, these administrative bodies can have enormous powers in imposing sanctions (i.e., closing an establishment harmful to the public health) or ordering abatement measures (i.e., draining standing water that can harbor mosquitoes and clearing away debris that attract vermin).

Whether a case is prosecuted criminally or handled in a regular civil or an administrative court depends on how the state and locality have defined jurisdiction for their courts. The person framing the case, whether a civil lawyer or a prosecutor, will consider the most important sanction (e.g., closure, fine, imprisonment) and will most likely steer the case into the forum that can most efficiently impose that sanction. Civil law sets the range of fines that each level of court can assess, and civil law will delineate the forms of relief in the civil and administrative courts in terms of compelling or prohibiting actions that affect the public health.

Law on the Books: Criminal Law and Public Health

Criminal Law Theories in Relation to Public Health Goals

Law plays many roles in public health practice. Law expresses the mission or agenda of public health agencies, and although it provides authority for action, it also sets limits on that authority. The law can act as a direct tool of disease and injury prevention and health promotion. The law also can educate the public and policymakers about important public health issues.[5] Criminal sanctions in public health usually are intended as a tool to change or avoid unhealthy behavior. To a lesser degree, such laws function as a means to educate the citizenry of the parameters of acceptable behavior. At least two theories are worth mentioning about how criminal law can change individuals' behavior: deterrence and norm-setting.

The theory of deterrence suggests that people obey the law primarily because they fear they will be caught and punished.[11,12] For example, deterrence supposes that persons who otherwise would not wear motorcycle helmets will change their behavior to avoid an expensive ticket. The theory that law sets or reflects community norms suggests, instead, that individuals obey the law because the law has influenced or reflects what they and their peers believe is right, regardless of the availability or likelihood of punishment.[13,14] In practice, norm-setting suggests that where most members of a community believe that driving drunk is wrong, then most will obey the law against driving under the influence, regardless of the likelihood of being caught or punished. In reality, both motivations probably influence individual behavior, and people may obey or disobey different laws for different reasons, or they may be motivated by a combination of fear of punishment and a desire to be seen as "law-abiding" or "upstanding" by adhering to community norms. That the citizens' perception of the law's fairness or their grasp of the importance of the law at issue affects their motivation and behavior cannot be ignored. The degree to which law affects behavior becomes important when we look more closely at specific kinds of criminal laws and the behavior they seek to prevent or change.

Public Health and Criminal Laws with Similar Goals

Public health practitioners should be aware of the wide variety of public health laws that potentially invoke criminal penalties. Many public health–related misdemeanors and felonies are codified in statewide public health statutes or local health codes. These include criminal penalties for air and water pollution, improper disposal of hazardous waste or sewage, contamination or adulteration of foods and drugs, and acts of bioterrorism. Laws with public health objectives that carry criminal penalties include provisions mandating the use of protective devices such as child safety seats in cars, seatbelts, and bicycle and motorcycle helmets; prohibitions of the sale of tobacco or alcohol to minors; and restrictions on the time and place of alcohol sales to adults (Table 6-1).

TABLE 6-1 Selected State Statutes Criminalizing Public Health Violations

Public Health Problem	Statute/Penal Code/ Public Health Code	Statute Summary	Penalty
Air pollution	O.R.S. (Oregon) §468.939 Unlawful air pollution, first degree	Unlawful to knowingly discharge, emit, or allow to be discharged or emitted any air contaminant into the atmosphere that recklessly causes substantial harm to human health or environment or knowingly disregards the law in committing violation.	Class B felony. On second conviction within 5-year period, the court may require polluter to pay an amount not exceeding $200,000 in addition to other sanctions.
Hazardous waste: unlawful disposal or abandonment	M.S.A. (Minnesota) §609.671 Environment; criminal penalties	Unlawful to knowingly dispose of or abandon hazardous waste or arrange for the disposal at a location other than one authorized by pollution control agency or Environmental Protection Agency, or in violation of terms of hazardous waste facility permit.	Felony. May be sentenced to imprisonment for not more than 5 years or to payment of a fine of not more than $50,000 or both.
Water pollution	O.R.S. (Oregon) §449.105 Placing polluting substances in waters, on highways or other property	Unlawful to discard any dead animal carcass, excrement, putrid, nauseous, noisome, decaying, deleterious or offensive substance into or in any other manner befoul, pollute or impair the quality of any spring, river, brook, creek, branch, well, irrigation drainage ditch, irrigation ditch, cistern, or pond of water. Unlawful to place any of these polluting substances into any road, street, alley, lane, railroad right-of-way, lot field, meadow, or common; and an owner thereof cannot knowingly permit any polluting substances to remain in any of the places to the injury of the health or to the annoyance of any citizen of the state.	Class A misdemeanor. Every 24 hours after conviction for violation of this during which the violator permits the polluting substances to remain is an additional offense.

Subject	Statute	Description	Penalty
Food/drug contamination or adulteration	West's Ann. Cal. Penal Code §383 Sale of adulterated or tainted food beverage, drug, or medicine	Unlawful to sell or keep or dispose of food, drink, drug or medicine, knowing that it is adulterated or otherwise unwholesome or unfit to be eaten or drunk, with intent to permit it to be eaten or drunk.	Misdemeanor. Must be fined not exceeding $1,000, or imprisoned in county jail not exceeding 6 months, or both.
Bioterrorism	West's Ann. Cal. Code, Article 4.6 The Herzberg-Alarcon California Prevention of Terrorism Act §11419 Possession of Restricted Biological Agents	Unlawful for any person or entity to possess any of the enumerated restricted biological agents.	Shall be imprisoned in state prison for 4, 8, or 12 years and fined not more than $250,000.
Sanitation	West's Ann. Cal. Penal Code §374.2	Unlawful to maliciously discharge or otherwise deposit, or to maliciously cause to be deposited, any substance capable of causing substantial damage or harm to the operation of a public sewer sanitary facility, or to deposit in commercial quantities any other substance into a place not intended for use as a point of deposit for sewage, which is connected to a public sanitary sewer system, without authorization.	Imprisonment in county jail for not more than 1 year or by fine of up to $25,000 or both. If a subsequent violation, punishment by imprisonment in county jail for not more than 1 year or imprisonment in the state prison for 16, 20, or 24 months, and by a fine of not less than $5,000 and not more than $25,000.
Preventing alcohol sales to minors	Conn. Gen. Stat 30-86	Prohibits sales of alcohol to minors.	Fine of not more than $1,500 or imprisonment up to 18 months, or both.
Preventing tobacco sales to minors	Cal. Penal Code 308 (California)	Prohibits sale of tobacco or smoking paraphernalia to minors, permits criminal or civil action.	Criminal action: Misdemeanor Civil action. First offense, $200; second, $500; third, $1,000.

(continued)

TABLE 6-1 (continued)

Public Health Problem	Statute/Penal Code/ Public Health Code	Statute Summary	Penalty
Control of paraphernalia used to inject illegal drugs	M.G.L.A. 94 C 38	Criminalizes possession of syringe, needles, or other drug paraphernalia without a prescription.	First offense punishable by imprisonment for not more than 1 year or by a fine up to $1,000 or both. Second offense punishable by imprisonment for 2 years or fine up to $2,000 or both.
Reducing drunk driving	Cal. Veh. Code §23550	Enhances penalties for multiple offenses of driving under the influence of drugs or alcohol.	Imprisonment for 180 days to 1 year and fine of $390 to $1,000.
Child abuse and neglect	NY Penal Law 260.10	Criminalizes endangering the welfare of a child.	Class A misdemeanor.
Transmission of HIV by persons who know they are infected	ILCS 5/12/16.2	Criminalizes many specific acts that could expose anther to HIV.	Class B felony.
Confidentiality of medical records and public health information	Arkansas Code Ann. 20-7-307	Prohibits violations of confidentiality of information in the collection or dissemination of public health data collected by the Health Department.	Misdemeanor punishable by a fine or by imprisonment.
Confidentiality of information in investigations of sexually transmissible diseases (incl. HIV)	410 ILCS 325/5.5(d)	Prohibits violations of confidentiality of information during the Department of Public Health process of investigating risks for transmission of HIV and notifying contacts of potential risk.	Class A misdemeanor.

Laws That Act as Barriers to Public Health Practices

Sometimes lawmakers enact provisions of law to address public health or criminal justice problems that eventually become barriers to effective public health efforts as circumstances change. During the course of the HIV/AIDS epidemic, one area of policy and practice that illustrates this dilemma is laws and practices governing access to sterile syringes and needles.

At the beginning of the 1990s, virtually all states had in place drug paraphernalia laws that criminalized the sale, purchase, and possession of syringes with the intent to use them to inject or ingest illegal drugs. A smaller number of states also had specific syringe-prescription laws that required a valid physician's prescription for all sales of syringes and needles. An intermediate number of states had pharmacy regulations that discouraged the sale of syringes to persons without a valid medical purpose. These provisions had been adopted in response to earlier "epidemics" of drug use, specifically the 1960s and 1970s (drug paraphernalia laws) and the early 1900s (syringe-prescription laws).[15] Beginning in the late 1980s, numerous studies indicated that the reuse of contaminated syringes by injection-drug users (IDUs) contributed significantly to the spread of HIV, hepatitis B and C, and other bloodborne diseases. In part, IDUs reuse contaminated injection equipment because of the scarcity of sterile syringes created by the criminal provisions described above. In 1995, a scientific panel of the National Academy of Sciences, Institute of Medicine, concluded that legal barriers to the purchase and possession of syringes were contributing to epidemics of bloodborne disease and should be rescinded.[16]

The original laws sought to discourage drug use by making syringes more difficult to obtain. This created a dilemma for policymakers who now faced a new, yet pressing, public health crisis: how to prevent the spread of HIV and other bloodborne diseases. All the federal agencies concerned (Centers for Disease Control and Prevention [CDC]; Health Resources and Services Administration; National Institute on Drug Abuse, Substance Abuse and Mental Health Services Administration), as well as national medical (American Medical Association), public health (Association of State and Territorial Health Officers, National Alliance of State and Territorial AIDS Directors), legal (American Bar Association), pharmaceutical (American Pharmaceutical Association), and pharmacy (National Association of Boards of Pharmacy) groups, have issued recommendations identifying the need for access to sterile syringes for IDUs who continue to inject drugs.[17,18] The prohibition on use of federal funds to support syringe-exchange programs remains in place, and most states still criminalize sale or possession of syringes for use with illegal drugs. At the same time, however, state, local, or private organizations continue to support syringe exchanges in all major cities and many localities. In addition, several states have deregulated sale of syringes (California [at pharmacies registered as part of the "Disease Prevention Demonstration Project"], Connecticut, Illinois, Maine, New York, New Hampshire, Rhode Island), or removed them from the definition of prohibited paraphernalia (Oregon, Wisconsin).[15,19]

Related to laws that create barriers to public health practice are law enforcement practices that do the same. Sometimes "policing" rather than law places individuals at risk or reduces the effectiveness of public health efforts. In Connecticut, even after deregulation of syringe sales, police in some cities continued to arrest IDUs who were carrying syringes. Public health advocates went to court to get an injunction to stop the practice.[20]

Public Health–Related Activities within the Criminal Justice System

The United States incarcerates a higher proportion of its population than does any other western democracy. An estimated 2.8% of the adult U.S. population is incarcerated or under court supervision at any one time.[21] Prison and jail populations have doubled and even quadrupled during the past 20 years in many places, in large part because of increased arrest and incarceration of persons accused of drug-related offenses (percentage of federal prisoners sentenced for drug offenses, 1970: 16.3%; 1980: 25.6%; 1990: 52.2%; 2000: 56.9%).[22] Minorities are disproportionately likely to be arrested and incarcerated in most state and the federal prison systems.[23,24] Although men still outnumber women 9:1, during 1990–2005, the number of adult women in jails increased faster than the number of men.[25] For a breakdown of prison populations for one year by race/ethnicity and sex, see Table 6-2.

When compared with the total population, incarcerated populations have disproportionately higher rates of some health problems. Rates of TB, HIV infection, hepatitis, and mental illness are many times higher among incarcerated than nonincarcerated persons, with HIV infection rates 12–17 times higher in prisons and jails.[26] The higher number of women in prison means increased need for basic and specialized gynecologic, obstetric, and pediatric care by correctional facilities. Prison health problems are public health problems, not only because of the high prevalence of communicable diseases traditionally associated with public health but also because prisoners disproportionately represent populations underserved by health services. Incarceration provides one opportunity to use public health interventions to improve health and, by extension, the health of the communities to which they belong. Almost 500,000 prisoners are released from state and federal prisons each year, and many more are discharged from city and county jails.[27] Failure to address their public health needs is a lost opportunity for public health.[28,29]

Law in Practice: The Intersection of Public Health and Criminal Investigations

This section gives an overview of the methods, definitions, and important legal issues emerging where public health and law enforcement personnel investigate events with public health significance that may also involve criminal activity. After describing key scientific methods used in conjunction with epidemiology, we discuss the evolving concept and definition of "forensic epidemiology," review a series of joint investigations that have been published, address selected legal issues arising or implicated in such investigations, and consider the challenges of using the language and findings of epidemiologic investigations in the courtroom.

TABLE 6-2   U.S. Resident Population of Sentenced Prisoners (Rates per 100,000) in State and Federal Correctional Authorities, as of July 1, 2004

Sex	Total*	White, non-Hispanic	Black, non-Hispanic	Hispanic
Male	926/100,000	463/100,000	3218/100,000	1220/100,000
Female	64/100,000	42/100,000	170/100,000	75/100,000

Source: Table 6.33.2004. Available at http://www.albany.edu/sourcebook/pdf/t6332004.pdf.

* Total includes all races/ethnicities, including American Indians, Alaska Natives, Asians, Native Hawaiians, other Pacific Islanders, and persons identifying with two or more races.

Scientific Methods Used by Both Public Health and Criminal Investigations

Public health authorities and criminal investigators can use many scientific techniques—from basic epidemiology to increasingly sophisticated genetic analyses. For example, genetic analyses are used in public health investigations to track the spread of specific strains of infectious diseases (e.g., different strains of *Mycobacterium tuberculosis*, hepatitis virus, or HIV), and criminal investigators use similar molecular biology techniques to include or exclude individuals as suspects in a case where biologic evidence has been collected. Whether a particular laboratory test is used as a part of an epidemiologic study, individual patient care, or a criminal investigation, adherence to proper technique in collecting, transferring, processing, and reporting results is essential. The consequences of the same test can vary profoundly depending on the context in which it is used, and different safeguards may be appropriate under different circumstances. For example, in a broad, population-level assessment of the prevalence of a specific gene or strain of infection in a specific population, maintaining an accurate link to the identity of the individual from whom the biologic sample was taken may not be necessary. In fact, it may be undesirable or even prohibited by research protocol or by law. In contrast, if the results of a laboratory test will be used to implicate a person in a criminal investigation, then everyone handling the sample must be able to demonstrate it is, and has been, identified as coming from the person in question to be admissible and probative in court. In legal terms, this is known as "maintaining the chain of custody" of the evidence. From a scientific perspective, such adherence to detail is part of the scientific method when testing certain hypotheses (i.e., what is the cause or source of *this particular* case of infection, rather than *the general nature of all these samples*). Careful tracking of samples and results ensures reproducibility of results and should be part of every well-established laboratory.

Epidemiology—the study of the distribution and determinants of disease (and health) in populations—can characterize health problems arising from criminal activity as well as the "natural" spread of diseases and determinants of risk. Insights gained from such investigations can be used to inform public policy, as in the epidemiologic assessment of alcohol use as a "risk factor" for homicide.[30] The techniques of field epidemiology traditionally used by public health agencies to investigate outbreaks of disease also can be applied to situations when disease clusters result from suspected criminal activity, as in the study of victims in a series of child murders in Atlanta during 1979–1981[31] or in clusters of illness or death in hospitals or other health-care settings where staff have been suspected of intentionally harming patients.

Increasingly, advances in molecular biology also are being used in criminal cases. The DNA testing of biologic evidence to support claims of guilt or innocence of a specific defendant is becoming widespread. Every state in the United States has some form of a "DNA data-banking" law, mandating that a biologic sample be obtained from prisoners convicted of specific felonies, which vary from state to state. The convicted offender's sample is analyzed and the results entered into a data bank for future reference. From a public health perspective, use of such banked information to rapidly identify repeat violent offenders could reduce the incidence of future violence.

The vast majority of U.S. courts will admit evidence obtained by standard molecular biology techniques. The use of molecular biology in this context is commonly referred to as "DNA evidence" or "DNA testing." Many prisoner advocates argue that failure to permit or require testing where biologic evidence exists but has not been previously analyzed or used may result in the frequent miscarriage of justice and even the execution of innocent individuals.[32,33] Other proposals, however, create different concerns. For example, should law enforcement agencies be allowed to conduct nationwide matches of evidence obtained from a crime scene against all stored and tested DNA samples to identify suspects in a case? These samples could include those obtained by the military, prisons, and other law enforcement agencies, or samples that an individual has given to exclude himself or herself from suspicion of another crime. Using molecular biology techniques of identification combined with personal information that may have been collected for non-criminal-justice purposes raises significant privacy concerns and deserves careful scrutiny to ensure that Constitutional rights are protected.

Forensic Epidemiology

Background

Since at least the mid-1970s, public health and law enforcement officials have conducted joint or parallel epidemiologic and criminal investigations of health problems possibly associated with criminal intent, or crimes having particular health dimensions.[34] However, the anthrax and other terrorist attacks of fall 2001 dramatically underscored the needs that public health and law enforcement officials have for clearer understanding of the goals and methods each discipline uses in investigating such problems, including and especially the potential use of biologic agents as weapons of mass destruction.[35,36] Recognition of these needs prompted some experts to call for the application of "forensic epidemiology" to such problems.[37,38] Even before the attacks of fall 2001, other problems, such as the detection of the West Nile virus in the United States and concerns that the emergence of this infectious agent was the consequence of a deliberate act, raised novel challenges to the combined interests of public health and criminal investigators.[39]

In addition to demonstrating both similarities and divergences in the investigative goals and methods used by public health and law enforcement, the 2001 events highlighted fundamental legal issues related to the conduct of such investigations, including statutory bases for legal action, and safeguards to individual rights and liberties.[40–42]

Defining "Forensic Epidemiology"

The term "forensic epidemiology" in relation to threats to public health was included in testimony given in October 1999 before a House Subcommittee by Dr. Ken Alibek, former first deputy chief of the Soviet Union's bioweapons program,[43] in reference to investigation of the recent West Nile virus outbreak and the need to distinguish between natural and human-made epidemics.[37] The term also was used in early 2002 by a senior CDC official who, in discussing evolving concepts of applied epidemiology in the aftermath of the fall 2001 attacks, noted that forensic epidemiology needed to become part of epidemiology training at CDC.[38] Following these uses of the term, this definition was developed for "forensic epidemiology": the use of epidemiologic methods as part of an ongoing investigation of a health problem for which there is suspicion or evidence regarding possible intentional acts or criminal behavior as factors contributing to the health problem. An alternative definition is: the use of epidemiologic and other public health methods in conjunction with or as an adjunct to an ongoing criminal investigation.[36]

Encompassed within the development of forensic epidemiology is the emerging and more specific focus of "microbial forensics," defined as an emerging discipline that "combines principles of public health epidemiology and law enforcement to identify patterns in a disease outbreak, determine the pathogen involved, control its spread and trace the microorganism to its source—the perpetrator(s)."[44]

A Record of Joint Epidemiologic and Criminal Investigations

A review of joint epidemiologic and criminal investigations conducted in North America that fit the definitions of forensic epidemiology was reported in late 2003.[36] That review summarized 12 reports published in the biomedical literature and/or in newspapers (see selected reports in Table 6-3[34,36,45–50]). For each of these problems, the investigations involved federal and/or state epidemiologists and law enforcement officials, sometimes working in parallel or independently, but other times working together.

The 12 problems occurred during 1975–2003, and the numbers of persons potentially affected for some of the episodes were substantial, including, for example, as many as 51 cardiopulmonary arrests in 35 patients in one hospital,[34] 751 persons with *Salmonella typhimurium* gastroenteritis,[46] and approximately 32,000 persons initiating post-exposure antibiotic prophylaxis in conjunction with the 2001 anthrax attacks causing 22 cases of cutaneous or inhalation anthrax.[49] The settings for these problems included hospitals and a nursing home, communities, restaurants, and other workplaces (e.g., media facilities, government offices, and postal facilities). The investigations examined a spectrum of problems considered at the time potentially to have involved criminal behavior, including murder, attempted murder, criminal assault, and bioterrorism.

TABLE 6-3 Selected Examples of Investigations Involving Public Health and Law Enforcement: United States and Canada, 1975–2003

Year, Author (Reference number)	Problem/Setting	Implicated or Suspected Disease- or Injury-Causing Agent	Magnitude/Scope of Problem	Epidemiologic Association	Outcome
1976, Stross[34]	Over 6-week period, occurrence of striking increase in incidence of cardiopulmonary arrests in Veterans Administration and teaching hospital	Pancuronium bromide	During 6-week period, 51 episodes of cardiac arrest in 35 patients	Cardiopulmonary arrests were disproportionately more likely during one specific shift	Two nurses indicted for murder, attempted murder, and conspiracy to commit murder
1980–1981, Buehler[45]	Nurse on cardiology ward of children's hospital was arrested and accused of administering overdoses of digoxin to four patients who had died	Digoxin	Over 9-month period, death rate for patients on ward was nearly four times that in preceding 54 months, with risk significantly increased during one specific shift	Strong association between infant deaths and duty times of particular nurse	Despite documented increased risks, cause of epidemic remained unclear
1984, Torok[46]	Outbreak of acute gastroenteritis among customers of multiple restaurants in one community	Salmonella typhimurium	Total of 751 persons with Salmonella gastroenteritis	Risk for illness associated with eating at salad bars, but investigators unable to implicate single food item(s) or commonly known mechanisms of contamination	Epidemiologic investigation did not fully explain outbreak and law enforcement criminal investigation followed; 2 persons indicted for conspiring to tamper with consumer products by poisoning food;

1985, Franks[47]	Nursing supervisor noted increase in number of cardiac arrests in surgical intensive-care unit patients during 3-week period	Undetermined, although suggestion of hyperkalemia in some patients	During epidemic period, nine arrests occurred in unit which averaged three to four arrests per month	Compared with exposure to other intensive-care unit nurses on duty during evening shift, risk associated with exposure to one specific nurse was infinitely large	Nurse who was epidemiologically associated with cluster was removed from intensive-care unit; same nurse was subsequently acquitted of murder charges but convicted for aggravated assault
1996, Kovalovic[48]	Over 3-day period, laboratory workers in a large medical center had severe gastroenteritis caused by rarely identified organism	*Shigella dysenteriae* type 2	Of 45 laboratory staff, 12 (27%) had severe acute, diarrheal illness	All 12 persons who ate pastries placed in lab staff break room became ill compared with none of 33 who did not eat, resulting in undefined relative risk	Pastries most likely contaminated by lab's stock culture; lab worker indicted and charged with first-degree felony of tampering with consumer product
2001, Jernigan[49]	After the terrorist attacks in fall 2001, envelopes containing *Bacillus anthracis* spores mailed to news media companies and government officials	*B. anthracis*	Total of 22 cases of anthrax (11 inhalational and 11 cutaneous), including five fatal cases; 20 cases were in mail handlers or worked in settings where mail processed; approximately 32,000 persons initiated antimicrobial prophylaxis	*B. anthracis* isolates from envelopes, patient specimens, and environmental samples indistinguishable by molecular subtyping	At time of press for this manuscript, no suspect(s) had yet been indicted under federal terrorism statutes for criminal use of biologic agents in this attack

(continued)

TABLE 6-3 *(continued)*

Year, Author (Reference number)	Problem/Setting	Implicated or Suspected Disease- or Injury-Causing Agent	Magnitude/Scope of Problem	Epidemiologic Association	Outcome
2003, CDC[50]	Supermarket notified state and federal agencies of planned recall of ground beef because of customer complaints of acute illness after eating product; supermarket's laboratory then identified nicotine as ground beef contaminant	Nicotine	At least 92 persons had illness meeting case definition, including one with atrial fibrillation and one with complaint of rectal bleeding	High concentrations of nicotine detected in ground beef samples submitted by families with ill persons	Grand jury indictment for arrest of person (supermarket employee) accused of poisoning meat with insecticide containing nicotine

The earliest report involved a 1975 incident in which an unexpected cluster of cardiopulmonary arrests occurred among patients in a U.S. Veterans Administration hospital.[34] In that situation, the concurrent epidemiologic and criminal investigations examined 51 episodes of cardiopulmonary arrest in 35 patients; and urine samples obtained from 3 patients after their cardiopulmonary arrests contained pancuronium bromide, a muscle paralyzing agent, that had not been prescribed for any of them. Two of the hospital's nurses subsequently were indicted for murder, attempted murder, and conspiracy to commit murder. In addition to the 1975 investigation, episodes of cardiopulmonary arrests and/or deaths in health-care facilities appeared to cluster in the mid-1980s.[36]

One final example highlighting forensic epidemiology was the large community-wide outbreak of salmonellosis in Oregon in 1984.[46] This outbreak probably was the first recognized, thoroughly investigated and documented, and reported instance of domestic bioterrorism in the United States. After the investigation, two persons were indicted for conspiring to tamper with consumer products in violation of the federal anti-tampering act. This episode also illustrates the concepts of "biocrime" and "microbial forensics" as described by the American Academy of Microbiology.[44]

Legal Issues in Joint Epidemiologic and Criminal Investigations

Practically, interactions between public health and law enforcement, especially during joint investigations of threatened or real bioterror attacks, have revealed a host of legal issues. Although we cannot address all the legal issues raised in joint investigations, we consider two in some detail, specifically the law regarding gathering of admissible evidence during public health investigations so as to comport with Fourth and Fifth Amendment requirements.

Gathering Admissible Evidence in Public Health Investigations

Successful prosecution of the perpetrators of crimes that use biologic or chemical agents requires admissible evidence. In gathering evidence, government agents must comply with, among other things, the Fourth Amendment prohibition against unreasonable searches and seizures and the Fifth Amendment protection against self-incrimination.

The Fourth and Fifth amendments to the U.S. Constitution apply only to government-sponsored actions;[51,52] therefore, public health officials, like all government agents, must conform their investigations to constitutional standards. Because public health officials typically do not investigate criminal activity, the greatest potential for the inadvertent gathering of evidence that later could be excluded from a criminal trial, or could become the focus of a civil suit against the public health official because of a constitutionally invalid search or seizure, may exist when a public health official is leading the investigation when evidence is obtained (i.e., investigation of a public health event by a public health official and law enforcement either is present but passive or is absent). Examples might include a public health investigation that is ongoing before authorities realize the particular public health event resulted from a potential criminal act; or conduct of parallel investigations by public health and law enforcement, even if a law enforcement official technically is in charge;

or conduct of an investigation by a public health official accompanied by a law enforcement officer who does not actively participate in the investigation at that time.

Common purposes of public health investigations include detecting and remediating biologic, chemical, or other threats to community health; developing information regarding risk factors for diseases, injuries, and disabilities; and providing a scientifically rational basis for implementing prevention and control measures. These purposes may require public health officials to enter residences and businesses to obtain samples of substances that may pose a threat to public health, to conduct inspections, or to alleviate hazardous conditions. Public health personnel also may seek entry to buildings in response to a complaint, in furtherance of a regulatory scheme, or pursuant to an enforcement provision in a statute or ordinance.

Entries, such as those described above, by representatives of a government public health agency generally are referred to as "administrative searches," to distinguish them from searches by law enforcement personnel seeking evidence of criminal activity for which the perpetrator can be prosecuted. Administrative search warrants often are viewed as requiring a "lower standard" of probable cause than criminal searches.[53] In administrative searches, probable cause is supported not by the traditional definition of likelihood to believe that evidence of a crime will be found in the area to be searched, but rather probable cause is satisfied by "reasonable legislative or administrative standards for conducting an area inspection . . . with respect to a particular dwelling."[54]

Whether the entry onto private property is for criminal investigative or administrative purposes, the overarching protection covering the expectation of privacy in homes, workplaces, and businesses is found in the Fourth Amendment's prohibition against "unreasonable searches and seizures."[51] A search is reasonable if performed pursuant to a warrant or pursuant to a judicial exception to the warrant requirement. Evidence gathered as the result of an unreasonable search is subject to the exclusionary rule, the remedy for which is generally the inadmissibility of that evidence in a criminal case (see *Weeks v. United States* and *Gouled v. United States*[55,56]).

In *Camara v. Municipal Court*, the U.S. Supreme Court expressly overruled its prior case, *Frank v. Maryland*, which had held that a city's health department inspectors did not need a search warrant to conduct routine health inspections. In so doing, the Court held that the "one governing principle . . . [is that] except in certain carefully defined classes of cases, a search of private property without proper consent is 'unreasonable' unless it has been authorized by a valid search warrant."[54] *Camara* and the case of *See v. City of Seattle* are companion cases: *Camara* addressed warrantless, unconsented entry into a residence, and *See* examined the same issue with regard to a business. After *See*, inspections of businesses that are not subject to specific and pervasive regulation must be conducted pursuant to a search warrant, unless some recognized exception to the warrant requirement applies.[58]

In considering whether a particular search was the product of a valid administrative search and not an unconstitutional warrantless search, a court will often find the purpose of the search the deciding factor. To be a valid administrative search, the search must rest on "a pre-planned and dispassionate administrative procedure" and not "direct criminal suspicion."[a]

For public health investigators, the difficulty arises when, in the course of an administrative search, evidence of a crime is found. Several court decisions have given direction on the admissibility of evidence of a crime discovered during an administrative search. In *Michigan v. Clifford*, when fire officials went to the scene of a fire to investigate the cause, they found evidence of arson. The Court set specific parameters for the administrative nature of the search as it evolved into the criminal arena and restated the requirement for a search warrant issued pursuant to probable cause, noting that the "plain view" doctrine might come into play, such that "[i]f evidence of criminal activity is discovered during the course of a valid administrative search, it may be seized under the 'plain view' doctrine. This evidence then may be used to establish probable cause to obtain a criminal search warrant."[59] Other cases have upheld or rejected the seizure of evidence uncovered during administrative searches.[60,61]

Courts have found that, in some circumstances, searches predicated on something besides a warrant also can be reasonable. In an epidemiologic investigation, three oft-used exceptions to the warrant requirement are likely to be (1) where a person with authority consents to the search; (2) where exigent circumstances compel immediate action on the part of the government agent; or (3) where the search is of a workplace or business that is part of a "pervasively regulated industry."[62–64]

Related Constitutional Considerations in Gathering Evidence

Other complex constitutional issues may arise when public health officials investigate public health problems possibly resulting from criminal behavior. Examples of such issues include "seizure" of a person, Fifth Amendment protections against self-incrimination, and the requirement to properly establish a chain of custody of evidence.

A public health official can effectuate a "seizure" of a person during an interview; generally, seizure or custody occurs during an interview when "in view of all of the circumstances surrounding the incident, a reasonable person would have believed that he was not free to leave."[65] A situation can readily be hypothesized where a public health official is leading an interview in the presence of law enforcement during an investigation of a suspected intentional event involving a biologic agent. In such a case, the argument would be that the interviewee was in custody and was unconstitutionally seized. The determination of whether the person was indeed in custody, such as he would not feel free to leave, would turn on the facts surrounding the interview, such as whether a law enforcement officer was present when the interview took place.

Finally, to be admissible in a criminal prosecution, evidence gathered during an investigation must be properly maintained from discovery until presentation in the courtroom. Uncertainty about how a particular sample was obtained, stored, maintained, or tested can result in the evidence being ruled inadmissible, or, even if admitted, in the jury discounting the evidence and questioning the credibility of the officials who handled the evidence.

Challenges to Understanding Science in the Courtroom

Analysis of the previously published accounts identified several key issues that might arise when epidemiology is used in conjunction with criminal investigations and prosecutions.[36] First are operational issues in such settings, including the unique approaches to investigation, use of data, and communications employed by epidemiologists, who are focusing on whether a public health problem exists, and by police, who are trying to gather evidence. Second, prosecutors face at least two related challenges in communicating epidemiologic data in the courtroom. They must deal with the differing languages of law and epidemiology. For example, epidemiologic conclusions usually are stated in terms of probabilities, whereas criminal law seeks evidence of causation in terms of "beyond a reasonable doubt." These differences in describing the nature of evidence and the standard of proof create the potential for mischaracterization or misunderstanding of epidemiologic data. Finally, courts may impose a spectrum of limitations on epidemiologic data offered as evidence during a trial. This spectrum ranges from exclusion of or uncertainty about admitting such evidence (e.g., on the basis of its being considered too speculative) to no limitations (e.g., a court permitting the prosecution to present epidemiologic evidence as long as such data are not viewed as definitively demonstrating guilt).

The difficulties in using epidemiology to meet the rigorous standard of proof in criminal cases contrast sharply with the role and use of epidemiology in class action product liability cases tried in civil courts. Civil courts have been far more receptive to the use of epidemiologic studies as evidence. For example, the plaintiffs used epidemiologic studies in the cases involving the putative association between Bendectin® (an antinausea drug commonly prescribed for pregnant women) and the risk for birth defects;[66] the putative association between silicone breast implants and autoimmune diseases;[67] and the putative association between paternal exposure to Agent Orange and birth defects.[68] The term putative is used deliberately because in each of these cases, although the epidemiologic data figured prominently in civil judgments in favor of the plaintiffs, the strength of the epidemiologic evidence was tentative or seriously questioned in subsequent proceedings. This demonstrates that juries and judges may interpret epidemiologic data differently than would most scientists.

Role of Laws That Criminalize Behavior That Harms the Public

Legislatures sometimes use criminal law to try to reshape behavior that harms the public health. This section begins with a discussion of one use of such laws, those criminalizing exposure or transmission of HIV. We also consider how modifications of existing public health law, sometimes intended to aid authorities investigating or controlling bioterror or public health emergencies, could be used in a variety of situations including against persons who might spread communicable diseases such as HIV. Finally, we examine the use of criminal prosecution for these offenses, considering how prosecution converges with or diverges from public health goals.

Policy and Statutory Context

Public health codes traditionally allowed prosecution of individuals for a misdemeanor for failure to adhere to disease-control laws. Violations could include failure to report a notifiable disease, breaches of confidential information, and maintenance of unsanitary premises. For food or health-care establishments or residences that pose a danger to the public health, failure to follow a "public health order" issued by the commissioner of health can result in closure of the facility. Violators usually incurred the mildest of misdemeanor sentences, up to $500 or six months in jail.[10]

The emergence of the HIV/AIDS epidemic led to use of criminal law to impose more serious penalties. These efforts have been motivated, in part, by public concern over highly publicized cases of frightening or morally reprehensible conduct on the part of a few HIV-infected persons, such as a father who injected his son with an HIV-infected syringe to avoid paying child support[69] or a young man, knowing of his HIV infection, who had unprotected intercourse with at least 47 young women without disclosing his HIV infection.[70]

Prosecutors have used two broad types of criminal provisions in these cases. In some, prosecutors used common law crimes—usually attempted murder, assault, aggravated assault, or reckless endangerment. These common law offenses require both a culpable state of mind (intent for attempted murder and assault; willful disregard of risk for reckless endangerment) and a wrongful act for conviction. Proving intent can be difficult, especially where the activity, such as having sexual intercourse, is otherwise legal and nonviolent. In an increasing number of states, prosecutors have the option of HIV-specific exposure and transmission laws for prosecution of these activities. Most HIV-specific laws do not require intent to cause harm, only knowledge that one is HIV infected and proof of the prohibited act for prosecution.

Research has uncovered at least 316 cases of prosecution of persons in the United States for knowing or willful exposure or transmission of HIV during 1986–2001.[71] Of those cases, at least 184 resulted in conviction based on some HIV-related charge. A total of 211 cases involved charges for sexual exposure. A significant number of prosecutions were for actions that were unlikely to cause infection, including 75 cases involving spitting, biting, or scratching, and 10 involving other activities (e.g., throwing a blood-soaked towel, throwing feces, or licking). Another 5 involved selling blood, and 12 involved actual or threatened injection with a syringe; in 2, the mode was unknown or uncharged. Although not available for all the cases, data on penalties reinforce earlier studies suggesting judges are willing to impose harsh sentences, even in cases involving little or no real risk for transmission.[72–74]

The particular characteristics of HIV-specific exposure and transmission laws vary significantly around the county. By the end of 2001, at least 26 states had at least one law specifically criminalizing HIV exposure in certain circumstances, while 15 states had statutes criminalizing exposure or transmission of HIV through sexual intercourse, intimate contact, or exposure to bodily fluids. Laws in 8 states criminalized use of needles, syringes, or other injection equipment that could transmit HIV, and laws in 12 others prohibited donation of blood, organs, or tissue by persons with HIV. In 3 states, laws criminalized behavior that poses little risk of infection including spitting, biting, or smearing, or throwing blood, saliva, semen, urine or feces. In 4 states, the person with HIV must have had the specific intent to infect another person for a crime to have occurred. For example, California's statute requires intent to infect:

> Any person who exposes another to the human immunodeficiency virus (HIV) by engaging in unprotected sexual activity when the infected person knows at the time of the

unprotected sex that he or she is infected with HIV, has not disclosed his or her HIV-positive status, and *acts with the specific intent to infect the other person* with HIV, is guilty of a felony punishable by imprisonment in the state prison for three, five, or eight years. *Evidence that the person had knowledge of his or her HIV-positive status, without additional evidence, shall not be sufficient to prove specific intent.*[75] (emphasis added)

Some states define prohibited sex acts and other activities that could transmit the virus (e.g., Michigan and Illinois statutes), while others are general (e.g., Florida statute). Michigan's statute provides:

(1) A person who knows that he or she has or has been diagnosed as having acquired immunodeficiency syndrome or acquired immunodeficiency syndrome related complex, or who knows that he or she is HIV infected, and who engages in sexual penetration with another person without having first informed the other person that he or she has acquired immunodeficiency syndrome or acquired immunodeficiency syndrome related complex or is HIV infected, is guilty of a felony.

(2) As used in this section, "sexual penetration" means sexual intercourse, cunnilingus, fellatio, anal intercourse, or any other intrusion, however slight, of any part of a person's body or of any object into the genital or anal openings of another person's body, but emission of semen is not required.[76]

Compare to Florida's more general prohibition:

It is unlawful for any person who has human immunodeficiency virus infection, when such person knows he or she is infected with this disease and when such person has been informed that he or she may communicate this disease to another person through sexual intercourse, to have sexual intercourse with any other person, unless such other person has been informed of the presence of the sexually transmissible disease and has consented to the sexual intercourse.[77]

Although the drafters of Michigan's law clearly meant to avoid vagueness in defining sexual exposure, one effect is the criminalization of some acts that are extremely low risk (e.g., oral sex involving an infected and an uninfected partner, with or without barrier protection) and others that pose zero risk (e.g., the use of sex toys for penetrative vaginal or anal sex).[78]

Laws also differ on whether they include consent of the other person (12 states) or use of condom (2 states) as an affirmative defense. Where these defenses are not included, or implied by interpretation, such laws effectively prohibit HIV-infected persons from engaging in a wide range of sexual activities for life. From a public health perspective, such laws reflect an unrealistic expectation and may be unenforceable.

Disclosure of Confidential Health Information by Public Health Agencies to Law Enforcement

In the aftermath of the September 2001 terrorist attacks, some state legislatures undertook assessment and revision of statutory provisions regarding the response capacities of public health and law enforcement agencies.[41] An example of an important issue at the intersection of protecting community health, safeguarding individual interests, and ensuring due process is whether, when, and how public health officials should be able to disclose to law enforcement confidential, personal information obtained by public health.

In North Carolina, the legislature addressed this issue in the context of joint public health and law enforcement investigations by enacting expanded powers for the state health director to investigate suspected terrorist incidents involving nuclear, biologic, or chemical (NBC) weapons.[79] The legislation also authorized the director to gather otherwise confidential medical information that might assist in the epidemiologic investigation of communicable diseases indicating a terrorist incident.[80] Part of the changes made to aid in the investigation of a terrorist incident reflected a recognition that otherwise confidential medical information protected by a strict confidentiality statute[81] may need to be shared with law enforcement to investigate, and perhaps prevent, a terrorist attack, or to allow law enforcement to assist the public health agency in preventing the spread of a communicable disease as the result of a terrorist incident.[80,81] Therefore, the legislature included a specific exception to its confidentiality statute that allows the sharing of otherwise confidential medical information with law enforcement officials regarding persons who have or may have a communicable disease. Such information may be shared with law enforcement officials only for enforcement of communicable disease–control statutes or of public health statutes specifically addressing the use of NBC agents as part of a terrorist incident, or when law enforcement is "investigating a terrorist incident using nuclear, biological, or chemical agents."[80,82] In addition, the law prohibits further disclosure of such information by law enforcement officials except "when necessary" to enforce the public health laws or to conduct an investigation of a terrorist incident involving NBC agents, or "when the Department or a local health department seeks the assistance of the law enforcement official in preventing or controlling the spread of the disease or condition and expressly authorizes the disclosure as necessary for that purpose."[82]

Restricting Freedom of Movement in Response to Public Health Emergencies

Bioterrorism and other public health emergencies also require law enforcement and public health officials to cooperate in the implementation of a variety of legal interventions. For example, another problem North Carolina's legislature addressed recently is the dilemma faced when a person violates a public health order restricting their freedom of movement because they have, or may have, been exposed to a communicable disease. Under North Carolina law, violation of such an order is a criminal act, punishable by up to two years' imprisonment.[83] If the person who has violated a public health order is in a communicable stage of a disease such as smallpox, then release on bail or detention within the jail population could pose serious adverse consequences. Therefore, the legislature included provisions allowing law enforcement to detain a person arrested for violation of such an order in the area designated by the state health director in his or her order until an initial appearance before a judicial official.[84] If a judicial official finds, by clear and convincing evidence, that the person posed a threat to the public's health, then the judicial official must deny bail and detain the person in an area designated by that official in consultation with the state health director.[85]

Even though North Carolina's provisions related to both sharing information and restricting freedom of movement clearly were intended to assist investigation and/or control of instances of suspected NBC-related outbreaks, they leave open the possibility that public health authorities will disclose confidential disease information to prosecutors or detain persons under a variety of other circumstances. One scenario is that public health officials, having identified an individual infected with HIV whom they believe is continuing to expose others, might disclose that information directly to prosecutors. Although this may be the only means to control spread of disease in some circumstances, in others it may lead to neglect of traditional public health efforts for outreach, education, and counseling of persons infected and their partners.

Congruence of Prosecution with and Divergence from Public Health Goals

Use of criminal law to prevent or deter behavior that endangers others provides some advantages over use of civil law. According to constitutional standards, criminal law is required to clearly define prohibited activity, provide fair procedures to defendants, and fix terms of punishment. It has clear goals: deterrence, punishment, incapacitation, and rehabilitation.[1] The process of making criminal law should also be transparent enough to allow public objection to laws widely perceived as unfair. Theoretically, criminal law can also set clear standards for what behavior society considers unacceptable and thus bolster normative standards of conduct. Most of these characteristics are congruent with public health goals and ideally could reinforce public health efforts in other areas. Moreover, even those who oppose widespread enforcement of these laws may agree that some public sanction is necessary to punish egregiously reckless or intentional acts of exposure or transmission.

Use of criminal law to punish individuals for exposure or transmission of HIV or other sexually transmitted diseases raises important issues of fairness and practicality in the field of public health. Many HIV-infected persons have engaged in some activity that could transmit the virus to another, without first disclosing their HIV status to that person.[86-88] Moreover, existing criminal HIV exposure laws do not distinguish between high- and low-risk activities. In some cases they could punish as felonies very low-risk alternative behaviors (e.g., oral sex with condoms or use of sex toys) that public health officials might support as "safer sex" practices. If law criminalizes behavior that is common or otherwise legal, or punishes that which poses little or no risk, then enactment of the law may do little to provide actual notice to those most likely to bear its consequences.[1] Without effective notice, the law cannot serve either its deterrent or norm-setting functions. Also, if many of the most highly publicized cases involve nonsexual behavior, even publicity around the prosecutions may not signify to most HIV-infected persons that their sexual conduct is covered by the law.[71]

Prosecutions also raise fundamental issues of fairness if prosecutors use the law to punish behaviors that are highly unlikely to result in transmission (e.g., spitting, biting, scratching, protected oral sex, or use of sex toys). These prosecutions are, by their nature, "exceptional," and those punished may justifiably believe they have been singled out for some reason unrelated to either law enforcement or public health goals. From a practical perspective, widespread enforcement of these provisions would create an incentive for intrusive surveillance of highly personal activities such as sexual relationships and drug use. This level of invasion into personal behaviors is unacceptable to many Americans and thus consistent enforcement of criminal provisions is unlikely.

Given the relatively small number of overall prosecutions for all types of exposure or transmission since the beginning of the HIV epidemic, the laws also appear to be selectively enforced. Selective enforcement raises the specter of abuse of discretion or prejudice on the part of those reporting, prosecuting, and adjudicating these cases. Commentators have suggested that enforcement of criminal law provisions motivated by prejudice or fear, rather than by legitimate efforts to protect society, "corrupts both citizenry and police and reduces the moral authority of the criminal law, especially among those portions of the citizenry—the poor and subcultural—who are particularly likely to be treated in an arbitrary fashion."[88] Finally, because all common law and HIV-specific criminal prosecutions depend on the defendant knowing his or her HIV status, enforcement of these statutes could deter persons who know they are at risk for infection from being tested. It also could deter those who test positive from revealing the names of their sex or needle-sharing partners for fear that one of them might become subject to criminal prosecution.[1,89] In these ways, use of criminal prosecutions may diverge from public health goals.

Conclusion: Utility of the Law in Relation to Public Health Practice

The current practice of public health and criminal law are intertwined more closely than most practitioners in either field realize. Our current bodies of "law on the books"—that is, the law as it is described in statutes, case law, and relevant regulations—include a variety of provisions across the codes of public health, the environment, regulation of drugs and foods, care and protection of children and the elderly, as well as the penal code that includes criminal penalties. Our practitioners of public health and related sciences often work closely with law enforcement personnel in specific areas of investigation. Legislators interested in promoting the public health (or in making a strong public statement) may adopt criminal sanctions without a clear sense of the possible unintended consequences.

Certain characteristics stand out as probable indicators of where the criminal law may be a useful public health tool. Where criminal enforcement is part of an overall strategy that involves a well-regulated system of relatively public activity—such as the operation of food establishments and health-care facilities, workplace safety, driving, and public sale or consumption of dangerous products—criminal law may function best in supporting public health objectives. Such a system usually includes established monitoring systems, well-known standards for compliance, and the absence of highly intrusive monitoring.

Other characteristics emerge that might make criminal enforcement less effective. Vague or broadly defined prohibited conduct, poor dissemination of information about the illegal nature of the conduct, and the need for highly intrusive monitoring to detect violations, all suggest that criminal enforcement will be rare, selective, or potentially biased against already disfavored individuals or populations.

However, even in some situations where laws could be abused, they may have symbolic or normative value that operates benignly. The normative impact of a law as well as its characteristics and scope need to be explored using empirical methods wherever possible. The symbolic importance of the laws needs to be weighed against their potential harms or unintended consequences.

Forensic epidemiology, where epidemiologic methods are used as part of an ongoing investigation of a health problem that may or may not include criminal acts, illustrates an emerging area of joint law enforcement and public health practice while raising important legal issues. These issues include the law of entry into residential, business, and workplace settings during concurrent epidemiologic and criminal investigations; legal and operational implications if law enforcement or public health first take charge of a scene; other Fourth and Fifth Amendment issues; and establishment of a chain of custody of evidence.

Science has far outstripped the law in the speed of scientific discoveries and advances. The HIV/AIDS epidemic has highlighted many stresses in the joining of criminal law and public health law, as has the recognition of bioterrorism as a real public health and criminal justice issue. Molecular biology technology systematically used for criminal justice purposes has the potential to eliminate the anonymity of rape, improving the apprehension of serial criminals and exonerating those falsely accused, but it also poses serious philosophic and privacy questions for which there are not easy answers.

When the practitioner reviews the public health and criminal laws of his or her state, many incongruities become evident. Many of the public health laws need revision to reflect changing priorities in public health, and many of the criminal laws affecting public health need to be modified to accommodate due process and avoid unfairly selective use. Properly regulating powerful technologies has never been easy because science is an intellectual activity that requires room for experimentation and exploration; nevertheless, fair regulation of scientific areas affecting public health and safety must be undertaken if appropriate safeguards do not exist.

Finally, in considering use of the criminal law in any area related to public health, policymakers and practitioners should be aware of the risk for unintended consequences. Examples of unintended actual and possible consequences abound, including those discussed in this chapter, such as the impact of syringe-prescription and drug-paraphernalia laws on the spread of bloodborne diseases among IDUs. Another controversial area that should be studied carefully is whether exposure and transmission laws create resistance to voluntary testing during the HIV epidemic. In the roil of human events, the search for ways to control public health brings imperfect solutions; yet sensitive study, analysis, and empirical experience may be able to minimize the undesirable, unintended consequences of modern public health measures.

We thank James W. Buehler, John Barkley, Sarah Scott, and Judith W. Munson.

Note

a. See *United States v. Johnson*, 408 F.3d 1313 (10th Cir.) (2005); compare *Ferguson v. City of Charleston*, 532 U.S. 67 (2001) (rejecting as unconstitutional administrative search the drug testing of obstetrics patients admitted to hospital because purpose of the testing, which constituted a seizure of the patient's fluids, was to gather evidence of violation of drug laws) with *United States v. Marquez*, 410 F.3d 612 (9th Cir. 2005) (upholding as product of valid administrative search illegal drugs uncovered during a airport security screening where the screener testified they were not instructed to look for drugs but only for security risk items).

References

1. Gostin LO. *Public Health Law: Power, Duty, Restraint.* Berkeley: University of California Press, 2000.
2. Institute of Medicine. *The Future of Public Health.* Washington, DC: National Academy Press, 1988.
3. *Bamford v Turnley*, 3 B & S 67, 122 Eng Rep 27 (Exch Ch 1862), summary of which appears in Dobbs DB, Hayden PT, eds. *Torts and Compensation: Personal Accountability and Social Responsibility for Injury.* 3rd ed. St Paul, MN: West Publishing, 1997.
4. Pincoffs EL. The problem of punishment. In: *Philosophy of Law: A Brief Introduction.* Belmont, CA: Wadsworth Publishing, 1991:9–19.
5. Gostin LO, Burris S, Lazzarini Z. The law and the public's health: a study of infectious disease law in the United States. *Columbia Law Rev* 1999;99:59–128.
6. *Greene v Edwards*, 263 SE 2d 661 (WVa 1980).
7. *Addington v Texas*, 441 US 418 (1979).
8. Saltzburg SA, Diamond JL, Kinports K, Morawetz TH. The nature and structure of criminal law. In: *Criminal Law: Cases and Materials.* 2nd ed. New York: Lexis Publishing, 2000:1–67.
9. *McCullough v State*, 657 P 2d 1157 (Nev 1983).
10. Grad FP. *Public Health Law Manual.* 2nd ed. Washington, DC: American Public Health Association, 1990.
11. Zimring FE, Hawkins GJ. *Deterrence: The Legal Threat in Crime Control.* Chicago: University of Chicago Press, 1973.
12. Becker G. Crime and punishment: an economic approach. *J Political Economy* 1968;76:169–217.
13. Kuperan K, Sutinen JG. Blue water crime: deterrence, legitimacy, and compliance in fisheries. *Law & Society Rev* 1998;32:309–37.
14. Tyler TR. *Why People Obey the Law.* New Haven, CT: Yale University Press, 1990.
15. Gostin LO, Lazzarini Z. Prevention of HIV/AIDS among injection drug users: the theory and science of public health and criminal justice approaches to disease prevention. *Emory Law J* 1997;46:587–696.
16. Normand J, Vlahov D, Moses LE, eds. *Preventing HIV Transmission: The Role of Sterile Needles and Bleach.* Washington, DC: National Academy Press, 1995.
17. CDC, Health Resources and Services Administration, National Institute on Drug Abuse,

Substance Abuse and Mental Health Services Administration. *HIV Prevention Bulletin: Medical Advice for Persons Who Inject Illicit Drugs.* Washington, DC: US Department of Health and Human Services, Public Health Service, 1997.

18. American Medical Association, American Pharmaceutical Association, Association of State and Territorial Health Officials, the National Alliance of State and Territorial AIDS Directors, National Association of Boards of Pharmacy. Access to sterile syringes. Joint statement encouraging state-level action to reduce the legal and regulatory barriers that currently restricts access to sterile syringes in nearly every state. Includes summary of (and link to) American Bar Association letter expressing similar support for reducing barriers. Available at http://www.ama-assn.org/ama/pub/category/1808.html. Accessed January 5, 2006.

19. American Bar Association. Burris S, ed. *Deregulation of Hypodermic Needles and Syringes as a Public Health Measure: A Report on Emerging Policy and Law in the United States.* Available at http://www.abanet.org/AIDS/publications/deregulation.pdf. Accessed May 25, 2001.

20. *Doe v Bridgeport Police Dept,* 198 FRD 325 (D Conn 2001), reported at http://ww.aclu.org/drugpolicy/harm/10884lgl20010118.html. Accessed January 19, 2006.

21. Bureau of Justice Statistics, US Department of Justice. Prison and jail inmates at mid-year 1999. (Bureau of Justice Statistics Bulletin NCJ-181643. 2000). Available at http://www.ojp.usdoj.gov/bjs/pub/pdf/pjim99.pdf. Accessed January 12, 2006.

22. Bureau of Justice Statistics. Sourcebook of criminal justice statistics. Table 6.51: Federal prison population, and number and percent sentenced for drug offenses (United States 1970–2001). Available at http://www.albany.edu/sourcebook/pdf/sb2001/sb2001–section6.pdf. Accessed January 12, 2006.

23. Freeman A. HIV in prison. In: Burris S, Dalton HL, Miller JL, eds. *AIDS Law Today: A New Guide for the Public.* New Haven, CT: Yale University Press, 1993:263–94.

24. Bureau of Justice Statistics, US Department of Justice. Sourcebook of criminal justice statistics. Table 6.33.2004: Rate (per 100,000 US resident population in each group) of sentenced prisoners under jurisdiction of state and federal correctional authorities. Available at http://www.albany.edu/sourcebook/pdf/t6332004.pdf. Accessed June 9, 2006.

25. Bureau of Justice Statistics, US Department of Justice. Jail populations, by age and gender, 1990–2005. Available at http://www.ojp.usdoj.gov/bjs/glance/jailag.htm. Accessed June 10, 2006.

26. US Department of Justice. 1994 Update: HIV/AIDS and STDs in correctional facilities. In: *Issues and Practices in Criminal Justice.* Washington, DC: National Institute of Justice, 1995.

27. Bureau of Justice Statistics, US Department of Justice. Sourcebook of criminal justice statistics. Table 6.68. Sentenced prisoners admitted to state and federal institutions for violation of parole or other conditional release. By whether new sentence was imposed, sex, region, and jurisdiction, 1995. Available at http://www.druglibrary.org/schaffer/Govpubs/sourcebook/1995/pdf/t668.pdf. Accessed January 12, 2006.

28. Burris S. Prisons, law and public health: the case for a coordinated response to epidemic disease behind bars. *University of Miami Law Rev* 1992;47:291–335.

29. Hammett TM, Rhodes W, Harmon P. HIV/AIDS and other infectious diseases among correctional inmates: a public health problem and opportunity [abstract 571]. National HIV Prevention Conference, Atlanta, GA, August 29–September 1, 1999. Available at http://www.aegis.com/news/PR/1999/PR990825.html. Accessed January 12, 2006.

30. Goodman RA, Mercy JA, Layde PM, Thacker SB. Case-control studies: design issues for criminological applications. *J Quantitative Criminology* 1988;4:71–84.

31. Blaser MJ, Jason JM, Weniger BG, et al. Epidemiologic analysis of a cluster of homicides of children in Atlanta. *JAMA* 1984;251:3255–8.
32. Christian K. And the DNA shall set you free: issues surrounding postconviction DNA evidence and the pursuit of innocence. *Ohio State Law J* 2001;62:1195–241.
33. Ryan GH. Innocent execution prevention. Testimony of Illinois Governor, George H. Ryan, before the US House Judiciary Crime Subcommittee, Chair Henry Hyde, on June 20, 2000. Federal Document Clearing House (2000 WL 19304891).
34. Stross JK, Shasby DM, Harlan WR. An epidemic of mysterious cardiopulmonary arrests. *N Engl J Med* 1976;295:1107–10.
35. Butler JC, Cohen ML, Friedman CR, et al. Collaboration between public health and law enforcement: new paradigms and partnerships for bioterrorism planning and response. *Emerg Infect Dis* 2002;8:1152–6.
36. Goodman RA, Munson JW, Dammers K, Lazzarini Z, Barkley JP. Forensic epidemiology: law at the intersection of public health and criminal investigations. *J Law Med Ethics* 2003;31:684–700.
37. US House. House Armed Services Committee. Hearing on Chemical and Biological Weapons, 20 October 1999. Washington, DC: Government Printing Office, 1999.
38. Altman LK, Kolata G. A nation challenged: anthrax—anthrax missteps offer guide to fight next bioterror battle. *New York Times* 2002 (January 6):A1.
39. Moscoso E. West Nile outbreak not terrorism, experts say—officials dismiss bioweapons theory. *Atlanta Journal-Constitution* 2002 (September 14):A5.
40. Model State Emergency Health Powers Act. December 21, 2001. Available at http://www.publichealthlaw.net/Resources/Modellaws.htm. Accessed January 7, 2006.
41. Gostin LO, Sapsin JW, Teret SP, et al. The Model State Emergency Health Powers Act: planning for and response to bioterrorism and naturally occurring infectious diseases. *JAMA* 2002;288:622–8.
42. Annas GJ. Bioterrorism, public health, and civil liberties. *N Engl J Med* 2002;346:1337–42.
43. Alibek K, Handelman S. *Biohazard.* New York: Random House, 1999.
44. American Society for Microbiology. *Microbial Forensics: A Scientific Assessment.* Washington, DC: American Society for Microbiology, 2003. Available at http://www.asm.org/ASM/files/CCPAGECONTENT/docfilename/0000018026/FOREN%20REPORT_BW.pdf. Accessed January 7, 2006.
45. Buehler JW, Smith LF, Wallace EM, Heath CW, Rusiak R, Herndon JL. Unexplained deaths in a children's hospital, an epidemiologic assessment. *N Engl J Med* 1985;313:211–6.
46. Torok TJ, Tauxe RV, Wise RP, et al. A large community outbreak of salmonellosis caused by intentional contamination of restaurant salad bars. *JAMA* 1997;278:389–95.
47. Franks A, Sacks JJ, Smith JD, et al. A cluster of unexplained cardiac arrests in a surgical intensive care unit. *Crit Care Med* 1987;15:1075–6.
48. Kolavic SA, Kimura A, Simons SL, et al. An outbreak of *Shigella dysenteria* type 2 among laboratory workers due to intentional food contamination. *JAMA* 1997;278:396–8.
49. Jernigan DB, Raghunathan PL, Bell BP, et al. Investigation of bioterrorism-related anthrax, United States, 2001: epidemiologic findings. *Emerg Infect Dis* 2002;8 [serial online].
50. CDC. Nicotine poisoning after ingestion of contaminated ground beef—Michigan, 2003. *MMWR* 2003;52:413–6.
51. US Constitution, Amendment IV.
52. US Constitution, Amendment V.
53. Christensen DA. Warrantless administrative searches under environmental laws: the limits to EPA inspectors' statutory invitation. 26 *Environ Law* 1996;26:1019–47.

54. *Camara v Municipal Court*, 387 US 523 (1967).
55. *Weeks v United States*, 232 US 282 (1914).
56. *Gouled v United States*, 255 US 298 (1921).
57. *Frank v Maryland*, 259 US 360 (1959).
58. *See v City of Seattle*, 387 US 541 (1967).
59. *Michigan v Clifford*, 464 US 287 (1984).
60. Wooster AK. Annotation, validity of warrantless administrative inspection of business that is allegedly closely or pervasively regulated: cases decided since *Colonnade Catering Corp v US*. *Am Law Rev Fed* 2002;182:467.
61. *United States v Branson*, 21 F 3d 113 (1994).
62. *Payton v New York*, 445 US 573 (1980).
63. *New York v Burger*, 482 US 691 (1987).
64. *Michigan v Tyler*, 436 US 499 (1978).
65. *United States v Mendenhall*, 446 US 544, 554 (1980).
66. Brent RL. Bendectin®: review of the medical literature of a comprehensively studied human nonteratogen and the most prevalent tortogen-litigen [review]. *Reprod Toxicol* 1995;9:337–49.
67. Angell M. Shattuck Lecture—Evaluating the health risks of breast implants: the interplay of medical science, the law, and public opinion. *N Engl J Med* 1996;334:1513–8.
68. Stephenson J. New IOM report links Agent Orange exposure to risk of birth defect in Vietnam vets' children [Medical News and Perspectives]. *JAMA* 1996;275:1066–7.
69. Associated Press. Father is accused of injecting son with HIV-infected blood. *Los Angeles Times* 1998 (April 24):A13.
70. CDC. Cluster of HIV-positive young women—New York. 1997–1998. *MMWR* 1999;48: 413–6.
71. Lazzarini Z, Bray S, Messing N, Burris S, Blankenship K. Criminal law and HIV transmission: an analysis of criminal law as a structural intervention to regulate behavior [poster no 873]. National HIV Prevention Conference, Atlanta: August 13–15, 2001.
72. Strader K. Criminalization as a policy response to a public health crisis. *J Marshall Law Rev* 1994;27:435–47.
73. *State v Smith*, 621 A 2d 493 (NJ Super Ct App Div), cert denied, 634 A 2d 523 (NJ 1993) (defendant convicted of attempted murder for biting a correctional officer).
74. *Weeks v Scott*, 55 F 3d 1059 (5th Cir 1995) (defendant convicted of attempted murder and sentenced to life in prison for spitting at a correctional officer).
75. Cal Health & Safety Code, Ch 4, §120291(a).
76. Michigan Compiled Laws §333.5210.
77. Fl Stat Ann Title XXIX Public Health, §384.24 Unlawful acts.
78. Galletly CL, Pinkerton SD. Toward rational criminal HIV exposure laws. *J Law Med Ethics* 2004;32:327–37.
79. NC Gen Stat §130A-475.
80. NC Gen Stat §130A-476.
81. NC Gen Stat §130A-143.
82. NC Gen Stat §130A-143(7).
83. NC Gen Stat §130A-25.
84. NC Gen Stat §15A-401(b)(4).
85. NC Gen Stat §15A-534.5.
86. Hays RB, Paul J, Ekstrand M, Kegeles SM, Stall R, Coates TJ. Actual versus perceived HIV status, sexual behaviors, and predictors of unprotected sex among young gay and bisexual men who identify as HIV-negative, HIV-positive, and untested. *AIDS* 1997;1: 1495–502.

87. Singh BK, Koman JJ 3rd, Catan VM, Souply KL, Birkel RC, Golaszewski TJ. Sexual risk behavior among injection drug-using human immunodeficiency virus positive clients. *Int J Addict* 1993;28:735–47.
88. Niccolai LM, Dorst D, Myers L, Kissinger PJ. Disclosure of HIV status to sexual partners: predictors and temporal patterns. *Sex Transm Dis* 1999;26:281–5.
89. Dalton H. Law and responsibility lecture series. Shaping responsible behavior: lessons from the AIDS front. *Washington and Lee Law Rev* 1999;56:931–52.

Chapter 7

INTERNATIONAL CONSIDERATIONS

David P. Fidler and Martin S. Cetron*

Public health literature of the past decade frequently identified globalization as one of the most important phenomena facing public health.[1] Experts differ on how they interpret the relationship between public health and globalization, but consensus exists that public health challenges transcend borders. The transnational nature of public health problems is not novel. Infectious disease specialists long have argued that "germs do not carry passports." Cross-border outbreaks of severe acute respiratory syndrome (SARS) in 2003, avian influenza (H5N1) in 2004–2005, and the polio and Marburg viruses in 2005 reinforce the critical importance of having global perspective on public health threats. The international threat posed by infectious diseases has raised public health's profile as a matter of U.S. foreign and national security policy.[2,3] The global nature of public health also has received renewed policy emphasis in recent reports on United Nations (UN) reform that make infectious disease surveillance and control a global action priority for the 21st century (Box 7-1).[4,5]

Although the globalization of public health has historical and contemporary significance, analysis of public health law generally has neglected international aspects of public health. Public health law texts in the United States from the 20th century, including those by Tobey (1939),[6] Wing (1990),[7] and Grad (1996)[8,a] contain little or no discussion of international considerations involving international law or comparative law. Even Gostin's *Public Health Law* (2000) does not address the global context of U.S. public health law.[9]

* The findings and conclusions in this chapter are those of the author(s) and do not necessarily represent the views of the U.S. Department of Health and Human Services or the Centers for Disease Control and Prevention.

BOX 7-1. Global Policy Emphasis on Infectious Disease Control and Prevention

United Nations Secretary-General's High-Level Panel on Threats, Challenges, and Change (December 2004)

"Over the past three decades, the world has seen the emergence of new infectious diseases, a resurgence of older diseases and a spread of resistance to a growing number of mainstay antibiotic drugs. Recent outbreaks of polio threaten to undermine its near eradication, which was one of the great accomplishments of the twentieth century. These trends signify a dramatic decay in local and global public health capacity. . . . The recent international experience in combating SARS shows how the spread of infectious disease can be limited when effective global institutions work in close partnership with capable national institutions. . . . No State could have achieved this degree of containment of the disease in isolation."[4]

United Nations Secretary-General (March 2005)

"The overall international response to evolving pandemics has been shockingly slow and remains shamefully underresourced. Malaria continues to rage throughout the tropical world. . . . Many infectious diseases that ravage developing countries today, notably HIV/AIDS and tuberculosis, pose severe risks for the entire world, particularly in light of emerging drug resistance. . . . To strengthen existing mechanisms for timely and effective international cooperation, I call on Member States to agree on the revision of the International Health Regulations at the World Health Assembly to be held in May 2005. To contain the risk of future outbreaks, greater resources should also be given to the WHO Global Outbreak Alert and Response Network so that it can coordinate the response of a broad international partnership in support of national health surveillance and response systems."[5]

In this chapter, we remedy the neglect of international considerations in the analysis of U.S. public health law. The first section focuses on the legal structure and sources of public health law viewed from an international perspective. The analysis concentrates on the legal structures created by the U.S. Constitution and international law. Next we review U.S. participation in international health diplomacy. This analysis looks at international health organizations and legal regimes to demonstrate the importance of these efforts to U.S. public health. This section mentions other international legal regimes relevant for public health in which the United States has played or is playing a leading role.

The next two sections address the law relevant to public health problems that U.S. public health officials and practitioners may face: public health threats that (1) originate outside the United States but come into the United States through people, animals, or goods and (2) flow out of the United States toward other countries. We also address public health controversies that result from the U.S. pursuit of liberalization in international trade and foreign investment through international law.

The chapter concludes with thoughts on the future importance of international considerations in U.S. public health law. Not only is international law becoming more important in thinking about public health in the United States, but also globalization generally is affecting how U.S. public health will evolve in coming decades. We call for public health lawyers, international legal practitioners and academics, and other experts to increase attention in their respective activities on the international and comparative features of U.S. public health and the law that serves the public's health.

Legal Structures and Sources for U.S. Public Health Law in the International Context

International relations experts argue that anarchy—the lack of any supreme, central power—characterizes international politics. Countries interact in this condition of anarchy as independent, sovereign states. This "anarchical society" of sovereign states creates a legal structure through which states pursue public health and other objectives.[10] Within the sovereign state, national law guides the pursuit of public health. If states desire to cooperate on public health problems, then international law becomes the mechanism through which they organize anarchy to reflect public health concerns. For U.S. public health practitioners, understanding the international context of U.S. public health law requires appreciation of (1) federalism and the U.S. constitutional structure (how public health law is organized within the United States) and (2) the structure of international law (how sovereign states legally cooperate in the international system).

U.S. Constitutional Structure and Domestic Sources of Public Health Law in the International Context

Scholars of U.S. public health law frequently note that federalism and the U.S. constitutional system leave most public health powers to the individual states of the Union. Although the federal government has enumerated powers, such as the powers to tax and spend and to regulate interstate commerce, which can be exercised for public health purposes, the states retain a great deal of sovereignty over public health. In the international public health context, however, the federal government has supreme power because of its constitutional monopoly in foreign affairs.

Under the Constitution, the federal government has the power to regulate commerce with foreign nations, to determine the conditions for immigration into the United States, and to make treaties with other countries (U.S. Constitution, Article I, §8, Cls. 3–4; and Article II, §2, Cl. 2). None of these powers is expressly a public health power; but the federal government uses these powers to achieve public health objectives, such as protecting the nation from the importation of foodborne pathogens, prohibiting the entry of immigrants with certain infectious diseases, and concluding agreements with other nations to achieve mutual public health goals. However,

federalism can affect the implementation of public health activities that involve foreign affairs and international law (Box 7-2).

The federal monopoly on foreign affairs powers means that the primary source
of public health law in U.S. international relations is federal law. Statutes, codified
in the United States Code (U.S.C.), and regulations, found in the Code of Federal
Regulations (C.F.R.), are important sources of public health law. In the public health
context, Congress often passes legislation delegating authority to the executive
branch, which then promulgates regulations to implement the law. The executive
branch's handling of public health can be confusing because many executive agencies implement statutory law. For example, the Department of Health and Human
Services is responsible for federal quarantine; the Department of Agriculture inspects imported food; and the Food and Drug Administration (an agency within
the Department of Health and Human Services) regulates pharmaceutical imports.
Because the federal government exercises numerous federal powers for public
health purposes through multiple executive agencies, federal law affecting public
health is scattered across the U.S.C. and C.F.R. in ways that make the composite
picture difficult to see.

The structure of the U.S. constitutional system also makes the judicial branch an
important source of public health law in the international context. The U.S. federal
courts have interpreted treaties, statutes, and regulations in cases involving U.S. public
health and foreign persons and products. Federal courts have also adjudicated cases
involving the boundaries between state and federal public health powers in connection with health threats from other countries.

Structure of International Law and Public Health

International law constitutes the rules that regulate the relations among sovereign
states and other actors (e.g., international organizations and individuals) in the international system. Many people think the rules of international law are not actually
"law" because they cannot be enforced the way domestic law is enforced. This attitude judges international law by the political conditions that characterize domestic
law, which include a central government with a mandate to make and enforce laws.
International law arises, however, in a political environment characterized by the
absence of any central law-making or law-enforcing authority. International law
should be judged, not by the criteria of domestic governance but by the circumstances
that characterize international relations.

Therefore, the sources of international law differ from the sources of domestic law.
The classic sources of international law are (1) treaties; (2) customary international law;
(3) general principles of law recognized by civilized nations; and (4) as supplementary
means for determining rules of international law, judicial decisions of national and
international tribunals, and the teachings of the most highly qualified publicists of various nations (Statute of the International Court of Justice, Article 38[1]).

Treaties

Treaties are written agreements between sovereign states, the obligations of which
are legally binding. Treaties do not bind states that do not ratify or otherwise accept

---

BOX 7-2. Potential U.S. "Federalism" Reservation to the New International Health Regulations

In conjunction with the World Health Assembly's May 2005 adoption of the new International Health Regulations (IHR) (see Box 7-5), the United States stated:

Federalism

For the record, the United States sought a provision that would explicitly recognize the right of federal states to implement the IHRs in a manner that is consistent with the division of rights and responsibilities existing in their constitutionally mandated systems of government. Unfortunately, the IGWG [Intergovernmental Working Group] did not accept this straightforward request.

Accordingly, the United States will submit a narrowly tailored reservation . . . that will clarify that the United States will implement the IHRs in a manner consistent with our federal system of government.

The United States also states for the record . . . that . . . the Federal government will implement the IHRs to the extent it exercises jurisdiction over the matters covered therein. Otherwise, our state and local governments will implement them. To the extent that state and local governments in the United States exercise jurisdiction over such matters, the Federal Government will take measures appropriate to our Federal system to facilitate the implementation of these Regulations.

Source: Statement for the Record by the Government of the United States of America Concerning the World Health Organization's Revised International Health Regulations, 23 May 2005.

---

them. Treaties have been analogized to contracts. Like treaties, contracts bind the persons involved but do not bind people who did not sign the contract. A large body of international law, now codified in the Vienna Convention on the Law of Treaties (1969), regulates the formation, implementation, interpretation, and termination of treaties. The treaty is a flexible instrument because states can use it for almost any purpose, and treaties can be bilateral or multilateral in membership.

Customary International Law

In contrast with treaties, customary international law (CIL) compromises unwritten rules that develop out of state interaction in the international system, and CIL forms when general and consistent state practice exists that is supported by the states' sense that following the practice is legally required.[11] General state practice refers to practice that is widespread in the international system. Consistent state practice requires state behavior that converges around a discernable principle. The sense of legal obligation means that states follow the principle and practice because they believe they are required to do so under international law. Rules of CIL are binding on all states in the international system except on those that have persistently objected to the rules' formation.

Although CIL is an important source of international law, it is problematic. Determining whether the criteria for CIL formation have been satisfied is fraught with difficulties.[12] Also, CIL rules tend to create general, ambiguous obligations about what states should do in specific situations. Some international lawyers argue, for example, that CIL imposes a duty on states to prevent, control, and reduce transboundary and maritime pollution.[13] Because this rule proves not very helpful, treaties are needed for states to craft more precise rules to reduce pollution.

General Principles of Law

The third primary source of international law is "general principles of law recognized by civilized nations," which are principles of domestic law that appear in national legal systems around the world. General principles of law have not been a robust source of international legal rules. International lawyers and tribunals dislike using rules taken directly from domestic law. General principles of law have been used most frequently when international tribunals confront issues, such as the admissibility of circumstantial evidence, for which no international law exists. The tribunals refer to how domestic legal systems handle such issues in order to complete their analysis.

Judicial Decisions and the Writings of Publicists

International lawyers use judicial decisions and the writings of scholars and practitioners to identify and interpret rules that arise from treaties, CIL, or general principles of law, which is why the International Court of Justice Statute refers to decisions and writings as "supplementary means" for determining rules of international law. However, sometimes these supplementary means are important in the creation and development of rules of international law. Historically, one drawback has been that decisions of international tribunals have been relatively few. As more international tribunals are established, such as the Dispute Settlement Body of the World Trade Organization (WTO), the importance of judicial decisions of international tribunals will increase.

Sources of International Law and Public Health

The bulk of international law that affects public health is found in treaties. One reason for this is that public health arose as an issue in international diplomacy only in the mid-19th century. When sovereign states discussed infectious disease control in the 19th century, no CIL rules existed to guide cooperation because no general and consistent practice on public health had developed. Nor was reliance on general principles of law possible to sustain multilateral efforts on public health. In addition, because science informs public health policies, treaties are better suited to crafting scientifically appropriate rules than CIL or general principles of law.

Globalization and National and International Law on Public Health

Globalization does not alter the national and international legal structures outlined above, but public health officials and legal experts believe that the law as traditionally produced has become anachronistic and requires reform. Much of the national and international law on controlling the international spread of infectious diseases, for example, developed during the time maritime commerce and travel was dominant and focused on control measures at points of entry and exit. Although public health capabilities at exit-and-entry points remain important, the speed and volume of international trade, travel, and migration made much of traditional national and international law on public health look inflexible in facilitating responses to rapidly changing global public health conditions.

Individuals and goods that can transmit public health threats now frequently bypass border control systems and, thus, require more-demanding public health action and cooperation among local, state, and federal governments (Box 7-3). Along with attention to traditional border strategies, public health experts perceive the need for regulatory approaches that deal with the threats to U.S. public health posed by mobile individuals, populations, animals, and goods.[14] This chapter mentions efforts to revise national and international legal regimes to make the law more flexible and responsive in light of the challenges that globalization presents.

The United States and International Health Diplomacy

The United States has been involved in international health diplomacy since the late 19th century, and it remains a key player in global public health. This section looks at U.S. participation in international health diplomacy to demonstrate how important the global context is for U.S. public health law.

Beginning of U.S. Involvement in International Public Health Efforts

International cooperation on public health began in 1851, when European states convened the first International Sanitary Conference to discuss cross-border transmission of cholera, plague, and yellow fever.[15] The 1851 conference launched a series of international sanitary meetings and treaties that continued until the formation of the World Health Organization (WHO) in 1948. The first U.S. participation in this process took place in 1881, when the United States hosted the fifth International Sanitary Conference, which marked the emergence of United States as an important player in international public health efforts, and continued when the United States became a state party to (i.e., formally agreed to be bound by) the treaty establishing WHO—the WHO Constitution.

In the years immediately before and after the 1881 conference, the federal government adopted legislation aimed at public health threats originating in foreign countries. Congress passed a national quarantine act in 1878, an action prompted by a yellow fever epidemic in the Western Hemisphere that reached the United States in 1878.[16] Congress enacted a statute in 1882 requiring the federal government to undertake medical inspection of aliens (defined as any person not a citizen or national of the United States [8 U.S.C. §1101(a)(3)]) seeking admission to the country. These laws suggested that the federal government appreciated threats to U.S. public health

---

BOX 7-3. Mobility and Infectious Disease Control: SARS and Polio

The outbreak and global spread of severe acute respiratory syndrome (SARS) in 2003 powerfully illustrated the vector that international trade and travel can be in spreading infectious disease around the world. The index patient with SARS traveled from Guangzhou Province in China to Hong Kong, triggering the serious SARS outbreak in Hong Kong. In Hong Kong, the SARS coronavirus also spread from the index patient to people who subsequently carried the pathogen to other countries, including Canada, Singapore, Vietnam, and Taiwan. Each of these countries then suffered outbreaks that proved difficult to control. In all, approximately 30 countries reported SARS cases to the World Health Organization before the outbreak was controlled in the summer of 2003.

Similarly, the spread of poliomyelitis across Africa to the Arabian peninsula and to Indonesia during 2004–2005 also demonstrated the capacities of pathogenic microbes to spread rapidly across borders in the early 21st century. Outbreaks of polio in Nigeria during 2003–2004 triggered the widespread geographic spread of the polio virus. As of the end of April 2005, 16 previously polio-free countries experienced polio importation since the outbreaks in Nigeria. The international spread of polio has adversely affected WHO's polio eradication strategy.

---

from foreign products and persons and moved to improve public health defenses at points of entry into the United States. These exercises of federal legislative power occurred simultaneously with the beginning of U.S. participation in international health diplomacy.

United States Participation and Leadership in Regional and International Efforts on Public Health

Once engaged, the United States deepened its participation in international cooperation on public health and emerged as a leader in this area. The United States was instrumental in the 1902 establishment of the first permanent international organization on public health—the Pan American Sanitary Bureau (PASB). The PASB supported hemispheric efforts to address infectious diseases through the development of important treaties, such as the Pan American Sanitary Code (1905, revised 1924) and the Pan American Sanitary Convention on Aerial Navigation (1928). The PASB also engaged in activities in other areas of public health, such as nutrition and noncommunicable diseases. The United States was also an original member state of the Office International de l'Hygiène Publique, established in 1907 to support international efforts against infectious diseases. The Office International de l'Hygiène Publique became important for international law on infectious disease control because it was central to the flow of global epidemiologic information and was responsible for overseeing the main international sanitary treaties.

The United States' refusal to join the League of Nations after World War I meant that the United States did not become a member of the Health Organization of the League of Nations in 1923. The United States played a leading role in WHO's establishment, hosting the conference in 1946 that created WHO. The United States pushed for inclusion in the WHO Constitution of innovative powers for WHO to adopt binding international legal regulations (WHO Constitution, articles 21–22). PASB was not absorbed by WHO, but instead retained its separate status while becoming WHO's regional office for the Americas.

The United States and the World Health Organization

The United States' relationship with WHO has been, and remains, complex and controversial. The United States is important to WHO because it provides a significant portion of WHO's budget; and U.S. experts have played important roles in WHO, for example, in the global eradication of smallpox. However, the relationship has often been contentious, especially when WHO moved beyond its technical and scientific roles into more political matters, such as connections between trade and public health. Against the advice and recommendations of U.S. public health officials, the United States opposed on trade-related grounds WHO's efforts to (1) regulate the quality of pharmaceuticals moving in international commerce, (2) oppose corporate marketing of breast-milk substitutes in developing countries, and (3) develop the program on essential drugs and vaccines.[17]

A key factor in the relationship between WHO and the United States is U.S. perceptions about international threats to U.S. public health. U.S. involvement in international health diplomacy from the late 19th century through WHO's formation drew strength from the belief that international cooperation was essential to protecting U.S. public health. Advances in U.S. domestic public health in the first half of the 20th century, and the development of antibiotics and vaccines after World War II, reduced the U.S. perception that it was vulnerable to imported infectious diseases, which had been the focus of international health cooperation. International health diplomacy lost its grounding in U.S. self-interest.

The emergence of public health as an important issue in U.S. foreign policy during the last decade has created its own complications and controversies for the relationship between the United States and WHO. During this period, the United States and WHO have disagreed about, among other things, (1) the protection of intellectual property rights and strategies to increase access to drugs and vaccines in developing countries; (2) HIV and AIDS prevention strategies in the developing world; and (3) WHO's potential role in investigating suspected intentional releases of biologic weapon agents.

Beyond WHO: United States Influence on Global Public Health through International Economics

United States power in global public health extends beyond WHO. The United States also affects public health globally through its support for the liberalization of trade and foreign investment and its leadership in international financial institutions. The United States played a key role in developing international trade law from the adoption of the General Agreement on Tariffs and Trade in 1947 through the creation of the WTO in 1995. Because WTO agreements affect many key public health issues, such as infectious disease control, food safety, tobacco control, access to drugs, health services, and biotechnology, they have become important components of national and international efforts on global health.[18]

Since 2000, the United States has started to pursue more aggressively regional and bilateral free-trade agreements, all of which also have implications for public health. In addition, through the exercise of U.S. power, institutions such as the World Bank and the International Monetary Fund wield influence in global public health because of their resources and willingness to demand that governments of developing countries change policies in return for financial assistance. Overseas development assistance from the United States also affects global public health, as illustrated by bilateral initiatives such as the President's Emergency Plan for AIDS Relief and to the Millennium Challenge Account. These indicators of U.S. economic and financial power in global public health suggest that U.S. involvement in international health diplomacy involves protecting not only U.S. public health but also how the exercise of U.S. power affects public health in other countries.

Prevention and Control of Public Health Threats Originating Outside the United States

The traditional justification for federal activity in international health—to protect U.S. public health from exogenous threats—explains why the federal government enacted legislation to prevent and minimize the importation of health threats (e.g., infectious diseases) through people, animals, and goods and entered treaties to cooperate on managing transboundary movement of such threats. This section looks at federal and international laws that connect with U.S. efforts to prevent and control the impact on U.S. public health from threats originating in other countries.

General Principles on Protecting Domestic Public Health from Outside Threats

General principles of international law hold that a state has sovereignty over its borders; it alone determines what goods, services, and people enter its territory. The only restrictions on this power are those the country imposes through constitutional or statutory law or accepts through treaties. For example, the United States has agreed to comply with the WTO Agreement on the Application of Sanitary and Phytosanitary Measures in how it seeks to ensure food safety for the U.S. population; and the United States supports the new International Health Regulations (IHR) adopted in May 2005. Thus, international law is used to discipline the exercise of sovereign power over human and commercial traffic crossing the state's border.

Public Health Threats from People

Federal Law on Public Health Criteria for Admission of Aliens

Federal law requires that aliens wanting to be admitted into United States as refugees or immigrants be screened for public health purposes (8 U.S.C. §1182 [a][1]; 42 C.F.R. Part 34; 8 U.S.C. §1222). Federal law also mandates medical examinations for public health purposes for aliens who want to change their immigration status from temporary to permanent residence (42 C.F.R. §34.1[d]).[19] Aliens seeking refugee status, immigrant visas, or adjustment of their immigration status are denied admission into the United States or a change in their immigration status on the following health-related grounds: (1) they have a communicable disease of public health significance (e.g., currently, active tuberculosis, HIV infection, syphilis, chancroid, gonorrhea, granuloma inguinale, lymphogranuloma venerum, and Hansen disease [i.e., leprosy] [42 C.F.R. §34.2[b]]); (2) they fail to present documentation of having received vaccination against vaccine-preventable diseases (e.g., currently mumps, measles, rubella, poliomyelitis, tetanus and diphtheria toxoids, pertussis, *Haemophilus influenzae* type B, and hepatitis B); (3) they have or have had a physical or mental disorder and behavior associated with that disorder that may pose a threat to the property, safety, or welfare of the alien or others; or (4) they are drug abusers or addicts (8 U.S.C. §1182 [a][1][A]). The Attorney General has discretion to waive certain of these provisions in specific circumstances (8 U.S.C. §1182 [g]). Aliens who seek entry into the United States through nonimmigrant visas (e.g., tourists) may be required to undergo a medical examination at the discretion of either U.S. consular officers overseas, U.S. immigration officers at the port of entry, or personnel at the Centers for Disease Control and Prevention (CDC), if these officials suspect an inadmissible health-related condition exists.[20]

United States experience with refugees suggests that enhanced health assessments of refugees before they depart foreign countries for resettlement in the United States can improve refugee health and protect U.S. public health. In 1997, CDC developed an enhanced health-assessment protocol for a portion of Barawan refugees from Somalia scheduled for resettlement in the United States.[21] In addition to the mandatory health assessment required by federal law, CDC also screened a portion of the Barawan refugees for malaria, intestinal parasites, and schistosomiasis. The enhanced health assessment produced results that led to pre-embarkation therapy for malaria and intestinal parasites for all the resettling Barawan refugees to reduce refugee morbidity and mortality and to reduce the introduction of parasitic infections into the United States. The approach, pioneered by the enhanced health-assessment protocol in the case of the Barawan refugees, provides a strategy to strengthen the traditional federal strategy to prevent the importation of diseases through aliens.

Federal Quarantine Law

The federal government can apprehend, detain, examine, and conditionally release individuals (aliens and U.S. citizens) entering the United States to prevent the introduction, transmission, or spread of certain infectious diseases from foreign countries into the United States (42 U.S.C. §264; 42 C.F.R. Part 71) (see also Chapter 2). Federal quarantine authority also exists to control infectious disease transmission between states of the Union (42 U.S.C. §264; 42 C.F.R. Part 70). The infectious diseases against which federal quarantine powers can be exercised are determined by executive order. President George W. Bush twice has revised the list of quarantinable diseases to add SARS and novel or re-emergent influenza viruses with pandemic potential (e.g., avian influenza [H5N1]) to the previous list of cholera, diphtheria, infectious tuberculosis, plague, smallpox, yellow fever, and viral hemorrhagic fevers (Lassa, Marburg, Ebola, Congo-Crimean, South American, and others not yet isolated or named) (Executive Order No. 13295, 68 F.R. 17255, 4 Apr. 2003; Amendment to Executive Order No. 13295, 70 F.R. 17299, 1 Apr. 2005).

The federal government also has the statutory power to prohibit introduction of persons from a foreign country when the Secretary of Health and Human Services determines that, by reason of the existence of any communicable disease in that country, serious danger exists of the introduction of such disease into the United States and the introduction of persons from such country increases this danger (42 U.S.C. §265). State governments in the United States also possess quarantine powers in their respective public health laws.[19]

In response to emerging and reemerging infectious diseases and the threat of biologic terrorism, state and federal governments have been reevaluating their quarantine powers, which have not been used frequently in the past few decades (Box 7-4). The Department of Health and Human Services is revising federal interstate and foreign quarantine regulations to produce a modernized legal framework for quarantine as a public health tool in the age of globalization. The principal changes being pursued in the revision of the federal quarantine regulations include due process provisions, expanded definitions of ill-passenger reporting requirements to close gaps in efficient contact tracing, and to standardize public health measures for disease containment with those in the new IHR.[b]

International Law and Public Health Criteria for Admission of Aliens

Four areas of international law relate to the exercise of U.S. public health sovereignty over the admission of aliens: (1) the IHR, (2) trade and investment treaties, (3) international human rights law, and (4) refugee treaties.

The IHR. In May 2005, WHO adopted a new set of IHR to replace the previous rules that had not been amended materially since 1969.[22] The new IHR differ significantly from the old IHR to make the regulations a more effective international legal framework against the international spread of disease (Box 7-5),[23] and the United States has expressed its support for the new IHR.[24] The new IHR contain provisions relevant to public health criteria the United States uses in connection with the admission of aliens. The new IHR prohibit states parties, for example, from requiring invasive medical examination, vaccination, or other prophylaxis as a condition of entry of any traveler, except when such an examination, vaccination, or other prophylaxis is necessary to determine the existence of a public health risk or as a condition of entry for any travelers seeking temporary or permanent residence (Article 31.1). In addition, the new IHR prohibit states parties from requiring health documents from travelers other than those documents provided for in the IHR or recommended by

BOX 7-4. Exercise of Federal Quarantine Authority

The exercise of federal quarantine authority during the last two decades has been limited to sporadic, isolated cases of disease or suspected disease on board airliners and vessels entering the United States from foreign countries. The only noteworthy exceptions were the mobilization of federal quarantine staff and resources in response to a plague outbreak in Sarat, India, in 1994 and to the SARS outbreak in 2003. Exercises of federal quarantine authority tend to fall into one of three categories.

Isolation, quarantine, or both of a conveyance or passenger(s) to prevent the possible spread of a communicable disease. In an ongoing effort to eliminate tuberculosis (TB), measles, and rubella in the United States, CDC's Division of Global Migration and Quarantine (DGMQ), National Center for Infectious Diseases, along with the Division of Tuberculosis Elimination of CDC's National Center HIV, STD, and TB Prevention and the National Immunization Program, established protocols to identify possible cases of measles, meningitis, Legionnaire disease, viral hemorrhagic fevers (e.g., Lassa), and pandemic influenza strains on board international flights and cruises. These protocols included isolation of possible cases, notification of passengers and crew, distribution of health and contact information, and coordination of the medical follow-up of any such cases.

The use of federal quarantine authority to stop a conveyance from moving passengers or cargo to prevent possible spread of communicable diseases. An example of this type of exercise of authority is the issuance of "No Sail Orders." From time to time, cruise ships on international itineraries visiting U.S. ports experience disease outbreaks on board (usually foodborne or waterborne infections). By law, these outbreaks are to be reported to CDC's Vessel Sanitation Program, National Center for Environmental Health, and the outbreaks addressed in collaborative manner by the cruise ship line and CDC. However, exceptions do exist.

In July 2001, CDC prohibited importation of *Dracaena* (bamboo) shipments in standing water that could have introduced mosquito species not widely seen in the United States. The Los Angeles district office of the U.S. Department of Agriculture notified CDC that it had identified maritime cargo containers of "lucky bamboo" (*Dracaena* species), an ornamental plant, that were infested with mosquitoes. CDC subsequently identified the Asian tiger mosquito (*Aedes albopictus*, a species previously not seen in California) and other species of mosquitoes associated with these cargo containers. *Dracaena* shipments in standing water appeared to pose a considerable risk of importing exotic mosquitoes into the United States. *Aedes albopictus* can transmit human diseases, such as western equine encephalitis, St. Louis encephalitis, and dengue viruses. CDC also has exercised federal quarantine powers to prevent the spread of communicable diseases by banning the importation into the United States of African rodents (2003, monkeypox), civet cats (2004, SARS), and birds from Southeast Asia (2004, avian influenza).

(continued)

Preventing persons from boarding a conveyance. In January 2005, a U.S. Department of State program to resettle 15,707 Hmong refugees from Laos living in Thailand was suspended because some refugees already resettled in the United States tested positive for multidrug-resistant strains of TB. After the suspension, CDC coordinated investigations in Thailand and the United States to identify and treat refugees who tested positive for TB. The intensified TB-control measures allowed the resettlement program to restart in February 2005.

WHO; but this prohibition does not apply to persons seeking temporary or permanent residence (Article 35).

International trade law. The United States has entered treaties that enable foreign business persons to live and work in the United States as part of the liberalization of trade and investment with other countries. These treaty provisions normally reserve to the United States the ability to deny temporary entry rights on the public health grounds provided in federal law. The North American Free Trade Agreement (NAFTA) provides, for example, that "[e]ach Party shall grant temporary entry to business persons who are otherwise qualified for entry under applicable measures relating to public health and safety and national security" (NAFTA, Article 1603). Thus, the United States could legitimately deny entry to a business person from Canada under NAFTA because the person has a communicable disease of public health significance, such as HIV infection and AIDS.

International human rights law. HIV infection's inclusion as a reason to deny aliens admission to the United States has been controversial. Experts have criticized the U.S. immigration policy on HIV as a violation of international human rights law, with commentators arguing, for example, that "denying entry to individuals based solely on HIV infection fundamentally infringes on human rights."[25.] However, the United States has not restricted its ability to deny entry to HIV-positive aliens in either treaty law or CIL. Whether denying entry to aliens with HIV infection makes public health sense remains controversial, but the United States does not violate international human rights law in denying aliens admission because they are infected with HIV. Although legislated to protect public health, the HIV exclusion increasingly functions to prevent immigrants with HIV from becoming a "public charge," which is a different rationale for exclusion than public health (8 U.S.C. §1182 [a][4]). Any HIV-positive immigrants who can show that they have the financial resources and access to a health-care provider can receive waivers to the HIV exclusion rule. Refugees for whom "public charge" is not an exclusionary criterion per se can more easily obtain waivers of the HIV exclusion rule.

International law on refugees. The United States is party to the UN Convention Relating to the Status of Refugees (UN Refugee Convention, 1951), and it has enacted legislation to implement its obligations under this treaty (Refugee Act, 1980). Basic disciplines required by the UN Refugee Convention are for parties to treat refugees no less favorably than they treat other aliens or their own nationals with respect

BOX 7-5. The New International Health Regulations

The International Health Regulations (IHR) originally were adopted by the World Health Assembly (WHA) in 1951 as the International Sanitary Regulations. In 1969, the WHA changed the name to the International Health Regulations. In response to growing concerns about emerging and reemerging infectious diseases, the WHA instructed the WHO Director-General in 1995 to revise the IHR in light of challenges generated by globalization. The WHA adopted the new IHR in May 2005.

The new IHR differ significantly from the old IHR and represent a historic development in the use of international law for public health purposes.[24] Some key features of the new IHR are as follows:

- *Purpose*: The purpose of the new IHR is to prevent, protect against, control, and provide a public health response to the international spread of disease in ways commensurate with and restricted to public health risks, and that avoid unnecessary interference with international trade and travel.
- *Scope*: Unlike the old IHR, which applied only to a limited number of infectious diseases, the new IHR apply to communicable and noncommunicable diseases, regardless of their origin or source, that could significantly harm humans through international spread. This scope includes biologic, chemical, and radiologic threats to public health originating from natural, accidental, or deliberate causes (Annex 2).
- *Incorporation of Human Rights Principles*: The new IHR incorporate principles from international law on human rights to balance effective public health responses to disease risks with respect for the dignity, human rights, and fundamental freedoms of individuals.
- *Surveillance and Response Capabilities*: The new IHR oblige states parties to develop, strengthen, and maintain core surveillance and response capacities (Annex 1). States parties have until 2012 to fulfill their surveillance and response capability requirements.
- *Notification Obligations*: The new IHR require states parties to notify WHO of all events in their territories that may constitute a public health emergency of international concern. A "decision instrument" (Annex 2) helps guide states parties through the process of determining whether a disease event must be reported to WHO.
- *Provisions on Information and Verification*: The new IHR allow WHO to account for epidemiologic information received from nongovernment sources and to request that governments verify such information.
- *Declaration and Recommendations Powers*: The new IHR grant WHO the power to (1) declare that a disease event constitutes a public health emergency of international concern, (2) make temporary recommendations on how states parties should respond to declared public health emergencies of international

(continued)

concern, and (3) issue standing recommendations on routine, periodic application of health measures for specific ongoing public health risks.

- *Rules on Permissible Health Measures*: The new IHR restrict states parties to the application of certain health measures concerning the treatment of travelers, goods, and means of transportation. Health measures that do not comply with the limitations provided in the new IHR must satisfy certain criteria to be legitimate (e.g., be based on a risk assessment and scientific principles and evidence and not be more restrictive of international traffic or more invasive or intrusive to persons than reasonably available alternatives that would achieve a similar or greater level of health protection).
- *Rejections and Reservations*: States have 18 months from the date of the new IHR's adoption by the WHA to reject the new regulations or formulate reservations to specific principles of them.

The new IHR will enter into force in June 2007 for WHO member states that have not rejected them.

to various public services and laws. The UN Refugee Convention requires, for example, national treatment for refugees in connection with public relief, labor laws, and social security, including provisions for occupational injury and disease, sickness, maternity, and disability (UN Refugee Convention, articles 23–24). Thus, in applying public health laws to refugees, the United States has agreed to implement such laws in a nondiscriminatory manner. The enhanced refugee assessment protocols developed by CDC respond to the United States' humanitarian responsibility to evaluate, diagnose, and treat U.S.-bound refugees for communicable diseases of public health significance, as well as other infectious conditions that impact refugee health.

Public Health Threats from Goods

Federal Law

Federal quarantine law gives the U.S. government the power to prevent the introduction, transmission, or spread of communicable diseases from foreign countries or between states of the Union through the importation or interstate movement of property, including animals (42 U.S.C. §§264–265; 42 C.F.R. Parts 70–71). The U.S. government has exercised these powers, for example, to ban the importation of African rodents, civets, and certain birds from southeast Asia and to prohibit the interstate sale and movement of various animals as part of efforts to prevent the introduction and spread of monkeypox, SARS, and avian influenza, respectively, in the United States (42 C.F.R. §71.32[b] and 42 C.F.R. §71.56 [banning importation of African rodents]; 21 C.F.R. §1240.23 [prohibition on capture, sale, transport, barter, or exchange concerning certain animal species related to spread of monkeypox];

Notice of Embargo of Civets, 13 Jan. 2004; Notice of Embargo on Birds [Class Aves] from Specified Southeast Asian Countries, 4 Feb. 2004 [subsequently lifted on 10 Mar. 2004]). The U.S. Customs Service and Department of Agriculture are also empowered to prevent the importation of products believed harmful to human, animal, or plant health (e.g., cattle potentially infected with bovine spongiform encephalopathy or foot and mouth disease).

These powers reflect Congress's exercise of its constitutional authority to regulate commerce with foreign nations and interstate commerce between states of the Union. Although the United States retains sovereignty over what goods from other countries enter its territory, international law affects this area more than it does the admission of foreign persons. The United States has played an influential role in the construction of international law that directly and indirectly affects U.S. efforts to keep health-threatening products out of the country.

International Trade Law

International trade law affects a variety of trade-restricting health measures that states can take to protect public health from communicable and noncommunicable disease threats.[26] This section focuses on the principles found in the WTO, but rules in regional trade agreements, such as NAFTA, and bilateral trade agreements tend to follow the pattern discernible in the WTO with respect to goods.

The General Agreement on Tariffs and Trade (GATT, 1994) permits WTO member states to restrict trade for health purposes. In the *EC* [*European Communities*]—*Asbestos* case (2001), the WTO Appellate Body ruled that health-threatening characteristics of a product could be considered in the "like product" analysis for purposes of applying the national treatment principle (GATT, Article III).[27] Thus, the Appellate Body held that products containing asbestos and products not containing asbestos were not "like products" because asbestos fibers threatened human health. The same reasoning applies to the interpretation of the "like products" requirement in the most-favored-nation principle (GATT, Article I).

The second set of rules in GATT that relate to public health involves GATT's recognition that WTO member states may legally violate a GATT obligation if the measure is necessary to protect human health (GATT, Article XX[b]). For example, if the United States banned importation of clothes impregnated with potentially carcinogenic chemicals, the prohibition would violate the GATT ban on quantitative restrictions (Article XI) but would be justifiable under Article XX(b) as necessary to protect health.

If the trade-restricting measure protects health from risks arising from additives, contaminants, toxins, or disease-causing organisms in foods, beverages, or feedstuffs, then WTO member states have to comply with the WTO Agreement on the Application of Sanitary and Phytosanitary Measures (SPS Agreement).[c] The SPS Agreement applies scientific and trade-related disciplines to trade-restricting food-safety measures. The scientific disciplines require that sufficient scientific evidence support the measures (Article 2.2) and that the measures be based on a scientific and policy risk assessment (Article 5.1). The SPS Agreement also mandates that WTO member states base their food-safety regulations on relevant international standards promulgated by competent international organizations, such as the Codex Alimentarius Commission (Codex) (Article 3.1). If a WTO member state applies measures more protective than applicable international standards, it may do so if it has a scientific justification (Article 3.3).

The SPS Agreement necessitates the involvement of public health experts and officials in various ways. The requirement for a trade-restricting health measure to be based on scientific evidence and a risk assessment calls for epidemiologic data. The importance of international standards, such as those developed by Codex, makes the standard-setting work of public health officials in WHO and elsewhere legally relevant. Settling disputes under the SPS Agreement between WTO member states requires scientific testimony and input from public health experts. In addition, WTO dispute settlement panels may call on independent experts to help the panels evaluate scientific and technical evidence presented by the disputing parties (SPS Agreement, Article 11.2).

The WTO Dispute Settlement Body interpreted the SPS Agreement in a dispute between the United States and the European Communities (EC) involving food safety in the *EC—Hormones* case (1998).[28] In this case, the WTO Appellate Body held that the EC violated Article 5.1 of the SPS Agreement because it had not shown that its ban on the importation of beef raised with growth-promoting hormones was based on a risk assessment. Codex had previously determined that the hormones in question posed no threat to human health, but the EC imposed a ban on beef grown with such hormones. Although not technically part of the WTO's holding, the decision also suggested that the EC had no scientific basis for its total prohibition on the importation of hormone-raised beef.[e]

Trade-restricting health measures that do not fall into the food-safety category of the SPS Agreement may be subject to the disciplines of the WTO Agreement on Technical Barriers to Trade. Technical regulations set out product characteristics or their related processes and production methods that products must meet before being sold to consumers (Annex 1). Health protection is a legitimate objective for applying technical regulations to imported products (Article 2.2), but such regulations must be applied in a way that does not violate either the most-favored-nation or national treatment principles (Article 2.1) or create unnecessary obstacles to international trade (Article 2.2). The Technical Barriers to Trade Agreement requires that WTO member states use relevant international standards as a basis for their technical regulations, unless such use would be inappropriate or ineffective (Article 2.4).

This overview of the complicated disciplines in international trade law and the WTO demonstrate that international trade law applies significant disciplines to the sovereign state's power to protect national public health from foreign products. Some experts have argued that the disciplines in the WTO system and regional agreements such as NAFTA reduce the United States' ability to protect itself from health-damaging foreign products in two respects: (1) trade liberalization fostered by free trade agreements overwhelms the U.S. capacity to inspect foreign food products at the border for possible health-damaging chemicals and organisms, and (2) the disciplines used in trade agreements weaken the United States' ability to protect the health of its population from dangerous foreign products.[29] The discourse between opponents and defenders of international trade law suggests that the debate is fundamental to how the United States will exercise its public health sovereignty in the years to come.

International Health Regulations

The purpose of the new IHR is to facilitate prevention of, protection against, and control and provision of responses to the international spread of disease in ways that avoid unnecessary inference with international trade (Article 2). The new IHR approaches this task in a manner that echoes the strategy used in international trade law, namely that trade-restricting health measures should be based on scientific principles and evidence and a risk assessment and be the least trade-restrictive measures possible to achieve the level of health protection desired (Article 43). These disciplines also apply to WHO's exercise of its authority to issue temporary or standing recommendations that might restrict the flow of international trade (Article 17). The new IHR's rules on health measures applied to ships, aircraft, trucks, trains, and containers (e.g., articles 25–29, 33–35, 37–39, and 41) also contribute to striking the balance between robust public health action and the need for international commerce to flow efficiently.

Public Health and Trade in Services

As a member state of the WTO, the United States also is bound by the rules of the General Agreement on Trade in Services (GATS), which provides the multilateral framework for the progressive liberalization of international trade in services. In many respects, GATS is a more complicated trade agreement than GATT because it allows WTO member states to make their own specific commitments on market access and on national treatment (GATS, articles XVI and XVII). This complexity has made controversies about the impact of GATS on health care and public health difficult to follow, particularly for those not trained in international trade law.[30] With negotiations on liberalization of trade in services occurring in the Doha Development Round of trade talks, how the United States and other states address health-related services will be an important issue for health policy communities to monitor.

Public Health Threats from Terrorism

Other chapters in this book address bioterrorism's impact on state and federal law in the United States (see Chapters 11 and 15), but U.S. homeland security concerns about bioterrorism and other forms of catastrophic terrorism also generate international considerations. One example can be found in the Public Health Security and Bioterrorism Preparedness and Response Act of 2002 (Public Law 107-188). Congress passed this legislation to protect the health and safety of the U.S. population from terrorist attacks on the nation's food supply. Under this act, the Food and Drug Administration must receive prior electronic notice for all food imported into the United States, subject to certain exceptions (21 U.S.C. §381[a]). United States interest in the new IHR includes the potential benefits the new Regulations could produce for public health responses to intentional uses of biologic, chemical, or radiologic agents.[24]

A different international consideration involves U.S. government plans to engage in novel research on dangerous biologic agents to engage in assessing what bioterrorist threats may yet emerge. Such plans have caused controversy because critics argue that the type of pathogen research envisioned would violate U.S. obligations under the Biological and Toxin Weapons Convention of 1972 and the statute implementing such obligations into federal law (18 U.S.C. §175).[31] How this convention and the implementing federal law are interpreted with respect to the kind of pathogen research proposed by the U.S. government will be critical arms control issues.

Exportation of Public Health Threats from the United States

General Principles on the Exportation of Public Health Threats

As a matter of constitutional law, Congress has authority to regulate commerce with foreign nations to restrict or prohibit the emigration of persons who, or the exportation of products that, may cause public health damage in foreign countries. Whether international law contains rules that regulate the emigration of people for public health purposes or the exportation of dangerous products is more complicated. The United States can enter, and has entered, treaties that contain provisions on preventing the disembarkation of persons with certain diseases (e.g., the IHR) and regulating the exportation of dangerous products (e.g., Montreal Protocol on Substances that Deplete the Ozone Layer).

In addition, CIL holds that states must not allow their territories to be used in ways that cause damage inside the territory of another state. This rule has most often been invoked in connection with transboundary air or water pollution than in the context of the movement of people or goods. The reason for this is that, unlike with transboundary pollution, the state importing goods and receiving refugees, immigrants, or tourists has sovereign power and border-control mechanisms to protect its public health from disease threats moving in international commerce. In other words, without specific treaty obligations, the legal onus falls on the importing state rather than the exporting state as a matter of international law. Public health practices do not, however, necessarily reflect this legal reality. Public health officials from different national governments cooperate and communicate to protect public health and do not restrict their collaborative efforts because, under international law, the legal onus to protect from threats falls on the importing state.

Exportation of Public Health Threats through People

Federal Law

Federal statutory law does not require the U.S. government to prevent people with diseases of public health significance from leaving the United States to travel to other countries. Such power exists in federal quarantine authority to prevent disease transmission between states of the Union (42 U.S.C. §264; 42 C.F.R. Part 70), but existing federal quarantine law relating to foreign countries focuses on preventing the introduction of diseases in the United States and does not mention preventing the exportation of diseases from the United States (42 U.S.C. §264; 42 C.F.R. Part 71). The proposed revisions to federal quarantine regulations may address this problem.

International Law

The new IHR do not explicitly require states parties to stop people infected with, or suspected of being infected with, diseases that could spread internationally from leaving their respective territories. Nor do the new IHR prohibit states parties from acting to prevent the international spread of disease by stopping the exportation of public health risks through people.

Most rules in the new IHR dealing with travelers address the entry of people into a state's territory rather than the exit of individuals from such territory. However, under the new IHR, states parties may (1) engage in "exit screening" and/or restrictions on persons coming from areas affected by disease events on their own or pursuant to WHO recommendations (Article 18.1), and (2) require information from travelers upon departure and a noninvasive medical examination that is the least intrusive examination possible that would achieve the public health objective in question (Article 23.1) The new IHR also permit states parties to implement additional health measures on departing or arriving travelers on the basis of evidence of a public health risk, as long as such additional measures are the least intrusive and invasive measures possible, are undertaken with the prior informed consent of the travelers, and involve informing travelers of any risks associated with vaccination or other prophylaxis recommended (articles 23.2–23.4).

The provision addressing compulsory health measures in situations involving imminent public health risks concerns only the entry of travelers, not their departure (Article 31.2); however, this situation does not prevent states parties to the new IHR from using compulsory measures, including isolation and quarantine, against persons departing for other countries. Also, WHO could recommend the use of compulsory measures against departing travelers (Article 18.1). Such compulsory measures on persons seeking to depart still would have to meet the new IHR requirements on treating all travelers with respect for their dignity, human rights, and fundamental freedoms (Article 32) and would need to be applied in a transparent, nondiscriminatory manner (Article 42).

Exportation of Public Health Threats through Goods

Federal Law

Congress has used its power to regulate commerce with foreign nations to restrict U.S. exports to foreign countries, mainly for reasons relating to national security. Federal law regulates, for example, the exportation and importation of pathogens and toxins as part of efforts to prevent proliferation of biologic weapons (e.g., 42 C.F.R. §73.14 [regulation of select agent importation] and 15 C.F.R. §742.2 [regulating exportation of pathogens]). In the public health context, federal law contains provisions that regulate the exportation of products that might be harmful to public health in other countries. For example, a food, drug, device, or cosmetic that cannot be sold in the United States because it is adulterated[e] or misbranded can be exported if the product (1) accords to the foreign purchaser's specifications, (2) does not conflict with the importing country's law, (3) is labeled as intended for export, and (4) is not sold or offered for sale in U.S. commerce (21 U.S.C. §381[e][1]).

Federal law also allows the exportation of drugs and devices not approved for sale or use in the United States if the drug or device complies with the laws of the importing country and has valid marketing authorization from the responsible government agency in that country (21 U.S.C. §382[a]–[b]). For countries other than Australia, Canada, Israel, Japan, New Zealand, Switzerland, and South Africa, and for those in the European Economic Area, unapproved drugs cannot be exported unless the laws of the importing country also meet certain substantive requirements relating to oversight of drug safety and effectiveness (21 U.S.C. §382[b][2][B]). Federal law also prohibits exportation of drugs and devices that, among other requirements, present an imminent hazard to the public health of the intended importing country (21 U.S.C. §382[f][4][B]), a determination made by the Secretary of Health and Human Services in consultation with the appropriate public health official of the importing country. Under federal law, neither the U.S. Export-Import Bank nor the federal government's Overseas Private Investment Corporation can support export or investment projects that may cause environmental or health damage in a foreign country (12 U.S.C. 635i-5[a][2]; 22 U.S.C. 2191[n]). Federal law does not, however, require that exported cigarettes comply with U.S. law on the manufacture, labeling, and packaging of cigarettes for domestic consumption (15 U.S.C. §1340).

International Law

Several treaties in international environmental law regulate the export of products deemed dangerous to health and the environment, including the Montreal Protocol on Substances That Deplete the Ozone Layer (1987), the Basel Convention on the Control of Transboundary Movements of Hazardous Wastes and Their Disposal (1989), the Rotterdam Convention on the Prior Informed Consent Procedure for Certain Hazardous Chemicals and Pesticides (1998), the Cartagena Protocol on Biosafety (2000), and the Stockholm Convention on Persistent Organic Pollutants (2001). Table 7-1 summarizes the export-related provisions of these agreements and the U.S. position on each.

The United States also has used international law to open foreign markets for products that can harm health. For example, the United States used federal law and GATT to open developing-country markets to tobacco exports from U.S. tobacco companies. In 1990, the United States prevailed against Thailand in a GATT case in which the GATT panel held that Thailand's ban on the importation of foreign-made tobacco products was not necessary to protect human health within the meaning of GATT Article XX(b).[32] In the 1990s, however, the U.S. government and tobacco companies came under criticism through WHO's effort to mount a global effort to reduce tobacco-related morbidity and mortality, an effort that included crafting a Framework Convention on Tobacco Control (FCTC), which was opened for signature in 2003 and entered into force in 2005 (Box 7-6). The FCTC contains provisions that would affect states parties that export and import tobacco (e.g., Article 5.3 [obligation to protect tobacco-control policies from commercial and other vested tobacco industry interests], Article 10 [regulation of tobacco product disclosures], Article 11 [packaging

TABLE 7-1   International Environmental Treaties on Substances Harmful
to Public Health or the Environment: Export Controls and U.S. Reaction

Treaty	Export-Related Provisions	U.S. Position
Montreal Protocol on Substances that Deplete the Ozone Layer	States parties must ban the export of certain ozone-depleting substances to non–states parties.	The United States has ratified the Montreal Protocol.
Basel Convention on the Control of Trans-boundary Movements of Hazardous Wastes and Their Disposal	The treaty bans the export of hazardous wastes from member countries of the Organization of Economic Co-operation and Development (OECD) to non-member OECD countries, to Antarctica, and to countries not party to the Basel Convention.	The United States has signed but has not ratified the Basel Convention.
Rotterdam Convention on the Prior Informed Consent Procedure for Certain Hazardous Chemicals and Pesticides	The treaty regulates the exportation of certain hazard-ous chemicals and pesticides from states parties through, among other things, the requirement of prior informed consent from the importing state party.	The United States has signed but not ratified the Rotterdam Convention.
Cartagena Protocol on Biosafety	The treaty applies an advanced informed agreement proce-dure to the exportation of living modified organisms.	The United States cannot join the Cartagena Protocol because it has not ratified the Convention on Biodiversity and is unlikely to do so in the near future.
Stockholm Convention on Persistent Organic Pollutants	The treaty prohibits states parties from exporting certain chemicals.	The United States has signed but not ratified the Stockholm Convention.

and labeling of tobacco products], and Article 15 [illicit trade in tobacco products]); thus far, the United States has signed but not ratified the FCTC and thus is not bound legally by those trade-related provisions.

The United States has opposed or raised questions about international public health efforts to regulate commerce (and thus U.S. exports) in pharmaceutical products, breast-milk substitutes, genetically modified organisms (GMOs), and processed food products. In the late 1960s and early 1970s, the United States opposed proposals to establish international monitoring of the quality of pharmaceuticals moving in international commerce. As a result of U.S. opposition, nonbinding guidelines on manufacturing, labeling, and quality control were adopted rather than internationally binding regula-tions. In the 1970s, public health experts argued that the marketing of breast-milk sub-

---

BOX 7-6. The WHO Framework Convention on Tobacco Control

In 1995, the World Health Assembly (WHA) asked the WHO Director-General to report to it in 1996 on the feasibility of developing an international instrument on tobacco control. In 1996, the WHA called on the WHO Director-General to begin developing the Framework Convention on Tobacco Control (FCTC). In 1999, the WHA established a working group to prepare for intergovernment negotiations on the FCTC; the working group completed its task in May 2000.

Three intergovernment negotiating sessions on the FCTC were held in Geneva, and WHO opened the FCTC for signature in June 2003. The FCTC was the first treaty negotiated under the treaty-making powers in Article 19 of the WHO Constitution. The FCTC entered into force on February 27, 2005. As of August 2005, 168 countries had signed the FCTC, and 76 had ratified the treaty.

The FCTC contains provisions that attempt to reduce both the demand for and supply of tobacco products and thus uses a different approach from other treaties on addictive substances that focus only on reduction of supply. In terms of reducing demand, the FCTC includes provisions on price and tax measures; on protection from exposure to tobacco smoke; on regulation of the contents, disclosure statements, and packaging and labeling of tobacco products; and on tobacco advertising, promotion, and sponsorship. Supply reduction provisions include obligations on illicit trade in tobacco products and sales to and by minors, and on support for economically viable alternatives to tobacco farming.

---

stitutes by Western international corporations in developing countries was detrimental to public health because such marketing reduced levels of breast feeding. The World Health Assembly adopted a nonbinding code on the marketing of breast-milk substitutes in 1981, with the United States casting the only negative vote.

The United States also has opposed international regulations on trade in GMOs, as evidenced during the Cartagena Protocol negotiations, in part because the United States does not believe that scientific evidence supports claims that GMOs threaten health. It is pursuing claims at the WTO that the EC's measures on GMOs violate WTO rules and are not justified by claims that the measures protect health.[f] The United States also raised concerns during WHO's development of a global strategy for fighting obesity and its related diseases (which eventually was adopted in May 2004),[33] concerns that critics believed were prompted by opposition of U.S. food companies to aspects of WHO's strategy.[34]

Intellectual Property Rights and U.S. Exports of Pharmaceuticals

U.S. positions on other areas of international law also have been part of global controversies. The United States remains embroiled in a global dispute that pits international legal protection of patent rights in pharmaceuticals against needs in many developing countries for affordable access to drugs and vaccines.[35] The dispute arose in the late 1990s when the United States, European countries, and multinational pharmaceutical companies opposed developing country efforts to engage in compulsory licensing and parallel importing under the Agreement on Trade-Related Aspects of Intellectual Property Rights (TRIPS) of patented antiretroviral drugs for treatment of HIV and AIDS. A global coalition of developing countries and nongovernment organizations managed to force the United States and European countries to accept the Doha Declaration on TRIPS and Public Health in November 2001.[36] The Doha Declaration provides that WTO member states "agree that TRIPS does not and should not prevent Members from taking measures to protect public health" (paragraph 4). The declaration also clarified that each WTO member has the right to (1) grant compulsory licenses on grounds its determines appropriate, (2) determine what constitutes a national emergency or other circumstances of extreme urgency for purposes of TRIPS, and (3) establish its own regime for parallel importing (paragraph 5).

However, the Doha Declaration did not put the controversy between "pharmaceutical patents v. access to medicines" to rest. Disagreements continued between the United States particularly and other WTO members on the creation of a mechanism to allow a "third party compulsory licensing" procedure for WTO developing countries that do not have domestic pharmaceutical manufacturing capacity. The WTO member states finally reached agreement on creating such a mechanism in August 2003.[37] Most recently, U.S. pursuit of protections for intellectual property rights that go beyond what TRIPS requires (so-called "TRIPS-plus" provisions) in bilateral and regional trade agreements has shifted this controversy from the multilateral TRIPS to a new international legal context in which the United States attempts to secure objectives related to protection of intellectual property rights it failed to achieve through TRIPS.[35]

Harmonization of Product Standards and U.S. Exports

A key strategy in balancing the needs of trade and health is the establishment of international product standards through standard-setting entities and processes. As noted earlier, the SPS Agreement and the Agreement on Technical Barriers to Trade of the WTO contain provisions that either require or encourage WTO members to adopt internationally recognized standards for products they export. For food safety standards, the Codex Alimentarius Commission (a joint venture of WHO and the Food and Agriculture Organization) plays the leading role in the process of setting internationally recognized standards. The United States participates actively in the work of Codex and other standard-setting processes, including the International Conference on Harmonization (with Japan and the European Union on harmonizing pharmaceutical regulatory review standards) and multilateral efforts to standardize safety standards for automobiles to help reduce the growing global problem of injuries and death related to road accidents.[38]

Conclusion

This chapter focused on international considerations that arise in the exercise of U.S. public health sovereignty. Our objective was to correct the traditional neglect of these considerations and to encourage public health practitioners, international legal experts, and scholars to view U.S. public health and public health law in their proper global context and to integrate international and comparative perspectives in their work. Public health and public health law in the United States are intertwined with U.S. participation in international politics and economics and have been since the Republic's founding. The federal powers to regulate foreign commerce and to enter into treaties have been and remain key legal instruments for the U.S. government's responsibility for the health of the U.S. population. The United States is a leading power in the "anarchical society" of sovereign states, and international law also has been and remains central to U.S. international activities that affect public health in the United States and beyond its shores.

The traditional neglect of international considerations in analysis of U.S. public health law leaves out an aspect that is important for not only historical understanding but also for an accurate picture of the global public health environment in which U.S. policy and law is embedded. In addition to international law, increasing interdependencies create opportunities for comparative law analyses to contribute to our understanding of the role of law in public health. As globalization continues to accelerate, international considerations in U.S. public health and U.S. public health law will only continue to become more important, whether the issues involve local communities, cross-border public health cooperation with neighboring countries, or the dynamics of global health governance.[39]

Notes

a. The third edition of *The Public Health Law Manual*, published in 2004, now includes a new chapter on international issues.

b. See Department of Health and Human Services, Control of Communicable Diseases (Proposed Rule) 42 C.F.R. Parts 70 and 71, 70 F.R. 71892–948 (November 30, 2005). For public comments on the proposed revisions, see Division of Global Migration and Quarantine, View Comments, at http://www.cdc.gov/ncidod/dq/nprm/viewcomments.html.

c. The SPS Agreement essentially replaces GATT Article XX(b) for purposes of trade-restricting food-safety measures imposed by WTO member states.

d. As of this writing, the EC's WTO challenge, filed in November 2004, against the continued application of trade sanctions the United States and Canada put in place pursuant to *EC—Hormones* was ongoing.

e. Certain adulterated drugs or devices cannot be exported (21 U.S.C. §382[F][2]).

f. The WTO dispute settlement panel issued its ruling in this case in February 2006, but as of this writing, the WTO has not publicly circulated the ruling.

References

1. Lee K. *Globalization and Health: An Introduction.* Basingstoke: Palgrave Macmillan, 2003.
2. The White House. *National Security Strategy of the United States.* Washington, DC: The White House, 2002. Available at http://www.whitehouse.gov/nsc/nss.html. Accessed October 17, 2005.

3. Fidler DP. Fighting the axis of illness: HIV/AIDS, human rights, and U.S. foreign policy. *Harvard Human Rights J* 2004;17:99–136.

4. United Nations General Assembly. *A More Secure World: Our Shared Responsibility. Report of the Secretary-General's High-Level Panel on Threats, Challenges, and Change.* New York: United Nations, 2004. Available at http://www.un.org/secureworld. Accessed October 17, 2005.

5. Secretary-General of the United Nations. *In Larger Freedom: Towards Development, Security, and Human Rights for All. Report of the Secretary-General.* New York: United Nations, 2005. Available at http://www.un.org/largerfreedom. Accessed October 17, 2005.

6. Tobey JA. *Public Health Law.* 2nd ed. New York: The Commonwealth Fund, 1939.

7. Wing KR. *The Law and the Public's Health.* 5th ed. Ann Arbor, MI: Health Administration Press, 1999.

8. Grad FP. *The Public Health Law Manual.* 2nd ed. Washington, DC: American Public Health Association, 1996.

9. Gostin LO. *Public Health Law: Power, Duty, Restraint.* Berkeley: University of California Press and the Milbank Memorial Fund, 2000.

10. Bull H. *The Anarchical Society: A Study of Order in World Politics.* London: Macmillan, 1977.

11. Brownlie I. *Principles of Public International Law.* 5th ed. Oxford: Oxford University Press, 1998.

12. Fidler DP. Challenging the classical concept of custom: perspectives on the future of customary international law. *German Yearbook of International Law* 1996;39:198–248.

13. Birnie PW, Boyle AE. *International Law and the Environment.* 2nd ed. Oxford: Clarendon Press, 1992.

14. Maloney SA, Cetron MS. Investigation and management of infectious diseases on international conveyances (airplanes and cruise ships). In: DuPont HL, Steffen R, eds. *Textbook of Travel Medicine and Health.* 2nd ed. London: BC Decker Inc, 2001:519–30.

15. Howard-Jones N. *The Scientific Background of the International Sanitary Conferences 1851–1938.* Geneva: World Health Organization, 1975.

16. Pan American Health Organization. *Pro Salute Novi Mundi: A History of the Pan American Health Organization.* Washington, DC: Pan American Health Organization, 1992.

17. Gordenker L. The World Health Organization: sectoral leader or occasional benefactor? In: Coate RA, ed. *U.S. Policy and the Future of the United Nations.* Washington, DC: The Twentieth Century Fund, 1994:167–91.

18. WHO, WTO. *WTO Agreements & Public Health: A Joint Study by the WHO and the WTO Secretariat.* Geneva: World Health Organization, 2002.

19. CDC, National Center for Infectious Diseases, Division of Global Migration and Quarantine. Technical Instructions for Medical Examination of Aliens in the United States, March 1998. Available at http://www.cdc.gov/ncidod/dq/pdf/ti-civil.pdf. Accessed April 25, 2005.

20. CDC, National Center for Infectious Diseases, Division of Global Migration and Quarantine. Medical Examinations. Available at http://www.cdc.gov/ncidod/dq/health.htm. Accessed April 25, 2005.

21. Miller JM, Boyd HA, Ostrowski SR, et al. Malaria, intestinal parasites, and schistosomiasis among Barawan Somali refugees resettling to the United States: a strategy to reduce morbidity and decrease risk of imported infections. *Am J Trop Med Hyg* 2000;62: 115–21.

22. World Health Assembly. Revision of the International Health Regulations, WHA58.3, 23 May 2005.

23. Fidler DP. From international sanitary conventions to global health security: The new International Health Regulations. *Chinese J Int Law* 2005;4:325–92.

24. US Department of State, Bureau of International Organization Affairs. US statement for the record concerning the World Health Organization's Revised International Health Regulations. May 23, 2005. Available at http://www.state.gov/p/io/rls/rm/46714.htm. Accessed October 17, 2005.

25. Gostin LO, Lazzarini Z. *Human Rights and Public Health in the AIDS Pandemic*. Oxford: Oxford University Press, 1997.

26. Shaffer ER, Waitzkin H, Brenner J, Jasso-Aguilar R. Global trade and public health. *Am J Public Health* 2005;95:23–34.

27. WTO. *European Communities—Measures Affecting Asbestos and Asbestos-Containing Products*. Appellate Body Report, issued 12 Mar. 2001. Geneva: World Trade Organization, 1998 (WTO Doc. WT/DS135/AB/R). Available at http://www.wto.org/english/tratop_e/dispu_e/135abr_e.doc. Accessed October 17, 2005.

28. WTO. *European Communities—Measures Concerning Meat and Meat Products (Hormones)*. Appellate Body Report, adopted 13 Feb. 1998. Geneva: World Trade Organization, 1998 (WTO Doc. WT/DS26/AB/R). Available at http://www.wto.org/english/tratop_e/dispu_e/cases_e/ds26_e.htm. Accessed October 18, 2005.

29. Public Citizen. *NAFTA's Broken Promises: Fast Track to Unsafe Food*. Washington, DC: Public Citizen, 1997.

30. Drager N, Fidler DP. Managing liberalization of trade in services from a health policy perspective. *WHO Trade and Health Notes 2004*; no. 1 (Feb). Available at http://www.who.int/trade/resource/en/GATSfoldout_e.pdf. Accessed October 17, 2005.

31. Cohen HW, Gould RM, Sidel VW. The pitfalls of bioterrorism preparedness: the anthrax and smallpox experiences. *Am J Public Health* 2004;94:1667–71.

32. *Thailand—Restrictions on Importation of and Internal Taxes on Cigarettes*. Adopted 7 Nov. 1990 (GATT Doc. DS10/R). Available at http://www.worldtradelaw.net/reports/gattpanels/thaicigarettes.pdf. Accessed October 18, 2005.

33. WHO. *Global Strategy on Diet, Physical Activity, and Health*. Geneva: World Health Organization, 2004 (WHA57.17). Available at http://www.who.int/gb/ebwha/pdf_files/WHA57/A57_R17–en.pdf. Accessed October 17, 2005.

34. The Fat of the Land [Editorial]. *New York Times* 2 Feb 2004: A20.

35. Abbot FM. The WTO medicines decision: World pharmaceutical trade and the protection of public health. *Am J Int Law* 2005;99:317–58.

36. WTO. Doha Declaration on the TRIPS Agreement and Public Health, WT/MIN(01)/DEC/2, 14 Nov. 2001. Available at http://www.wto.org/english/thewto_e/minist_e/min01_e/mindecl_trips_e.htm. Accessed October 17, 2005.

37. WTO. Implementation of Paragraph 6 of the Doha Declaration on the TRIPS Agreement and Public Health, WT/L/540, 1 Sept. 2003. Available at http://www.wto.org/english/tratop_e/trips_e/implem_para6_e.htm. Accessed April 25, 2005.

38. WHO. *World Report on Road Traffic Injury Prevention*. Geneva: World Health Organization, 2004. Available at http://www.who.int/world-health-day/2004/infomaterials/world_report/en/. Accessed October 17, 2005.

39. Surgeon General of the United States. Call to action on global health, 5 June 2005. Proceedings of the Global Health Summit. *Mil Med*. In press.

Section II

The Law and Core
Public Health Applications

Chapter 8

LEGAL COUNSEL TO PUBLIC HEALTH PRACTITIONERS

Wilfredo Lopez and Thomas R. Frieden

Public health practitioners within a government agency constitute a broad array of titles and functions—positions ranging, for example, from the U.S. Secretary of Health and Human Services, the Surgeon General of the United States, and the Director of the Centers for Disease Control and Prevention to the commissioner of a state or local health department, deputy and assistant commissioners, bureau directors, epidemiologists, public health advisors, and inspectors. All are integral to the practice of public health. Legal advisors to these practitioners can be internal or external to the agency and may comprise one or more lawyers with limited or broad roles. It is not uncommon, for example, for lawyers to work within the office of a state attorney general and be assigned to provide legal services to the state health department, either exclusively or as one of several agencies within a portfolio. Similar arrangements can be found with regard to local health departments, with lawyers working out of a county or city law department. Smaller jurisdictions even may have law firms on retainer to the local government.

The implications of these various arrangements can be significant and, in some situations, can seriously limit the effectiveness of a health officer's mission to protect the public's health. As will be evident in the following discussion, public health law can be nuanced and require specialized knowledge. Whether in the context of an urgent epidemiologic investigation to detect and contain a possible disease outbreak requiring issuance of a subpoena, or with regard to an order to abate an imminent health hazard, public health practice often needs immediate access to expert legal advice. A lawyer in a remote location and perhaps with other priorities cannot always provide the kind of service or the degree of specialized legal professionalism necessary in public health practice.

Medical schools and even schools of public health address the roles and activities of government public health agencies with only a limited curriculum. Similarly, law schools rarely provide insight into the field of public health law. Therefore, many public health practitioners and their attorneys, even those with considerable experience in the fields of health-care delivery or health-care financing, find themselves needing on-the-job training regarding the relation between the practitioner and legal counsel. The purpose of this chapter, therefore, is to provide a practical framework for understanding and guiding the relationship between public health practitioners and legal counsel. We first suggest issues to be reviewed when a public health practitioner and his or her legal counsel initially meet or when the legal counsel writes the practitioner an introductory memo; we then describe in detail the different roles and responsibilities of the legal counsel in relation to the practitioner-client.

For simplicity in illustration, this chapter focuses primarily on the relationship between the head of a state or local health agency and its chief legal officer who supervises an internal counsel's office. Legal citations will focus on New York City and New York State to accommodate the authors' areas of expertise and to emphasize that the heart of public health law and practice is at the local and state levels. However, the concepts addressed here most likely apply to any practitioner and can, or should be made to, apply to any level of legal advisor, whether internal or external. Because law is so fundamental to public health—and because public health is so grounded in law—we believe the optimum arrangement is for a public health practitioner to have an internal lawyer to provide readily available and expert legal services.

Initial Encounter between Public Health Practitioner and Legal Counsel

The Statutory Framework

As administrative agencies, state and local health departments are creatures of statute. The state laws and the city charters that create state and local health departments usually will have particular sections that set forth the powers, functions, and duties of the health commissioner, sometimes called the "health officer," or of the health department.[1-4] Because the health officer can exercise all the powers of the health department, the terms are interchangeable.[3,5] These jurisdictional statutes and the court decisions that have interpreted them are a good place for counsel to start elucidating what the practitioner can do and why.

One possibility is for counsel to provide a memorandum to a new health commissioner as part of an introductory or transition document. The memorandum should point out where the law states the prime directive is to protect the health of the public,[1,2,4] or what might be thought of as the "three-M theory" of public health: to mitigate morbidity and mortality.[6,7] The document should explain that these jurisdictional statutes set forth the agency's core activities of "assessment, policy development, and assurance."[8] Assessment mandates requiring the department to supervise the reporting of vital events, such as births and deaths, or to supervise the reporting and control of communicable and chronic diseases. Policy development mandates to regulate many activities through the issuance of permits to safely operate hospitals, health centers, clinical and environmental laboratories, food-service establishments, radiation facilities, and others. Assurance mandates safeguarding of the food and drinking water supply and generally developing programs and interventions that will reduce morbidity and mortality. These statutes also will provide the authority, if not the mandate, for the health agency's other activities related to personal health issues, such as health-care access, maternal and child health, school health, and correctional health.

The Police Power

Health departments, along with police, fire, and sanitation departments, are fundamental to the exercise of the state's police power. Indeed, most constitutions declare that the reason for government's existence is to provide for the *health,* safety, and welfare of the people.[9] The introductory memorandum should clearly indicate to the health *officer* that he or she is constitutionally and legislatively charged with the exercise of the police power. Simply put, the police power is the power to issue orders. In New York City, the breadth and depth of this authority is extraordinary and includes the powers to do the following:

- Regulate commercial and noncommercial activities as the Permit Issuing Official
- Issue Commissioner's Orders to abate environmental nuisances and, when not obeyed, to actually abate the nuisance and impose a lien on the offending premises
- Issue Commissioner's Orders to individuals to cease and desist from committing a nuisance, i.e., something dangerous to life or detrimental to health[a] and, if not complied with, to prosecute the person civilly or criminally
- Compel the attendance of witnesses and the production of records through the issuance of subpoenas in any matter before the health officer, including to subpoena records necessary to the conduct of an epidemiologic investigation
- Isolate individuals, quarantine premises, and even detain persons who present a danger of transmitting disease to others

These sorts of police powers, which have long protected the health of the populace, are reserved to the states by the Tenth Amendment to the federal Constitution because they have not been delegated to the federal government. However, since September 11, 2001, concerns about the threat of bioterrorism or of naturally occurring infectious diseases, such as severe acute respiratory syndrome (SARS) or pandemic influenza, have increasingly made traditional public health activities, such as isolation and quarantine or even disease surveillance, appear as national security matters. In recognizing that national security falls squarely within the federal government's jurisdiction, counsel and the practitioner should be aware of and sensitive to these areas of increasing jurisdictional blurring, with their potential for confusion and unintended consequences.

For example, in the area of disease surveillance and public health investigations, state and local health departments have established relationships with the disease-reporting community of hospitals and laboratories. They are struggling mightily to build trust and encourage the rapid reporting of unusual manifestations of disease, which often are mere suspicions and case-by-case judgment calls, particularly on the part of infectious disease personnel in hospitals. (Only an alert reporter will recognize a fever and a rash as a possible case of smallpox or recognize flu-like symptoms as possible inhalational anthrax.) Local authorities, exercising their extraordinary public health investigative police powers, quickly can investigate potentially threatening occurrences and ascertain the existence (or nonexistence) of outbreaks. The federal government, through its public health or law enforcement agencies, also might have a legitimate need to know and to investigate public health occurrences that may have national security or other clearly federal implications. However, if the federal government were to initiate unilateral epidemiologic investigations without the involvement of state and local public health authorities, confusion and possible irreparable harm to the local reporting relationship easily could result, particularly if the federal response turns out to be unwarranted. Working together, lawyers and practitioners at different levels of government, or in different jurisdictional spheres (such as public health and law enforcement), can avoid these pitfalls by fashioning agreements for information sharing and joint investigations, if necessary, thereby preserving an appropriate balance of police powers. Such an agreement was entered into between New York City and the federal government in 2004.[10]

The Rulemaking Power of Boards of Health and Health Officers; Overview of Boards of Health

States mandate and outline the authority of health agencies within their jurisdiction. Other state mandates define the roles and responsibilities of the governing bodies for health agencies. In most states, the governing body is called the board of health. Approximately 3,186 local boards of health and approximately 20 state boards of health exist in the United States.

Boards of health often provide a vital link in the public health system—boards of health represent the public in public health. In many cases, board of health members are citizen volunteers committed to enhancing and achieving the public health goals and objectives that will make their communities safer and healthier places in which to live. Most local boards of health are affiliated with a local health department that serves jurisdictions comprising either counties or townships. They perform multiple functions, including some combination of advisory, governance, and policymaking. Specific responsibilities of most boards of health include recommending public health policies; proposing, adopting and enforcing public health regulations; approving health department budgets; and approving the strategic plan developed by and for their health department. Usually, board of health oversight includes environmental health programs; some also may oversee mental health programs.

The composition of boards of health varies according to the dictates of the governing statutes. Most local boards of health have three to seven members; these members can be elected, appointed, or both, but usually are appointed. To set the stage for a successful board appointment, the individuals responsible for appointing board members should fully understand the roles and responsibilities of board members and should communicate these directives to candidates before their appointment. Once members are appointed, formal orientation and ongoing education and training are essential to provide the tools needed. Boards of health are the liaisons between the health department and the communities being served. Ideally, they work cohesively with the director of the health department to improve health outcomes for their constituents.

The New York City Board of Health

Boards of health, like legal advisors, may follow different models and have varying roles and functions. In New York State, Article 3 of the New York State Public Health Law sets forth the powers and duties of local health officers and of local boards of health. The state law also provides for the State Health Commissioner to exercise general supervision over local health officers and boards of health. However, as with many other parts of the state Public Health Law, Article 3 itself specifies that its provisions, except for one section, do not apply in New York City. The laws establishing the New York City Board of Health—which first met on April 3, 1805—and providing for its appointment, composition, jurisdiction and authority are found in Chapter 22 of the New York City Charter. The Board currently comprises 11 members. The City Commissioner of Health is the ex officio chair. Of the other 10 members, 5 must be physicians with at least ten years' experience in specified fields; the other 5 must have at least a master's degree in certain fields such as environmental, biologic, veterinary, physical, or behavioral science and at least ten years' experience in those fields. They are appointed by the mayor with the advice and consent of the local legislature for a six-year term and serve without compensation.

The Board is not the governing body of the Department of Health and Mental Hygiene and does not approve its budget. Rather, the board is a body of experts whose main function is to enact the New York City Health Code. The Board of Health may embrace in the Health Code all matters and subjects within the jurisdiction of the Department. The Board of Health also can declare a state of great and imminent peril and, with the approval of the mayor, take such measures and order the Department to take such actions as it deems necessary to protect the public health, including taking over buildings to use as temporary hospitals. However, this authority is somewhat redundant with the governor's and the mayor's authorities to declare states of emergency under state law. Finally, the Board acts in a quasi-judicial capacity with authorization to hear appeals from certain commissioner of health decisions, such as permit denials or revocations. The traditional role for most boards, however, is to promulgate a health code. We focus here on this latter function.

The Quasi-Legislative Function

An initial memorandum from counsel should explain to the public health practitioner the parameters of the authority vested in the particular jurisdiction's board of health and how that authority differs from the practitioner's inherent authority to promulgate rules. Commissioner's regulations generally fill in the details necessary to implement a state or local law. However, a board of health enactment, depending on the nature of the board's underlying authority, may have a vastly different force and effect. Extensively elaborating in the memorandum on the role of a board and illustrating its value to the practitioner may be worthwhile.

In New York City, the Board of Health has been accorded the ability to legislate in the area of health through the promulgation of the Health Code, which to some extent has the force and effect of state law and otherwise may be viewed as equivalent to a local law.[11] The force and effect of state law may result from either the state legislature enacting or amending the City Charter directly or from the fact that a state law may exempt the city from its application. (The parallel to local law stems from several provisions of the Charter and is discussed in more detail below.) The courts long ago found this extraordinary delegation of legislative authority to be constitutional as a time-honored exception to the principle that the power to legislate cannot be delegated.[12] The rationale for the delegation is that public health requires the exercise of professional and expert judgment and that it often needs to be exercised more quickly than what a typical city council or state legislative process would permit. The result is that similar boards of health can swiftly enact provisions that have greater force and effect than mere regulations. Counsel should impress on the practitioner the opportunity that such a board presents as a tool to protect the health of the public.

Health officers might choose to accomplish their goals by administrative regulations, which most agency heads have the authority to promulgate, rather than by working through their board of health. However, this approach carries several risks. First, an administrative regulation generally needs specific enabling legislation. A commissioner's regulation that cannot demonstrate its enabling source risks being easily challenged. In contrast, when a board has broad legislative power, no specific enabling legislation is necessary in a particular case before action can be taken. In effect, the above-cited New York City Charter's legislative delegation is the enabling authority for all of the board's Health Code enactments. This principle is not as arcane as it may appear. For example, during the 1990s, New York City wanted to codify the ability of domestic partners, legally registered as such, to have the same rights as spouses. The concept applied to many aspects of life, requiring the local legislature, known as the City Council, to amend many local laws and other affected agencies to change regulations. However, because it needed no enabling legislation, the New York City Board of Health quickly was able to change the Health Code to put domestic partners on the same priority footing as spouses with regard to claiming the bodies of deceased loved ones and the issuance of burial permits.[13]

A second risk associated with the use of a commissioner's regulation, rather than board of health enactments, is that the courts generally grant greater deference and weight to the provisions of the Health Code than to commissioner's regulations.[14] Some proposals need to be enacted by a board, rather than by a commissioner, because they need the greater authority and deference to survive legal challenge. For example, if a board of health has the authority to enact laws requiring reporting of individualized medical information to the health officer for surveillance purposes, then the law should be at a level sufficient to establish the confidentiality of that information. In our view, such a confidentiality provision should be at least a board of health enactment, if not a statute. However, it should not be the subject of a mere administrative regulation, as such a rule will most likely not be sufficient, for example, to form the basis for a motion to quash a judge-signed subpoena seeking the inappropriate disclosure of confidential information.

Furthermore, the confidentiality of public health information should be the province of at least a board of health enactment, not of a commissioner's regulation, to better protect such information from the incursions of "data snoopers" using freedom of information laws (FOIL). A somewhat subliminal principle that underlies much of public health is that individualized health information, once reported to the health officer, should be accorded a higher level of confidentiality than that accorded the same information in the hospital or physician's office. If a physician believes that public health reporting may result in the compromise of his or her patient's confidentiality (or, to use FOIL terminology, invasion of the patient's personal privacy), then the physician may be less willing to report completely and promptly.

The centralized, population-wide nature of public health information makes health agencies an increasingly attractive target of data miners and information manipulators. Parenthetically, by obtaining supposedly de-identified information (i.e., apparently redacted of personal identifiers), it also is possible, through the use of other easily available data bases, to link "de-identified" information to an individual.[15] Therefore, a reporting requirement established by a board of health should be associated with a provision that addresses the confidentiality of that information, such as a provision specifying the information will not be disclosed even with the consent of the subject of the report, that it will not be subject to disclosure under FOIL, or that disclosures under FOIL will be limited to aggregated data. However, depending on the language of a particular state's information laws, even a board of health enactment might not be sufficient to adequately protect individualized medical information, and a state law might be required.[16]

The Line between a Board of Health and a Local Legislature

Counsel also should advise the health officer about the limits of a board of health's jurisdiction. Although no bright line separates the authority of a city council from that of a board of health with regard to public health regulations, the following analysis as it relates to New York City also may illustrate similar dichotomies in other jurisdictions.

The government of New York City, like that of many other municipalities, is modeled on the tripartite distribution of powers among the three branches of government: executive, legislative, and judicial.[17] Despite this functional separation, the Court of Appeals has recognized that "the duties and powers of the legislative and executive branches cannot be neatly divided into isolated pockets."[18] Many public health-related matters may be common to the powers and authority of both the City Council and the Board of Health.[19] "Public health" is not an easily defined term; the scope of what may be considered "public health," is constantly evolving. For example, sanitation, water supply and quality, and public hospital administration were core public health functions in past decades; most are now the purview of other agencies. The difficulty in reconciling the relative jurisdictions of the Board of Health and of the City Council regarding authority to enact health regulations is reflected in the New York City Charter Revision Commission Report (dated August 17, 1936), which provides that "the charter, effective January 1, 1938, is intended to confer 'extraordinary' and 'plenary' powers of legislators for the protection of health upon the Board of Health." The courts have quoted from the report to support the Board's authority, pointing out that the report states that "[t]he Board of Health exercises extraordinary police powers affecting the health of the city. By its power to adopt a Sanitary Code the Board has plenary powers of legislation."[20] Cases also cite the report to buttress the role of the City Council, acknowledging that the report stated: "The Council is the legislative body and is vested with the entire legislative power of the City."[21]

We can reasonably postulate that certain areas of public health regulation are exclusively within the domain of the New York City Board of Health and for which only the Board would be authorized to enact health regulations. Examples of such areas are the control of communicable diseases and requirements concerning the detention of noncompliant patients with tuberculosis (TB). These areas of public health regulation constitute the essence of a health department's role.[22,b]

An assessment of the appropriateness of a law enacted by the City Council rather than by the Board of Health shows that, in vesting the City Council with legislative authority, the City Charter stipulates that the Council may enact only local laws that are not inconsistent with the charter.[23] Legislative action taken by the City Council in certain areas (e.g., those identified above) would be inconsistent with the Charter by usurping the authority vested in the Board of Health. For example, the Council could pass a law limiting the number of swimming pools or restaurants within a geographic area but could not specify the temperature at which hot foods must be maintained in a restaurant because that probably would be the prerogative of the Board of Health.

For other areas, such as domestic violence, in New York City and probably other places as well, both the Board and the City Council could have jurisdiction. The Board of Health clearly would have authority to issue regulations in this area. If the City Council wished to enact a local law addressing domestic violence, such legislation also would seem to be appropriate. If, however, the Board of Health amended the Health Code with regard to domestic violence in a manner that was stricter than a local law enacted by the City Council, then the Health Code provision would take precedence. That is, if the City Council proposed legislation regarding a public health matter not exclusively vested in the Board of Health, then the Board would continue to be authorized to impose more stringent requirements at its discretion. To hold otherwise would be inconsistent with and impede the required and statutory mission of the New York City Department of Health.[21] (As of July 1, 2002, the former New York City Department of Health became the New York City Department of Health and Mental Hygiene as a result of a merger with the city's former mental hygiene agency.) Furthermore, a decision to the contrary would be inconsistent with the Charter, which specifically grants the New York City Board of Health the authority to "publish additional provisions for security of life and health in the City. . . ."[11] The delegation of legislative authority to a board of health should not be taken for granted. Current legislators seem less inclined to cede such authority to a nonelected body, such as a board of health. The line between public health policy, which should be the province of a board of health, and social engineering, which should be a legislative prerogative, has never been clear. Examples of such issues are whether requirements for window guards in multiple dwellings where children reside should be set forth in a health code; whether the board should determine the degree of abatement necessary to render a lead paint hazard safe; and whether prohibiting smoking in restaurants is more appropriate for the legislature because it affects broader social and economic policies. Myriad similar issues exist about which counsel can provide only advice, and not definitive answers, on the basis of applicable statutes and case law.[24] Even though public health practitioners must understand the principles underlying such questions, the legislature and the Board of Health also must be attuned to these matters so that they both can act effectively without interfering with one another.

Overlapping Jurisdictions: The Example of Lead

One example of the difficulty of sorting out the overlapping jurisdictions of a local legislature, such as the New York City Council, and a board of health is the class action suit involving lead abatements in multiple dwellings. Although this case involved many issues, the key point regarding counsel's advice to the public health practitioner concerns a direct inconsistency between the city's Administrative Code, enacted by the City Council, and the Health Code.

For many years, the Health Code had defined lead-based paint as interior paint containing 0.5% metallic lead or more and that a reading on an x-ray fluorometer of 0.7 micrograms of lead per square centimeter ($\mu g/cm^2$) would be deemed the equivalent of 0.5%. In 1981, the City Council amended the part of the city's Administrative Code known as the Housing Maintenance Code to create a lead-abatement mechanism in multiple dwellings where children aged 6 years or younger resided. The Council defined lead-based paint in a similar manner to the Board by using the 0.5% by weight or the 0.7 $\mu g/cm^2$ lead standard. Although the Administrative Code did not mention whether intact, rather than peeling, paint was a hazard, a court in the course of the litigation had required the abatement of intact lead-based paint. In 1996, the Board of Health focused on two points that were particularly within its field of expertise: (1) the x-ray fluorometer machine was not reliable at readings of less than 1.0 $\mu g/cm^2$, and (2) disturbing intact lead-based paint in the course of abatement was more hazardous for children than abating the peeling or damaged paint only. Therefore, the Board amended the Health Code by changing the definition of lead-based paint to reflect the 1.0 $\mu g/cm^2$ threshold and by requiring abatement only when the health department found lead-based paint that was peeling; on a window friction surface; or on any surface where a hazard exists because of the paint's condition, location, or accessibility to children.

The Board's determination created a direct contradiction between the Health Code and Administrative Code. The court, in an unpublished order, struck down the Health Code amendment on the ground that it violated the Administrative Code provisions. The city appealed this ruling, vigorously defending the Board's authority. By then, however, the 15-year-old class action suit was so mired in other issues that the appeal was denied with no mention of the relative authority of the two legislative bodies.[25] Subsequently, the City Council passed Local Law 38 of 1999, amending the Administrative Code in a manner that adopted the Board of Health's position relative to not disturbing intact lead-based paint and as to the 1.0 $\mu g/cm^2$ threshold. The litigation continued with the courts nullifying that law on unrelated grounds; but its successor, Local Law 1 of 2004, retained the Board of Health's position on these two points.

In an area as unique and sensitive as this, another important function of a legal advisor to a health department is to educate the litigating attorney—whether it be a corporation counsel or an attorney general—for who delegated legislative authority is counterintuitive, with regard to the extraordinary authority of a board of health. Such an effort will assist in providing a vigorous defense to uphold this fundamental and necessary legislative power vested in some boards of health.

Modernizing Public Health Powers: Detention for Tuberculosis Control

Counsel should help the health officer understand that the fundamental public health laws that constitute a public health agency's statutory framework are usually among the oldest in the annals of state and local laws and must be interpreted carefully. In some respects, such laws may seem overly vague, but they may need to be left alone to provide the health officer with the flexibility and authority to act. For example, the ability to order an individual or an entity to cease and desist from committing or maintaining a nuisance and to order the abatement and correction of the nuisance is crucial. Given the broad definition of a nuisance, one might be tempted to seek specificity. However, establishing an all-encompassing list of specific public health nuisances is not possible. Efforts to attempt to define a health nuisance more specifically than "anything that is dangerous to life or detrimental to health" most likely would limit the health officer's ability to protect the public from some unforeseen risks.

Nevertheless, the broad authority conferred by these statutes must be exercised with restraint and with due consideration, particularly when individual civil liberties need to be limited for the public's health and safety. And, in some cases, they may require updating to strengthen the public health infrastructure. These principles are illustrated through a review of how the city reacted to an epidemic of drug-resistant TB during the early 1990s. This case study demonstrates how law can assist the public health practitioner's efforts to protect the public in a manner that safeguards it against the arbitrary and capricious use of the police power. It also illustrates how both the practitioner and counsel can fully engage the communities affected by a proposed public health intervention in the context of rulemaking.

For many years, New York City's Health Commissioner had the authority—on determining that the health of others is endangered by a case, contact, or carrier of a communicable disease—to order such an individual to be removed and detained in a hospital.[26] However, although a detained patient could, in theory, petition the Commissioner for release and file a writ of habeas corpus in the courts, the patient had no meaningful way to access an attorney. Section 11.55 of the New York City Health Code contained none of the protections that one associates with modern concepts of due process in the context of civil detention.

In addition, the necessity of completion of treatment to control the epidemic became clear. This recognition led to the innovative program of directly observed therapy (DOT). However, options were unclear for those with noninfectious TB and a history of noncompliance with traditional therapy or DOT. Modern concepts of due process held that, to sustain civil detention, an individual had to constitute a clear and present danger to others. At first blush, patients with noninfectious TB might appear to present no immediate danger to others. Discussions catalyzed by the counsel's office at the city health department ensued and included representatives of the New York Civil Liberties Union, the city's Corporation Counsel, and others.

The process was one of mutual education not without points of serious contention. One area of initial disagreement involved the ability of a health commissioner (rather than a judge) to order someone detained. Ultimately, the practicalities of the situation prevailed; allowing an individual leave a hospital and petition a court for a detention order, only to then have to find and seize the person, simply was not practical. Another area of contention involved the government's right to civilly detain a noninfectious person until completion of therapy, particularly when such therapy could last 6–24 months or longer. This option seemed counterintuitive to many who were grounded in the due process principles of least-restrictive alternatives and the need for clear and convincing evidence of imminent danger.

However, dialogue led to recognition that public health is preventive. This idea was illustrated by the well-recognized, although still-challenged, right to exclude unvaccinated children from school. Such children do not present a danger to others until they become infected by and are contagious with a vaccine-preventable disease. Yet, because the great majority of children must be vaccinated if the community is to be protected, the proposition that unvaccinated persons present a risk to the public is accepted. Similarly, because a person with noninfectious active TB who does not complete therapy can, at any time, relapse into infectiousness and possibly transmit a drug-resistant strain, the argument held that such a person constitutes a current and significant threat to the public health.

The result was a Health Code enactment by the New York City Board of Health that allowed for Commissioner-ordered detention of patients with either infectious or noninfectious TB. The provision (New York City Health Code §11.47), which is limited to TB, also incorporates many due process protections, such as requiring the department to seek a court order within three business days of a request for release by the detained person. The patient cannot be held for more than 60 days without a court order, regardless of whether he or she has requested release. The detained person has a right to be represented by counsel and, on request of the person, the city must provide and pay for counsel. In a related resolution, the Board of Health found that patients who fail to adhere to their prescribed course of TB treatment constitute a public health nuisance.[c] Section 11.47 has survived legal challenge and has been upheld at the appellate level.[27]

Although Section 11.55, applicable to other communicable diseases, remained on the books in its antiquated fashion for a number of years, it too was amended in a similar manner and with a similarly inclusive process during 2003 in the midst of the SARS outbreak. These changes demonstrate how a fundamental public health police power such as detention still can be exercised practically, with due restraint and safeguards, and how a law can be updated to strengthen the public health infrastructure.

The Role of Counsel to a Public Health Agency

An attorney to a health department needs to be experienced in the distinct field of public health law. The concepts of public health law may be known to some lawyers, particularly academicians, but public health law is not a field of law practiced outside of government. Furthermore, as demonstrated in the preceding discussions, it is broad and complicated. Therefore, expertise in the practice comes only from years of work in the field itself—meaning that the health commissioner or the chief counsel (hereinafter "counsel") would be well advised to hire attorneys at entry-level positions to develop their exposure to the breadth and depth of the practice over time. Such development and expertise will enhance the ability of an attorney to render accurate legal advice spontaneously at a meeting. Finally, because a counsel's office relates to every part of the agency and often is involved in the most pressing issues at a high policy level, the role of counsel often evolves to include that of the institutional memory. The value of institutional memory should be considered in regard to attorney hiring, retention, and development practices.

As any public health practitioner knows, many crucial decisions are made quickly in response to an emergent situation. Whether that situation is an outbreak of communicable disease or an immediately dangerous environmental health risk, rarely does sufficient time exist to ask for a legal opinion if a question arises about the legality of a particular public health intervention. In times of crisis, which are invariably frequent, access to a knowledgeable public health lawyer is necessary. To ensure immediate access to such, an attorney should be available in house.

The role of in-house counsel should not be confused with that of a private lawyer to the public health practitioner. As a government lawyer, counsel's duty as a matter of legal professionalism is to report wrongdoing. Therefore, the limits of attorney-client privilege should not be crossed or compromised. For example, if a practitioner finds himself or herself the target of an Inspector General investigation, the practitioner should not ask counsel to represent him or her at a sworn interview before the investigators. Fortunately, such complications rarely, if ever, intrude into the relationship.

The day-to-day operational interactions between counsel and the various public health practitioners within a health department are numerous and varied. They involve many kinds of legal skills, activities, and areas for which legal counsel is required. The remainder of this section illustrates counsel's role in several key functional areas.

Legal Advisor

The core function of counsel is to provide legal advice and to render legal opinions. Typically, this function involves two kinds of activities: (1) participating in policy planning discussions and (2) researching and providing legal opinions. In a narrow but important sense, the role of a lawyer at a policy meeting is to advise on matters such as the agency's legal authority to undertake a particular course of action, the exposure to liability inherent in the action or intervention, and the procedural requisites involved.

Policy meetings can be challenging in that focusing on the line between legal advice and programmatic direction is sometimes difficult. In addition to the role of advising on whether something can be done, the risks associated therewith, and the legal requirements for doing it, lawyers often are asked for advice on which course of action to take. This can be a slippery and perhaps dangerous road. Ideally, the practitioner with decision-making responsibility will know and be sufficiently confident to set forth what needs to be done. Certainly a practitioner can ask a high-ranking attorney for a policy recommendation from among possibilities. However, asking an open-ended question about what should be done in a particular situation is another matter entirely and can too easily result in inappropriate transfer of decision-making authority. For example, a public health practitioner might ask about dealing with mold in an apartment that is a potential health risk, and the lawyer might reply that the practitioner can issue a vacate order. The practitioner then should weigh in with his or her own professional judgment about whether the health risk warrants that kind of intervention or whether a more appropriate remedy (e.g., bleaching the walls) exists that would adequately mitigate an immediate danger. Without such an exchange, there is a danger that the lawyer's initial advice will be blindly accepted without benefit of the practitioner's independent technical assessment, especially if the query to the lawyer is by a lower echelon practitioner. Thus, counsel should be cognizant of situations where appropriate legal advice becomes inappropriate programmatic direction and decision-making.

The above word of caution is not intended to minimize the important role of policy advisor that counsel often plays. The point is to keep an eye on what is purely legal counsel and what may be considered sage advice. A relatively new iteration of the policy advisor role for counsel is found when counsel has an established place in the Incident Command Systems (ICSs) that many agencies have organized to more effectively respond to emergencies, such as bioterrorist threats. Counsel clearly can be useful in an emergency by, for example, pointing out the jurisdictional boundaries of the various responding agencies. However, in the midst of working through an emergency, high-level personnel are expected to contribute whatever skills or insight they may posses. Much like the public relations person who may be at the table because of his or her role in risk communication but whose advice is valued, counsel is there as both a legal and policy advisor.

Of course, not all legal questions can be answered on the spot. Many issues—such as the health officer's emergency powers or a physician's duty to warn his or her patient's contacts—are complex and evolving. Researching the applicable law and writing a legal opinion often are necessary to render legal advice adequately.

For several reasons, opinions should be requested in writing. First, a written request assists inquirers in determining whether they are asking a legal question or a programmatic one. Second, it creates a record that connects the question to the answer, thereby minimizing dangerous extrapolations of legal answers to fact patterns that were not contemplated when the answer was developed. Such unwarranted extrapolations can lead to mistakes and subsequent recriminations such as "Legal said it was okay." Maintaining a database of legal questions and answers also is advisable to facilitate future research. Past opinions in the database should be used only as a starting point and not as the absolute answer in every instance because statutory, regulatory, or common law changes might produce a different legal answer at a later time.

Although written and catalogued legal opinions approved by the chief legal officer are the ideal, today's fast-paced electronic world is making such organization difficult to achieve. Electronic mail makes legal advice accessible to all levels of public health practitioners because they can simply e-mail whichever attorney may strike their fancy. The perceived need for instantaneous legal feedback creates an expectation of, and a temptation to provide, "off-the-cuff" legal opinions without the benefit of legal research. Counsel must be vigilant to the danger of rendering quick—but wrong—advice and must caution subordinates to take the time to research when necessary.

A further point about attorney/client e-mail communications is that such communication in theory is entitled to the same confidentiality privileges as a written memorandum or oral advice. However, the technologic ease of wide distribution of e-mail communications can result in unintentionally making recipients privy to counsel's advice, with significant negative consequences. And although confidentiality notices have become standard practice on e-mail communications generally, both the client and the attorney should consider making special mention of confidentiality concerns in the e-mail message itself. For example, pointing out that a person who may have been copied on an "e-mail string" is not being copied in the attorney's response because that individual is outside the agency and not within the client's "zone of privilege" would be advisable.

Protector of Confidentiality

The public health practitioner needs to have broad and easy access to individualized medical and demographic information to protect the population at large. For example, statutes and regulations that authorize such access necessarily must be open ended to allow the practitioner conducting an epidemiologic investigation to demand more information than is initially required to be reported. However, the corollary to such broad authority is an increased obligation to protect such information. Of course, different levels of confidentiality apply to different kinds of information in the custody of a health department. In addition to the FOIL forays discussed above, counsel must be vigilant to subpoenas that seek protected information.

For example, the results of a lead hazard inspection of an apartment obviously would be readily available to the landlord of the dwelling, the tenant of the unit, or their attorneys. The blood lead level of a child residing therein would not be available to the landlord except with the consent of the tenant-parent or on the issuance of an appropriate subpoena. In New York State, the disclosure of confidential HIV information under circumstances not specified in the statute requires a specialized court order[28] and HIV-related information reported to the practitioner is accorded an even higher level of protection.[29,30] Sexually transmitted disease information in the custody of the health department, whether obtained through surveillance or through the provision of clinical services by the department, is protected similarly and not subject to disclosure by regular subpoena.[31] Obviously, the disclosure of information by a health agency is a complicated matter that requires the review, and often the intervention, of an attorney. Relevant, common activities for counsel include discussions with lawyers seeking information and with judges signing subpoenas and the development and arguing of motions to quash or motions for protective orders.

Compliance with the requirements of confidentiality is not a matter just for lawyers. Program staff and their supervising practitioners need to be trained in and familiar with the nuances of confidentiality to appropriately use and maintain the protected information. Because the laws that apply to public health information differ from those that govern clinical information in a hospital or physician's office, the training of personnel needs to be specialized and can be provided only by attorneys familiar with these principles and experienced in their application. This need underscores the importance of developing expertise in the distinct field of public health law within a health agency.

Another example of how confidentiality laws differ in a public health context can be found in the privacy rules developed pursuant to the federal Health Insurance Portability and Accountability Act of 1996. When the privacy rule first became effective in 2003, many entities covered by the rules, such as hospitals, doctors and laboratories, believed they no longer could report personal health information with identifiers to the health department. Substantial educational outreach was required to convince these covered entities that such was not the case. Indeed, the regulations contain specific provisions making it clear that the prohibitions on the disclosure of personal health information do not apply when disclosure of such is required by law, as is the case with public health surveillance laws, or when necessary for authorized public health activities such as epidemiologic investigations.[32]

Contracts

Increasingly, health departments are forming partnerships with medical and academic institutions for the delivery of clinical or research services, with community-based organizations for outreach and education, with technology companies for specialized software, or with other vendors for myriad activities and services, such as pesticide spraying to control mosquitoes to prevent arthropod-borne diseases. Although the process-related functions associated with contracting (e.g., ensuring competition through bids or requests for proposals) may be the province of non-legal procurement specialists, the drafting of contract language remains largely a legal function that is best met by attorneys within the health agency.

Historically, health-related services have not been easy to quantify, resulting in contracts that reimburse contractors for actual expenses. However, in recent years the philosophy of government contracting has shifted toward presumably more accountable approaches, such as performance-based contracting or outcome funding. Vendors, particularly community-based organizations with few resources and little familiarity with such approaches, need to be given a clear and early understanding of the contractual expectations. Negotiating and drafting such contracts in the "human services" arena require close collaboration between the attorney drafting the agreement and the departmental programs that need outside services.

As government downsizing continues, the need for outsourcing will increase. However, because a health department is a police power agency, it should be careful not to contractually vest a non-government entity with the police power. Sometimes keeping this bright line in focus is not easy. For example, in this era of electronic reporting, a health department might be tempted to contract with a company to electronically receive and sort mandated surveillance reports. Aside from issues of confidentiality, the line can become blurred if the contractor is assigned the responsibility to call a physician to advise him or her that the report was not complete and to *demand* additional information. Such a contract can be viewed as an unconstitutional delegation of the police power. In 1996, the U.S. Department of Defense gave considerable thought to the inappropriateness of contracting out "inherently governmental functions."[33]

Legislative and Regulatory Counsel

Public health practice often requires legislative or regulatory action. Topics covered vary from regulation of food and water to establishment of smoke-free workplaces. Future potential areas for legislative or regulatory action include food content, labeling, pricing, and marketing practices in the context of the epidemic of obesity; tobacco and alcohol taxation; advertising and sales restrictions on harmful products; and health-care delivery and financing policy.[34] A significant role for counsel is to ensure that health code changes or agency head rules are within the statutory authority of the health board or commissioner to adopt and that they are enacted in compliance with laws that dictate the procedures to be followed in the promulgation process. The following typical process illustrates an appropriate interaction between counsel and practitioner.

The practitioner (e.g., a program director or a deputy commissioner) prepares a Certificate of Necessity that describes the problem that needs to be addressed by rulemaking and the proposed solution and suggests the language of a proposed rule. The certificate then is transmitted to counsel's office for analysis of the statutory basis and legal viability of the proposal. Counsel then prepares a document setting forth the basis and purpose of the rule and the actual resolution language to be promulgated. After preliminary approval by the board or commissioner, the information is published, and notice of the proposal is provided to known interested parties (e.g., licensees or trade associations) to give them an opportunity to comment. Also, a public hearing may be held during which testimony may be taken. The proposal may be amended to reflect comments and then submitted to the board or commissioner for adoption. The final rule is then published. In addition, board of health meetings are subject to the Open Meetings laws. Counsel must ensure compliance with all of these procedural requisites.

Another function of counsel relative to legislation and regulations is to coordinate the agency's comments on legislation or regulations proposed at the federal or state level or by sister agencies. Such coordination may involve tracking and distribution of proposals within the agency, synthesizing various internal comments, and drafting the agency's position.

Enforcement

As previously mentioned, one of the basic ways a health agency exercises its police power is through issuance of valid and enforceable orders. These can take the form of commissioner's orders issued to TB patients who persistently do not adhere to therapy, compelling them to complete their medical regimen, or detention orders such as those issued in 2003, isolating two suspected SARS patients to hospitals in New York City. Or they can be subpoenas issued to a physician who refuses to disclose information necessary to an epidemiologic investigation. More typically, however, commissioners' orders are issued to landlords (or others in control of property or premises), requiring abatement of a health nuisance that presents a danger, or to restaurants, ordering cleanup or closure. Such orders can be standardized, as in the case of orders to abate peeling lead paint in an apartment in which a lead-poisoned child resides, to install window guards where a child aged 10 years or younger lives, or to clean a vacant lot strewn with garbage that provides harbor for rats. Individualized commissioner's orders also can be issued to others, such as a dry-cleaning establishment releasing dangerous fumes to adjoining residential units, to require cessation of operations until the activity can be safely conducted.

Drafting orders, whether standardized or individualized, requires close working relationships between the practitioner and the attorney. The issuance of an order should be taken seriously. Program experts should be clear on the existence of a danger. The practitioner should direct the attorney drafting an order regarding the appropriate remedy to be required—for example, whether a lead hazard should be abated by wet-scraping and repainting, by encapsulation, or by complete removal are scientific or technical, not legal, decisions necessitating professional public health judgment combined with environmental and engineering input. Once the practitioner articulates the nature of the danger and the means of abatement, the attorney can draft an order that provides adequate notice to the subject of the order.

Due process usually requires an opportunity to be heard, although the opportunity need not be a full-scale hearing. Such a requirement can be met by affording the subject of an order the ability to call or appear before a supervising practitioner, such as an assistant commissioner, to challenge the scientific underpinnings of the order or to dispute ownership or control of the offending premises. Training by, and consultation with, an attorney is useful to make the opportunity to be heard fair and meaningful.

Issuance of an order is many times the beginning of an arduous process to achieve compliance. Follow-up inspections to ascertain compliance are necessary. If no action has been taken, a notice of violation may be issued that charges the responsible party with disobeying a commissioner's order and with maintaining a nuisance, requiring appearance before an administrative tribunal and resulting in the possible imposition of a fine. Some nuisances, however, are too dangerous to leave at that, for a fine is not abatement and does not by itself render a dangerous situation safe. Therefore, an order may need to be executed by the health agency directly or through another government agency. For example, a lot providing a rat harborage or with conditions conducive to water accumulations and mosquito breeding can be cleaned by the health department or, if heavy equipment is necessary, by the sanitation department. In New York City, lead hazards are corrected and window guards are installed by the housing agency. These other units of government act as agents of the health officer in the execution of proper orders. The cost of the abatement work performed by the health agency and its agents is calculated and, pursuant to provisions of several local laws (enacted by the city council) that are specific to the authority of the health department, a tax lien is imposed on the premises.[35]

Sometimes access to offending premises is not possible without breaking down an obstruction such as a fence. When a condition does not rise to the level of an imminent health hazard necessitating an immediate intervention, New York City seeks access warrants from the courts to forcibly gain entry for inspecting or abating these types of conditions. All these activities attendant to the issuance and enforcement of orders require close interaction between the program and legal staffs of a health agency.

Institutional Review Board

To ensure that research involving living persons is subjected to an ethical review that evaluates the risks and benefits associated with a proposed study, the federal government and some states require that institutions engaging in such human subjects research establish review boards, called institutional review boards (IRBs) or human research review committees.[36,37] In addition to determining whether the potential benefit of the research to "generalizable" knowledge outweighs the risk that may be associated with it, one of the primary functions of an IRB is to ensure an appropriate informed consent process is used when necessary.[38] The role of an IRB Chair is to lead the board in its mission. Often the Chair is called on to make independent judgments without the benefit of a full-board review, such as when determining whether certain research is exempt or can be expedited.[39] To determine whether research is worth the risk, some understanding of the science underlying the research is necessary, and some ability to distinguish good science from bad is useful. These determinations do not require legal judgments as much as scientific and ethical ones.

Most institutions that engage in human subjects research, whether they are medical, academic or some other kind of entity, do not have the chair or the office of the IRB report to counsel. However, one exception is the New York City Department of Health and Mental Hygiene, where the IRB has reported to counsel's office since 2002. At least two reasons support such an organizational structure. First, in a public health agency, unlike medical or academic institutions, an issue that often comes up is whether a particular matter is a public health practice activity, for which IRB review is not applicable, or whether it is human subjects research requiring IRB approval.[40] One of the prime determinants of what constitutes a public health activity is whether it is mandated or authorized by law.[41,42] Such a determination does necessitate some legal expertise. Although it may seem counterintuitive, the fact is that what may be research if conducted by a medical institution or laboratory could be an epidemiologic investigation and a public health activity if conducted by a public health authority. For example, during and after the blackout of 2003, the health department in New York City reviewed the medical records of emergency department visits to ascertain whether an outbreak of foodborne illness resulted from people eating spoiled food. If a private researcher wanted to undertake such an analysis, IRB review and approval would have been necessary. However, because a health officer has an affirmative obligation to ascertain the existence of outbreaks,[43] the exercise constituted public health practice, which did not require IRB review.

Second, the day-to-day function of an IRB is to some extent legalistic. All IRB members, and particularly IRB chairs, need to have an intimate working understanding of the federal and state laws and regulations governing human subjects research. For example, deciding that a particular research protocol can be deemed exempt research, or that its review can be expedited, and capable of being approved by the Chair alone without full board review, requires a finding that the research falls within one or more categories specified in the federal regulations and documentation of the specific applicable subdivision(s).[44] Easy access to legal advice, indeed perhaps legal supervision, often is useful to correctly determine and document the appropriate regulatory provision. However, counsel must take care not to cross the line from administrative and legal supervision to inappropriate interference into scientific and ethical determinations.

Conflicts of Interest

Among government agencies, health departments in particular have a high percentage of professional staff with a concomitant high degree of outside interests. For example, some may be medical doctors with positions at area hospitals or doctors of public health teaching at universities, others may sit on boards of directors of health-related organizations, and some may collaborate with outside entities in the conduct of research. All these raise conflicts with regard to potential misuse of "city time" or, of greater concern, relative to relationships with entities that do business with the city or department. To help staff avoid difficulties after unknowingly entering into questionable activities, counsel can act as an advisor and a liaison to a central authority such as a conflicts of interest board. Employees can request approval from the agency head and, if necessary, from the central board. Counsel advises the agency head about the propriety of the activity.

Disciplinary Matters

Counsel also may be responsible for investigating and prosecuting wrongdoing by agency employees, other than criminal or corrupt behavior that usually is within the jurisdiction of an inspector general. Such allegations may relate to time and leave abuse, incompetent performance, insubordination, fights, arguments, or harassment.

If the allegations are borne out, charges are brought against an employee who, by virtue of civil service status or contractual rights, is entitled to be served with charges and afforded a hearing to determine whether he or she should be terminated, suspended, or fined. Legal staff will work closely with the inspector general in situations of overlapping jurisdiction, with the employee's supervisory chain of authority and the human resources department and will represent the agency in the prosecution of the charges before administrative bodies authorized to hear and determine such cases.

Human Rights Cases

Counsel's office, as representative of the agency, will investigate the matter when employees or other parties bring formal charges before the local, state, or federal human rights agencies accusing the department of unlawful discrimination, usually in the context of employment practices, or of condoning sexual harassment. If the charges are substantiated, the agency may settle the matter with the aggrieved party and may bring disciplinary charges against an employee who committed the wrongful act. If, after investigation, the charges are deemed to be inaccurate, agency legal staff will defend the department before the administrative human rights bodies. If these bodies find probable cause to believe that the allegations are true, or if the aggrieved party takes his or her claim to court, then the matter is turned over to the city's law department to represent the department in court.

Litigation Liaison

Except for perhaps motions to quash subpoenas, as discussed above, most internal counsel's offices—including that in New York City—do not engage in litigation. However, counsel's office is integrally involved as liaison to the litigating attorneys at the municipal Corporation Counsel's Office or Law Department. Whether the litigation is against the health agency—for example, as in the case of a coalition of plaintiffs suing to stop the city's spraying of pesticides to prevent West Nile virus infection—or the city is suing lead paint or tobacco manufacturers affirmatively, the legal staff at the health department serves various functions. In such cases, legal staff may facilitate the gathering of information from the agency that may be necessary to defend or prosecute the case or respond to discovery demands. In addition, staff may explain the nuances of public health law to the litigating attorneys, often conducting legal research, for example, as discussed above in relation to lead litigation, explaining the authority of a board of health to the litigating and appellate lawyers. Counsel also explains the nuances of legal theories and strategies to the public health practitioner so that the client can be an active and informed participant in the litigation.

Conclusion

Law is fundamental to the practice of public health. Public health, at its most effective, changes social structures or contexts so that healthier behavior becomes the natural course of action and does not rely on exhortation or clinical intervention. Classical examples include mandates to chlorinate and fluoridate water, restrict unsafe housing, and require seat-belt use. Control of communicable disease outbreaks often requires mandatory reporting, examination, isolation, or exclusion from work of infectious persons. Control of vaccine-preventable diseases relies on mandatory school entry vaccination requirements. Vaccination requirements are in the interest of society but from the perspective of any one individual, being a "free rider" would be safer if all other people were vaccinated. Regulation of public facilities such as restaurants, beaches, and daycare facilities can establish a basic level of safety. Focused legal action can control specific health problems with interventions ranging from taxation of tobacco and alcohol to restriction of the places where tobacco can be consumed or alcohol purchased. Oversight of medical-care institutions can include mandates to increase the effectiveness of preventive interventions. Public health is often in the position of taking action that discomfits a small number of people, for the greater good of society. Ensuring that the smaller number of people who oppose public health action can be compelled to comply, yet have adequate recourse against arbitrary and capricious implementation, requires a careful legal balancing act.

The legal advisor must caution the practitioner to exercise public health authority with restraint in relation to the possible primacy of other units of government. Potential exists for overlap between health departments and other agencies, at both the state and local levels, such as departments of environmental protection with regard to environmental and chemical hazards, departments of sanitation relative to rodent or vector control, and housing agencies concerned with lead paint. Therefore, the fundamental, jurisdiction-setting public health statutes cannot be read as a simple list of absolute mandates, but rather should be viewed as an aggregation of the areas where the health officer can act. For example, a health officer always will have the authority to control and abate public health nuisances, generally accepted to be anything that is dangerous to life or detrimental to health. However, even the simplest act or condition can be converted into a public health issue by, for example, asking whether it is safe. If other agencies have greater primacy, then the health officer may not need to act. However, if other agencies do not have the authority or the resources to implement the appropriate remedy, then the health department's participation may be brought in to ensure the public's health.

The interaction between the public health practitioner and legal counsel is as broad and deep as the field of public health. The practice of public health is inextricably tied to law because so much of the health officer's powers, functions, and duties are founded in law. The requirements of law in public health practice represent a distinct specialty practiced only within a health agency, and expertise in the field can be developed only from within. The day-to-day role of counsel to a health agency touches every aspect of the practice of public health. Understanding and appreciating the role of law in the practice of public health will help a practitioner better achieve the agency's mission of protecting the public's health.

We thank Roslyn Windholz, Deputy General Counsel, New York City Department of Health and Mental Hygiene, for her many years of research into the history of the

New York City Board of Health's authority. We also thank Marie Fallon, Executive Director of the National Association of Local Boards of Health, for her assistance with the overview of boards of health and other contributions.

Notes

a. The New York City Administrative Code, §17-142, defines a public health nuisance as follows: "The word 'nuisance' shall be held to embrace public nuisance, as known at common law or in equity jurisprudence; whatever is dangerous to human life or detrimental to health; whatever building or erection, or part or cellar thereof, is overcrowded with occupants, or is not provided with adequate ingress and egress to and from the same or the apartments thereof, or is not sufficiently supported, ventilated, sewered, drained, cleaned, or lighted in reference to its intended or actual use; and whatever renders the air or human food or drink, unwholesome. All such nuisances are hereby declared illegal."

b. "The protection from a disease which actually exists and kills a number of persons each year is a *function of the board of health*" (emphasis added).

c. See notes to 24 RCNY §11.47.

References

1. New York State Public Health Law, §201.
2. New York State Public Health Law, §206.
3. New York City Charter, §555. Available at http://www.nyc.gov/html/charter/downloads/pdf/citycharter2004.pdf. Accessed October 19, 2005.
4. New York City Charter, §556. Available at http://www.nyc.gov/html/charter/downloads/pdf/citycharter2004.pdf. Accessed October 19, 2005.
5. New York State Public Health Law, §204.
6. New York State Sanitary Code, 10 NYCRR, §2.6
7. New York City Health Code, 24 RCNY, §11.03(b).
8. Institute of Medicine, Committee for the Study of Future Health. *The Future of Public Health*. Washington, DC: National Academy Press, 1988.
9. New York State Constitution, Article XVII, §3.
10. Centers for Disease Control and Prevention. *Public Health Legal Preparedness Manual*. General Legal Materials. New York City [first mention]. Available at http://www2.cdc.gov/phlp/phlegalresponse.asp. Accessed November 8, 2005.
11. New York City Charter, §558.
12. *People v Blanchard*, 288 NY 145, 42 NE 2d 7 (1942).
13. New York City Health Code, 24 RCNY, §205.01(d).
14. *Grossman v Baumgartner*, 17 NY2d 345, 218 NE 2d 259 (1966).
15. Lane E. A question of identity—computer-based pinpointing of "anonymous" health records prompts calls for tighter security. *Newsday* 2000 (Nov 21):C8.
16. New York State Public Officers Law, Article 6.
17. *Kelly v Dinkins*, 155 Misc 2d 787, 590 NY S 2d 166 (1992).
18. *Bourquin v Cuomo*, 85 NY 2d 781, 652 NE 2d 171 (1995).
19. *Knoblauch v Warden of the Prison*, 216 NY 154, 110 NE 451 (1915) (which addressed the authority of the board of health and the board of aldermen—the body replaced by the city council).

20. *Paduano v City of New York*, 45 Misc 2d 718, 257 NYS 2d 531, 535 (1965), aff'd, 17 NY 2d 875, 218 NE 2d 339, 271 NYS 2d 305 (1966).
21. *LaGuardia v Smith*, 176 Misc 482, 27 NYS 2d 321, 325 (1941), aff'd, 288 NY 1 (1942).
22. *Knoblauch v Warden of the Prison*, 89 Misc 243, 245, 153 NYS 463 (1915).
23. New York City Charter, §28.
24. *Boreali v Axelrod,* 71 NY 2d 1, 523 NYS 2d 464 (1987).
25. *New York City Coalition to End Lead Poisoning et al v Giuliani*, 248, AD 2d 120 (1st Dept 1998).
26. New York City Health Code, 24 RCNY, §11.55. In 2003, this section was significantly amended.
27. *City of New York v Mary Doe*, 205 AD 2d 469, 614 NYS 2d 8 (1st Dept 1994).
28. New York Public Health Law, §2785.
29. New York Public Health Law, §2135.
30. New York State Health Department regulations, 10 NYCRR §63.4(c).
31. New York Public Health Law, §2306.
32. 45 CFR Subdivisions 164.512(a) and (b).
33. 48 CFR Subpart 7.5.
34. Frieden TR. Asleep at the switch: local public health and chronic disease. *Am J Public Health* 2004;94:2059–61.
35. New York City Administrative Code, §17-145 *et seq.*
36. 45 CFR Part 46.
37. New York Public Health Law, Article 24-A.
38. 45 CFR §46.111(a)(2).
39. 45 CFR §§46.101(b), 46.110, respectively.
40. Fleming DW. CDC Efforts to Protect Human Subjects Participants [memorandum]. Atlanta, GA: US Department of Health and Human Services, Public Health Service, Centers for Disease Control and Prevention, 2001 (June 8). Available at http://72.14.207.104/search?q=cache:UlTR2Nn0ywYJ:www.washington.edu/research/hsd/form.php%3Fid%3D7+Efforts+to+protect+Human+Subjects+participants&hl=en. Accessed November 8, 2005.
41. Centers for Disease Control and Prevention, Office of the Chief Science Officer. *Guidelines for Defining Public Health Research and Public Health Non-Research*. October 4, 1999. Accessed September 24, 2006. Available at http://www.cdc.gov/od/ads/opspoll1.htm.
42. Hodge JG Jr, Gostin LO, CSTE Advisory Committee. *Public Health Practice vs Research: A Report for Public Health Practitioners Including Cases and Guidance for Making Distinctions*. May 24, 2004. Available at http://www.cste.org/pdffiles/newpdffiles/CSTEPHResRptHodgeFinal.5.24.04.pdf. Accessed October 19, 2005.
43. New York State Sanitary Code, 10 NYCRR, §2.16.
44. 45 CFR §§46.101(b) and 46.110.

Chapter 9

FRONTLINE PUBLIC HEALTH: SURVEILLANCE AND FIELD EPIDEMIOLOGY

Verla S. Neslund,* Richard A. Goodman,* and James L. Hadler

Public health surveillance and field epidemiology—including investigation of disease outbreaks and clusters—are critical, basic functions carried out by public health agencies at local, state, and federal levels. Each of the 50 states operates and maintains public health surveillance systems, not only to monitor notifiable disease conditions caused primarily by infectious pathogens but also to monitor noninfectious disease conditions and public health indicators, such as behavioral risk factors for injuries and chronic conditions.[1,2] Along with the traditional collection and analysis of vital records, state-level surveillance forms the foundation for national-level surveillance systems, which may be coordinated by federal agencies such as the Centers for Disease Control and Prevention (CDC) and the National Institutes of Health.[1–3]

In addition to conducting surveillance, local, state, and federal public health agencies that are engaged in field epidemiology must be able to respond to disease threats by investigating the hundreds of outbreaks and disease clusters that occur in the United States each year. Outbreak response relies not only on the legal authorities necessary for public health agencies to conduct surveillance and, therefore, to detect such problems but also on the authorities and assurances required for carrying out the steps of an investigation and implementing appropriate control measures. Specifically, these legal authorities enable public health officials to obtain clinical specimens and data

* The findings and conclusions in this chapter are those of the author(s) and do not necessarily represent the views of the U.S. Department of Health and Human Services or the Centers for Disease Control and Prevention.

from persons affected by an outbreak; collect environmental samples; protect the privacy of information; conduct analytic studies (e.g., case-control or cohort studies) to test hypotheses about sources for pathogens and modes of spread; and implement and enforce control measures, such as vaccination, chemoprophylaxis, quarantine, or even seizure or destruction of property.

This chapter provides an overview of the legal issues relating to public health surveillance and field epidemiology. It discusses the general legal authorities for surveillance and public health investigations provided by the U.S. Constitution and by state laws; legal milestones in the evolution of public health surveillance, outbreak investigations, and disease control in the United States; and legal issues related to the collection, analysis, and dissemination of surveillance data. In addition, the chapter presents information about new surveillance challenges beyond traditional infectious disease models, including the influence of bioterrorism preparedness on surveillance activities. Related aspects of legal authorities and issues bearing on surveillance and public health investigations also are addressed in other chapters in this book, especially those covering criminal law (Chapter 6), foodborne diseases (Chapter 15), and sexually transmitted and bloodborne infections (Chapter 16).

General Legal Authorities for Surveillance and Public Health Investigations

Both federal and state governments have inherent powers to protect the public's health. Article 1, Section 8, of the U.S. Constitution authorizes Congress to impose taxes to "provide for the general [w]elfare of the United States" and to regulate interstate and foreign commerce. The Public Health Service (PHS) and CDC are examples of federal activities that may be generally supported by the authority of the Welfare Clause. Under the authority of the Commerce Clause of the Constitution, the federal government oversees such health-related activities as the licensing and regulation of drugs, biologic products, and medical devices. Although the provisions in the federal Constitution are broad, the activities of the federal government relating to health and welfare nonetheless must fit within the enumerated powers.

By contrast, the public health powers of a state are extensive, rooted in its inherent powers to protect the peace, safety, health, and general welfare of its citizens. The Tenth Amendment to the U.S. Constitution specifically reserves all powers not expressly granted to the federal government nor otherwise prohibited by the Constitution to the states. Unlike the federal government, the states have vast, sovereign authority, including public health powers that are not limited to specific constitutional provisions. The states' police powers include the intrinsic right to pass laws and to take other measures necessary to protect the citizenry. In many instances, states have delegated their public health responsibilities to county or municipal governments, which likewise exercise the state's broad authority to examine, treat, and in the case of certain contagious diseases, even to quarantine citizens to protect the public health. The state's public health laws include not only the established statutes of the state but also regulations, executive orders, and other directives from health authorities that may have the force of law.

The exercise of the states' police powers with respect to public health matters has limitations. The U.S. Constitution provides procedural safeguards to ensure the exercise of these powers is not excessive or unrestrained. The Fourth Amendment protects citizens from unlawful searches and seizures, and the Fifth Amendment prohibits the federal government from depriving any persons of life, liberty, or property without due process of law. The Fourteenth Amendment imposes similar due process obligations on states. Due process demands the government use even-handed and impartial procedures in exercising its police power. The basic elements of such due process include notice to the person involved, opportunity for a hearing or similar proceeding, and the right to representation by counsel. In addition, the exercise of the state's police power necessitates the principle of using the least restrictive alternative that would achieve the state's interest, particularly when the exercise involves limitations of the individual's personal liberty.

Public health surveillance systems in the United States are established as an exercise of the states' police powers. These state-based systems are designed for reporting of diseases and conditions of public health interest by health-care professionals and laboratories. State laws and regulations mandate the reporting by physicians and other specified entities of a list of diseases and conditions, as well as timing and nature of information to be reported, and may prescribe penalties for noncompliance with the reporting laws. Required disease reporting varies greatly among states and territories. In some states, disease reporting is mandated by statutes that have not been reviewed by legislatures in decades. Other states have general statutes that empower the health commissioner or state boards of health to create, monitor, and revise the list of reportable diseases and conditions.[4] Some states require reports under both statutes and health department regulations.[5]

Similar to the public health activities discussed above, the states' inherent powers to protect the public's health provide the general authority for laws and regulations that empower health officials to conduct epidemiologic investigations.[6,7] Although cooperation of institutions and individuals in epidemiologic investigations is usually voluntary, the intervention of state or local officials is within the scope of government legal authority. Furthermore, either specific legislation and/or the police power of the state provide the necessary authority to compel cooperation in such investigations in instances where individuals or institutions are reluctant to grant access to certain properties, records, or individuals associated with information essential to the investigation.

Outbreaks and epidemics are terms well known to the public, and problems for which the public expects aggressive responses. Regardless of the dimensions of any given outbreak, most health authorities employ a standard approach for investigating the problem. The goals of investigation are to provide a scientifically rational basis for identifying the source and for implementing measures to terminate the outbreak and to prevent recurrences in as timely a manner as possible.[8] The elements of a typical outbreak investigation highlight many of the basic functional activities used more generally for the control and prevention of reportable conditions. In addition, both outbreak investigations as overall exercises in disease control, and their component parts, invoke a multitude of legal issues.

The basic steps of an investigation are detecting and confirming the occurrence of an outbreak; identifying and characterizing cases; developing and testing hypotheses regarding potential explanations for the outbreak; and implementing control measures.[8,9] In addition to the legal authorities that both compel and enable health agencies to undertake such investigations, myriad related considerations exist regarding responsibilities and authorities for the individual elements of an investigation. Such considerations encompass the authorities necessary to obtain microbiology cultures and other laboratory specimens from hospitals and private laboratories; review patients' medical records kept in the offices of physicians, dentists, and other health-care providers; administer questionnaires to and collect specimens from persons affected in the outbreak, as well as unaffected persons who may be important sources of information for solving the outbreak; retain information about medical histories and laboratory results; protect confidentiality; and implement a variety of measures intended to control the immediate problem and prevent recurrences. Such measures may include the ongoing collection of additional data, recall of an implicated product, closure of a business or restriction of activities relating to the source of an outbreak, isolation or other forms of restriction of activities of affected persons, quarantine of exposed persons, vaccination of or administration of antibiotics to exposed groups, and even compulsory treatment of some individuals or groups with antibiotics and other medications.

A measles outbreak in Iowa in 2004 illustrates several of the response and control measure options employed by state public health agencies, including some relying even more directly on specific legal instruments and procedures.[10] In that outbreak, in which large numbers of persons in an insular community with low vaccination rates were exposed to measles-infected patients, the public health response included voluntary isolation of the patients, as well as offering post-exposure vaccination prophylaxis to exposed community members who were deemed susceptible. In addition, when some of those who potentially had been exposed to measles first refused post-exposure prophylaxis and then were unwilling to comply with voluntary quarantine, those persons were served with state-issued involuntary home quarantine orders by the local public health nurse, in some instances with the assistance of local law enforcement officers.[a] The health department monitored compliance with quarantine orders through daily, unannounced home visits or telephone calls.

Certain statutory provisions may be absolutely necessary for epidemiologists to complete critical steps of outbreak investigations. Accordingly, epidemiologists need to be aware of any state laws—including statutes or regulations—that could affect their ability to investigate an outbreak. For example, in one of the largest foodborne infectious disease outbreaks in U.S. history, the manufacturers of the implicated product (ice cream) agreed to disclose manufacturing and product distribution information only after Minnesota's public health legal counsel provided written confirmation of state statutory provisions protecting corporate trade secrets.[11] Similarly, in an investigation of an infectious disease outbreak involving meals served to passengers of an international airline, the airline disclosed flight manifests only after learning of the state health commissioner's subpoena power to obtain such data.[11]

The Role of Surveillance in Public Health

Public health surveillance is a cornerstone activity for virtually all public health programs and activities. Although the definition of public health surveillance has changed during the past century, the definition applicable to this discussion is the one first discussed by Alexander Langmuir in the 1960s.[12] Langmuir redefined surveillance as the ongoing, systematic collection of public health data with analysis and dissemination of results and interpretation of these data to those who contributed them and to all others who "need to know."[13] Accordingly, an effective surveillance system includes both the capacity for data collection and the ability to disseminate the data to persons who can undertake prevention and control activities.[14] The public health surveillance definition employed by CDC includes the concept of using the data for "planning, implementation, and evaluation of public health practice."[15]

Surveillance has played an especially vital role in the control and prevention of infectious diseases. For example, surveillance can be instrumental in detecting outbreaks of infectious diseases, then triggering the elements of an investigation, as described in the preceding section, and finally monitoring the long-term effectiveness of control measures put in place as a result of the investigation. In addition to the detection of epidemics, other examples of roles for surveillance systems in controlling infectious diseases include determining trends and risk factors for disease occurrence, evaluating the impact of control and prevention programs, monitoring the natural history of certain diseases, assessing more-slowly-occurring changes in the interactions between organisms and populations over time, and monitoring changes in the biology of infectious agents.

The collection of vital records and other data for public health surveillance and during epidemic investigations may involve a variety of legal issues and considerations, which also are relevant to information gathering necessary for other basic disease-control activities (e.g., surveys, special studies, and categorical disease-control programs). Increasingly, surveillance is used for investigating the range of conditions affecting health, including, for example, injuries, chronic diseases, environmental exposures, and maternal and child health activities.[12] The underlying issues attendant to data collection in these situations are balancing the need for access to medical and other records against individuals' interests in privacy through the imposition of strict limits on access (see also Chapter 10). These legal considerations, most of which are addressed by statutes or regulations, include protections available during and after investigations for records developed in relation to the investigation; special privacy provisions for medical and other information; and mandated reporting of specific infectious conditions, as noted above.

Legal Milestones in the Evolution of Public Health Surveillance, Outbreak Investigations, and Disease Control

Legal Milestones in Public Health Surveillance

A form of surveillance was employed in colonial America as early as 1741, when the colony of Rhode Island passed an act requiring tavern keepers to report contagious diseases among their patrons.[15] Two years later, the colony enacted a law requiring the reporting of smallpox, yellow fever, and cholera. In 1874, systematic reporting of disease in the United States began when the Massachusetts State Board of Health initiated voluntary weekly reporting of common diseases by physicians who used a postcard reporting format.[16] The collection of morbidity data to be used by the U.S. Marine Hospital Service, the forerunner to PHS, for quarantine measures against selected diseases (e.g., cholera and yellow fever) was authorized by Congress in the Quarantine Act of 1878.[17] Fifteen years later, Michigan became the first jurisdiction in the United States to require reporting of specific infectious diseases.[15]

The federal Quarantine Act of 1893 authorized the weekly collection of data from all states.[18] By 1901, all states required that selected infectious diseases be reported to local health authorities. As the result of the intervening epidemic of polio in 1916 and pandemic of influenza in 1918, all states were participating in national morbidity reporting by 1925.[16] In 1961, CDC—at that time bearing the name "Communicable Disease Center"—became responsible for receipt of reports of notifiable conditions and for weekly dissemination of such data through the *Morbidity and Mortality Weekly Report*, a publication that by 1994 had begun to make these data available online. The Public Health Service Act authorized CDC to collect, collate, and analyze notifiable disease data at the national level; but in fact, state health agencies provide these data to the federal government on a voluntary, cooperative basis. Moreover, and as noted above, each state promulgates its own set of conditions by legislative enactment or regulation.[16,19]

Influence of Smallpox on Public Health Laws

Smallpox, the only disease to have been eradicated from the world, played an especially profound role in influencing the evolution of the legal basis for the control of infectious diseases in the United States; many of the key developments have been reported by Dr. Donald R. Hopkins.[20] An early example of the use of the functional strategies of local quarantine and isolation to prevent the spread of smallpox during the colonial era was an order issued in East Hampton, Long Island, in 1662. In 1676, the colony of Virginia legislated mandatory home isolation of persons with smallpox. During a protracted outbreak in 1702, Massachusetts Bay Colony enacted a law authorizing selectmen of local towns to carry out isolation and quarantine; this act superseded vaguer authority previously delegated by the governor to selectmen. Massachusetts Bay Colony authorized additional measures in 1731 with enactment of "An Act to Prevent Persons from Concealing the Small Pox," which required household heads to report cases to selectmen and to display a red flag on the home to warn others.[20]

As part of a more concerted effort to control smallpox, in 1813, the U.S. Congress established a National Vaccine Agency as part of the "An Act to Encourage Vaccination"; however, the Agency was closed and the act repealed in 1822 at the recommendation of a Congressional committee investigating a cluster of deaths in persons who inadvertently had been vaccinated with real smallpox scabs.[20–22] As the 19th century progressed, legislators were faced with the challenge of balancing the need for control measures, such as vaccination to protect communities, against evolving beliefs regarding personal freedom of choice. However, in the setting of an epidemic in Boston during 1855, the state legislature enacted "the first mandatory school vaccination law in the United States," although this law was not enforced until an epidemic wave in the early 1880s.[20] Similarly, in Atlanta, regulations mandating vaccination of schoolchildren were enforced only months before an outbreak in that city in 1882. Improvement in the smallpox situation led to public resistance to vaccination and vaccination laws in the early 1900s, and California went so far as to repeal its law mandating vaccination for schoolchildren. However, in 1922, after a resurgence of smallpox beginning in 1920, the U.S. Supreme Court held that school authorities could mandate vaccination for school entry, regardless of whether an immediate local smallpox threat existed.[20,23]

Smallpox precipitated one of the most important, if not *the* most important, appellate decisions involving U.S. public health practice—the 1905 U.S. Supreme Court case of *Jacobson v. Massachusetts*.[24] In that case, the facts of which emerged during a smallpox epidemic in 1902, the defendant, Henning Jacobson, refused smallpox vaccination as ordered by the Cambridge Board of Health pursuant to its authorities under Massachusetts law. Jacobson was found guilty of violating the law and appealed the verdict first to the state's Supreme Judicial Court, and then to the U.S. Supreme Court. In its opinion, the Supreme Court upheld the validity of the Massachusetts statute and stated that "[u]pon the principle of self-defense, of paramount necessity, a community has the right to protect itself against an epidemic of disease which threatens the safety of its members." The impact of this case on public health practice has endured for over a full century, and the holding has provided constitutional support not only for vaccination laws but also for many other public health laws.[25]

As a historical footnote, in addition to prompting laws and other control measures, smallpox affected the legislative and judicial processes in colonial America in other ways. For example, in 1636 and 1659, the General Court of Massachusetts Bay Colony was forced to convene in locations outside of Boston, where it usually met, to escape smallpox outbreaks in the city. Similarly, in 1696, an outbreak in Jamestown, Virginia, caused the colony's assembly to recess; and in 1702, smallpox in Manhattan caused both the assembly and supreme court to adjourn to Long Island.[20]

Impact of Other Infectious Disease Influences on Present-Day Laws

Although smallpox represents one of the earliest of the infectious disease problems prompting legislative responses in the United States, many other infectious diseases fundamentally influenced present-day laws related to infectious diseases.[26] For example, epidemics of yellow fever and cholera during the 1800s also led to enactment of state and local disease-control laws providing for sanitation, quarantine, and isolation. Recognition of the impact of tuberculosis led to changes in disease reporting and surveillance, including establishment of case reporting in New York in the 1890s; and syphilis-control initiatives in the early 1900s prompted enactment of laws for premarital screening, reporting, contact tracing, and involuntary treatment.[26] The federal government had only limited early involvement in public health, including the control and prevention of infectious diseases; examples of such involvement included "An Act relative to Quarantine," passed in 1796 and authorizing the President to direct federal officials "to aid in the execution of quarantine, and also in the execution of the health laws of the states"; and the 1813 act to encourage smallpox vaccination, as noted above.[21,27]

Some of the earliest sanitary legislation in the American colonies was enactment in 1647 or 1648 by the General Court of Massachusetts Bay Colony that provided for maritime quarantine against ships from the yellow fever-affected West Indies.[28] In 1678, local regulations against smallpox were adopted in Boston, Salem, and Plymouth, and in 1742, Massachusetts Bay Colony passed a law to prevent smallpox and other infectious sickness. The first local boards of health in the United States were created during 1793–1794 in Baltimore and Philadelphia as a consequence of a yellow fever epidemic.[28]

Mandatory Reporting of Diseases and Conditions

All states have legislatively specified requirements for reporting of specified notifiable or infectious conditions.[16] These requirements may be enumerated directly by statute, through authorities delegated to state boards of health, and under health department regulations. Reporting may be required of a variety of professionals and organizational entities, including physicians and other health-care providers, diagnostic laboratories, clinical facilities, and schools and daycare centers.[14,16,29] Although state disease reporting generally is mandated by law or regulation, reporting of disease and death information by the state or territorial health department to CDC is voluntary.

The scope and nature of reporting requirements vary considerably by state, differing, for example, by the number of conditions required for reporting, time periods within which conditions must be reported, agencies to which reports must be submitted, and persons or sources required to report. Moreover, despite the legal requirements for reporting, adherence to and completeness of reporting also vary substantially by infectious disease agent, ranging from 6% to 90% for different common infectious conditions.[30] The deficiencies in reporting by physicians are accounted for, in part, by limitations in physicians' knowledge of reporting requirements and procedures, as well as the assumption that laboratories have reported cases of infectious diseases.[16,31]

Since the early 1900s, PHS has attempted to collect disease information from all states about certain infectious diseases.[1,15] Beginning in 1951, the Council of State and Territorial Epidemiologists (CSTE) was authorized by its parent body, the Association of State and Territorial Health Officials, to decide what diseases states should report to PHS and to recommend reporting procedures. CSTE meets annually and, in consultation with CDC, recommends additions and deletions to the list of diseases and conditions.

An assessment of state laws and regulations in 1989 highlighted an important impediment to the surveillance and control of infectious diseases—namely, variations in case definitions the states used for identifying and acting on reports of cases and the effect of lack of uniformity on limiting the ability to compare patterns of infectious disease occurrence between states. For example, some states required reporting of any person with a positive culture for *Salmonella*, whereas others required reporting of only culture-positive persons who were symptomatic.[16] To address these differences and to facilitate comparison of surveillance between states, CSTE and CDC developed and update standardized case definitions for the nationally notifiable infectious diseases.[32] Implementation of uniform case definitions and related procedures was expected to provide for interstate reciprocal notification for cases of infectious disease when onset was in one state but the patient was hospitalized in or transferred to another state, and cases for which public health action (e.g., contact tracing) might be involved in different states. However, reporting requirements by state continue to differ: as of January 1999, of the 52 infectious conditions agreed on for national surveillance, only 19 were reportable in all states.[14]

In 1995 and 1996, CDC and CSTE expanded the list beyond the traditional collection of infectious diseases, recommending that elevated blood lead levels, silicosis, and acute pesticide poisoning be added.[14] The number of diseases and conditions on the list varies from year to year but is usually 65–75. The list of diseases and conditions under national surveillance is published each year in the annual summary of notifiable diseases in the *Morbidity and Mortality Weekly Report*. CSTE also keeps information about state disease and condition reporting requirements on its website, http://www.cste.org/NNDSSHome.htm.

Even though few states choose to penalize physicians for not reporting notifiable conditions, disciplinary measures may be invoked in instances when failure to report has serious untoward effects. For example, the California Board of Medical Quality Assurance took action against a physician in that state for "gross negligence and incompetence, failure to report to local health authorities a suspected case of an infectious disease in a known food handler."[33] At that time, California law set forth legal responsibility of physicians, dentists, nurses, and others to notify local health authorities of persons ill with specified infectious diseases. In this instance, the physician had examined a patient he knew to be a food handler. Although the physician recognized the patient was jaundiced and possibly had hepatitis, he failed to report the patient's condition to local public health authorities. An outbreak of foodborne hepatitis followed in which at least 62 cases of hepatitis were associated with the food handler; one person died. In suspending the physician's license for one year (the suspension was stayed and the physician was placed on five years' probation), the California Board of Medical Quality Assurance declared that the "failure to report a suspected if not a known case of an infectious disease in a food handler was an extreme departure from the standard practice of medicine."[33] More recently, in Minnesota, a small proportion of physicians initially refused to report the identity of HIV-positive persons to the state health department as required, even though violation of any health department rule represented a misdemeanor.[34]

Interplay of Federal and State Laws in Field Epidemiology

When an outbreak of disease or other event threatens public health, state or local public health authorities are responsible for investigating it because of their inherent police powers. In practice, institutions and individuals generally cooperate voluntarily in epidemiologic and outbreak investigations. However, if investigators meet with resistance, local or state public health officials can take legal actions, such as applying to a court with jurisdiction over the institution (or individual) for a subpoena or court order to compel the institution (or individual) to grant investigators access to the premises or records at issue. An individual can be compelled by court order to provide the information necessary to the public health investigation.

By contrast to the broad state public health authorities, federal public health officials have limited statutory authorities to initiate independent epidemiologic investigations. For epidemiologists and public health officials employed by the federal government, the laws relating to the general powers and duties of PHS for research and investigation are found in Title III of the Public Health Service Act. The general statutory authority that applies to federal epidemiologic investigations is Section 301(a) of the Public Health Service Act, 42 U.S.C. Section 241(a):

> The Secretary shall conduct in the Service, and encourage, cooperate with, and render assistance to the other appropriate public authorities, scientific institutions, and scientists in the conduct of, and promote the coordination of, research, investigations, experiments, demonstrations, and studies relating to the causes, diagnosis, treatment, control, and prevention of physical and mental diseases and impairments of man. . . .

In addition, subsection 6 of Section 301(a) indicates that the Secretary is authorized to "make available to health officials, scientists, and appropriate public health and other nonprofit institutions and organizations, technical advice and assistance on the application of statistical methods to experiments, studies, and surveys in health and medical fields." Although these provisions are broadly worded and are permissive rather than compulsory, they nonetheless give legal authority for intervention by federal epidemiologists in disease outbreaks and other instances in which such assistance is requested. In practice, local and state public health officials may request federal assistance in the epidemiologic or field investigation. Federal public health employees who collaborate with state and local public health authorities in such investigations generally are not exercising specific federal authority but rather are assisting the state or local investigation.

Legal Issues Related to Data Collection, Analysis, and Dissemination

The processes of collecting data for public health surveillance, as part of an outbreak investigation or for other field epidemiology activities, may implicate numerous legal considerations, including (1) protection available under state or federal law during and after the investigation for records collected and generated in relation to the investigation; (2) privacy provisions for medical and other information; (3) required reporting of particular diseases or conditions; (4) status of information in investigative files under the federal Freedom of Information Act (5 U.S.C. §552) or state Freedom of Information Act counterparts; and (5) the possible applicability of federal or state human subjects research regulations, including the need for review of study protocols by institutional review boards and the need for informed consent for participation in the investigation or for procedures related to the investigation.

To determine what records will be kept or generated and where and how such records will be stored, federal, state, and local public health officials need to be familiar with legal protections applicable to documents and other records that will be examined, extracted, and compiled in association with the surveillance activity or outbreak investigation. Most states provide specific statutory and regulatory privacy protection over medical and public health records. In general, the privacy protection prevents disclosure of a name-identified record without the consent of the person on whom the record is maintained. Accordingly, state law generally protects such medical records in the hands of an investigator. Furthermore, such state laws frequently require that only certain authorized personnel have access to such private records and that such records be maintained in a secure manner. Public health investigators usually would be authorized access to such records for surveillance and related public health activities but would be bound to maintain the records in a manner that would protect the privacy of the identifiable information from unauthorized or inadvertent disclosure.

In the course of an outbreak investigation or surveillance activities, investigators may create or compile a variety of documents, including questionnaires, forms, investigative notes, copies or extractions of patient or other records, letters, reports, memoranda, drafts, manuscripts, and final reports. Depending on the nature of the records and the status of the investigation, these documents may not be protected from disclosure to the public by state or federal laws. Except for records afforded specific protection by state or federal laws (such as state laws protecting medical records), public health investigators should assume that all records collected may at some point be open to public scrutiny. This may include personal notes by the public health investigator, drafts of documents retained in the files, and other related information that is within the scope of the request. A more detailed discussion of the topics related to data collection, analysis, and dissemination is contained in Chapter 10.

Emerging Developments in Public Health Surveillance, Investigation, and Response

Newer Surveillance Concepts

Historically, public health surveillance was largely for infectious diseases and based on mandatory reporting of individual cases of disease. Increasingly, in the past decade, use of mandatory reporting as a surveillance method has been expanded through changes in state public health reporting statutes, regulations, or executive orders to include conditions and syndromes that fall outside more traditional infectious diseases. These especially include environmental and occupational health conditions, emerging infectious diseases, and diseases that may be due to bioterrorism.

In addition, through collaboration between CSTE and CDC, newer methods have been developed as a basis for state and national public health surveillance. These include use of the Behavioral Risk Factor Surveillance System to monitor prevalence of health risk behaviors such as tobacco smoking[35] and a variety of methods to monitor occupational disease, chronic conditions, and injuries. Methods range from telephone surveys (Behavioral Risk Factor Surveillance System) to the development and maintenance of cancer and birth defect registries, to use of hospital discharge databases. Similar to updating the national list of notifiable infectious diseases and case definitions, a collaborative process exists to develop, define, and update a national list of chronic disease indicators.[36] CSTE maintains information on its website identifying indicators for chronic disease surveillance, including access to current data to assist public health practitioners assess indicators for their locales. In addition, publication of data on matters such as firearm-related injuries has significantly increased awareness of these public health issues, as well as the importance of surveillance to the consideration of law and policy interventions.

With the exceptions of tumor and birth defect registries, these newer surveillance methods do not use mandatory reporting and do not depend highly on state or federal law. They either use voluntary processes, such as willingness of the public to respond to a telephone survey, or employ existing databases from which individual identifier information usually is removed. However, their public health use is facilitated by the broad authority of state public health officials to obtain public health surveillance data.

In recent years, CSTE and CDC have cooperated in publishing numerous surveillance summaries about a broad spectrum of problems, including hazardous substances and emergency events, infant mortality, childhood lead poisoning, low birthweight, neural tube defects, occupational asthma, occupational hazards, and smoking. Perhaps even more than traditional reportable disease surveillance reports, the analysis of these surveillance summaries has provided essential information at both the state and national levels for developing policy and for evaluating programs.

Bioterrorism-Related Surveillance and Investigation

Terrorism-related concerns have led to efforts to examine the adequacy of disease reporting laws and disease-specific surveillance to meet the challenge of detecting acts of bioterrorism as rapidly as possible to minimize their health, social, and psychological consequences. In 2002, CDC reported on an examination of disease reporting laws of 54 jurisdictions, including all 50 states, to determine how many had laws mandating the reporting of diseases caused by "critical biological agents"[37]—agents designated by CDC with the potential for use in a bioterrorist weapon. The study showed that particular deficiencies existed for the immediate reporting of diseases associated with Category A agents (i.e., anthrax, botulism, viral hemorrhagic fevers, plague, smallpox, and tularemia). Although anthrax, botulism, and plague were immediately reportable in most jurisdictions, tularemia was immediately reportable in less than half of the jurisdictions. The findings underscored the need for states and other jurisdictions to review existing disease reporting laws to determine whether they include the most critical biologic agents associated with bioterrorism,[37] an activity that has become a requirement of federal public health preparedness funding.[38]

To speed up reporting of some diseases and laboratory findings, use of electronic data captured from laboratories (electronic laboratory reporting) and Web-based clinical facility and provider reporting increasingly are replacing paper and mail-based reporting.[39–41] In some states, disease reporting regulations have been modified to provide a legal basis for such electronic reporting.[b]

In addition, syndromic surveillance—use of real-time data from existing systems that record events such as emergency department visits, 911 calls, and pharmacy purchases—is being explored at both the state and national levels to detect unusual disease activity up to several days before reporting of any specific diagnostic information by providers and to help monitor the scope and duration of outbreaks, including those detected by other means.[42–44] Although participation in these systems by health-care facilities and providers has been mostly voluntary, questions have been raised regarding whether state and local jurisdictions have the legal authority to obtain personal identifying information when necessary to investigate increases in any given syndrome.[45,46] An analysis of statutes and regulations in New York City and New York State led to the conclusion that New York City had ample authority for its syndromic surveillance activities.[45] At least three states (Iowa, Nevada, and Arizona) have passed explicit statutory language authorizing syndromic surveillance.[47–49]

The anthrax attacks of 2001 and increased recognition of the potential for criminal behavior and other deliberate actions to cause disease outbreaks have crystallized the concept of "forensic epidemiology" (see also Chapter 6). Forensic epidemiology has been characterized as "the use of epidemiologic methods as part of an ongoing investigation of a health problem for which there is suspicion or evidence regarding possible intentional acts or criminal behavior as factors contributing to the health problem."[50] The operational challenges during joint public health and law enforcement investigations of such problems implicate several relatively new legal issues that, in turn, have stimulated development of new legal frameworks for interdisciplinary collaboration, such as the "agreement regarding joint field investigations following a suspected bioterrorist incident" entered into by the City of New York Department of Mental Health and Hygiene, the City of New York Police Department, and the Federal Bureau of Investigation field office in New York City.[51]

State and Federal Cooperation in Emergency Responses

Beginning in 1999, federal government initiatives designed to improve national public health capabilities to respond to acts of chemical and biologic terrorism raised questions about the adequacy of state quarantine, isolation, and other compulsory public health powers. Preliminary review of state quarantine, isolation, and other critical agent laws conducted informally by CDC in 2000 showed that most of these laws had not been revised since the 1940s—probably because voluntary cooperation of the public and advances in medical interventions used compulsory actions less frequently. However, in the context of public health threats related to potential bioterrorism events, the infrequent use of such actions also presented the possibility that public health officials were inexperienced or unfamiliar with the proper procedures for invoking the compulsory powers. Accordingly, CDC and other federal officials involved in bioterrorism preparedness have suggested that states examine public health laws—including quarantine and isolation powers—that affect their abilities to effectively respond to potential chemical and biological threats. Such assessments can help ensure that the laws enable public health officials to act promptly while providing adequate due process protections for individuals who may be detained as part of a bioterrorism response. In addition, bioterrorism initiatives increasingly focus on the need for advance coordination, planning, pharmaceutical stockpiling, and training that involves public health officials and officials from various law-enforcement, emergency-response, and other civilian agencies, as well as military intelligence experts.

The events following the September 11, 2001, attacks in New York City and Northern Virginia illustrate both the strengths of and challenges to traditional concepts of primary state and local responsibility for public health investigations. The catastrophic nature of the events rapidly taxed the ability of local and state public health officials to respond to the needs for surveillance of hospital and emergency department admissions, injuries, hospital-based syndromic surveillance, and various environmental monitoring activities. Resources from CDC and other public health agencies had to be deployed to help gather this important surveillance information. Yet, the legal authority and oversight for most of these public health activities remained with local and state public health officials. The consistency in training, advance planning, and prior collaborative relationships between state, municipal, and local public health practitioners made possible an effective response during this emergency situation. In the aftermath of the events of September 11 and the anthrax attack in the United States, a draft model law (The Model State Emergency Health Powers Act) was created for public review and use to strengthen preparedness (see Chapter 11).

We acknowledge David W. Fleming, whose work on Chapter 7, "Frontline Public Health: Surveillance and Outbreak Investigations," in the first edition of this text contributed in part to this chapter.

Note

a. Examples of Iowa's quarantine orders are available at http://ww.idph.state.ia.us/adper/cade.asp; see also Iowa Code §135.144 (2003 Suppl.), 139A.4, 139A.9, and 641 Iowa Administrative Code, Ch 1.

b. See, for example, 33 Pennsylvania Bulletin (Pa.B.) 2439 (effective Nov. 16, 2003) (under authority of 28 Pa.Code §27.4); 6 Code of Colorado Regulations (CCR) 1009–1, Reporting of Selected Cases of Morbidity and Mortality (effective September 30, 2004); Administrative Rules of South Dakota (ARDS) 44:20:02:06 (under authority of SDCL 34-22-9) (effective Dec. 7, 2003); Washington Administrative Code (WAC) 246-101-110(2).

References

1. CDC. Summary of notifiable diseases, United States, 2003. *MMWR* 2005;52:2–3.
2. CDC. Surveillance for certain health behaviors among selected local areas—United States, Behavioral Risk Factor Surveillance System, 2002. *MMWR* 2004;53(SS05):2–3.
3. Ries LAG, Eisner MP, Kosary CL, et al, eds. *SEER Cancer Statistics Review, 1975–2001*. Bethesda, MD: National Cancer Institute. 2004 Available at http://seer.cancer.gov/csr/1975_2001. Accessed November 16, 2005.

4. Gen Stat of Conn (revised to January 1, 2005), §19a-2a, Powers and duties, Volume 6, 787.
5. Public Health Code (revised through Sept. 21, 2004). Reportable Diseases and Laboratory Findings, §19a-36-A7, Diseases not enumerated, p. 529. Available at http://www.dph .state.ct.us/phc/phc.doc. Accessed November 16, 2005.
6. Iowa Code, Title 4, Subtitle 2, Ch 139, §139A.3A (2005).
7. Conn Public Health Code §19a-36-A6 (2005).
8. Goodman RA, Buehler JW, Koplan JP. The epidemiologic field investigation: science and judgment in public health practice. *Am J Epidemiol* 1990;132:9–16.
9. Gregg MB. Conducting a field investigation. In: Gregg MB, ed. *Field Epidemiology*. New York: Oxford University Press, 2001:62–77.
10. CDC. Postexposure prophylaxis, isolation, and quarantine to control an import-associated measles outbreak—Iowa, 2004. *MMWR* 2004; 53:969–71.
11. Fidler DP, Heymann DL, Ostroff SM, O'Brien T. Emerging and reemerging infectious diseases: challenges for international, national, and state law. *International Lawyer*. 1997; 31:773–99.
12. Birkhead GS, Maylahn CM. State and local public health surveillance In: Teutsch SM, Churchill RE, eds. *Principles and Practice of Public Health Surveillance*. 2nd ed. New York: Oxford University Press, 2000;253–9.
13. Langmuir AD. The surveillance of communicable diseases of national importance. *N Engl J Med* 1963;268:182–92.
14. Rousch S, Birkhead GS, Koo D, Cobb A, Fleming D. Mandatory reporting of diseases and conditions by health care professionals and laboratorians. *JAMA* 1999;282:164–70.
15. Thacker SB. Historical development. In: Teutsch SM, Churchill RE, eds. *Principles and Practice of Public Health Surveillance*. 2nd ed. New York: Oxford University Press, 2000:1–16.
16. Chorba TL, Berkelman RL, Safford SK, Gibbs NP, Hull HF. The reportable diseases: I. Mandatory reporting of infectious diseases by clinicians. *JAMA* 1989;262:3018–26.
17. Act of Apr 29, 1878, Ch 66, 20 Stat 37.
18. Act of Feb 15, 1893, Ch 114, 27 Stat 449, *amended by* Act of June 19, 1906, Ch 3433, 34 Stat 299.
19. Koo D, Wetterhall SF. History and current status of the National Notifiable Diseases Surveillance System. *J Public Health Manag Pract* 1996;2:4–10.
20. Hopkins DR. *Princes and Peasants: Smallpox in History*. Chicago: University of Chicago Press, 1983.
21. Act of Feb 27, 1813, Ch 37, 2 Stat 806, *repealed by* Act of May 4, 1822, Ch 50, 3 Stat 677.
22. Furman B. *A Profile of the United States Public Health Service, 1798–1948*. Washington, DC: US Department of Health, Education, and Welfare, 1973 (DHEW publication no [NIH] 73–369).
23. *Zucht v King*, 260 US 174 (1922).
24. *Jacobson v Massachusetts*, 197 US 11 (1905).
25. Parmet WE, Goodman RA, Farber A. Individual rights versus the public's health—100 years after *Jacobson v Massachusetts*. *N Engl J Med* 2005;352:652–54.
26. Gostin LO, Burris S, Lazzarini Z. The law and the public's health: a study of infectious disease law in the United States. *Columbia Law Rev* 1999;99:59–128.
27. Act of May 27, 1796, Ch 31, 1 Stat 474, repealed by Act of Feb 25, 1799, Ch 12, 1 Stat 619.
28. Tobey JA. *Public Health Law*. 3rd ed. New York: Commonwealth Fund, 1947.
29. Thacker SB. Surveillance. In: Gregg MB, Dicker RC, Goodman RA, eds. *Field Epidemiology*. New York: Oxford University Press, 1996:16–32.

30. Thacker SB, Berkelman RL. Public health surveillance in the United States. *Epidemiol Rev* 1988;10:164–90.
31. Konowitz PM, Petrossian GA, Rose DN. The underreporting of disease and physicians' knowledge of reporting requirements. *Public Health Rep* 1984;99:31–5.
32. CDC. Case definitions for infectious conditions under public health surveillance. *MMWR* 1997;46(RR10):1–64.
33. California Department of Health Services. Disciplinary action by Board of Medical Quality Assurance for failure to report a reportable infectious disease. *California Morbidity* 1978 (August 11).
34. Fidler DP, Heymann DL, Ostroff SM, O'Brien T. Emerging and reemerging infectious diseases: challenges for international, national, and state law. *International Lawyer.* 1997;31:773–99.
35. CDC. Addition of prevalence of cigarette smoking as a nationally notifiable condition— June 1996. *MMWR* 1996;45:537.
36. CDC. Indicators for chronic disease surveillance. *MMWR* 2004;53(no RR11):1–8.
37. Horton H, Misrahi JJ, Matthews GW, Kocher PL. Critical biological agents: disease reporting as a tool for bioterrorism preparedness. *J Law Med Ethics* 2002;30:262–66.
38. CDC. *Continuation Guidance—Budget Year 5. Attachment B. Focus B: Surveillance and Epidemiology Capacity.* June 14, 2004:1–8. Available at http://www.bt.cdc.gov/planning/continuationguidance/pdf/epidemiology_capacity_attachb.pdf. Accessed September 4, 2005.
39. Effler P, Ching-Lee M, Bogard A, Ieong M, Nekomoto T, Jernigan D. Statewide system of electronic notifiable disease reporting from clinical laboratories. *JAMA* 1999;282:1845–50.
40. Backer HD, Bissel SR, Vugia DJ. Disease reporting from automated laboratory-based reporting system to a state health department via local health departments. *Public Health Rep* 2001;116:257–65.
41. Jernigan DB. Electronic laboratory-based reporting: opportunities and challenges for surveillance. *Emerg Infect Dis* 2001;7(3 Suppl):538.
42. Henning K. What is syndromic surveillance? *MMWR* 2004;53(Suppl):7–11.
43. CDC. Framework for evaluating public health surveillance systems for early detection of outbreaks: recommendations from the CDC working group. *MMWR* 2004;53(RR5):2–3.
44. Loonsk J. Biosense—a national initiative for early detection and quantification of public health emergencies. *MMWR* 2004;53(Suppl):53–5.
45. Lopez W. New York City and state legal authorities related to syndromic surveillance. *J Urban Health* 2003;80(2Suppl 1):i23–4.
46. Drociuk D, Gibson J, Hodge JG Jr. Health information privacy and syndromic surveillance systems. *MMWR* 2004;53(Suppl):221–5.
47. Iowa Code, Title 4, Subtitle 2, Ch 139, §139A.3A (2005).
48. Nev Rev Stat, Ch 441A, §441 A.125 (2003).
49. Ariz Rev Stat, Title 36, §36-782 (2005).
50. Goodman RA, Munson JW, Dammers K, Lazzarini Z, Barkley JP. Forensic epidemiology: law at the intersection of public health and criminal investigations. *J Law Med Ethics* 2003a;31:684–700.
51. Agreement regarding joint field investigations following a suspected bioterrorist incident. Available at http://www2a.cdc.gov/phlp/docs/Investigations.pdf. Accessed November 16, 2005.

Chapter 10

IDENTIFIABLE HEALTH INFORMATION AND THE PUBLIC'S HEALTH: PRACTICE, RESEARCH, AND POLICY

James G. Hodge, Jr., Richard E. Hoffman,
Deborah W. Tress,* and Verla S. Neslund*

Responsible data-sharing practices are a dominant health policy objective in a new millennium in which billions of individually identifiable health data are exchanged annually as part of the ongoing development of a national electronic health information infrastructure.[1] These multi-purpose, rapid exchanges of electronic health data of varying sensitivities are essential to support health-care services, conduct health research, and promote the public's health. Yet, the acquisition, use, disclosure, and storage of health data contribute to individuals' concerns about their privacy and security. Responding to Americans' fears and perceptions of actual and potential privacy abuses, lawmakers and policymakers have developed new, modern privacy and data-sharing protections through legislation and regulations, as well as ethical and industry codes and standards.[2]

Central to modern (and historic) data-sharing laws and policies is the need to balance individual and communal interests in health data. Striking an appropriate balance is not easy. Privacy and security advocates consistently seek to limit the acquisition, use, and disclosure of identifiable health information in government and private-sector settings to avoid potential inadvertent or wrongful releases, acquisitions, uses, or disclosures of data that can lead to individual discrimination and other harms. Conversely, federal, tribal, state, and local health authorities seek regular access to and use of identifiable health information to conduct important public health practice and research activities.

---

* The findings and conclusions in this chapter are those of the author(s) and do not necessarily represent the views of the U.S. Department of Health and Human Services or the Centers for Disease Control and Prevention.

Despite the traditional acceptance of public health functions that rely on exchanges of health data, privacy and public health proponents continue to debate the extent to which public health needs for health data should take priority over legitimate privacy and security interests of individuals. This debate tends to frame individual privacy and public health objectives as conflicting. In fact, they are synergistic. Protecting the privacy of identifiable health data is critical to reaching public health goals. Failing to respect the sensitivity and privacy of a person's health information can lead some people to avoid, or limit their participation in, public health programs, human subjects research, and clinical care. Collectively, these decisions can skew the accuracy of public health information across populations, in turn affecting public health programs and outcomes. Protecting privacy is thus essential to protecting the public's health.[3]

On the other hand, adherence to privacy and other data principles cannot trump public health needs.[2] Just as privacy is a shared goal, so is communal health. Protecting the public's health through practice and research activities requires cooperation and participation by each individual as a member of society. For everyone to benefit, people must recognize some diminution in their informational privacy expectations to allow data sharing that furthers the public's health. This theme pervades the Federal Policy for the Protection of Human Subjects (Common Rule)[4] and the Privacy Rule of the U.S. Department of Health and Human Services (DHHS),[5] promulgated pursuant to the Health Insurance Portability and Accountability Act of 1996 (HIPAA).[6] At balance in these (and other) data-sharing laws is the societal goal of protecting the public's health with individual desires to maximize informational privacy interests.[7]

In this chapter, we examine some of the difficult issues at the intersection of public health, data uses, and individual interests. We describe some of the fundamental uses and disclosures of identifiable health data for public health practice and public health research. Next, we present legal structures and challenges that underlie public health data uses and disclosures. We briefly explore relevant constitutional sources of public health powers and privacy. Core statutory and regulatory legal protections for data uses related to public health research (i.e., federal, state, and local human subjects research protections) and public health privacy (i.e., privacy laws at the federal, state, and local levels) are examined. This includes core analysis of the public health implications of the HIPAA Privacy Rule. We conclude by addressing one of the key questions critical to each of these legal approaches: What are the distinctions between public health practice and research activities? We set forth enhanced methodology on the basis of a 2004 report of the Council of State and Territorial Epidemiologists (CSTE) for distinguishing these activities.[8]

Fundamental Uses and Disclosures of Identifiable Public Health Data

Public Health Practice

Federal, tribal, state, and local public health agencies engage in a wide array of activities—many of which are considered public health practice activities—in the interest of protecting the public's health. Public health functions involve the collection, use, and analysis of health data from health-care providers, insurers, laboratories, other government agencies, and individuals. These include activities such as surveillance (e.g., reporting requirements, disease registries, sentinel networks), epidemiologic investigations (e.g., disease outbreak investigations), and evaluation and monitoring activities (e.g., public health program development and analysis, oversight functions). Tracking disease and injury in the population and providing well-targeted prevention services are significant factors in reducing public health threats and improving community health.

Each of these activities may require the collection and use of individually identifiable health information. This information is the lifeblood of public health practice.[3] Once aggregated by the public health authority, data are used to monitor the incidence, patterns, and trends of injury and disease in populations. Carefully planned surveillance or epidemiologic investigations or studies facilitate rapid identification of health needs, including (1) the spread of communicable or sexually transmitted infection or disease (e.g., HIV, tuberculosis, hepatitis B virus); (2) clusters or outbreaks of bacterial or viral infection (e.g., Legionnaire disease, hantavirus, *Escherichia coli*) from naturally occurring sources or bioterrorism; (3) risk behaviors in subpopulations (e.g., smoking among adolescents or ethnic minorities); and (4) other harmful conditions (e.g., child or spouse abuse, lead poisoning, environmental exposures).

Of course, health data are not the only types of information that public health authorities gather. In the course of an outbreak investigation, investigators may create or compile a variety of documents, including questionnaires, forms, investigative notes, copies or extractions of other records, letters, reports, memoranda, drafts, and manuscripts. The processes of collecting identifiable data for public health surveillance activities or epidemiologic outbreak investigations implicate numerous legal considerations, including (1) protections available under federal or state laws for records produced during or after the public health activity; (2) privacy provisions for identifiable information in the records; (3) legal reporting requirements for particular diseases or conditions to federal, tribal, state, or local public health, environmental, law enforcement, or intelligence agencies; and (4) potential applicability of federal or state human subjects research regulations.[9] As discussed in sections below, a host of legal protections regulate how records will be kept, generated, shared, or stored in association with public health activities.

Public Health Research

In addition to practice activities conducted by public health agencies at all levels of government are activities that involve or resemble human subjects research. "Human subjects research" is defined in the Common Rule as "a systematic investigation, including research development, testing, and evaluation, designed to develop or contribute to generalizable knowledge" that involves human subjects.[10] The same definition of research also is featured in the HIPAA Privacy Rule (although its meaning may be interpreted differently under privacy norms).[8] As defined, human subjects research is not limited to any particular actor or setting. A person engaged in human subjects research may be a public- or private-sector individual, an institution, an agency, or a corporation, including a public health agency.

Research activities may supplement public health practice or be engaged independently to enhance public health knowledge. Examples include clinical trials to evaluate new medications, laboratory investigations to identify a new or previously unrecognized pathogen, formal surveys of physicians to assess the barriers to implementing a new vaccine recommendation, or behavioral interventions to reduce risky behaviors.[11] For example, in response to a suspected population-based health problem, a public health agency may hypothesize, design, and conduct a double-blinded, placebo-controlled study to assess the efficacy of a new vaccine or medication among a randomly selected group of persons within the affected population. The study's hypothesis, methods, implementation, and underlying intent conclude the activity is research.[8] As a result, the public health agency must adhere to a series of protections and procedures pursuant to the Common Rule. These protections (e.g., individual informed consent) and procedures (e.g., review by an institutional review board [IRB]), as discussed below, are designed to protect the health and safety of human subjects.

Legal Frameworks Underlying Public Health Data Uses and Disclosures

Constitutional Principles

Constitutional principles are at the source of public health powers and privacy expectations. However, the federal Constitution neither guarantees the provision of public health services[12] nor strongly protects informational privacy.[13] Rather, federal, tribal, state, and local governments are constitutionally vested with the ability to regulate, protect, and promote the public's health, restricted only by minimal privacy requirements. The federal government draws on its enumerated powers, specifically the powers to tax, spend, regulate interstate commerce, and protect national security. These powers are wielded to promote the public's health and safety through laws executed by federal public health, health care, environmental, security, and other agencies.

Though federal public health power is expansive, primary responsibility for protecting the public's health is held by the sovereign states. The Tenth Amendment reserves extensive and broad powers to the states (and local governments through delegated state authority). Commonly known as the police powers, they represent the inherent authority of the state to enact laws and promulgate regulations to protect, preserve, and promote the health, safety, morals, and general welfare of the people.[14] Police powers justify virtually any exercise of state or local government in the interest of public health that does not infringe constitutionally protected individual or community rights or federal powers.[15]

Corresponding to the constitutional conceptions of police powers is an array of public health powers and duties authorized under state and local laws. Among other functions, public health laws authorize vaccination, isolation and quarantine, inspection of commercial and residential premises, abatement of public health nuisances, regulation of air and surface water contaminants, standards for pure food and drinking water, fluoridation of municipal water supplies, and licensure of health-care facilities and workers.[14] Each of these and other public health functions may be supported by state and local efforts to gather identifiable health data.

The U.S. Constitution supports, but does not expressly provide, individuals' privacy rights in their identifiable information. The Supreme Court has recognized a limited right to health information privacy as a liberty interest within the Fifth and Fourteenth amendments.[13] In *Whalen v. Roe*, the Court considered whether the constitutional right to privacy was infringed by New York state reporting law requiring physicians to relay the names and other information of persons receiving prescriptions for certain addictive drugs to the state health department.[16] The Court found no breach of individual privacy rights as a result of the reporting requirement because the state had adequate standards and procedures to protect the confidentiality of the information.[17] Measures taken by the state health department, including limited access to information and the prevention of online interception of computer databases holding such information, were deemed sufficient to protect individual privacy. Rather than prescribing exacting constitutional standards to protect individual privacy, the Court deferred to the government's judgment on how to protect private information.

Other courts have relied on state constitutional provisions in support of such rights.[13] Courts regularly allow privacy infringements through the administration of a flexible test that balances the invasion of privacy against the strength of the government interest.[a] Provided the government articulates a valid societal purpose[b] and employs reasonable security measures, courts typically do not interfere with traditional government health information collections. Individuals asserting a constitutional right to information privacy are unlikely to succeed except where the state fails to assert any significant interest or is particularly careless in disclosing highly sensitive information.[c]

Legal Protections of Human Subjects in Research

As discussed above, substantial public health research activities involve the acquisition or use of identifiable health data. Unlike the constitutional norms that underlie public health data collections and corresponding privacy expectations, identifiable data for public health research are acquired under different legal and ethical structures.[8] Research is not always tied to grants of legislative authority and could operate unchecked absent legal protections. Public health researchers, unlike public health practitioners, must adhere to regulations including advance written and informed consent of subjects (and sometimes their communities) that are codified in a series of federal regulations known collectively as the Common Rule.[4] The Common Rule applies to virtually all research involving human subjects and federal funding. For most activities determined to be human subjects research (as defined above), the Common Rule requires a prospective review by an IRB or medical ethics board in compliance with various specifications.[18] IRBs review research proposals to assess the extent to which research subjects are protected during the course and aftermath of the research activities.

The Common Rule requirements for IRB review are triggered only when an institution seeks federal funding to engage in human subjects research or when it decides to apply the same requirements in reviewing all its human subjects research pursuant to a multi-project or federal-wide assurance. Five key questions underlie the application of the Common Rule in any setting:

- Is the activity research?
- Does the research involve human subjects?
- Is the research supported in whole or part by federal funds?
- Is the research subject to exemption?
- Is the research entitled to expedited review by an IRB?[8]

Key Questions That Underlie Application of the Common Rule

Is the activity research? Whether an activity is research (or not) is not always easy to determine from a review of the Common Rule definition of research (stated above). Yet, this determination is essential to properly apply research protections to activities involving identifiable data. The Common Rule concerns only research activities; anything that is not a research activity is obviously not covered. Specifically, the acquisition of identifiable health data by public health authorities for public health practice is not subject to the Common Rule. In its guidance documents, the federal Office for Human Research Protections (OHRP) clarifies that identifiable private information or specimens may be acquired and used without IRB review if they are released "to a State or Local Health Department or its agent for legitimate *public health purposes* within the recognized authority of that Department. However, utilization of such information or specimens by Department investigators for *research purposes* would constitute engagement in research, and would require an Assurance from the Department" (italics added).[19] Thus, any activity that *is* classifiable as research requires further assessment.

Does the research involve human subjects? An institution is engaged in human subjects research when the researcher obtains (1) data through intervention or interaction with a living person (e.g., gathering data pursuant to a clinical examination) or (2) individually identifiable, private information about a living person (e.g., reviewing a person's existing medical records). "Individually identifiable" means the identity of the subject about whom the private information pertains is or may readily be ascertained by the investigator or associated with the information.[20] These criteria do not themselves define an activity as research; they merely identify whether it is *human subjects* research. If the research does not involve human subjects, the Common Rule does not apply. In clear cases, this determination need not be made by an IRB. In cases of ambiguity, responsibility for determining whether human subjects are involved may best be determined by the IRB.[21] Only if the research involves human subjects does the inquiry proceed.

Is the research funded by a federal source? If human subjects research receives funding or support from any federal agency (that has adopted the Common Rule—and most federal agencies have) or is performed directly by a federal agency, the Common Rule applies. Even if federal funding or support is not involved, institutions may choose to apply the Common Rule. Similar human subjects protections also may be required by other public- or private-sector funding organizations, regardless of federal funding. For these reasons, the Common Rule nearly universally applies to all research settings in the United States.[8]

Is the research subject to exemption? If an activity meets all the first three criteria, it is covered by the Common Rule, unless specifically exempted. Unlike with the prior questions, those conducting the activity cannot determine the exemption. Rather it should be submitted to the IRB or some authority other than the principal investigator. The Common Rule specifically exempts the following:

- Research on common educational practices in educational settings;[22]
- research involving educational tests (cognitive, diagnostic, aptitude, achievement), surveys, or observations of public behavior that are not recorded in an identifiable format and could not place participants at risk for liability or damage their reputation, employability, or financial standing;[23]
- research involving educational tests (cognitive, diagnostic, aptitude, achievement), surveys, or observations of public behavior involving elected or appointed public officials or candidates, or information required under federal statute to be kept confidential throughout the research and thereafter;[24]
- research involving existing data, documents, records, pathological specimens or diagnostic specimens, if these sources are publicly available or if the information is recorded by the investigator in such a manner that participants cannot be identified directly or through identifiers linked to the participants;[25]
- research conducted by agency/department heads to evaluate public benefit or service programs; procedures for obtaining benefits or services; possible changes or alternatives to the programs or procedures; possible changes in payment levels; and methods for services under these programs. The research must be conducted pursuant to specific federal statutory authority;[26] and
- taste and food-quality examinations and consumer acceptance studies.[27]

Applying these exemptions can be problematic. The National Bioethics Advisory Committee recommends an exemption not be based merely on a technical review of the research methods. Rather, other factors should be assessed such as whether any risks exist to participants or subjects have a right to refuse to participate.[28]

Is the research entitled to expedited review? An activity determined to be nonexempt human subjects research may be entitled to expedited IRB review if it involves minimal risks to participants and fits among a list of categories provided by DHHS.[29] The IRB chair usually determines whether a research protocol undergoes either expedited or full review when the protocol is submitted. Expedited review does not require review and approval by the fully convened board. The objective is to more rapidly evaluate the proposal consistent with the Common Rule. Research categories relevant to public health activities that may be subject to expedited review (as described by the OHRP) include the following:

- Clinical studies of new applications of drugs and medical devices when the drug or device is already being marketed;
- collection of blood samples by finger stick, heel stick, ear stick, or venipuncture;
- prospective collection of biologic specimens for research purposes by noninvasive means;

- collection of data through noninvasive procedures (not involving general anesthesia or sedation) routinely employed in clinical practice, excluding procedures involving x-rays or microwaves. Where medical devices are employed, they must be cleared/approved for marketing;
- research involving materials (data, documents, records, or specimens) that have been or will be collected solely for nonresearch purposes (such as medical treatment or diagnosis); and
- research on individual or group characteristics or behavior (including research on perception, cognition, motivation, identity, language, communication, cultural beliefs or practices, and social behavior) or research employing survey, interview, oral history, focus group, program evaluation, human factors evaluation, or quality assurance methodologies.[30]

Each of these categories may enhance the ability of public health practitioners to more efficiently gain IRB approval for a range of research activities that may be commonly performed to promote the public's health.

Functions and Responsibilities of Institutional Review Boards

As noted, the Common Rule vests authority within the IRBs to approve, disapprove, or require modifications of all federally funded human subjects research. An IRB must approve human subjects research before an investigator contacts human participants unless such research is specifically exempt by the regulations. In some state or local public health agencies, if uncertainty exists regarding whether an activity is research or practice, or whether it is exempt from the Common Rule, the IRBs may be asked to make the determination.

All IRBs comprise at least five members with diverse backgrounds, at least one of whom is a nonscientist and another of whom is not otherwise affiliated with the IRB's institution. IRBs review research proposals to assess the extent to which research subjects are protected during the course and aftermath of the research activities. They have a range of authority to approve research, require modifications to a research protocol, or disapprove of the proposed research entirely. Among other things, IRBs must examine whether

- Individual or guardian consent for data collection appropriately meets all of the Common Rule requirements;[31]
- the privacy of individuals and confidentiality of their identifiable information are protected;[32]
- the research design is sound, safe, and effective;[33]
- research subjects are equitably selected;[34]
- data safety is appropriately monitored;[35] and
- vulnerable populations (e.g., children, prisoners, mentally disabled persons) are protected.[36]

One of the most critical roles of IRBs is to review the appropriateness and adequacy of the research subject's informed consent. In this context, informed consent refers to the entire process of securing legal and ethical consent, including (1) who is seeking the informed consent, (2) where it is being sought, (3) when it is being sought, and (4) the method used to convey information that underlies individual consent. After what often can be an exhaustive review, IRBs approve only consent procedures that are voluntary and informed. The informed consent document must accurately and clearly state the risks and benefits of participation in straightforward and comprehensible language—typically at an eighth-grade reading level or lower. Additionally, federal regulations require inclusion of eight specific elements in all informed consents, including "a statement describing the extent, if any, to which confidentiality of records identifying the subject will be maintained."[37]

Although IRBs must review active protocols at least annually, some of these protocol reviews may be eligible for expedited review if the protocol previously was approved by the fully convened IRB. Although the process of obtaining and confirming IRB approval may be time-consuming for investigators, it is grounded in the need to ensure adequate protection of participants.

State/Local Human Subject Protections

Despite the nearly universal application of the Common Rule, state and local public health laws and regulations may additionally protect human subjects in public health research activities. A myriad of state regulations mimic core protections provided by the Common Rule. The degree and means of protection vary greatly from state to state. According to one commentator, some states (e.g., New York, California, and Virginia) have laws that specifically govern human subjects research, or explicitly address research design, but not at the level of specificity of the Common Rule. Most states' research protections are embedded within their public health regulations, authorizing statutes, and case law. Different oversight mechanisms are employed by states to hold public health officials accountable for compliance with the relevant state protections of human participants in public health activities.[38]

Health Information Privacy and the Public's Health

Protecting the privacy, confidentiality, and security of health data, whether in a research or public health activity, is fundamental to responsible data-sharing practices. Although often used interchangeably, the terms *privacy*, *confidentiality*, and *security* have distinct legal and ethical meanings as relates to identifiable health information.[3] Health information *privacy* broadly refers to individuals' rights to control the acquisition, uses, or disclosures of their identifiable health data. The closely related concept of *confidentiality* refers to the obligations of those who receive information to respect the privacy interests of individuals who are the subjects the data. In a legal sense, duties of confidentiality arise from specific relationships (e.g., doctor-patient, researcher-subjects). From an ethical perspective, health information privacy rights (grounded in individual autonomy) include a corresponding duty of confidentiality to which others must adhere.

Security is altogether different. It refers to technologic or administrative safeguards or tools to protect identifiable health data from unwarranted access or disclosure. Maintaining information security may become increasingly more difficult in the modern era of digitized exchanges and large electronic databases that can be hacked or infiltrated through unlawful invasions. However, electronic health systems also hold great promise for improving health care and public health efficiency as well as for protecting privacy and security.[1] The following statement is thus consistent with these definitions: "[I]f the *security* safeguards in an automated system fail or are compromised, a breach of *confidentiality* can occur and the *privacy* of data subjects invaded").[39]

Varied privacy and security laws and policies for sharing health data reflect the fragmented nature of legal protections of health information privacy. Neither constitutional principles nor judicial decisions (focused on common law conceptions of duties of confidentiality) support an individual's broad expectation of health information privacy. Rather, federal and state statutes and regulations are the dominant basis for health information privacy protections in the United States.[3] An array of significant federal and state laws, briefly discussed below, are intended to safeguard health information privacy.

Federal Privacy Laws and Policies

Before the introduction of the HIPAA Privacy Rule, no comprehensive federal health information privacy law existed. Rather, federal privacy laws generally applied to certain types of health information collected, maintained, or funded by the federal government through its specific agencies (e.g., Centers for Medicare and Medicaid Services, National Institutes of Health, Centers for Disease Control and Prevention [CDC]). These laws, some of which seem unrelated to health information privacy, protect the privacy of an individual's health information in various ways.

The federal Privacy Act of 1974 applies whenever information is collected and maintained by a federal agency in a system of records (e.g., Medicare records) in which the information is retrieved by an individual's name, identification number, or other identifier.[40] The Privacy Act was the first national law to introduce fair information practices that allow individuals to access their own government-held information. A person also may seek amendments to information that is not accurate, relevant, or complete. Among other things, the Privacy Act protects individual privacy by (1) specifying the situations in which a person's health information may be disclosed without that person's consent, and requiring consent in all other situations; (2) proscribing government maintenance of identifiable health information that is irrelevant and unnecessary to accomplish the agency's purposes; (3) requiring agencies to publish a notice about each record system describing its purpose and identifying disclosures outside the agency (e.g., "routine uses") that the agency has chosen administratively to make; and (4) requiring agencies to inform individuals of the statutory basis for collecting health information, purposes for which it is used, and consequences for not supplying the information.

The Freedom of Information Act (FOIA) provides that agency records created or maintained by an agency and under its control are available to the public unless specifically exempted from disclosure.[41] The Act contains nine exemptions, several of which help protect the privacy of some public health data, including the following:

- *Interagency and intra-agency communications.* Exemption (b)(5) permits the federal government to withhold from disclosure interagency and intra-agency memoranda or letters that would not be available "to a party other than an agency in litigation with the agency." This exemption may be used by the agency data holder, for example, to protect from disclosure a draft memorandum written by the investigator to his or her supervisor describing the early findings of an epidemiologic investigation.
- *Personnel and medical records.* Exemption (b)(6) permits an agency data holder to withhold from mandatory disclosure "personnel and medical files and similar files the disclosure of which would constitute a clearly unwarranted invasion of personal privacy." This exemption may be invoked to protect confidential medical information about a person contained in an agency record.
- *Information otherwise exempt from disclosure by statute.* Exemption (b)(3) provides that a federal agency may withhold from disclosure information "specifically exempted from disclosure by statute." For example, if a federal epidemiologic investigation is conducted under an assurance of confidentiality authorized by a federal statute (discussed below) the information collected pursuant to the confidentiality assurance may be exempted from disclosure under FOIA.[9]

Specific provisions of the E-Government Act of 2002 protect the confidentiality of federal government statistical collections of identifiable information, including health information.[42] The act restricts the use of information gathered for statistical uses to the purposes for which it is gathered and penalizes unauthorized disclosures. It also requires federal agencies to conduct "privacy assessments" before developing or procuring information technology that collects, maintains, or disseminates identifiable information.

Whereas the Privacy Act, FOIA, and the E-Government Act apply to all federal agencies, other federal privacy laws and regulations relate to particular government programs or agencies. For example, a federal statute protects the privacy of health information generated in federally assisted specialized substance abuse facilities.[43] The Common Rule, as noted above, requires that the privacy of human research subjects be reviewed in research proposals and that subjects be informed of existing confidentiality protections. Additional privacy protections for research and other health data are found in the Public Health Service Act (PHSA).[44] Sections 308(d) and 924(c) of the PHSA provide strong protection for identifiable information collected respectively by CDC's National Center for Health Statistics and DHHS's Agency for Healthcare Research and Quality.[45] Assurances of confidentiality under Section 308(d) can be used to protect individuals and institutions providing information. Section 308(d) provides that: "No [identifiable] information . . . may be used for any purpose other than the purpose for which it was supplied unless such establishment or person has consented. . . ."

Certificates of confidentiality, available to researchers within and outside government, are authorized under PHSA Section 301(d). DHHS can grant these certificates to to protect research participants from legally compelled disclosures of identifiable health information. Section 301(d) provides that health researchers may "protect the privacy of [research participants] by withholding from all persons not connected with the conduct of such research the names or other identifying characteristics of such [participants]." Researchers generally seek this confidentiality protection only when the health information collected is so sensitive (e.g., related to sexual practices or illegal conduct) that research subjects probably either would not participate or would provide inaccurate or incomplete responses without such protections.

State and Local Public Health Information Privacy Laws

Although many states have statutory laws similar to the federal Privacy Act and FOIA, and a few (e.g., California, Rhode Island, Maryland, Montana, and Washington) have passed additional privacy protections, most do not have comprehensive statutes regulating the acquisition, use and disclosure of individual health data.[3] Rather, state privacy laws tend to regulate specific data recipients (e.g., public health agencies, health insurers); certain medical tests, diseases, or conditions (e.g., genetic tests, HIV status, mental disorders); or particular data sources (e.g., nursing or health-care facilities).

State public health statutes feature the typical balance of privacy protections with the need to share identifiable health data for the public's health. For example, Colorado statutorily authorizes its board of health to require reporting of individual cases of disease (including the patient's name, address, age, sex, diagnosis, and other relevant information) to state and local health departments by any person having knowledge. Individual consent is not required. However, identifiable health data reported may not be disclosed except in limited, enumerated circumstances (e.g., to the extent necessary for the treatment, control, investigation, and prevention of conditions dangerous to the public health; or to the person who is the subject of a medical record or report).[46] State laws also may designate particular disease-related data as deserving additional, higher levels of privacy protections. Most states require the named reporting of HIV, for example, but some (e.g., Maryland) permit the use of unique identifiers.[47] Failure to maintain the confidentiality of individuals in reporting registries or other public health activities in violation of these legal protections may subject responsible persons to criminal and civil sanctions.[48]

Despite some important privacy safeguards, extant state laws concerning public health information privacy often are inconsistent, fragmented, and inadequate. These laws differ significantly in the degree of privacy protections afforded, give varying rights to access identifiable data, and allow multiple exceptions to disclosure prohibitions outside public health agencies. They may support in principle that public health records are private but (1) are silent about the degree of privacy protections, (2) fail to define narrowly who may have access to such data, (3) lack specificity about when information can be disclosed, (4) permissively allow disclosures to persons or for purposes that are inconsistent with public health (e.g. disclosure in legal settings through court orders or subpoenas), or (5) fail to address secondary disclosures of information for reasons that do not relate to their acquisition.[49] Significant, additional privacy protections of public health data are featured in the Model State Public Health Information Privacy Act of 1999, and, most recently, the Turning Point Model State Public Health Act of 2003.[49,50] Both acts introduce modern privacy language to protect the privacy and security of identifiable health data acquired, used, disclosed, or stored by state public health agencies while preserving the ability of state and local health departments to use health data responsibly for the common good.

The HIPAA Privacy Rule and the Public's Health

A significant development in the national protection of the privacy of medical information came in December 2000 with DHHS's publication of its "Standards for Privacy of Individually Identifiable Health Information"[5] pursuant to HIPAA.[6,d] Commonly referred to as the Privacy Rule, these regulations provide the first national standards for the protection of identifiable health information as applied to three types of covered entities: health plans, health-care clearinghouses, and health-care providers who conduct certain health-care transactions electronically.[7,51] Although the Rule sets a national floor of privacy protections for many exchanges of identifiable health data, it does not preempt more stringent state and local privacy laws.[3] The Privacy Rule took effect on April 14, 2001, with compliance required for most covered entities by April 14, 2003 (and small health plans by April 14, 2004).[2,e]

In general, the Privacy Rule establishes standards for covered entities to use and disclose "protected health information" (PHI), which includes individually identifiable health information.[52] A covered entity may use or disclose PHI only as required or permitted by the Privacy Rule. It requires disclosures (without written authorization) in only two instances: to the individual and to DHHS for compliance investigations, reviews, or enforcement actions. Permitted disclosures without individual authorization include those made (1) directly to the individual; (2) for treatment, payment, and health-care operations; (3) for specific purposes for which an individual must be given an opportunity to agree or object (such as inclusion in a health-care facility directory); (4) incident to an otherwise permitted use and disclosure; (5) for designated public interest; and (6) as a limited data set for research, public health, or health-care operations.[7] Any PHI that is de-identified consistent with the Rule no longer is covered and may be used or disclosed for any purpose.[52] Covered entities must adhere to additional requirements under the Rule, including the following:

- The need to obtain individual authorization that complies with the Privacy Rule for disclosures (other than those discussed above)[53]
- Release of the minimum necessary amount of PHI to accomplish the purpose of the disclosure[54]
- Provision of notice of privacy practices to individuals[55]
- Account of many disclosures of PHI when an individual requests an accounting[56]
- Establishment of privacy polices, procedures, and training for the covered entity and its workforce[57]

The primary intent of the Privacy Rule is to regulate the use and disclosure of PHI by covered entities. Nevertheless, the Rule has internal and external implications for public health practice. From an internal perspective, public health authorities may have to adhere to the Privacy Rule's requirements if they carry out "covered functions" (or functions that assimilate the activities of health plans, health-care clearinghouses, or health-care providers who perform certain electronic transactions).[58] For example, a local public health agency that operates a community health clinic providing basic health-care services for disadvantaged citizens may be considered a health-care provider if the agency electronically bills for its services.[7] As a result, the local public health agency must adhere to the full gamut of the Privacy Rule's requirements.

However, the local agency can simultaneously use PHI for public health purposes. The Rule specifically provides that such entities may "use protected health information in all cases in which it is permitted to disclose such information for public health activities. . . ."[59] The local agency also has the option to hybridize under the Privacy Rule.[7] By designating hybrid status, the agency may identify its covered and noncovered functions. Covered functions, like the operation of the clinic, must be conducted consistent with the Privacy Rule's requirements. Noncovered functions, such as the agency's surveillance activities, are not subject to these requirements.[7,60] Most public health agencies that conduct covered functions elect hybrid status.

Externally, public health authorities conduct many activities that require the acquisition, use, or disclosure of PHI from covered entities. The Privacy Rule's requirements apply to the disclosure of health data from a covered entity to a public health authority. Disclosures for public health purposes are established clearly among the 12 national priority purposes for which disclosures are permitted without individual authorization.[52,60] According to HIPAA, which essentially required permitted disclosures for state public health purposes: "Nothing in this part shall be construed to invalidate or limit the authority, power, or procedures established under any law providing for the reporting of disease or injury, child abuse, birth, or death, public health surveillance, or public health investigation or intervention."[61] Specifically, the Privacy Rule provides that covered entities may disclose PHI (without individual authorization) to the following:

- Public health authorities authorized by law to collect or receive such information for preventing or controlling disease, injury, or disability and to public heath or other government authorities empowered to receive reports of child abuse and neglect. Although undefined in the Privacy Rule, DHHS addressed the broad scope of the phrase "authorized by law" in the preamble to the final rule, which states, "When we describe an action as 'authorized by law,' we mean that a legal basis exists for the activity. [This] includes both actions that are permitted and actions that are required by law."[62]
- Entities subject to Food and Drug Administration (FDA) regulations regarding FDA-regulated products or activities for purposes such as adverse events reporting, tracking and recalls of FDA-regulated products, and postmarketing surveillance
- Individuals who may have contracted or been exposed to a communicable disease when notification is authorized by law
- Employers concerning a work-related illness or injury of an employee or workplace-related medical surveillance when needed by the employer to comply with the Occupational Safety and Health Act or other statute (e.g., state workers' compensation laws)[52,61]

The Privacy Rule broadly defines "public health authority" as "an agency or authority of the United States, a State, a territory, a political subdivision of a State or territory, or an Indian tribe, or person or authority acting under a grant of authority from or contract with such public agency, including the employees or agents of such public agency or its contractors or persons or entities to whom it has granted authority, that is responsible for public health matters as part of its official mandate."[63] This definition is based on the functions carried out by the entity and is intended to cover traditional public health authorities, such as CDC and tribal, state, and local health departments, as well as other agencies that have public health functions as part of their responsibilities, such as the Environmental Protection Agency or National Institutes of Health.[7] As defined, public health authorities also include persons, contractors, or other entities (e.g., academic institutions) to which a government agency has granted authority. The Rule's definition of public health authority thus encapsulates traditional government entities and their public- and private-sector partners.

Through additional guidance, DHHS has provided examples of language to verify that a person or entity is acting with a grant of public health authority for a particular activity.[7] To facilitate disclosures by a covered entity to traditional and nontraditional public health authorities, the authority may need to provide information that (1) verifies the identity and status of the individual or entity as a public health authority, (2) identifies the authorities' legal empowerment to acquire PHI for public health purposes, (3) cites applicable provisions of the Privacy Rule permitting the disclosure, (4) demonstrates the information requested is the minimum necessary needed, and (5) helps the covered entity comply with the Rule's accounting requirements. Alternatively, a public health authority may seek disclosures of de-identified data (under methods set out in the Rule) or limited data sets (in which specific, direct identifiers are removed from the PHI), or execute data-use agreements that allow exchange of PHI for limited purposes.

A separate provision of the Privacy Rule addresses disclosures by covered entities to public health authorities and others for research purposes.[64,f] Covered entities may disclose PHI to public health authorities for research purposes under several scenarios. This includes disclosures for research purposes (1) with individual authorization, (2) of de-identified information, (3) within a limited data set pursuant to a data-use agreement with the recipient, or (4) without individual authorization if the covered entity obtains documentation that an IRB or Privacy Board has waived the requirement for authorization or allowed an alteration pursuant to standards similar to those found in the Common Rule (discussed above). The Rule also describes how PHI can be used or disclosed for activities preparatory to research and for research on decedents' information, as well as how to apply the Rule's requirements to research that was ongoing before the compliance dates of the Rule.[65]

Distinguishing Public Health Practice and Research[g]

One of the core premises of privacy laws, policies, and ethics is that health information for public health or research purposes should be disclosed or used under clearly defined standards. This presumes that disclosures for public health practice are neatly distinguishable from disclosures for other purposes, such as research. This premise, however, is debatable.[66] Considerable uncertainty exists regarding how to distinguish research and nonresearch activities. The Common Rule and the Privacy Rule systematically require public health authorities to distinguish human subjects research activities from clinical care and public health practice. Yet, neither regulation provides clear guidance on what distinguishes these activities. As a result, researchers, practitioners, IRB members, and others may struggle to classify these activities under the applicable rules, potentially resulting in confusion, inconsistency, and breaches of confidentiality arising from poor, improper, and questionable decisions.

Public health activities (such as surveillance, epidemiologic investigation, and program evaluation) often are confused with human subjects research because both may involve the systematic acquisition and use of identifiable health data for health-related purposes. For example, an acute epidemiologic investigation of airline passengers possibly exposed to the virus that causes severe acute respiratory syndrome (SARS) may be viewed as a quintessential public health activity necessary to protect their and their contacts' health.[8] Yet if the investigation continues to collect data from asymptomatic passengers after incubation periods have expired, the data collection serves no health purpose for those persons, even though it may help public health officials assess important, generalizable characteristics about the disease. Public health practitioners at the federal, state, and local levels have struggled with these and other examples to determine whether their activities are public health practice or research.

In 2003, CSTE assembled an expert committee to improve guidance on the distinctions between human subjects research and public health practice activities. This work led to the production of CSTE's report, *Public Health Practice vs. Research: A Report for Public Health Practitioners Including Case Studies and Guidance*, which proposed a two-stage framework for classifying these activities.[8] As organized in the accompanying checklist (Table 10-1), the first stage draws on key assumptions and foundations of public health practice and research to distinguish these activities in relatively easy cases by reviewing those parameters that are exclusive to each activity. Eliciting essential characteristics, or foundations, of public health practice and research helps separate the easy and difficult cases, and eliminate some cases altogether from further need for classification.

Essential characteristics of public health practice (defined in the report as the collection and analysis of identifiable health data by a public health authority for the purpose of protecting the health of a particular community, where the benefits and risks are designed primarily to accrue to the participating community), include the following:

- Specific legal authorization for conducting the activity as public health practice at the federal, state, or local level. Although subject to interpretation, the intent of this parameter is to identify specific legislative or regulatory support for the public health activity (e.g., "the state department of health is authorized to conduct name-based reporting for HIV/AIDS disease among the population")
- A government obligation to perform the activity to protect the public's health
- Direct performance or oversight by a government public health authority (or its authorized partner) and accountability to the public for its performance
- Involvement of people who did not specifically volunteer to participate (i.e., they did not provide informed consent)

TABLE 10-1 Checklist for Distinguishing Public Health Practice and Human Subjects Research

This working model can help public health practitioners determine whether an activity is public health practice (practice) or human subjects research (research) consistent with the Common Rule and the HIPAA Privacy Rule. To use this checklist, answer the key Assumptions [As] and Questions [Qs] in Steps 1–4 below, proceeding in accordance with your responses, to reach the Conclusions in Step 5. In some cases, this process will not require addressing all of the steps; in others, each step may help clarify the distinction.

Steps and Related Assumptions and Questions	Next Action	
	If Yes, then	If No, then
Step 1: Check Key Assumptions		
Assumption 1.A: Are you a government public health official, agent, or agency, at the federal, tribal, state, or local level (or an authorized partner conducting public health activities through contract or other agreement)?	Go to **A 1.B.**	**Stop.** This Checklist does not apply.
Assumption 1.B: Does your activity involve the acquisition, use, or disclosure or identifiable health data (i.e., individually identifiable data that relate to a person's past, present, or future physical or mental health or condition or provision or payment of health care, or identifiable body tissues or biologic samples)?	Go to **Step 2.**	**Stop.** This Checklist does not apply.
Step 2: Assess the Foundations of Public Health Practice		
Assumption 2.A: In general, does your activity involve collection and analysis of identifiable health data for the purpose of protecting the health of a particular community, where the benefits and risks are designed primarily to accrue to the participating community?	Go to **Q 2.A.**	Go to Step 3.
Question 2.A: Do a *specific* legal authorization (through statute, administrative regulation, or other law) and corresponding government duty exist for using identifiable health data for a public health purpose that underlies the activity?	**Stop.** This activity is practice.	Go to **Q 2.B.**
Question 2.B: Does your activity involve direct performance or oversight by a government public health authority (or its authorized partner) and accountability to the public for its performance?	Go to **Q 2.C.**	Go to **Step 3.**
Question 2.C: Does your activity legitimately involve persons who must participate in the activity or did not specifically volunteer to participate (i.e., they did not provide informed consent absent a waiver under the Common Rule?)	**Stop.** This activity is practice.	Go to **Step 3.**

254

Step 3: Assess the Foundations of Human Subjects Research

Assumption 3.A: In general, does your activity involve the collection and analysis of identifiable health data for the purpose of generating knowledge that will benefit those beyond the community of persons who bear the risks of participation?

Question 3.A: Does your activity involve living individuals?

	Go to **Q 3.A.**
	The activity most likely is practice. Go to **Step 4.**
	Go to **Q 3.B.**
	Stop. This is not human subjects research.

Question 3.B: Does your activity involve, in part, private information as defined in the Common Rule?

	Go to **Q 3.C.**
	Stop. This is not human subjects research.

Question 3.C: Does your activity involve persons who voluntarily participate through informed consent or the consent of their guardians, absent a waiver of informed consent under the Common Rule?

	Go to **Step 4.**
	Stop. This activity is practice.

Step 4: Consider Enhanced Guidance

Question 4.A: *General Legal Authority:* Does *general* legal authorization exist (through statute, administrative regulation, or other law), as well as a corresponding government duty supporting the use of identifiable health data for a legitimate public health purpose?

	The activity is most likely practice. Go to **Q 4.B. 1-2**
	Go to **Q 4.B. 1-2**

Question 4.B.1: *Specific Intent:* Does any intent underlie the activity to test a hypothesis and seek to generalize the findings or acquired knowledge beyond the activity's participants?

	The activity is most likely research. Go to **Q 4.C.**	Go to **Q 4.B.2.**

Question 4.B.2: *Specific Intent:* Is the primary intent underlying the activity to ensure the conditions in which people can be healthy through public health efforts that are primarily aimed at preventing known or suspected injuries, diseases, or other conditions, or promoting the health of a particular community?

	The activity is most likely practice. Go to **Q 4.C.**	Go to **Q 4.C.**

Question 4.C: *Responsibility:* Is responsibility for the health, safety, or welfare of the participants vested or assigned to an identified person, such as a principal investigator?

	The activity is most likely research. Go to **Q 4.D 1-2**	Go to **Q 4.D.1.**

Question 4.D.1: *Participant Benefits:* Is the activity designed to provide some benefit to the participants or their population as a whole?

	The activity is most likely practice. Go to **Q 4.E.**	Go to **Q 4.D.2.**

255

(continued)

TABLE 10-1   *(continued)*

Steps and Related Assumptions and Questions	Next Action	
	If Yes, then	If No, then
Question 4.D.2: *Participant Benefits*: Does the activity involve additional risks imposed on participants to make the results generalizable beyond the participants themselves?	The activity is most likely research. Go to **Q 4.E.**	Go to **Q 4.E.**
Question 4.E: *Experimentation*: Is the activity designed to introduce nonstandard or experimental elements or methods to the research subjects or the analysis of their identifiable health data?	The activity is most likely research. Go to **Q 4.F.**	Go to **Q 4.F.**
Question 4.F: *Subject Selection*: Are the participants in the activity selected randomly so the results of the activity can be generalized to a larger population?	**Stop.** The activity is most likely research.	**Stop.** The activity is most likely practice.

Step 5: Conclusions

Conclusion 5.A: *Public Health Practice*. If your responses affirm that your activity (or some part thereof) is or most likely is public health practice, the activity is not subject to the Common Rule. However, it still must be conducted consistent with principles of law and ethics designed to protect individuals and their privacy while furthering the public's health. In addition, even though the HIPAA Privacy Act allows sharing of identifiable health data without written authorization for public health purposes, the Rule does not require data sharing. Authorization for disclosures from covered entities under the Rule derives from other public health laws or policies. For helpful guidance on the impact of the HIPAA Privacy Rule on public health practice, please see HIPAA Privacy Rule and Public Health: Guidance from CDC and DHHS, available at: http://www.cdc.gov/privacyrule/Guidance/Content.htm.

Conclusion 5.B: *Human Subject Research*. If your responses affirm that your activity (or some part thereof) is or most likely is human subjects research, the Common Rule may apply, subject to an exemption. In addition, the activity may be entitled to expedited review under the Common Rule. For additional guidance and a helpful flowchart, please see the Guidelines for the Conduct of Research published by the Office for Human Subjects Research at the National Institutes of Health: http://www.nihtraining.com/ohsrsite/guidelines/graybook.html.

- Adherence to principles of public health ethics that focus on populations while respecting the dignity and rights of individuals

Essential characteristics of human subjects research (defined in the report as the collection and analysis of identifiable health data for the purpose of generating knowledge that will benefit those beyond the participating community who bear the risks of participation) include these parameters:

- The subjects of the research are living individuals
- Identifiable private health information is gathered and produced
- Research subjects participate voluntarily, or participate with the consent of a guardian, absent a waiver of informed consent
- The researchers adhere to principles of bioethics that focus on the interests of individuals while balancing the communal value of research

These characteristics help distinguish public health practice from research in many of the easy cases. For example, a public health reporting requirement may be specifically authorized by state legislation or administrative regulation. Laws may require the public health agency to perform the activity to protect the public's health. Some states—for example, New York—statutorily clarify that epidemiologic investigations or other common public health practices are not human subjects research.[67] These activities are public health practice as long as their design and implementation do not cross over into research. In addition, if an activity may lawfully require the nonvoluntary compliance of autonomous individuals, it probably is not classifiable as research because voluntary consent is a foundation of research. Only through the waiver of the consent requirement—which requires IRB approval—may persons engage in federally funded human subjects research without providing informed consent. Furthermore, if an activity is designed as research but does not involve identifiable health data, it is not included in this analysis because it does not implicate the Privacy Rule.

The second stage of analysis proposed in the CSTE analysis introduces and explains enhanced principles of guidance to draw distinctions in more difficult cases. These include the following principles:

- *General legal authority*. Public health authorities may conduct activities pursuant to general legal authorization (e.g., the state department of health is authorized to "supervise and control communicable and chronic diseases") that may justify classifying an activity as public health practice subject to additional analysis.
- *Specific intent*. The intent of human subjects research is to test a hypothesis and generalize findings or acquired knowledge beyond the activity's participants. Conversely, the intent underlying public health practice is to ensure the conditions in which people can be healthy through public health efforts that are aimed primarily at preventing known or suspected injuries and diseases, or promoting the health of a particular community.
- *Responsibility*. Responsibility for the health, safety, and welfare of human participants in research falls on a specific individual, typically the principal investigator.

Public health practice, however, does not always vest responsibility for participants' welfare in individuals, but rather in government agencies or authorized
partner entities.

- *Participant benefits.* Public health practice should contribute to improving the
  health of participants and populations. In contrast, research might, but does not
  necessarily, benefit participants. Such is the nature of risk in research studies.
- *Experimentation.* Research may involve the application of something nonstand-
  ard or experimental in nature to human subjects or their identifiable health data.
  Public health practice is dominated by the use of standard, accepted, and proven
  interventions to address known or suspected public health problems.
- *Subject selection.* To reduce the possibility of bias in their studies, and to generalize their results, researchers may select human subjects randomly. Participants in public health practice activities are self-selected persons with, or at risk
  for, an affected disease or condition who can benefit from the activity.

No set of principles will completely distinguish between human subjects research,
public health practice, and other related activities. However, these principles may
help resolve most cases, provide consistency in rational decision-making, and improve application of privacy protections in public health and research settings.[66]

Conclusion

Protecting individual privacy and the public's health are indispensable objectives
within a national health infrastructure that increasingly exchanges health data through
electronic means. Neither goal can be neglected because privacy and public health
are synergistic. Individuals rely on public health authorities to protect the health of
communities, which requires access to identifiable health data. Public health authorities rely on individuals to participate in research studies or provide timely and accurate health data through covered entities and others, which requires privacy protections
for health information. Modern privacy laws and protections, such as the HIPAA
Privacy Rule, recognize this synergy, balancing essential disclosures for public health
and research purposes with individual privacy interests.

   However, challenges remain. The digitization of health records continues to stretch
existing conceptions of responsible data practices. Privacy laws can impede legitimate data flows to public health authorities. Research protections can limit acquisitions or uses of identifiable health data by public health authorities, even for laudable
purposes. Distinguishing public health practice and research activities is complicated
by existing, variant standards among public health agencies, private sector partners,
and research institutions. Conversely, potential abuses in the sharing of individual
health data can lead to individual and communal harms. Although the informational
landscape for data uses in public health practice is by no means perfect, it is improving through greater efforts to explore the need for workable standards of privacy
protections for public health data in all their many uses.

We acknowledge Nanette R. Elster and John R. Livengood, whose work on Chapter
8, "Public Health Research and Health Information," in the 1st edition of this text

contributed in part to this chapter. We thank James Buehler for his expert reviews of the outline and draft of this chapter, as well as Erin Fuse Brown and Jessica O'Connell for their research and reviews of various drafts of this chapter.

Notes

a. In *United States v. Westinghouse Electric Corp.*, 638 F.2d 570, 578 (3d Cir. 1980), the Third Circuit enunciated five factors to be balanced in determining the scope of the constitutional right to informational privacy: (1) the type of record and the information it contains, (2) the potential for harm in any unauthorized disclosure, (3) the injury from disclosure to the relationship in which the record was generated, (4) the adequacy of safeguards to prevent nonconsensual disclosure, and (5) the degree of need for access (i.e., a recognizable public interest).

b. See, for example, *Westinghouse*, 638 F.2d at 578–9 (noting strong public interest in facilitating research and investigations of CDC's National Institute for Occupational Safety and Health); *Barry v. City of New York*, 712 F.2d 1554, 1560 (2d Cir. 1983) (finding city's financial disclosure law furthered a substantial state interest in deterring corruption and conflicts of interest); *Schacter v. Whalen*, 581 F.2d 35, 37 (2d Cir. 1978) (finding information crucial to implementation of sound state policy of investigating licensed physicians for medical misconduct).

c. See *Doe v. Borough of Barrington*, 729 F. Supp. 376 (D.N.J. 1990) (holding that a police officer violated constitutional right to privacy by disclosing that a person was infected with HIV); *Woods v. White*, 689 F. Supp. 874 (W.D. Wis. 1988) (extending constitutional right to privacy to disclosure of prisoner's HIV status by prison medical service personnel), affirmed, 899 F.2d 17 (7th Cir. 1990); *Carter v. Broadlawns Medical Ctr.*, 667 F. Supp. 1269 (S.D. Iowa 1987) (holding that giving chaplains open access to patient medical records violated privacy rights of patients), cert. denied, 489 U.S. 1096 (1989).

d. The Final Rule was published on December 28, 2000, by the outgoing administration of President Clinton. DHHS subsequently reopened the comment period and published an amended Final Rule on August 14, 2002.

e. The text of the Privacy Rule, detailed guidance material, and answers to frequently asked questions are available on the official Web site for the DHHS Office for Civil Rights, the agency responsible for interpreting and enforcing the Rule (http://www.hhs.gov/ocr/hipaa).

f. Official DHHS guidance on the research implications for the Privacy Rule is available at http://privacyruleandresearch.nih.gov.

g. The methodologies and principles discussed in this section have not been adopted or endorsed by DHHS's Office for Human Research Protections.

References

1. Hodge JG Jr, Gostin LO, Jacobson P. Legal issues concerning electronic health information. *JAMA* 1999;282:1466–71.
2. Gostin LO, Hodge JG Jr. Personal privacy and common goods: a framework for balancing under the National Health Information Privacy Rule. *Minn Law Rev* 2002;86:1439–80.
3. Hodge JG Jr. Health information privacy and public health. *J Law Med Ethics* 2004;31: 4:663–71.
4. 45 CFR 46 *et seq* (1993).

5. 45 CFR 160.101 *et seq* (2004).

6. Pub L 104-191, 110 Stat 1936 (1996).

7. CDC. HIPAA Privacy Rule and public health: guidance from the Centers for Disease Control and the Department of Health and Human Services. *MMWR* 2003;52(Supp):1–20.

8. Hodge JG Jr, Gostin LO, CSTE Advisory Committee. *Public Health Practice vs. Research: A Report for Public Health Practitioners Including Case Studies and Guidance.* May 17, 2004. Available at http://www.cste.org/pdffiles/newpdffiles/CSTEPHResRptHodgeFinal .5.24.04.pdf. Accessed July 10, 2005.

9. Neslund VS, Goodman RA, Fleming DW. Frontline public health: surveillance and outbreak investigations. In: Goodman RA, Rothstein MA, Hoffman RE, Lopez W, Matthews GW, eds. *Law in Public Health Practice.* New York: Oxford University Press, 2003:143–59.

10. 32 CFR 219 (1991).

11. Elster NR, Hoffman RE, Livengood JR. Public health research and health information. In: Goodman RA, Rothstein MA, Hoffman RE, Lopez W, Matthews GW, eds. *Law in Public Health Practice.* New York: Oxford University Press, 2003:160–74.

12. *DeShaney v Winnebago County Dept of Soc Services*, 489 US 189 (1989).

13. Gostin LO. Health information privacy. *Cornell Law Rev* 1995;80:451–507.

14. Hodge JG Jr. The role of new federalism and public health law. *J Law Health* 1998;12:309–57.

15. Gostin LO. *Public Health Law: Power, Duty, Restraint.* Berkeley: University of California Press, 2000:48.

16. 429 US 589 (1977).

17. 429 US 589, 593–594 (1977).

18. 45 CFR 46.103 (1991).

19. Office for Human Research Protection. Engaging in Human Subjects Research by Institutions. [Memorandum of January 26, 1999]. Available at http://www.hhs.gov/ohrp/humansubjects/assurance/engage.htm. Accessed January 23, 2004; November 1, 2005.

20. 45 CFR 46.102(f) (1991).

21. National Institutes of Health. Regulations and Ethical Guidelines. *Guidelines for the Conduct of Research Involving Human Subjects at the National Institutes of Health.* Available at http://www.nihtraining.com/ohsrsite/guidelines/graybook.html. Accessed January 23, 2004.

22. 45 C.F.R. §46.101(b)(1) (1991).

23. 45 C.F.R. §46.101(b)(2) (1991).

24. .45 C.F.R. §46.101(b)(3) (1991).

25. .45 C.F.R. § 46.101(b)(4) (1991).

26. 45 C.F.R. § 46.101(b)(5) (1991).

27. 45 C.F.R. § 46.101(b)(6) (1991).

28. National Bioethics Advisory Commission. *Ethical and Policy Issues in Research Involving Human Participants.* Available at http://www.georgetown.edu/research/nrcbl/nbac/pubs .html. Accessed November 5, 2003.

29. 45 CFR 46.110 (1991).

30. Office for Human Research Protection. *Categories of Research that May Be Reviewed by an Institutional Review Board (IRB) through an Expedited Review Procedure.* November 9, 1998. Available at http://www.hhs.gov/ohrp/humansubjects/guidance/expedited98 .htm. Accessed January 23, 2004.

31. 45 CFR 46.111(a)(4)–(5) (1991).

32. 45 CFR 46.111(a)(7) (1991).

33. 45 CFR 46.111(a)(1)–(2) (1991).

34. 45 CFR 46.111(a)(3) (1991).

35. 45 CFR 46.109(e) (1991); 46.111(a)(6) (1991).
36. 45 CFR 46.111(b) (1991); 45 CFR 46.201 (1991); 45 CFR 46.301(1991); 45 CFR 46.401 (1991).
37. 45 CFR 46.116(d)(1)–(4) (2001).
38. Burris S, Gable L, Stone L, Lazzarini Z. The role of state law in protecting human subjects of public health research and practice. *J Law Med Ethics* 2004;31:654–62.
39. Ware W. Lessons for the future: dimensions of medical record keeping. In: *Health Records: Social Needs and Personal Privacy 43*. Conference proceedings. 1993. Available at http://aspe.hhs.gov/pic/pdf/4441.pdf. Accessed July 11, 2005.
40. 5 USC 552(a) (1988).
41. 5 USC 552 (1988).
42. Pub L 107-347 (2002).
43. 42 USC 290dd-2 (Supp V 1993).
44. 42 USCA 242m(d) (1997).
45. 42 USC 242m(d) and 299c-3 (2001).
46. Colo Rev Stat Ann 25-1-122.
47. Gostin LO, Hodge JG Jr. The "names" debate: the case for national HIV reporting in the United States. *Albany Law Rev* 1998;61:679–743.
48. Gostin LO, Lazzarini Z, Neslund VS, Osterholm MT. The public health information infrastructure: a national review of the law on health information privacy. *JAMA* 1996;275:1921–27.
49. Gostin LO, Hodge JG Jr, Valdiserri RO. Informational privacy and the public's health: the model state public health privacy act. *Am J Public Health* 2001;91:1388–92.
50. The Center for Law and the Public's Health. Model state public health laws. Turning Point Model State Public Health Act. September 16, 2003. Available at http://www.publichealthlaw.net/Resources/Modellaws.htm. Accessed November 24, 2004.
51. 45 CFR §164.502(a)(2) (2003).
52. DHHS. OCR Privacy Brief. *Summary of the HIPAA Privacy Rule: HIPAA Compliance Assistance, 2003*. Available at http://www.hhs.gov/ocr/privacysummary.pdf #search='OCR%20Privacy%20Brief.%20Summary%20of%20the%20HIPAA%20Privacy%20Rule'. Accessed September 12, 2005.
53. 45 CFR §164.508 (2003).
54. 45 CFR §164.502 (2003).
55. 45 CFR §164.520 (2003).
56. 45 CFR §164.528 (2003).
57. 45 CFR §164.530 (2003).
58. 45 CFR §164.500 (2003).
59. 45 CFR §164.512(b)(2) (2003).
60. 45 CFR §§164.103 and 164.105 (2003).
61. Pub L 104-191, 110 Stat 1936, §1178(b) (1996).
62. 64 Fed Reg 59929 (November 1999).
63. 45 CFR 164.501 (2003).
64. 45 CFR §164.512(o) (2003).
65. 45 CFR §164.532(c) (2003).
66. Hodge JG Jr. An enhanced approach to distinguishing public health practice and human subjects research. *J Law Med Ethics* 2005; 33:1:125–41.
67. NY Public Health Law §2441(2) (McKinney 2002).

Chapter 11

LEGAL AUTHORITIES FOR INTERVENTIONS IN PUBLIC HEALTH EMERGENCIES

Gene W. Matthews, Ernest B. Abbott,
Richard E. Hoffman, and Martin S. Cetron*

> Every imaginable threat from civil suits to cold-blooded murder when they
> got an opportunity to commit it, was made by the writhing, cursing, strug-
> gling tramps who were operated upon, and a lot of them had to be held
> down in their cots, one big policeman sitting on their legs, and another
> on their heads, while the third held the arms, bared for the doctors.
> Account of the 1901–1903 smallpox epidemic in Boston[1]

The public health measures used to control the 1901–03 outbreak of smallpox in
Boston no doubt appear draconian to a modern-day public health officer. Recently,
however, public health officers, academics, and government policymakers, motivated
by concerns about the threat of bioterrorism, have grappled with the complex public
policy and risk-communication issues involved in planning a widespread, rapid
smallpox vaccination program. Moreover, since 2000, the public health community
has faced a cascade of new and emerging infection threats, including West Nile virus,
"mad cow" disease, severe acute respiratory syndrome (SARS), monkeypox, and
avian influenza. In 2005, the troubled response to Hurricane Katrina at all levels of
government not only revealed the fragility of the country's emergency preparedness
and response systems but also demonstrated how quickly a natural catastrophe could

* The findings and conclusions in this chapter are those of the author(s) and do not necessarily represent the views of the U.S. Department of Health and Human Services or the Centers for Disease Control
and Prevention.

create a public health crisis. These events underscore the importance of public health officers understanding their legal authorities to ensure an effective, well-reasoned, and appropriate response that will respect individual rights in a public health emergency. These recent experiences also have drawn new attention to this sector of law that is used in preparing for and handling such public health emergency episodes.

In this chapter, the term "public health emergencies" encompasses the broad spectrum of natural and environmental problems, as well as deliberate and other human-made problems, often acute and affecting the public's health on a relatively large scale. We first provide the historical context to the current revision of legal authorities that may be needed in public health emergencies. We then describe the array of legal authorities available to practitioners, including the traditional public health powers to manage property and protect persons, as well as the federal and state emergency management laws and structures that must be brought carefully to bear during a public health emergency. Finally, we highlight cutting-edge emerging issues that are likely to challenge public health officials and stakeholders as the demands of 21st century public health emergency practice continue to unfold.

Historical Perspective: Sources of Legal Authority for Public Health Emergency Situations

Context: State Public Health Laws and Federal Assistance

In the United States, the major source of legal authority for public health interventions historically has been the police power, defined as the inherent authority of all sovereign governments to enact laws and promote regulations that safeguard the health, welfare, and morals of citizens (Table 11-1). Under the authority of the police power, for example, states have enacted laws for nuisance abatement, traffic safety, and firearms safety. During colonial times, public health interventions were exercised primarily at the local level, with some of the earliest municipal ordinances enacted by Boston in 1647 and New York in 1663. Local boards of health eventually were organized, leading to more extensive state public health laws and regulations in the late 18th and early 19th centuries. At the time the Constitution was framed, such public health powers as quarantine were well established.[2] The Tenth Amendment reserves to the states all powers not expressly granted to the federal government nor otherwise prohibited by the Constitution, including the police power.

Even though the Constitution reserves the police power to the states, the federal government nonetheless has extensive authority over public health by virtue of the Commerce Clause, which grants it the exclusive power to regulate interstate and foreign commerce.[3,4] Under this authority, for example, the federal government has enacted such diverse laws as those prohibiting racial discrimination, mandating environmental cleanup, and criminalizing certain activities such as loan sharking.[2] In the area of public health, the federal government has authority under the Constitution to medically examine immigrants seeking entry into the United States and to quarantine infectious persons when they are about to move from one state to another.[5–7]

TABLE 11-1   State Emergency Public Health Powers

Power	Source	Restriction
Disease reporting and medical surveillance	Police power reserved to states under Tenth Amendment	Constitutionally recognized right to privacy; state statutes covering medical privacy
Subpoena of business information (e.g., customer lists, shipping information)	Derived from state statute	Fourth Amendment right against "unreasonable" searches and seizures; trade secrets and other information may be viewed as "property" under the Fifth and Fourteenth amendments
Commandeer private buildings and seize pharmaceuticals	Police power	Fifth and Fourteenth amendments' requirements of due process and just compensation
Abate nuisances	Police power	No compensation required if deemed a "nuisance," otherwise a "taking" requiring compensation
Personal-control measures (e.g., quarantine, compelled medical testing, mandatory vaccination)	Police power	Considered a significant deprivation of "liberty" requiring due process; Equal Protection Clause implicated if applied in a discriminatory manner; possibly First Amendment Freedom of Religion Clause
Legal immunity	State statute may provide legal immunity from lawsuits under state law	42 USC §1983 authorizes damage awards for violation of rights under the Constitution subject to doctrine of "qualified immunity"
Dissemination of public health information	Unclear whether the police power authorizes control of media outlets	First Amendment doctrine of "prior restraint" generally prohibits government from censoring information in advance of publication

The federal government also may significantly affect public health policy under its constitutional authority to tax and spend. Article I, Section 8, of the U.S. Constitution states that "Congress shall have the power to lay and collect taxes . . . and provide for the common defense and general welfare of the United States." While recent Supreme Court decisions may have limited the scope of Congress's Commerce Clause power, courts have remained deferential to Congress's use of the tax-and-spend power. Beginning in the 1960s, Congress used its tax-and-spend power to enact an array of categorical grant programs to state and local governments to support prevention efforts for such politically popular programs as childhood vaccination, environmental protection, sexually transmitted disease control, tuberculosis control, occupational health, and injury prevention. After the events of September 11, 2001, Congress has used this same tax-and-spend authority to reallocate federal resources to state and local governments to improve response capabilities to handle terrorism threats, including bioterrorism.

Organizational Scope of Public Health Emergency Law

Traditionally, "public health" distinguishes itself from medical care by its focus on the community as a whole rather than on the individual patient. Accordingly, public health emergency laws must initially facilitate the joint efforts of local and state health departments, federal agencies, and public or private health-care facilities. State public health organizational structures may have separate legal authorities for public health, mental health, Medicaid services, and emergency management services. On the other hand, some states may place all such community service units organizationally inside a single "umbrella agency" containing overlapping legal jurisdiction.

The concept of a public health emergency covers a spectrum of contexts in modern society. In the narrow context, a public health emergency may be a stand-alone event that requires only the narrow legal authority necessary to handle a single public health event, such as the traditional response to a community outbreak of viral encephalitis or influenza. In the broader context, practitioners may encounter a combination of events that require more careful legal coordination with many other disciplines, such as law enforcement, emergency management, labor, transportation, social services, military, and health-care services.

The Rise of the 20th-Century "Silos" and Homeland Security Agencies

During the last half of the 20th century, state and federal civil defense agencies evolved into all-hazard agencies that also prepared for and coordinated response to natural catastrophes. Furthermore, federal ad hoc response authorities were consolidated with the enactment of the Disaster Relief Acts of 1969 and 1974 and the Robert T. Stafford Disaster Relief and Emergency Assistance Act of 1988 (Stafford Act).[8] These laws encouraged the independent development and training of a new emergency management chain of command at the local, state, and federal levels. This legislative initiative also included a clear federal funding stream that was separate from the appropriations used to support public health agencies. One long-range impact of the latter was the steady evolution over the last 40 years of independent emergency management agencies (EMAs) inside governments, and such separate EMAs were not closely linked organizationally, financially, or legislatively with the comparable public health agency. Separate institutional cultures evolved over time.

Most recently in this evolutionary process, as a direct consequence of the terrorist attacks in 2001, elected officials responded by creating various homeland security agencies at the local, state, and federal levels. Accordingly, many of the comprehensive sets of skills and laws needed to handle the complexities of modern public health emergencies are diffused across an array of organizational "silos" that include public health, fire and emergency medical services, homeland security, emergency management, law enforcement, food protection, and agricultural agencies (Figure 11-1). Furthermore,

Figure 11-1. The Silos of Federal, State, and Local "Legal Preparedness"

each of these "silos" also contains internal organizational layering and legal stratification at the local, state, and federal levels.

One key legal challenge confronting any public health emergency response is the need for rapid coordination of the complex legal authorities and jurisdictions within a sometimes-confusing matrix of government partners. The aftermath of Hurricane Katrina demonstrated that improving such coordination among these "silos" remains a work in progress for all levels of government, including public health.

Legal Authorities Used in Public Health Emergencies

Traditional Public Health Powers

Public health practitioners have retained a sense of practical experience in the use of traditional public health powers to control the behavior of individual persons on a case-by-case basis. For example, most public health jurisdictions are familiar with the application of a gradually escalating series of control measures to restrict the risk of a noncompliant patient with tuberculosis from spreading an active case of disease to other contacts. Such specific controls usually are imposed with procedural respect for the legal rights of the individual involved.[2]

Although the handling of health risks posed by *individual persons* has remained within the skill set of most public health departments, few situations have occurred during the past several decades when a health department had to impose legally enforced *communitywide* restrictions to prevent the spread of an infectious disease. However, the dual threats of bioterrorism and emerging infections now present officials with the dilemma of imposing communitywide control measures (that most recently were practiced widely during the first half of the 20th century), while still respecting the procedural rights and civil liberties to which our society has become accustomed to expect during the latter part of the 20th century.

The Emergency Management System

Although emergency management organizations at the local, county, and state levels may be known by different official titles and have varying organizational structures, each organization performs the basic functions of emergency management: coordinating the efforts of all government agencies (and even private and volunteer actors); responding to an incident to stabilize the incident; and protecting life, property, and the environment. For command, control, and coordination, EMAs at all levels of government now generally use the Incident Command System (ICS). Under the ICS, the local incident commander is in charge at an event, and other agencies provide resources to support the actions of the incident commander. To ensure these ICSs are compatible with each other—so resources drawn from multiple jurisdictions can work effectively together in response to an incident—the federal Department of Homeland Security has developed the National Incident Management System (NIMS). All agencies of the federal government require a local government adopt NIMS to be eligible to receive federal preparedness grants.[a]

The Department of Homeland Security also has developed the National Response Plan, signed by all cabinet agencies of the federal government, establishing the framework for how federal agencies will interact with each other and with state, local, and tribal governments; the private sector; and nongovernment organizations. The National Response Plan defines and specifies roles and responsibilities for domestic incident prevention, preparedness, mitigation, response, and recovery activities. In the basic response structure under the National Response Plan, federal assistance is provided through 15 different support functions (e.g., "communications," "transportation," and "mass care"), staffed as appropriate for the nature of the incident.[b] To ensure coordination, state assistance is organized into the same support functions, and the state and federal coordinators are located in the same joint field office. As an indication of the significance of electronic communication in a 21st century emergency situation, a joint information center also is established to allow spokespersons from all levels of government to share and disseminate to the media and the public reliable and consistent information about an incident.[c]

During the past half-century, public health officials have had extraordinary success in preventing outbreaks of communicable diseases in the United States from rising to emergency levels. Vaccination programs have eradicated smallpox, nearly eradicated polio and guinea worm disease, and addressed tuberculosis (TB) and acquired immunodeficiency syndrome (AIDS) without generally involving the emergency management system. However, larger incidents may require emergency resources, as well as the police or National Guard, which sometimes are brought to bear during natural disasters. Such resources could be needed, for example, to provide shelters and emergency food and housing for displaced persons in the event homes or businesses become contaminated by radiation or infectious agents, to put in place new facilities and personnel, to distribute drugs on a mass scale, and to enforce evacuation or quarantine orders. In these situations, effective coordination of public health responses through established emergency response systems—including NIMS and the National Response Plan—can try to ensure that the different organizational silos, which must participate in the response, can communicate and coordinate with each other.

Emergency Declarations

Public health officials at the local, state, and federal levels generally have the authority to exercise principal control measures to prevent the spread of communicable disease without declaring a public health emergency, including (1) quarantine and isolation, (2) travel restrictions, (3) contact tracing, and (4) medical examinations and treatment. Indeed, in two well-known recent disease incidents that provoked major government action and widespread media attention (the anthrax envelopes found in offices and mail facilities in Washington, Florida, and New Jersey in late 2001 and the SARS outbreak in 2003) federal, state, and local public health and emergency management officials did not officially declare an emergency. Yet, as the potential severity of incidents increases, requiring improved coordination of response resources from multiple agencies and multiple levels of government, understanding the relevance of declarations to emergency response becomes more important.

Declaring a disaster or emergency is much more than a public announcement, even though such a declaration usually is accompanied by a press release or televised announcement advising the public that an emergency situation exists and that emergency plans, resources, and EMA authorities are being activated to address it. A declaration also is a formal legal document or determination made by an authorized official, in accordance with criteria specified by law, which has the particular effect specified in the governing law: a declaration may (1) trigger special emergency powers, (2) allow expenditure of emergency funds or expenditure of funds in advance or in lieu of appropriation, or (3) waive or modify normal legal requirements.

Several types of declarations exist that mirror the possible ways in which state and federal legislatures can provide special powers to government officials who face and declare publicly the existence of varying types of emergencies covering particular geographic areas (states or counties) or involving particular types of problems (such as drought or transportation emergencies).

State Emergency Declarations

For state emergency declarations, state law determines such factors as (1) who can issue a declaration order (governor, state public health officer, or local official), (2) what factual findings the official must make and procedures the official must follow in issuing a declaration, (3) how long a declaration can last before being renewed or before being ratified by the legislature, and (4) what emergency powers can be exercised once the declaration is in effect. A declaration of emergency by a governor frequently bestows substantial powers on officials delegated by the governor. For example, in Florida, the governor has the power, after declaring a state of emergency, to suspend the effect of any statute, rule, ordinance, or order of any state, regional, or local government entity as needed to cope with the disaster;[d] to direct all state, regional, and local government agencies, including law enforcement agencies;[9] to confiscate any private property needed to address the disaster;[10] to order the evacuation of all persons from any part of the state and regulate the movement of persons and traffic within the state;[11] and to re-delegate his or her powers to subordinates by designating one or more deputy state coordinating officers and alternate authorized representatives to act in his or her absence.[12] These authorities then can be exercised for the duration of the emergency, regardless of whether it was caused by a hurricane or other natural event or by a chemical spill or terrorist attack involving a biologic weapon.

Federal Declarations

Two federal declarations involving two separate federal agencies are particularly important in the context of public health emergencies. First, the Secretary of Health and Human Services can declare a public health emergency covering a designated area.[13] This declaration authorizes the Secretary to "take such action as may be appropriate to respond to the public health emergency," including mobilizing the Public Health Service Corps, suspending various Medicare and Medicaid requirements that become impractical during an emergency, providing emergency approvals for the use of unapproved or experimental drugs, and granting assistance (when funds have been appropriated). Second, the President can, at the request of a governor,[e] declare an "emergency" under the Stafford Act,[f] allowing the Federal Emergency Management Agency (FEMA) to direct any federal agency, using any federal resources and authority, to take action "in support of state and local emergency assistance efforts to save lives, protect property and the public health and safety, and lessen or avert the threat of a catastrophe."[14] The Stafford Act declaration is particularly important because it allows the federal government to fund its response actions from the Disaster Relief Fund, a large standing appropriation available for response to declared major disasters and emergencies.

Management of Property: Seizures, Takings, Nuisances, and Coordination

Public health officers retain traditional legal authorities concerning the control of private property. In general, state laws authorize health departments to take, destroy, or restrict the use of private property to protect the health and safety of the community. These powers often include the authority to enter suspicious premises, close facilities on an emergency basis, and seize and destroy contaminated articles.

These historical police powers (Table 11–1) flow out of the constitutional and statutory sources by which the government protects the public. This same fundamental framework of authority also contains constitutional and statutory restrictions to safeguard certain personal rights of the property owners, such as the rights of due process and just compensation when the government commandeers property during an emergency. Despite the historical constitutional grounding of these powers over property, even an abstract discussion about these traditional powers can touch on current public sensitivities regarding the proper role of government in controlling privately owned property.

A bioterrorism event, large-scale epidemic, or other public health emergency nonetheless can require even greater government control of private property than that to which the public is accustomed. For example, public health officers may have to designate certain hospitals to receive infected patients and transfer uninfected patients to other facilities. In addition, health officers may have to redirect medicines from local hospitals and pharmacies; establish priorities for the use of limited stockpiles of pharmaceuticals among the population; and temporarily commandeer additional private facilities, such as hotel rooms that operate on separate ventilation systems and drive-through restaurant facilities that easily can be used to dispense medication. The disposal of human corpses may differ radically in a large-scale epidemic, and public health officers may be required to issue orders directing how corpses should be treated.[15,16]

One fundamental factor that clearly raises the sensitivity regarding government control over private property is whether the private owner will be compensated for the loss of his or her property. In general, the government does *not* provide compensation when exercising its police power to close or regulate property to protect the public from unsafe conditions or nuisances. Accordingly, governments can close a restaurant because of unsanitary conditions or condemn an unsafe structure after an earthquake without compensating the owner because the purpose of the closing is to protect the public.

On the other hand, when government "takes" a person's property for a government purpose, such as using a private facility during an emergency, then the owner generally *is* entitled to compensation for such loss. Accordingly, in a "takings" situation, the major legal constraints on a public health department's use of private property are the constitutional requirements of due process and just compensation. The Constitution states that the government may not take private property for public use without compensating the owner.[17] Similarly, the government generally must provide notice and an opportunity for a hearing before depriving a landowner of the use of private property.[18] Although the concept of compensation for public use appears simple, under what circumstances the government must compensate private landowners has been the subject of extensive litigation.

Even though government may legitimately abate nuisances, it may not avoid paying compensation to private property owners by simply declaring their activities to be nuisances. Rather, the U.S. Supreme Court has held that government must rely on "background principles of nuisance and property law" requiring that government find some precedent, either in common law or in the law pertaining to private nuisance suits, that allows it to declare an activity to be a nuisance.[19] Some legal commentators have argued that this approach unduly hampers public health departments because it forces health officers to rely on often vague and outdated concepts of what constitutes a public health threat.[2]

Management of Persons: Quarantine, Detention, and Treatment

The modern developments of new emerging infections and terrorism activity also require some understanding of the historical context of measures used to reduce public health threats from individual persons who pose a risk to others (Box 11-1). As with property matters, management of people in such emergencies requires careful balancing of the risk to the community and protection of the rights of the individual.

Legal Authorities

In some narrow contexts, Americans are familiar with the state's authority to restrain personal liberty to protect the public health and safety. For example, state and local police have authority to restrain individuals where necessary to protect the public health and safety. This "police power" is exercised frequently in natural disaster settings; it is used to order evacuation from areas rendered unsafe by the derailment and rupture of a chemical tank car or from a low-lying area threatened by a major hurricane; it is used to close a road that has become unsafe because of threat of avalanche or mudslide or even to prohibit entry into a crime scene. Similarly, public health officials in every state have authority, when faced with an outbreak of a communicable disease, to order a specific individual who poses a real threat to undergo a physical examination, to provide information, and even to detain that person in a medical or other public facility or in his or her own home.[2]

Exercise of compulsory public health powers—whether through quarantine, isolation, mandatory vaccination, or mandatory treatment—invariably restricts an individual's liberty and implicates constitutional rights. In 1905, in *Jacobson v. Massachusetts*, the Supreme Court upheld a mandatory vaccination law despite its impact on individual's rights. The Court noted that "[r]eal liberty for all could not exist if each individual can use his own, whether in respect of his person or property, regardless of the injury that may be done to others. . . . Upon the principle of self defense, of paramount necessity, a community has the right to protect itself against an epidemic of disease which threatens the safety of its members." Thus, the Supreme Court held that the police power of a state embraces compulsory public health measures required to protect the public health and safety. However, this power is not absolute; it is limited to "reasonable" regulations, and the measures cannot "contravene the Constitution of the United States, or with any right which that instrument gives or secures."[20] Exercise of compulsory public health powers must therefore provide "due process" and cannot deny "equal protection" to affected individuals.

Due Process Protections

In contrast to situations involving control of specific individuals, no major outbreak of a highly communicable disease has occurred in the United States since the polio outbreaks of the early 1950s that required quarantine or other such communitywide control measures limiting movement or public gatherings. Hence, how contemporary courts may react to a communitywide quarantine on the scale of the historic Boston smallpox outbreak is unclear. However, courts do closely scrutinize government actions that result in the involuntary commitment of individuals. For example,

BOX 11-1. Public Health Powers Protecting Individuals

Cordon sanitaire: Literally a "sanitary cord" which, by tradition, is placed by health authorities around an infected area to control, restrict, or prohibit the movement of persons and articles into or out of a location where a contagious disease exists.

Isolation: The separation, for the period of communicability, of *known infected persons* in such places and under such conditions as to prevent or limit the transmission of the infectious agent.

Quarantine: The restriction of the activities of *healthy persons* who have been exposed to a communicable disease, during its period of communicability, to prevent disease transmission during the incubation period if infection should occur.

Shelter in place: A modern concept to decrease the level of personal exposure in a community by asking individuals to remain in their homes, schools, or work locations while a chemical, radiologic, or biologic threat exists. Shelter in place sometimes is referred to as "snow day."

Work quarantine: A measure developed by Toronto health officials during the 2003 SARS epidemic to relieve hospital staff shortages by asking certain health-care workers who had been exposed to SARS but showed no signs of infection to agree voluntarily to work in certain hospital units while wearing recommended personal protective equipment. Such persons in work quarantine continued to maintain the standard quarantine procedures in their homes and avoided public transportation when moving between homes and work.

courts have held, in the context of civil commitment to mental hospitals, that involuntary commitment is a significant deprivation of liberty requiring both procedural and substantive due process of law.[21] In the context of detaining infectious persons, procedural due process requires the state to provide written notice of the behavior or condition that allegedly poses a risk to the community, access to counsel, a full and impartial hearing, and an appeal.[g] Even though the state ordinarily must provide notice and a hearing before detaining someone, the law recognizes that, just as police may detain rioters without a warrant to protect the public safety, so can the state temporarily detain persons who may spread disease during the interim required for a hearing. In such cases, however, the government must arrange for a fair hearing as soon as practicable after the detention—generally within one or several days. These hearings present significant logistical challenges, both in numbers and in ensuring the hearing itself does not spread disease, in any situation requiring mass quarantine and isolation. Public health and emergency management officials should carefully prepare their plans for due process hearings and coordinate with the judiciary.

Substantive due process for a deprivation of liberty requires the state to show it has a compelling interest in the detention: that its detention is "reasonable" (in the words of the Supreme Court in *Jacobson*), and that society's interest in the confinement outweighs the individual's liberty interest.[2] In nonemergency civil commitment cases, the courts have held that the state must show that confinement is necessary by "clear and convincing evidence," a legal standard somewhat greater than a "preponderance of the evidence" but less than "beyond a reasonable doubt." This may require, for example, that the state prove the person is infected or actually has been exposed to an infectious disease and that alternatives to confinement that would protect the public from the disease were not available. Furthermore, where the state compels an individual to a detention facility, substantive due process also requires that the state provide adequate food, shelter, medicine, and medical care.[22] Finally, where public health control measures appear to single out particular racial or ethnic groups because of a conclusion that they had a high incidence of or susceptibility to disease, courts will give those measures "strict scrutiny," the most rigorous and least deferential standard of review.

One of the most significant disconnects in current public health law arises from the remarkable coincidence that the modern legal tapestry that protects individual liberties has evolved in the past 50 years, during the exact same time when public health officials (because of the arrival of modern drugs and vaccines) have not had to exercise communitywide control measures significantly limiting these individual liberties. As a society, we are only now beginning to reconnect the legal and policy circuitry between modern individual liberties and traditional public health control.

As this reconnection process unfolds, many states have adopted into their state health codes procedural and substantive due process protections, such as those incorporated into the Model State Public Health Emergency Powers Act, which requires, for example, that quarantine or isolation be imposed only if it is the "least restrictive alternative" available to control a public health emergency.[16] Initially, courts may be likely to defer to the medical judgment of public health officials about whether options short of confinement would effectively control the spread of infectious disease. Nevertheless, in large-scale quarantine, public health officials and emergency managers still have strong practical and logistical reasons to control disease without taking custody of and providing food, shelter, and medical care to tens of thousands of people.

Operational Considerations

The practical complexity of large-scale detention is exacerbated by the need to account for individual differences of the population. For example, how will the quarantine allow for continuation of essential public services (communications, water, power, sanitation)? How will food and medicine be provided to the quarantined population? How will religious and cultural dietary restrictions be accommodated? How will authorities communicate to the substantial segment of the population that does not speak English? How will authorities provide for special needs populations, such as the elderly and disabled at home and those hospitalized or residing in sanitaria, nursing homes, and even prisons? Some of these issues may appear superficially to be simplified by drawing a line around an area where infection is known to exist—*cordon sanitaire*—and prohibiting movement of persons into or out of the zone. But even in this case, our just-in-time supply chain economy will require authorities immediately to provide the food, medicine, and services required for those within the zone to survive. The law enforcement aspects of obtaining voluntary citizen cooperation in such a cordon sanitaire remain untested in modern times, and international attempts in the past decade to apply a cordon sanitaire during the Ebola virus outbreaks in central Africa proved to increase panic and be counterproductive.

During a bioterrorism event, theoretically the best control option is to require exposed persons to accept chemoprophylaxis or vaccinations, despite personal and religious objections, to ensure they do not become contagious and infect others.[23] However, the U.S. Supreme Court has recognized a constitutionally protected right of competent persons to refuse medical treatment, which derives from the common-law concept of informed consent.[24] The state can require medical treatment only if it can show its need to act to protect public health outweighs this liberty interest. In *Washington v. Harper*, for example, the U.S. Supreme Court held in the context of prisoners that the state's interest in preventing dangerously mentally ill prisoners from harming themselves or others outweighed the prisoner's interest in refusing antipsychotic medications.[25]

As a practical matter, a public health department may have to provide an exposed person with the choice of either accepting preventive therapy or being isolated until the incubation period passes, and he or she no longer is at risk of becoming contagious. Indeed, a number of state laws specify that a person refusing mandatory treatment or vaccination can be quarantined or isolated until the risk of spreading disease passes.[26]

Mutual Aid Assistance and Volunteer Resources

Mutual aid is assistance provided by one government to another government, building from a people-helping-people tradition that extends to colonial times in the United States. Early mutual aid was usually informal and event driven: neighbors and neighboring communities would run to join fire lines when they saw a fire. Informal mutual aid provided without compensation or paperwork remains common among adjacent communities for purely local emergencies and operational issues.[27] However, mutual aid has become more formal when used as part of major responses involving extended and substantial commitments of resources, cost reimbursement, significant potential liabilities, and multijurisdictional professional licensing issues. Mutual aid is now a major component of NIMS, and jurisdictions that do not include mutual aid in their emergency preparedness planning may lose their eligibility for federal preparedness grants.[h]

Mutual aid now includes systems of mutual aid agreements between states; between local governments within a state; between local governments in a multistate region; and even between the federal government and other nations, states and Canadian provinces, and local communities across the international border. Some agreements are broadly drafted to cover all types of emergencies; others address only particular emergencies, such as fires or disease outbreaks. Despite this variety, a number of elements are common to mutual aid agreements. First, mutual aid agreements for major emergency responses now are generally performed only pursuant to written agreements specifying their scope; how the agreement is activated; and covering issues of liability, employment, and licensing. Second, mutual aid agreements do not require that jurisdictions provide resources when requested (no jurisdiction can commit to send resources that might be required for its own emergency needs). Instead, agreements state an intent to provide resources where possible and specify procedures under which assistance will be requested and provided. Third, mutual aid agreements specify whether the requesting jurisdiction will pay for the resources provided. Compensation traditionally is not provided in operational mutual aid agreements covering small-scale incidents in which each community might help the other with some frequency. However, in virtually all mutual aid agreements applicable to major responses, the requesting jurisdiction reimburses the costs of the responding jurisdiction. Not only is it financially difficult for responding jurisdictions to provide significant resources for an extended period without reimbursement but also, in declared disaster events, the costs incurred by requesting jurisdictions for emergency measures performed by a mutual aid resource are eligible for federal reimbursement provided the mutual aid agreement requires payment for mutual aid.[i]

The Emergency Management Assistance Compact (EMAC) is the principal mutual aid agreement at the state level. Congress approved this compact in 1996,[j] and all 50 states and several territories have adopted it. When the governor declares an emergency, EMAC permits the exchange of personnel, equipment, and supplies and generally imposes liability and responsibility for reimbursement and compensation on the state requesting assistance from other states. Even in the absence of a declaration, EMAC permits planning, information sharing, training, and execution of supplementary agreements between cooperating states.

Emergency situations frequently elicit the best instincts in people. Volunteers and voluntary organizations, such as the American Red Cross, are an integral part of emergency response. In public health emergencies, ensuring that volunteers who assert they have medical or other professional training are in fact so qualified, while relaxing normal state-specific medical license requirements, is particularly important. The Health Resources and Services Administration within the U.S. Department of Health and Human Services sponsors an Emergency System for Advance Registration of Volunteer Health Professional. This system has identified legal and regulatory issues that states need to resolve when using the volunteer services of health-care professionals from other states. Included among those issues are civil and criminal liability, workers' compensation, and licensing, privileging, and credentialing of those professionals. Among others, Good Samaritan and licensing reciprocity laws must be reviewed carefully and adopted or modified when necessary.

The Role of the Military

The largest source of equipment, supplies, trained personnel, and specialized resources that can be made available in catastrophic events is the nation's military. The Stafford Act specifically authorizes the President to use resources of the U.S. Department of Defense to assist state and local authorities in responding to major disasters and emergencies, and the Department of Defense regularly supplies resources and personnel.[28] For example, the Army Corps of Engineers frequently helps remove debris or even uses its Prime Power unit to restore power in remote areas; helicopters are used for rescue missions; satellite photography is obtained to assess damage; and specialized military teams are trained and equipped to respond to chemical, radiologic, or biologic hazards.

Nonetheless, two important legal restrictions exist on the use of the military: the Posse Comitatus Act and the Insurrection Act. The Posse Comitatus Act generally prohibits the use of military for law enforcement purposes: military personnel cannot be used to make arrests, and the military cannot be tasked to ensure law and order in a disaster zone unless accompanied by badged civilian law enforcement under whose authority people can be arrested.[29] Only a few exceptions exist to this requirement. First, of importance to public health officials, military officers at points of entry are specifically authorized to enforce a state or local quarantine.[k] Second, the Insurrection Act authorizes the President to use the armed forces to suppress an insurrection on request of a governor, or even without a request from the governor, to "suppress the rebellion" when "unlawful obstructions, combinations, assemblages, or rebellion against the authority of the United States" make normal enforcement through judicial proceedings impracticable.[30] For these reasons, use of the military for law enforcement, in comparison with the multitude of other disaster response missions traditionally assigned to the military, is rare. Indeed, these legal restraints help explain why National Guard forces are not federalized when called to assist in disaster response. Not only does the EMAC make federalization unnecessary (National Guard in other states can be called up by their governor and sent to a state suffering from disaster), but federalization would convert guard forces—which *can* be used for law enforcement—into "armed forces," which are barred from doing so.

Emerging Issues in Public Health Emergency Law

When considering emerging issues in public health law in the 21st century, practitioners face at least two major challenges: coordinating animal control globally and recognizing the usefulness of a "leaky" quarantine.

The Global Challenges of Legal Systems for Animal Control

The recently emerging infectious threats of SARS, the Ebola and Marburg viruses, and avian influenza underscore the serious threats from zoonotic diseases created by increased proximity and concentration of humans to animals, as well as the increased ability of such diseases to spread because of easier international travel. In addition, the monkeypox experience during summer 2003 served as a warning of the threats to humans caused by the relatively unregulated commerce in exotic pets that has developed during the past two decades. Unfortunately, the evolution of legal mechanisms to protect against the spread of zoonotic diseases has not kept pace with these transformations in population concentration, travel speed, and social interactions.

Most of the laws that might be used to control a threat caused by infected animals may apply only to one facet of a problem, can limit agency jurisdiction, and can be antiquated. For example, during the monkeypox emergency in 2003, the federal response was complicated by the legislative authority of *five* different cabinet-level agencies relevant to the control of animal populations (Table 11-2). The dates of enactment of these *nine* different federal statutes span nearly a century, and none of these laws contain any comprehensive approach to the modern public health problems encountered in controlling an acute or emerging disease threat from animals to humans. For example, none of these laws effectively focus on the current threat to humans posed by the increasing global exotic-pet trade.

Similarly, the states that attempted using their own laws to handle the monkeypox outbreak found wide variation in the applicability of their specific authorities. In particular, laws varied from state to state and from species to species as to whether an owner of an animal was entitled to compensation when the animal needed to be destroyed as a preventive measure.

Finally, at the international level, both the World Health Organization and the Food and Agriculture Service of the United Nations have only limited authority to identify or control the reservoirs of disease residing in animal populations that pose a threat to humans.[31] Future pressures caused by emerging zoonotic diseases are likely to point out the current legal and policy gaps and to demand rapid changes at the local, state, federal, and international levels.

Recognizing the Usefulness of a Leaky Quarantine

A second emerging challenge in public health emergency law in the 21st century is whether public health officials can communicate effectively to political leaders the important practical value that sustaining even a leaky quarantine (i.e., a quarantine that has gaps in its implementation) can have in quenching an emerging epidemic. One key history lesson learned from public health experiences is that 100% compliance with a communitywide quarantine may *not* be necessary to effectively lower the rate of spread of a communicable infectious epidemic. The important implication for 21st century policymakers, legal experts, and enforcement personnel is to understand an apparent paradox—that certain legal control measures, even if not perfectly implemented in the community, in the aggregate still can lead to a decrease in the rate of transmission, resulting in the extraordinary public health benefit of the epidemic burning itself out. From the perspective of modern quarantine, epidemics can be quenched with practical control measures that temporarily increase "social distance" within the community. Thereafter, health officials can focus limited resources on the targeted use of more restrictive control measures, such as the rapid effective isolation of actual contagious cases and limited quarantines on the contacts of such cases.

The emerging challenge for community leaders in such a situation will be to sustain communication and legal strategies to maintain public support for such legal control measures that will require individuals, at least temporarily, to cooperate in limiting their full range of social activity to permit the epidemic to quench itself. This citizen cooperation may be motivated less by any concern about the punitive consequences of violating a quarantine order and more on the public's sense of civic duty to help resolve the situation.[32]

Although the mathematics of a leaky quarantine can be clear and predictable, the patterns of social compliance in such an emergency situation are less certain but

TABLE 11-2   Federal Agencies with Responsibilities for Preventing and Controlling Monkeypox

Agency	Statutes	Actions	Scope	Subject Matter	Citation
Fish & Wildlife Service, US Department of Interior	Lacey Act Amendments of 1981	Enforcement	Intrastate Interstate Import/Export	Wildlife; Violation of federal, state, tribal, foreign laws	16 USC 3371 et seq
	Lacey Act (1900) (Listing in CFR with notice and comment)	Destruction Enforcement	Interstate Import	Wildlife injurious to humans, animals, plants (non-native)	18 USC 42 50 CFR Part 16
	Endangered Species Act (1973)	Reporting Licensing	Import/Export	Engagement in business importing/exporting wildlife	16 USC 1538(d–f) 50 CFR Part 14
Animal & Plant Health Inspection Service, US Dept of Agriculture	Animal Health Protection Act (2002)—Veterinary services	Enforcement Surveillance Inspection Detention Quarantine Destruction Remedial measures	Intrastate in extraordinary emergency Interstate Export	Pest or disease livestock	7 USC 8301 et seq
	Animal Welfare Act (1966)—Animal-care servicesAnimal Damage Control Act (1931)—Wildlife services	Recordkeeping Licensing Inspection Surveillance Destruction Fee-for-Service Agreements	Intrastate Interstate Intrastate Interstate	Exhibitors/Dealers/Handlers nonlivestock animals "Nuisance" animals and/or reservoir zoonotic disease	7 USC 2131 7 USC 426, 426c

Agency	Authority	Activities		Purpose	Legal citation
Centers for Disease Control and Prevention *and* Food and Drug Administration, US Department of Health and Human Services	Public Health Service Act (1942)	Public health surveillance Inspection Detention Quarantine Destruction Enforcement (FDA)	Intrastate Interstate Import (CDC)	Prevention of communicable diseases affecting human health	42 USC 264; 21 CFR 1240; 42 CFR Parts 70, 71
Customs and Border Protection, Department of Homeland Security (Plant Protection Quarantine Service [formerly USDA])	Tariff Act of 1930	Inspection Seizure Destruction Enforcement	Import	Import prohibited by law	19 USC 1499; 19 USC 1595a; 18 USC 545; 19 CFR Part 151
US Department of Transportation	Federal Hazardous Materials Transportation Law (1994)	Approval for transport of infected animals Enforcement	Intrastate Interstate Import Export	Hazardous materials	49 USC 5101 et seq; 49 CFR Parts 171–180

Source: Adapted from similar CDC information posted as Version.5 (July 14, 2003).

equally critical. For example, in a disease emergency, identification and criticism of the apparent holes in the government's legal implementation of a control strategy may be relatively easy for the media. Accordingly, preparedness efforts need to understand in advance the aggregate value of even a leaky quarantine. An understanding of this subtle but valuable concept is critical not only to the public health officials responding to an epidemic but also to law enforcement, emergency management, political leaders, legal experts, and the media, all of whom will play an equally vital role in influencing the degree of community compliance with this legal tool during an emergency.

Conclusion: Anticipating the Next Moment When Laws and Policy Change after a Public Health Emergency

We have advanced the concept of public health emergency law as a new and rapidly developing area of public health practice. Public health practitioners and legal experts in the 21st century will need to master the various legal tools and policies that exist to competently handle an emergency situation. In addition, however, leadership requires the capacities to anticipate and capitalize on the window of opportunity for law and policy change that could occur after the next public health emergency. Many sensitive and complex societal issues, such as government resource allocations, liability, compensation, and individual rights, are extremely difficult to change during normal times. Change naturally is resisted by such factors as gridlock of opposing vested interests, limited resources, and the difficulty in achieving broad-based political consensus. However, a public health emergency also can create two important opportunities: a temporary increase in social cohesion and a desire on the part of public leaders to take immediate remedial action. These two phenomena create an important window of opportunity immediately after the emergency during which significant changes in law and policy often take place. Public health practitioners should prepare in advance for such moments.

The temporary increase in social cohesion during an emergency repeatedly has been demonstrated in the context of hurricane damage to a region, the terrorism attacks in the United States in September 2001, and the SARS epidemic in Toronto in 2003. On the other hand, in certain severe situations when basic services are not available, social cohesion can break down temporarily, as shown during Hurricane Katrina in 2005. Similarly, after such events, the political systems respond by quickly changing laws through appropriating emergency relief assistance, updating state emergency public health laws, and providing compensation for individuals in quarantine.[33–35] In fact, most of the increases in public health funding to state and local governments in recent years have been based on a preparedness rationale of protecting the public from emerging infections and bioterrorism.

The continuing likelihood of new emerging infections, as well as the ongoing threats of future terrorism events, also carries the potential that additional windows of opportunity for future law and policy change will temporarily open during and immediately after such events. At such moments, public health practitioners cannot realistically devote much attention to shaping legislative and policy changes when their immediate priority is addressing the more urgent community demands to quickly bring the epidemic or emergency under control. Accordingly, public health practitioners must begin now to apply the obvious construct that another emergency eventually *will* occur; using that assumption, practitioners and legal experts should develop now the necessary legal analysis, policy justifications, and professional networks to effectively respond to those windows of opportunity that will open suddenly when public health laws, policies, and resource allocations can undergo significant alteration. Public health emergency preparedness includes being ready to reshape public health laws and policies, both rapidly and competently, when such moments of change suddenly arrive.

We gratefully acknowledge the assistance of James J. Misrahi, J.D., CDC Branch, Office of the General Counsel, U.S. Department of Health and Human Services, Atlanta, for his work in the initial development of Table 11-2; Daniel Stier, J.D., Public Health Law Program, Centers for Disease Control and Prevention, Atlanta, for his contributions on interstate mutual aid assistance agreements; and Samantha D. Harrykisson, M.P.H., Georgia State College of Law, Atlanta, for her valuable research contributions and the final development of Table 11-2.

Notes

a. In Homeland Security Presidential Directives 5 and 8 (issued February 28, 2003, and December 17, 2003, respectively), President Bush directed all federal agencies to require state and local organizations to adopt NIMS to receive federal preparedness grants and contracts by fiscal year 2005. (HSPD-5 is available at http://www.whitehouse.gov/news/releases/2003/02/20030228-9.html; HSPD-8 is available at http://www.whitehouse.gov/news/releases/2003/12/print/20031217-6.html.) Adopting the basic tenets of the ICS constitutes initial compliance; the Department of Health and Human Services is to publish additional standards, guidelines, and compliance protocols. See "NIMS Alert," August 17, 2005, issued by NIMS Integration Center (Department of Homeland Security/FEMA [Federal Emergency Management Agency]) and available at http://www.oes.ca.gov/Operational/OESHome.nsf/PDF/NIMSAlert8-05/$file/NA008.05.pdf.

b. The emergency support functions (ESFs) are as follows: ESF 1: Transportation; ESF 2: Telecommunications and Information Technology; ESF 3: Public Works and Engineering; ESF 4: Firefighting; ESF 5: Emergency Management; ESF 6: Mass Care, Housing, and Human Services; ESF 7: Resource Support; ESF 8: Public Health and Medical Services; ESF 9: Urban Search and Rescue; ESF 10: Oil and Hazardous Materials Response; ESF 11: Agriculture and Natural Resources; ESF 12: Energy; ESF 13: Public Safety and Security; ESF: 14 Community Recovery, Mitigation, and Economic Stabilization; and ESF 15: Emergency Public Information and External Communications.

c. The National Response Plan is available at http://www.dhs.gov/interweb/assetlibrary/NRP_FullText.pdf, and NIMS is at http://www.fema.gov/pdf/nims/nims_doc_full.pdf. Changes to the National Response Plan are anticipated as the Administration and the Congress respond to widespread criticism of the government's response to Hurricane Katrina.

d. Fla. Stat. 252.36(5)(a), 252.46(2) (2004); see Fla. Exec. Order No. 04-192 (Sept. 1, 2004) (Hurricane Frances). This discussion of Florida authorities is based on a more detailed discussion of the emergency powers of the Governor of Florida found in Bragg AO, Experiencing the

2004 Florida hurricanes: a lawyer's perspective. In: Abbott EB, Hetzel OJ, eds. *A Legal Guide to Homeland Security and Emergency Management for State and Local Governments*. Chicago: ABA Press, 2005.

e. The President could declare an emergency without the request of a governor if the situation involves an area that is the preeminent responsibility of the United States. This most likely would apply to a foreign terrorist attack (federal power over national defense) but not to a natural disease outbreak.

f. Pub. L. 93-288, as amended and codified at 42 U.S.C. §5121-5206. Most Stafford Act authorities are bestowed on the President, who has delegated them to the Department of Homeland Security and re-delegated to the Undersecretary for Emergency Preparedness and Response (and the Director of FEMA).

g. See, for example, *Best v. St. Vincent's Hospital*, No. 03 CV.0365 RMB JCF, 2003 WL 21518829 (S.D.N.Y. July 2003—Magistrate's opinion); affirmed, *Best v. Bellevue*, 2003 WL 21767656 (S.D.N.Y. July 2003—District Judge); affirmed in part, vacated in part, dismissed in part, *Best v. Bellevue*, 2004 WL 2166316 (2d Cir. 2004)—all opinions are unpublished. This case involved involuntary confinement of a patient with drug-resistant TB until completion of the treatment regimen.

h. See note a, above.

i. See FEMA Policy 9523.6 Mutual Aid Agreements for Public Assistance and Fire Management Assistance (Sept. 22, 2004) and Mutual Aid Policy Clarification Memorandum (Mar. 15, 2005).

j. Pub. L. 104-321, Oct. 19, 1996, 110 Stat. 3877. The Constitution requires Congressional approval for interstate compacts of this type. Article 1, Cl. 10.

k. 42 U.S.C. §97. State health laws observed by United States officers. "The quarantines and other restraints established by the health laws of any state, respecting any vessels arriving in, or bound to, any port or district thereof, shall be duly observed . . . by the military officers commanding in any fort or station upon the seacoast; and all such officers of the United States shall faithfully aid in the execution of such quarantines and health laws, according to their respective powers and within their respective precincts, and as they shall be directed, from time to time, by the Secretary of Health and Human Services."

References

1. Albert MR, Ostheimer KG, Bremen JG. The last smallpox epidemic in Boston and the vaccination controversy, 1901–1903. *N Engl J Med* 2001;344:375–9.
2. Gostin LO. *Public Health Law: Power, Duty, Restraint*. Berkeley: University of California Press, 2000.
3. Hodge JG Jr. The role of new federalism and public health law. *J Law Health* 1998; 12:311–2.
4. 8 USC §1222.
5. US Constitution Article I, §8.
6. 8 USC §1222.
7. 42 USC §264.
8. Pub L 93-288, as amended and codified at 42 USC §5121-5206.
9. Fla Stat 252.36(5)(b), 252.36(6) (2004).
10. Fla Stat 252.36(5)(d), 252.43(1), 252.43(3) (2004).
11. Fla Stat 252.36(5)(e), 252.36(5)(f) (2004).
12. Fla Stat 252.36(4), 252.36(8) (2004).
13. Section 319 of Public Health Service Act, codified at 42 USC 247d.

14. Stafford Act §502(a) 42 UCS §5192(a).
15. Cantigny Conference Series. *State Emergency Health Powers and the Bioterrorism Threat.* Cantigny Conference on State Emergency Health Powers and the Bioterrorism Threat, April 26–27, 2001, Chicago IL.
16. Model State Emergency Public Health Powers Act. December 21, 2001. Available at http://www.publichealthlaw.net/Resources/Modellaws.htm#MSEHPA. Accessed November 8, 2005.
17. US Constitution, Amendment V.
18. US Constitution, Amendments V and XIV.
19. *Lucas v South Carolina Coastal Council*, 505 US 1003, 1031 (1992).
20. *Jacobson v Massachusetts,* 197 US 11 (1905) at 24–27.
21. Mindes P. Quarantine law. Tuberculosis quarantine: a review of legal issues in Ohio and other states. *J Law Health* 1995;10:408–13.
22. Prison conditions as amounting to cruel and unusual punishment, 51 ALR 3d 111.
23. Kayyem J. US preparations for biological terrorism: legal limitations and the need for planning. BCSIA (Belief Center for Science and International Affairs) Discussion Paper 2001-4, ESDP (Executive Session on Domestic Preparedness) Discussion Paper EDSP-2001-02. Boston: John F. Kennedy School of Government, Harvard University, 2001.
24. *Cruzan v Director, Missouri Department of Health*, 497 US 261, 278 (1990).
25. 494 US §210, 227 (1990).
26. ICA §135.144 (Iowa).
27. Cohn A. Mutual aid: intergovernmental agreements for emergency preparedness and response. *Urban Lawyer* 2005;37:1–51.
28. 42 USC §5170b©; see also §5170.
29. 18 USC §1385.
30. 10 USC §§331, 332.
31. World Health Organization. *Zoonoses and Veterinary Public Heath.* Available at http://www.who.int/zoonoses/vph/en/. Accessed October 4, 2005.
32. DiGiovanni C, Conley J, Chiu D, Zaborski J. Factors influencing compliance with quarantine in Toronto during the 2003 SARS outbreak. *Biosecurity and Bioterrorism* 2004;2:265–72.
33. Federal Emergency Management Agency. Federal Disaster Aid Programs. Available at http://www.fema.gov/rrr/fdap.shtm, Accessed October 4, 2005.
34. The Center for Law and the Public's Health. *The Model State Emergency Health Powers Act: State Legislative Activity*. Available at http://www.publichealthlaw.net/MSEHPA/MSEHPA%20Leg%20Activity.pdf. Accessed November 10, 2005.
35. Rothstein MA, Alcalde MG, Elster NR, et al. *Quarantine and Isolation: Lessons Learned from SARS—A Report to the Centers for Disease Control and Prevention.* Louisville, KY: Institute for Bioethics, Health Policy and Law, University of Louisville School of Medicine; 2003.

Chapter 12

CONSIDERATIONS FOR SPECIAL POPULATIONS

T. Howard Stone, Heather H. Horton,*
Robert M. Pestronk, and
Montrece M. Ransom*

This chapter focuses on laws that pertain to special populations and their public health needs. We consider as "special populations" persons with mental disabilities; persons involved with the criminal justice system; homeless persons; children, including children who may be disproportionately affected by disparities in public health–related intervention; and undocumented immigrants. At first glance, persons who are similarly situated with regard to one or more characteristics relevant to public health—such as persons with sexually transmitted diseases, drug dependency, or diabetes—might at one time or another be considered a special population. These persons may share attributes that facilitate identification and public health intervention. Our concept of special populations, however, includes the additional attribute of vulnerability and therefore comprises persons who not only are underserved with regard to public health intervention but who also may be disenfranchised with respect to the legal status or social regard that is generally accorded our citizens.

Public health concerns about special populations are not new. Undocumented immigrants and homeless persons generally are transient populations who always have been difficult to reach for public health surveillance and service. Many of these persons try to avoid contact with public authorities at all costs, including the cost of their own health. Services for children and persons with mental disabilities are critical because these populations are situated at the nexus of the heightened value of early public health intervention and the potential for diminished capacity. For these persons, cost as well as

---

* The findings and conclusions in this chapter are those of the author(s) and do not necessarily represent the views of the U.S. Department of Health and Humans Services or the Centers for Disease Control and Prevention.

nonfinancial barriers often prevent more timely and appropriate access to needed health services. In addition, the health needs of undocumented immigrants, persons with mental disabilities, and persons involved in the criminal justice system may be confounded by histories of past abuse or neglect. Added to this history is the matter of legal capacity because many of these persons have reduced civil liberties and diminished legal rights to shape or determine the course of their treatment. To more effectively intervene with the public health needs of all persons, public health professionals should familiarize themselves with special populations and with laws relevant to them.

This is not an exhaustive list of special populations and related concerns; limitations of space permit only a brief review of the public health issues and relevant laws pertaining to these special populations. This chapter is divided into sections, each focused on a special population. Each section begins with a case study of a member of a special population and his or her public health needs. Analysis of the pertinent legal issues follows each case study. Each section closes with practice pointers that incorporate the pertinent legal issues in the context of the case study.

Persons with Mental Disabilities

Case Study 1

At the other end of the phone is an attorney who tells you he represents the wife of John H. The attorney states that John's recent behavior has left his client's health and welfare at risk. The attorney asks you to provide him with copies of your public health agency's treatment records for John, who, the attorney asserts, has previously received mental health and substance-abuse treatment from one of your agency's facilities or programs. The attorney states that you should in fact take action to prevent John from further harming himself or others, including his wife. You are not aware of whether John has actually received any treatment through your agency or any of its contracting health service providers. Should you ask staff to search the department's files to produce the documents? Should you request the files from the contract agency? If you find the files, should you release them to the attorney? Whose rights are paramount? Whose are subsidiary?

Legal Analysis

At first, this case appears largely concerned with the confidentiality of health information for patients undergoing mental health and substance-abuse treatment, and whether you should or are required to disclose such information in these circumstances. However, it also raises the important issue of John's dereliction and its attendant risks to John, his wife, or other persons, as well as the apparently conflicting responsibility of public health agencies or professionals to intervene.

Confidentiality of Health Records

Patient health information is protected by a mixed bag of state and federal laws—including statutes, regulations, court cases, and agency rules—the predominant characteristics of which are lack of uniformity and questionable effectiveness. A number of federal laws and regulations pertain to the confidentiality of patient health information. Perhaps most pertinent to this case study is the federal law and regulation pertaining to substance-abuse programs and to the confidentiality of records created or maintained therein. The authority of the federal government to mandate these confidentiality requirements with regard to substance-abuse health information is based on the federal government's funding or regulating authority: health facilities or professionals who are either "directly or indirectly assisted by any department or agency of the United States" government are subject to these confidentiality regulations, as is any program conducted or regulated by any department or agency of the U.S. government. Under federal law, "[r]ecords of the identity, diagnosis, prognosis, or treatment of any patient which are maintained in connection with the performance of any program or activity relating to substance abuse education, prevention, training, treatment, rehabilitation, or research . . . shall . . . be confidential and disclosed only for the purposes and under the circumstances expressly authorized. . . ."[1] One circumstance is when there is prior written consent from the patient about whom the records are maintained. Other purposes and circumstances include disclosure to medical personnel to the extent necessary in a medical emergency; disclosure for research or program evaluation in which the records are unidentifiable; or disclosure by order of a court after demonstration of good cause, such as the need to avert a substantial risk for death or serious bodily injury.

Federal regulations protect information about persons who have applied for or been given diagnoses or treatment for alcohol or drug abuse at a federally assisted program.[2] Where state and federal laws overlap, specific provisions apply: where disclosure permitted under federal law is nonetheless prohibited by state law, then federal regulations may not "be construed to authorize any violation of that state law." Conversely, these federal regulations provide that "no State law may either authorize or compel any disclosure prohibited by these regulations."[3] In this regard, the law of the jurisdiction with the strictest safeguards for patient health information confidentiality will prevail over the law with lesser safeguards.

Another significant federal confidentiality regulation is the Privacy Rule, promulgated pursuant to the Health Insurance Portability and Accountability Act, which, with some exceptions, restricts the use and disclosure of identifiable health information.[4] Under the Privacy Rule, covered entities (i.e., persons or organizations subject to the Privacy Rule, such as certain health-care providers) may not use or disclose patients' protected health information except where permitted, such as when authorized by the patient, or where the use or disclosure does not require a patient's authorization, such as when the protected health information will be used to carry out treatment or where the disclosure is required by law for public health purposes. Under the Privacy Rule, public health entities may be considered health-care providers and therefore prohibited from disclosing protected health information absent specific exceptions that provide otherwise. Such permissible conditions include disclosure of a patient's protected health information by a health-care provider to other public health authorities for preventing or controlling disease, injury, or disability, or disclosure of a patient's protected health information by a public health authority otherwise permitted by law to persons who may have been exposed to or are at risk of contracting or spreading a communicable disease.[5]

Medicare regulations are another federal source of laws pertaining to confidentiality that apply to public hospitals. Medicare regulations require that all hospitals—which would include public health agency facilities—that participate in the Medicare program have procedures "for ensuring the confidentiality of patient records."[6] In addition, because most hospitals participate in the Medicare program, most hospitals have instituted the requisite confidentiality procedures.

In addition to federal laws, state laws also address the confidentiality of patient information. State laws about health information confidentiality are based on a state's "police powers," which are a form of expansive sovereign authority intended in part to secure and protect public safety and are reserved to the 50 states under the U.S. Constitution.[7,a] Many laws that address confidentiality actually are situated within broader state laws whose main purpose is to accomplish something other than protecting patient health information but that happen to include some level of protection for patient health information. For example, most state licensing laws or "practice acts" require—in addition to training in approved professional programs or continuing education—that health professionals observe or adhere to certain practice standards, including maintaining the confidentiality of their patients' health information. Professional licensees may have their licenses or privileges to practice revoked or suspended, or may be subject to other disciplinary actions, for failing to protect their patients' confidences.[8,9,b] For example, the "willful or negligent violation of the confidentiality between physician and patient, except as required by law" is one of the grounds for disciplinary action against physicians in North Dakota,[10] while "willfully or negligently violating the confidentiality between advanced practice nurse, collaborating physician, and patient, except as required by law" can be the basis for disciplinary action against nursing professionals in Illinois.[11] Other health professionals also are subject to sanctions for violating patient confidences.[12]

Health institutions and agencies also may be legally obligated to protect the confidentiality of patient health information. These obligations often are subsumed under a state's health facility licensing authority. Under this scheme, a health facility may be required, as a condition of receiving an operating license, to provide its patients with certain rights, including the right to "confidentiality of all information and records pertaining to the patient's treatment. . . ."[13] A health facility's failure to provide these rights to its patients or to adequately protect patient health information from being impermissibly divulged may cost the health facility its operating license or result in some other sanction. In many states, the use and disclosure of patients' mental health information may be subject to even greater restrictions, given concerns about the sensitivity of mental health information and the potential for harm that may result from its unauthorized use or disclosure.

Mitigating Risks Posed by Persons with Mental and Substance-Abuse Disorders

In most states and for many people, the only meaningful mental health or substance-abuse programs are provided or coordinated through the state or local public health authority through such providers as community mental health clinics or chemical dependency programs, crisis intervention, the inpatient and outpatient services of a local public psychiatric hospital, or the psychiatric service of a local public hospital. In particular, for persons with severe mental disorders, mental health care often occurs pursuant to law enforcement arrest or referral. For persons with substance-abuse disorders, the first encounter with substance-abuse treatment often results from a drunk driving or drug-related arrest.

The power of state or local authorities, including public health authorities, to compel mental health or substance-abuse treatment has a long history. For many years, the typical public health response to persons with mental disabilities was institutionalization, which transformed during the past few decades into civil commitment in only the most egregious cases of mental disability and the need for treatment coupled with some indication of a mentally disordered person's dangerous behavior or the risk for harm or injury posed thereby. In some jurisdictions, the lack of mental health and substance-abuse programs has resulted in arrest and jailing in lieu of treatment. Spurred by increasing public alarm over substance abuse, especially the abuse of drugs other than alcohol, some jurisdictions have tailored civil commitment laws that provide for the legally authorized confinement of substance abusers, sometimes in lieu of criminal prosecution.[14–17]

Civil commitment is essentially a statutorily structured process by which persons with qualifying conditions are legally confined within a mental health or substance-abuse treatment milieu for their own good or for the safety of others. Civil commitment laws usually are subsumed under state mental health laws and generally include provisions for referral, evaluation, treatment, release, notice, hearing, right to counsel, and the right to be present at the commitment hearing.[18–20] In fact, some state court decisions have indicated that the criteria for commitment of drug-dependent persons are guided by the same concerns for safeguarding public safety, the individual's health, and the individual's liberty interest under mental health laws.[21]

Civil commitment is intended to prevent persons with qualifying conditions from harming themselves and others and to provide them with treatment. In particular, drug-dependency civil commitment laws require sufficient evidence to establish the person to be committed has "lost the power of self-control" with respect to the use of a controlled substance or is "incapable of self-management or management of personal affairs" by reason of the habitual and excessive use of drugs.[22,23] Most civil commitment statutes also require the person for whom commitment is sought to actually pose a danger or substantial likelihood of *physical harm* to himself or herself or others. Furthermore, the likelihood of this harm must be shown by clear and convincing evidence.[c] Finally, some states require that proper treatment programs be available and that a likely benefit from such treatment to the person being committed be shown before commitment will be effected, an especially interesting requirement because mental health and substance-abuse treatment programs are in notoriously short supply.[24,25] Generally, courts will strictly construe the statutory provisions pertaining to civil commitment before permitting states to use their legal authority to take the drastic action of legally confining persons into such treatment settings.

Practice Pointers

Confidentiality of Health Records

Under the facts presented in Case Study 1, federal law pertaining to the confidentiality of health information under the Privacy Rule, and federal regulations pertaining to records of alcohol- and drug-abuse patients—including mental health and substance-abuse treatment records—apply. Providing John's mental health and substance-abuse records to his wife's attorney may fall outside the boundary of permissible disclosure. No indication exists that John has consented to or authorized such a disclosure, and, without that consent or authorization, John's treatment records can be released only for one of several enumerated exceptions, none of which appear to apply here on the basis of the facts provided. The attorney is not a medical professional, so the exception for disclosing health information to further John's treatment is not applicable. In addition, the circumstances do not suggest that a medical emergency exists or that John poses an imminent risk of serious harm to himself or to others, which are common exceptions to the rule against disclosure. Finally, no court order has authorized disclosure of John's treatment records, even if, as the attorney alleges, a potential risk exists to the attorney's client, John's wife. Even if the attorney were to invoke a state law that allowed the release of John's health records, less protective state law gives way to the more protective federal law, and the disclosure of John's records still is impermissible.

An exception may exist if John exposed his wife to a communicable disease, such as HIV infection, hepatitis C infection, or tuberculosis (TB). In that case, federal and state law might permit the public health department, as long as the department is so authorized under state laws, to notify John's wife of his communicable disease status for public health information or investigation. Even so, federal law permits only the disclosure of the minimum health information necessary for the public health department to intervene or investigate, so disclosures in this case may be limited to John's communicable disease status and not his mental health and substance-abuse treatment records.

Mitigating Risks Posed by Mental Disorders and Substance-Abuse Dependency

The attorney's statement that more should be done to prevent further harm from John's mental health status and substance abuse raises a number of concerns. First, the existence of a potential for harm, the nature of the harm, and legal steps to mitigate such harm need to be determined. This is a calculus that should take place independently of the attorney's request for copies of John's treatment records, although the attorney's request actually may be part of a legal action of which the purpose is to initiate civil commitment. John's records may need to be reviewed to ensure the agency or contractor is discharging its treatment responsibilities. If past or current treatment is inadequate, and John's potential for harm is evident, then the agency may be required to take additional steps to safeguard public safety and John's own welfare. These steps might include enlisting John's wife to help guide subsequent agency intervention, but this still does not necessarily permit disclosure to the attorney of John's confidential health information. Even without the assistance of John's wife, public health officers are authorized to petition a court for a hearing to effect John's civil commitment. Depending on the jurisdiction, other petitioners may include the director of a community mental health center, a peace officer, the court, or the physician of the person for whom commitment is sought. The law's intent is to ensure that all persons who may have police powers or firsthand knowledge, including knowledge arising from the course of treatment, are permitted to ask a court to determine whether persons in John's situation should be civilly committed for evaluation or treatment. Under these circumstances, the requisite "emergency" or other need for hospitalization may exist that would permit disclosure of confidential health information, and a reviewing court may even order that John's health records be provided to the court. Both the potential for risk and the need for a court hearing on the matter of civil commitment may suffice as an exception to the limits on disclosure of John's substance-abuse records.

Persons Who Are Criminal Justice–Involved

Case Study 2

Jack T. recently was released from state prison. Now unemployed and living temporarily on public assistance and the services of local charities, he has been searching for a job. He stops by the local health department requesting medical services for chronic hepatitis C and HIV infections, for which he received treatment while incarcerated. Services of this nature are not available at the health department, so he is referred to the local emergency department, and from there, to a free medical clinic that operates just once a week. The free medical clinic does not provide Jack with the full range of services he received in prison. Why was Jack's care better when he was a prisoner than when he is a free citizen? What are his rights to care in both environments?

Legal Analysis

This case illustrates an irony that often is difficult to explain: once incarcerated, prisoners have a federal constitutional right to health care that is not accorded to nonprisoners, but that health care need not necessarily measure up to the standard of medical care for nonprisoner patients who are similarly situated. In the landmark 1976 decision of *Estelle v. Gamble*, the U.S. Supreme Court declared that governments have an "obligation to provide medical care for those whom it is punishing by incarceration . . . ," the denial of which violates a prisoner's rights under the Eighth Amendment of the U.S. Constitution.[26] The Court's reasoning, which in part appears deceptively simple, is that prisoners are essentially wards of the state: prisoners rely on prison officials for their most basic needs, including medical care, and if prison officials do not provide this care, the health-related needs of prisoners will not be met. Nonprisoners, on the other hand, generally do not stand in the same position as prisoners as wards or as subject to government constraint; their limited or lack of access to health care is irrelevant to this concept. More fundamentally, denying medical care to prisoners may be tantamount to inflicting pain and suffering, which is essentially punishment without any legitimate penological purpose that the Court construes is "inconsistent with contemporary standards of decency."

The *Estelle* case is unquestionably the progenitor of most improvements in prison-based health-care services in the United States; understandably, prisoners rely on its pivotal place in modern Eighth Amendment jurisprudence to assert other claims regarding their medical care, such as the right to psychiatric services, care ordered by a physician, exercise and recreational opportunities, housing that is free of environmental tobacco smoke (i.e., secondhand smoke), and follow-up health visits. Included among these is the government's obligation to screen or test prisoners for certain infectious diseases, the failure of which may be construed by a court as a negligent and reckless disregard of a known and obvious risk for contagion. In *DeGidio v. Pung*, for example, the Circuit Court of Appeals for the Eighth Circuit found fault with prison officials who failed to implement TB testing and control procedures, despite a TB outbreak among over 200 prisoners, and concluded that prison officials had violated the Eighth Amendment right of prisoners who had acquired TB while incarcerated.[27,d,e]

The public health implications of decisions such as these are profound; they may be interpreted as imposing on state and local prison officials an obligation—a violation of which could be punishable—to undertake public health measures to identify and prevent communicable diseases within jail and prison populations. In fact, prison officials who have taken an aggressive public health approach toward screening and testing prisoners for certain health conditions have been accorded substantial discretion by courts that have addressed prisoners' claims that such screening and testing violate a number of their legal rights. Courts generally have found that imposing mandatory screening and testing of prisoners for conditions, such as communicable diseases, furthers a government's "compelling interest in protecting inmates and [correctional] staff . . ."[28,f] and is permissible under the government's public health authority to take reasonable measures to prevent transmission of communicable diseases.[29] In fact, in cases where inmates have sued prison officials over mandatory screening and testing, the legality of the screening and testing is not itself at issue, but rather whether the means used by prison officials impermissibly burdened prisoners' other rights, such as loss of certain prison privileges, when prisoners refused such testing.

The case of *Funtanilla v. Campbell* illustrates how courts have approached the tension between the government's public health authority and the rights of prisoners.[30,g] In *Funtanilla*, a prisoner sued a number of prison officials, claiming that they violated his federal constitutional rights by placing him in segregation for four months, limiting his visitation privileges, and restricting exercise privileges because he refused to have a tuberculin test or chest radiograph. The Ninth Circuit Court observed that prisoners may be provided with visitation and exercise privileges, but the court stated that "preventing disease and protecting the health of visitors and inmates are unquestionably legitimate penological goals." The court found that restrictions imposed on the prisoner's privileges while prison officials assessed his TB status were reasonable in light of these penological goals. The court concluded that prison officials did not violate the prisoner's federal constitutional rights.

Less clear cut than cases involving a government's abject failure to provide prisoners with medical care are cases in which prisoners allege that prison officials provide *inadequate* health care. The precise parameters of the government's federal constitutional obligation to provide prisoners with medical care rarely have been clearly spelled out, often leaving government officials ambivalent about the nature, frequency, and degree of medical care for any particular condition. Paradoxically, the *Estelle* case involved a prisoner's claim that prison officials had failed to provide the prisoner with adequate medical treatment after a back injury caused by a prison farm accident, a claim the Supreme Court ultimately rejected, even while the Court cloaked prisoners' right to health care within federal constitutional protection. In relevant part, the Court observed that the decision to order diagnostic tests or other forms of treatment is "a classic example of a matter for medical judgment" and that a decision based on such judgment does not represent an Eighth Amendment violation but, at most, medical malpractice, where the proper forum is state court.

A more recent case vividly demonstrates the limits of prisoners' federal constitutional right to health care—and the considerable discretion accorded by courts to clinical decision-making. In this case, a court decided that, for a prisoner's Eighth Amendment rights, the medical care due incarcerated patients does not need to mirror the standard of medical care for nonprisoners who are similarly clinically situated. In *Perkins v. Kansas Department of Corrections*, an HIV-infected prisoner claimed that prison physicians should have provided him with protease inhibitor therapy instead of treatment only with zidovudine (AZT) and lamivudine (3TC), which the prisoner considered an inadequate treatment and one that would lead to drug resistance.[31] Despite mounting evidence at the time that established appropriate treatment for HIV infection and AIDS (which was what the prisoner had requested), the court rejected the prisoner's claim, observing that prison officials were aware of and treating the prisoner's condition and stating that "a prisoner who merely disagrees with a diagnosis or a prescribed course of treatment does not state a constitutional violation." The court, similar to the Supreme Court in *Estelle,* explicitly maintained that these types of claims are medical malpractice issues for which federal constitutional protection is unavailing. In sum, in situations where prisoners are provided with a modicum of health care, even if that care departs from what may be provided to nonprisoners with similar clinical indications, prison officials do not fail in their federal constitutional obligations unless the prison officials are found to be deliberately indifferent to prisoners' medical needs.[h]

Practice Pointers

Given the conceptual underpinnings of the government's obligation to provide prisoners with health care, the predicament arising in Case Study 2, involving Jack's diminished access to medical services for his chronic hepatitis C and HIV infections, becomes easier to understand, although no easier to resolve. When he was a prisoner, Jack's condition could not have been ignored by prison officials, including prison health professionals. That he received regular and excellent primary and specialty medical care during his incarceration is noteworthy, especially because much of prison health care is, at best, minimally adequate given the health condition of prisoners and the resources of prison officials. Even if Jack's care while incarcerated was less than regular or not up to the prevailing standard of care for persons similarly situated clinically, prison officials' federal constitutional obligations still might have been discharged. Once Jack was released from prison, however, the state or local government's federal constitutional obligation under the Eighth Amendment to provide Jack or any other nonprisoner with public health intervention or with primary or specialty services for their health condition abruptly ceased.

If Jack is to continue to receive services, or receive medical attention for his chronic hepatitis C and HIV infections, then he must find an alternative right or privilege unrelated to his status as an "ex-convict," such as eligibility for state or federal insurance or services related to his medical circumstances or other qualifying conditions (e.g., long-term disability, age, armed services), or seek care as an indigent patient. Without eligibility or qualifications for these programs, Jack may have almost no right that would obligate or compel a government or health professional to provide him with care. One notable exception is Jack's rights pursuant to the Emergency Medical Treatment and Active Labor Act (EMTALA), which covers hospitals that participate in the federal Medicare program. Under EMTALA, if Jack comes to a covered hospital emergency department requesting examination or treatment for a medical condition, he has a right to receive a medical screening examination to determine whether an emergency medical condition exists, and, if such an emergency condition exists, to receive treatment for that condition.[32]

Homeless Persons

> [H]omelessness and healthcare . . . interact in three ways: (1) health problems cause homelessness; (2) homelessness causes health problems; and (3) homelessness makes health problems harder to treat.
>
> P. E. Phillips[33]

Case Study 3

Marie R. has been abused repeatedly by her husband. She and her 3-year-old son, Sean, are now homeless. They live in and out of supervised charitable settings but have settled for a time in the local women's shelter. While in the shelter, Marie tests positive for TB. She is reluctant to sign a release-of-information-and-consent form, which would allow medical information about her and Sean to be shared with local health department staff. Marie fears the loss of confidentiality and the intervention of agencies outside the shelter may bring her in contact with staff of the local social services agency with whom she has had a difficult relationship over time. Marie also fears the loss of her son. The director of the shelter is an acquaintance of the director of the health department. During a meeting at the shelter, the shelter director mentions to the health department director that a shelter resident tested positive for TB. While at the meeting, the health director notices that conditions at the shelter, both in the kitchen and in the living areas, appear unsanitary. What legal damage has the shelter director done? What legal obligation does the health director have to intervene at the shelter and with the TB-positive resident or her family? What are Marie and Sean's rights? What about cleaning up the shelter?

Legal Analysis

From a public health standpoint, homeless persons are a special population. Because of their socioeconomic status, poor lifestyle choices, lack of adequate health care, transient living conditions, or a combination of these factors, homeless persons are characterized by poor health status and therefore face an elevated risk of contracting some infectious diseases such as TB. A highly communicable disease once thought to have been largely eliminated from the United States, TB has returned with a vengeance—especially in its multidrug-resistant form—and is now the world's leading cause of death.[34,i] The resurgence of TB is attributed in part to persons at high risk both for acquiring and spreading the disease, including persons who are homeless. Compared with nonhomeless persons, homeless persons are considered to suffer disproportionately from TB.[35] When homeless persons are placed in such congregate settings as shelters or temporary housing, their risk increases for TB and other communicable diseases.

In almost all states, public health officials are accorded broad powers under state law to act to protect the public from highly infectious diseases (such as TB) or to take measures to protect the public from unhealthy or unsanitary conditions. This expansive authority was acknowledged long ago in the U.S. Supreme Court case of *Jacobson v. Massachusetts*, in which the Court recognized the authority of city health officials to curtail the spread of smallpox by requiring all city inhabitants to undergo smallpox vaccination.[29] One inhabitant refused the vaccination, suggesting a prior vaccination had caused him injury and compulsory vaccination violated his federal constitutional rights to due process under the Fourteenth Amendment. The *Jacobson* case has been invoked many times since then to vindicate similar public health measures undertaken to address serious risks to public health, such as the obligation of health professionals to report communicable disease cases or the right of state and local officials to inspect public accommodations, services, or venues (e.g., water service, sewage and waste treatment, restaurants, other retail establishments) for health and sanitation reasons. Such legal intervention is considered by many to be particularly appropriate in the case of homeless persons (and public shelters) because of their higher incidence rates for TB and the difficulty of reaching this population for screening and treatment.

Many states have laws specific to the control of TB because of its communicable nature. Although states differ in their approach to controlling TB, some consistency exists. For example, one important intervention provided for by all states is the requirement that suspected or confirmed cases of TB be reported to state or local public health officials by health professionals (e.g., physicians, laboratory directors, and public health nurses) or other persons who have knowledge of such cases. Additionally, some states require reporting of TB patients who refuse treatment, and a few states require notification of the state health department when a patient has completed treatment for TB. Most states consider the deliberate failure to report TB a criminal misdemeanor and impose fines. Almost all state laws require reporting of TB within a specific time frame, ranging from immediately to within one week after diagnosis. Federal guidelines, however, recommend states require reporting of TB within two working days of diagnosis.[36]

State laws also permit public health officials to place TB-infected persons in isolation or quarantine under certain conditions. For example, most states provide for isolation of anyone refusing TB treatment. Although many persons with TB may be subject to isolation within their own homes, many states designate appropriate residence facilities, including homeless shelters, for the care of homeless persons infected with TB. State laws also may permit public health officials to forcibly treat TB-infected persons, such as requiring them to undergo directly observed therapy, in which public health workers observe the taking of TB medications. However, state laws that permit public health officials to intervene in TB cases do not exist in a total legal vacuum. Cases such as *Jacobson* clearly establish public health officials' legal authority to compel compliance with public health measures, but these measures can neither be taken arbitrarily nor violate other rights that persons may have. In fact, public health measures must usually be balanced against a number of rights that have been accorded to persons over time to protect them from abuses of power by state officials. Even in *Jacobson,* the Court was careful to note that local health officials were acting within authority delegated to them by the state legislature and that even if the health officials had acted arbitrarily by, for example, requiring vaccination without regard to a person's individual health condition or irrespective of the presence of smallpox, then their action would have been impermissible. More importantly for this case, the Court observed that if local health officials had "picked out one class of persons arbitrarily for immediate vaccination, while indefinitely postponing action toward all others," their action might violate the U.S. Constitution.[29]

Within the context of state intervention regarding persons who may test positive for TB, competing individual rights may include a person's right to privacy and to refuse medical treatment, both of which are well grounded in state and federal law. For example, state law may require public health officials to provide "proof of actual danger to the community" before a homeless person with TB can be involuntarily civilly committed for isolation or TB treatment. Ultimately, whenever legal interventions such as detention, quarantine or isolation, forcible treatment, or directly observed therapy are imposed, public health officials walk a fine line between acting in the interest of the TB-infected person and the public's health and impermissibly burdening a person's fundamental rights of liberty and privacy.

Practice Pointers

The rapid and accurate reporting of TB cases is critical to managing TB patients. Thus, health professionals and health facilities, and sometimes human services professionals (such as social workers), may be obligated to report known or suspected TB cases to local or state public health officials, the disclosure of which usually is an exception to laws regarding the confidentiality of a person's health information. The reporting obligation is generally a condition of the privilege of licensing or certification accorded health professionals or health facilities by state authorities. Reporting these cases not only alerts local and state public health officials to a TB incident for statistical purposes but also may be used by local or state public health officials to effect an infected person's isolation, confirmatory testing in cases of suspected TB infection, and treatment and monitoring.

Shelters such as described in this case, which often are regulated by local and state authorities, also may be required to report TB cases, particularly given the homeless state of their residents, congregate setting, residents' poor health status, and consequent risk for contagion. Even if Marie is unwilling to sign a release-of-information-and-consent form, shelter staff may be required by law to report her case to the local health department. Any court would be unlikely to find that Marie's right *not* to sign any release or consent outweighs a state's public health interest in TB prevention and the means for accomplishing its objective through such devices as mandatory reporting, testing, and isolation.

Marie's fears about losing her son might be addressed by making Marie aware that further withholding of information about her infectiousness, and thus the opportunity for local health officials to provide treatment or other intervention for Marie or testing for Sean, may be considered evidence of child neglect, which would almost certainly jeopardize her custody of Sean. In fact, Marie's willingness to disclose her TB status and seek treatment would speak far more positively of her ability to care for Sean than would her reluctance to be so forthcoming with shelter or health department staff.

The shelter director's disclosure to the health department director that a shelter resident has tested positive for TB is unlikely to be construed as a violation of law. The disclosure did not divulge the resident's identity, was directed toward an official to whom such disclosures usually are required, and—even if disclosed unwisely or in passing—actually may be legally mandated and require the identity of the infected person. Not only may the disclosure be permitted or required, but depending on state law, such a disclosure may compel action by the local health department, such as confirmatory testing (depending on when Marie was originally tested and who performed the testing), detention, isolation, follow-up treatment, and testing of other residents (including Marie's son, Sean) or shelter staff. However, the federal due process protections discussed above may require a public health officer who wants to impose isolation or treatment on Marie pursuant to a state law first establish by clear and convincing evidence that Marie actually poses a serious risk of transmitting TB to others. Moreover, the health officer may be required to use the least restrictive means possible to achieve the clearly confined public health goal of preventing the spread of TB. For example, the involuntary commitment of Marie to a hospital may be appropriate only if no question exists about the diagnosis and, because she is homeless, no other place she could stay would be less restrictive than a hospital. In this case, confining Marie until her TB is no longer active may be permissible and necessary.

The health department director's observation about the shelter's unsanitary condition, although perhaps related to the issue of TB control, simply provides the health department with an independent basis for taking action to ensure the shelter does not pose a risk to public health, particularly to the health of the shelter's residents. Similar to health facilities, the privilege of operating a shelter or other public accommodation generally is conditioned on conformity to state laws, particularly laws pertaining to public safety such as sanitation. Any report made to local or state officials about the sanitation of public accommodations, reasonable or not, may be used to take official action, such as a site visit to ascertain any public health risks. In this case, the health department director's observation alone may justify action by the local health department, such as inspecting the shelter kitchen and living areas and requiring corrective action if necessary.

Children—Part I: Child Nutritional Status and Child Maltreatment

Case Study 4

Sharie W., a 3-year-old child, is one of many participants in the county's Supplemental Feeding Program for the Women, Infants, and Children (WIC) program. Her mother, Martha, received coupons for healthy foods, referrals for medical visits, and nutrition information and counseling during her pregnancy with Sharie. Sharie now eats well and nutritiously each morning before she leaves for preschool. Additionally, Sharie has had access to pediatric services from the time of her birth.

As part of the WIC program, Sharie is weighed and measured weekly at the WIC clinic. Unlike Sharie's prior visits to a variety of other local medical clinics—which did not yield careful and sequential monitoring of Sharie's growth and development—her mother's now-regular visits to pick up coupons at the WIC clinic have made that site an ideal setting at which to monitor Sharie's health. However, abuse of Sharie is now suspected. During a recent WIC visit, severe facial bruising and welts were visible on Sharie. When asked about the bruises and welts by WIC staff, Sharie's mother left the clinic nervously. Clinic staff called the local child protective services agency (CPS) immediately, and CPS workers responded by visiting Sharie's house and removing Sharie to foster care.

Legal Analysis

Children are a special population from a public health standpoint because of their status as some of the most vulnerable members of society. Children depend on their parents or legal guardians for virtually all of their health and human services needs. If parents or legal guardians fail to discharge their parental responsibilities, their children's needs will not be met. In these circumstances, the government may be authorized or compelled to provide for these children's needs. This section focuses on two important roles of the law in promoting the health and welfare of U.S. children: (1) improving the nutritional status of children and (2) combating child maltreatment.

Child Nutritional Status

The nutritional status of children is measured in a number of ways, including one described as "food security" or by the percentage of children under age 18 years who live in households that experience food insecurity, with moderate or severe hunger.[37]

Nearly 4% of all children, and almost 12% of children classified as poor, experience moderate or severe hunger. Many children have a diet that is poor or needs improvement, and, not unexpectedly, children in families below poverty are less likely than children in higher-income families to have a diet rated "good" under the federal government's Healthy Eating Index.

One federal program intended to improve children's nutritional status is the Women, Infants, and Children (WIC) program, an excellent example of law as a tool to improve the health status of children. Established by Congress in 1972 as an amendment to the Child Nutrition Act of 1966, WIC provides federal grants to states for supplemental food, nutrition counseling, and access to health-care services for certain pregnant, breastfeeding, and nonbreastfeeding postpartum women, and to infants and children. Administered by the Food and Nutrition Service of the U.S. Department of Agriculture, WIC is available in each state, the District of Columbia, 32 Indian Tribal Organizations, Puerto Rico, the Virgin Islands, American Samoa, and Guam.

As with many federally funded programs, WIC gives states and local agencies substantial discretion in the administration of the program. Federal law authorizes the Secretary of Agriculture to make grants to state public health agencies, and states in turn contract with local agencies to effectuate the delivery of WIC services. States may choose to provide WIC services at county health departments, hospitals, mobile clinics, community centers, schools, public housing sites, migrant health centers and camps, and Indian Health Service facilities.[38] State WIC agencies and their local WIC service providers may design programs appropriate for their particular WIC caseloads. Normally, WIC is administered through statewide community networks, and the program's success relies on the coordinated efforts of local programs, sites, and retail food stores. In fact, one of the most successful models for providing children with WIC benefits is by combining public health programs for mothers and their children with an onsite WIC program component and allowing WIC-eligible persons to obtain needed services in one visit.[39,40]

Child Maltreatment

Child maltreatment (including physical, sexual, and emotional abuse, as well as physical and emotional neglect) traditionally has been in the province of social services or the criminal justice system. However, child maltreatment is also a substantial public health problem, as evidenced by the detrimental health and psychosocial effects faced by abused and neglected children. The grave public health consequences of child abuse and neglect include depression, suicidal ideation, violent behavior, physical injuries, substance abuse, and chronic low self-esteem. Sexually abused children may engage in premature sexual activity, increasing their risk for unintended pregnancies or sexually transmitted diseases.[41]

Each year, in the United States, approximately 1 million children are the victims of maltreatment, and approximately 1000 children die from abuse or neglect. In 1998, the most recent year for which data are available, there were 12.9 victims of maltreatment per 1000 children, and 1.6 child maltreatment fatalities per 100,000 children. Specified goals of Healthy People 2010—health objectives for the United States to achieve over the first decade of the 21st century—are to reduce child maltreatment to 10.3 victims per 1000 children and to reduce child maltreatment fatalities to

1.4 per 100,000 children.[42] Improved understanding and use of public health law can help meet these important public health goals.

Federal public health laws, in the form of statutes and administrative regulations, serve as effective interventions to combat child abuse and neglect. The U.S. Congress recognized the seriousness of child maltreatment when they enacted the Adoption and Safe Families Act of 1997 (ASFA), establishing explicitly for the first time in federal law that a child's health and safety are of paramount importance for the nation's health. This federal legislation prioritizes safety and permanence for children who have been removed from their homes because of abuse or neglect.

Ostensibly, ASFA was enacted to promote the adoption of children in foster care; however, ASFA goes beyond this narrow goal to address comprehensively the public health concern of child maltreatment. Specifically, ASFA helps public officials and CPS professionals combat child abuse and neglect by specifying the circumstances under which, before placing an abused or neglected child in temporary foster care or with a permanent adoptive family, reasonable efforts need not be made to preserve or reunify the family (i.e., if parents pose a serious risk to a child's health or safety); giving incentives to states for providing adoptive families for children whose parents' rights have been permanently terminated because of abuse or neglect; and requiring that states move to terminate the parental rights of parents whose children have been in foster care for 15 of the last 22 months.[43]

Other, more recent federal legislation has been enacted in part to reduce the incidence of child abuse and neglect. Under these federal laws, funds are appropriated to enforce existing child abuse and neglect laws (including laws protecting against child sexual abuse) and to promote programs designed to prevent child abuse and neglect.[44,45] The U.S. Department of Health and Human Services (DHHS) issued child welfare regulations establishing a federal review process where state outcomes for children are measured in terms of safety, permanency, and family well-being. Under these regulations, federal funds are withheld from and financial penalties are imposed on states failing to improve outcomes for abused and neglected children.[46]

Federal legislation and guidelines for combating child maltreatment notwithstanding, state and local public health officials often must rely on their own state laws to address this public health problem. For example, legislatively mandated surveillance of child maltreatment by state or local health departments may reduce morbidity and mortality associated with child abuse and neglect. For surveillance purposes, all states have laws requiring the reporting of suspected or confirmed child maltreatment to public health agencies. Public health practitioners who are mandated reporters generally include physicians, mental health workers, social workers, and nurses. State licensing requirements for these public health professionals may include training in identifying and appropriately reporting suspected child maltreatment. All states have statutes specifying procedures for mandated reporters to follow when reporting child maltreatment. Reports typically are made by telephone to CPS; the reports generally include age and address of the child, name and address of the parent or guardian, information about the alleged perpetrator, and type of suspected maltreatment (e.g., physical abuse, sexual abuse, or neglect). Almost all states have laws and regulations providing for immunity from civil and criminal liability for individuals (including public health practitioners) making good-faith reports of suspected instances of child maltreatment.

Unfortunately, many cases of child maltreatment are neither reported nor investigated, even when suspected by public health professionals. To help address this underreporting and lack of investigation, nearly every state imposes civil or criminal penalties on health professionals for the knowing of but intentional failure to report suspected cases of child maltreatment. Some states (i.e., Alabama, California, Delaware, Michigan, Minnesota, New Jersey, Rhode Island, South Carolina, and Wisconsin) impose sentences of imprisonment for failure to report. Other states (i.e., Maine, Massachusetts, Oregon, Vermont, and Virginia) penalize nonreporters with a fine. Additionally, many states (e.g., Arkansas, Colorado, Iowa, Montana, and New York) mandate that nonreporters be civilly liable for damages caused by the failure to report.[47–49]

Early identification of child maltreatment is necessary to intervene and prevent further abuse. However, the highest goal of the public health community and of laws related to child maltreatment should be intervention *before* abuse or neglect occurs. State laws may set aside funds and establish programs to serve families with multiple risk factors (including poverty, unintended or teen pregnancy, substance abuse, child with disabilities, or parents who were abused as children) that may lead to the abuse or neglect of children.[50]

Practice Pointers

Case Study 4 demonstrates what may appear to be an awkward dilemma for many public health professionals: incurring and discharging a legal obligation to report suspected child abuse or neglect that arose from a public health encounter. In this particular case, Sharie's mother, Martha, left the WIC clinic when questioned by clinic staff about Sharie's visible bruises and welts. Subsequently, the clinic staff reported their suspicions to a CPS, and Sharie was removed from her mother's custody. Unquestionably, clinic staff are responsible for contacting a CPS once they suspect child abuse or neglect. However, the facts of the case do not indicate whether, pursuant to an investigation, CPS workers suspect abuse by Martha or by someone else in Sharie's family or household. Alternatively, Sharie's bruises and welts may not be the result of child abuse or neglect at all, and Sharie might have been removed from her mother's custody on an entirely unrelated basis. Regardless of the basis for revoking Martha's custody of Sharie, clinic workers may believe that, by reporting the suspected child abuse or neglect, they may have deterred Martha from ever again obtaining WIC benefits for Sharie. Such a belief might be reinforced in the event that Martha and Sharie are never again seen at the clinic, and WIC clinic workers are not informed about whether their suspicions had a basis in fact.

These concerns, although understandable, should not diminish the vigilance with which public health professionals tend to cases in which they suspect child abuse or neglect among their clients or patients. On the contrary, under circumstances such as these, public health professionals should exercise their continuing responsibilities pursuant to their authority under programs such as WIC. In other words, suspected or actual child abuse or neglect, failure of Martha or Sharie to return to the WIC clinic, or removal of Sharie from Martha's custody does not necessarily terminate Sharie's need for the nutrition made possible through the WIC program.

Rather, the WIC clinic staff should take steps to ensure (if appropriate) that Martha and Sharie continue to receive WIC benefits to which they may be entitled. This will require that the WIC clinic staff develop and maintain effective communication with CPS staff. Otherwise, malnutrition may be added to Sharie's already difficult situation.

Children—Part II: Health Disparities and Lead Poisoning

Case Study 5

Carl J S., aged 4 years, is being seen by a primary-care physician at the local public health department's clinic as part of a preschool physical required for Carl J to attend daycare. Carl J lives with his mother and siblings, an African-American family, in substandard housing in an urbanized, densely populated neighborhood. Carl J is Medicaid-eligible, but because his family does not have a primary-care physician, Carl J is seen at the local public health department's clinic for certain primary-care needs. During the visit with the physician, Carl J's mother tells the physician that Carl J sometimes complains of stomach aches and has constipation. Over-the-counter medicines seem to work for these problems, and other than what she considers normal hyperactivity, Carl J's mother tells the physician that she is confident Carl J is healthy. The physician notes that Carl J is very active and that his attention span is noticeably short. Carl J's vision and hearing are normal, and despite lack of continuous health-care coverage, his vaccinations are up to date. The physician further notes that, even though Carl J seems to have reached some of the most important developmental milestones for a child his age, he appears to have slightly delayed language and social skills. Considering Carl J's circumstances, the physician is concerned about possible lead poisoning. Because the physician has no indication that Carl J previously was screened for lead exposure, the physician has Carl J tested. Carl J has a blood lead level (BLL) of 23 micrograms per deciliter (μg/dL); an acceptable BLL is below 10 μg/dL. Such elevated levels of lead in blood can cause serious problems, including neurologic damage, learning disabilities, and behavioral problems. When informed about Carl J's condition, his mother asks the physician what might be done to improve Carl J's health and the health of her other children.

What steps might Carl J's mother take with regard to her children's apparent exposure or risk of exposure to lead? What steps might the public health clinic physician take with regard to Carl J's elevated BLL or to the risk for lead exposure among Carl J's siblings?

Background

Lead is one of society's oldest known and most thoroughly studied environmental hazards.[51] The devastating effects of lead exposure can include serious damage to the central nervous system and red blood cells.[52] High levels of exposure can result in coma, convulsions, and death.[53] Levels as low as 10 μg/dL—an amount the Centers for Disease Control and Prevention considers "lead poisoning"—do not cause any distinctive symptoms but are associated with decreased intelligence and impaired neurobehavioral developments.[53] Lead exposure is particularly harmful to children aged 6 years and under, whose developing nervous systems and rapid metabolism are particularly vulnerable to adverse effects of lead.[54]

During 1999–2002, the overall prevalence of elevated BLL for children aged 1–5 years was 1.6%, indicating approximately 310,000 children in that age range were at risk for exposure to harmful BLLs.[55] Before lead's harmful effects were known more widely and federal legislation restricted the use of lead or products containing lead, lead was used in residential paint, gasoline, water pipes, and other products. Today, childhood lead poisoning is known or suspected to be associated with exposure to lead-contaminated drinking water,[56] litargirio[57] and other folk remedies,[58] imported tamarind candies,[58] and certain imported spices.[59] In addition, certain industrial workers (particularly those working in smelters) may be exposed to lead and may take lead home on their clothes, skin, hair, and tools and in their vehicles, potentially also exposing family members to lead.[60] The primary source of harmful environmental lead exposure is considered to be lead-contaminated household dust in homes built before widespread restrictions on the use of lead-based paint: about 75% of housing built before 1978 contains lead paint.[61]

Despite the dramatic decline in the prevalence of elevated BLLs among children, those similarly situated to Carl J—children in minority, impoverished households who live in older, substandard housing—disproportionately bear the burden of environmental lead exposure.[62] Nationally, children in low-income households are eight times more likely than children in higher-income households to have elevated BLLs, and black children are twice as likely as white children to have elevated BLLs. Impoverished, minority families—similar to Carl J's—are more likely than their higher-income nonminority counterparts to suffer a variety of health disparities, possibly reflecting a lack of continuous health insurance or coverage; lack of access to appropriate health-care providers; and poor nutrition. Health disparities may contribute to higher levels of morbidity, lower life expectancy, decreased quality of life, loss of economic opportunities, and perceptions of injustice.[63]

Legal Analysis

As early as 1971, the U.S. government began to recognize the serious health threat posed by lead in the environment and, in response, enacted various laws to mitigate lead hazards. For example, the Lead Based Poisoning Prevention Act of 1971 included a call for research into the extent of the lead-related hazards, and for the development of local lead poisoning prevention programs.[64,65] In 1988, the U.S. Congress amended the Safe Drinking Water Act to include the Lead Contamination Control Act; this act provided for programs intended to reduce lead contamination in drinking water.[66] In 1992, Congress enacted the Residential Lead-Based Paint Hazard Reduction Act (or Title X of the Housing and Community Development Act), which addresses lead poisoning prevention in residential property, as well as the training and certification related to lead risk assessment, abatement, inspection, and accreditation of training programs.[67] One of Title X's most important provisions is the requirement that known lead hazards be disclosed to prospective home buyers at the time of sale or lease of a home built before 1978.[68] Many state governments have enacted their own laws related to notification and disclosure of known lead hazards in home sale or rental transactions.[69,70] Since enactment of laws related to the mitigation of lead hazards, the prevalence of elevated BLL cases has steadily and dramatically decreased. Nonetheless, lead poisoning still exists, and the prevalence of elevated BLL cases among segments of the U.S. population still exceeds DHHS's goal of eliminating child lead poisoning as a public health problem by 2010.[42,71]

Screening

Young children such as Carl J are considered at higher-than-average risk for lead poisoning: eight of ten lead-poisoned children are Medicaid-eligible. Under Medicaid's Early and Periodic Screening, Diagnostic and Treatment program, participating states are required to provide for the screening of all Medicaid-eligible children and to provide for the education of these children and their families about the potential hazards of lead exposure.[72] Some state governments have passed their own, sometimes more stringent, laws related to lead poisoning screening.[73] For example, under New Jersey law, physicians, nurse practitioners, and health facilities are required to conduct lead exposure screening for all of their patients (not just Medicaid-eligible children) under the age of 6 years.[74] Massachusetts law requires that children aged 9–13 months be screened for lead exposure, with subsequent screening at ages 2 and 3 years.[75] Massachusetts children in households living in what are considered to be high-risk communities—those with a significant number of older homes—also must be tested at age 4 years. A few states require blood lead screening as a requirement for school or daycare entry.

Despite federal and state screening laws, lead screening rates among children remain low. The U.S. General Accounting Office (now the Government Accountability Office) has reported that, although Medicaid-eligible children account for approximately 60% of all children with lead poisoning, only 20% of Medicaid-eligible children actually are screened for lead poisoning. Several factors may account for low rates of lead poisoning screening, including lack of federal oversight to ensure screening policies are fully implemented; low levels of compliance with screening laws or requirements among health-care providers; and general difficulties in providing services to Medicaid-eligible persons.[76,77] The failure to adhere to Medicaid regulations on BLL screening was the subject of the 2004 case of *Memisovski v. Marman,* in which the Illinois Supreme Court ruled that state officials violated the rights of Medicaid-eligible children in Illinois by failing to provide for their lead poisoning screening as required under Medicaid regulations. Although all Medicaid-eligible children aged 11–23 months in Illinois should have received at least one blood lead screening, nearly 80% were not screened at all. In its decision, the Illinois Supreme Court observed that although the state's participation in the federal Medicaid program may be voluntary, once the state chose to participate, the state was required to comply with Medicaid regulations. This case may be the broadest challenge so far against any state for its administration of the federal Medicaid program.[78,j]

Legal Remedies

Persons who believe they have been harmed as a result of exposure to lead hazards have filed lawsuits against their landlords, owners of property and businesses with lead hazards, and managers and insurers of such properties. Such lawsuits have been based on claims that landlords, owners, managers, or insurers have breached their contracts or warranties of habitability; are negligent; or have violated consumer protection laws or lead paint poisoning prevention acts.[79]

Individuals and governments also have sued lead paint manufacturers, although such lawsuits are difficult to pursue because of challenges in ascertaining which lead paint manufacturer actually produced the paint that caused the lead poisoning.[80] However, the landmark Wisconsin case of *Thomas v. Mallet* suggests that some courts may not require such a clear connection between actual lead poisoning and a specific lead paint manufacturer. In that case, the court noted that lead paint manufacturers continued to produce and market lead paint pigment despite industry knowledge of its hazards dating back to 1904.[81] On this basis, the court decided to broaden its definition of liability in this case to include the lead paint manufacturers that were sued and allowed the lawsuit against these manufacturers to proceed.[k]

In addition to individual lawsuits, another legal remedy for mitigating the risk of lead exposure is the government's enforcement of existing local, state, and federal laws pertaining to lead poisoning prevention. Examples are the successful collaborations of federal agencies such as the Environmental Protection Agency, the Department of Housing and Urban Development, and the Department of Justice in investigating reports of Title X noncompliance, and in enforcing the Title X requirement that known lead hazards be disclosed. In addition to receiving tips and complaints from the public, officials from the Environmental Protection Agency and the Department of Housing and Urban Development regularly conduct onsite inspections of locations such as property management firms and rental offices to review sales contracts and leases involving housing that may pose lead hazards.[82,83] Violations of Title X may result in fines up to $11,000 per violation and criminal sanctions.[84]

Practice Pointers

Despite the attention paid to lead hazards, particularly lead poisoning among children—including enactment of related laws at the local, state, and federal levels—the response to Case Study 5 is not straightforward. Carl J's mother might be able to have her other children screened for BLLs, assuming they also are Medicaid eligible and, absent a primary-care physician, the local public health department is able to provide such screening. Because the health department already has provided screening for Carl J, BLL screening of Carl J's siblings probably is available. Of course, in the event treatment is required for Carl J or his siblings, Carl J's mother will still need a referral to a health-care provider for appropriate services.

Even though screening and detection are important, the primary intervention for lead poisoning is to stop further lead exposure. If Carl J's house is the suspected source of lead exposure, then his mother may decide she must move her family out of the home. Given her circumstances, however, she may not be able to secure more suitable housing. Whether the household remains or leaves, the source of lead exposure in the home needs to be abated. Because of the known association between older and substandard housing and the increased risk for lead exposure, public health departments need to work with housing and property code inspectors to identify the source of lead hazards in Carl J's home and secure the professional abatement services necessary to remove or mitigate the lead hazard. For example, in Manchester, Connecticut, the property maintenance code requires that interior and exterior lead-based paint be "maintained in a condition free from peeling, chipping, and flaking" or such paint must "be removed or covered in an appropriate manner."[85] If a child under age 6 years resides in a home with such conditions, the ordinance requires code officials to collect dust-wipe samples and refer the test results along with a report of conditions (at 7-305.4.2). Should the "sample test exceed safe conditions as determined by the Director of Health based on state and federal standards," the health departments will pursue compliance with federal and state regulations.[85]

A public health agency's response to a child in Carl J's circumstances can vary depending on the state or locality. When a child's BLL is mildly elevated (e.g., 10–19 μg/dL), public health regulations typically call for dietary counseling aimed at reducing the child's absorption of lead.[77,86] Other suggested measures might include frequent wet cleaning and hand-washing to help reduce lead dust, and follow-up testing for BLLs. With a BLL of 20 μg/dL or higher, the primary public health response will include a home inspection.[l] In a few states, this inspection is required when levels as low as 10 μg/dL are reported.[m] Inspectors may take paint samples from various places in the home, particularly in areas with paint chipping or peeling or in which paint chips might be considered chewable by children; samples also may be taken from "friction surfaces" where one painted surface rubs against another and creates dust. If hazardous levels of lead paint are found, the health department may be authorized by law to order the landlord or property owner to abate the property within a specific time (e.g. 30 days for nonimminent hazards).[87] Lead paint usually is abated by (1) stripping the lead paint from painted surface; (2) removing the surface containing lead paint; or (3) covering the paint-covered area.[88] Because of the environmental dangers associated with disturbing or removing lead-based paint, states often require training and certification of persons who perform lead abatement.[89,90]

Other public health responses to cases such as Carl J's include interim measures such as securing or making referrals for house-dust control by professional cleaners, and relocating a lead-poisoned child and the child's family to reduce ongoing lead exposure. In cases where housing agency responses or interim measures are not effective, public health officials may need to work with their legal counsel or the local housing agency's counsel to consider or pursue legal action in local courts, such as administrative enforcement proceedings, contempt judgments, and civil penalties. Such recourse may be necessary if, for example, the landlord or property owner refuses to comply with an abatement order. Some states have passed laws making as a misdemeanor the failure to abate a lead hazard as required in an abatement order in a home in which a minor resides.[91]

To facilitate property owners' compliance with lead abatement laws, some jurisdictions provide owners with financial incentives and other assistance. For example, in Milwaukee, certain property owners may be eligible for assistance in removing lead hazards created by lead dust in window troughs and dust created from the opening and closing of windows.[92] The city of Milwaukee works with licensed contractors who repair such windows to lead-safe conditions at minimal costs. Property owners who delay removing such lead hazards and wait until a child is lead poisoned automatically lose eligibility for city assistance on that particular housing unit. In Massachusetts and New Jersey, certain property owners may be eligible to apply for financial assistance—including grants, lower interest loans, and tax credits—if they are not financially able to perform essential lead abatement. In cases where property owners refuse to abate lead hazards, the local health department may be able to arrange for abatement and charge the property owner for the costs; the health department may secure a lien on a property for which abatement services were provided if the property owner fails to reimburse the department for costs of abatement.[93]

In addition to a treatment response, either Carl J's mother or the health department should consider contacting the local housing agency to determine whether a lead hazard inspection and, where appropriate, abatement services are available to remove lead hazards in Carl J's home. Depending on the jurisdiction and circumstances, the physician or other clinic staff might be able to facilitate such a referral, such as providing a report to the local housing agency that may be authorized by law to initiate or perform an inspection or abatement of Carl J's home. Because the authority to address lead hazards may be spread among several local agencies, public agencies should develop agreements to coordinate their lead hazard programs with other local agencies, such as housing or property agencies and housing courts, to ensure continuity between lead screening programs for children and effective lead abatement in homes where lead-poisoned children reside.[94]

Undocumented Immigrants

> Germs do not check for green cards.
> S. B. Drake[95]

Case Study 6

Artel M. is a 25-year-old man who legally entered the United States on a student visa as an 18-year-old. Artel has overstayed his visa and no longer is a student. Artel works in a local small business that does not provide him with health benefits; he and his wife are raising two children, both of whom are foreign-born and will soon enter a public school. On the basis of the local school district's recommendation, Artel's youngest child is taken to the local health department's well-child clinic, where the child is found to need vaccinations and other physical and mental health services. During the visit, the staff determines that, on the basis of Artel's salary, Artel and his children are qualified to receive publicly funded health services. However, the staff also learn that neither Artel nor his children are legal residents of the United States, and they bring these findings to the attention of the department's director. What services may the health department provide to Artel and his family? Who will pay for these services? Should other local, state, or federal agencies be notified about Artel and his family's undocumented status?

Legal Analysis

Undocumented immigrants[n] are a special population from a public health perspective: this population is characterized by relatively poor health and high rates of untreated communicable disease. For example, compared with U.S. citizens, undocumented immigrants have slower rates of declining infant mortality; lower rates of vaccination; and higher rates of dental disease, delayed growth and development, poor mental health, and infectious diseases such as TB.[o] Moreover, many undocumented immigrants have severely limited access to public and primary-care health services because of their lower socioeconomic status and because of lack of familiarity with public health services and other nonfinancial barriers such as language and culture. Confounding their poor health status, undocumented immigrants are at all times at risk for detention and deportation because of their unresolved legal status.

These facts and the above case study illustrate an increasingly common dilemma for many public health officials: how to balance the seemingly conflicting obligations to (1) promote the public's health and prevent the spread of disease by providing preventive and other health services, without regard to immigration status or ability to pay, and to (2) report undocumented immigrants who request or receive department services, at the risk of discouraging undocumented immigrants from seeking needed services. This section describes the legal considerations pertaining to public health and undocumented immigrants.

Federal Law

The federal government, acting through Congress, has plenary authority over immigration matters. As the U.S. Supreme Court stated many years ago, "The Federal Government has broad constitutional powers in determining what aliens shall be admitted to the United States, the period they may remain, regulation of their conduct before naturalization, and the terms and conditions of their naturalization."[96] The authority of the U.S. Congress with regard to matters involving aliens was elaborated further in the 1976 case of *Matthews v. Diaz*; in this case, the U.S. Supreme Court ruled that the federal government may discriminate against immigrants and among different groups of immigrants regarding eligibility for federal benefits.[97] Relying on its broad authority over immigrations, the federal government enacted the Personal Responsibility and Work Opportunity Reconciliation Act of 1996 (PRWORA), significantly limiting the rights of illegal immigrants to receive public health services.[98] This law restricts undocumented immigrants' access to many federally funded health services and requires states to deny many state and local benefits to undocumented immigrants. Specifically, the PRWORA eliminated the eligibility of undocumented immigrants (with certain exceptions, described below) for "any State or local public benefit," defined as including "any . . . health . . . benefit for which payments or assistance are provided . . . [by] a State or local government or by appropriated funds of a State or local government."[99] For example, under this act, undocumented immigrants are excluded from Medicaid (except emergency Medicaid), and undocumented immigrant children are excluded from the State Children's Health Insurance Program, which, under Title XII of the Balanced Budget Act of 1997, allows states to develop programs that provide health-care coverage for uninsured children from low-income families. Importantly, however, states may choose to reject the general federal provision barring state assistance to undocumented immigrants as long as they pass affirmative legislation to that effect.[100,101] One of the most controversial restrictions of the PRWORA may be the denial of federally funded prenatal care for undocumented immigrants. Prenatal care for a mother undisputedly increases the likelihood of a healthy life for the child, and, as acknowledged in the 2001 case of *Lewis v. Thompson*, no doubt exists that a "child suffers after birth from lack of prenatal care in the womb."[102,p] On the basis of these considerations, plaintiffs in *Lewis* argued that denying prenatal care for a pregnant undocumented immigrant violates a born child's right to equal protection of the laws under the Fourteenth Amendment to the Constitution. The Court in the case disagreed and ruled that denying federal funding for prenatal care does not violate the Constitution. First, the Court stated that deterring illegal immigration is a rational basis for denying federal funding for prenatal care because Congress explicitly intended as one purpose of the Act to remove the incentive for illegal immigration that might be occasioned by federal assistance. The Court also stated that a fetus is not a "person" for equal protection purposes and therefore lacks the "constitutional protection to assure it enhanced prospects of good health after birth."

Despite restrictions in the PRWORA, a range of *both* federally funded and state-funded health services are available to undocumented immigrants. For example, undocumented immigrants may be provided with public health services such as child vaccinations; HIV- and AIDS-related care and treatment; TB screening, diagnosis, and treatment; screening, diagnosis, and treatment for sexually transmitted diseases; and testing and treatment of symptoms of other communicable diseases (regardless of whether those diseases are actually present).[103] Federal law also designates community programs, services, and assistance for which all immigrants, regardless of legal status, are eligible. These include (1) ambulance, sanitation, and other widely available services; (2) crisis counseling and intervention programs, including services related to child protection, violence and abuse prevention, and treatment for mental illness or substance abuse; (3) shelter and housing assistance for the homeless, for victims of domestic violence, and for abused or abandoned children; (4) community nutritional services, including food banks and senior nutrition programs; and (5) public health services that protect life and safety by preventing disease and injury.

Federal law also ensures that emergency health care and short-term, noncash disaster relief (including food, clothing, and shelter) are available to all persons without regard to their immigration status.[104] Emergency Medicaid, which pays for treatment of emergency medical conditions,[105,106,q] is available to undocumented immigrants who otherwise qualify for Medicaid and meet state residency requirements.[107] Undocumented immigrants also can access emergency care under the Emergency Medical Treatment and Active Labor Act (EMTALA),[108] which requires that Medicare-participating hospitals with an emergency department must triage incoming patients to determine whether they have an emergency medical condition or are in active labor and, if so, to provide stabilizing treatment. These hospitals are prohibited from transferring patients before stabilization unless the physician on duty certifies the medical benefits of transfer outweigh the increased risks to the individual. These obligations exist without regard to a patient's immigration status.

Emergency health services for undocumented immigrants also may be provided pursuant to Section 1011 of the Medicare Prescription Drug, Improvement and Modernization Act of 2003.[109] Section 1011, entitled "Federal Reimbursement of Emergency Health Services Furnished to Undocumented Aliens," provides $250 million per year for fiscal years 2005–2008 for payments to eligible providers for emergency health services provided to undocumented immigrants. Reimbursement under Section 1011 is targeted to otherwise uncompensated care and therefore is not available for services provided to undocumented immigrants who are eligible for Medicaid or emergency Medicaid or who have other insurance. Unlike emergency Medicaid, Section 1011 does not provide insurance coverage to undocumented immigrants and does not guarantee coverage of their emergency bill. Additionally, reimbursement under Section 1011 is limited to the services necessary to "stabilize" the emergency condition. Undocumented immigrants seeking services under Section 1011 are not required to provide immigration documents or to disclose their immigration status to receive emergency treatment or to be claimed for Section 1011 reimbursement.

Federal law also may make available to some undocumented immigrants certain nonemergency health services. The Hill-Burton Act requires hospitals and nursing homes, in return for federal construction and renovation grant funds, to undertake a community service obligation.[110,r] This obligation prohibits Hill-Burton facilities from discriminating on any ground unrelated to an individual's need for services or the availability of the needed services in the facility. Hill-Burton facilities must accept all persons, including undocumented immigrants, who are able to pay for their care either directly or indirectly through insurance coverage or through state or local government programs.

State Law

States have no authority over immigration. The U.S. Supreme Court has indicated clearly that "the regulation of aliens is so intimately blended and intertwined with responsibilities of the national government" that federal laws regarding immigration will always take precedence over state laws.[111] Despite the federal government's broad power over immigration, states are not prohibited from enacting public health laws specifically directed at immigrants as an exercise of their broad power to protect the health and welfare of their citizens. A state statute directed at *immigrants*, as long as it is not a regulation of *immigration* (i.e., a regulation determining who should or should not be admitted into the country or the conditions under which an immigrant may remain), will not be preempted.

Some states have made generous choices in providing health services to undocumented immigrants. For example, even though federal law excludes undocumented immigrant children from coverage under the State Children's Health Insurance Program, several states (e.g., Washington) have chosen to use state funds to provide health care to these children. Additionally, several states have enacted laws that specifically provide public funding for prenatal care for undocumented immigrants. Many states mandate that pregnant immigrants are presumptively eligible[s] for publicly funded prenatal services. Nebraska law, for example, provides that, although undocumented immigrants are eligible for emergency medical care only, pregnant immigrants have "presumptive eligibility" for prenatal services.[112] A pregnant immigrant may apply for ambulatory prenatal services, and the provider makes a presumptive determination of eligibility on the basis of income only. The provider is not required to investigate other eligibility requirements, such as immigration status. The provider must notify the applicant that to continue receiving prenatal care, she must apply for the Nebraska Medical Assistance Program by the last day of the month after the month of presumptive eligibility. If the woman fails to apply, prenatal care ends on the last day of the month after the month of the presumptive eligibility determination. If she applies within the required time, her presumptive eligibility continues through the day on which her continued eligibility is determined.

On the other hand, some states acted quickly pursuant to the PRWORA's passage to establish regulations consistent with the federal law in limiting benefits for undocumented immigrants. For example, California issued emergency regulations rendering undocumented immigrants ineligible for state or local public benefits. When public health organizations filed suit against the state, arguing that promulgating emergency regulations to hastily comply with federal law was an abuse of discretion, a California Court of Appeal held that the emergency regulations should be enforced. The court reasoned that because California's program providing state funding for undocumented immigrants' prenatal care—a subject over which federal government has plenary jurisdiction—was rendered immediately illegal by the Act, prompt compliance with the federal law justified the emergency regulations.[113] The court specifically held that the state did not abuse its discretion in issuing emergency regulations because the state lacked the time to promulgate regular regulations before the Act went into effect.

Practice Pointers

An important determinant of the extent of the services that may be provided to Artel and his children under the facts presented in Case Study 6 depends on the state in which Artel and his family reside. This is due primarily to provisions of the PRWORA, which generally restrict undocumented immigrants' access to state and locally funded health services. If Artel's family lives in a state that has enacted a law affirmatively rejecting the Act's restrictive provisions, then obtaining the needed vaccinations and other physical and mental health services for which Artel and his children may otherwise be eligible presents no real problem.

The conclusion is entirely different if Artel's family lives in a state that has *not* enacted a law affirmatively rejecting the PRWORA's restrictive provisions. Under these circumstances, Artel's family may be entitled only to needed health services specifically delineated under the Act or to health services not otherwise covered by the Act. For example, undocumented immigrants may receive public health assistance for vaccinations. Thus, the health department can provide Artel's child with needed vaccinations. Whether the department may provide Artel's child with other physical and mental health services depends on the nature of those needed services. For example, although the case study does not specify these other needed services, if Artel's child required hospitalization or treatment for an emergency medical condition, or treatment for a communicable disease (e.g., TB infection or positive skin test), then the health department may provide such services. Additionally, a hospital or other provider may provide emergency treatments to Artel's family and most likely will be reimbursed pursuant to Section 1011 of the Medicare Prescription Drug, Improvement and Modernization Act of 2003 (discussed above).

Moreover, Artel and his family may be eligible for *federally* funded benefits or programs that are not subject to the Act, including benefits or services enumerated in the discussion section above. Careful screening by health department staff of the needs of persons such as Artel and his family, and matching those needs to available federal programs, may help offset some of the restrictions imposed by the Act.

Nonetheless, undocumented immigrants' eligibility for public health services does not necessarily ensure access to or use of these services. Other significant barriers may contribute to underutilization of public health services by undocumented immigrants, including language and cultural differences or misunderstandings, as well as lack of knowledge about or familiarity with public health programs. Fear of apprehension by immigration authorities also may contribute to underutilization of public health services by undocumented immigrants. The fear of apprehension may be heightened because federal law prevents states from restricting government entities or officials from reporting to the U.S. Department of Homeland Security's Immigration and Customs Enforcement the immigration status of persons with whom they may come into contact.[114] To address the more general problem of underutilization of health services by undocumented immigrants, public health officials may consider educational programs for the undocumented immigrant community about their eligibility for emergency, nonemergency, and preventive health services. Undocumented immigrants also should be reassured that they cannot be deported solely for seeking and receiving publicly funded health services.

Additionally, the health department director might review his or her state's policies and application forms to determine whether they obstruct or facilitate undocumented immigrants' access to services. To encourage undocumented immigrants to access available and needed public health services without fear of reporting or deportation, neither application and enrollment forms nor health department staff should require social security numbers, immigration status, or unnecessary documentation if this information is not required by state law or essential to providing such services. Although state law may not *require* reporting of immigration status by health department staff, it also, as discussed above, may not *prohibit* such reporting.

Conclusion

Unquestionably, public health intervention may provide untold benefits for many persons. However, providing needed health services for some of these persons may require public health professionals to consider carefully laws outside those generally considered "public health law." In fact, public health laws may fail to either improve or sustain intervention for the most needful or vulnerable persons in society, who are included in special populations. Outside of public health practice and the laws specifically intended to support such practice exists a body of laws implicated when special populations are at issue. Some of these laws, although generally applicable, may appear to limit significantly the work of public health practice, such as laws that constrain the sharing of protected health information under most circumstances; in these cases, public health professionals must act quickly and prudently to conform their practice to new and changing civil liberties and other rights accorded to persons in the pursuit of competing values such as privacy. At the same time, public health professionals should recognize that these competing values are generally carefully balanced and, in the case of confidentiality of health information, will permit public health professionals to vigorously pursue the health and well-being of a larger society when those interests are deemed more important.

Other laws, such as those limiting the eligibility of undocumented immigrants to certain public benefits, may be so onerous that little if anything can mitigate the law's impact on the health and welfare of undocumented immigrants. However, public health professionals can take solace in the many exceptions to the restrictions on public benefits for undocumented immigrants. Most of these exceptions are crafted in response to concerns that no person—not even those who are accorded fewer civil rights than others—be denied services considered vital to preventing disease and promoting public health. In this regard, special populations may be served best by public health practitioners making every effort to ensure persons in need are identified, carefully evaluated, and referred to the available programs.

Notes

a. For an example of a court case, consider *Tarasoff v. Regents of the University of California*, 551 P.2d 334 (1976), in which the California Supreme Court carefully weighed the state's interest in protecting the health information of psychiatric patients against the state's interest in protecting the public from harms that may be posed by patients with mental disorders. For an interesting discussion of competing state interests in health information privacy and protecting the public from harm, see Gostin LO, Hodge JG Jr. Piercing the veil of secrecy in HIV/AIDS and other sexually transmitted diseases: theories of privacy and disclosure in partner notification. *Duke J Law Gender* 1998;5:9–88.

b. Article 4495b, §5.08(a), of the Texas Medical Practice Act (Physician-Patient Communication) states that "communications between one licensed to practice medicine, relative to or in connection with any professional services as a physician to a patient, is confidential and privileged and may not be disclosed except as provided in this section."

c. The element of "dangerousness" as a criterion for commitment obtained its initial dimensions in the U.S. Supreme Court's decision in *O'Connor v. Donaldson*, 422 U.S. 563 (1975). There, the Court stated, "a State cannot constitutionally confine without more a nondangerous individual who is capable of surviving safely in freedom by himself or with the help of . . . family or friends" (ibid., at 576). The Court left unsaid what it meant by "nondangerous" and even stated it would "not decide whether, when, or by what procedures" a state may justify confinement to prevent a person's injury to the public, ensure the person's own survival or safety, or to alleviate or cure his or her illness (ibid., at 573–4). Judging by the wide range of what states have construed as "dangerousness," state legislatures and courts have had to devise their own definitions. See, for example, Fla. Stat. Ann. §397.675(1) (requiring that a petition to involuntarily treat a drug-dependent person shall allege that the drug-dependent person "[h]as lost the power of self-control with respect to the use of such controlled substance"); see generally Hafemeister and Amirshahi (reference number 18, at 49–50) (providing other examples of how the term "dangerousness" resulting from drug dependency is defined by various state statutes). See, for example, Minn. Stat. Ann. §253B.02 Subd. 13(a) (providing that substantial likelihood of physical harm can be demonstrated by recent attempts or threats to physically harm herself or others, evidence of recent serious physical problems, or failure to obtain necessary food, clothing, shelter, or medical care). The "clear and convincing" standard of proof for commitment purposes was established as a constitutional minimum in the U.S. Supreme Court's decision in *Addington v. Texas*, 441 U.S. 418, 431, 433 (1979).

d. But compare *Africa v. Vaughn*, No. CIV. A. 96–649, 1996 WL 677515 (E.D. Pa.), at *4 (Nov. 21, 1996) (commenting, in denying an inmate's First Amendment claim resulting from ten-week confinement in restrictive housing for refusing TB test, that prison authorities may not "indefinitely segregate an asymptomatic inmate who refuses on religious grounds to take a tuberculosis skin test").

e. Prison officials do not necessarily violate the Eighth Amendment for every failure to test for infectious diseases. See, for example, *Doe v. Wigginton*, 21 F.3d 733, 738–39 (6th Cir. 1994), and *Feigley v. Fulcomer*, 720 F.Supp. 475, 481 (M.D. PA. 1989) (*not* screening prisoners for HIV infection in the absence of indication of risk does not violate other prisoners' Eighth Amendment rights). But compare *Lassiter v. Buskirk*, No. CIV. A. 03-5511, 2005 WL 1006313 (E.D. Pa.), at *6 (Apr. 28, 2005) (denying defendant prison officials' motion to dismiss complaint of prisoner who alleged that he was exposed to HIV cellmate when prison personnel were aware of cellmate's HIV status).

f. See also *Harris v. Thigpen*, 941 F.2d 1495, 1501 (11th Cir. 1991) (concluding that Alabama's law mandating the testing of all prisoners for sexually transmitted diseases, including testing for HIV, does not violate prisoners' U.S. Constitutional or statutory rights).

g. See also *Davidson v. Kelly*, No. 96-2066, 1997 WL 738109 (2nd Cir. [N.Y.]) (Nov. 24, 1997) (finding no Eighth Amendment, due process, or equal protection violation where an inmate was placed in keeplock for three days after refusing tuberculin testing). Religious objections also have been the basis for challenging mandatory tuberculin testing. Unlike prison privileges such as visitation, the right to freely exercise one's religion is carefully regarded by the courts because the right is considered a fundamental civil liberty that is retained by individuals notwithstanding their imprisonment. For example, in *Williams v. Scott*, No. 97-1223, 1998 WL 152969 (7th Cir. [Ind.]) (Mar. 27, 1998), an inmate sued a number of prison employees, claiming that his federal constitutional right to freely exercise his religion was violated when he was placed in "restrictive medical separation" for approximately 1 month for refusing to take a purified protein derivative (PPD) test to determine his latent TB status. The inmate argued that his Muslim religious tenets did not permit the injection of "unnatural substances" into his body and that, as an alternative, he had offered to undergo a chest radiograph. The inmate also alleged that while in medical separation, he was denied regular visits, telephone calls, showers, and recreation. The inmate believed he and others of his faith who also had refused PPD testing were placed in medical separation on the basis of their religious beliefs rather than, as argued by prison officials, on their refusal to undergo testing. The court sided with prison officials and stated that prison officials need only demonstrate their decision to segregate was rationally related to a proffered and legitimate government interest and concluded prison officials' objective of "protecting other prisoners from an outbreak of TB" that may be posed by prisoners who refuse tuberculin testing was just such an interest.

h. Generally, for a characterization of "deliberately indifferent," evidence must show that prison officials—including medical professionals—knew of and disregarded an excessive risk to inmate health and safety on the basis of their awareness of facts on which an "inference could be drawn that a substantial risk of serious harm exists" and that such an inference was made. *Farmer v. Brennan*, 511 U.S. 825, at 837 (1994). A "serious medical need" is a need that has been diagnosed by a physician as mandating treatment or a need so obvious that even a lay person would easily recognize the necessity for a doctor's attention. *Van Riper v. Wexford Health Sources*, 2003 U.S. App. LEXIS 9628 (10th Cir.), at *7 (May 19, 2003) (citing *Riddle v. Mondragon*, 83 F.3d 1197, 1202 [10th Cir. 1996]) .

i. Rothstein MA, Epps PG, Wang JJ, Stone TH. Legal analysis of the Institute of Medicine recommendations to expand testing for and treatment of latent tuberculosis 1. Unpublished report, 2001.

j. The Natural Resources Defense Council, the National Association for the Advancement of Colored People Legal Defense and Education Fund, the American Civil Liberties Union, and the Legal Aid Society of Alameda County, California, argued that the state of California failed to conduct blood lead screening as mandated by Medicaid law, winning an out-of-court settlement worth up to $20 million for a program to test blood levels. See http://www.goldbergkohn.com/CM/PressReleases/PressReleases461.asp.

k. Under a risk contribution theory fashioned, the plaintiff can still collect damages if he or she can prove the product was dangerous, it caused or created the injuries in question, and the defendant negligently produced or marketed the product.

l. Depending on the level of lead in the blood, a child may also need to undergo chelation therapy to bind the lead and reduce its toxicity. In more severe cases, 65 µg/dL or higher, hospitalization may be required.

m. See, for example, N.C. Gen. Stat. §§130(A)–131.9(A). Under N.C. regulations, 20 µg/dL constitutes lead poisoning. Levels 10–19 µg/dL are considered dangerous, and health officials can inspect at these levels but only with the consent of the landlord or tenant. See also: Ashburn E. Laws limit action on lead cases. *Greensboro News and Record* 1999(January 30):A1.

n. An undocumented immigrant is an immigrant who is not a U.S. citizen and who has entered the United States (or has remained) without the proper documentation and who does not have legal status for immigration purposes. According to one report, approximately 20% of the immigrant population is undocumented. See Figures 7 and 8 in The Kaiser Commission on Medicaid and the Uninsured. *Immigrants' Healthcare: Coverage and Access* (August 2000). Another report found the estimated number of undocumented persons in the United States is 10.3 million. See: Passel JS. Estimates of the size and characteristics of the undocumented population. *Pew Hispanic Center Report, 2005* (March 21. Available at http://pewhispanic.org/files/reports/44.pdf. Accessed May 30, 2006).

o. For example, TB rates among immigrants have remained constant, while rates among citizens have declined considerably. Undocumented immigrants are particularly vulnerable to TB partly because of the high concentration of undocumented migrant farm workers; substandard living conditions of many undocumented immigrants; and malnourishment. See Johns KA, Varkoutas C. The tuberculosis crisis: the deadly consequence of immigration policies and welfare reform. *J Contemp Health Law Policy* 1998;15:101–30. Many public health leaders consider immigration the primary force behind the TB resurgence during the late 20th century. See Martin JA. Proposition 187, tuberculosis and the immigration epidemic. *Stanford Law Policy Rev* 1996;7:89, 90 (noting that for the first time in more than 50 years, the number of TB incidents is increasing in the United States).

p. The court reasoned that if, under *Roe v. Wade* (410 U.S. 113 [1973]), a fetus lacks constitutional protections to ensure it an opportunity to be born, then it must also lack constitutional protections to ensure it an opportunity for good health after birth.

q. An emergency medical condition is defined as the sudden onset of a medical condition—including labor and delivery—manifesting itself by acute symptoms of sufficient severity such that the absence of immediate medical attention could reasonably be expected to result in placing the person's health in serious jeopardy; serious impairment to bodily function; or serious dysfunction of any bodily organ or part. See 42 U.S.C., Ch 7, Subch XIX, §1396b(v)(3) (2005).

r. Some Hill-Burton facilities also have an uncompensated-care obligation, which generally lasts for 20 years after the date of the federal grant. Many facilities no longer have this obligation; those that still do are required to post notices—which must be easy to read and printed in languages other than English if a significant part of the community has limited English proficiency—explaining their obligation.

s. "Presumptive eligibility," in the context of state laws providing public funds for undocumented immigrants' prenatal care, generally means that income-eligible pregnant immigrants will be presumed eligible for prenatal care until they are determined to be ineligible because of their undocumented status.

References

1. 42 USC, §290dd-2 (2005).
2. 42 CFR Part 2 (2005).
3. 42 CFR, Ch I, Subch A, Part 2, §2.20 (2005) (relationship to state laws).
4. 45 CFR, Subch C, Part 160, §160 *et seq* and §164 *et seq* (2005); §164.512.(b)(1)(i), (iv).
5. 45 CFR, Subch C, Parts 160, 164 (2005).
6. 42 CFR, Ch IV, Subch G, Part 482, §482.24(b)(3) (2005).
7. Wing KR. The power of the state governments in matters affecting healthcare. In: *The Law and the Public's Health*, 6th ed. Chicago: Health Administration Press, 2003:19–46.
8. Cal Business and Professions Code §2878 (2005) (vocational nursing, disciplinary proceedings, grounds for suspension or revocation).
9. Tex Rev Civil Stat, Article 4495b, §5.08(a) (2005) (Medical Practice Act, physician-patient communication).
10. ND Cent Code 43-17-31(13) (2005) (physicians and surgeons, grounds for disciplinary action).
11. Ill Comp Stat Ann, Ch 225, Title 15, §65/15–50(a)(7) (2005) (advanced practice nurses, grounds for disciplinary action).
12. Ann Code of Md §14-5A-17(a)(12) (2004) (health occupations, physicians, respiratory care practitioners).
13. NY Codes, Rules & Regulations, Title 10, Ch V, Subch A, Article 2, Part 405, §405.7(b)(13), (c)(13) (2005) (Department of Health, medical facilities, minimum standards, patient rights).
14. Fla Stat Ann, Title 29, Ch 397, Part VII, §397.705 (2005).
15. Cal Welfare & Institutions Code, Div 3, Ch 1, Article 3, §3106.5 (2005).
16. Fla Sta Ann, Title 29, Ch 397, Part VII, §397.706 (2005).
17. Or Rev Stat, Title 35, Ch 430, §430.485 (2003).
18. Hafemeister TL, Amirshahi AJ. Civil commitment for drug dependency: the judicial response. *Loyola of Los Angeles Law Rev* 1992;26:39–104.
19. *Jackson v Indiana*, 406 US 715, 731, 738 (1972).
20. *Addington v Texas*, 441 US 418, 423, 425, 432 (1979).
21. *State of Oregon v Smith*, 692 P 2d 120, 122–4 (1984) (criteria of commitment for drug addicts same as criteria for commitment as with other mental disorders).

22. Fla Stat Ann, Title 29, Ch 397, Part VII, §397.675(1) (2005).

23. Minn Stat Ann, Ch 253B, §253B.02 Subd 2 (2004).

24. Fla Stat Ann §397.334(2) (2005).

25. Cal Welfare & Institutions Code, Div 3, Ch 1, §§3000, 3006, 3055 (2005).

26. *Estelle v Gamble*, 429 US 97, 103 (1976).

27. *DeGidio v Pung*, 920 F 2d 525, 533 (8th Cir 1990).

28. *Jolly v Coughlin*, 76 F 3d 468, 483 (2d Cir 1996) (affirming lower court's grant of preliminary injunction to plaintiff inmate who argued for release from medical keeplock imposed for refusing screening test for latent TB).

29. *Jacobson v Massachusetts*, 197 US 11 (1905).

30. *Funtanilla v Campbell*, No 96-15439, 1996 WL 481710 (9th Cir [Cal]) (Aug. 26, 1996).

31. *Perkins v Kansas Department of Corrections*, 165 F 3d 803, 811 (10th Cir 1999) appeal after remand No 97-3460-GTV, 2004 US Dist LEXIS 6546 (DC Kan 2004).

32. 42 USC, Ch 7, Title XVIII, Part E, §1395dd (2005).

33. Phillips PE. Adding insult to injury: the lack of medically-appropriate housing for the homeless HIV-ill. *University of Miami Law Rev* 1991;45:567–615 (citing a study by Sutherland AR. Healthcare for the homeless. *Issues Sci Technol* 1988:79).

34. Kuszler PC. Balancing the barriers: exploiting and creating incentives to promote development of new tuberculosis treatments. *Washington Law Rev* 1996;71:919–67. 35. Kong PM, Tapy J, Calixto P, et al. Skin-test screening and tuberculosis transmission among the homeless. *Emerg Infect Dis* 2002;8:1280–4.

36. Advisory Committee for the Elimination of Tuberculosis. Tuberculosis control laws—United States, 1993. *MMWR* 1993;42(RR-15). Available at http://www.cdc.gov/MMWR/PDF/rr/rr4215.pdf. Accessed December 15, 2005.

37. Federal Interagency Forum on Child and Family Statistics. *America's Children: Key National Indicators of Well-Being, 2001*. Washington, DC: National Institute of Child Health and Human Development, 2001.

38. 42 USC, Ch 13A, §1786 (2005).

39. US Department of Agriculture. *Coordination Strategies Handbook: A Guide for WIC and Primary Care Professionals*. Alexandria, VA: US Department of Agriculture, 2000. Available at http://www.fns.usda.gov/wic/resources/strategies.htm. Accessed December 15, 2005.

40. Lipsky M, Thibodeau MA. Domestic food policy in the United States. *J Health Polit Policy Law* 1990;15:319–39.

41. Hutchinson J, Langlykke K. Adolescent maltreatment: youth as victims of abuse and neglect. In: *Maternal and Child Health Technical Information Bulletin*. Arlington, VA: National Center for Education in Maternal and Child Health, 1998.

42. US Department of Health and Human Services. *Healthy People 2010*. Available at http://www.health.gov/healthypeople. Accessed December 15, 2005.

43. Adoption and Safe Families Act of 1997, Pub L 105-89, 111 Stat 2115 (1997).

44. The Child Abuse Prevention and Enforcement Act, Pub L 106-77, 114 Stat 35 (2000).

45. Keeping Children and Families Safe Act of 2003, Pub L 108-36, 117 Stat 800 (2003).

46. Foster Care Eligibility Reviews and Child and Family Services State Plan Reviews; Final Rule, 65 Fed Reg 4,020, 4,075 *et seq* (January 25, 2000) (to be codified at 45 CFR Parts 1355, 1356, and 1357).

47. National Clearinghouse on Child Abuse and Neglect Information, Children's Bureau, Administration for Children and Families. US DHHS. *Definitions of Child Abuse and Neglect*. Available at http://nccanch.acf.hhs.gov/general/legal/statutes/define.pdf. Accessed July 10, 2005).

48. National Clearinghouse on Child Abuse and Neglect Information, Children's Bureau,

Administration for Children and Families. US DHHS. *Mandatory Reporters of Child Abuse and Neglect.* Available at http://nccanch.acf.hhs.gov/general/legal/statutes/manda.pdf. Accessed July 10, 2005).

49. National Clearinghouse on Child Abuse and Neglect Information, Children's Bureau, Administration for Children and Families. US DHHS. *Reporting Penalties.* Available at http://nccanch.acf.hhs.gov/general/legal/statutes/report.pdf. Accessed July 10, 2005.

50. Or Rev Stat, Title 34, Ch 417, §417.775 *et seq* (2003).

51. Yassi A, Kjellstrom T, De Kok T, Guidotti TL. *Basic Environmental Health.* Oxford: Oxford University Press, 2001:344–9.

52. Centers for Disease Control and Prevention. *CDC's Lead Poisoning Prevention Program.* Available at http://www.cdc.gov/nceh/lead/factsheets/leadfcts.htm. Accessed September 9, 2005.

53. Lanphear B, Hornung R, Ho M. Screening in housing to prevent lead toxicity in children. *Public Health Rep* 2005;120:305–10.

54. Centers for Disease Control and Prevention. Backgrounder: CDC Releases New Guidance on Lead Screening, November 3, 1997. Available at http://www.cdc.gov/nceh/lead/guide/1997/docs/backgr.htm. Accessed September 9, 2005.

55. Centers for Disease Control and Prevention. Blood lead levels—United States, 1999–2002. *MMWR* 2005;54:513–6. Available at http://www.cdc.gov/mmwr/preview/mmwrhtml/mm5420a5.htm. Accessed December 15, 2005.

56. Environmental Protection Agency. Mid-Atlantic Region: Lead in Washington D.C. Drinking Water. Available at http://www.epa.gov/dclead/faq.htm. Accessed December 15, 2005.

57. Centers for Disease Control and Prevention. Lead poisoning associated with use of litargirio—Rhode Island, 2003. *MMWR* 2005;54:227–9. Available at http://www.cdc.gov/mmwr/preview/mmwrhtml/mm5409a5.htm. Accessed December 15, 2005.

58. Centers for Disease Control and Prevention. Childhood lead poisoning associated with tamarind candy and folk remedies—California, 1999–2000. *MMWR* 2002;51:684–6. Available at http://www.cdc.gov/mmwr/preview/mmwrhtml/mm5131a3.htm. Accessed December 15, 2005.

59. Woolf AD, Woolf NT. Childhood lead poisoning in two families associated with spices used in food preparation. *Pediatrics* 2005;116:314–8. Available at http://pediatrics.aappublications.org/cgi/content/full/116/2/e314. Accessed December 15, 2005.

60. Centers for Disease Control and Prevention. NIOSH Safety and Health Topic: Lead. Available at http://www.cdc.gov/niosh/topics/lead. Accessed September 9, 2005.

61. State Bar of Texas. Information for clients of Texas attorneys: lead poisoning and you. *Texas Bar J* 2003;66:533. Available at http://www.texasbar.com/Template.cfm?Section=Texas_Bar_Journal1&Template=/ContentManagement/ContentDisplay.cfm&ContentID=3631. Accessed December 15, 2005.

62. Daghlian KK. Lead-based paint: the crisis still facing our nation's poor and minority children. *Dickinson J Environ Law Policy* 2001;9:535–51.

63. Centers for Disease Control and Prevention. Health disparities experienced by racial/ethnic minority populations. *MMWR* 2004;53:755. Available at http://www.cdc.gov/mmwr/PDF/wk/mm5333.pdf. Accessed December 15, 2005.

64. 42 USC §4822 (2005).

65. Requirement of Removal of Lead-Based Paint under Provisions of Lead-Based Paint Poisoning Act. 70 *Am Law Rep Fed* 358 (1997).

66. 42 USC §§300(j)(21)–(j)(26) (2005).

67. 42 USC §4851 (2000) *et seq* (2005).

68. 42 USC §4852(d) (2005).

69. Wis Stat Ann §709.02 (2005) (disclosures by owners of residential real estate).

70. Mass Gen Laws Ann, Ch 84, h 111 §197(A)(b) (2005) (requiring agents to disclose the presence of lead-based paint on residential property to be sold).

71. US Department of Health and Human Services. *Healthy People 2010: Environmental Health.* Available at http://www.healthypeople.gov/Document/HTML/Volume1/08Environmental .htm. Accessed September 9, 2005).

72. 42 USC §1396(d)®(1) (2005).

73. National Conference of State Legislatures. Lead Statutes Database. Available at http:// www.ncsl.org/programs/environ/envhealth/leadStatutesdb.cfm. Accessed September 9, 2005.

74. NJ Admin Code §8:51-2.1 (2005) (certification required).

75. Mass Ann Law, Ch 111 §193 (2005) (requiring the director to establish a program to screen all children under age 6 years, and others at high risk, for lead poisoning).

76. US General Accounting Office. *Lead Poisoning: Federal Healthcare Programs Are not Effectively Reaching At-Risk Children. Report to the Ranking Minority Member, Committee on Government Reform, House of Representatives.* Washington, DC: US General Accounting Office, 1999:33–42 (GAO/HEHS-99-18). Available at http://www.gao.gov/ archive/1999/he99018.pdf#search='GAO%2FHEHS9918'. Accessed December 15, 2005.

77. Farmer C. *Lead Screening for Children Enrolled in Medicaid: State Approaches* 5 (Forum for State Health Policy Leadership National Conference of State Legislatures, 2001). Available at http://www.ncsl.org/programs/health/forum/leadscreening.pdf. Accessed December 15, 2005.

78. *Memisovsk v Maram,* 2004 US Dist Lexis 16772 (ND Ill Aug 23, 2004);

79. Larson S. Landlord's liability for injury or death of tenant's child from lead paint poisoning. 19 *ALR* 5th 405 (2005).

80. *Santiago v Sherwin-Williams Co,* 794 F Supp 29, 31 (D Mass 1993); aff'd, 3 F 3d 546 (1st Cir 1993) (rejecting the application of the concert of action and enterprise liability tort recovery theories to an action filed against several lead-based paint manufacturers because the plaintiff could not identify the manufacturer which produced the paint that caused his injury).

81. *Thomas v Mallet,* 2005 WI 129 (Wis 2005); see also *State of Rhode Island v Lead Industries Association, Inc,* no. 99-5226 (RI Super Ct, Feb 22, 2006), 15-5 *Mealey's Litig Rep Lead 2* (March 2006).

82. Walker CE. The lead based paint real estate notification and disclosure rule. *Buffalo Environ Law J* 2000;8:65–98.

83. US Department of Housing and Urban Development. Compliance Assistance and Information. Available at http://www.hud.gov/offices/lead/compliance/index.cfm. Accessed September 9, 2005.

84. Environmental Protection Agency. *Section 1018—Disclosure Rule Enforcement Response Policy B4.* December1999. Available at http://www.epa.gov/compliance/resources/policies/ civil/tsca/lead.pdf. Accessed December 15, 2005.

85. Town of Manchester Prop Maint Code (Conn) §§305.4-7–305.7.

86. Centers for Disease Control and Prevention. *Managing Elevated Blood Lead Levels Among Young Children: Recommendations from the Advisory Committee on Childhood Lead Poisoning Prevention.* Available at http://www.cdc.gov/nceh/lead/CaseManagement/ caseManage_chap2.htm. Accessed September 9, 2005.

87. Wis Stat Ann §709.02 (2005).

88. City of St. Louis Department of Health. *Childhood Lead Poisoning Annual Report: 1999.* Available at http://stlouis.missouri.org/citygov/health/lead99.pdf. Accessed December 15, 2005.

89. Mich Comp Laws §333.5461 (2005).

90. NJ Admin Code §5:17-2.1 (2005).
91. McDiarmid H. Lead law has its first charge. *Detroit Free Press* 2005 (Feb 25):14e.
92. US Housing and Urban Development. *Ten Effective Strategies for Preventing Child-hood Lead Poisoning through Code Enforcement*. Available at http://www.hud.gov/offices/lead/lhc/startup/CodeEnforcementStrategies.doc. Accessed September 9, 2005.
93. Philadelphia Code and Charter, Title 6 (Health Code), §6-403(4)(b)(1) (2005).
94. Centers for Disease Control and Prevention. *Preventing Lead Poisoning in Young Children*. Available at http://www.cdc.gov/nceh/lead/publications/books/plpyc/chapter5.htm. Accessed September 9, 2005.
95. Drake SB. America's newcomers: healthcare issues for new Americans, In: Tomasi LF, ed. *In Defense of the Alien*. No 17. New York: Center for Migration Studies, 1994:35–41.
96. *Takahashi v Fish and Game Commission*, 334 US 410, 419 (1948).
97. *Matthews v Diaz*, 426 US 67 (1976).
98. Personal Responsibility and Work Opportunity Reconciliation Act of 1996, Pub L 104-193, 110 Stat 2105 (1996).
99. Personal Responsibility and Work Opportunity Reconciliation Act of 1996, Pub L 104-193, 110 Stat 2105 (1996) at §411(a), (c)(1)(B) (codified at 8 USC, Ch 14, Subch II, §1621(a),(c) *et seq.*
100. Personal Responsibility and Work Opportunity Reconciliation Act of 1996, Pub L 104-193, 110 Stat 2105 (1996) at §411(d) (codified at 8 USC Ch 14, Subch II, §1621[d]).
101. Stubbs E. Welfare and immigration reform: refusing aid to immigrants. *Berkeley Women's Law J* 1997;12:151–57.
102. *Lewis v Thompson*, 252 F 3d 567 (2d Cir 2001).
103. 8 USC, Ch 14, §1611(b)(1)(C) (2005).
104. 8 US, Ch 14, §1611(b)(1)(A), (B) (2005).
105. 42 USC, Ch 7, Title XVIII, §1395dd (2005) (setting forth requirements for hospitals' examination and treatment of patients with emergency medical conditions and women in labor).
106. 42 USC, Ch 7, Title XIX, §1396a *et seq* (2005) (establishing requirements for states' administration of Medicaid programs).
107. 8 USC, Ch 14, §1611(b)(1)(A) (2005) (providing for an exception to the general ineligibility of aliens to federal benefits where care and services are necessary for the treatment of an alien with an "emergency medical condition").
108. 42 USC, Ch 7, Title XVIII, §1395dd (a) (which requires that hospitals provide for the examination and treatment of patients with emergency medical conditions and women in labor whether such patients are otherwise "eligible for benefits").
109. 42 USC §1395dd NOTE (2005) (federal reimbursement of emergency health services furnished to undocumented aliens).
110. 42 USC Title 6A, §291 *et seq* (construction and modernization of hospitals and other medical facilities) (2005).
111. *Hines v Davidowitz*, 312 US 52, 66 (1941).
112. Neb Admin Code Title 468, Ch 2-000 *et seq*, and Ch 4, §001 *et seq* (2002).
113. *Doe v Wilson*, 57 Cal App 4th 296, 311 (1997), rev denied, 1997 Cal LEXIS 7717 (1997).
114. 8 USC §1644 (2005).

Section III

The Law in Controlling and Preventing Diseases, Injuries, and Disabilities

Chapter 13

INTEGRATING GENETICS INTO PUBLIC HEALTH POLICY AND PRACTICE*

Ellen Wright Clayton and Mark A. Rothstein

Since the Human Genome Project began in 1990, our understanding of the contributions of genetics to health and disease has increased substantially. Announcements of new discoveries appear daily in the news, often accompanied by claims of imminent therapeutic benefit. Because much genome research has been publicly funded, public and scientific interest has been considerable in translating these advances into health benefits at both the clinical and public health levels. Concurrent with excitement at the prospect of new diagnoses and therapies is concern by much of the public that genetic information could be used in ways that harm the interests of individuals and groups.

The role of genetics in improving public health is complex. A committee of the Institute of Medicine defined "the mission of public health as fulfilling society's interest in assuring conditions in which people can be healthy."[1] Within this broad remit, genetics is only one of many factors that influence health and illness. The public's health can be promoted through the actions of numerous entities throughout society that function outside, but often in coordination with, the traditional public health sector. The private health-care sector is perhaps the most obvious example of an institution that affects public health, but others include housing agencies, water departments, sewage disposal systems, and corporate enterprise generally. As a result, the

* This chapter is based, in part, on a revision of Ellen Wright Clayton. Genetics, Public Health, and the Law. In: Khoury MJ, Burke W, Thomson E, eds. *Genetics and Public Health in the 21st Century: Using Genetic Information to Improve Health and Prevent Disease.* New York: Oxford University Press, 2000:489–503.

committee concluded that the core functions of government entities in public health are "assessment, policy development, and assurance."[1] Yet the government's role necessarily extends beyond these goals because it is the only institution in society empowered to alter behaviors that affect health. The government's authority to promote the public health, however, is not unlimited but rather is both based on and limited by the law.[2,3] In addition, public health agencies continue to play an important role in directly providing genetic services.

In this chapter, we explore the complex patchwork of federal and state laws applicable to the evolving relation between genetics and public health practice. We focus on two major genetics-associated challenges for public health law and public health agencies at all levels. The first challenge involves the ability of the medical and public health sectors to assess the effect of genetic variation on health, a task made more difficult by tensions between the government's need for information and the public's concerns about privacy, confidentiality, and discrimination. The second challenge is ensuring the appropriate translation of genetic discoveries into the clinical setting.

Legal Authorities

Given the public attention devoted to genetics in recent years, the fact that legislators, regulators, and the courts have addressed only a fraction of the issues raised is a bit surprising. Many other countries have far more comprehensive regulatory regimes than does the United States. Even so, the number of genetics-related issues considered by legislatures has expanded so dramatically in recent years that numerous Web sites now are devoted to tracking them.[46] Groups such as the National Conference of State Legislatures have worked hard to educate legislators and to compile and update lists of state laws concerning genetics. States, however, often vary widely in their approaches to genetics, reflecting the impact of diverse values and political advocacy.

State Level

Reproductive Genetics

The earliest public health effort based on genetics was the adoption of eugenics programs during the first third of the 20th century.[7,8] These took two forms: positive eugenics (encouraging the reproduction of people deemed genetically superior), and negative eugenics (prohibiting or limiting the reproduction of people deemed genetically inferior). The most infamous examples of negative eugenics in the United States were eugenic sterilization laws, which led to involuntary sterilization of tens of thousands of people believed to be unfit to procreate. These laws fell into disfavor after World War II for a host of reasons—the science that underlies these practices was flawed, horror at abuses by the Nazis, and a growing culture of individual rights in this country—but the shadow cast by this union of "genetics" and public health law has been long indeed.[9] A more recent example of an ill-advised public health genetics program was the enactment of laws in the 1970s in many states to require screening for sickle cell trait. Although intended to help carriers of this mutation, the effect instead was confusion and stigmatization, raising the specter of the earlier eugenics programs. As a result, almost all of these laws were repealed.[10]

The current debate is about access to reproductive genetic testing services (e.g., prenatal genetic testing for Tay-Sachs disease and cystic fibrosis), a colloquy profoundly influenced by deeply divided opinions about abortion.[11] The issue now is framed as whether prospective parents should be able to obtain such tests and, if so, under what conditions. A few states have chosen to provide these services or to require third-party payers to provide coverage (subject, of course, to the Employee Retirement Income Security Act preemption of employer-funded health plans). Many more states, however, have passed laws prohibiting the use of state funds for abortion and, in some cases, for reproductive genetic testing as well. A few states have tried to ban selective abortion altogether, but these efforts have been struck down as unconstitutional.[12,13] A main driver of reproductive genetic testing has been the willingness of many state courts to impose liability on clinicians who negligently fail to provide tests and counseling to their patients, but an increasing number of states, either through legislative action or judicial decision, have banned such lawsuits.

Newborn Screening

The first population-wide programs in public health genetics were state-run newborn screening programs. Since their inception during the 1960s, newborn screening programs have been, by far, the most common clinical genetic testing program in this country.[14] Beginning with screening for phenylketonuria (PKU), these programs spread rapidly throughout the country and then evolved slowly for many years. This growth was governed for the most part by widely held views of policy and ethics analysts that screening is appropriate only to detect serious disorders that can be ameliorated only by early intervention before symptoms become apparent.[15,16] During the last decade, however, legislative and regulatory activity have exploded in response to the development of tandem mass spectrometry (MS/MS), a technology that can detect dozens of metabolites (products of biochemical reactions) that are altered in metabolic diseases.[17] The pressure to adopt MS/MS has been intense, but it is expensive, and only some of the detectable variants meet the criteria for screening.

Federal Level

Surveillance, Policy Development, and Assessment

Congress created the Public Health Service near the beginning of the 20th century. Its functions, now including research and surveillance, are performed both by an array of federal agencies (such as the Centers for Disease Control and Prevention [CDC] and the National Institutes of Health) and by state agencies and private entities through grants and contracts, funding of hospital construction and undergraduate and graduate medical education, and direct provision of health services.[18] Within this extremely broad and complex mandate, Congress has said almost nothing specifically about genetics. In 1978, Congress directed the Secretary of what is now Health and Human Services to use "an identifiable administrative unit" to

(1) conduct epidemiological assessments and surveillance of genetic diseases to define the scope and extent of such [genetic] diseases and the need for programs for the diagnosis, treatment, and control of such diseases, screening for such diseases, and the counseling of persons with such diseases;

(2) on the basis of the assessments and surveillance described in paragraph (1), develop for use by the States programs which combine in an effective manner diagnosis, treatment, and control of such diseases, screening for such diseases, and counseling of persons with such diseases; and

(3) on the basis of the assessments and surveillance described in paragraph (1), provide technical assistance to States to implement the programs developed under paragraph (2) and train appropriate personnel for such programs.[19]

Traditionally, surveillance has been a state public health activity, and therefore no systematic, national system of surveillance existed for genetic diseases. Nevertheless, CDC, through its National Center on Birth Defects and Developmental Disabilities, has surveillance-based research projects in a limited number of states to study birth defects, muscular dystrophy, and newborn screening.[20]

Parts of the federal government have tried to develop policy recommendations for the use of screening and diagnostic techniques for genetic diseases, evidently relying on the broad authority of the Public Health Service Act. The Secretary's Advisory Committee on Genetic Testing was convened in 1998 and followed in 2003 by the Secretary's Advisory Committee on Genetics, Health, and Society.[21] Both entities were charged with advising the Secretary on clinical genetics and, later, on the use of genetic information in a variety of settings. The Maternal and Child Health Bureau (MCHB) of the Health Resources and Services Administration convened its own advisory panel, the Advisory Committee on Heritable Disorders and Genetic Diseases in Newborns and Children[22] and funded the American College of Medical Genetics to propose national guidelines for newborn screening.[23]

CDC has established a far-reaching agenda to develop policy regarding public health and genetics. In its 1997 planning document, CDC indicated its fundamental assumption that "the use of genetic information in public health is appropriate in promoting health and in diagnosing, treating, and preventing disease, disability, and death among people who inherit specific genotypes. Such prevention concerns the use of medical, behavioral, and environmental interventions to reduce the risk for disease among people susceptible because of their genetic makeup. It does not include efforts to prevent the birth of infants with specific genotypes."[24] Beyond prenatal testing, CDC recently published recommendations for newborn screening for cystic fibrosis, which, by identifying mutation carriers, may indirectly affect reproduction by the carriers identified through testing.[25] CDC also has held numerous conferences and recently convened a project to evaluate the use of genetic tests.[26]

Direct Regulation of Genetic Tests and Services

The Food and Drug Administration (FDA) has far-reaching authority to regulate the safety and efficacy of drugs and medical devices sold to the public. As more has been learned about the impact of genetic variation, FDA has developed guidance regarding submission of data about pharmacogenetics in applications for drug approval.[27] Under the authority of the Clinical Laboratory Improvement Amendments,[28] FDA regulates genetic testing kits, recently approving the Roche AmpliChip for detection of cytochrome P450 variants.[29]

Delivery of Services Using Federal Funds

Although the primary goals of public health now are surveillance, policy development, and assessment, the public health sector for years has directly provided services for certain segments of the population. In 1976, as part of the National Sickle Cell Anemia, Cooley's Anemia, Tay-Sachs, and Genetic Diseases Act, Congress directed the Secretary to "establish a program within the [Public Health] Service to provide voluntary testing, diagnosis, counseling, and treatment of individuals respecting genetic diseases."[30] In 1978, the Senate Human Resources Committee stated these services were to include "1. Early detection of disease: (a) Newborn screening, (b) Prenatal screening, (c) Prenatal diagnosis; (d) Screening at later ages; 2. Carrier detection; 3. Counseling; 4. Diagnosis and monitoring of effectiveness of treatment; and 5. Information and education."[31] These requirements were embodied in the federal regulations found at 42 C.F.R. Part 51f.[32] At the same time, Congress provided that "[t]he participation by any individual in any program or portion thereof under this part [addressing genetic diseases] shall be wholly voluntary and shall not be a prerequisite to eligibility for or receipt of any other service or assistance from, or to participation in, any other program."[33]

In 1981, these programs were rolled into block grants administered by the MCHB, which provide funding only for "special projects of regional and national significance, research, and training."[32] In addition, the National Institutes of Health funds the National Newborn Screening and Genetic Resource Center, Gene Tests–Gene Clinics, grants to assist states to conduct universal newborn hearing screening, and the Advisory Committee on Heritable Disorders and Genetic Diseases in Newborns and Children.[34] When the funding for genetic testing was shifted to block grants to the states, the types of services that could be provided by genetics programs receiving federal funds were limited seriously because of a requirement banning abortion except when the life of the pregnant woman is in danger or when the pregnancy results from rape or incest.[35]

Privacy and Discrimination

Of the various aspects of privacy relevant to genetics, the most important is informational privacy—the right to keep certain information from disclosure to others.[36] Privacy encompasses an individual's right to decide whether to receive certain information, as well as the circumstances under which the individual shares information with others, such as family members, health-care providers, or entities with a financial interest in the individual's current or future health, including an employer or insurer. Privacy has both an intrinsic and an instrumental value to individuals, and the latter is linked closely to possible discrimination.[37]

The most important law protecting health privacy, including genetic privacy, is the Health Insurance Portability and Accountability Act (HIPAA)[38] and its Privacy Rule.[39] Under the Privacy Rule, uses and disclosures of protected health information (individually identifiable health information) beyond routine uses for treatment, payment, and health-care operations generally require a HIPAA-compliant authorization signed by the individual (see also Chapter 10). Because HIPAA was intended to regulate financial transactions in health care, the Privacy Rule applies only to the following covered entities: health-care providers, health plans, and health clearinghouses.[40] The Act does not cover private health information, including genetic information, in the possession of other entities, including schools, employers, and insurers. Nor does HIPAA prohibit noncovered entities from making the signing of an authorization for the release of health information a lawful condition of employment, insurance, or other transactions. Finally, legally mandated or permissive disclosures by covered entities to public health agencies (e.g., certain infectious diseases, suspected child abuse) are not subject to the authorization requirement.[41]

The two areas of greatest public concern about possible genetic discrimination are health insurance and employment. Important legal developments have occurred in both areas. With regard to health insurance, HIPAA prohibits employer-sponsored group health plans from charging individuals higher rates or excluding certain medical conditions from coverage on the basis of an individual's current health or "genetic information."[42] Thus, genetic discrimination concerns center on individual health insurance policies and nonemployer group plans to which HIPAA does not apply. In response to these concerns, many states have enacted legislation prohibiting genetic discrimination in health insurance.[43] These laws, however, protect only asymptomatic persons— meaning protection no longer exists once individuals develop gene-based disorders.[44]

The Americans with Disabilities Act of 1990 (ADA)[45] is the primary federal law prohibiting discrimination on the basis of disability, including employment discrimination. In 1995, the Equal Employment Opportunity Commission issued an interpretation that individuals subject to employment discrimination because they are at a genetically increased risk for future illness are covered under the ADA.[46] This interpretation never has been challenged in court, but most commentators do not believe it would be upheld if challenged. In a series of Supreme Court decisions, beginning with *Sutton v. United Air Lines, Inc.*,[47] the Court, although not specifically considering genetic predisposition, adopted narrow rules for coverage under the ADA.

With disability discrimination law inapplicable to asymptomatic persons at genetically increased risk for illness, most state legislatures have enacted laws prohibiting genetic discrimination in employment.[48] The laws generally prohibit employers from requesting or requiring genetic testing as a condition of employment and discriminating on the basis of genetic information. The laws do not change the current law under the ADA, which permits employers, after a conditional offer of employment, to require individuals to sign an authorization to release all their medical records to the employer. Because these records can contain genetic information and genetic test results, at-risk persons might be reluctant to have genetic tests because prospective employers could get the results. Both the executive order, issued in 2000 (applicable to employment with the federal government),[49] and bills introduced in Congress,[50] which would ban genetic discrimination in employment, contain similar provisions.

Legal Issues and Controversies

Several important threads run through this patchwork of laws, regulations, and cases.

Genetic Exceptionalism

The term "genetic exceptionalism" generally describes laws, policies, and attitudes that genetic information differs from other health information and therefore should be treated separately for legal and other purposes. Much of the impetus for genetic exceptionalism is that genetic information, the topic of much media attention, is seen as particularly powerful. The public overwhelmingly is concerned that genetic information will be used to limit access to employment and various types of insurance,[51–53] even though actual evidence of adverse use is mixed.[54,55]

Scientifically, in almost all cases, human health and disease are the products of interactions among our own genes, the genes of other organisms, and the environment. Thus, genetic factors usually are only one element in a chain of disease causation.

Given the complex etiology of most diseases, the fundamental question is why, and to what extent, special efforts are warranted to limit the use of genetic information. To be sure, people have no control over the genes they were born with, and information about one person's genetic variants has implications for his or her relatives as well, but the lack of individual responsibility for these variants does not necessarily warrant a complete ban on any consideration of this information. Indeed, a real risk of enacting specific regulations on the use of genetic information is that such regulation makes genetics appear more determinative than it actually is. Furthermore, segregating genetic information from other medical information in typically voluminous medical records is practically impossible—assuming doing so is desirable. This is one reason the effectiveness of genetics-specific legislation has been questionable.[56] Ultimately, in debates about "genetic" discrimination, we must balance the interests of users of the information and those of individuals to decide what information can be used and how.

Control of Information: Surveillance versus Research

A major function of public health is surveillance, which requires access to data (see also Chapter 10). However, people in the United States are concerned deeply about protection of their privacy.[57] The resulting tension affects all of public health practice but often is highlighted when genetics is involved. Nonetheless, the HIPAA Privacy Rule permits covered entities to disclose protected health information to public health agencies without consent or authorization by the patient for surveillance purposes.

Given the current understanding of the contributions of genetic factors to disease, some activities that federal agencies will undertake are likely to be more research than surveillance. Determining the type of activity in any particular case requires analysis of the agency's intentions, methodology used, and preexisting scientific knowledge. The distinction between surveillance and research is important because, to the extent that CDC and other government agencies engage in the latter, their actions are governed by the regulations for protecting human subjects, requiring at least review by an institutional review board and in many cases consent of the individuals to participate in the study and authorization for use and disclosure of protected health information.[57]

Oversight of Genetic Technologies

The incorporation of new technologies into clinical care predictably poses an array of issues. Is evidence of safety and efficacy sufficient to support their use? Do patients and providers understand the risks and benefits of using new diagnostics and therapeutics? Is access sufficiently equitable (always a difficult question in a fragmented health-care system such as ours)? Do direct-to-consumer advertising and sales and political advocacy lead to overuse? Who will address these issues, using what criteria? Is testing appropriate only when the results will alter medical management? Are other goals, such as informing or assisting another person, ever relevant or sufficient to justify testing? What is the appropriate role of regulation? These and similar questions have been posed on numerous occasions in the context of genetics.[14,15,58–62] New discoveries in genetics will not alter the questions, but they will increase the frequency in which the questions arise and the importance of systematically resolving them.

Practice Considerations

Newborn Screening

Virtually all babies born in the United States are screened for a variety of metabolic, endocrine, and infectious disorders in state-run programs that are mandatory as a matter of practice and usually mandatory as a matter of law. Until recently, these programs generally have sought only disorders for which early detection and intervention dramatically improves the outcomes of affected children. These programs have confronted a number of issues over the years.

One of the most longstanding is how to ensure that affected children receive appropriate treatment because simply diagnosing a condition will not improve health. Improving health is a matter of not only sending affected children to the optimal specialist but also ensuring their access to needed medical interventions. The latter is less complicated for disorders such as congenital hypothyroidism, for which therapy is relatively inexpensive, than it is for diseases such as PKU that require expensive specialized diets, for which insurers often deny coverage. States have attempted various means to ensure access to treatment, ranging from including the cost in the charge for the screening to requiring insurers to provide coverage (to the extent the Employee Retirement Income Security Act does not preempt such laws).

Ensuring adequate follow up also requires tracking and coordination of care.[63] However, computer technology, which makes tracking and coordination possible in ways previously inconceivable, raises concerns about privacy. Both HIPAA and, more significantly, the Family Educational Rights and Privacy Act (applicable to school records, including school health records)[64] impose substantial requirements for parental permission for the creation of useful databases.

At least one state retains newborn screening samples during childhood for use in identifying missing children.[65] This decision raises at least three serious concerns. First, it conflicts with widespread concerns about privacy and is imposed without notice or consent. Second, many adults would object to creating a universal DNA-identification bank involving their own samples. Using newborn screening samples for this purpose flies in the face of these concerns. Finally, such a program is over-broad. States could address the identification of missing children by other means. The possible use of newborn screening samples for research, both in anonymous form[66] and in identifiable form with consent also has been discussed.[67]

As noted previously, the most prominent issue currently is the appropriate use of MS/MS. This technology is now the optimal method for screening for PKU and a number of other treatable, serious disorders, but it can detect metabolites associated with untreatable disorders and some disorders that do not always have clinical mani-festations. Although some states adhere to generally accepted criteria for screening in their use of MS/MS, other states are adopting much more expansive programs. Several factors have contributed to this dramatic expansion. A private company has been aggressively marketing expanded screening, at times convincing legislatures to use its product in addition to or instead of the state-run program.[68] Parent and cli-nician advocates also have argued for much broader criteria for screening, urging that greater knowledge and avoiding the "diagnostic odyssey" (caused when a de-finitive diagnosis is lacking) are valuable per se and that newborn screening is ap-propriate to identify the parents' reproductive risk, benefit the family more generally and identify subjects for research.[23] In addition, of course, the threat of litigation always is present if available technologies are not adopted.[69] Aside from the pos-sible harms to families who receive unwanted and, in the case of inevitable false-positives, ultimately unfounded news, a real dilemma posed by deciding to report all variations detectable by MS/MS is that policymakers are left without any criteria to make decisions in the future.

Direct-to-Consumer Advertising and Sales

Anyone who watches television or reads magazines is aware of drug advertising. Not surprisingly, consumers tend to see more benefits from these ads than do physi-cians.[70–72] Evidence also suggests that these ads affect prescribing patterns, not al-ways optimally.[73] Use of traditional print, radio, and television advertising has expanded to genetic testing. During the time that Myriad Genetics engaged in a direct-to-consumer ad campaign for testing for breast cancer gene mutations (*BRCA1* and *BRCA2*) in the Denver area, referrals for evaluation increased dramatically, but a much larger percent-age of those referred were not appropriate candidates for testing.[74]

Most direct-to-consumer advertising and sales of genetic tests occur on the Internet. Some sites offer tests for clinically relevant variants conducted in Clinical Labora-tory Improvement Amendments–approved laboratories,[75] and a few provide genetic experts for assistance.[76] Ironically, some of the tests are more readily available to consumers over the Internet than they are through physicians' offices. Other sites focus on nutraceuticals and skin care, for which the scientific basis is much less estab-lished.[77,78] Although some of these sites state a physician's prescription is required, such prescriptions are easy to obtain at other Web sites.

The growth of direct-to-consumer advertising and direct sales appears to under-cut the ability of clinicians to counsel their patients before and after testing, as well as to increase patient demand to incorporate the tests into clinical care regardless of whether the test's clinical validity and utility are known. As a result, many commentators have called for greater regulation in this area.[79] FDA and the Federal Trade Commission, however, have been reluctant to act, citing both their hesitation to move into new areas and First Amendment limits on regulating commercial speech.[80]

Genetic Discrimination

Public health practitioners and public health lawyers need to recognize the deep concern of many members of the public about "genetic discrimination" in employment, insurance, and other third-party uses of genetic information. Consequently, in the informed consent process for public health research or public health screening involving genetics, individuals need to be apprised of the social risks of learning genetic information, including the risk for adverse treatment because the individual is considered at genetically increased risk for illness.

In designing the disclosures in genetic testing protocols, however, the risks for genetic discrimination should not be overstated. Even though legal protections often are lacking, few cases of genetic discrimination have been reported in health insurance or employment—the two areas of greatest concern to the public. If people are led to believe genetic testing carries a significant risk for genetic discrimination, then many people will refuse testing, thereby precluding the possible benefits of testing both for individual and public health.

Emerging Issues

Although progress has been astonishing in deciphering genomic structure and the functions of genes, the future lies in understanding the interactions among genes of individuals and other organisms, as well as with the environment. From such research will emerge greater insight into opportunities for improving health at the individual and population levels. Some of these approaches will involve directed therapies; others will entail environmental remediation or avoidance. The challenges will not be particularly new, but surmounting them will present new difficulties.

Clinicians' Obtaining and Responding to Information

Before clinical care and public health practice can change, research using large, robust databases that include both clinical and DNA information will be essential. Use of these databases will require not only sophisticated informatics but also ongoing consideration of the requirements of HIPAA and the federal regulations for research on human subjects (Common Rule).

To fully use the research, clinicians will need access to much more complete information about individual patients, which electronic medical records could provide. Clinicians also may be able to rely on electronic decision–support systems. State privacy laws and HIPAA will be major factors in developing these systems. These tools, however, are not substitutes for clinician training, and clinicians will need to know more about genetics and how to think "genetically." The experience of the National Coalition for Health Professional Education in Genetics demonstrates that continuing education of professionals is difficult, and will become more so given the pace of discovery.

Behavior Change

Any intervention to improve health entails behavior change, whether submitting to surgery, taking medications, avoiding a hazardous workplace, or exercising and eating well. Although the promise is almost surely overstated that increased understanding of genetics will make possible the correct diagnosis of a condition and identification of the best intervention the first time, more knowledge will permit more accurate risk stratification and detection of prevention and therapeutic strategies. The policy challenges of this increased knowledge are myriad. One will be to identify behaviors that, across the board, ought to be encouraged (e.g., exercise) or discouraged (e.g., smoking). Another will be ways to create incentives for more targeted risk-reducing behaviors without invading privacy or crossing the often blurry line between health promotion and discrimination. For example, people are unlikely to participate in cholesterol screening, diabetes control, or other measures if identifying individual risk factors will adversely affect their employment, insurance, and other matters.

Reproductive Genetic Testing

The debate in this country about the moral status of the embryo/fetus has intensified in light of recent developments in stem cell research. Increasingly, this attention will spill over into the discussion about reproductive genetic testing, and the impact is not completely clear. The conjunction of the embryo debate and reproductive genetic testing is clearest in the case of preimplantation genetic diagnosis, in which embryos are created in vitro and then tested to determine which do, and do not, have a particular desired or feared trait. The existence of these embryos ex vivo makes particularly stark the questions about which are implanted and which are not and for what reasons. These questions may invite a degree of regulation of assisted reproductive technologies that has not previously been seen in this country. Any discussion could then extend into the larger and longstanding debate about the appropriate role of reproductive genetic testing.

Conclusion

Maximizing the health benefits of genetic knowledge in U.S. society will require creation of extensive but secure databases, robust informatics tools, evidence- and value-based incorporation of tests and therapeutics into clinical care and public health practice, and creation of appropriate but not overly intrusive incentives for health promotion, creating an environment in which this information does not result in unwarranted discrimination. Public health has an important role in every aspect of this complex problem.

The authors acknowledge Laura M. Beskow, M.P.H., and Marta Gwinn, M.D., M.P.H., who wrote the genomics chapter in the first edition of this book. Dr. Gwinn also provided input into this current chapter.

References

1. Institute of Medicine. *The Future of Public Health*. Washington, DC: National Academy Press, 1988.
2. Wing KR. *The Law and the Public's Health*. 5th ed. Chicago: Health Administration Press, 1999.
3. Gostin LO. *Public Health Law: Power, Duty, Restraint*. Berkeley: University of California Press, 2000.
4. National Conference of State Legislatures. Genetics Legislation Database. Available at http://www.ncsl.org/programs/health/genetics/geneticsDB.cfm. Accessed June 4, 2005.
5. National Human Genome Research Institute. Policy and Legislation Database. Available at http://www.genome.gov/PolicyEthics/LegDatabase/pubsearch.cfm. Accessed June 3, 2005.
6. Council for Responsible Genetics. Genetics and the Law. Available at http://www.genelaw.info/. Accessed June 4, 2005.
7. Duster T. *Backdoor to Eugenics*. New York: Routledge, 1990.
8. Kevles DJ. *In the Name of Eugenics: Genetics and the Uses of Human Heredity*. New York: Knopf, 1985.
9. Pernick M. Eugenics and public health in American history. *Am J Public Health* 1997;87: 1767–72.
10. Reilly P. *Genetics, Law, and Social Policy*. Boston: Harvard University Press, 1977.
11. Clayton EW. What should be the role of public health in newborn screening and prenatal diagnosis? *Am J Prevent Med* 1999;16:111–5.
12. *Jane L v Bangerter*, 809 F Supp 865 (D Utah 1992); aff'd in part, rev'd in part, 61 F 3d 1493 (10th Cir 1995); judgment rev'd and remanded sub nom, *Leavitt v Jane L*, 518 US 137 (1996); on remand aff'd in relevant part sub nom, *Jane L v Bangerter*, 102 F 3d 1112 (10th Cir. 1996).
13. *Margaret S v Edwards*, 488 F Supp 181 (D La 1980).
14. National Newborn Screening and Genetics Resource Center. 2005. Available at http://genes-r-us.uthscsa.edu. Accessed June 4, 2005.
15. Wilson JM, Jungner G. *Principles and Practice of Screening for Disease*. Geneva: World Health Organization, 1968.
16. Committee for the Study of Inborn Errors of Metabolism, National Research Council. *Genetic Screening: Programs, Principles, and Research*. Washington, DC: National Academy of Sciences, 1975.
17. CDC. Using tandem mass spectrometry for metabolic disease screening among newborns. A report of a work group. *MMWR* 2001;50 (RR3):1–22. Available at http://www.cdc.gov/mmwr/PDF/rr/rr5003.pdf. Accessed January 25, 2006.
18. 42 USC §§201–300aaa (2005).
19. 42 USC §300b-6 (2005).
20. CDC. Monitoring Birth Defects. Available at http://www.cdc.gov/ncbddd/bd/monitoring .htm. Accessed July 27, 2005.
21. Secretary's Advisory Committee on Genetics, Health, and Society. Available at http://www4.od.nih.gov/oba/sacghs.htm. Accessed June 4, 2005.

22. Health Resources and Services Administration. Advisory Committee on Heritable Disorders and Genetic Diseases in Newborns and Children. Available at http://mchb.hrsa.gov/programs/genetics/committee/. Accessed June 4, 2005.
23. Health Resources and Services Administration, Maternal and Child Health Bureau. *Newborn Screening: Toward a Uniform Screening Panel and System—Report for Public Comment.* Available at http://mchb.hrsa.gov/screening. Accessed July 27, 2005.
24. CDC. *Translating Advance in Human Genetics into Public Health Action: A Strategic Plan.* 1997. Available at http://www.cdc.gov/genomics/about/strategic.htm. Accessed June 4, 2005.
25. CDC. Newborn screening for cystic fibrosis. Evaluation of benefits and risks and recommendations for state newborn screening programs. *MMWR* 2004;53(RR13). Available at http://www.cdc.gov/mmwr/preview/mmwrhtml/rr5313a1.htm. Accessed July 27, 2005.
26. CDC. *Evaluation of Genomic Applications in Practice and Prevention (EGAPP): Implementation and Evaluation of a Model Approach.* Available at http://www.cdc.gov/genomics/gtesting/egapp.htm. Accessed June 5, 2005.
27. FDA. *Guidance for Industry: Pharmacogenomic Data Submissions.* Available at http://www.fda.gov/cder/guidance/6400fnl.htm. Accessed June 5, 2005.
28. Clinical Laboratory Improvement Amendments, 42 CFR 493 (2005).
29. FDA. New Device Clearance: Roche AmpliChip Cytochrome P450 Genotyping Test and Affymetrix GeneChip Microarray Instrumentation System—K042259. Available at http://www.fda.gov/cdrh/mda/docs/k042259.html. Accessed June 5, 2005.
30. 42 USC §300b-4 (2005).
31. Senate Report No 95-860, 95th Congress, 2d Sess, at 33–34 (May 27, 1978), in 1978 USC Cong Ad News 9134, 9166–67 (1978).
32. 42 CFR 51f, removed as obsolete, 53 Fed Reg 27859 (July 25, 1988).
33. 42 USC §300b-2 (2005).
34. Health Resources and Services Administration, Maternal and Child Health Bureau. Programs. Available at http://mchb.hrsa.gov/programs/. Accessed June 4, 2005.
35. 42 CFR Part 51a (2004).
36. Allen AL. Genetic privacy: emerging concepts and values. In: Rothstein MA, ed. *Genetic Secrets: Protecting Privacy and Confidentiality in the Genetic Era.* New Haven, CT: Yale University Press, 1997:31–59.
37. Anderlik MR, Rothstein MA. Privacy and confidentiality of genetic information: what rules for the new science? *Ann Rev Genomics Hum Genet* 2001;2:401–33.
38. 42 USC §§300gg–300gg-2 (1996).
39. 45 CFR Parts 160, 164 (2005).
40. 45 CFR §160.103 (2005).
41. 45 CFR §164.512(b) (2005).
42. 42 USC §§300gg (b)(1)(B), 300gg-1(a)(1)(F).
43. National Conference of State Legislatures, Genetics and Health Insurance. State Anti-Discrimination Laws. Available at http://www.ncsl.org/programs/health/genetics/ndishlth.htm. Accessed January 17, 2006.
44. Rothstein MA. Genetic privacy and confidentiality: why they are so hard to protect. *J Law Med Ethics* 1998;26:198–203.
45. 42 USC §§12101–12213.
46. 2 EEOC Compliance Manual (CCH), §§902–945 (March 14, 1995), reprinted in *Daily Labor Rep* (March 16, 1995), E-1, E-23.
47. *Sutton v United Air Lines, Inc,* 527 US 471 (1999).
48. National Conference of State Legislatures. State Genetics Employment Laws. Available at http://www.ncsl.org/programs/health/genetics/ndiscrim.htm. Accessed July 27, 2005.

49. Executive Order 13145. To Prohibit Discrimination in Federal Employment Based on Genetic Information. Available at http://www.eeoc.gov/abouteeoc/35th/thelaw/13145.html. Accessed January 17, 2005.

50. Genetic Information Nondiscrimination Act of 2005, S 306, 109th Congress, 1st Sess (2005); HR 1227, 109th Congress, 1st Sess (2005).

51. Hall MA, McEwen JE, Barton JC, et al. Concerns in a primary care population about genetic discrimination by insurers. *Genet Med* 2005;7:311–6.

52. Lapham EV, Kozma C, Weiss JO. Genetic discrimination: perspectives of consumers. *Science* 1996;274:621–4.

53. Rothstein MA, Hornung CA. Public attitudes about genetics and life insurance. In: Rothstein MA, ed. *Genetics and Life Insurance: Medical Underwriting and Social Policy.* Cambridge, MA: MIT Press, 2004:1–25.

54. Billings PR, Kohn MA, De Cuevas M, et al. Discrimination as a consequence of genetic testing. *Am J Hum Genet* 1992;50:476–82.

55. Hall MA, Rich SS. Patients' fear of genetic discrimination by health insurers: the impact of legal protections. *Genet Med* 2000;2:214–21.

56. Rothstein MA. Genetic exceptionalism and legislative pragmatism. *Hastings Cent Rep* 2005;35:2–8.

57. Federal Policy for the Protection of Human Subjects, 45 CFR Part 46, Subpart A (2005).

58. Committee on Assessing Genetic Risks, Institute of Medicine. *Assessing Genetic Risks: Implications for Health and Social Policy.* Washington, DC: National Academy Press, 1994.

59. Holtzman NA, Watson MS, eds. *Promoting Safe and Effective Genetic Testing in the United States: Final Report of the Task Force on Genetic Testing.* September 1997. Available at http://www.genome.gov/10001733; 1997. Accessed January 17, 2006.

60. Task Force on Newborn Screening. Serving the family from birth to the medical home. A report from the Task Force on Newborn Screening. *Pediatrics* 2000;106(2 Pt 2):383–427.

61. Burke W, Zimmern RL. Ensuring the appropriate use of genetic tests. *Nat Rev Genet* 2004;5:955–9.

62. Burke W, Atkins D, Gwinn M, et al. Genetic test evaluation: information needs of clinicians, policy makers, and the public. *Am J Epidemiol* 2002;156:311–8.

63. Pass KA, Lane PA, Fernhoff PM, et al. US newborn screening system guidelines II: follow-up of children, diagnosis, management, and evaluation. Statement of the Council of Regional Networks for Genetic Services (CORN). *J Pediatr* 2000;137(4 Supp.):S1–46.

64. Family Educational Rights and Privacy Act, 20 USC §1232g, 34 CFR Part 99 (2005).

65. Michigan Commission on Genetic Privacy and Progress. *Final Report and Recommendations: February 1999.* Available at http://www.michigan.gov/documents/GeneticsReport_11649_7.pdf. Accessed January 19, 2006.

66. Fitzgerald T, Duva S, Ostrer H, et al. The frequency of *GJB2* and *GJB6* mutations in the New York State newborn population: feasibility of genetic screening for hearing defects. *Clin Genet* 2004;65:338–42.

67. Wion E, Brantley M, Stevens J, et al. Population-wide infant screening for HLA-based type 1 diabetes risk via dried blood spots from the public health infrastructure. *Ann NY Acad Sci* 2003;1005:400–3.

68. About Pediatrix. Available at http://www.pediatrix.com/body.cfm?id=48&oTopID=517. Accessed May 30, 2005.

69. Hehmeyer CP. The case for universal newborn screening. *Exceptional Parent* 2002; 31(8):88.

70. Murray E, Lo B, Pollack L, et al. Direct-to-consumer advertising: physicians' views of its effects on quality of care and the doctor-patient relationship. *J Am Board Fam Pract* 2003;16:513–24.
71. Murray E, Lo B, Pollack L, et al. Direct-to-consumer advertising: public perceptions of its effects on health behaviors, health care, and the doctor-patient relationship. *J Am Board Fam Pract* 2004;17:6–18.
72. Robinson AR, Hohmann KB, Rifkin JI, et al. Direct-to-consumer pharmaceutical advertising: physician and public opinion and potential effects on the physician-patient relationship. *Arch Intern Med* 2004;164:427–32.
73. Zachry WM 3rd, Shepherd MD, Hinich MJ, et al. Relationship between direct-to-consumer advertising and physician diagnosing and prescribing. *Am J Health Syst Pharm* 2002;59: 42–9.
74. Mouchawar J, Hensley-Alford S, Laurion S, et al. Impact of direct-to-consumer advertising for hereditary breast cancer testing on genetic services at a managed care organization: a naturally-occurring experiment. *Genet Med* 2005;7:191–7.
75. Genelex. Available at http://www.genelex.com. Accessed June 5, 2005.
76. DNAdirect: Your genes in context. Available at http://www.dnadirect.com. Accessed June 5, 2005.
77. Genovations: Predictive Genomics for Personalized Medicine. Available at http://www.genovations.com/. Accessed June 5, 2005.
78. GeneLink: Genetic BioSciences for Improving the Quality of Life. Available at http://www.bankdna.com. Accessed June 5, 2005.
79. Gollust SE, Hull SC, Wilfond BS. Limitations of direct-to-consumer advertising for clinical genetic testing. *JAMA* 2002;288:1762–7.
80. Javitt GH, Stanley E, Hudson K. Direct-to-consumer genetic tests, government oversight, and the First Amendment: what the government can (and can't) do to protect the public's health. *Oklahoma Law Rev* 2004;57:251–302.

Chapter 14

VACCINATION MANDATES: THE PUBLIC HEALTH IMPERATIVE AND INDIVIDUAL RIGHTS

Kevin M. Malone* and Alan R. Hinman

In 1796, Edward Jenner demonstrated that inoculation with material from a cowpox (vaccinia) lesion would protect against subsequent exposure to smallpox. This began the vaccine era, although nearly 100 years passed until the next vaccine (against rabies) was introduced. In the 20th century, many new vaccines were developed and used, with spectacular impact on the occurrence of disease. The Centers for Disease Control and Prevention (CDC) declared that vaccinations were one of the ten great public health achievements of the 20th century.[1,2]

This chapter describes the impact of vaccines in dramatically reducing infectious diseases in the United States, the role of legally mandated vaccination in achieving and sustaining that impact, and the constitutional basis for those mandates. The chapter also includes a brief overview of the federal role and its legal foundations in immunization practices.

Background

Concept of Community Disease Prevention

Garrett Hardin's classic essay "The Tragedy of the Commons" describes the challenges presented when societal interest conflicts with the individual's interest.[3] Hardin

---

* The findings and conclusions in this chapter are those of the author(s) and do not necessarily represent the views of the U.S. Department of Health and Human Services or the Centers for Disease Control and Prevention.

notes the incentives present when the cattle of a community are commingled in a common pasture. When the pasture reaches capacity, each owner retains an incentive to add additional cattle to the common herd because, even though the yield from each animal decreases with the addition of more cattle, the additional animal offsets the decrease for the individual owner. With this incentive, individual owners continue to add cattle to the commons to reap their individual benefit, leading to the inevitable failure of the common from overgrazing. The community interest in maximizing food production, therefore, can be achieved only by controlling the interests of the individual owners in favor of those of the community.

Analogously, a community free of a communicable disease because of a high vaccination rate can be viewed as a common. As in Hardin's common, the very existence of this common leads to tension between the best interests of the individual and those of the community. Increased immunization rates result in significantly decreased risk for disease. Although no remaining unimmunized individual can be said to be free of risk from the infectious disease, the herd immunity effect generated from high immunization rates significantly reduces these individuals' risk for disease. Additional benefit is conferred on the unimmunized person because avoidance of the vaccine avoids the risk for any adverse reactions associated with the vaccine. As disease rates drop, the risks associated with the vaccine come even more to the fore, providing further incentive to avoid immunization. Thus, when an individual in this common chooses to go unimmunized, it only minimally increases that person's risk for illness, while conferring on that person the benefit of avoiding the risk for vaccine-induced side effects. At the same time, however, this action weakens the herd-effect protection for the entire community. As more and more individuals choose what is in their "best" individual interest, the common eventually fails as herd immunity disappears and disease outbreaks occur. To avoid this "tragedy of the commons," communities (and, in recent times, states) have imposed legal requirements to mandate particular vaccinations.

Vaccine Safety and Effectiveness

Vaccines are safe and effective. However, they are neither perfectly safe nor perfectly effective. Consequently, some people who receive vaccines will be injured as a result, and some persons who receive vaccines will not be protected. Most adverse events associated with vaccines are minor and involve local soreness or redness at the injection site, or perhaps fever, for a day or so. Rarely, however, vaccines cause more serious adverse events. Whether an adverse event that occurs after vaccination was caused by the vaccine or was merely temporally related and caused by some totally independent (and often unknown or unidentified) factor often is difficult to ascertain. This is particularly problematic during infancy, when a number of conditions may occur spontaneously. In a given instance, determining whether vaccine was responsible may be impossible.[4] Particularly when dealing with rare events, large-scale case-control studies or reviews of comprehensive records of large numbers of infants may be necessary to ascertain whether those who received a vaccine had a higher incidence of the event than those who did not. In support of such research, CDC operates a large linked database involving a number of large health-maintenance organizations. This Vaccine Safety Datalink project includes more than 7 million persons (approximately 2% of the U.S. population) and has proven invaluable for attempting to determine causality.[5]

Decisions about use of vaccines are based on the relative balance of risks and benefits. This balance may change over time. For example, recipients of oral polio vaccine (OPV) and their close contacts have a risk of developing paralysis associated with the vaccine of 1 in approximately every 2.4 million doses of vaccine distributed. This risk is small and certainly was outweighed by the much larger risk for paralysis from wild polioviruses when they circulated in the United States. However, because wild polioviruses no longer circulate in the United States, and the global effort to eradicate polio has greatly reduced the risk for importation of wild viruses, the balance has shifted. Paralysis from indigenously acquired wild poliovirus has not occurred in the United States since 1979, and the entire Western Hemisphere has been free from wild poliovirus circulation since 1991.[6] The Advisory Committee on Immunization Practices (ACIP), an advisory group to CDC, recommended in 1997 that children receive a sequential schedule with two doses of inactivated polio vaccine (IPV) (which carries no risk for paralysis but is slightly less effective in preventing community spread of wild poliovirus), followed by two doses of OPV. In 2000, the ACIP recommended an all-IPV regimen.[7]

An important characteristic of most vaccines is that they provide both individual and community protection. Most of the diseases against which we vaccinate are transmitted from person to person. When a sufficiently large proportion of individuals in a community are vaccinated, those persons serve as a protective barrier against the likelihood of transmission of the disease in the community, thus indirectly protecting those who are not vaccinated and those who received vaccine but are not protected (i.e., vaccine failures). The proportion of the population that needs to be immune to provide this "herd immunity" varies according to the infectiousness of the agent. For poliomyelitis, that proportion is considered around 80%, whereas for measles, it exceeds 90%.

When a community has a high level of vaccination, an individual might decide to not be vaccinated to avoid the small risk for adverse events while benefiting from the vaccination of others. Of course, if a sufficient number of individuals make this decision, the protection levels in the community decline, the herd immunity effect is lost, and the risk increases for transmission of disease.

Impact of Vaccines

The introduction and widespread use of vaccines has profoundly affected the occurrence of several infectious diseases. Smallpox was eradicated from the world (onset of the last naturally occurring case was in 1977), and vaccination against smallpox stopped. Poliomyelitis is on the verge of eradication. The last indigenous case in the United States associated with wild poliovirus occurred in 1979, and only six countries were still reporting endemic transmission as of the end of 2003, although several countries were subsequently re-infected as a result of temporary cessation of vaccination in northern Nigeria.[8]

In the United States, infants and young children are vaccinated against 13 diseases: diphtheria, *Haemophilus influenzae* type b (Hib), hepatitis A, hepatitis B, influenza, measles, mumps, pertussis, poliomyelitis, rubella, *Streptococcus pneumoniae*, tetanus, and varicella.[9] Meningococcal vaccine also is recommended for adolescents. Except for tetanus, each of these diseases is spread from person to person by direct contact or by aerosol droplet transmission. Most of the diseases historically have had very high incidence in school-aged children because of the high potential for transmission in the congregate setting. With more children in preschool programs, outbreaks have occurred among children at earlier ages. By contrast, hepatitis B has its highest incidence in young adulthood as a result of transmission through sexual contact or needle sharing. Tetanus is acquired by contamination of wounds and is not transmitted from person to person.

Vaccination coverage in the United States among 19- to 35-month-old children is at an all-time high (Table 14-1).[10] However, vaccination coverage is not static. Maintaining high coverage rates is an ongoing challenge because approximately 11,000 infants, all vulnerable to communicable diseases, are born every day in the United States. In addition, the threat remains of importation of infectious diseases from other countries.

Vaccines have had a major impact on the occurrence of disease (Table 14-2), as illustrated by the representative annual morbidity (typically, average morbidity reported in the three years before introduction of the vaccine) in the 20th century and the number of cases reported in 2004 for diseases against which children have been routinely vaccinated.[11] Most diseases have declined by 99% or more (pneumococcal disease and varicella are not reportable conditions) and are at all-time lows. However, disease can rebound quickly if parents do not vaccinate their children.

Modern Federal Government Role in Immunization

Vaccines are subject to licensure in the United States by the Food and Drug Administration (FDA) after studies that address safety and efficacy.[12,13] With declining vaccine production capacity in the United States, Congress approved the National Childhood Vaccine Injury Act (NCVIA) in 1986.[14] This comprehensive law established the National Vaccine Program within the U.S. Department of Health and Human Services to coordinate and oversee all activities within the U.S. government related to vaccine research and development, vaccine-safety monitoring, and vaccination activities. In addition, the Act established the National Vaccine Injury Compensation Program (VICP) to compensate for injuries associated with routinely administered childhood vaccines (42 U.S.C. §§300aa-10–300aa-23). At least some of the decline in the number of vaccine producers in the United States had been attributed to liability costs. The VICP effectively removes this as a significant consideration.

Acknowledging that vaccines, as with any medication, are not without risk to the patient, that vaccines, unlike other medications, are a medical intervention generally given to healthy people, and that vaccination has benefits beyond the individual by significantly benefiting the public health through creation of herd immunity, the VICP was established to shift the monetary costs of vaccine injuries from vaccine recipients and manufacturers. Using a vaccine injury table and a simplified administrative process through the U.S. Court of Federal Claims, this no-fault system is designed to fairly compensate children and their families (along with adult recipients of the

TABLE 14-1   Vaccination Coverage Levels among Children Aged 19–35 Months—United States, 2003

Vaccine—Doses	Percent
DTP—3	96.0
DTP—4	84.8
Polio—3	91.6
Hib—3	93.9
MMR—1	93
Hep B—3	92.4
Varicella	84.8
Combined series	
4 DTP/3 Polio/1 MMR	82.2
4 DTP/3 Polio/1 MMR/3 Hib	81.3
4 DTP/3 Polio/1 MMR/3 Hib/3 Hep B	79.4

Abbreviations: DTP—diphtheria and tetanus toxoids and pertussis vaccine; Hib—*Haemophilus influenzae* type b vaccine; MMR—measles-mumps-rubella vaccine; Hep B—hepatitis B vaccine.

covered vaccines) for the costs associated with the rare injuries related to vaccination. An excise tax on each dose of covered vaccine funds the compensation program.

Individuals alleging vaccine injury must go through the VICP before filing any tort action against the administering health-care provider or the vaccine manufacturer. If the judgment of the court is accepted, further actions against the provider and manufacturer are barred. Even if the judgment is declined, the NCVIA significantly narrows the scope of any tort action against the manufacturer. Liability costs of the vaccine manufacturers have dropped dramatically since establishment of the VICP.

With the product liability incentive for vaccine improvement substantially reduced by the existence of the VICP, the role of the government in monitoring vaccine safety becomes more prominent. Beyond post-licensure surveillance requirements of FDA, the NCVIA also established the Vaccine Adverse Event Reporting System (VAERS), which requires reporting of adverse events by vaccination providers and vaccine manufacturers (42 U.S.C. §300aa-25). Providers also must record lot numbers of vaccines administered. Furthermore, various federal agencies, including CDC, have expanded vaccine-safety activities. In addition, with diminished liability costs, more pharmaceutical companies have entered the vaccine production arena with the resultant competition leading to further vaccine improvements and development of new vaccines against other diseases.

The NCVIA also seeks to improve the knowledge level of parents through its requirements for CDC to produce vaccine information materials for mandatory distribution by all providers, public or private, to patients or parents before administration of VICP-covered vaccines (42 U.S.C. §300aa-26). Through these materials, called Vaccine Information Statements, parents/patients are informed about the schedules for administration of the vaccines, are alerted to contraindications that dictate against administration to particular individuals, and are informed about potential adverse reactions to encourage timely medical intervention, as needed.

Table 14-2   Comparison of 20th-Century Annual Morbidity and Current Morbidity for Vaccine-Preventable Diseases of Children—United States

Disease	20th Century Annual Morbidity*	2004†	Percentage Decrease
Smallpox	48,164	0	100.00
Diphtheria	175,885	0	100.00
Measles	503,282	37	99.99
Mumps	152,209	236	99.85
Pertussis	147,271	18,957	87.13
Polio (paralytic)	16,316	0	100.00
Rubella	47,745	12	99.97
Congenital rubella syndrome	823	0	100.00
Tetanus	1,314	26	98.02
Haemophilus influenzae type b and unknown (children <5 years)	20,000	172	99.14

* Typical average during the three years before vaccine licensure.
† Provisional data.

Most U.S. children receive their vaccinations in the private sector from pediatricians or family physicians, while others receive vaccinations in the public sector, typically from local health departments; however, there is considerable variation around the country.[15] At current prices, the cost for vaccines alone (irrespective of physician fees) is approximately $770 in the private sector.[16] Most employer-based insurance plans now cover childhood vaccinations.

Since 1962, the federal government has supported childhood vaccination programs through a grant program administered by CDC.[17] These "317" grants, named for the authorizing statute, support purchase of vaccine for free administration at local health departments and support vaccination delivery, surveillance, and communication and education. As of 2005, CDC purchased approximately half the childhood vaccine administered in the United States through two federally overseen, state-administered programs. In addition to the 317 program, in 1994 the Vaccines for Children Program (VFC) began, under which Medicaid-eligible children, uninsured children, American Indian and Alaska Native children, and insured children whose coverage does not include vaccinations (with limitations on the locations where this last group can receive VFC vaccine) qualify to receive routine childhood vaccines at no cost for the vaccine.[18] The VFC program operates in both public health clinics and private provider offices. The 317 grant program provides additional vaccines to the states for administration to adults and to children who do not qualify for VFC vaccine. Additional federal assistance for vaccination is provided by the Children's Health Insurance Program through expanded Medicaid eligibility for low-income children.[19] Many states use state funds to purchase additional quantities of vaccine.[20]

The ACIP determines the vaccines to be administered in the VFC program and the schedules for their use. In addition, the ACIP issues recommendations for use of adult and pediatric vaccines in the United States and, generally in coordination with the American Academy of Pediatrics and the American Academy of Family

Physicians, establishes a recommended schedule for administration of routine childhood, adolescent, and adult vaccines.[9,21] The ACIP recommendations often are considered by states as they determine which vaccinations to mandate for school attendance.

To assist parents in complying with the often complex vaccination schedules, many states and localities, with the assistance of CDC and professional organizations, have established immunization registries to remind parents when their children's vaccines are due. In a mobile era when families move often and frequently change healthcare providers, these registries also help avoid over-vaccination and ensure catch-up vaccination when needed.[22]

School and Daycare Vaccination Laws

School vaccination laws have played a key role in the control of vaccine-preventable diseases in the United States. The first school vaccination requirement was enacted in the 1850s in Massachusetts to prevent smallpox transmission in schools.[23] By 1963, 20 states, the District of Columbia, and Puerto Rico required children to be vaccinated before entering school, with a variety of different vaccines being mandated.[24] However, enforcement was uneven.

In the late 1960s, efforts were undertaken to eradicate measles from the United States. Transmission in schools was recognized as a significant problem.[25] In the early 1970s, states that had school laws mandating measles vaccination had measles incidence rates 40%–51% lower than states without such laws.[26] In 1976 and 1977, measles outbreaks in Alaska and Los Angeles, respectively, led health officials to strictly enforce the existing requirements.[27] Advance notice was given that the laws were to be enforced, and major efforts were undertaken to ensure that vaccination could be obtained easily. In Alaska, on the announced day of enforcement, 7,418 of 89,109 students (8.3%) failed to provide proof of vaccination and were excluded from school. One month later, fewer than 51 students remained excluded. No further cases of measles occurred.[28] In Los Angeles, approximately 50,000 of 1,400,000 students (<4%) were excluded; most were back in school within a few days, and the number of measles cases dropped precipitously. These experiences demonstrated that mandatory vaccination could be enforced and was effective.

Because of declining vaccination levels in children, a nationwide Childhood Immunization Initiative was undertaken in 1977 to raise vaccination levels in children to 90% by 1979. An important component of this initiative was to support enactment and enforcement of school vaccination requirements. During a two-year period, 28 million records were reviewed, and children in need were vaccinated.[29]

An analysis of 6 states that strictly enforced comprehensive laws (affecting all grades) beginning with the 1977–1978 school year compared with the rest of the country showed that in the 1975–1976 school year, they had comparable incidence rates of measles. However, in the 1977–1978 school year, the 6 states that strictly enforced the laws had incidence rates less than half those of the rest of the country; and in the 1978–1979 school year, the incidence rates were less than one-tenth those of the rest of the country.[30] An analysis of states with the highest and lowest incidences of measles in 1979–1980 found that states with the lowest incidence rates were significantly more likely to have laws covering the entire school population (rather than just first entrants) and more likely to be strictly enforcing the laws.[31]

By the 1980–1981 school year, all 50 states had laws covering students first entering school. In most states, these laws affected children at all grade levels, as well as those involved in licensed preschool settings. Some of the laws specify the particular vaccines required (and the numbers of doses of each); others authorize the state health officer (or public health board) to designate which vaccines (and number of doses) will be required, often after a public rulemaking process.

As of the 2003–2004 school year, all states but 4 (Louisiana, Michigan, South Carolina, and West Virginia) had requirements covering all grades from kindergarten through twelfth grade. In all 50 states, the District of Columbia, and Puerto Rico, the requirements covered daycare centers; in 48 states (all but Iowa and West Virginia), the requirements covered Head Start programs. In 30 states, the District of Columbia, and Puerto Rico, some requirements covered college entrance. In all 50 states, the requirements included diphtheria and tetanus toxoids, and polio, measles, and rubella vaccines. In addition, 47 required mumps vaccine, 44 required pertussis vaccine, 44 required hepatitis B vaccine, 42 required varicella vaccine, and 7 required hepatitis A vaccine.[32] All 50 states required Hib vaccine for entry to licensed daycare settings and 48 for entry to Head Start programs.

Since 1981, vaccination levels in school entrants have been 95% or higher for diphtheria and tetanus toxoids and pertussis vaccine (DTP), polio vaccine, and measles vaccine. All states require vaccination for children attending licensed daycare centers, and as a result, such children have vaccination levels 90% or higher. Nonetheless, overall levels in preschool-aged children have not been as high, as manifested by the resurgence of measles during 1989–1991, primarily affecting unvaccinated preschool-aged children.[33] Levels in these children recently have been raised to their currently high levels as a result of major efforts (and major infusions of resources) directed at this population.[15]

The Task Force on Community Preventive Services is an independent body carrying out evidence-based reviews of the literature to assess the strength of evidence that preventive interventions directed to populations are effective. One of the 17 interventions reviewed for vaccine-preventable diseases was mandatory vaccination requirements. The task force found that sufficient evidence existed to demonstrate the effectiveness of these requirements in increasing vaccine coverage, thereby reducing disease incidence, and so recommended their use.[34]

Historical Context

John Duffy's description of smallpox vaccination in early American history highlights both the significant positive public health impact of vaccines and the ongoing challenges that this success presents:

> Smallpox . . . was the great scourge of the American colonies until the introduction of inoculation or variolation, and the subsequent discovery of vaccination in 1796 relegated it to minor importance among the great epidemic diseases. As memories of the horrify-

ing outbreaks of smallpox gradually faded, and a generation appeared which had had little contact with its victims, vaccination was neglected, and the incidence of smallpox began to rise. Beginning in the 1830s its attacks gradually intensified, and by the time of the Civil War the disorder was once again a serious problem.

By chance, the rise of smallpox coincided with the enactment of compulsory school attendance laws and the subsequent rapid growth in the number of public schools. Since the bringing together of large numbers of children clearly facilitated the spread of smallpox, and since vaccination provided a relatively safe preventive, it was natural that compulsory school attendance laws should lead to a movement for compulsory vaccination. . . .[23]

Many other childhood diseases for which vaccines were developed also frequently occurred in school-based outbreaks; consequently, when polio and measles vaccines were introduced in 1955 and 1963, respectively, adding them to the list of requirements for school entry was a logical consideration. The 1963 survey of state laws found that, of 20 states with requirements, 18 included smallpox, 11 included diphtheria, 10 included polio, 7 included tetanus, and 5 included pertussis. Measles requirements soon were added. By 1970, 20 states required measles vaccination, and by 1983, all 50 states did.[35]

Legal Authorities: Constitutional Basis of Mandatory Vaccination

Police Power

The first state law mandating vaccination was enacted in Massachusetts in 1809; in 1855, Massachusetts became the first state to enact a school vaccination requirement. The constitutional basis of vaccination requirements rests in the police power of the state. In 1905, the U.S. Supreme Court issued its landmark ruling in *Jacobson v. Massachusetts* upholding the right of states to compel vaccination.[36] The Court held that a health regulation requiring smallpox vaccination was a reasonable exercise of the state's police power that did not violate the liberty rights of individuals under the Fourteenth Amendment to the U.S. Constitution. The police power is the authority reserved to the states by the Constitution and embraces "such reasonable regulations established directly by legislative enactment as will protect the public health and the public safety" (197 U.S. at 25, 25 S. Ct. at 361).[a]

In *Jacobson*, the Commonwealth of Massachusetts had enacted a statute that authorized local boards of health to require vaccination. Jacobson challenged his conviction for refusal to be vaccinated against smallpox as required by regulations of the Cambridge Board of Health. While acknowledging the potential for vaccines to cause adverse events and the inability to determine with absolute certainty whether a particular person can be safely vaccinated, the Court specifically rejected the notion of an exemption based on personal choice.[b] To do otherwise "would practically strip the legislative department of its function to [in its considered judgment] care for the public health and the public safety when endangered by epidemics of disease" (197 U.S. at 37, 25 S. Ct. at 366). The Court elaborated on the tension between personal freedom and public health inherent in liberty: "The liberty secured by the Constitution of the United States to every person within its jurisdiction does not import an absolute right in each person to be, at all times and in all circumstances, wholly freed from restraint. There are manifold restraints to which every person is necessarily subject for the common good. On any other basis, organized society could not exist with safety to its members" (197 U.S. at 26, 25 S. Ct. at 361).

School Vaccination Laws

The Supreme Court in 1922 addressed the constitutionality of childhood vaccination requirements in *Zucht v. King*.[37] The Court denied a due process Fourteenth Amendment challenge to the constitutionality of city ordinances that excluded children from school attendance for failure to present a certificate of vaccination, holding that "these ordinances confer not arbitrary power, but only that broad discretion required for the protection of the public health" (260 U.S. at 177, 43 S. Ct. at 25).[c]

More recently, in the face of a measles epidemic in Maricopa County, Arizona, the Arizona Court of Appeals rejected the argument that an individual's right to education would trump the state's need to protect against the spread of infectious diseases short of confirmed cases of measles in the particular school. Given the nature of the spread of measles and the lag time in getting laboratory confirmation of cases, the court in *Maricopa County Health Department v. Harmon*[38] was satisfied that taking action to combat disease by excluding unvaccinated children from school was prudent when a reasonably perceived, but unconfirmed, risk exists for the spread of measles (156 Ariz. at 166, 750 P.2d at 1369). Although the court considered the right to education under Arizona's constitution, the decision is instructive in showing the reach of the police power to ensure the public health. The court in *Maricopa* specifically noted that *Jacobson* did not require that epidemic conditions exist to compel vaccination (156 Ariz. at 166, 750 P.2d at 1369).

Parens Patriae

Further authority to compel vaccination of children comes under the doctrine of *parens patriae* in which the state asserts authority over child welfare. In the 1944 case of *Prince v. Massachusetts*,[39] which involved child labor under an asserted right of religious freedom, the U.S. Supreme Court summarized the doctrine, noting that

> [n]either rights of religion nor rights of parenthood are beyond limitation. Acting to guard the general interest in youth's well being, the state as *parens patriae* may restrict the parent's control by requiring school attendance, regulating or prohibiting the child's labor, and in many other ways. Its authority is not nullified merely because the parent grounds his claim to control the child's course of conduct on religion or conscience. Thus, he cannot claim freedom from compulsory vaccination for the child more than for himself on religious grounds. The right to practice religion freely does not include liberty to expose the community or the child to communicable disease or the latter to ill health or death. (321 U.S. at 166–67, 64 S. Ct. at 442)[d]

Legal Issues and Controversies: Exemptions to Mandatory Vaccination

Although vaccines are safe and effective, as previously noted, they are neither perfectly safe nor perfectly effective. Some people who receive vaccines will have an adverse reaction, and some will not be protected. In developing vaccines, the challenge is to minimize the likelihood of adverse effect while maximizing effectiveness. Some people have medical conditions that increase the risk for adverse effect, and therefore they should not receive vaccines. Recognizing this fact, all state vaccination laws provide for exemptions for persons with contraindicating conditions.

The religious beliefs of some people oppose vaccination, and other people oppose vaccination on other grounds, including philosophic. In addition, some people are not opposed to all vaccines but oppose the concept of mandatory vaccination or mandates for specific vaccines. In the latter case, they may believe they (or their children) are not at risk for a particular disease or that, if contracted, the disease is not severe. If the disease in question is uncommon (as in the United States today for most vaccine-preventable diseases), people with philosophic opposition might not be willing to undertake any level of risk for adverse effect.

Forty-eight states allow religious exemptions (all but Mississippi and West Virginia) and at least twenty permit philosophic exemptions.[32] The criteria for allowing these exemptions vary greatly. Some states require membership in a recognized religion,[e] whereas others merely require an affirmation of religious (or philosophic) opposition. During the 1997–1998 school year, fewer than 1% of school entrants nationwide had any kind of exemption to mandatory vaccination. Only 7 states had more than 1% with exemption; Michigan had the highest level of exemption at 2.3%. By contrast, during the 2003–2004 school year, 4 states had more than 1% with religious exemptions, and 10 states had more than 1% with philosophic exemptions. The highest rates for religious and philosophic exemptions were 3.2% in Wyoming and 3.6% in Washington.[32]

During 1985–1994, 13 outbreaks of measles were identified in religious groups opposing vaccination. These outbreaks resulted in 1200 cases and 9 deaths. Outbreaks of polio (in the 1970s), pertussis, and rubella have been documented among Amish groups.[40] During 1985–1992, persons with religious or philosophic exemptions were 35 times more likely to contract measles than were vaccinated persons.[41] In addition, persons living in communities with high concentrations of exemptors were themselves at increased risk for measles because of increased risk for exposure. Another study found that children with personal exemptions were 22 times more likely than vaccinated children to have measles and that children with personal exemptions were 5.9 times more likely than vaccinated children to have pertussis. This study also found that the frequency of exemptors was associated with the incidence of both measles and pertussis in vaccinated children.[42]

A study of the processes required to obtain religious and philosophic exemptions to school vaccination laws found an inverse correlation between the complexity of the exemption process and the proportion of exemptions filed.[43] None of the 19 states with the highest level of complexity in gaining exemptions had more than 1% of students exempted, compared with 5 of 15 states with the simplest procedure. Other studies have found variations among states in the approaches to exemption.[44]

Results of the studies cited above indicate the need for states to develop policies and procedures for requesting and granting exemptions, and to ensure that school personnel and local health departments fully understand and implement these policies and procedures.[32] The policies and procedures certainly vary on the basis of state laws and regulations but as some commentators have suggested, "[I]t should not be easier to obtain an exemption than it is to have a child immunized."[45]

Is There a Constitutional Right to a Religious Exemption from Mandatory Vaccination?

Challenges to mandatory vaccination laws based on religion or philosophic belief have led various courts to hold that no constitutional right exists either to religious or philosophic exemptions.

First Amendment: Free Exercise Clause

Freedom to believe in a religion is absolute under the First Amendment.[f] However, freedom to act in accordance with one's religious beliefs "remains subject to regulation for the protection of society."[46] In the 1963 case of *Sherbert v. Verner*, the U.S. Supreme Court established a balancing test for determining whether a regulation violated a person's First Amendment right to free exercise of religion.[47] The test, which prevailed until 1990, required the government to justify any substantial burden on religiously motivated conduct by a compelling government interest and by means narrowly tailored to achieve that interest (374 U.S. at 406–8, 83 S. Ct. at 1795–96).

Notwithstanding the state's power as *parens patriae*, instances occur in which a parent's claim of religious freedom under the Free Exercise Clause will prevail, as in *Wisconsin v. Yoder*.[48] In *Yoder*, Amish parents challenged a Wisconsin law that required formal education of children to age 16 years. The parents asserted that formal schooling beyond the eighth grade would gravely endanger the free exercise of their religion because of their belief that values taught in higher education, including exposure to worldly influences, vary markedly from Amish values and the Amish way of life. While acknowledging the state's interest in universal education, the U.S. Supreme Court, in applying the *Sherbert* compelling interest test, rejected Wisconsin's argument of a compelling state interest in requiring formal education of the Amish beyond eighth grade given the strong religious interference of such a requirement and the provision of adequate alternative informal vocational education by the Amish. The Court in *Yoder* articulated its application of the compelling interest test: "[W]here fundamental claims of religious freedom are at stake," the Court will not accept a state's "sweeping claim" that its interest in compulsory education is compelling. "[D]espite its admitted validity in the generality of cases, we must searchingly examine the interests that the State seeks to promote . . . and the impediment to those objectives that would flow from recognizing the claimed Amish exemption" (406 U.S. at 221, 92 S. Ct. at 1536).

Free Exercise Standard

Little recent case law directly addresses the existence of a First Amendment free exercise right to a religious exemption from mandatory vaccination because 48 states have provided by statute for religious exemptions to school vaccination laws.[32]

However, dicta in both *Sherbert*[49] and *Yoder*,[50] referring to the *Jacobson* and *Prince* decisions, clearly indicate that both on *parens patriae* and police power grounds, the U.S. Supreme Court sees a compelling state interest in mandating vaccination of children because of the health threat to the community and to the children themselves. With little practical alternative to vaccination to avoid or be a disease risk (e.g., inability to avoid contact with other persons, except for those totally isolated from society), mandatory vaccination of all schoolchildren should also meet the "narrowly tailored" criterion of *Sherbert*.

In addition, in a case that predates the *Yoder* decision and enactment of a statutory religious exemption by Arkansas, the Arkansas Supreme Court in *Wright v. DeWitt School District*[51] held that no First Amendment right existed to a religious exemption given the state's compelling interest in mandating vaccination under its police power to protect the public health (238 Ark. at 913, 385 S.W.2d at 648).[g] Significantly, the U.S. Supreme Court in *Yoder* referenced the *Wright* decision in dicta regarding cases in which the health of the child or public health are at issue, with the implication that a vaccination mandate providing no religious exemption would meet the compelling state interest test (406 U.S. at 230, 92 S. Ct. at 1540–1).

Current Free Exercise Standard

Whether a vaccination law that does not provide for religious exemptions would meet the compelling state interest test essentially is moot now because of a U.S. Supreme Court ruling that significantly lowers the bar for states to prevail. In its 1990 decision in *Employment Div., Dept. of Human Resources of Oregon v. Smith*,[52] the Supreme Court rejected the compelling interest test and established a new standard that holds "the right of free exercise does not relieve an individual of the obligation to comply with a 'valid and neutral law of general applicability on the ground that the law proscribes (or prescribes) conduct that his religion prescribes (or proscribes)'" (494 U.S. at 879, 110 S. Ct. at 1600 [quoting *United States v. Lee*, 455 U.S. 252, 263, n. 3, 102 S. Ct. 1051, 1058, n. 3 (1982)]).

Congress attempted to legislatively override the ruling in *Smith* by enacting the Religious Freedom Restoration Act of 1993, which reestablished the compelling interest test as the standard for considering the constitutionality of free exercise claims.[53] However, the U.S. Supreme Court in *City of Boerne v. Flores*[54] struck down the Religious Freedom Restoration Act of 1993, holding that Congress had exceeded its constitutional authority in implementing the statute (521 U.S. at 510–37, 117 S. Ct. at 2160–72). Thus, the *Smith* standard is the current law. Whether judged under the neutral law of general applicability test of *Smith* or the compelling interest test of *Sherbert*, it is reasonable to conclude that no First Amendment free exercise right exists to an exemption from mandatory vaccination requirements.

Is a Statutory Religious Exemption Constitutional?

With no First Amendment free exercise right to a religious exemption, the next question is whether the states have the discretion to allow such exemptions by statute. The court decisions are mixed. The Establishment Clause[h] of the First Amendment establishes the constitutional limits within which a state may accommodate a religious exemption to a law of general application, including whether such an exemption is allowed and how inclusively the exemption must be defined. As noted above, 48 states provide by statute for religious exemptions to school vaccination laws.[32]

In *Brown v. Stone*,[55] the Mississippi Supreme Court struck down the religious exemption that appeared in the Mississippi school vaccination statute, holding that the statutory religious exemption violated the Equal Protection Clause of the Fourteenth Amendment because it would "require the great body of schoolchildren to be vaccinated and at the same time expose them to the hazard of associating in school with children exempted under the religious exemption who had not been immunized" (378 So. 2d at 223). Thus, the *Jacobson* argument comes full circle. The fact that no vaccine confers immunity on all persons who receive it illustrates the point that even people who comply with vaccination statutes can be placed at increased risk by exposure to individuals never vaccinated because of exemptions.

First Amendment: Establishment Clause

Most challenges to religion-based vaccination exemptions have been decided by the courts on establishment grounds and concern the inclusiveness of such exemptions rather than their existence. The U.S. Supreme Court in *Lemon v. Kurtzman*,[56] a case involving state supplementation of parochial school salaries, defined a three-pronged test for determining whether a state religious accommodation complies with the Establishment Clause: "First, the statute must have a secular legislative purpose; second, its principal or primary effect must be one that neither advances nor inhibits religion; finally, the statute must not foster 'an excessive government entanglement with religion'" (403 U.S. at 612–3, 91 S. Ct. at 2111 [citation omitted] [quoting *Walz v. Tax Commission*, 397 U.S. 664, 674, 90 S. Ct. 1409, 1414 (1970)]).

Scope of Statutory Exemptions: Sincerely Held Religious Belief

In *Sherr v. Northport-East Northport Union Free School District*,[57] the plaintiffs had been denied an exemption under the state's religious exemption statute by the school district because, although they claimed religious opposition to vaccination, they were not "bona fide members of a recognized religious organization" whose teachings oppose vaccination, as required by New York law (672 F. Supp. at 84 [quoting subsection 9 of N.Y. Pub. Health L. §2164]). The U.S. District Court for the Eastern District of New York found that New York's limitation of the religious exemption violated both the Establishment and Free Exercise clauses of the First Amendment.[i] The court found that this limitation violated the Establishment Clause by running afoul of at least the last two prongs of the *Lemon* test: (1) by inhibiting the religious practices of individuals who oppose vaccination of their children on religious grounds but are not members of a religious organization recognized by the state and (2) by restricting the exemption to "recognized religious organizations" requires that the government involve itself in religious matters to an inordinate degree through such government approval (672 F. Supp. at 89–90).[j] In addition, the court held that the limiting language violated the Free Exercise Clause because no compelling societal interest existed to justify the burden placed on the free religious exercise of "certain individuals while other persons remain free to avoid subjecting their children to a religiously objectionable medical technique because they may belong to a particular religious organization to which the state has given a stamp of approval" (672 F. Supp. at 90–91). There "surely exist less restrictive alternative means of achieving the state's aims than the blatantly discriminatory restriction . . . the state has devised" (672 F. Supp. at 91). Striking down New York's limitation, the court found that "sincerely held religious beliefs" in opposition to vaccination, whether or not as part of a recognized religion, should suffice (672 F. Supp. at 98).

Similarly, two U.S. District Courts in Arkansas, in *McCarthy v. Boozman*[58] and *Boone v. Boozman*,[59] while upholding that state's underlying immunization statute, in 2002 struck down as violating the Establishment and Free Exercise clauses the state's religious exemption that had been limited to members or adherents of a church or religious denomination recognized by the state.

After the *Sherr* decision, the New York legislature revised that state's immunization statute to provide an exemption for persons who "hold genuine and sincere religious beliefs" that are contrary to immunization.[60] The courts have upheld this revised exemption. The U.S. District Court for the Eastern District of New York, in *Berg v. Glen Cove City School District*,[61] described a two-step analysis for determining whether a person qualifies for the exemption. First, there must be a determination whether the beliefs are religious. If they are, the genuineness and sincerity of those beliefs must be established (853 F. Supp. at 655). In *Turner v. Liverpool Central School*,[62] the U.S. District Court for the Northern District of New York held that New York's revised exemption complies with all three prongs of the *Lemon* test. Of particular note, the court observed that violation of *Lemon*'s excessive entanglement of church and state prong is avoided by the state not assessing the validity of the individual's religious beliefs but rather determining only whether those beliefs are genuine and sincere (186 F. Supp.2d at 193).

Do Statutory Religious Exemptions Encompass Philosophic Opposition?

Strength of convictions aside, defining "religious" belief can be difficult, and understanding its implications for philosophic exemptions that a state may or may not wish to voluntarily confer is a challenge. As the Supreme Court noted in *Yoder*: "[T]o have the protection of the Religion Clauses, the claims must be rooted in religious belief" (406 U.S. at 215, 92 S. Ct. at 1533). Decisions by the U.S. Supreme Court in two conscientious objector cases indicate that a bright line may not always exist between the religious and the philosophic and that at least some amount of philosophic opposition to vaccination may rise to the level of being religious and therefore incorporated into a voluntarily conferred religious exemption, regardless of whether the state explicitly provides for a philosophic exemption.[k] In *United States v. Seeger*[63] and *Welsh v. United States*,[64] the Court interpreted "religious," as it appeared in a federal statutory religious-based conscientious objector exemption from military conscription, expansively to extend beyond traditional religious beliefs. *Seeger* defined the test as "[a] sincere and meaningful belief which occupies in the life of its possessor a place parallel to that filled by the God of those admittedly qualifying for the exemption" (380 U.S. at 176, 85 S. Ct. at 859). The Court elaborated in *Welsh*: "[T]o be 'religious' . . . this opposition . . . [must] stem from . . . moral, ethical, or religious beliefs about what is right and wrong and that these beliefs be held with the strength of traditional religious convictions" (398 U.S. at 340, 90 S. Ct. at 1796).

However, the Court in *Welsh* clarified that "moral, ethical, or religious principles" do not incorporate "considerations of policy, pragmatism, or expediency" (398 U.S. at 342–3, 90 S. Ct. at 1798). *Yoder* provides further illumination: "A way of life, however virtuous and admirable, may not be interposed as a barrier to reasonable state regulation of education if it is based on purely secular considerations. . . . [T]he very concept of ordered liberty precludes allowing every person to make his own standards on matters of conduct in which the society as a whole has important interests. Thus, if the Amish asserted their claims because of their subjective evaluation and rejection of the contemporary secular values accepted by the majority, much as Thoreau rejected the social values of his time and isolated himself at Walden Pond, their claims would not rest on a religious basis. Thoreau's choice was philosophical and personal rather than religious, and such belief does not rise to the demands of the Religion Clauses" (406 U.S. at 215–16, 92 S. Ct. at 1533). Thus, the U.S. Court of Appeals for the Second Circuit in *Mason v. General Brown Central School District*[65] rejected fear of the possible side effects from vaccination, although based on strong convictions, as rising to the level of religious beliefs because of evidence that the plaintiff's beliefs were "simply an embodiment of secular chiropractic ethics" (851 F.2d at 51–2). *Mason* and similar decisions indicate that the expansive religious interpretation of *Seeger* and *Welsh* should not be read too broadly.

Impact of Evolving Privacy Rights

Finally, the general concept of a liberty interest in bodily integrity first was articulated by then Judge, later Justice, Cardozo in *Schloendorff v. Society of New York Hospital*: "Every human being of adult years and sound mind has a right to determine what shall be done with his own body" regarding medical needs.[66] Recognition by the courts in recent years of a liberty right, or right to privacy, in medical decision-making emanating from the Due Process Clause of the Fourteenth Amendment and noted most prominently by the U.S. Supreme Court in its 1973 decision *Roe v. Wade*[67] might be used as the basis of a claimed privacy right by a college student subject to mandatory vaccination. However, the Court in *Roe*, referencing *Jacobson*, noted that the medical privacy right is not unlimited and must be balanced against important state interests in regulation (410 U.S. at 154, 93 S. Ct. at 727). More recently, in dicta in the 1990 "right to die" case of *Cruzan v. Director, Missouri Dept. of Health*,[68] the U.S. Supreme Court again acknowledged the viability of the *Jacobson* holding, leading to the conclusion that, as long as the public health need for widespread vaccination exists, the courts will not recognize a privacy right to refuse state-mandated vaccination and will uphold the police power of states to mandate vaccination.

Practice Considerations and Emerging Issues

As new vaccines have been introduced and recommended for universal use in infants and children, states have responded by expanding the scope of their vaccination laws.

Vaccination laws were first enacted to control epidemic diseases. Now they also are used to increase coverage with vaccines deemed important to protect the public's health even in the absence of epidemics.[69] This practice is increasingly subject to challenge, particularly with varicella vaccine. Varicella typically is a mild disease in children, although nationwide it accounts for more than 50 deaths each year. Some parents have argued that no compelling state interest exists in preventing this disease.

With hepatitis B vaccine, the argument has been that most hepatitis B occurs in adults whose sexual or drug-using behavior puts them at risk and that schoolchildren should not be forced to be vaccinated against a disease that often results from voluntary behavior of adults. However, in the second 2002 decision striking down the Arkansas religious exemption but upholding the underlying immunization law, the U.S. District Court for the Eastern District of Arkansas, in *Boone v. Boozman*,[59] acknowledged that hepatitis B vaccination mandates for children have a "real and substantial relation" to the protection of public health. Because the groups at highest risk for hepatitis B are unlikely to self-identify and pursue the vaccine, vaccinating those individuals as children is likely to stem the spread of hepatitis B (217 F. Supp.2d at 954). In addition, high-risk behavior is not the only risk factor for hepatitis B, a disease that has severe health consequences. Globally, hepatitis B is second only to tobacco in causing cancer.[70] Yet, it is highly preventable through immunization with hepatitis B vaccine, the first anticancer vaccine.[71]

Publicity about adverse events alleged to be caused by vaccine fuels controversy about the wisdom or necessity of requiring vaccination, particularly in absence of visible threat from disease. In the 1970s, concern about the possibility of pertussis vaccine causing sudden infant death syndrome or infantile spasms led to debate about pertussis vaccination requirements, even though studies showed the vaccine caused neither event.[72] More recently, concern that measles-mumps-rubella vaccine (MMR) or thimerosal (a mercury-based preservative used in some vaccines) might cause autism led to congressional hearings and challenges to requirements for vaccination. Reviews by the Institute of Medicine have failed to show such an association.[73,74]

Also, with the growing list of recommended childhood vaccines and the availability of expanded information sources of varying quality created through the Internet, theories regarding potential risk factors associated with vaccines can drive concerns about vaccines and at times can outstrip the ability of scientific inquiry to provide clear-cut answers regarding those concerns. That feeds an anxiety among some that vaccines may be associated with other yet undiscovered risks.

The appearance of new adverse events caused by vaccines further feeds the controversy. For example, the occurrence of intestinal intussusception following administration of rotavirus vaccine, soon after its licensure, led to withdrawal of the vaccine and lent some support to the arguments of those opposed to vaccination.[75]

Even though vaccines are not risk free, immunization remains one of the most effective tools of infectious disease prevention. In a time of diminished personal experience with these infectious diseases, primarily because of the immense success of vaccination programs, concerns about potential adverse effects of vaccines can rise to the fore and appear to drive at least some philosophic opposition to vaccination. The public health key is to ensure that parents and others facing concerns regarding vaccine safety are informed about the facts regarding those vaccines.

The Arkansas state legislature responded to the court decisions striking down that state's religious exemption by reinstating a religious exemption that presumably is constitutional because it no longer is restricted to recognized religions. In addition, the list of exemptions was broadened to allow for philosophic opposition. However, that did not complete their revision of the Arkansas vaccination mandate statute. Interestingly, among other new requirements, the state legislature added a requirement that anyone seeking a medical, religious, or philosophic exemption must complete an educational component that includes information about the risks and benefits of vaccination.[76]

Most parents today, and even many health-care providers, often have more direct experience or knowledge regarding side effects of vaccines, both known and alleged, than they do of the devastating effects of infectious diseases avoided by such vaccines. Ensuring that parents are fully informed about both vaccine risks and disease risks is critical to maintaining historic lows of these diseases. When a parent asserts an exemption, the high stakes of reducing herd immunity through such exemptions demands "informed refusal" as the standard for claiming a religious, philosophic, or medical exemption.

Conclusion

School vaccination requirements have been a key factor in the prevention and control of vaccine-preventable diseases in the United States. Their constitutional basis rests in the police power of the state, as well as the *parens patriae* doctrine. No constitutional right exists to either a religious or philosophic exemption to these requirements, although most states allow religious exemptions and a number allow philosophic exemptions. The courts generally have upheld these exemptions. Most litigation regarding exemptions has focused on the scope of the exemption, with courts holding that religious exemptions may not be limited to members of organized religions but rather must allow all who have sincerely held religious beliefs opposing vaccination to qualify. "Religious" may be defined broadly enough to incorporate some amount of philosophic opposition but has not been interpreted to bring purely secular-based "philosophic" opposition to vaccination within the meaning of religion.

With the increasing numbers of vaccines being introduced and the generally low level of visible threat from disease, continued challenges to school vaccination requirements are expected. School vaccination laws continue to play a central role in avoiding "the tragedy of the commons" by preventing disease through high vaccination coverage.

But challenges remain. For example, experience in the United States has shown that, although measles is no longer endemic in this country, measles is imported each year. These importations typically result in few secondary cases given the high vaccination levels in the vast majority of American communities.[77] However, 1 measles case importation in an unvaccinated child in 2005 resulted in one of the largest measles outbreaks in the United States since the early 1990s, producing a three-generation outbreak of 34 cases in 3 states; 70% among children whose parents objected to vaccination. The impact of this single measles case importation extended beyond the community of vaccination objectors to impact exposed hospitalized children who were too young to be vaccinated and hospital employees whose vaccination status was unknown. This resulted in a situation requiring mass screening for immunity, administration of immune globulin, exclusion from work and other costly measures.[78,1]

Lowered vaccination coverage levels in the United States would create an even greater risk. In the United Kingdom, where coverage with MMR fell from 90%–93% in 1991–1997 to 80% in 2003 as a result of publicity about the alleged causal role of MMR in autism, importations have resulted in significant secondary transmission.[79,80]

These experiences demonstrate the necessity of maintaining very high immunization levels. With the threat of reintroduction of communicable diseases literally only an airplane ride away, school vaccination requirements remain an important component of our national defense against vaccine-preventable diseases. School vaccination laws can be expected to be upheld by the courts as long as the task of protecting the public health is achieved by mandating such requirements.

Notes

a. Compulsory vaccination is not beyond the police power without arbitrariness or extreme injustice under particular facts. (See note b, below, regarding medical-based exemption.) In *Jacobson*, the Court—in addition to holding that providing for compulsory vaccination is within the police power of a state—held that such authority may be delegated to a local body (197 U.S. at 25, 25 S. Ct. at 361).

b. In dicta, the Court in *Jacobson* indicated, however, that a liberty right would exist to an exemption on the basis of known medical contraindication "to protect the health and life of the individual concerned" (197 U.S. at 39, 25 S. Ct. at 366). (Dicta is discussion in a court decision that addresses an issue outside the direct facts presented by the case and therefore outside the court's holding and thus is of no precedential value in directing future court decisions.)

c. See also *Brown v. Stone*, 378 So. 2d 218, 222–3 (Miss. 1979), *cert. denied* 449 U.S. 887 (1980) for discussion regarding the logical nexus between mandatory vaccination and school attendance: "[O]verriding and compelling public interest . . . [in] exclusion of a child until such immunization has been effected, not only as a protection of that child but as a protection of the large number of other children comprising the school community and with whom he will be daily in close contact in the school room."

d. See also *In re: Christine M.*, 157 Misc. 2d 4, 595 N.Y.S.2d 606 (N.Y. Fam. Ct. 1992) in which the court, citing to *Prince*, held that a father's knowing failure to have his child vaccinated against measles in the midst of a measles outbreak, and not qualifying for a statutory religious exemption, caused the child to be a "neglected child" under state law. However, the court declined to order vaccination because the measles outbreak had ended by then, and the child was not yet old enough to be subject to the school attendance law.

e. But see discussion regarding holding in *Sherr* striking down state religious exemption requirement that an individual be a "bona fide member of a recognized religious organization."

f. The First Amendment to the U.S. Constitution states in pertinent part: "Congress shall make no law respecting an establishment of religion, or prohibiting the free exercise thereof. . . ." The Free Exercise and Establishment clauses have been held applicable to the states through the Due Process Clause of the Fourteenth Amendment.[46]

g. See also *Cude v. State*, 237 Ark. 927, 377 S.W.2d 816 (Ark. 1964) (upholding ruling of neglect and appointment of temporary guardian to consent to vaccination of children despite parents' good-faith religious beliefs in opposition).

h. See note f, above.

i. See also *Davis v. State*, 294 Md. 379, 451 A.2d 107 (Md. 1982), which held that limiting religious exemption to children whose parents were "members" (as statute provided) or "adherents" (as health department regulation further attempted to narrow qualification) of a "recognized church or religious denomination" opposing vaccination violated the Establishment Clause. On the basis of rules of statutory construction in Maryland, the court severed the offending religious exemption from the statute and upheld the conviction of Davis under the remaining statute that compelled vaccination (294 Md. at 382–5, 451 A.2d at 114–5). Rules of statutory construction vary, so that in the *Sherr* case, the court struck down the limiting "bona fide members of a recognized religious organization" language but otherwise upheld the religious exemption. In addition, the court enjoined enforcement of the "bona fide" language as to one of the two sets of plaintiffs, who otherwise qualified, and further enjoined the state from enforcing the offending language in the future (672 F. Supp. at 97–99).

j. The court in *Sherr*, having noted the constitutional infirmity of the "bona fide" limitation under the other two prongs of *Lemon*, did not resolve whether the "bona fide" portion of the religious exemption possessed a secular purpose as required under the first prong. However, in dicta, the court noted that the legislature may have had a number of secular purposes for adopting such language, including "as a guard against claims of exemption on the basis of personal moral scruples or unsupported fear of vaccinations, as a means of allowing certain exemptions without risking lessened effectiveness of the state's inoculation program due to the granting of a large number of exemptions, or perhaps because of the difficulties inherent in devising a legally workable definition of religion" (672 F. Supp. at 89).

k. Twenty states provide a separate philosophic exemption to school attendance vaccination laws, in addition to religious exemptions (CR Wolfe, National Immunization Program, CDC, personal communication, 2006); also see reference 32.

l. CW LeBaron, National Immunization Program, CDC, personal communication, 2005.

References

1. CDC. Ten great public health achievements—United States, 1900–1999. *MMWR* 1999;48: 241–3.
2. CDC. Impact of vaccines universally recommended for children—United States, 1900–1998. *MMWR* 1999;48:243–8.
3. Hardin G. The tragedy of the commons. *Science* 1968;162:1243–8.
4. Advisory Committee on Immunization Practices. Update: vaccine side effects, adverse reactions, contraindications, and precautions. Recommendations of the Advisory Committee on Immunization Practices (ACIP). *MMWR* 1996;45(RR12):1–35.
5. Institute of Medicine. *Vaccine Safety Research, Data Access, and Public Trust*. Washington DC: National Academies Press. 2005.
6. Robbins FC, de Quadros CA. Certification of the eradication of indigenous transmission of wild poliovirus in the Americas. *J Infect Dis* 1997;175(Suppl 1):S281–5.
7. ACIP. Poliomyelitis prevention in the United States. Updated recommendations of the Advisory Committee on Immunization Practices (ACIP). *MMWR* 2000;49(RR05): 1–22.
8. CDC. Progress toward interruption of wild poliovirus transmission—worldwide, January 2004–March 2005. *MMWR* 2005;54:408–12.

9. CDC. Recommended childhood and adolescent immunization schedule—United States, 2006. *MMWR* 2006;54:Q1–Q4.

10. CDC. National, state, and urban area vaccination coverage levels among children aged 19–35 months—United States, 2003. *MMWR* 2004;53:658–61.

11. Orenstein WA, Douglas RG, Rodewald LE, Hinman AR. Immunizations in the United States: success, structure, and stress. *Health Aff* 2005;24:599–610.

12. Section 351 of the Public Health Service Act, 42 USC §262.

13. 21 USC §321 *et seq* (Federal Food, Drug and Cosmetic Act).

14. 42 USC §300aa-1 *et seq* (National Childhood Vaccine Injury Act).

15. Orenstein WA, Hinman AR, Rodewald LE. Public health considerations—United States. In: Plotkin SA, Orenstein WA, eds. *Vaccines.* 4th ed. Philadelphia: WB Saunders, 2004; 1357–86.

16. Hinman AR, Orenstein WA, Santoli JM, Rodewald LE, Cochi SL. Vaccine shortages: history, impact, and prospects for the future. *Annu Rev Public Health* 2006;27:11.1–11.25.

17. Section 317 of the Public Health Service Act, 42 USC §247b.

18. Section 1928 of the Social Security Act, 42 USC §1396s.

19. 42 USC §§1397aa–1397jj.

20. Hinman AR, Orenstein WA, Rodewald LE. Financing immunizations in the United States. *Clin Infect Dis* 2004;38:1440–6.

21. CDC. Recommended adult immunization schedule—United States, October 2004–September 2005. *MMWR* 2004;53:Q1–Q4.

22. National Vaccine Advisory Committee. Development of Community- and State-Based Immunization Registries. Approved January 12, 1999. Available at http://www.hhs.gov/nvpo/report071100.pdf. Accessed June 10, 2006.

23. Duffy J. School vaccination: the precursor to school medical inspection. *J Hist Med Allied Sci* 1978;33:344–55.

24. Hein FV, Bauer WW. Legal requirements for immunizations: a survey of state laws and regulations. *Arch Environ Health* 1964;9:82–5.

25. Sencer DJ, Dull HB, Langmuir AD. Epidemiologic basis for eradication of measles in 1967. *Public Health Rep* 1967;82:253–6.

26. CDC. Measles—United States. *MMWR* 1977;26:101–9.

27. Orenstein WA, Hinman AR. The immunization system in the United States—the role of school immunization laws. *Vaccine* 1999;17:S19–24.

28. Middaugh JP, Zyla LD. Enforcement of school immunization law in Alaska. *JAMA* 1978;239:2128–30.

29. Hinman AR. A new US initiative in childhood immunization. *Bull Pan Am Health Organ* 1979;13:169–76.

30. CDC. Measles and school immunization requirements—United States. *MMWR* 1978;27: 303–4.

31. Robbins KB, Brandling-Bennett D, Hinman AR. Low measles incidence: association with enforcement of school immunization laws. *Am J Public Health* 1981;71:270–4.

32. Hinman AR. Overview of court challenges of vaccine exemptions. In: *Proceedings of the 39th National Immunization Conference.* Atlanta: US Department of Health and Human Services, CDC, 2005. Available at http://cdc.confex.com/cdc/nic2005/techprogram/paper_8761.htm. Accessed June 10, 2006.

33. National Vaccine Advisory Committee. The measles epidemic: the problems, barriers, and recommendations. *JAMA* 1991;266:1547–52.

34. Task Force on Community Preventive Services. Recommendations regarding interventions to improve vaccination coverage in children, adolescents, and adults. *Am J Prev Med* 2000;18(1S):92–6.

35. CDC. *State Immunization Requirements*. Atlanta: US Department of Health, Education, and Welfare, Public Health Service, CDC, 1983.

36. *Jacobson v Massachusetts*, 197 US 11, 25 S Ct 358 (1905).

37. *Zucht v King*, 260 US 174, 43 S Ct 24 (1922).

38. *Maricopa County Health Dept v Harmon*, 156 Ariz 161, 750 P 2d 1364 (Ariz Ct App 1987).

39. *Prince v Massachusetts*, 321 US 158, 64 S Ct 438 (1944).

40. Hinman AR. How should physicians and nurses deal with people who do not want immunizations? *Can J Public Health* 2000;91:248–51.

41. Salmon DA, Haber M, Gangarosa EJ, et al. Health consequences of religious and philosophical exemptions from immunization laws: individual and societal risk of measles. *JAMA* 1999;282:47–53.

42. Feiken DR, Lezotte DC, Hamman RF, et al. Individual and community risks of measles and pertussis associated with personal exemptions to immunization. *JAMA* 2000;284:3145–50.

43. Rota JS, Salmon DA, Rodewald LE, et al. Processes for obtaining nonmedical exemptions to state immunization laws. *Am J Public Health* 2001;91:645–8.

44. Salmon DA, Omer SB, Moulton LH, et al. Exemptions to school immunization requirements: the role of school-level requirements, policies, and procedures. *Am J Public Health* 2005;95:436–40.

45. Santoli JM, Hinman AR. Nonmedical exemptions to state immunization laws [letter]. *Am J Public Health* 2002;92:8.

46. *Cantwell v Connecticut,* 310 US 296, 303–4, 60 S Ct 900, 903 (1940).

47. *Sherbert v Verner*, 374 US 398, 83 S Ct 1790 (1963).

48. *Wisconsin v Yoder*, 406 US 205, 92 S Ct 1526 (1972).

49. 374 US at 402–03, 83 S Ct at 1793.

50. 406 US at 229–30, 233–34, 92 S Ct at 1540–42.

51. *Wright v DeWitt School District*, 238 Ark 906, 385 SW 2d 644 (Ark 1965).

52. *Employment Div, Dept of Human Resources of Oregon v Smith*, 494 US 872, 110 S Ct 1595 (1990).

53. 42 USC §§2000bb–2000bb-4 (Religious Freedom Restoration Act of 1993).

54. *City of Boerne v Flores*, 521 US 507, 117 S Ct 2157 (1997).

55. *Brown v Stone*, 378 So 2d 218 (Miss 1979), *cert denied* 449 US 887 (1980).

56. *Lemon v Kurtzman*, 403 US 602, 91 S Ct 2105 (1971).

57. *Sherr v Northport-East Northport Union Free School District*, 672 F Supp 81 (EDNY 1987).

58. *McCarthy v Boozman,* 212 F Supp 2d 945 (WD Ark 2002), *appeal dismissed as moot by McCarthy v Ozark School District*, 359 F 3d 1029 (8th Cir 2004).

59. *Boone v Boozman,* 217 F Supp 2d 938 (ED Ark 2002), *appeal dismissed as moot by McCarthy v Ozark School District*, 359 F 3d 1029 (8th Cir 2004).

60. NY Public Health Law, §2164, Subsection 9.

61. *Berg v Glen Cove City School District*, 853 F Supp 651 (EDNY 1994).

62. *Turner v Liverpool Central School*, 186 F Supp 2d 187 (NDNY 2002).

63. *United States v Seeger*, 380 US 163, 85 S Ct 850 (1965).

64. *Welsh v United States*, 398 US 333, 90 S Ct 1792 (1970).

65. *Mason v General Brown Central School District*, 851 F 2d 47 (2d Cir 1988).

66. *Schloendorff v Society of New York Hospital*, 211 NY 125, 129, 105 NE 92, 93 (NY 1914).

67. *Roe v Wade*, 410 US 113, 93 S Ct 705 (1973).

68. *Cruzan v Director, Missouri Dept of Health*, 497 US 261, 278, 110 S Ct 2841, 2851 (1990).

69. Averhoff F, Linton L, Peddecord KM, et al. A middle school immunization law rapidly and substantially increases immunization coverage among adolescents. *Am J Public Health* 2004;94:978–4.

70. World Health Organization/Department of Vaccines and Biologicals. *Hepatitis B Immunization*. Geneva: World Health Organization, October 2001. Available at http://www.who.int/vaccines-documents/DocsPDF01/www598.pdf. Accessed January 12, 2006.

71. World Health Organization. *Fact Sheet No. 204: Hepatitis B*. Geneva: World Health Organization, October 2000. Available at http://www.who.int/mediacentre/factsheets/fs204/en/. Accessed January 12, 2006.

72. Hinman AR. The pertussis vaccine controversy. *Public Health Rep* 1984;99:255–9.

73. Institute of Medicine. *Measles-Mumps-Rubella Vaccine and Autism. Report by the Immunization Safety Review Committee, Institute of Medicine*. Washington, DC: National Academy Press, 2001.

74. Institute of Medicine. *Immunization Safety Review: Vaccines and Autism. Report by the Immunization Safety Review Committee, Institute of Medicine*. Washington, DC: National Academy Press, 2004.

75. CDC. Withdrawal of rotavirus vaccine recommendation. *MMWR* 1999;48:1007.

76. Ark Code Ann §6-18-702.

77. CDC. Measles—United States, 2000. *MMWR* 2002;51:120–3.

78. CDC. Import-associated measles outbreak—Indiana, May–June 2005. *MMWR* 2005;54:1073–5.

79. World Health Organization (WHO)/United Nations Children's Fund (UNICEF). Review of National Immunization Coverage, 1980–2003. United Kingdom, August 2004. Available at http://www.who.int/immunization_monitoring/en/globalsummary/countryprofileselect.cfm. Accessed November 5, 2005.

80. Jansen VAA, Stollenwer N, Jensen HJ, et al. Measles outbreaks in a population with declining vaccine uptake. *Science* 2003;301:804.

Chapter 15

CONTROL OF FOODBORNE DISEASES

Leslie Kux,* Jeremy Sobel,*
and Kevin M. Fain*

Successes in controlling foodborne diseases, due in large part to public health laws, ranks among the great achievements of public health during the past 100 years. At the beginning of the 20th century, infectious foodborne diseases, including typhoid fever, tuberculosis, botulism, and scarlet fever, were leading causes of mortality in the United States. The passage of the Pure Food and Drug Act and the Meat Inspection Act in 1906 signified the government's new role in ensuring the safety of the nation's food supply. During the next half-century, implementation of various food-safety laws and related advances in science and technology resulted in new food-protection measures, such as milk pasteurization and the inspection and improved sanitization of slaughter plants, canneries, and other processing factories. These measures, along with better care of farm animals and improved living standards and personal hygiene, dramatically decreased the societal costs of foodborne diseases. In 1900, the incidence of typhoid fever in the U.S. population was about 100 per 100,000 persons; by 1950, it had decreased to 1.7 per 100,000 persons.[1]

From 1950 to 2000, food-safety laws, scientific understanding, and technologic capabilities continued to evolve. Despite these improvements, foodborne diseases continue to significantly burden the United States at the beginning of the 21st century. Approximately 76 million cases of foodborne illness occur each year in the United States, including 323,000 hospitalizations and 5200 deaths. The economic

*The findings and conclusions in this chapter are those of the author(s) and do not necessarily represent the views of the U.S. Department of Health and Human Services, the Centers for Disease Control and Prevention, or the Food and Drug Administration.

361

cost may be as high as $24 billion per year.[2] Since the terrorist attacks of September 11, 2001, attention has focused on whether terrorists could perpetrate contamination of food and on ways to reduce such a threat. This focus on possible intentional contamination adds a new dimension to food-safety efforts, which previously aimed to avoid unintentional contamination.

Government agencies at the federal, state, and local levels are charged with applying food-safety laws. These agencies generally fall within two distinct categories: public health nonregulatory agencies (i.e., public health agencies) and food-safety regulatory agencies (i.e., regulatory agencies). Public health agencies usually are responsible for disease control through surveillance and investigation of individual cases of illness and outbreaks of disease and with scientific research into the host- and pathogen-specific risk factors for foodborne diseases. Regulatory agencies usually are responsible for issuing and enforcing food-safety requirements with respect to the processors and handlers of food; by ensuring the safety of the nation's food supply, regulatory agencies also are responsible for protecting the public health.

However, the specific duties and responsibilities of public health and regulatory agencies differ because of their respective enabling statutes and legal authorities. The duties of public health agencies generally focus on human illness resulting from foodborne pathogens. By contrast, the duties of regulatory agencies generally focus on the behavior of the regulated entities and on the food products themselves.

Despite these differences in duties and responsibilities, the goals of public health and regulatory agencies complement each other. Public health officials use surveillance reports of foodborne illness from physicians and laboratories to identify and investigate specific cases and outbreaks of illness. These investigations aim to identify a contaminated food so it can be removed from circulation. Additionally, public health officials may identify unsafe practices that allowed the contamination at various stages of the human food chain, from the farm to the dinner table, and suggest ways to correct these practices. Regulatory agencies promulgate and enforce regulations that aim to ensure the safety of food along the extremely complex human food chain, which includes farms, animals and their feed, slaughterhouses, packing and processing plants, transport vehicles, storage and retail facilities, and commercial food establishments. Ensuring compliance includes inspection of facilities and testing of product. In turn, surveillance by public health agencies for human illness and outbreaks then indicates whether these regulations accomplish their intended purpose of reducing disease. Rapid changes in the food supply constantly produce new modes of contamination, which require vigilant disease surveillance and investigation and frequent adjustment of the regulatory framework.[3]

As with all laws, public health law governing the prevention of foodborne disease is shaped by the political process. Participants in this process include the agricultural sector, the food industry, public interest and consumer groups, and academic and professional health associations. Not surprisingly, the promulgation, application, and interpretation of food-safety laws reflect the interplay between expert scientific opinion and the goals of various political interests. Additionally, coordination of food-safety activities between government agencies at the federal, state, and local levels shapes the application of these laws to specific settings, such as outbreak investigations. The jurisdictions of both public health and regulatory food-safety agencies intersect at times, and the division of authority at these intersections may be subject to interpretation.

Federal, state, and local regulatory and nonregulatory agencies face significant challenges in ensuring food safety because of the complexity of the scientific and political issues that shape food-safety laws, as well as the logistical difficulties in quickly and effectively investigating outbreaks. To the extent that these agencies can interpret and apply their relevant authorities collaboratively, their efforts to protect public health will be optimized, particularly in the context of specific outbreak investigations.

Legal Authorities

Various federal, state, and local authorities implement the statutes, regulations, and codes that govern food safety.

Federal Authorities

At the national level, agencies charged with ensuring the safety of the nation's food supply include the Food and Drug Administration (FDA) and the Centers for Disease Control and Prevention (CDC), both within the U.S. Department of Health and Human Services; the U.S. Department of Agriculture (USDA); and the U.S. Environmental Protection Agency (EPA). These agencies together administer the following food-safety laws: the Federal Food, Drug, and Cosmetic Act (FFDCA);[4] the Public Health Service Act;[5] the Federal Meat Inspection Act;[6] the Poultry Products Inspection Act;[7] the Egg Products Inspection Act;[8] and the Federal Insecticide, Fungicide, and Rodenticide Act.[9] FDA, USDA, and EPA exercise their authority primarily as food-safety regulatory agencies; CDC exercises its authority primarily as a public health nonregulatory agency.

These federal regulatory agencies exercise their authority over food safety at three general stages along the farm-to-table continuum: on the farm itself, during subsequent processing of the food, and at distribution (Table 15-1). On the farm, FDA has authority over the safety of food, feed, and animals, including live food animals (e.g., cattle) before slaughter. USDA's Animal and Plant Health Inspection Service (APHIS) has the authority to protect plant and animal health on the farm and to ensure the safety of animal vaccines. EPA has authority over pesticide use on the farm.

FDA has authority over all food processing, except the slaughter and processing of meat and poultry products from domesticated animals and certain egg products, over which USDA's Food Safety Inspection Service (FSIS) exercises jurisdiction. Thus, FDA and USDA both may have authority over a processing plant if it makes both meat or poultry or non-meat or non-poultry products. For example, FDA inspects the cheese pizza operations at a facility, and FSIS inspects the pepperoni pizza operations. Furthermore, EPA sets limits for pesticide residues in food (so-called "tolerances"), which FDA and USDA then enforce. Additionally, under the Agricultural Marketing Act, both USDA and the Department of Commerce run fee-for-service inspection programs for food quality (such as the "Grade A" rankings) at

TABLE 15-1 Federal Regulatory Agencies Involved with Food-Safety Protection, by Stages of Jurisdictional Responsibility on the Farm-to-Table Continuum

Regulatory Agency	Farm	Slaughter	Processing	Labeling	Transport	Storage	Retail
Food Safety Inspection Service (FSIS)		✓ (meat, poultry)	✓ (meat, poultry)	✓	✓	✓	✓
Food and Drug Administration (FDA)	✓	✓ (seafood, game)	✓	✓	✓	✓	✓
Animal and Plant Health Inspection Service (APHIS): animal health	✓						
Environmental Protection Agency (EPA): pesticide use	✓						

processing facilities.[10] At the post-processing stage, FDA has authority over labeling, transportation, storage, and retail sale of all food. When meat, poultry, or egg products are involved, however, FDA defers to USDA on these matters.[11]

These agencies exercise their food-safety authority primarily by inspecting facilities (and, on some occasion, farms) involved in the production and distribution of food products, as well as approving substances and establishing tolerances for use in food (such as pesticides by EPA and "food additives" and "new animal drugs" by FDA). These inspections allow the agency to determine whether the farm or facility, as well as the food product at issue, complies with applicable legal requirements. These inspections can focus on the product itself by sampling and testing for foodborne pathogens (when such tests are available).

In the arena of foodborne disease, CDC functions as an expert scientific agency, providing consultative support to state health departments. CDC exercises its authority as a public health agency by monitoring the number and causes of various types of foodborne diseases in the United States using data submitted voluntarily by state health departments; by assisting, on request, state health departments investigating outbreaks of disease in humans; and by making recommendations for disease prevention. Other than the rarely exercised authority to quarantine immigrants with communicable diseases, CDC does not exercise regulatory authority, particularly with respect to farm, facilities, and food product. CDC investigates disease outbreaks, including acquisition of records of human illness, at the request of the states. To exercise effectively its surveillance and investigation authority, CDC relies on the cooperation of state and local health agencies to provide data on human illness and to invite CDC to conduct specific investigations. In practice, in an outbreak affecting resident of several states, CDC plays an indispensable role in coordinating the investigation and analyzing sand interpreting the data needed to guide public health action, including regulatory action.

CDC also has authority over cruise ships. This authority is governed by the Public Health Service Act (42 U.S.C. §264. Quarantine and Inspection—Regulations to control communicable diseases), which permit the taking of measures necessary to prevent the introduction, transmission, and spread of communicable diseases into the United States from a foreign country. Regulations promulgated to carry out these duties authorize the Public Health Service to conduct sanitary inspections on carriers traveling to U.S. ports from foreign areas (42 C.F.R. §71.41. General Provisions, Foreign Quarantine Regulations). CDC and the cruise ship industry collaboratively have developed a manual of procedures for prevention and monitoring of foodborne diseases and other sanitary concerns that exceeds the requirements of law, and the industry voluntarily complies with these standards.[12]

State and Local Authorities

State and local agencies also play an important role in protecting the nation's food supply. These agencies, both regulatory and public health, share numerous responsibilities with the above-described federal agencies in exercising food-safety authority. For example, numerous states have laws governing the processing and distribution of food products that are similar to laws administered by FDA and FSIS,[13] and state officials conduct inspections and sampling. Furthermore, as noted above, although FDA has jurisdiction over restaurants, groceries, and other retail establishments, it generally defers to state and local agencies to enforce their own requirements through inspections.

FDA publishes a model food code and encourages state and local governments to adopt it. The "Food Code" is developed by the Conference on Food Protection, which comprises representatives from federal agencies, state and local governments, industry, and academia.[14] FDA also participates in two other cooperative programs that rely on state and local health agencies: one for Grade A milk[15] and one for molluscan shellfish.[16] Finally, unlike CDC, state and local public health agencies exercise the authority to collect information about ill persons for disease surveillance and to directly investigate outbreaks of illness in humans along the farm-to-table continuum, from interviewing patients to inspecting facilities.[a] Under the health codes of same states, the state health department can seize food that threatens human health.[17]

FDA as an Example of a Food-Safety Regulatory Agency

An analysis of FDA's regulatory authority provides a useful framework in considering relevant legal issues facing federal, state, and local food-safety agencies. FDA is charged with implementing the FFDCA, as well as various parts of other statutes, such as the Public Health Service Act. The FFDCA is the primary legislation by which FDA exercises authority over food, and the statute sets forth applicable standards for food safety. (USDA operates under different statutes and therefore has a different inspection framework and operating culture.) The FFDCA 21 U.S.C. §342 defines certain categories of food as "adulterated," and 21 U.S.C. §331 sets forth "prohibited acts." Furthermore, 21 U.S.C. §331(a) prohibits the introduction of adulterated food into interstate commerce, and 21 U.S.C. §331(k) prohibits any act that results in the adulteration of food while it is held for sale after shipment in interstate commerce. These two provisions, working together, cover the stages of the farm-to-table continuum from the food producer to the retailer. However, the statute requires interstate commerce for FDA to exercise jurisdiction. This requirement supplements the interstate commerce requirement of the U.S. Constitution, which limits all federal regulatory agencies' jurisdiction.[18] Food produced, distributed, and eaten only within one state does not, therefore, fall under FDA's jurisdiction pursuant to the FFDCA.

Food is deemed "adulterated" under 21 U.S.C. §342(a)(1) if it "bears or contains any poisonous or deleterious substance which may render it injurious to health." This provision applies to the presence in food of pathogens, such as *Salmonella* and *Listeria*, that cause illness in humans. Additionally, a food is deemed adulterated under 21 U.S.C. §342(a)(2) if it bears or contains a food additive, new animal drug, or pesticide chemical residue that is unapproved or above the tolerances established by FDA and EPA, respectively, as safe for use in food. Furthermore, food is deemed adulterated under 21 U.S.C. §342(a)(3) if it "consists in whole or in part of any filthy, putrid, or decomposed substance, or if it is otherwise unfit for food." This provision applies to the presence in food of excreta from rodents or insect fragments, for example. Even though the provisions discussed above focus on the condition of the food product itself, the definition of adulterated food also includes the conditions of manufacturing and handling of the food product. Food is deemed adulterated under 21 U.S.C. §342(a)(4) if "it has been prepared, packed, or held under insanitary conditions whereby it may have become contaminated with filth, or whereby it may have been rendered injurious to health." This provision applies where a food processor, retailer, or other establishment has failed, for example, to maintain a clean facility or to handle product at the proper temperatures.

If an individual or a farm or facility commits a prohibited act under 21 U.S.C. §331 with respect to a food considered adulterated under 21 U.S.C. §342, then such an act is subject to legal penalties and enforcement action under the FFDCA. These remedies allow FDA to enforce the legal requirements of those programs that it is charged by statute to administer. For example, FDA can pursue criminal action under 21 U.S.C. §333(a) against an individual or company for any violations of the FFDCA, such as the introduction by a farm or facility of food that is adulterated because of filth, contamination by a substance that may render it injurious to health, or inadequate processing and handling of food by the facility. These criminal remedies, as punitive measures, are intended to punish individuals and companies for past violative behavior.

FDA also can pursue civil remedies, such as an injunction under 21 U.S.C. §332, against individuals and companies that commit a prohibited act under 21 U.S.C. §331, such as, for example, the distribution of adulterated food. An injunction action is based on FDA's evidence of past food contamination or inadequate food handling practices at the defendant's facility. However, the goal of an injunction is forward-looking in that FDA seeks an order from a federal district court that would require a violative facility's operations to cease until FDA determines the facility, by addressing its inadequacies, is ready to resume operations. FDA pursues injunction actions when, for example, a current and definite health hazard (such as food with *Listeria*) exists; or chronic violative practices exist that, although not having produced a clear health hazard, have not yet been corrected.[19] If FDA concludes from an inspection that an immediate shutdown of the facility is warranted, then it may seek more expedient relief in the form of a preliminary injunction or temporary restraining order from a court. Thus, an injunction action is a tool FDA can wield to ensure a facility or farm does not continue to distribute adulterated food.

Additionally, FDA may pursue civil remedies with respect to the violative product itself. For example, in an injunction proceeding, FDA also may legally seek an immediate recall of product when it has concluded that such product may injure the health of consumers. Furthermore, the statute provides in 21 U.S.C. §304 for the civil remedy of seizure of an adulterated food "when introduced into or while in interstate commerce or while held for sale (whether or not the first sale) after shipment in interstate commerce." A seizure action allows FDA to remove a specific lot or lots of adulterated food from the farm-to-table continuum. A seizure action is an "in rem" proceeding against the adulterated food itself in which the U.S. Marshal's Office typically holds the product in its protective custody until the federal district court decides the outcome of the case and the product's disposition. The applicable rules of procedure provide for individuals with any property interest in the food, known as "claimants," to enter the case against the government and argue for the release of the goods.[20] Typically, if the court rules that the food is "adulterated," then the court will order destruction of the food.[21] In addition, under the authority added to the FFDCA by the Public Health Security and Bioterrorism Preparedness Act of 2002 (BT Act) (21 U.S.C. §334[h]),[22] FDA can detain food by administrative order for a short time (not more that 30 days), without going to court. However, this administrative detention authority does not apply to all adulterated food; FDA can administratively detain food only when FDA has credible evidence indicating the food threatens serious adverse health consequences or death to humans or animals. Table 15-2 provides an overview of FDA's and FSIS's compliance and enforcement tools.

State agencies are not limited by the jurisdiction requirement of the FFDCA for interstate commerce. Furthermore, in some instances, the enforcement tools available to the states can be swifter, even than FDA's expanded authority under the 2002 BT Act. For example, the state law of Florida authorizes its food-safety agencies to issue temporary "stop-sale" orders and embargos using less stringent standards than those imposed on FDA by the BT Act.[17,23]

In applying the statutory adulteration standard, FDA has implemented regulations that detail the legal requirements for facilities that process foods. Specifically, the regulations at 21 C.F.R. Part 110 specify the requirements of "current good manufacturing practice" in manufacturing, packing, and holding human food. The provisions of this regulation require, among other things, that food facilities maintain clean equipment and grounds and ensure their employees maintain good sanitation practices.[24]

Additionally, FDA has enacted specific regulations for the seafood industry at 21 C.F.R. Part 123. The core of these regulations requires each seafood firm to maintain and follow a Hazard Analysis and Critical Control Point Plan (HACCP) to ensure that seafood is held, processed, and shipped at proper temperatures and times to prevent contamination by food pathogens.[25]

A firm must identify in its HACCP the relevant food-safety hazards that are reasonably likely to occur during the storage, processing, and shipping of its product and identify the "critical control points" designed to control these hazards that could be introduced in the processing plant environment. Furthermore, the firm must identify the "critical limits" required at these points to prevent contamination by food pathogens and to monitor production for these limits.[26] For example, the processors of ready-to-eat crabmeat typically will set specific minimum and/or maximum times and temperatures for the cooking and handling of the product. Finally, FDA has enacted similar regulations with respect to specific high-risk food products, such as juice,[27] low-acid canned foods,[28] and acidified food.[29]

FDA also has enacted procedures and standards for the recall of adulterated product at 21 C.F.R. Part 7. A recall is advantageous to FDA because it allows the agency to ensure the immediate withdrawal of a dangerous food from the marketplace without taking the various legal steps and procedures for a court-ordered seizure. Although these regulations allow FDA to request the immediate recall of a food product with a pathogen, recall ultimately is voluntary on the part of the firm (except with respect to infant formula under 21 U.S.C. 350a[e]). However, FDA may notify the public of problems, which can persuade firms to recall product by focusing public scrutiny on the firm's response.[30]

FDA periodically inspects regulated facilities to ensure they follow the relevant statutory and regulatory requirements.[31] Typically, FDA initiates these inspections

TABLE 15-2   Overview of Food and Drug Administration (FDA) and Food Safety Inspection Service (FSIS) Compliance and Authorities

Authority	FDA*	FSIS*
Registration	§350d	§643; §460(c), (e)
Facility Inspection	§374	§455; §603-06, 608; §1034
Required Premarket Inspection	N/A	§455; §603-06, 608; §1034
Withdrawal of Inspection	N/A	§467(a); §671; §1047
Records Inspection	§350c	§460(b); §642; §1040
Administrative Detention	§334(h)	§467a; §672; §1048
Mandatory Recall	§350a(e) (infant formula)	N/A
Judicial Seizure	§334	§467b; §673; §1049
Injunction	§332	§467c; §674; §1050
Prosecution	§333	§461; §676; §1041
Debarment (prohibits from engaging in debarred activity)	§335a(b)(3) (importing food)	N/A
Civil Money Penalties	§333(f)(2) (pesticide residue violations)	N/A
Imports	§381	§466; §620; §1046

* All references are to Title 21 of the United States Code.

as part of its routine, risk-based inspection program rather than by the discovery of human illness from pathogens in food handled or processed by the facility. Given its limited resources, FDA focuses its food-inspection resources on high-risk establishments, aiming to inspect these establishments once a year.[32] Other facilities are inspected much less frequently. (By contrast, for the food under FSIS jurisdiction, FSIS inspectors must be present when slaughter or processing facilities are operating.) During inspections, FDA investigators observe and record the processing and handling of food products and take product and environmental samples to be tested by FDA laboratories for filth and pathogens. If a facility fails to maintain adequate sanitary conditions at the plant or if samples of product test positive for filth or pathogens, then FDA can consider its options for bringing enforcement actions for civil or criminal relief. FDA also may request a firm immediately recall violative product.

Increasingly, our food is produced not just domestically but also in every corner of the world. Although imported food is in "interstate commerce" under 21 U.S.C. §321(b), the FFDCA also contains provisions, under 21 U.S.C. §381(a), that authorize FDA, in conjunction with Customs and Border Protection in the Department of Homeland Security, to "refuse admission" to food imports that "appear, based on physical examination or otherwise," to be adulterated or produced under insanitary conditions. This evidentiary standard, the "appearance" standard, is much lower than the standard that applies in seizures. The phrase "based on physical examination or otherwise" allows FDA to rely on a broad range of evidence when taking import actions, including sample results, product exams, and product or firm's history. The refusal process is an informal administrative process set out both in 21 U.S.C. §381 and in FDA's regulations at 21 C.F.R. Part 1, Subpart E. The lower standard and streamlined administrative process allows FDA to deal expeditiously with an ever-increasing volume of imported products.

Legal Issues and Controversies

Many of the legal issues and controversies in the realm of food safety have arisen in the context of enforcement actions brought by regulatory agencies against members of industry or their product. FDA, in particular, brings numerous seizure actions each year against adulterated food, including product that has tested positive for a pathogen, as well as injunction actions against food processors that distribute adulterated food, under 21 U.S.C. §342(a)(1), and fail to follow good sanitary practices, under 21 U.S.C. §342(a)(4). FDA has faced two general types of challenges in these actions: factual and legal.

First, claimants in seizure actions and defendants in injunction actions have challenged the adequacy of FDA's sampling and testing methods in detecting the pathogen or the accuracy of its inspectional findings at the facility in question. Thus, FDA has developed internal guidance for its investigators in collecting samples of food, documenting the chain of custody from the time of collection to the time of testing, and recording the testing of product and the results.[33] Additionally, FDA ensures that the tests used at its regional laboratories are accepted throughout the scientific community as valid methods.[34] These procedures help ensure the accuracy and validity of the test results in each individual case, as well as the sufficiency of evidence under the Federal Rules of Civil Procedure. Furthermore, these procedures ensure that FDA handles the sampling and testing uniformly across the food industry.

While conducting an inspection, an FDA investigator accompanies a responsible individual at the facility in observing all of the relevant manufacturing and processing functions.[35] The investigator takes detailed notes and photographs of the sanitary conditions. At the conclusion of the inspection, the investigator notes all observed violations of good manufacturing practices at the facility, such as failure to maintain clean equipment or lack of controls to ensure adequate cooking time and temperature. The investigator lists these violations in a written report and reviews them with the facility's responsible individual, who then verifies and signs the report.[36] These steps help ensure FDA is prepared to support the facts of its cases with sufficient evidence.

Second, claimants in seizure actions and defendants in injunction actions often challenge whether FDA's inspection findings and test results, even if accurate and valid, actually show the food in question is adulterated under the applicable legal standard. The courts have considered many such issues related to the presence of pathogens in food and the insanitary conditions at food facilities. For example, courts have considered the scope of 21 U.S.C. §342(a)(1) in defining an adulterated food as a "poisonous or deleterious substance which may render it injurious to health." Courts have held specifically that the presence of a pathogen, such as *Salmonella*, in a food product satisfies this definition, even though the pathogen's harmful effects can be avoided by proper cooking and handling.[37,38] To satisfy this legal standard, courts have found that FDA does not have to identify persons who have become sick as a result of eating the contaminated product at issue.[39]

Furthermore, courts have considered the proof required by FDA to bring an adulteration claim under 21 U.S.C. §342(a)(4) on the basis of its findings of insanitary conditions at a facility. Courts have held that FDA is not required to show that any individual food product would be injurious to health (i.e., by the presence of a contaminant, such as *Salmonella*). Instead, FDA must show only that the insanitary conditions at a facility are such that they are reasonably likely to result in the production of contaminated food product.[40–42] This standard, by placing the burden on the food processor to maintain sanitary conditions at all stages and locations of production, provides greater protection for the consumer in preventing the reasonable possibility of contamination. By shifting the focus of inquiry from specific product test results to the general conditions at a plant, this statutory standard allows FDA to bring enforcement actions in circumstances where a real probability exists of future harm to the consumer but no specific evidence of contamination or incidences of human illness have been documented. This legal requirement also helps FDA to protect the public health because, as a practical matter, the agency has neither the resources nor the time to test for a pathogen a representative sample of every product lot that is distributed each day from a food facility. This legal analysis concerning FDA's adulteration standard demonstrates that the agency's primary focus and authority is preventing contamination of food product before distribution. Thus, a significant part of FDA's food-safety programs are based on its inspection of facilities and testing of product to determine industry compliance with the relevant legal standards applicable to that facility and product. Of course, the effectiveness of the statute in protecting the public depends on the compliance by industry and the efficiency and resources of FDA's enforcement programs. The effectiveness of the public health system in investigating and determining the causes of foodborne disease outbreaks is a key to identify circumstances in which the statutes themselves or their enforcement still permit food contamination and require updating.[43–45]

FDA has adopted this forward-looking approach in its HACCP regulations, as illustrated in the regulations governing seafood safety. These regulations, 21 C.F.R. Part 123, as described briefly above, additionally are intended to protect consumers by requiring seafood facilities to establish written critical control points in a HACCP for the various steps in processing (such as cooking, preparing, and packing) and to record the relevant critical control point measurements (such as actual times and temperatures) for each batch of product at the various stages. Failure to follow these HACCP requirements, in itself, constitutes an insanitary condition that causes the food to be adulterated under 21 U.S.C. §342(a)(4).[46] USDA also has implemented similar regulations requiring an HACCP for meat packers, with dramatic results.[47] However, parts of FSIS's implementation of its HACCP program have been challenged in court and overturned.[b]

During FDA inspections under the HACCP program, the investigator reviews the records to ensure compliance with the firm's HACCP. HACCP regulations ease the burden on the regulatory agency to conduct inspections because the burden lies on the individual firm to ensure its food products will not become contaminated by following its individual HACCP. FDA initiates injunction proceedings against seafood firms that have repeatedly failed to follow such plans.[48]

Practice Considerations

Using Epidemiologic Data as the Basis for Regulatory Actions

In the outbreak setting, an epidemiologic investigation can provide strong scientific evidence linking illness to a particular food.[49] The strength of the association, in terms of its probability of being true and not a statistical fluke, is quantifiable. Epidemiologic analysis involves assessment of the various possible exposures to a pathogen in individual patients in an outbreak. Laboratory results sometimes can confirm such an epidemiologic association between an exposure and a disease. For example, in an outbreak investigation, the isolation of indistinguishable pathogens from a patient sample and from an implicated food confirms the statistical association.[43,50–55] However, for several reasons, the agent responsible for an outbreak may not be isolated from or identified in the implicated food. Some organisms and toxins are difficult or impossible to detect in food. Agents may have been reduced or eliminated from food samples by freezing, temperature abuse, or overgrowth by other microorganisms. In many outbreaks, samples of implicated foods no longer exist.

If epidemiologic data obtained from the study of an illness in humans implicate a specific type of food or food producer, then food-safety regulatory agencies can initiate or participate in a "traceback" investigation. Successful tracebacks typically depend on an epidemiologic assessment of traceback data to optimally link the findings of human illness with food distributor records and plant or farm evaluation. Public health agency epidemiologists and regulatory agency investigators at this stage often negotiate informally the details of their interaction.

In some outbreak investigations, human illness still may be occurring when epidemiologic methods identify a suspected food, so quick public health action is necessary to end the outbreak. Such action may entail issuing a press release that warns the public to avoid ingesting a specific food, requesting a product recall, or initiating legal action to shut down a production facility. Strong epidemiologic data that implicate a contaminated food vehicle can be the basis for rapid, targeted, and carefully applied control measures to prevent further illness and death, even without laboratory confirmation.

For example, in 1997, an outbreak of *Escherichia coli* O157:H7 infections caused 70 illnesses, including 14 cases of hemolytic uremic syndrome and 1 death. Epidemiologic data strongly linked these illnesses with ingestion of a particular brand of unpasteurized apple juice. State, local, and CDC investigators concluded that the most effective response would be to warn the public and recall the implicated juice. Because of FDA's authority in regulating food products, such as the juice at issue, the investigators presented their findings and conclusion to FDA staff in an emergency session. FDA then issued public notice of the implicated apple juice and requested the manufacturer immediately recall all lots of the juice. The manufacturer complied with FDA's request. Later, laboratory tests confirmed the epidemiologic findings by isolating indistinguishable strains of *E. coli* O157:H7 in patient samples and in the implicated juice. This sequence of events demonstrates successful regulatory action based on the use of epidemiologic data.[43] CDC's and FDA's prompt actions in responding to the outbreak probably prevented additional cases of illness and possibly deaths. In the longer term, the outcome of this and a series of similar investigations resulted in more rigorous regulation of unpasteurized juice production and retail, with subsequent elimination of disease outbreaks from fruit juices in recent years.[c] This illustrates the cycle of disease surveillance, outbreak detection, implementation of acute and longer-term regulatory control measures and demonstrates the interventions' effectiveness through ongoing disease surveillance.

However, despite the success of such multiple agency efforts, the potential remains for inefficiency when public health and regulatory agencies act on epidemiologic data in exigent circumstances. Such inefficiency is caused, in large part, by the legal and administrative divisions of authority between public health and regulatory agencies for the pursuit of outbreak investigations, particularly for the use of epidemiologic data. As a result of these limitations and the exigency of circumstances, government officials at various agencies often must implement ad hoc procedures in coordinating each individual outbreak investigation and the use of epidemiologic data. Both public health and regulatory agencies might be able to act more quickly and coordinate more effectively their responses if these agencies would collaborate prospectively in developing specific guidelines for the shared use of epidemiologic data in certain types of investigations.

Coordinating Outbreak and Traceback Investigations

In an outbreak of foodborne disease, a traceback investigation attempts to determine the source of the disease by tracking the food vehicle to its origins to determine the source of contamination. Investigators often review the records of vendors, shippers, producers, and processors involved in handling the implicated food and may inspect their facilities. These activities are within the jurisdiction of local, state, and federal government regulatory agencies that exercise regulatory authority over the particular industries. Because the traceback is often an integral part of the outbreak investigation, epidemiologists can and should participate in the traceback investigation.

Analysis of the epidemiologic data, combined with the results of the traceback and environmental investigation, can allow the investigators to determine where contamination is likely to have occurred at the distributor, processing facility, or farm. Relevant information gathered in the course of a traceback investigation includes the volume of food produced at a facility or farm and the area in which it was distributed; other foods that might contain the contaminated ingredient of a multi-ingredient food; the growth, production, or transportation stages at which contamination may have occurred; and the specific practice or circumstance that allowed for contamination. For example, in an investigation of a multistate outbreak of *Salmonella* serotype Agona from toasted oats cereal, traceback was facilitated by epidemiologists determining the dates of production of contaminated cereal from cereal boxes collected at patients' homes.[51] These findings are relevant both to control the acute outbreak and to identify and ultimately change farming, production, or transport processes that allowed for food contamination.[56]

Because of the need to provide continuity between the epidemiologic data and the product information, the respective responsibilities of public health and regulatory agencies overlap. Agencies often handle this overlap by making ad hoc arrangements in each circumstance. Public health epidemiologists may be invited to accompany regulatory investigators in the field or go under the authority of state agencies. Otherwise, they must await a written report from the regulatory agency, which typically is issued months after the investigation and may not address all their concerns. Optimally, epidemiologists from either the public health or regulatory agency participate personally and directly in the traceback investigation. One approach to maximize the effectiveness of such outbreak investigations in controlling foodborne diseases would be to establish a standing group of investigators from regulatory agencies whose principal responsibility is outbreak investigation to work with public health epidemiologists on traceback investigations.

Sharing Information about Products and Producers among Investigators

Public health officials at CDC and state and local health departments must know the identity and brand names of suspected foods to confirm or dismiss the role of those foods in an outbreak investigation. For example, in investigating an outbreak in which ground meat is suspected, health officials often will identify stores at which patients purchased meat and then may request the help of regulatory agencies to assist in tracing the implicated meat to the distributor(s) and the processor. Brand name identities are necessary to determine whether the implicated meat indeed came from the same source and, if so, to focus the investigation on implicating or excluding that particular source as the cause of the outbreak. Public health officials have a strong incentive not to publicly identify prematurely any foods generically or by brand name because this identification might bias members of the public being questioned during the investigation about foods they ate, resulting in the failure to reach scientifically valid results. Regulatory agencies frequently obtain production records, distribution information, and other documents related to food products from members of industry. These agencies are not generally legally prohibited from disclosing the identity of products in communicating with other federal agencies during an outbreak investigation, although such disclosure usually is conditioned on the satisfaction of certain requirements.

On the other hand, these regulatory agencies are limited by specific confidentiality rules that prohibit them from sharing certain other types of information with officials from other agencies, such as a public health agency, who are not bound by these rules.[57] For example, the FFDCA and other laws generally prohibit FDA from disclosing trade secret information to the public and others, including other government agencies outside of the Department of Health and Human Services.[58–60] Furthermore, these laws prohibit FDA from disclosing confidential commercial information to state and local government agencies that fail to satisfy certain conditions.[61,62] FDA may happen to observe and record such information during its inspection of facilities, such as the method of processing a specific food, and thus may share such information with state and local public health agencies only if such conditions are satisfied. This information can be critical for public health agencies in identifying a specific source of pathogen and cause of contamination.

Similarly, the ability of public health and regulatory agencies to share information with each other may be asymmetric. Public health agencies generally are allowed, pursuant to their laws, to share any information with other agencies after removing names and other personal identifiers. Regulatory agencies, on the other hand, may be reluctant to share information that potentially constitutes part of a legal enforcement action, particularly a criminal case against an industry member. For example, in a 1999 investigation of an outbreak of *E. coli* O157:H7 in patrons of a national fast-food chain, CDC suspected that ground beef had been contaminated and requested that USDA determine the distribution of meat from the processor. USDA dispatched a large team of investigators to the meat-processing facility, where initial findings reportedly suggested a violation of law. After becoming involved in the case, USDA would not share data on its findings because of its concern with compromising evidence in a potential criminal case.[d] Similar incidents have occurred in investigations pursued by CDC and by FDA and other regulatory agencies. These scenarios illustrate different interests driving government agencies with broadly complementary, but at times divergent, missions. Public health agencies sometimes can negotiate with regulatory agencies to obtain a limited sharing of their information, but the resulting delays in reaching such agreements can compromise implementation of appropriate public health responses. More explicit authority for agencies to share such information in these circumstances could assist in the conduct of outbreak investigations.

Finally, the focus on bioterrorism since 2001 has raised new information-sharing issues. Both FDA and FSIS are assessing the food under their jurisdiction to determine how susceptible to tampering products may be at various points along the farm-to-table continuum. For obvious reasons, much of the information derived from these investigations is classified. However, classification makes sharing any information with industry difficult, even though sharing some of the information would help the food industry take steps that could make tampering with the food supply more difficult.

Laboratory Testing Issues

Another practical issue facing food-safety agencies with legal implications involves laboratory testing of food or environmental specimens and use of the results in public health investigations or enforcement actions. In the case of regulatory agencies, laboratory testing generally is conducted in U.S. government or other authorized laboratories. In the context of enforcement litigation, regulatory agencies such as FDA usually would not rely on a foreign laboratory's results because of the procedural requirements applicable to the sampling and testing of evidence, particularly when the product has not been in that agency's custody and control. In a multinational outbreak of *Salmonella* Agona in the early 1990s, a public health laboratory in the United Kingdom identified the pathogen at issue in the implicated food. FDA could not rely on the laboratory results because these findings were not from a U.S. government or other authorized laboratory.

A regulatory agency's choice of laboratory tests can affect how the test results can be used. The agency bases its choice on its goals for such testing, on the investigations themselves, and on related actions of public health agencies. For example, the finding of *Salmonella* serotype Enteritidis in eggs, poultry, or the environment at a poultry farm typically is sufficient to trigger regulatory action, regardless of whether human illness resulted. Therefore, agency laboratories in many instances do not further subtype *Salmonella* Enteritidis isolates in these samples, although such subtyping might help confirm the epidemiologic link between eggs from the farm and illness in the humans who ate them. This subtyping is important to epidemiologic investigators because the findings confirm the validity of the epidemiologic methods and may contribute to understanding of the mechanisms of contamination and transmission.

Federal Agency Regulation of Farms: Effect of Interstate Commerce Requirements

Finally, the regulatory status of farms identified as the possible source of contaminated food, where no interstate commerce is involved, represents a potential difficulty for federal agencies in outbreak investigations. If an epidemiologic investigation identifies a farm as the possible source of an outbreak, investigation of the farm would be important so any problem on the farm can be identified and corrected, and such information subsequently could be used to prevent similar contamination events on other farms. Where no interstate commerce has occurred—that is, eggs from the farm have not been shipped over state lines—jurisdiction over the farm may rest solely with the state agriculture department. The resources of some state agricultural departments, which can be politically influenced because of their contradictory dual role of both promoting and regulating agriculture, may limit their effectiveness in carrying out investigations.

In one example, epidemiologic investigation of a statewide outbreak of *Salmonella* Enteritidis infections strongly implicated eggs from a cooperative supplied by five chicken farms.[63] The state agriculture department was asked to perform microbiologic testing on the farms to confirm the source of the outbreak. A standardized, validated FDA protocol for such sampling existed; however, the state agriculture department obtained less than 5% of the number of samples specified in the FDA protocol. Tests on these samples did not detect *Salmonella*, and the state agriculture department announced that the epidemiologic findings thereby were invalidated. The subsequent discovery of interstate commerce in the suspected eggs triggered federal jurisdiction and allowed FDA to investigate and sample the farms more thoroughly, which showed heavy contamination at one of these egg farms. In another example, a commercial dairy was implicated in a multistate outbreak of *Salmonella* serotype Typhimurium infections from contaminated milk. The dairy had passed regular inspections by the state agriculture department. However, FDA inspectors then found gross violations of the sanitary code sufficient to close the dairy.[64]

Emerging issues

Implications of the Changing Locus of Outbreaks and Public Health Legal Authority

The locus of legal authority for public health agencies is at the local and state levels. This focus was specified when most foodborne disease prevention measures were local because food was produced mostly within individual states, and disease outbreaks typically occurred in small groups of people who knew each other, so the outbreaks were readily detectable. However, in the opening years of the 21st century, food-safety issues are increasingly national—and even international—because of the extensive international food trade, consolidation of food manufacturing and processing, and widespread distribution of food products. These conditions have resulted in large, diffuse outbreaks affecting people in many states and even countries. These outbreaks may be difficult to detect at the state level because the diffuse distribution of ill persons may result in initially imperceptible increases in infections.

Additionally, differences in state public health laws may impede response to foodborne disease. For example, individual states determine which diseases must be reported by laboratories and physicians and, in turn, voluntarily report these cases to CDC. Even though an estimated 27% of deaths from foodborne disease in the United States result from *Listeria monocytogenes*, this infection is not reportable in 13 states. Two large outbreaks of *L. monocytogenes* resulting from contaminated commercially produced hot dogs were detected only through collation of surveillance data from several states because cases occurred in many states with no geographic clustering and during several months.[65,66]

Another difficulty facing public health authorities is that reporting of foodborne disease outbreaks is voluntary. Although such voluntary reporting is widely practiced, no standard exists for the immediate reporting by states to CDC of outbreaks that may extend beyond one state or even beyond the national borders (suggestive features would include a large number of infected persons within a state, wide geographic distribution of cases, involvement of travelers, implication of a food imported into or exported from the involved state, or relation to a dining facility near a state border). Rapid, efficient investigation of the growing proportion of outbreaks that involve multiple states would be facilitated by uniform rapid reporting standards. As foodborne disease outbreaks become less of a local and more of a national or international phenomenon, appropriate revision of the public health legal structure should be considered. Such restructuring might be considered a public health corollary of the authority of federal regulatory agencies under the interstate Commerce Clause of their respective enabling statutes—when events affecting human health extend beyond a single state or extend to the international arena, they would fall under the jurisdiction of federal public health agencies rather than the individual states alone.

Food Disparagement Laws

Another emerging issue for the regulation of food safety involves passage of a unique class of state laws that restrict discussion of food-safety issues. These so-called food disparagement laws enacted in the 1990s in 13 states make persons legally liable for asserting that certain foods are unsafe for human consumption.[67] These laws burden critics of foods with the requirement that they demonstrate that their claims are backed by scientific data of high reliability. Thus, for several reasons, these laws are restrictive in a manner unparalleled in the United States. First, the food disparagement laws cover generic classes of products, such as "perishable foods," rather than the product of an individual enterprise. Second, the laws require the critic to demonstrate not simply good faith in his or her information but rather satisfy a uniquely high standard of proof. One of the most far-reaching of these laws is in Colorado.[68] Under its provisions, critics are subject to criminal prosecution for food disparagement. Although these laws exist in a minority of states, they exert a nationwide effect because national publishers and electronic media purveyors fear they might be sued in any such state where their publications or broadcasts are available to the public.

The best-known case involving food disparagement laws was the $10 million lawsuit by the Texans Cattlemen's Association against the television talk-show host Oprah Winfrey for her allegedly disparaging comments about hamburgers and the risk for *E. coli* O157:H7 infection.[69] Although the court dismissed the suit because the state failed to make its case under the standards of the Texas food disparagement law, the court did not question the constitutionality of the statute. Despite its seemingly favorable outcome, this litigation illustrates the dangerous potential of food disparagement laws. These laws, in effect, can allow for the organized intimidation of any perceived critics of the food industry by the filing of multimillion-dollar lawsuits for exercising what in many other forms would be considered constitutionally protected speech. This effect is likely to inhibit most critics who lack Ms. Winfrey's resources from engaging in debate. The limitation of free public discussion on general issues of food safety can inhibit the development of sound public health policy in this area. The great public debate on food safety that resulted in the passage of the Pure Food and Drug Act in 1906 was launched by Upton Sinclair's description of insanitary and poor working conditions in Chicago's meat-packing plants in *The Jungle*.[70] Oddly enough, under today's food disparagement laws, he may well have had difficulty finding a publisher.

Regulation of Food Production

Another crucial issue recently emerging for food safety involves the differences between regulation of food production at the farm and at the remaining stages of the farm-to-table continuum. Many agencies at the federal, state, and local levels generally regulate processed foods like any other consumer product subject to government regulation. Thus, these agencies view foods contaminated by pathogens essentially as defective products under their respective laws (such as under FDA's adulteration provisions). FDA inspections of facilities and food products, as well as any resulting enforcement action, place the burden on the facility and individuals to comply with the law and absorb the loss of any noncompliance. When contaminated food is defined as a defective product, that is, "adulterated" under the FFDCA, the manufacturer bears monetary losses from destruction of condemned product, shutdown of a plant, or loss of sales. Thus, this burden creates a strong incentive on regulated industries to comply with regulations and produce safe foods. Similarly, restaurants are subject to licensing, regulation, inspection, and sanctions for violations by state and local agencies.

On the other hand, farms and farm produce enjoy a different regulatory standard, particularly at the state level. At the level of the farm, contamination of animal-derived foods with organisms pathogenic to humans is often considered a "no-fault" event in which the state assumes the cost by indemnifying the farmer for financial losses and upgrading safety standards. Regular inspection, mandatory safety plans, and sanctions for farms are generally not widely employed by states in improving the safety of animal-derived foods. Agriculture in the United States, however, is increasingly characterized by industrial scale animal and produce production.[71,72] Thus, from a public health perspective, farm produce, as part of the farm-to-table continuum, should be treated under the law as a consumer product, just like processed food or a restaurant meal, and should be regulated with similar rigor.

Bioterrorism

After September 11, 2001, concern heightened about the possibility of contamination of the food supply by terrorists using chemical or biologic agents. Before 2001, food-safety laws and regulations aimed to prevent or mitigate inadvertent contamination, not secure the food supply from intentional acts of contamination. Although inadvertent contamination remains a focus, the federal government has turned its attention to food security as well. Its response has been multifaceted.[73] FDA and FSIS have been conducting threat assessments to determine the scope of the risk and ways to mitigate it. FDA and FSIS have issued food security guidance to sectors of the food industry to help industry identify steps to mitigate risk.[74–78] In the immediate aftermath of the terrorist attacks of September 2001, Congress increased FDA's funding for food safety, focusing on inspections of imported food. In addition, FDA requested, and Congress granted, new statutory tools to address food-safety risks. The new authorities contained in the BT Act update FDA's basic food-safety authorities, which had not significantly changed since 1938.

Although the BT Act contains several new food-safety provisions, none of the authority in these provisions is revolutionary: the new food-safety regulatory powers specified in the BT Act tend to be tools previously granted to FSIS for meat, poultry, and egg products or tools that FDA has with regard to other product areas it regulates (e.g., drugs and devices). The most significant provision in the BT Act includes the following: registration of food facilities with FDA; recordkeeping requirements for certain distribution records; record inspection authority for FDA; administrative detention authority for potentially harmful food; advance notice to FDA for shipments of imported food; and the authority to mark imported food indicating it has been refused admission.

Before enactment of the registration provision, the responsibility of identifying firms subject to FDA regulation rested on the agency; an individual firm was not required to make its existence known to FDA. FDA field staff compiled the agency's inventory of firms subject to FDA regulation in a given area from a variety of sources, including state inventories and phone books. The new 21 U.S.C. §350d authorizes FDA to issue regulations requiring facilities that manufacture, process, pack, or hold "food for consumption in the United States" to register with FDA. Both domestic and foreign firms must register—although the statute 21 U.S.C. §350d(b)(3) limits the foreign facilities subject to registration to those that manufacture, process, pack, or hold food that "is exported to the United States without further processing or packing outside the United States." FDA's rules implementing 21 U.S.C. §350d (which can be found at 21 C.F.R. Part 1, Subpart H) went into effect on December 12, 2004. Registration will allow FDA to compile a more complete list of domestic and foreign firms that make food for the U.S. market, and will make finding and communicating with firms in tracebacks and other emergencies faster and more effective.

Unlike FSIS, which long has had authority over record inspection and record-keeping for the foods it regulated, FDA did not have any general authority to require food manufacturing or processing firms to keep distribution records or review production records until the BT Act. FDA has issued several food-safety regulations (e.g., seafood and juice HACCP) that impose recordkeeping and record inspection requirements but otherwise has not been able to require firms to keep records and allow FDA to inspect them. The provision 21 U.S.C. §350c(a) authorizes FDA inspection of records (except at farms and restaurants) when FDA has a "reasonable belief that an article of food is adulterated and presents a threat of serious adverse health consequences or death to humans or animals. . . ." Moreover, 21 U.S.C. §350c(b) authorizes FDA to promulgate regulations requiring persons (except farms or restaurants) to keep records "to allow [FDA] to identify the immediate previous sources and the immediate subsequent recipients. . . ." FDA published a rule implementing the recordkeeping provision on December 9, 2004, which becomes effective within 12–24 months after publication, depending on business size.[79]

Maintenance of complete and readily available records can be critical to identification of the source of contaminated food in an outbreak of intentional or unintentional nature and, if rigorously implemented with proper scope, could substantially improve the ability of government to protect the population from foodborne disease. The newly granted authority to require records inspection and recordkeeping is limited, however. Under 21 U.S.C. §350c, the recordkeeping provision requires only that facilities keep records of where food comes from and where it was sent (referred to as "one up, one back"), and FDA can use the record inspection authority only when it reasonably believes a food is adulterated and presents a threat of serious adverse health consequences or death to humans or animals. The extent of the code's impact on public health will be tested in coming years. Many foodborne disease outbreak investigations have failed to identify the cause of contamination of the implicated food because of incomplete recordkeeping. Furthermore, in outbreaks of unintentional origin in which incomplete but legally permissible recordkeeping impairs identification of food lot or production unit, regulatory control action is usually limited and consequently contaminated food may remain on the market. In a bioterrorism event, inability to narrowly identify affected lots or other units of production could result in designation of entire food product lines as associated with illness. Meticulous recordkeeping allowing rapid identification of affected lots or shipments of food would allow rapid, targeted interventions that would enhance protection of the public and protect the food industry from additional economic loss.

In fiscal year 2002, FDA estimated there were 6.1 million "line entries" of food,[80,e] and the number is growing. (A "line entry" refers to a line on an invoice.) Even before the events of September 2001, attention was devoted to the safety of food imports. However, the BT Act focused particularly on imports. For example, 21 U.S.C. §381(m) provides that FDA was to promulgate regulations by December 12, 2003, to require certain information about food imports (e.g., identity of the product, manufacturer, shipper) before arrival in the United States to determine whether FDA would inspect the food or take other action. FDA's prior notice regulations can be found at

21 C.F.R. Part 1, Subpart I. Other provisions added by the BT Act also are intended to help FDA better control food imports. For example, on occasion, food that has been refused admission into the United States under 21 U.S.C. 381(a) has been offered for re-import (usually at a different port)—a practice often referred to as "port shopping." Two provisions in the BT Act address port shopping. First, 21 U.S.C. §381(n) provides that FDA may require food that has been refused to be marked "United States: Refused Entry." If notice has been provided to the importer or consignee that marking is needed and that the food presents a threat of serious adverse health consequences or death, but the refused food is not so marked, the food is "misbranded" under 21 U.S.C. §343(v) and can be seized by FDA. Second, 21 U.S.C. §342(h) provides that food that has been refused is "adulterated" unless the importer shows the food complies with the FDCA.

Conclusion

Public health and food-safety regulatory agencies face many challenges today in ensuring the safety and security of the U.S. food supply. The emergence of new pathogens and sources of transmission, the rapidly changing practices for food production and distribution, the practical difficulties in responding to foodborne disease outbreaks, and the concern about the possibility of deliberate contamination of food are issues that federal, state, and local government agencies must address in protecting the public health. These agencies rely on their scientific and administrative capabilities, within the boundary of their legal authorities, in crafting general programs and specific actions to handle these food-safety issues. As food-safety challenges evolve, so must agencies' legal authorities, along with their scientific and administrative capabilities. This dynamic has been illustrated during the last century by the evolution of laws, and scientific and administrative advancements, in response to emerging food-safety threats. This dynamic is likely to continue throughout the 21st century, as public health and food-safety regulatory agencies require new legal authorities to employ more advanced and effective scientific and administrative tools against ever-changing food-safety dangers.

Notes

a. For example, Cal. Health and Safety Code, Div. 101 (Administration of Public Health), Part 3 (Local Health Departments); Div. 102 (Vital Records and Health Statistics); Div. 104 (Environmental Health), Part 7 (Retail Food); West's Ann. Cal. Health & Safety Code (2001).

b. *Supreme Beef Processors, Inc. v. USDA*, 295 F.3d 432 (5th Cir. 2001), held that *Salmonella* in meat was not necessarily indicative of conditions in the plant and that the tense of the word "rendered" in 21 U.S.C. §601(m)(4) precluded USDA regulation of pre-existing characteristic of product that was not affected by the processor.

c. CDC, unpublished data, 2004.

d. CDC, unpublished data, 1999.

e. A "line entry" refers to a unique item (on an invoice, usually). A shipment might consists of several different products and, thus, have several different line entries.

References

1. CDC. Achievements in public health, 1900–1999: safer and healthier foods. *MMWR* 1999;48:905–13.
2. Mead P, Slutsker L, Dietz V, et al. Food-related illness and death in the United States. *Emerg Infect Dis* 1999;5:607–25.
3. Sobel J, Swerdlow DL, Parsonnet J. Is there anything safe to eat? In: Remington JS, Schwartz MN, eds. *Current Clinical Topics in Infectious Diseases*. Vol. 21. Boston: Blackwell Scientific Publications, 2001:114–3.
4. Act of June 25, 1938, Ch 675, 52 Stat 1040 (codified at 21 USC §§301–97 [2005]).
5. Act of July 1, 1944, Ch 373, 58 Stat 682 (codified at 42 USC §§201–300qq-91 [2005]).
6. Pub L 90-201, 81 Stat 584 (1967) (codified at 21 USC §§601–91 [2005]).
7. Pub L 85-172, 71 Stat 441 (1957) (codified at 21 USC §§451–71 [2005]).
8. Pub L No 91-597, 84 Stat 1620 (1970) (codified at 21 USC §§1031–56 [2005]).
9. Federal Insecticide, Fungicide and Rodenticide Act of Oct 30, 1947, Ch 125, 61 Stat 163 (codified at 7 USC §§136–136y [2005]).
10. Act of August 14, 1946, Ch 966, Title II, 60 Stat 1087 (codified at USC §§1621–37b [2005]).
11. FDA. *Compliance Policy Guide*. Sec. 565.100. Available at http://www.fda.gov/ora/compliance_ref/cpg/cpgfod/cpg565–100.html. Accessed July 9, 2005.
12. CDC. Vessel Sanitation Program Operations Manual. August 2005. Available at http://www.cdc.gov/nceh/vsp/operationsmanual/OPSManual2005.pdf. Accessed October 26, 2005.
13. Cal Health & Safety Code, Div 104 (Environmental Health), Part 5 (Sherman Food, Drug, and Cosmetic Laws), West's Ann Cal Health & Safety Code §111150 *et seq* (2001).
14. FDA. *Food Code*. (2001). Available at http://www.cfsan.fda.gov/~dms/fc01-toc.html. Accessed July 9, 2005.
15. FDA. National Shellfish Sanitation Program. Guide for the Control of Molluscan Shellfish (2003). Available at http://www.cfsan.fda.gov/~ear/nss2-toc.html. Accessed July 9, 2005.
16. FDA. Grade "A" Pasteurized Milk Ordinance. 2003 Revision. Available at http://www.cfsan.fda.gov/~ear/pmo03toc.html. Accessed July 6, 2005.
17. Fla Stat Ann, Title XXIX (Public Health), Ch 381(6) (Imminent Dangers, Stop-Sale Orders), West's FSA §381.0072 (2004).
18. US Constitution, Article I, §8, Subsec 3.
19. FDA. *Regulatory Procedures Manual*, Ch 6, Subch Injunctions (2004). Available at http://www.fda.gov/ora/compliance_ref/rpm/. Accessed July 9, 2005.
20. Federal Supplemental Rules for Certain Admiralty and Maritime Claims, Rule C.
21. 21 USC §334(d)(1) (2005).
22. Pub L 107-188 (2002).
23. Fla Stat Ann, Title XXXIII (Trade, Commerce, and Investments), Ch 500(172) (Embargoing, detaining, or destroying food or food processing equipment that is in violation), West's FSA §381.0072 (2004).
24. 21 CFR §§110.10, 110.35, 110.37, 110.40 (2005).
25. 21 CFR §123.6 (2005).
26. 21 CFR §123.6(c) (2005).
27. 21 CFR Part 120 (2005).
28. 21 CFR Part 113 (2005).
29. 21 CFR Part 114 (2005).

30. 21 CFR §7.50 (2005).

31. FDA. *Investigations Operations Manual,* Chapter 5 (2005), available at http://www.fda .gov/ora/inspect_ref/iom/Contents/ch5_toc.html. Accessed July 9, 2005.

32. FDA. *CFSAN 2004 Program Priorities Report Card.* Assuring Food Safety and Security: Domestic Inspections. Available at http://www.cfsan.fda.gov/~dms/cfsan105.html#part1. Accessed July 9, 2005.

33. FDA. *Investigations Operations Manual* (2005). Chapter 4. Sampling. Available at http: //www.fda.gov/ora/inspect_ref/iom/Contents/ch4_toc.html. Accessed July 9, 2005.

34. FDA. *ORA Laboratory Manual* (2004). Available at http://www.fda.gov/ora/science_ref/ lm/default.htm. Accessed July 9, 2005.

35. FDA. *Investigations Operations Manual* (2005). Subchapter 511, Notice of inspection. Available at http://www.fda.gov/ora/inspect_ref/iom/ChapterText/510part1.html#511. Accessed July 9, 2005.

36. FDA. *Investigations Operations Manual* (2005). Subchapter 512, Reports of observations. Available at http://www.fda.gov/ora/inspect_ref/iom/ChapterText/510part2.html#512. Accessed July 9, 2005.

37. *Continental Seafoods, Inc v Schweiker*, 674 F 2d 38 (DC Cir 1982).

38. *United States v 1200 Cans . . . Pasteurized Whole Eggs*, 339 F Supp 131 (ND Ga 1972).

39. *Continental Seafoods, Inc v Schweiker*, 674 F 2d at 43–44.

40. *United States v 1200 Cans . . . Pasteurized Whole Eggs*, 339 F Supp at 141.

41. *United States v International Exterminator Corporation*, 294 F 2d 270, 271 (5th Cir 1961).

42. *Berger v United States*, 200 F 2d 818, 821 (8th Cir 1952).

43. Cody S, Glynn K, Farrar JA, et al. An outbreak of *Escherichia coli* O157:H7 infection from unpasteurized commercial apple juice. *Ann Intern Med* 1999;130:202–9.

44. St. Louis ME, Morse DL, Potter ME, et al. The emergence of grade A eggs as a major source of *Salmonella* Enteritidis infections: implications for the control of salmonellosis. *JAMA* 1988;259:2103–7.

45. Sivapalasingam S, Barrett E, Kimura A, et al. A multistate outbreak of *Salmonella enterica* serotype Newport infection linked to mango consumption: impact of water-dip disinfestation technology. *Clin Infect Dis* 2003;37:1585–90.

46. 21 CFR §123.6(g) (2005).

47. 9 CFR Part 417 (Hazard Analysis and Critical Control Point Systems) (2005).

48. *United States v Blue Ribbon Smoked Fish, Inc*,179 F Supp 2d 30 (EDNY 2001).

49. Goodman RA, Buehler JW. Field epidemiology defined. In: Gregg MB, ed. *Field Epidemiology.* New York: Oxford University Press, 2002:3–7.

50. Riley LW, Remis RS, Helgerson SD, et al. Hemorrhagic colitis associated with a rare *Escherichia coli* serotype. *N Engl J Med* 1983;308:681–5.

51. CDC. Multistage outbreak of *Salmonella* serotype Agona infections linked to toasted oats cereal. *MMWR* 1998;47:462–72.

52. Hennessy TW, Hedberg CW, Slutsker L, et al. A national outbreak of *Salmonella* Enteritidis infections from ice cream. *N Engl J Med* 1996;334:1281–6.

53. CDC. Outbreak of *Salmonella* serotype Muenchen infections associated with unpasteurized orange juice—United States and Canada, June 1999. *MMWR* 1999;48:582–5.

54. Cody SH, Glynn MK, Farrar JA, et al. An outbreak of *Escherichia coli* O157:H7 infection from unpasteurized commercial apple juice. *Ann Intern Med* 1999;130:202–9.

55. Villar R, Macek MD, Simons S, et al. Investigation of multidrug-resistant *Salmonella* serotype Typhimurium DT104 infections linked to raw-milk cheese in Washington State. *JAMA* 1999;281:1811–6.

56. Tauxe RV. The role of epidemiology in the detection and prevention of foodborne dis-

ease. In: *Issues in Food Safety: Proceedings of Joint Meeting of the Toxicology Forum and the Chinese Academy of Preventive Medicine, Beijing, October 16–20, 1988*. Washington, DC: Toxicology Forum, 1989:40–6.

57. 21 CFR §20.85 (2005).
58. 21 USC §331(j).
59. 18 USC §1906.
60. 5 USC §552(b)(4).
61. 21 CFR §20.88 (2005).
62. 5 USC §552(b)(4).
63. Sobel J, Hirshfeld AB, McTigue K, et al. The pandemic of *Salmonella* Enteritidis phage type 4 reaches Utah: a complex investigation confirms the need for continuing rigorous control measures. *Epidemiol Infect* 2000;125:1–8.
64. Olsen SJ, Ying M, Davis MF, et al. Multistate outbreak of multidrug-resistant *Salmonella* serotype Typhimurium infections due to post-pasteurization contaminated milk. *Emerg Infect Dis* 2004;10:932–5.
65. CDC. Update: multistate outbreak of listeriosis—United States, 1998–1999. *MMWR* 1998;47:1117–32.
66. CDC. Update: multistate outbreak of listeriosis—United States. *MMWR* 1999;47:1085.
67. Jones EG. Forbidden fruit: talking about pesticides and food safety in the era of agricultural product disparagement laws. *Brooklyn Law Rev* 2001;66:823–59.
68. Colo Rev Stat Ann §§35-31-01 and 35-331-01 (West 1999).
69. *Texas Beef Group v Winfrey*, 11 F Supp 2d 858, 864–5 (ND Tex 1998); aff'd, 201 F 3d 680 (5th Cir 2000).
70. Sinclair U. *The Jungle*. New York: Bantam Books, 1981.
71. USDA, APHIS. Current trends and uncertainties for the future of agriculture, 2000. Available at http://www.aphis.usda.gov/vs/ceah/cei/EmergingMarketConditions_files/market.htm#trends. Accessed October 17, 2005.
72. Rogue A, White P, Petter-Guard J, et al. Epidemiology and control of egg-associated *Salmonella* Enteritidis in the United States of America. *Rev Sci Off Int Epiz* 1997;16:542–53.
73. Sobel J, Khan AS, Swerdlow DS. The threat of a biological terrorist attack on the United States food supply: the CDC perspective. *Lancet* 2002;359:874–80.
74. FDA. Food Producers, Processors, and Transporters: Food Security Preventive Measures Guidance. Available at http://www.cfsan.fda.gov/~dms/secguid6.html. Accessed May 31, 2005.
75. FDA. Importers and Filers: Food Security Preventive Measures Guidance, Available at http://www.cfsan.fda.gov/~dms/secguid7.html. Accessed May 31, 2005.
76. FDA. Retail Food Stores and Food Service Establishments: Food Security Preventive Measures Guidance. Available at http://www.cfsan.fda.gov/~dms/secgui11.html. Accessed May 31, 2005.
77. USDA. FSIS Safety and Security Guidelines for the Transportation and Distribution of Meat, Poultry, and Egg Products. Available at http://www.fsis.usda.gov/oa/topics/transportguide.htm. Accessed May 31, 2005.
78. USDA. FSIS Security Guidelines for Food Processors. Available at http://www.fsis.usda.gov/oa/topics/securityguide.htm. Accessed May 31, 2005.
79. Establishment and Maintenance of Records Under the Public Health Security and Bioterrorism Preparedness and Response Act of 2002, 69 Fed Regist 71,561 (Dec. 9, 2004).
80. 68 Fed Reg 58,975, 59,024 (2003).

Chapter 16

BLOODBORNE AND SEXUALLY TRANSMITTED INFECTIONS

Edward P. Richards III
and Guthrie S. Birkhead

This chapter focuses on legal tools for controlling sexually transmitted infections (STIs) and certain related bloodborne infections for which sexual transmission is important. Sexually transmitted infections pose difficult legal and public policy issues in public health law practice. Sex and procreation are the most intimate of human activities; thus, prevention and control activities aimed at STIs present difficult privacy and personal freedom issues. Sex is also a primal biologic drive that is particularly difficult to influence or modify through rational argument and education. The second major route of transmission for some STIs is blood-to-blood contact, such as that which occurs among drug users during injection of narcotics and other drugs. Drug-use behaviors are complex, are wrapped in the psychology and physiology of addiction, and present similar challenges as STIs to public health prevention and control. More than in many other areas of public health, knowledgeable professionals are deeply divided about the correct approach to STI control, with the greatest diversity of opinion over the control of HIV infection.

Many human diseases can be spread by sexual contact, including those caused by bacteria (e.g., bacterial vaginosis, chancroid, gonorrhea, granuloma inguinale, and syphilis), chlamydia (i.e., genital chlamydia, lymphogranuloma venereum), mycoplasma, protozoa (e.g., trichomoniasis), and viruses (i.e., hepatitis B virus [HBV], hepatitis C virus, herpes simplex virus, HIV, and human papilloma virus). Other diseases can be transmitted by genital contact during sexual activity (e.g., phthiriasis [crab lice]) or oral-anal-genital contact (e.g., hepatitis A virus [HAV] and a myriad of enteric infections). These diseases run the spectrum from simply irritating (crab lice) to fatal (HIV infection). Asymptomatic infection may occur for some or be the rule for others. Curative treatment is available for some (syphilis, gonorrhea, and some cases of chronic HBV infection) but not others (e.g., HIV infection). Early preventive therapy sometimes can prevent infection altogether (e.g., syphilis). Some STIs are associated with significant bloodborne transmission (HIV, HBV, and hepatitis C virus infections). Finally, several STIs can also be transmitted from mother to child (syphilis, gonorrhea, HIV, HBV). Perinatal transmission can occur in utero, during delivery, or postpartum (e.g., through breast feeding).

This chapter focuses on the public health and legal response to four selected STIs that also are associated with significant bloodborne or perinatal transmission: HIV, gonorrhea, syphilis, and HBV. Together, these pose the key legal questions common to all STIs.

The core public health activities in STI and bloodborne infection control are (1) identification of index cases through public health surveillance (mandated reporting to the health department of persons with infection); (2) treatment and counseling of index patients; (3) identification, notification, prophylaxis or treatment, and counseling of sex or needle-sharing (blood-to-blood) contacts of the index patients; (4) mandated prevention measures (e.g., postpartum eye drops to prevent gonorrheal eye infections, mandated hepatitis B vaccination for school entry, and mandated condom availability in schools in Los Angeles, New York City, and elsewhere); (5) mandated education (required school curricula in some states); (6) mandated screening for infection (e.g., mandated prenatal screening for syphilis and HBV infection and premarital screening for syphilis [not a common practice currently]); (7) closing of institutions and businesses that promote the spread of infection, such as bathhouses and crack houses; (8) in rare cases, detention of persons who pose a threat to the community through their unwillingness or inability to desist from unsafe practices; and (9) regulation of blood and blood products to prevent the spread of STIs. Carrying out these activities demands a careful balancing between state police power and individual privacy.

Legal Authorities

Public health law is primarily state and local government law. The U.S. Constitution reserved the police powers, which include the power to protect the public from communicable diseases, to the states. Thus, under the Constitution, even though STI and bloodborne infection control activities receive important financial and technical assistance support from the federal government, primary control and prevention efforts are carried out by state and local public health agencies acting under the authority of the police powers.

Federal Powers and Approaches

Congress can address public health problems that involve interstate commerce or otherwise fall under other enumerated powers. For example, the Public Health Service has authority over the control of diseases related to interstate commerce and international shipping,[1] and the Food and Drug Administration (FDA) and the Department of Agriculture (USDA) share some authority over foodborne-illness control. FDA's regulation of blood products and management of transfusion-related transmission of infectious agents are the only areas with significant direct federal regulation of STIs. Congress has passed antidiscrimination laws (such as the Americans with Disabilities Act) and privacy laws that affect some public health STI services, but Congress has not passed any national STI-control legislation that preempts state authority in this area.

Outside direct regulatory authority, the federal government exercises significant control over all aspects of public health through the spending power. When Congress establishes programs such as the Ryan White Comprehensive AIDS Resources Emergency (CARE) Act to address the health needs of HIV-infected persons, it may attach conditions to receipt of the money and uses those conditions to control state public health services. For example, the 1996 reauthorized CARE Act required states to demonstrate a "good faith effort" to conduct partner notification of spouses of persons with HIV infection as a condition of receipt of funding to states under Title II of the Act.

Because most states depend on the federal government for substantial financial support of their public health efforts, federal funding priorities often shape state public health efforts. For example, for many years the federal government provided funds for syphilis case finding and partner notification and thus were able to achieve a certain consistency and uniformity among states' approaches to syphilis even though states each rely on their own laws to authorize and enforce partner-notification activities. When HBV was recognized as a major U.S. public health problem in the 1970s, the federal government did not provide funds for case finding and partner notification, and few states funded these programs on their own—probably at least partially because "serum hepatitis," as HBV was previously known, was not widely recognized to be sexually transmitted before the mid-1970s[2] nor was any preventive therapy for contacts available, therefore partner notification was not used as a control strategy.

The Police Power

Control of STIs tests the limits of public health authority under the police power more than most areas of public health practice. Understanding the breadth of the police power is critical because STI control requires the state to intrude on the most intimate relationships and to collect the most private information. This chapter discusses the U.S. Constitutional limitations on state authority and how, within the constitutional limits, states have approached STI-control laws. State laws on STI control, especially HIV control, differ substantially, representing different political and epidemiologic conditions in the states. Public health professionals implementing STI-control programs must work with lawyers in their individual state to ensure they work within that state's statutory framework.

Police powers are derived from the doctrine of societal self-defense.[3] Society has almost unlimited powers to protect itself because, in the classic Hobbesian view, life is nasty, brutish, and short without society. The U.S. Constitution and the state constitutions limit the power of the state and give individuals some rights against state action. When drafted, the U.S. Constitution protected individuals only from the actions of the federal government, but most of its protections subsequently were extended to the states. These protections are strongest when the state is prosecuting an individual for a crime with possible imprisonment as the punishment, and they are weakest when the state is restricting the liberty of individuals to protect others in society. The U.S. Constitution provides persons accused of a crime a right to counsel, protection from searches and seizures, right to trial by jury, and other procedural rights. These constitutional rights are the subject of popular discourse ranging from television police shows to newspaper editorial pages and have entered the popular consciousness as applying to all persons at all times.

Many people—including some lawyers and public health professionals—are surprised to learn that individual rights are attenuated when the state acts to protect itself or its citizens from future harm, as opposed to punishing criminals or taking property for state use. Under some circumstances, when the public health is threatened, a person can be detained without a trial, premises can be searched without a probable-cause warrant, and property can be destroyed without compensation. Because of the breadth of these powers, it is important they not be abused. Public health officials may not use their police powers to accomplish nonpublic health objectives, such as clearing prostitutes from the streets before a convention, nor may they use these powers to circumvent criminal law protections. Because states criminalize many activities involved with the spread of STIs, such as prostitution, illicit drug use, and sexual activity with children under the age of consent, public health officials receiving disease reports, investigating cases, and delivering services often learn of criminal behavior. Although police officials sometimes are tempted to use public health authority to bolster criminal law enforcement, this is an unconstitutional deprivation of criminal due process rights and should be opposed by public health officials.

Protection of STI Information

Both state and federal courts have ruled that using the police power to circumvent the constitutional protections against unreasonable search and seizure is unconstitutional. For example, public health inspectors can enter private property to look for rats without procuring a criminal search warrant. If the search for vermin results in evidence of a crime, this evidence would not be admissible in a criminal proceeding because investigators had no proper search warrant. A recent U.S. Supreme Court case applied this principle to the screening without consent of pregnant women for drug use. The information from the screening was used to threaten the women with criminal prosecution for endangering their unborn children. The court ruled that such screening was an improper use of the public health authority, and the information could not be used by law enforcement.[4] The court was careful to distinguish this from acceptable public health testing. It found that testing would have been constitutional if the information had been used to improve the medical care of the women or their babies or for some other legitimate public health purpose.

Much of the information that public health professionals collect about STIs is not constitutionally protected. For example, if an index patient names a contact and identifies that contact as a crack dealer, that information would not be protected and could be provided to law enforcement. Doing so, however, would make carrying out many public health investigations impossible. Recognizing this, many states have laws that limit the use of information gained through public health reporting and investigations to public health purposes. Even states that do not enact this protection into a specific law recognize its importance and do not force public health officials to provide information to law enforcement agencies, except under limited circumstances. This is important because many STI measures rely on the voluntary cooperation of individuals with diseases or risk factors of public health interest. For example, obtaining the names of sex or needle-sharing partners of persons with HIV or HBV infection is inherently voluntary. Coercion or the threat of legal action to obtain partner names may result only in producing false names or names of nonpartners, wasting public health resources at best or confounding of public health efforts at worst. Voluntarism also is important because public health efforts are not only reactive (e.g., following up after the report of a case of disease) but also aimed at preventing future disease. Counseling a person with syphilis or HIV infection to prevent future sexual exposure to disease requires a supportive, voluntary approach to succeed.

The privacy of public health information depends on the specific provisions of the applicable state laws. Most of these laws, which generally provide strong protection for public health information, allow disclosure in two circumstances. First, the person who is the subject of the report may release the information in the report that concerns his or her own conduct and medical condition, although the courts limit this disclosure in many situations.[5] In contrast, at least one state—Colorado—bans the release of public health department case-investigation information to the individual and thus prevents coerced release.[6] Because public health department case-investigation records are not the patient's primary medical records, they do not contain information relevant to medical treatment not otherwise available to the patient. Banning the release of public health investigation data to the individual provides useful protection of records containing information about sexual activity and drug use without depriving the individual of necessary information for personal medical needs.

Second, most state public health confidentiality laws allow disclosure when necessary to serve the ends of justice. An example is the New York State HIV confidentiality statute, which permits a court-ordered release of HIV information if there exists "a clear and imminent danger to an individual whose life or health may unknowingly be at significant risk as a result of contact with the individual."[7] This exception comes into play when no other less-intrusive way exists to protect persons at risk and the court determines that disclosure of the information is in the public's interest.[8,9] In practice, this sort of provision is used very rarely.

State Administrative Process

Public health law is administrative law, meaning that it is enforced by state and local administrative agencies rather than by the police or sheriff's department. Although the U.S. Constitution does not explicitly provide for administrative agencies, the courts have allowed Congress to delegate its power to agencies administered by the President. All states have a similar administrative agency structure, although the extent to which legislative power can be delegated to an agency, and the type of executive and judicial oversight of agencies allowed, varies substantially among the states. Traditionally, legislatures did not specify the details of public health programs and enforcement, leaving that to the discretion of the health officer. In many states, public health statutes said little more than that the health department is directed to protect the citizens of the state from threats to the public health. Such vague delegation passes Constitutional muster because agencies need flexibility to respond to changing threats and to change their regulations as better science becomes available. The courts recognize that the expert agency staff are in a better position than the judges and the legislature to determine the details of public health practice. Thus when controversy arises over whether the public health agency has made the correct decision, the courts will defer to the agency.[10]

This deference has become more controversial with the advent of HIV infection and the growing political pressure of civil liberties organizations. For example, in a case involving the closing of a gay bathhouse, the court reiterated that this deference to the health agency decision-maker includes decisions about STI control that potentially interfere with personal freedom:

> [D]efendants and the intervening patrons challenge the soundness of the scientific judgments upon which the Health Council regulation is based. . . . They go further and argue that facilities such as St. Mark's, which attempts to educate its patrons with written materials, signed pledges, and posted notices as to the advisability of safe sexual practices, provide a positive force in combating AIDS, and a valuable communication link between public health authorities and the homosexual community. While these arguments and proposals may have varying degrees of merit, they overlook a fundamental principle of applicable law: "It is not for the courts to determine which scientific view is correct in ruling upon whether the police power has been properly exercised. The judicial function is exhausted with the discovery that the relation between means and end is not wholly vain and fanciful, an illusory pretense."[11]

Administrative Regulations and Orders

Because the statutes that delegate the authority for conducting STI control are generally broad, the details of enforcement are developed by the agency. These enforcement polices are embodied in formal regulations, promulgated under the state's Administrative Procedure Act, or in informal guidance documents and administrative orders. For example, listing HIV infection as a reportable disease subject to contact tracing may require a formal regulation subject to notice and comment (see Chapter 3). The process for reporting and contact tracing may be specified in internal health department policies that are not subject to notice and comment, although they are subject to Freedom of Information Act requests in most states.

Formal regulations and informal guidance documents apply to the population in general; they are not directed at the activities of specific persons or institutions. Public health agencies also issue orders to specific businesses or individuals, such as an order to a restaurant to eliminate a rat infestation to avoid closure. When these policies and procedures apply to third parties, they are administrative orders, sometimes called "health-hold orders." Administrative orders vary in formality and specificity, with some applying to many persons rather than one individual or institution. The bathhouse closing case discussed above illustrates an administrative order to close a facility. Administrative orders also have been used to require that arrested prostitutes be screened for gonorrhea before being released.[12] Unless restricted by a specific state statute, the federal and most state constitutions give health departments broad authority to use administrative orders without getting a court order, even when the order involves individual restrictions.

To survive a constitutional challenge in the courts, administrative orders to control STIs should:

1. Address a real problem that poses a direct threat to the public health
2. Be based on a rational scientific control strategy, although there need not be scientific consensus on the strategy chosen
3. Implement that strategy with the least restrictions consistent with the resources available and other public health policy concerns
4. Include periodic program evaluation to show that the strategy is working
5. Provide for phasing out the program when it is no longer epidemiologically sound[13]

When the courts review administrative orders, they recognize that public health decision making is based on risk analysis, and solutions accepted by all members in the community seldom are clear and unambiguous. The courts do not demand perfection and do not require that the strategy be the least restrictive alternative, only that it be reasonably related to legitimate public health objectives.

Legal Issues and Controversies

Core STI public health control functions, which include primary reporting and partner notification, pose four types of legal issues: (1) invasion of privacy, (2) invasion of the person, (3) nuisance abatement (closures), and (4) regulation of interstate commerce (blood). Because legal prostitution is limited in the United States, this section does not discuss STIs as an occupational problem. Some of these issues, as they relate to requirements for proof of vaccination to attend school or as a condition of employment, and the right to conduct newborn screening, have been covered in other chapters and do not pose special issues for STIs. This section focuses on issues that either pose special problems in STI control, such as infection reporting and partner notification, or issues not covered elsewhere, such as blood products.

The central controversy in STI law is whether STI law in particular and public health law in general are individual-based or societal-based. Before the 1970s, public health law and STI-control law were seen as protecting society through the control of infection in individuals. Even though some concern always existed about the rights of infected persons, these rights were viewed as secondary to the right of society to control the spread of the diseases. The combination of the patient empowerment movement that started in the 1970s, the individual autonomy model of medical care promoted by bioethicists in the 1980s, and the flooding of health departments with medical-care professionals who delivered personal medical services such as prenatal care and indigent health care, so blurred the line between personal medical care and public health that many health directors and their staffs no longer recognized the difference between the law and ethics of the physician-patient relationship and those shared by a public health enforcement officer and a disease carrier. This shift from public health to personal health law was evidenced by the failure to close bathhouses in the 1970s,[14] despite the spread of HBV infection and other communicable diseases, then was reflected in the different approaches states took to HIV-control strategies such as reporting, contact tracing, and partner notification, as well as to whether HIV-related medical information was treated differently from other medical information.

Invasion of Privacy

Almost all STI control since the 1930s has been conducted through epidemiologic investigation, partner notification and education, and voluntary treatment and testing. Although these methods invade personal privacy, they do not restrict the person; thus, most of the legal controversies surrounding STI control have been driven by privacy concerns. Case identification through physician reports and contact investigation is the keystone of epidemiology and communicable disease control. Reporting allows the identification of infected individuals so that they can be treated (if treatment is available) and counseled in the prevention of the spread of the disease, but this is only part of the role of reporting. Reporting is critical to surveillance and enables identification of emerging and reemerging infections; spread of infections into new communities; changes in the incidence and prevalence of diseases in defined communities; new avenues of infection, such as the link between crack cocaine and STI; and, of increasing importance, changes in patterns of antimicrobial resistance.

The U.S. Supreme Court addressed the legality of public health reporting in *Whalen v. Roe*,[15] a case involving another controversial issue, the reporting of controlled substances prescriptions to identify physicians writing illegal prescriptions and patients seeking improper medication. This case directly confronted the claim that reporting might deter individuals from seeking diagnosis and treatment:

> Unquestionably, some individuals' concern for their own privacy may lead them to avoid or to postpone needed medical attention. Nevertheless, disclosures of private medical information to doctors, to hospital personnel, to insurance companies, and to public health agencies are often an essential part of modern medical practice even when the disclosure may reflect unfavorably on the character of the patient. Requiring such disclosures to representatives of the State having responsibility for the health of the community, does not automatically amount to an impermissible invasion of privacy. (p. 602)

This was based on an earlier ruling upholding reporting and record keeping requirements for abortion, which is the most legally protected area in medical and public health jurisprudence.[16] In each of these cases it is assumed the state will use reasonable measures to protect the privacy of the information it requires from negligent disclosure.

Invasion of the Person

Personal restrictions are used infrequently in STI control. Such restrictions are constitutional and were litigated in the STI landmark case, *Reynolds v. McNichols*,[17] which involved an administrative order to check arrested prostitutes for gonorrhea as part of the longest running epidemiologic study and control program for gonorrhea.[12,18] These orders required prostitutes arrested as part of routine police activity to be detained until examined and/or treated for gonorrhea. The court found that this temporary detention for the diagnosis and treatment of gonorrhea was a proper response and did not violate the plaintiff's constitutional rights. This is consistent with current case law, recognizing the constitutional limits that such restrictions cannot be used as a subterfuge for criminal enforcement and that the restricted individual always has access to habeas corpus proceedings to review the restriction. If persons infected with a STI violate the criminal law, such as prohibitions on reckless endangerment or specific laws criminalizing the spread of STIs, they can be prosecuted by the police who must provide them with full criminal due process protections. Such measures are not a public health action and should not involve public health personnel.

Nuisance Abatement

Public health officials have broad powers to close establishments that threaten the public health (see Chapter 3). This power has been routinely used in the past to close down houses of prostitution. Although such authority has not been employed routinely for STI control in recent times, it is within the powers of the health department as was reiterated in the St. Mark's Baths case discussed earlier. However, this power has been used to close adult book stores[19] and video arcades that permit unsafe sex practices, and could be used to close crack houses and other facilities that foster the unsafe use of illegal drugs. Such closing should be done by the police, however, because health departments are not staffed to deal with criminal enterprises, and involvement in police raids may undermine the credibility of the health department.

Regulation of Interstate Commerce

Bloodborne STIs raise special legal issues because they are subject to significant federal regulation under congressional power to regulate interstate commerce. Blood and blood products are classic commercial goods that are part of interstate commerce. Illegal intravenous drug use, which also spreads bloodborne STIs, is regulated because the illegal drugs pass over state lines and international boundaries. Two classes of legal issues surround bloodborne infections: those that involve illegal drug use and those that result from exposure to blood and body fluids as part of medical, emergency, and custodial care. Many public health professionals consider that policies prohibiting the use, possession, and sale of illegal drugs give little consideration to the prevention of bloodborne infections. The often severe penalties for drug possession and the related laws on drug paraphernalia make it difficult for public health personnel to identify and work with drug users and to help them prevent transmission of communicable diseases.

   Exposure to blood and body fluids in medical care, as well as in custodial care, sports, and other nonmedical settings, was recognized as a potentially important risk associated with the spread of HBV during the 1970s. Concerns about HIV transmission escalated this to a high profile issue during the 1980s. Except for regulations on blood products, public health officials have acted in an advisory and educating role on managing these risks but have only a limited regulatory role. Litigation in this area has been considerable under the federal disability laws and under state tort laws, with some large judgments against health-care providers for negligence in diagnosis and treatment of HIV.[20] Most of the litigation has been against blood banks for failing to screen for HIV in a timely manner.[21] The provision of whole blood and blood products is an interstate business, now heavily regulated by FDA. Although blood banks and blood products manufacturers were slow to recognize the risks posed by HBV and HIV, the combination of government regulation and private tort litigation substantially increased their sensitivity to the prevention of bloodborne infections.

Practice Considerations

Physician and Laboratory Reporting

Reporting of communicable diseases identified through the provision of personal medical services in the private community has been a key component of public health surveillance and practice for more than 100 years. These reports first came from physicians, and as the formal system of laboratories evolved and more diseases of public health interest were diagnosed directly by laboratory tests, laboratory directors also were required to report communicable diseases. Before 1983, such reporting was not controversial, and states had a list of more than 50 diseases and conditions that required reporting to the health department, including syphilis, gonorrhea, viral hepatitis, and later hepatitis A and B, with identifying information about the individuals reported.

When AIDS was recognized in 1981, states quickly instituted reporting of AIDS cases by name. Much information about the epidemiology of AIDS was worked out through this surveillance system. The AIDS reporting continued even after HIV, the virus that causes AIDS, was identified in the mid-1980s and became the focus of surveillance because AIDS case surveillance provides valuable information on the progression of the disease. AIDS case data also are used to determine federal funding formulas for AIDS care, and the AIDS case definition has been used in other areas, such as, for example, to determine eligibility for disability compensation. While some states did not move to HIV reporting in the first decade the HIV diagnostic test was available, all states now have some form of HIV reporting. In 2005, 39 states reported the names of HIV-infected persons in the same manner as other communicable diseases; 5 states and the District of Columbia report using a unique identifier code, based on elements such as initials, sex, and the last four digits of the social security number; and 5 states have a name-to-code reporting system. The code-based reporting systems give some useful HIV data but do not allow duplicate HIV surveillance reports on the same person to be removed (unduplicated) with certainty or to be easily linked to other sources of surveillance and medical information. The Centers for Disease Control and Prevention (CDC) does not currently report data from non-name reporting states in its summaries of national HIV statistics.

Although physician reporting in the modern era generally had not been controversial until the HIV/AIDS epidemic, it often is not complete or timely. For example, one study in the late 1970s showed that only 10%–20% of gonorrhea cases were reported by physicians and that many physicians never reported cases.[22] Many reasons existed for the failure to report, including administrative time and costs, which have only worsened recently. One legal reason for the failure to report is that, except for failure to report child abuse, physicians are seldom disciplined or prosecuted for failing to report communicable diseases. As a result, public health increasingly has depended on legally mandated laboratory reporting for surveillance purposes because it is much more effective. Physician reporting is still critical for conditions that do not have a specific laboratory diagnosis and for emerging conditions that are not yet reportable, as with the original reports of AIDS in 1981. Mandated physician reporting also may be the only source of detailed medical information about cases of illness, such as nature and date of onset of symptoms and details of treatment.

Laboratories can automate the reporting process, and they are subject to certification and accreditation procedures that help ensure they comply with the law. Effective laboratory reporting depends on the laboratory getting proper identifying information on the person whose specimen is being tested.

To remove all barriers to persons obtaining an HIV test, many states allow anonymous testing for HIV, which does not directly permit identified reporting. However, some states have developed successful programs that will convert an anonymous HIV test result to a confidential (identified) result, permitting both rapid entry into health care of the infected person and reporting to the health department for surveillance purposes. For example, New York State permits such an option and most persons testing HIV positive in the anonymous HIV testing program choose to convert their test result, even after HIV reporting by name was instituted in the state. Anonymous testing programs also make it difficult to contact persons who test positive but never return for their test results. However, this problem almost has been eliminated by the widespread offering of rapid HIV tests, with results available in 20 minutes, in anonymous testing programs.

Some states impose special requirements on HIV testing, such as requirements for counseling and written informed consent, which may be a barrier to the routine offering of HIV testing in medical settings. In many cases, these requirements were instituted early in the HIV epidemic when concerns about confidentiality, stigma, and discrimination, combined with lack of specific treatment for HIV, led to an uncertain balance between the risks and benefits of testing. Even in the current era of highly active antiretroviral therapy for HIV, some public health professionals remain concerned that persons undergoing HIV testing be aware of the risks of stigma and discrimination that accompany an HIV diagnosis, as well as that specific written consent be maintained as a safeguard against unauthorized or surreptitious testing. In addition, counseling after HIV testing remains an important preventive intervention for persons testing HIV negative and is critical for persons testing HIV positive to gain quick entry into medical care and supportive services. Nevertheless, anecdotal concerns remain about the barrier to testing that counseling and legally mandated written informed consent may create. Some states, such as New York, have attempted to streamline the HIV testing process within the current legal structure of required counseling and written consent; in New York, pretest counseling may be carried out by providing patients with a brochure covering the required counseling elements, asking if they have any questions, and having them sign a simplified, one-page consent form. CDC has recommended an approach of "opt-out" testing in prenatal care where testing is done unless the woman specifically declines in writing. Even this approach requires some communication with the woman that HIV testing is recommended and should be done, as well as giving her an opportunity to decline testing. This clearly is an evolving area of public health law.

Mandatory Screening, Treatment, and Vaccination

Mandatory screening, treatment, and vaccination for STIs is uncommon in the United States and, except for prenatal screening discussed below, almost always relies on obtaining a court order for a specific circumstance. At one time, mandatory screening of adults for syphilis to obtain a marriage license was common in the United States. The principle that screening is constitutionally permissible was upheld in the *Ferguson* case discussed above, even though the case rejected the screening program at issue because it was not for public health purposes. Screening for STIs has fallen out of favor for epidemiologic and cost-effectiveness reasons, although several states still have premarital screening requirements. The most common STI screening mandate for adults is testing pregnant women for syphilis, and to a lesser extent, hepatitis B. Syphilis, like HIV, can pass to the fetus and cause congenital infection. Perinatal infection with syphilis may cause congenital malformations and severe mental retardation. Perinatal HIV infection results in about one in four newborns becoming infected with HIV, with the eventual development of AIDS. For all three diseases, early detection of the disease in the mother allows intervention that dramatically reduces the likelihood that the baby will be infected. Although most states require syphilis screening for pregnant women, fewer require hepatitis B screening, and none require HIV screening. Connecticut[23] and New York[24] require that the person providing prenatal care also counsel the patient about HIV screening, but HIV testing still is done only with the mother's consent. The Connecticut statute mandates that a syphilis test be run on the same blood sample and the woman can refuse this only if she has religious objections to all medical testing. Both New York and Connecticut require neonatal screening for HIV, if the mother was not tested during prenatal care. In New York, maternity hospitals are required to conduct rapid HIV testing, with results available in 12 hours, for women in labor, with their consent, or for the newborn after birth for all women without confirmation of an HIV test during prenatal care. Such a testing program permits women and their infants to be treated immediately to prevent perinatal HIV transmission.[25,26]

Involuntary treatment is not a major issue for diseases such as syphilis and gonorrhea because the treatment is quick and simple, so few people refuse it. The HIV infection is more problematic, however, because it requires ongoing treatment, sometimes with substantial side effects. The only situation in which involuntary treatment for HIV infection has been raised is for pregnant women, where treatment can reduce the risk for transmission to the child. Such treatment is probably constitutional, in that the courts have found that a woman's right to privacy does not include harming her fetus; however, this is controversial and is not recommended by public health experts at this time because ultimately the woman's cooperation is necessary for any successful treatment regimen. HBV vaccine was the first vaccine for an STI; its widespread use worldwide has dramatically reduced the incidence of HBV and may nearly eliminate it in future generations in the United States. Mandatory school entrance requirements for HBV vaccination are an important tool in the eventual control and potential eradication of HBV in the United States.

Partner Identification and Notification

Disease reporting provides valuable epidemiologic information, but it is only the first step in public health intervention efforts to prevent STIs. When epidemiologically justified, the next step is to interview the reported (index) patient to identify other potentially infected contacts. These contacts are then located and interviewed. Depending on the nature of the disease, they are educated about testing and treatment and about ways to avoid spreading the diseases. In addition, they are asked about their contacts, and these also may be investigated. Contact tracing is legally justifiable because it is critical to elucidating the epidemiology of a disease and to mapping its spread, and it provides valuable benefits to the potentially infected persons, including early diagnosis and treatment in the case of HIV, gonorrhea, and syphilis. Individuals and businesses have no constitutional right to withhold information from public health investigators and could be ordered by a court to provide information necessary for a public health investigation. However, public health personnel always treat contact tracing and partner notification as a voluntary activity because contacts cannot be notified without the index patient's cooperation. To emphasize this aspect, CDC has adopted the terminology "partner counseling and referral services" (PCRS) to refer to partner notification or contact tracing for HIV. To help preserve the public's trust in the public health workers, public health personnel should not be involved in any forensic investigation when a criminal prosecution is contemplated, such as in child abuse cases.

Keying off of an index patient to identify other persons with a common exposure to track disease spread and offer preventive or curative treatments is a common public health strategy to control infectious diseases (e.g. tuberculosis, bacterial meningitis, foodborne illness). However, this strategy poses special challenges for STIs because individuals must disclose intimate and sometimes illegal behavior. (Recognizing the difference between the casual spread of tuberculosis and the intimate nature of STIs, STI investigators usually refer to partners, rather than contacts.) Contact tracing and partner notification are used for syphilis to try to locate and treat contacts during the three-week incubation period, and for gonorrhea to identify asymptomatic female contacts. This approach has been particularly effective in identifying core group members who are disproportionably responsible for spreading STIs.

When HIV first was discovered, some health departments treated it the same as syphilis and investigated cases and notified partners from the beginning. In other places, including the most populous states, investigation and notification was controversial because it had limited benefits to the individual. By the early 1990s, all states offered HIV partner notification services as a condition of receipt by the states of CDC HIV-prevention grant funding. In some states the program was passive whereas in others it was linked to HIV reporting. Many health departments that employed partner notification found it was justified as a very personal form of education because many contacts are not yet infected when first identified and because it helped prompt individuals to get tested and to obtain counseling about how to prevent the spread of the disease.[27,28] Now, with the availability of treatments that slow the course of the disease, early diagnosis is valuable to the individual as well as to society. This has made investigation and notification much less controversial, and these steps are specifically mandated by law in some states such as New York.[29]

Contact information must be treated as confidential by public health personnel, and is often protected by statute or regulation and cannot be released without a court order or statutory authorization to do so. Because of these legal restrictions, partner notification programs have developed procedures to interview named contacts without divulging the source of the information. The typical text of a public health worker's speech to a contact is: "You have been named as a contact of someone with an STI. You need to be screened and treated, if necessary." The identity of the index patient never is revealed in this process. Unfortunately, if the contact has few or only one sex or needle-sharing partner, preventing the contact from guessing who must have exposed him or her is impossible. The investigator must resist all entreaties to confirm the interviewee's suspicions, but this may not have a practical effect in some cases. Contact tracing raises difficult ethical questions, especially if a chance exists that the interview will trigger a violent reprisal from the suspected partner. The New York State HIV reporting and partner notification statute required that all persons reported to have HIV be screened for domestic violence risk from any partner named for subsequent notification.[30] When a risk for domestic violence is identified, referral for domestic violence prevention services is required, and if the risk is deemed great enough in the judgment of the responsible public health official, partner notification can be deferred. During 2001–2003, the first three years of the New York program, notification was deferred in less than 2% of named partners because of an identified risk for domestic violence.[31]

Prostitution and Illegal Drug Use

Prostitution and illegal drug use generally are linked in that they involve overlapping populations on the fringe of the law and because prostitutes are often drug users. Thus, bloodborne STIs are spread both through sexual activity to get drugs and, for intravenous drugs, through the use of the drugs themselves. Public health services are complicated because both activities are illegal and possession and sale of intravenous drugs carry draconian penalties under state and federal laws. Prostitutes and drug users may be suspicious of government officials and may not participate in programs that they feel might increase their chances of arrest. Laws criminalizing possession of drug paraphernalia make using effective bloodborne infection–control strategies such as needle exchange difficult or impossible. In addition, the federal government has not allowed states to use federal funds to support syringe exchange. In many jurisdictions that do not criminalize possession and sale of needles and syringes, it may be politically difficult for the health departments to provide assistance to intravenous drug users. However, syringe exchange programs have been authorized in a number of states and, in part, are responsible for the dramatic reduction in HIV transmission due to injection drug.[32]

Legal Issues in Personal Medical Services

Health department personnel have significant immunity when performing core public health functions, such as case finding, partner notification, basic STI treatment intended to protect the public, and general epidemiologic investigations (see Chapter 9). Health departments often provide personal medical services beyond these core public health functions, the most common being prenatal care. In many states, however, because no sovereign immunity exists for personal medical-care services, personnel may be exposed to medical malpractice litigation. This is further complicated when health departments use contract personnel to deliver medical services. Such personnel have few of the legal protections of a state employee. More problematically, most state laws regarding privacy of public health records do not apply to personal medical records. Health department personnel who deliver both personal medical services, such as prenatal care, and interview persons about their exposure to STIs must be careful to keep public health information, such as the identity of sexual contacts or other disease investigation information, separate from the patient's personal medical records. Thus the patient's medical record might contain the information that the patient had six sexual contacts in the last month, but it should not contain the names of the contacts. These would be maintained in a separate disease-control investigation file. This is especially important in small departments where each staff member has multiple job responsibilities.

In addition to liability concerns, personal medical services are covered by many state and federal laws such as the Americans with Disabilities Act and the Health Insurance Portability and Accountability Act of 1996 that do not apply to data collected as a part of authorized public health programs and disease-control investigations.

Emerging Issues

Surveillance for Treatment for HIV Infection

The emerging problem of drug-resistant strains of HIV developing from poorly designed treatment regimens or failure to promote patient adherence to treatment regimens is focusing attention on the role of public health in conducting surveillance of HIV treatment and antiviral resistance. In the spring of 2005, in response to a report of a patient with recent infection with an strain of HIV resistant to all major antiretroviral drug classes and with apparent rapid progression to AIDS in New York City,[33] New York added HIV genotypic viral resistance laboratory results to the list of legally reportable conditions. Such surveillance will allow monitoring of HIV resistance patterns in the population and will be helpful to guide treatment decisions and adherence programs. In addition, a number of states now require reporting of all viral load and CD4-cell-count (a measure of immune system function) laboratory results to ensure complete reporting of all HIV cases. These data carry the potential for public health agencies to monitor antiviral control of HIV and preservation of immune function on a population level, an important new tool to monitor and guide health-care quality programs. However, this purpose for collecting surveillance data often is not spelled out in the statutes and regulations governing disease reporting.

Vaccines for STIs

Although an effective vaccine for HIV would transform the control of the disease throughout the world, an HIV vaccine remains elusive. A vaccine that is significantly less than 100% effective paradoxically could increase the risk for transmission by causing people to think they are protected from disease. If such a vaccine were recommended for use in groups at high risk for HIV, such as gay men and injection-drug users, its use would have to be coupled with effective education on its limitations.[34] Whether such concerns would apply to the routine use of a vaccine in children or adolescents is not clear.

Legal questions—such as whether to require vaccination for school entry, as is done for many other routinely recommended vaccines—will need to be dealt with in the future. This issue is likely to be faced more imminently with human papilloma virus vaccines, which have been approved by FDA.[35] These vaccines prevent genital warts but have a much broader benefit in preventing cervical cancer later in life. They would ideally be used in preadolescents to prevent primary infection with human papilloma virus that occurs very rapidly in most people after sexual debut. The question of mandating vaccination for school attendance in adolescents also will be complicated by whether the requirements would apply to female only or to both males and females. As in other areas of public health law, the epidemiologic, medical evidence, and cost-benefit considerations should play an important role in determining the legal approach to these issues.

References

1. 42 USC 264 (regulations to control communicable diseases).
2. Benenson AS, ed. *Control of Communicable Diseases in Man*. 11th ed. Washington, DC: American Public Health Association, 1970: 105–10.
3. Richards EP. The jurisprudence of prevention: society's right of self-defense against dangerous individuals. *Hastings Constitutional Law Q* 1989;16:329–92.
4. *Ferguson v City of Charleston*, 532 US 67 (2001).
5. *Grattan v People*, 65 NY 2d 243, 480 NE 2d 714, 491 NYS 2d 125 (NY 1985).
6. Richards EP. Colorado public health laws: a rational approach to AIDS. *Dev ULR* 1988;65:127.
7. NYS Public Health Law Sec 2785.2. *McKinney's Consolidated Laws of New York, Annotated*. St Paul, MN: West Publishing, 1993.
8. *Westchester County v People*, 504 NYS 2d 497, 498, 122 AD 2d 1, 2 (NY AD 2 Dept 1986).
9. *McBarnette v Sobol*, 610 NYS 2d 460, 462, 632 NE 2d 866, 868, 83 NY 2d 333, 339, 62 USLW 2623, 2623 (NY 1994).

10. *Jacobson v Massachusetts*, 197 US 11 (1905).
11. *City of New York v New St Mark's Baths*, 130 Misc 2d 911, 497 NYS 2d 979 (1986), citations omitted.
12. Potterat JJ, Rothenberg RB, Muth JB, Woodhouse DE, Muth SQ. Invoking, monitoring, and relinquishing a public health power: the health hold order. *Sex Transm Dis* 1999;26: 345–9.
13. Richards EP 3rd, Rathbun KC. The role of the police power in 21st century public health. *Sex Transm Dis* 1999;26:350–7.
14. Thompson JR. Is the United States country zero for the First-World AIDS epidemic? *J Theor Biol* 2000;204:621–8.
15. *Whalen v Roe*, 429 US 589 (1977).
16. *Planned Parenthood of Central Missouri v Danforth*, 428 US 52 (1976), at 81.
17. *Reynolds v McNichols*, 488 F.2d 1378 (10th Cir. 1973).
18. Potterat JJ, Rothenberg R, Bross DC. Gonorrhea in street prostitutes: epidemiologic and legal implications. *Sex Transm Dis* 1979;6:58–63.
19. *Arcara v Cloud Books, Inc*, 478 US 697 (1986).
20. *Doe v McNulty*, 630 So 2d 825 (La Ct App 4th Cir 1993).
21. *Snyder v American Association of Blood Banks*, 676 A 2d 1036 (1996).
22. Rothenberg R, Bross DC, Vernon TM. Reporting of gonorrhea by private physicians: a behavioral study. *Am J Public Health* 1980;70:983–6.
23. Conn Gen Stat Ann §19a-90 (2001).
24. NY Comp Codes Rules & Regulations, Title 10, §754.7 (1997).
25. Wade NA, Birkhead GS, Warren BL, et al. Abbreviated regimens of zidovudine prophylaxis and perinatal transmission of the human immunodeficiency virus. *N Engl J Med* 1998;339:1409–14.
26. Wade NA, Zielinski MA, Butsashvili M, et al. Decline in perinatal HIV transmission in New York state (1997–2000). *J Acquir Immune Defic Syndr* 2004;36:1075–82.
27. Holtgrave DR, Valdiserri RO, Gerber AR, Hinman AR. Human immunodeficiency virus counseling, testing, referral, and partner notification services. A cost-benefit analysis. *Arch Intern Med* 1993;153:1225–30.
28. Varghese B, Peterman TA, Holtgrave DR. Cost-effectiveness of counseling and testing and partner notification: a decision analysis. *AIDS* 1999;13:1745–51.
29. New York HIV Reporting and Partner Notification Statute, section requiring reporting of partner names. New York State Public Heath Law Article 21, Title 3, §2130, ¶3. Available at http://public.leginfo.state.ny.us/menugetf.cgi. Accessed January 10, 2006.
30. New York HIV Reporting and Partner Notification Statute, section requiring domestic violence screening. New York State Public Health Law Article 21, Title 3, §2133, ¶1, and §2137. Available at *http://public.leginfo.state.ny.us/*. Accessed June 10, 2006.
31. Birkhead GS. HIV partner counseling and referral services in New York State. In: *Program and Abstracts of the 2005 National HIV Prevention Conference, Atlanta, GA. June 12–June 15, 2005.* Abstract # M3–B1603.
32. Des Jarlais DC, Parlis T, Arasteh K, et al. HIV incidence among injection drug users in New York City, 1990 to 2002: use of serologic test algorithm to assess expansion of HIV prevention services. *Am J Public Health* 2005;95:1439–44.
33. Santora M, Altman LK. Rare and aggressive HIV strain reported in New York City. *New York Times* 2005 (February 12):A1.
34. Hu DJ, Vitek CR, Bartholow B, Mastro TD. Key issues for a potential human immunodeficiency virus vaccine. *Clin Infect Dis* 2003;36:638–44.
35. Grady D. Vaccine works to prevent cervical cancer. *New York Times* 2004 (November 2).

Chapter 17

PREVENTION AND CONTROL OF CHRONIC DISEASES

Angela K. McGowan,* Ross C. Brownson,
Lynne S. Wilcox,* and George A. Mensah*

The origins of modern public health can be traced to infectious disease epidemics of now-uncommon diseases such as cholera, plague, and leprosy;[1] however, chronic noncommunicable diseases now are the leading cause of death and disability worldwide.[2,3] In 1900, the three leading causes of death—pneumonia and influenza; tuberculosis; and gastritis, enteritis, and colitis—accounted for nearly one-third of all deaths in the United States. In 2003, heart disease, cancers, stroke, chronic obstructive pulmonary diseases, diabetes, and Alzheimer disease accounted for almost 70% of all deaths (Table 17-1).[4,5] In 2002, the World Health Organization estimated that chronic diseases were responsible for 59% of global mortality (33.1 million deaths).[2] These diseases are leading causes of disability, poor quality of life, and health disparities.[6–10]

Chronic diseases can be defined according to a set of clinical and epidemiologic characteristics. In this chapter, we characterize chronic diseases as having a complex and multiple set of risk factors, a noncontagious origin, a long latent period between risk factor exposure and clinical occurrence of disease, and a long period of illness.[11] Because chronic diseases rarely are cured, public health has focused on disease control, prevention and control of risk factors, and secondary and primary prevention. Common preventable risk factors for chronic diseases include tobacco use, unhealthy diet, low levels of physical activity, obesity, high blood pressure, and high total cholesterol.

* The findings and conclusions in this chapter are those of the author(s) and do not necessarily represent the views of the U.S. Department of Health and Human Services or the Centers for Disease Control and Prevention.

TABLE 17-1   The Ten Leading Causes of Death—United States, 2003

Cause of Death	Death Rate*	Percentage of Total Deaths†
All causes	840	100.0
Diseases of heart	235	28.0
Malignant neoplasms	191	22.7
Cerebrovascular diseases	54	6.4
Chronic obstructive pulmonary disease	43	5.1
Accidents (unintentional injuries)	36	4.3
Diabetes mellitus	25	3.0
Influenza and pneumonia	22	2.6
Alzheimer disease	22	2.6
Nephritis, nephritic syndrome, and nephrosis	15	1.8
Septicemia	12	1.4
All other causes	184	21.9

Source: Hoyert DL, Kung HC, Smith BL. Deaths: preliminary data for 2003. *Natl Vital Stat Rep* 2005;53:1–48.

* Per 100,000 population.
† Percentages do not add up to 100 because of rounding.

Attention has increased on how legal and policy interventions can affect chronic disease in the context of an ecologic framework.[12–15] These models increasingly are viewed as having the largest potential to improve health on a population basis, and they have been applied to numerous chronic disease risk factors and conditions. These frameworks include individual, interpersonal, community, organizational, and legal/government attributes. They highlight the importance of addressing problems at multiple levels, and emphasize the interaction and integration of factors within and across all levels.

The legal/government level is particularly important because of its impact on large populations and because most research has focused on the individual and interpersonal levels of the ecologic framework. Policy and environmental changes, as well as legal tools, remedies, and mechanisms, can complement existing strategies for preventing and controlling chronic diseases and their risk factors.[4,16]

Here we describe legal authorities and controversies, then cover practice considerations in relation to three examples: cardiovascular health, diabetes, and physical activity. We conclude by briefly discussing several emerging issues that should be considered as this topic continues to evolve. As previously demonstrated, law can be an effective tool for preventing chronic diseases and expanding the range of effective public health strategies.[10,11]

Legal Authorities

An important goal in facilitating the prevention and control of chronic diseases is creating a healthier environment and making easier the living of a healthy life. Legal and policy solutions provide the opportunity to modify the environment or to reduce or eliminate risk factors for diseases. These strategies can be applied at the federal, state, and local or community levels.

Similarities in and Differences between Infectious and Chronic Diseases

Similarities exist between the legal sources and authorities used to prevent and control infectious diseases and chronic conditions. Both the U.S. Constitution and state constitutions provide the general legal authority to address infectious diseases and chronic diseases. In addition, both the executive branch and the legislative branch tend to actively address emerging public health problems. For both chronic diseases and infectious diseases, individual interests and rights must balance with societal interests to protect the public's health. As described in the U.S. Supreme Court case *Jacobson v. Massachusetts*, the police powers of the state extend to passing "health laws of every description" and this includes both laws that will protect the public's health and reasonable related regulations. *Jacobson* also held that local entities could be invested with authority to act to safeguard the public health and safety.[17]

The important differences between chronic diseases and infectious diseases derive from the primarily noncommunicable nature of chronic diseases and the long-term nature of chronic conditions. Because the immediate harm to society from a chronic disease may not be apparent, public health actions taken by governments may not appear to meet the legal burden of proof required for infectious diseases. Within the past few decades, attention granted by courts since *Jacobson* to protecting individual rights and due process may reduce the acceptability of government action previously considered appropriate.

Federal Authorities

Even though the U.S. Constitution confers limited powers on the federal government and leaves much of the authority to protect the public's health to the states, the federal government does have the ability to act in some areas.[18] The main authorities include the powers to tax and spend and to regulate interstate commerce (Article 1, §8).[19] The authority to tax and spend can allow the government to encourage or discourage behaviors or actions and thus is an important tool for chronic disease prevention and control. Taxes, subsidies, and federal spending can encourage healthier actions by directly providing health education or through communication efforts or even medical treatments. The power to regulate interstate commerce also may affect chronic diseases because it allows some actions, such as regulating the sale of tobacco products or alcohol, or regulating medications for weight loss or other chronic diseases, which may affect the health of persons with potential or identified chronic diseases. This is a limited power, though, and states still are primarily responsible for the health of their citizens through the Tenth Amendment's explicit reservation of powers (Table 17-2).

Congress has authorized the U.S. Department of Health and Human Services (DHHS) in Title 42 of the United States Code (U.S.C.) (the Public Health Service

TABLE 17-2 Selected Federal Legal Actions Regarding Chronic Disease Prevention and Control

Chronic Disease Focus Area	Year	Summary of Legal Intervention
General Authority to Act		
Public Health Service Act (PL 78-410), USC Title 42, §241—Public Health and Welfare	1946	General authorization for federal legal actions (Research and Investigations generally, Part 301, PHS, and DHHS).
CFR, Title 42—Public Health	Frequent updates	Administrative regulations to guide PHS and DHHS.
Department of Health, Education and Welfare created	1953	Federal Department of Health Education and Welfare created by Eisenhower through his presidential reorganization authority. DHEW remains the only agency to be created through reorganization authority. Became the Department of Health and Human Services (DHHS) in 1980.
Americans with Disabilities Act (PL 101-336)	1990	Prohibits discrimination against persons with disabilities in education or the workplace. May apply to persons with chronic conditions. The Americans with Disabilities Act does not cover some conditions that can be treated by medication (e.g., some diabetes cases, *Sutton v United Airlines*).
*Diabetes Prevention and Control**		
Omnibus Medical Research Act (1950) (PL 81-692)	1950	Established the National Institute of Arthritis and Metabolic Diseases in the Public Health Service. Expanded to include clinical investigation in diabetes. Section 431 authorized the surgeon general to establish a national advisory council.
National Diabetes Mellitus Research and Education Act (PL 93-354)	1974	Created the National Commission on Diabetes Act, which called for centers for research and training on diabetes and establishment of an intergovernment diabetes coordinating committee.
National Commission on Diabetes Report	1975	Investigation into epidemiology and nature of diabetes mellitus and public hearings throughout the United States. National Commission on Diabetes delivered its report, *Long-Range Plan to Combat Diabetes*, to Congress.
Arthritis, Diabetes and Digestive Diseases Amendments of 1976 (PL 94-562)	1976	Established the National Diabetes Advisory Board to advise Congress and DHEW on implementation of *Long-Range Plan to Combat Diabetes*.

(continued)

TABLE 17-2 (continued)

Chronic Disease Focus Area	Year	Summary of Legal Intervention
National Diabetes Education Program	1997	Announced in 1997, a joint NIH & CDC initiative, lead by National Institute of Diabetes & Digestive and Kidney Diseases to reduce the rising prevalence of diabetes, morbidity and mortality of the disease and its complications.
Children's Health Act of 2000 (PL 106-310)	2000	Includes a section on diabetes in children and youth (Public Health Service Act §317H(c), 42 USC 247b-9).
Physical Inactivity		
Land and Water Conservation Fund	1964	Established to create parks and open spaces, protect wilderness and enhance recreational activities.
Individuals with Disabilities Education Act Amendments of 1997 (PL 105-17)†	1997	Related to special education, or specially designed instruction, offered for free for children with disabilities, including instruction in physical activity.
Transportation Equity Act for the 21st Century (1998, PL 105-178)†	1998	Expands the ISTEA requirement that bicycling and walking are considered as transportation plans are assembled and eligibility for funds determined.
National Policy Athletic League Youth Enrichment Act of 1999†	1999	Provides grants to create or expand police athletic leagues. Funded chapters must have at least four nonschool programs including at least two with mentoring, academic assistance, recreational and athletic activities, or technology training.
Children's Health Act of 2000 (PL 106-310)†	2000	Comprehensive bill includes section on childhood obesity prevention. Bill establishes grant program whereby CDC awards grants to states and political subdivisions of states for development of intervention programs to promote good nutrition and physical activity in children and adolescents.
Consolidated Appropriations Act 2001/ Physical Education for Progress Act of 2000‡ (PL 106-554)	2000/2001	Established in part a program to assist local schools and organizations to upgrade their physical education programs and equipment.
No Child Left Behind Act of 2001/ Carol M. White Physical Education Program (PEP)†	2001	Awards grants and contracts for initiating, expanding, and improving physical education programs for all K–12 students. The Secretary of Education may give grants to local schools and community-based organizations for training for staff and teachers, fitness assessments, sports equipment, instruction, and so on.
Department of the Interior and Related Agencies Appropriations Act, 2001†	2001	Calls for funding of trails, to remain available until expended. No more than 20% of the Roads and Trails Fund may be used for indirect obligations.

406

Cardiovascular Health

State Heart Disease and Stroke Prevention Program[‡]	1998	Support from Congress led to creation by CDC of the State Heart Disease and Program ($43.2 million appropriated to implement this program in fiscal year 2003).
Women's Cardiovascular Diseases Research and Prevention Act[‡]	1998	Created a program to fight heart disease, stroke, and other CVDs in women. Expanded heart and stroke research, and created information and education programs for women and health-care providers on risk factors for CVD and stroke.
Cardiac Arrest Survival Act of 2000[‡]	2000	Required federal guidelines re: automated external defibrillators in federal buildings, also "Good Samaritan" provisions for persons using and purchasing automated external defibrillators.
Rural Access to Emergency Devices Act of 2000[‡]	2000	Authorized expenditure of funds in rural areas to purchase automated external defibrillators and provide training.
Paul Coverdell National Acute Stroke Registry of 2000[‡]	2000	Authorized CDC to develop and test systems to track acute stroke patients and their care. Four sites were funded initially and four additional in 2002.
Community AED Act[‡]	2002	Funds authorized to establish public access defibrillation programs in communities.
Medicare Cholesterol Screening Coverage Act of 2003[‡]	2003	Part of Medicare Prescription Drug and Modernization Act of 2003. Allows Medicare recipients to receive cholesterol and other CVD screenings.

* National Institute of Diabetes and Digestive and Kidney Diseases. http://www.niddk.nih.gov/.
† From National Coalition for Promoting Physical Activity. *Physical Activity Policy in Action: Scanning the Landscape* (June 9, 2004). Legislative reference manual.
‡ From the American Heart Association.

Abbreviations: CDC—Centers for Disease Control and Prevention; CFR—Code of Federal Regulations; CVD—cardiovascular disease; DHEW—US Department of Health, Education, and Welfare; DHHS—US Department of Health and Human Services; ISTEA—Intermodal Surface Transportation Efficiency Act; PHS—Public Health Service; PL—Public Law; USC—United States Code; §—Section.

Act) to protect the health of the public.[20] Several agencies within DHHS have been tasked with preventing and controlling chronic diseases. For example, the Centers for Disease Control and Prevention has extensive resources devoted to conditions such as arthritis, cancer, diabetes, epilepsy, heart disease, and stroke, as well as adolescent health, reproductive health, and oral health, and risk factors such as aging, nutrition, physical activity, smoking and alcohol use.

Many diseases have their own statutes and/or funding streams. For example, the National Breast and Cervical Cancer Early Detection Program of the Centers for Disease Control and Prevention was created and funded by the Breast and Cervical Mortality Prevention Act of 1990 (Public Law 101-354). This program helps low-income, uninsured, and underserved women gain access to screening programs to facilitate early detection, as well as follow-up for women with abnormal results through education and service referrals. An estimated 20%–21% of eligible women aged 50–64 years have received Pap tests or mammograms through this program.[21] Additional public health programs or services may be created as a result of a perceived need and may be addressed in the Congressional budgeting process through appropriation of specific designated or general funds.

The Food and Drug Administration (FDA) of DHHS also plays an important role in chronic disease control and prevention.[22] FDA began with the Federal Food and Drug and Cosmetic Act of 1906 (amended in 1938). This law authorized FDA to regulate food, drugs, and cosmetics to ensure their safety for the U.S. population. An example of recent law with chronic disease implications is the Nutrition Labeling and Education Act of 1990, which allows FDA to require nutrition labeling on most food items.[23] Nutrition labeling provides a powerful tool in educating consumers about the calorie and fat content of their diets.[23,24] FDA's final administrative rule, entitled the Food Labeling Regulations, was published in 1993.[25] FDA evaluates the costs and benefits of a drug in comparison with the risks to individuals and approves new drugs related to chronic disease prevention and control.

Congress authorizes the National Institutes of Health (NIH) of DHHS (in Title 42) to conduct research related to many chronic diseases, support nonfederal research, provide training, and communicate research findings.[26] NIH includes programs devoted to alcohol abuse and alcoholism, arthritis, musculoskeletal and skin diseases, dental and craniofacial research, diabetes, digestive and kidney diseases, and other chronic conditions.

The Centers for Medicare and Medicaid Services provides health insurance for many low-income, disabled, and elderly citizens. As the U.S. population ages and Medicare covers more individuals, chronic conditions will account for an increasing percentage of health-care costs. The Centers for Medicare and Medicaid Services also makes important coverage and spending decisions related to screening and preventive care for chronic diseases.

Departments other than DHHS also play an important role in prevention and control of chronic diseases. For instance, the U.S. Department of Agriculture ensures the safety of the food supply, national forests, water supply, and other requirements for health. This agency leads the nation's hunger prevention programs and coordinates food assistance programs such as Food Stamps, the Special Supplemental Nutrition Program for Women, Infant and Children (WIC), and the School Lunch

Program. These federally subsidized programs ensure that families who meet a low-income threshold receive supplemental food and healthy meals.[27]

Thus, the federal authority related to chronic diseases is varied and broad. Many programs have been established through either their own funding language or a delegation of legislative authority.

State Authorities

The states' police powers allow them to promulgate regulations and laws that promote the health, safety, morals, and general welfare of the people.[17,19] In addition, some state constitutions specifically charge the states with protecting their citizens' health.[a] Other states have legislated the duty to protect the public's health to the executive branch, and these duties usually are carried out by implementing existing statutes or by creating new administrative regulations to define roles and responsibilities. State governments may provide health care to citizens, whether through insurance; directly as a provider, such as for government employees or for Medicaid recipients; or through requiring coverage of certain treatments, screenings, or other care for insurers doing business in the state (e.g., the state insurance commissioner's office). Different state priorities create variation in states' laws, regulations and policies, reflecting their varying values, needs and requirements. Even though in most states a public health or other health agency is primarily responsible for chronic disease programs, other agencies—such as the environmental protection agency, state department of agriculture, health-care financing organization—agencies devoted to aging issues or youth health concerns, and the education department will have crucial roles (Table 17-3).

States' Ability to Address Chronic Diseases and Risk Factors

States approach the treatment and prevention of chronic diseases in various ways. Their actions may address one problem or disease or take a more comprehensive approach. For example, Delaware created the Delaware Cancer Consortium in 2003 through legislative efforts. The consortium addresses cancer-related issues, such as treatment, screening, and prevention. On the basis of recommendations by the Task Force on Cancer Incidence and Mortality, the Delaware Health and Safety Code was amended in 2002 to allow for better cancer registry reporting.[28] This legislation allowed regulations created by the Delaware Department of Health and Social Services.[29] Delaware also has implemented policies to address one of the major risk factors for cancer—tobacco use—which included strengthening the Delaware Clean Indoor Air Act.

Another example of a comprehensive state effort is the new Healthy Arkansas initiative initiated by Governor Mike Huckabee in 2004.[30] This plan addresses tobacco use, obesity, and physical inactivity to improve the health of citizens. It includes the Arkansas Diabetes Control Program, legislation to collect the body mass index (BMI) scores for all youth, measures to restrict smoking in public places, increased insurance coverage for smoking cessation measures, and increased physical activity requirements for students.

States also may address specific chronic diseases or issues related to screening for diseases or treating them. Examples related to cardiovascular disease (CVD) include

TABLE 17-3   Selected State and Local Legislative Actions Regarding Chronic
Disease Prevention and Control

Chronic Disease Subject	State and Local Actions
Cardiovascular disease and stroke	• Florida created the Women and Heart Disease Task Force (2000 Fla. Laws, Ch 199) to identify where education, research, and coordination is lacking. A report was required for the governor in 2002. • Tennessee (Tenn. Code Ann. §68-1-1901) now requires the Ccommissioner of Health to establish a stroke care, education, and outreach collaborative in each division of the state and to help develop "stroke centers" within community hospitals. • Colorado (Co. Rev. Stat. §24-75-1104) provides tobacco litigation settlement payments to many prevention programs and groups, including the Stroke Prevention and Treatment Cash Fund. • Texas (HB 580 in 1999) now gives immunity from liability for AED use by those meeting criteria (e.g., training), unless they are willfully or wantonly negligent (Health & Safety Code, Ch 779). • Many cities, localities, and private places (e.g., worksites) have established smoke-free air ordinances or policies that address secondhand smoke, a major risk factor for CVD.
Diabetes prevention and control	• Alaska now requires that diabetes treatment, including medication, equipment, and supplies, be covered by all health insurance plans, including up to $1500 per year for diabetes outpatient self-management training or education. (HB 298 of 2000). • Virginia amended its law to protect school employees assisting in diabetes treatment and insulin delivery during school from liability if parental consent and follows medication schedule (S 889 of 1999). • New York City has a current proposal to require reporting of A1C (average glucose measure) by labs for better tracking, support, and surveillance of diabetes patients. Voluntary opt-out anticipated.
Physical inactivity	• Healthy Arkansas—BMI measurements (Act 1220 of 2003), overall plans to increase physical activity. • West Virginia's Healthy Lifestyles Act of 2005 (HB 2816)— set into motion the state's Healthy Start Initiative: putting physical education back into K–12 curriculum, requiring 50% healthy items in vending machines for those with soft drink vending contracts, and establishing a governor's recognition program for restaurants that voluntarily label menus so children and adults can identify healthier choices. • Kentucky (HB 221 of 2000) created a state Rails-to-Trails development office. • Michigan (Act 451 of 1994) Department of Natural Resources appropriation for recreation improvement fund grants and national recreational trails.

TABLE 17-3   (*Continued*)

Chronic Disease Subject	State and Local Actions
	• Missouri metro park and recreation district: develops public system of interconnecting parks and trails. • "Step Up to Health . . . It Starts In Parks," a National Parks and Recreation program to train 1500 agencies to be magnet centers to help create a healthy community. Funding in 2005 for 500 additional communities. • Clovis/Fresno Old Town Trail (Rails-to-Trails) conversion. In 1997, these California cities purchased old railway right of way.

Sources: American Heart Association; the National Conference of State Legislatures Health Promotion; National Coalition for Promoting Physical Activity, *Physical Activity Policy in Action: Scanning the Landscape* (June 9, 2004), legislative reference manual.

Abbreviations: AED—Automatic external defibrillator; BMI—body mass index; CVD—cardiovascular disease; HB—House Bill; SB—Senate Bill.

laws requiring automated external defibrillators in state or other facilities and providing for Good Samaritan protection to volunteers by granting them immunity from liability for using this equipment to assist someone in cardiac distress. Actions to address diabetes might include identifying people with diabetes through implementing screening or providing specialized plans for children to allow participation in routine school activities.

At times the public health community focuses on risk factors for chronic diseases rather than the diseases themselves. Addressing a risk factor for one chronic disease may help decrease or prevent one or more other chronic diseases. For example, increasing physical activity may reduce the incidence and effects of CVD or diabetes. In particular, states have made major strides to curb one major risk factor for chronic disease: tobacco use.[31] Tobacco-control measures have included enforcing access laws, such as setting minimum purchasing ages; restricting or limiting advertising; reducing tobacco exposure through clean indoor air ordinances or laws;[32] increasing taxes on tobacco products; and subsidies to help tobacco farmers decrease production or change to other crops. (See also Chapter 18.) Although many of these tools are available to address other chronic conditions, they need to be tailored to each risk factor and to balance the societal good with the intrusion on individuals' rights and choices.

Another risk factor that influences chronic diseases is alcohol consumption. States may pass mandates to reduce access to alcohol by minors and to reduce driving under the influence of alcohol. Increased taxes for alcoholic beverages also can decrease consumption. A newer measure, for persons found guilty of driving under the influence, is mandated breathalyzers placed on car ignitions. States may pass laws in this area, but enforcement frequently is left to local authorities.

Reporting of and Surveillance for Chronic Diseases

States are responsible for requiring reporting of certain health conditions and diseases and for conducting health surveillance. Even though state law or regulation requires reporting of many infectious diseases, reporting of chronic health conditions is less frequently mandated. Some state laws have established cancer registries; these registries enable states to track the prevalence and incidence of cancer to plan for services and treatment and to identify unusual clusters of disease. For example, Louisiana's statewide cancer registry program (La. Rev. Stat. 40:1299.80 *et seq.*) specifies that health-care providers diagnosing cancer or treating cancer patients shall report each case within six months after diagnosis or each patient after hospital admission. In addition to establishing reporting requirements, administrative changes, such as rulemaking or policy guidance, may be necessary to educate health-care providers, health-care facilities, laboratories, or other groups to report information, as well as to prescribe the best methods of reporting.

However, concern regarding protection of the privacy of individual health information accompanies the benefits of population health monitoring. Most state laws or regulations provide for the protection of personal health information and specify penalties for violations (see also Chapter 10). In addition, federal legislation such as the Health Insurance Portability and Accountability Act of 1996 provides uniform protection among states for health information and assures citizens their information will be protected nationally.[34,b] For reported information in schools, federal laws such as the Family Educational Rights and Privacy Act (20 U.S.C. §1232g; 34 C.F.R. Part 99) protects the privacy of student education records.

A recent issue regarding the collection and reporting of health information addresses measuring students' BMIs. This has been proposed in several states, including Arkansas, Georgia, West Virginia, and Pennsylvania. Arkansas passed legislation in 2003 to allow for the collection of all students' BMIs and reporting of this information to parents.[35] This legislation was amended in 2004 to more clearly specify how this information should be collected and divulged to parents while protecting and supporting the students. This amendment called for sending a letter home to the parents and including educational materials to explain this measure and describe ways to address weight issues for children.

Local Authorities

Laws passed by the state legislature or regulations promulgated from state agencies may create the authority or provide the funding for local health departments or other entities to act to protect the public's health. Local governments may implement the regulations and requirements of the state or federal government by passing their own ordinances to provide for health or to regulate the health environment, issuing policy statements, and providing services.

One arena in which local health authorities have discretion is shaping the environment, sometimes termed the "built environment." Frequently, legislatures create broad policies regarding the built environment that are left to local entities (e.g., planning boards, school boards, zoning boards, and administrative agencies) to implement.[36] An example is zoning ordinances that require playgrounds or sidewalks in new communities to facilitate physical activity. One of the most well known of these local policies has been the use of clean indoor air ordinances that prohibit smoking in certain environments to protect citizens from secondhand smoke. One locality with great success in this area has been New York City, which passed a strict smoke-free air law in 2002 for almost all workplaces, which was later amended when New York State passed a similar law a year later.[37] Some states have preempted local authorities by passing laws that directly control actions regarding a particular health topic, such as smoking, but usually local authorities are free to act as long as they do not directly conflict with guidance from state or federal entities. Additionally, the enforcement of many public health laws is left to local officials.

Legal Issues and Controversies

Legal issues and controversies related to chronic diseases involve many different areas, including the need to balance individual rights and societal interests, shaping a healthier environment, health-care financing, and treatment concerns.[38,39]

Individual Rights versus Societal Interests

The tension between individual rights and societal interest tends to be especially contentious for some chronic disease prevention activities. For example, the decision to tax goods that are seen to be "unhealthy," such as cigarettes, alcohol, and foods of minimal nutritional value (i.e., "junk foods"), restricts an individual's personal choice to enjoy these activities. The benefit to society of the measure must be weighed against the restriction of personal freedom or choice. Measuring the benefits and costs should include reviewing the scientific evidence surrounding a particular legal or policy intervention, as well as its effects on health outcomes. Restricting indoor smoking curtails the choice of citizens to smoke when and where they choose. The harm of tobacco and secondhand smoke is well documented and has been fairly well disseminated to the public, but for other risk factors, the individual rights or freedom argument may seem stronger. For obesity or other nutritional problems, the line is less clear because most foods are not inherently dangerous; the combination of readily available excess food and calories and decreased physical activity have contributed to increased obesity in the U.S. population. Thus laws and policies aimed at reducing obesity and modifying eating behaviors are more controversial.

Nevertheless, legal options exist to address the growing problem of obesity. Taxes on foods of no or low nutritional value may discourage consumption of these foods. However, such a directed tax also may keep persons with lower incomes from enjoying certain foods. Food can be an important part of social activities, such as birthday cakes for special occasions, and this tax could be seen as an intrusion. A food tax may be regressive and most impact people with lower incomes who can least afford healthier alternatives.[40] Moreover, low-income areas may not be served by stores that provide healthier options, such as fruits and vegetables, and this measure could be punitive.[36]

Another option is direct government assistance, such as subsidies to encourage healthier behaviors (e.g., encouraging healthier foods in cafeterias at schools, assisting grocery stores to enter low-income areas that are underserved, and providing sidewalks to facilitate physical activity or incentives for alternate transportation). This approach, like the food stamp program or the National School Lunch Program, may be less controversial, but also may be considered paternalistic or costly. Measures focusing on children, such as modifying the food served in school cafeterias or mandating physical activity for students, usually are less controversial because children are minors and considered legally deserving of the state's protection.

Shaping a Healthier Environment

Legal or policy measures may be used to modify the environment and make it more conducive to health and healthy behaviors. These include policies that reduce exposure to secondhand smoke or encourage positive behaviors such as physical activity.[32] Universal fluoridation of water is considered one of the most successful public health policies of the 20th century.[41] Eleven states mandate water fluoridation of some variety through legislation, other states accomplish this through administrative regulations, and some states have allowed municipalities or communities to decide fluoridation.[42] Although fluoridation has been challenged on the basis of individual rights and less-intrusive means of obtaining fluoride (e.g., through toothpaste use and other sources), most courts have found that fluoridation is a valid use of the state police power and that the protection of oral health is a valid state purpose.[41]

Financing Chronic Disease Care

States face many issues related to the funding or financing of health care for chronic diseases.[43] In 2001, the United States spent around $1.4 trillion on health care—an average of $5,039 per person.[44] The direct medical care costs of chronic diseases account for at least 60% of the nation's annual health-care expenditures.[43] Legal issues related to the funding of health care surround the government's role in providing and financing services. The federal government sometimes funds health services directly through Medicare, through programs such as the National Breast and Cervical Cancer Early Detection Program, or by support for specific medical services, such as experimental treatment for cancer. Often, federal dollars are given to states, municipalities, and other groups as grants to encourage programs to prevent or control chronic diseases. One example is funding for state comprehensive cancer control programs. Requirements usually accompany these funds, such as specifying the services that must be provided; however, states or localities are left to implement the programs within their jurisdictions.

Treatment

Treatment of chronic diseases also involves legal and policy decisions. Governments frequently make decisions regarding covered services under health insurance policies, services by state-provided programs such as Medicaid, and services by plans insuring state employees. States have control over health insurance coverage plans offered within each state through a state health insurance commissioner or similar office and can require coverage of items such as gastric surgery for obese persons, specific chronic disease-related treatments, or screening tests (e.g., those for colorectal or prostate cancer).

Liability issues related to treatment for chronic diseases pose concerns for many states. Most states require medications be delivered by certain medical personnel, such as physicians, nurses, or pharmacists, but this approach may not be practicable for chronic diseases. One example of recent legal issues is the ability of students to self-medicate in schools. Some children with asthma or diabetes are not able to participate in traditional schooling if they are required to have a nurse or other responsible adult oversee every dose of medication. In most states, legislation allows students to self-medicate at school, and 23 states have enacted laws that allow students to carry their medications and to self-administer them at school with consent from parents and permission from a specified health-care provider.[45] For schools, training adults or teachers to supervise students' self-medication may be problematic if formal medical supervision is necessary. Untrained staff or adults must be taught to recognize the problems and address emergency situations.

Three important federal laws protect students with diabetes: the Americans with Disabilities Act (42 U.S.C. §12101 *et seq.*);[46] Section 504 of the Rehabilitation Act of 1973 (29 U.S.C. §794); and the Individuals with Disabilities Education Act (20 U.S.C. §1400 *et seq.*). Together these laws protect against discrimination for almost all students with diabetes and require accommodations as needed so students can safely participate in school activities.

Practice Considerations

We consider here the use of regulatory and legal approaches in chronic disease prevention using as examples two chronic diseases—cardiovascular disease and diabetes —and one risk factor for chronic diseases—physical inactivity.

Cardiovascular Disease

The major risk factors for most CVD are known.[47,48] Strategies and best practices for prevention and control of these risk factors and the principal CVDs they cause also are well established. Most of these risk factors have social and environmental origins requiring social, environmental, and policy change. Thus, they constitute fertile ground for law as a tool in their prevention and control.[4,16]

Advancing age, for example, is the most powerful independent risk factor for CVD in both men and women. Accordingly, the Welcome to Medicare Physical Examination program, a part of the Medicare Modernization Act[8] that authorizes Medicare reimbursement for CVD, cancer, and diabetes screening of all eligible persons on attainment of age 65 years, provides legal-based intervention for preventing and controlling major chronic diseases. This legislation affects all three levels of CVD prevention approaches—health promotion, primary prevention, and secondary prevention—in a high-risk population.[49]

Tobacco use is the next most common cause of CVD-related death and the single most preventable cause of morbidity and mortality in the United States.[50] During

1997–2001, smoking caused an estimated average of 259,494 deaths annually among men and 178,408 deaths among women in the United States. Most of these deaths resulted from chronic diseases, and CVD alone contributed 35% of the total attributable deaths.[51] The Pro-Children's Act of 1994[52] and the World Health Organization's Framework Convention for Tobacco Control[53] represent, respectively, examples of national and international application of legal tools, remedies, and interventions to address the burden and health impact of tobacco use.

Other major risk factors that contribute to CVD include physical inactivity, poor nutrition, obesity, hypertension, and high total blood cholesterol. Decreasing levels of physical activity and increasing prevalence of poor nutrition continue to fuel the epidemic of obesity and diabetes in the United States.[54] Legal interventions for prevention and control of diet- and nutrition-related morbidity and mortality require a more nuanced approach those for tobacco control.[55] In 2004, the U.S. House of Representatives overwhelmingly approved a bill to ban lawsuits by obese customers who blame their obesity on fast-food restaurants.[56] Even though this legislation did not pass the Senate and become enacted law, states have proposed—and in some cases passed—similar legislation.

Examples of current legislative interventions in the secondary prevention of CVD focus on the management of acute heart attack, stroke, cardiac arrest, and heart failure. At the federal level, legislative tools enable FDA and the Centers for Medicare and Medicaid Services to play a crucial role in the regulation and reimbursement for the use of automated implantable defibrillators in eligible persons.[57] At the state and local levels, legislative and policy interventions may include creation of or support for existing quality improvement organizations to identify needs for education, training, and advocacy related to secondary prevention practices and measurement of quality care. The CVD collaborative projects of the Health Resources and Services Administration within the Federally Qualified Health Centers represent another example in the area of heart failure and heart attack management.

Diabetes

Diabetes has been diagnosed in an estimated 14.6 million Americans. Diabetes has two major forms: type 1, which usually is diagnosed in childhood, and type 2, which usually appears in adults and represents about 90% of all diabetes cases. A major public health concern is the primary prevention of type 2 diabetes through proper nutrition and physical activity. However, this discussion focuses on legal issues for people in whom the disease already has been diagnosed.

Serious medical complications of diabetes include CVD, stroke, blindness, kidney disease, and limb amputations. Thus, funding health-care services is a critical aspect of legal issues regarding this disease. Medicare provides services for the elderly and for persons with certain disabilities. The program covers diabetes screening, diabetes-related medical supplies, therapeutic shoes, self-management training, nutritional counseling, influenza and pneumoccocal vaccinations, glaucoma screening, and end-stage renal dialysis. Medicaid, which is provided from a combination of state and federal budgets, pays for medical assistance for families with low incomes and resources. Coverage differs by state but generally covers both pregnant women and newborn care related to diabetes and adult diabetes care.

Although private health insurance plans vary widely in the level of diabetes-specific benefits they offer, they are subject to government regulation and must meet certain standards, particularly at the state level. Forty-six states and the District of Columbia have enacted legal protections requiring or related to coverage of diabetes supplies and services in state-regulated plans. In 2005, the Government Accountability Office reported that health plans not subject to state regulation usually cover some of the diabetes supplies and services required at the state level.[16,58]

Law and regulation at the state level also include health tracking authority. State health departments and vital statistics offices examine trends in diabetes prevalence using surveys—such as the Behavioral Risk Factor Surveillance System, which includes modules on diabetes and death certificates—that may indicate diabetes as the cause of mortality. These data inform policy decisions on programs that prevent diabetes or pay for its care.

At the local and community levels, "appropriate" school health measures allow students with diabetes to self-manage their disease to the extent they are able and to have trained adults present to provide care when needed. As previously discussed in this chapter, federal laws prohibit discrimination against schoolchildren with diabetes, and schools face multiple issues in addressing these needs, including limited resources for school nurses and lack of diabetes management information for teachers. Diabetes health-care professionals have responded by developing tools to provide basic information about diabetes to all school personnel and to train selected school personnel who are not nurses to provide diabetes care in the absence of a school nurse. However, in some instances, state laws regarding delegation of nursing tasks present barriers. In response, some states (e.g., Virginia, North Carolina, Washington, Tennessee, and Texas) have passed comprehensive diabetes school-care legislation, and other states have passed laws specific to certain aspects of diabetes care, such as administration of emergency medications.

The previous discussion provides only a partial list of diabetes-related laws and policies. For example, the American Diabetes Association has worked closely with the Transportation Security Administration to protect people passing through airport security screening from being retained or having their supplies confiscated on the basis of their diabetes. Additionally, education of all personnel who provide service to the public will be an essential aspect of developing appropriate laws and regulations for people with diabetes.

For workers with diabetes, the Americans with Disabilities Act, the Rehabilitation Act of 1973, and the Congressional Accountability Act (2 U.S.C. §1301 *et seq.*) protect against discrimination based on disability. These laws not only prohibit discrimination, but also require employers to provide reasonable accommodations. The Americans with Disabilities Act also prohibits discrimination in places of public accommodations, such as restaurants, amusement parks, and concert venues.

Finally, federal constitutional and statutory law addresses the rights of people with diabetes in correctional institutions. Barriers to appropriate care in these settings range from losing access to food and medication during initial police detainment (see, e.g.,

Flowers v. Bennett, 123 F. Supp. 2d 595 [N.D. Ala. 2000]) to lack of access to blood glucose monitoring and treatment of long-term complications in the context of long-term confinement (see, e.g., *Hunt v. Uphoff*, 199 F.3d 1220 [10th Cir. 1999], and *Howard v. City of Columbus*, 521 S.E.2d 51 [Ga. Ct. App. 1999]).

Physical Activity

A range of legal issues relevant to promotion of physical activity largely derive from research in urban planning and travel behavior.[59,60] To identify effective legal/policy approaches for promoting physical activity, researchers have examined the relation between community design variables and walking or cycling for transportation. The urban landscape has changed dramatically during the past 50 years.[61] The period from 1945 to the present has been described as the "Freeway Era," in which the automobile has changed from a luxury to a necessity for commuting, shopping, and socializing.[62] This trend also contributed to the advent of the suburban ring, and the accompanying freeway segments, which now girdle most central cities in the United States. The migration to suburban environments is linked closely with the evolution of zoning policies over the past century.[63] For example, landmark cases such as *Euclid v. Amber Realty* (1926)[64] established the importance of local zoning laws in shaping the patterns of growth in urban areas.

The *Guide to Community Preventive Services* identified two effective types of interventions through urban planning and policy.[65] The first set of strategies involves street-scale changes—urban design and land-use policies—that support physical activity in small geographic areas, generally limited to a few blocks. Another closely related group of interventions focus on community-scale changes that are similar to street-scale changes but involve a larger geographic area (e.g., an entire community).

Transportation policy also can substantially influence travel choice (e.g., walking versus driving). Changes in transportation policy may influence the rate of physical activity and may benefit air quality and traffic congestion. These interventions rely on policy measures, such as roadway design standards, expansion of public transportation services, and subsidization of public transportation (i.e., transit passes). In the review of the *Guide to Community Preventive Services*, only three studies were identified for this intervention strategy. However, because of the limited number of qualified studies, this intervention strategy has insufficient evidence to provide recommendations.

Legal issues affecting physical activity encompass three main areas: (1) formal written codes, regulations, or decisions bearing on relevant legal authority; (2) written standards that guide choices; and (3) unwritten norms that influence behavior. Perhaps more so than for many other public health issues, the legal issues affecting physical activity behavior are likely to be most important and relevant at the local level, rather than federal or state levels.

First, legal codes and regulations tremendously affect the physical activity environment. With the goal of creating environments less reliant on the automobile and more conducive to walking and bicycling, a growing number of cities throughout the United States have revised, are revising, or are considering revising, their land development codes, which regulate land use mix and density, design and configuration of streets, and other aspects of the built environment. Revised zoning and building codes may support a wider range of housing types and mixed use (e.g., residential and business). These code revisions are based largely on professional judgment of their benefits rather than empirical evidence and on a limited understanding of the degree of change necessary to significantly increase the likelihood of walking. At the same time, cities directly change the built environment through their capital improvement programs. For the most part, infrastructure improvements, such as the construction of sidewalks or a new park in older areas of the city or construction of a pedestrian bridge over a highway, are prioritized using criteria that reflect assumptions about the possible change in behavior those investments may trigger. State and federal agencies also can influence local land use and transportation policies through advisory and, in certain cases, regulatory approaches.

Second, written standards and guidelines also can influence physical activity patterns. Although land development codes and capital improvement programs are a decentralized form of policy, organizations such as the American Planning Association and the Institute of Transportation Engineers influence these efforts in a more centralized way by disseminating guidelines and best practices. At the local level, the utility of roads is described by their "level-of-service" (e.g., a facility is safe for all age groups versus one that is not suitable for pedestrians or cyclists). These standards may be influenced by studies that define the key attributes of the built environment crucial for promotion of physical activity. Most state health departments have, or are developing, state plans addressing physical inactivity and obesity; these plans may be important in highlighting the role of these standards and guidelines.

Finally, norms within communities and business practices may influence rates of physical activity. These unwritten norms may include the expectations or collective efficacy of a community (e.g., trust and informal social control).[66] Private businesses, such as housing developers, often adopt informal standards of practice—written or unwritten. These have been articulated as "new urbanist" principles, with the idea that development and re-development may positively affect residents' health and quality of life.[67]

Emerging Issues

Legislative and Regulatory Actions

Recent legislative and regulatory changes to address chronic diseases should be monitored and evaluated using traditional public health tools to assess their impact on health outcomes. For example, in the area of obesity prevention, bills have passed that focus on the school population by, for example, eliminating foods of minimal nutritional value from school cafeterias, requiring education in either nutrition or physical education, providing for teachers and equipment for physical activities, and measuring and reporting students' BMIs. Additionally, litigation has been proposed as one way to address the obesity epidemic, whether through suing manufacturers or restaurants for contributing to obesity in this country or through requiring insurance companies or other payers to cover obesity treatment programs or surgical options, such as gastric bypass. Litigation, however, is more controversial, and some states have reacted by passing "commonsense consumption" bills to protect sellers and restaurants from what can be viewed as a personal decision.[68] Agencies in charge of education, health, and agriculture have made additional efforts.

Legislative intervention to enforce compulsory vaccination of eligible persons has contributed to the remarkable success of immunization programs for controlling communicable diseases in the United States.[69] Similar interventions for large-scale prevention and control of CVD do not exist. However, an intriguing issue is emerging regarding use of a proposed "polypill" that theoretically appears to be a vaccine equivalent for CVD prevention. For example, one proposal calls for a single pill comprising aspirin (75 mg), statin, three blood pressure-lowering drugs (at half-dose), and folic acid (0.8 mg) that could reduce the incidence of coronary heart disease by 88% and stroke by 80%, if taken by all persons aged 55 years and older and by persons of any age who have existing CVD or diabetes.[70–72] This proposal concludes that "no other preventive method would have so great an impact on public health in the western world."[70] If clinical trials substantiate the polypill claim, then federal, state, and local authorities may play a role in ensuring widespread use of this intervention.

Disparities in Health Care and Status

The elimination of heath disparities is one of the two overarching goals of the Healthy People 2010 national health agenda.[73] Despite remarkable advances in improving overall health of the American public, marked disparities persist in the prevalence, morbidity, and mortality associated with chronic diseases and their major risk factors.[9,74] In general, the population subgroups most significantly and adversely affected by disparities include blacks, Hispanics/Mexican Americans, American Indians/Alaska Natives, persons with low socioeconomic status, persons without health insurance, and residents of the southeastern United States and the Appalachians.[9,73] Similarly, persons with less than a high school education tend to have a higher burden of the major chronic diseases regardless of race/ethnicity.

The causes of these disparities are complex and include individual as well as institutional and societal factors. Although access to care, cultural practices, and patient behaviors often are highlighted, other key determinants of disparities include regulations, policies, and systems of care that directly or indirectly lead to disparities in quality of care delivered.[75] In addition, differences in income and educational level and existence of prejudice, discrimination, and provider bias have been suggested.

Legal frameworks have the potential to affect many of these determinants. Enforcement of existing laws against discrimination in health care and enforcement of the community services provisions of Title VI of the Civil Rights Act of 1964[76] and the Hill-Burton Act's Community Services Assurance provision[77] can significantly reduce health disparities. Legislation to support or provide incentives for cultural competence training for health providers and improve access to quality care for poor, indigent, or inadequately insured persons will similarly help reduce disparities. Regulations and policies providing constraints on individual choices and institutional behavior can benefit health. Thus, legal and policy interventions can be used to improve access, financing, and quality of care and to help eliminate health disparities.

Chronic Disease Financing and Insurance Coverage

Financing and ensuring access to treatment for persons with chronic conditions remains a critical issue. Identifying ways to increase access to health-care providers, providing screening tests to identify those with chronic conditions, and requiring the best possible treatment for persons with these conditions is crucial. As the U.S. population ages, funding for health care will remain a large portion of federal and state budgets.

One investigator recently reported that addition of a fixed dose of isosorbide dinitrate plus hydralazine (BiDil) to standard therapy for heart failure is efficacious and increases survival among black patients with advanced heart failure. Previous studies had shown no benefit of this combination in the total population of heart failure patients. However, in this study, the rate of death from any cause decreased 43%, there was a 33% relative reduction in the rate of first hospitalization for heart failure, and the quality of life in blacks improved.[78] In part on the basis of these data, FDA recently approved BiDil for use in heart failure patients who self-identify as black.[79] This emerging issue has implications at the federal and state levels for reimbursement, as well as on appropriations for race-based, personalized drug development and treatment for chronic diseases.[78,80,81]

Policies recently introduced to modify health insurance premiums for people living healthier lifestyles by, for example, choosing not to smoke, increasing their physical activity, or staying within a certain weight range may provide incentives. These policies have been suggested as an increased premium for people who have poor health habits or a benefit for people who have healthier lifestyles. Georgia recently passed such legislation, and three other states already have implemented this approach.[c] Starting in July 2005, state employees in Georgia who smoke or who have family members on their health plan who smoke pay an additional $40 a month for health insurance premiums. Although this could encourage employees and their families to quit smoking, issues arise regarding whether these higher premiums may make insurance unaffordable for some people or whether enough assistance, such as smoking cessation tools, counseling, and products, has been made available to affected persons.

As genetic testing becomes more pervasive, legal approaches need to ensure that anyone identified with a genetic predisposition to a chronic condition or disease is not barred from receiving health coverage. Along with advances in the field, this matter may necessitate federal or state action to ensure that citizens are treated fairly and equitably.

Public Health Emergencies

The massive destruction from Hurricane Katrina in 2005 and other public health emergencies demonstrate the need to address legal concerns related to chronic conditions during disasters. The multitude of these issues—such as the ability to monitor chronic conditions, monitoring medical records and information, treating affected persons, or ensuring that prescriptions and medications can be obtained and dispensed rapidly—must be considered in advance to best protect the public's health.

Conclusion

Preventing and controlling chronic diseases represents a long-term and difficult challenge for the public health system. We have explored some ways that legal and policy interventions can be important weapons in this fight, and have attempted to provide a broad view of how to approach law and chronic diseases by focusing on a selection of diseases and risk factors. Addressing multiple level or ecologic frameworks allows practitioners to consider a wide range of options and interventions. Recent frameworks have focused on the built environment,[36] prevention and control of obesity and overweight, and cardiovascular diseases.[83] Through emerging legal interventions, as well as scientific and programmatic efforts, prevention and control of chronic diseases may succeed in increasing quality of life and reducing mortality and morbidity as previous infectious disease efforts have succeeded.

We thank Shereen Arent, J.D., managing director of legal advocacy from the American Diabetes Association, and Frank Vinicor, M.D., M.P.H., formerly the director of the Division of Diabetes Translation at CDC, for their valuable assistance in preparing this chapter.

Notes

a. Examples of this include (1) New York State, Article XVII,§3: "The protection and promotion of the health of the inhabitants of the state are matters of public concern and provision therefore shall be made by the state and by such of its subdivisions and in such manner, and by such means as the legislature shall from time to time determine," and (2) South Carolina, Article XII, §1: Matters of public concern; General Assembly to provide appropriate agencies; "The health, welfare, and safety of the lives and property of the people of this State and the conservation of its natural resources are matters of public concern. The General Assembly shall provide appropriate agencies to function in these areas of public concern and determine the activities, powers, and duties of such agencies."

b. The Health Insurance Portability and Accountability Act is a baseline; states with laws that are more protective of health information still will be controlling.

c. These states are West Virginia, Alabama, and Kentucky.

References

1. Turnock BJ. *Public Health: What It Is and How It Works*. Gaithersburg, MD: Aspen Publishers, 2001.
2. World Health Organization. *The World Health Report 2003: Shaping the Future*. Geneva: World Health Organization, 2003.
3. Murray CJ, Lopez AD. Mortality by cause for eight regions of the world: Global Burden of Disease Study. *Lancet* 1997;349:1269–76.
4. Mensah GA, Goodman RA, Moulton AD, et al. Law as a tool for preventing chronic diseases: expanding the range of effective public health strategies. *Prev Chronic Dis* [serial online] 2004;1:1–8.

5. Hoyert DL, Kung HC, Smith BL. Deaths: preliminary data for 2003. *Natl Vital Stat Rep* 2005;53:1–48.
6. Lillie-Blanton M, Maddox TM, Rushing O, Mensah GA. Disparities in cardiac care: rising to the challenge of Healthy People 2010. *J Am Coll Cardiol* 2004;44:503–8.
7. US Commission on Civil Rights. *The Health Care Challenge: Acknowledging Disparity, Confronting Discrimination, and Ensuring Equality. Volume I: The Role of Governmental and Private Health Care Programs and Initiatives*. Washington, DC: US Commission on Civil Rights, 1999.
8. Medicare Prescription Drug, Improvement, and Modernization Act of 2003, §611, Coverage of an initial preventive physical examination (Pub L 108–173). Available at http://frwebgate.access.gpo.gov/cgi-bin/getdoc.cgi?dbname=108_cong_public_laws&docid=f:publ173.108.pdf. Accessed January 4, 2006.
9. Liao Y, Tucker P, Okoro CA, Giles WH, Mokdad AH, Harris VB. REACH 2010 Surveillance for Health Status in Minority Communities—United States, 2001–2002. *MMWR Surveill Summ* 2004;53(SS6):1–36.
10. National Center for Health Statistics. *Health, United States, 2004. With Chartbook on Trends in the Health of Americans*. Hyattsville, MD: US Department of Health and Human Services, Centers for Disease Control and Prevention, National Center for Health Statistics, 2004.
11. McKenna MT, Taylor WR, Marks JS, Koplan JP. Current issues and challenges in chronic disease control. In: Brownson RC, Remington PL, Davis JR, eds. *Chronic Disease Epidemiology and Control*. 2nd ed. Washington, DC: American Public Health Association, 1998:1–26.
12. McLeroy KR, Bibeau D, Steckler A, Glanz K. An ecological perspective on health promotion programs. *Health Edu Q* 1988;15:351–77.
13. Simons-Morton DG, Simons-Morton BG. Influencing personal and environmental conditions for community health: a multilevel intervention model. *Fam Community Health* 1988;11:25–35.
14. Breslow L. Social ecological strategies for promoting healthy lifestyles. *Am J Health Promot* 1996;10:253–7.
15. Stokols D, Allen J, Bellingham, RL. The social ecology of health promotion: implications for research and practice. *Am J Health Promot* 1996;10:247–51.
16. Mensah GA, Goodman RA, Moulton AD, et al. Law as a tool for preventing chronic diseases: expanding the range of effective public health strategies. Part 1. *Prev Chronic Dis* [serial online]. 2004;1:1–8.
17. *Jacobson v Massachusetts*, 197 US 11 (1905).
18. Goodman RA, Kocher PL, O'Brien DJ, Alexander FS. The structure of law in public health systems and practice. In: Goodman RA, Rothstein MA, Hoffman RE, Lopez W, Matthews GW, Foster KL, eds. *Law in Public Health Practice*. 2nd ed. New York: Oxford University Press, 2007 (in press).
19. Gostin LO, Koplan JP, Grad FP. The law and the public's health: the foundations. In: Goodman RA, Rothstein MA, Hoffman RA, Lopez W, Matthews GW, Foster KL, eds. *Law in Public Health Practice*. New York: Oxford University Press, 2003 (in press).
20. Public Health Service Act, Pub L 78-410, 58 Stat 682 (1946).
21. Centers for Disease Control and Prevention. *2004/2005 Fact Sheet, The National Breast and Cervical Cancer Early Detection Program: Saving Lives through Screening*. 2005. Available at http://www.cdc.gov/cancer/nbccedp/about2004.htm. Accessed August 7, 2005.
22. FDA. Mission Statement. Available at http://www.fda.gov/opacom/morechoices/mission.html. Accessed November 15, 2005.

23. Nutrition Labeling and Education Act of 1990, Pub L 101–535, 21 USC, Ch 9 (1990).
24. Committee on Prevention of Obesity in Children and Youth. *Preventing Childhood Obesity: Health in the Balance*. Washington, DC: National Academies Press, 2004.
25. Food Labeling Regulations, 21 CFR §§101.1–101.108 (1993).
26. National Institutes of Health. Mission Statement. Available at http://www.nih.gov/about/. Accessed November 12, 2005.
27. US Department of Agriculture. Food and Nutrition. Available at http://www.usda.gov/wps/portal/!ut/p/_s.7_0_A/7_0_1OB?navtype=SU&navid=FOOD_NUTRITION. Accessed August 7, 2005.
28. An Act to amend Title 16 of the Delaware Code related to health and safety in order to implement recommendations of the Task Force on Cancer Incidence and Mortality and Improve the Quality of Cancer Registry Reporting, Delaware Senate Bill B 372 (2002). Available at http://www.legis.state.de.us/LIS/LIS141.NSF/vwLegislation/SB+372?Opendocument. Accessed January 5, 2006.
29. Delaware Regulations, 6 DE Reg 958 (2005).
30. Arkansas Department of Health and Human Services. Healthy Arkansas. Available at http://www.arkansas.gov/ha/home.html. Accessed November 12 2005.
31. Warner KE. Tobacco policy in the United States: lessons for the obesity epidemic. In: Mechanic D, Rogut LB, Colby DC, Knickman JR, eds. *Policy Challenges in Modern Health Care*. New Brunswick, NJ: Rutgers University Press, 2005:99–114.
32. Centers for Disease Control and Prevention. State smoking restrictions for private-sector worksites, restaurants, and bars—United States, 1998–2004. *MMWR* 2005;54:649–53.
33. Malek SH, Vollinger RE Jr, Sneegas KS, Shopland DR. Public and private policy interventions. *Monograph 16: ASSIST*. Rockville, MD: National Institutes of Health, National Cancer Institute, 2005:167–282. Available at http://cancercontrol.cancer.gov/tcrb/monographs/16/m16_6.pdf. Accessed November 15, 2005.
34. Health Insurance Portability and Accountability Act of 1996, Pub L 104-191, 110 Stat 1936.
35. An Act to Create a Child Health Advisory Committee, Arkansas General Assembly, Act 1220 (2003).
36. Perdue WC, Stone LA, Gostin LO. The built environment and its relationship to the public's health: the legal framework. *Am J Public Health* 2004;93:1390–4.
37. New York City Smoke-Free Air Act of 2002, Local Law 47 (2002).
38. Mensah G, Perdue WC, Plescia M. Legal frameworks for chronic disease prevention. *J Law Med Ethics* 2004;32(4 Suppl):35–7.
39. Perdue WC, Mensah GA, Goodman RA, Moulton AD. A legal framework for preventing cardiovascular diseases. *Am J Prev Med*. 2005 (in press).
40. Kuchler F, Golan E, Variyam JN, Crutchfield SR. Obesity policy and the law of unintended consequences. *Amber Waves* 2005;3:26–30.
41. American Dental Association. *Fluoridation Facts*. 2005. Available at http://www.ada.org/public/topics/fluoride/facts/. Accessed November 15, 2005.
42. National Conference of State Legislators. Community water fluoridation. *State Health Lawmakers Digest* 2005;3(2). Available at http://www.ncsl.org/programs/health/forum/shld/32.htm. Accessed January 4, 2006.
43. Robert Wood Johnson Foundation. *Annual Report 1994: Cost Containment*. Princeton, NJ: Robert Wood Johnson Foundation, 2005.
44. Heffler S, Smith S, Won G, et al. Health spending projections for 2001–2011: the latest outlook. *Health Aff* 2002;21:207–18.
45. Jones SE, Wheeler L. Asthma inhalers in schools: rights of students with asthma to a free appropriate education. *Am J Public Health* 2004;94:1102–8.

46. Americans with Disabilities Act, Pub L 101–336, 42 USC 12101 *et seq* (1990).

47. Yusuf S, Hawken S, Ounpuu S, et al. Effect of potentially modifiable risk factors associated with myocardial infarction in 52 countries (the INTERHEART study): case-control study. *Lancet* 2004;364:937–52.

48. Kannel WB. Bishop Lecture. Contribution of the Framingham Study to preventive cardiology. *J Am Coll Cardiol* 1990;15:206–11.

49. Mensah GA, Collins JL, Dietz WH, et al. Prevention and control of coronary heart disease and stroke: nomenclature for prevention approaches in public health. A statement for public health practice from the Centers for Disease Control and Prevention. *Am J Prev Med* 2005 (in press).

50. Centers for Disease Control and Prevention. *Best Practices for Comprehensive Tobacco Control Programs—August 1999*. Atlanta: US Department of Health and Human Services, Centers for Disease Control and Prevention, National Center for Chronic Disease Prevention and Health Promotion, Office on Smoking and Health, 1999.

51. Centers for Disease Control and Prevention. Annual smoking-attributable mortality, years of potential life lost, and productivity losses—United States, 1997–2001. *MMWR* 2005; 54:625–8.

52. Pro-Children's Act of 1994, Pub L 103–229, 20 USC 6081 *et seq*.

53. World Health Organization. *WHO Framework Convention on Tobacco Control*. Geneva: World Health Organization, 2003.

54. Mokdad AH, Bowman BA, Ford ES, Vinicor F, Marks JS, Koplan JP. The continuing epidemics of obesity and diabetes in the United States. *JAMA* 2001;286:1195–200.

55. Yach D, Hawkes C, Epping-Jordan JE, Galbraith S. The World Health Organization's Framework Convention on Tobacco Control: implications for global epidemics of food-related deaths and disease. *J Public Health Policy* 2003;24:274–90.

56. Barrett T. House bans fast-food lawsuits. CNN (online). Available at http://www.cnn.com/2004/LAW/03/10/fat.lawsuits/. Accessed November 12, 2005.

57. Barold HS. Using the MADIT II criteria for implantable cardioverter defibrillators—what is the role of the Food and Drug Administration approval? *Cardiol Electrophysiol Rev* 2003;7:443–6.

58. Government Accountability Office. *Managing Diabetes: Health Plan Coverage of Services and Supplies*. 2005. Washington, DC: Government Accountability Office, 2005 (Report no GAO-05–210). Available at http://www.gao.gov/new.items/d05210.pdf. Accessed November 15, 2005.

59. Handy SL, Boarnet MG, Ewing R, Killingsworth RE. How the built environment affects physical activity: views from urban planning. *Am J Prev Med* 2002;23(2 Suppl):64–73.

60. Hoehner CM, Brennan LK, Brownson RC, Handy SL, Killingsworth R. Opportunities for integrating public health and urban planning approaches to promote active community environments. *Am J Health Promot* 2003;18:14–20.

61. Brownson RC, Boehmer TK, Luke DA. Declining rates of physical activity in the United States: what are the contributors? *Annu Rev Public Health* 2005;26:421–43.

62. Muller PO. Transportation and urban form: stages in the spatial evolution of the American metropolis. In: Hanson S, ed. *The Geography of Urban Transportation*. New York: Guilford Press, 1995:26–62.

63. Schilling J, Linton LS. The public health roots of zoning: in search of active living's legal genealogy. *Am J Prev Med* 2005;28(2 Suppl 2):96–104.

64. *Village of Euclid, OH v Ambler Realty Co*, 272 US 365 (1926).

65. Heath GW, Brownson RC, Kruger J, et al. The effectiveness of urban design and land use and transport policies and practices to increase physical activity: a systematic review. *Journal of Physical Activity and Health* 2005 (in press).

66. Baker EA, Brennan LK, Brownson R, Houseman RA. Measuring the determinants of physical activity in the community: current and future directions. *Res Q Exerc Sport* 2000;71:146–58.

67. Congress for the New Urbanism. *The Coming Demand.* San Francisco: Congress for the New Urbanism, 2001. Available at http://www.cnu.org/cnu_reports/Coming_Demand .pdf. Accessed August 20, 2005.

68. Health Policy Tracking Service. *State Actions to Promote Nutrition, Increase Physical Activity and Prevent Obesity: A Legislative Overview.* July 11, 2005. Available at http: //www.rwjf.org/files/research/July%202005%20–%20Report.pdf. Accessed August 10, 2005.

69. Colgrove J, Bayer R. Manifold restraints: liberty, public health, and the legacy of *Jacobson v Massachusetts. Am J Public Health* 2005;95:571–6.

70. Wald NJ, Law MR. A strategy to reduce cardiovascular disease by more than 80%. *BMJ* 2003;326:1419–23. [correction *BMJ* 2003;327:586].

71. Law MR, Wald NJ, Morris JK, Jordan RE. Value of low dose combination treatment with blood pressure lowering drugs: analysis of 354 randomized trials. *BMJ* 2003;326: 1427–31.

72. Law MR, Wald NJ, Rudnicka AR. Quantifying effect of statins on low density lipoprotein cholesterol, ischemic heart disease, and stroke: systematic review and meta-analysis. *BMJ* 2003;326:1423–29.

73. US Department of Health and Human Services. *Healthy People 2010.* 2nd ed. Washington, DC: US Department of Health and Human Services, 2000.

74. Mensah GA, Mokdad AH. State of disparities in cardiovascular health in the United States. *Circulation* 2005;111:1233–41.

75. Mensah GA. Eliminating disparities in cardiovascular health: six strategic imperatives and a framework for action. *Circulation* 2005;111:1332–6.

76. Civil Rights Act of 1964, Pub L 88-352, 42 USC 2000e *et seq* (1964).

77. The Hospital Survey and Construction Act (the "Hill-Burton" Act), Pub L 79-725, 60 Stat 1040 (1946).

78. Taylor AL, Ziesche S, Yancy C, et al. Combination of isosorbide dinitrate and hydralazine in blacks with heart failure. *N Engl J Med* 2004;351:2049–57.

79. FDA. FDA Approves BiDil Heart Failure Drug for Black Patients. June 23, 2005. Available at http://www.fda.gov/bbs/topics/NEWS/2005/NEW01190.html. Accessed November 15, 2005.

80. Aronow WS. Race, drugs, and heart failure. *Geriatrics* 2005;60:8–9.

81. Kahn JD. Pharmacogenetics and ethnically targeted therapies: racial drugs need to be put in context. *BMJ* 2005;330:1508.

82. Badertscher N, Salzer J. State workers who smoke will pay more for insurance. May 12, 2005. *Atlanta Journal-Constitution* [online]. Available at http://www.ajc.com/metro/content/metro/0505/12smoke.html. Accessed November 15, 2005.

83. Stroup DF, Perdue WC, Richards EP, Acree KH. Legal frameworks for preventing chronic disease. *J Law Med Ethics* 2005 (in press).

Chapter 18

PREVENTION AND CONTROL OF DISEASES ASSOCIATED WITH TOBACCO USE THROUGH LAW AND POLICY

Richard A. Daynard, Mark A. Gottlieb,
Edward L. Sweda, Jr., Lissy C. Friedman,
and Michael P. Eriksen

Tobacco use causes an estimated 42,000 deaths each year in the United States.[1] The worldwide toll from tobacco-attributable disease is about 4 million per year and is expected to rise to 10 million per year by 2030.[2] Annually, about 1 million young Americans become regular smokers; for many, breaking their nicotine addiction will be extremely difficult, and about half of those who become lifelong smokers eventually will die prematurely from tobacco-caused disease. Furthermore, smoking causes about 50,000 deaths each year among nonsmokers exposed to secondhand smoke (SHS), in other words, passive smoking.[3] Prevention efforts, many of which do not raise legal issues, are proceeding on many fronts. Important elements of comprehensive tobacco-control programs include school- and community-based education programs; "counter-advertising" campaigns in the mass media, financed either through tobacco excise taxes or proceeds from the 1997 and 1998 settlements of the state lawsuits against the tobacco companies; and counseling and treatment for tobacco dependence.

Policies that discourage tobacco use and protect nonsmokers from exposure to SHS are also key elements of comprehensive tobacco-control programs. These policies typically are grouped into the categories of price policy (mainly referring to tobacco excise taxation), restrictions on tobacco advertising and promotion, restrictions on smoking in public places and work sites, restrictions on youth access to tobacco, government-mandated health warnings and disclosures on tobacco packaging and advertisements, and tobacco product regulation.[4] Such policies can be adopted through legislation or regulation at the federal, state, and local levels. Important tobacco-control policies also can be promulgated by private entities, such as employers, professional sports associations, and health-care organizations (e.g., accreditation bodies such as the Joint Commission on Accreditation of Healthcare Organizations, which requires that hospitals be smoke-free as a condition of accreditation). These policies, whether promulgated in the public sector or the private sector, along with tort litigation, result in the majority of legal disputes and controversies in tobacco control.

Legal Authorities

In this section, we review legal authorities that affect tobacco use at the federal, state, and local levels. Because litigation has figured prominently in the interpretation and application of those authorities, and because it forms the legal basis of many new "public policies," such as through the Master Settlement Agreement (MSA), we also review key developments in tobacco litigation.

Federal Authorities

Considering the amount of harm attributed to tobacco use, tobacco products are under-regulated. In the United States, the Food and Drug Administration (FDA), the Consumer Product Safety Commission, and the Occupational Safety and Health Administration are among the federal agencies that have not successfully regulated tobacco products. Starting in 1994, FDA sought to regulate the sale and marketing of cigarettes and smokeless tobacco products under the federal Food, Drug, and Cosmetic Act (classifying nicotine as a drug and treating these tobacco products as drug-delivery devices). However, the tobacco industry prevailed in a five-to-four Supreme Court decision in May 2000, in which the Court held that, although tobacco products deserved regulation, Congress had not authorized FDA to assert jurisdiction over tobacco products.[5] Nevertheless, several sources of federal legal authority exist over tobacco products.

The most significant federal statute is the Federal Cigarette Labeling and Advertising Act (FCLAA).[6] Enacted in 1965, in the wake of the first U.S. Surgeon General's report on smoking and health (released in 1964),[7] and amended several times, the FCLAA requires one of four rotating warnings to appear on each pack of cigarettes and on all cigarette advertising. It preempts any state or local cigarette warning requirements or advertising restrictions based on smoking and health. In 1971, Congress banned broadcast advertising for cigarettes.[8] Similarly, the Comprehensive Smokeless Tobacco Education Act of 1986 approached smokeless or "spit" tobacco products by mandating three rotating warnings on packaging and advertisements and banning broadcast advertising for this category of tobacco products.[9] Like the FCLAA, it preempted state and local efforts to restrict advertising or require warnings for smokeless tobacco products. Five rotating warnings are required on cigar packaging for 95% of the U.S. cigar market under consent decrees resulting from Federal Trade Commission actions taken against seven U.S. cigar companies.[10] The only categories of tobacco product left completely unregulated by warning requirements are pipe tobacco and "roll-your-own" cigarette tobacco.

Federal laws also address smoking in public places. In 1990, Congress banned smoking on all domestic airline flights of six or fewer hours (and since then, most airlines have extended the ban to include all flights).[11] International flights to or from the United States also are subject to the smoking ban.[12] In addition, the Pro-Children's Act of 1994 prohibits smoking in facilities in which federally funded children's services are regularly or routinely provided.[13] Another federal legal authority affecting tobacco products is an amendment to the federal Alcohol, Drug Abuse and Mental Health Administration Reorganization Act of 1992, known as the "Synar Amendment."[14] The statute provides for federal substance abuse block grants to states. The Synar Amendment requires each recipient state to enact a state law proscribing the sale of tobacco products to minors or the purchase of tobacco products by minors and to establish a compliance testing and reporting system as a condition of receiving the block grants.

State and Local Authorities

Individual states can use many legislative and regulatory approaches to reduce the prevalence of tobacco use and the harm it causes. The range of options available to a state depends largely on how state legislative, regulatory, and police powers are configured under a state's constitution and various state statutes.

The most notable limitation on state authority to regulate tobacco stems from the FCLAA, the federal law that requires rotating Surgeon General's warnings on every pack of cigarettes sold or advertised. The FCLAA contains a preemption clause that states: "No requirement or prohibition based on smoking and health shall be imposed under State law with respect to the advertising or promotion of any cigarettes the packages of which are labeled in conformity with the provisions of this Act."[15] The FCLAA defines "State" to include political subdivisions of the state. Even though this preemption generally does not affect state action on substantive regulatory areas such as SHS and youth access to tobacco, it profoundly affects state and local measures to restrict cigarette advertising and promotion.

Beyond the restrictions imposed on state action through the preemptive effect of the FCLAA, the primary means of enacting measures to control tobacco at the state level is through legislation. Every state legislature has the power to pass laws to, for example, restrict minors' access to tobacco products, prohibit smoking in public places, and increase tobacco excise taxes. Such legislation also may contain provisions that preempt localities from acting on such matters. Such local preemption generally is counterproductive from a public health standpoint because it prevents localities from passing more rigorous measures.[16,17] State health departments usually have explicit regulatory and enforcement powers that can be applied to tobacco control. In some instances, a state health department may be authorized to promulgate regulations pursuant to particular statutes, such as clean indoor air or tobacco youth-access legislation. In other states, such authority may be reserved for or shared with local health boards at the municipal or county level under a general grant of regulatory authority from state statute related to public health.

The power of municipalities and local boards of health to further the public health varies from state to state. The legal variables include whether the state constitution has a Home Rule provision granting legislative powers to municipalities so they can enact local tobacco-control measures or whether the state provides statutory authority to local health boards so they can enact reasonable health regulations to protect the public health (see also chapters 2 and 8). Such constitutional or statutory grants of authority, if available, provide a solid foundation for public health agencies to promulgate regulations implementing a wide range of tobacco-control provisions. On the other hand, state statutes "regulating" smoking in workplaces and restaurants, cigarette vending machines, sales to minors, and other tobacco-control subjects frequently combine weak substantive provisions with clauses preempting local action. Indeed, courts sometimes infer such preemption even in the absence of explicit preemption clauses.

In addition to state legislatures, health departments, and municipal legislation, state attorneys general have some enforcement authority—and, in some cases, regulatory authority—over tobacco. The range of civil and criminal law enforcement powers granted to state attorneys general varies significantly from state to state. Generally, state attorneys general can enforce state laws on unfair and deceptive acts and practices. Such laws may be targeted at tobacco industry marketing and sales activities where appropriate. In some states, the attorney general has rule-making powers.

The attorney general of Massachusetts attempted to exercise such powers in 1999 by promulgating regulations restricting outdoor tobacco advertising within 1000 feet of schools and playgrounds.[18] The restrictions were designed to eliminate deception and unfairness in the way cigarettes and smokeless tobacco products were marketed, sold, and distributed to reduce cigarette smoking and smokeless tobacco use by minors. The regulations were not premised on "smoking and health" concerns and therefore were not preempted by the FCLAA, according to the Massachusetts attorney general. However, on June 28, 2001, the U.S. Supreme Court disagreed with the attorney general's contention and struck down most of the Massachusetts attorney general's regulations.

In 46 states, the state attorneys general have enforcement power stemming from the MSA between the states and the major U.S. tobacco manufacturers.[19] The remaining 4 states (Florida, Minnesota, Mississippi, and Texas) have separate settlement agreements with tobacco manufacturers that likewise are enforceable by the state attorneys general in the court that approved the settlement and consent decree in each state.

Litigation against the Tobacco Industry

Litigation against the tobacco industry can have several effects. Lawsuits can force tobacco companies to reveal incriminating internal documents, weakening their ability to oppose effective regulation. Lawsuits also increase public discussion about the dangers of tobacco use and help to stimulate the media debates about whether people who develop tobacco-caused diseases should be compensated for their own poor judgment in relying on the industry's assurances that the risks were merely hypothetical.[20] Lawsuits also have the potential to force the industry to change its behavior, either through settlements or "voluntarily" to avoid future punitive damage awards. By forcing the industry to pay even a modest fraction of the medical and personal costs that their products and behavior cause, lawsuits can drive up the price of tobacco products, reducing use, particularly among youth. Finally, lawsuits can produce settlements or verdicts that can help fund tobacco-control programs.[21,22]

The most impressive demonstration of the regulatory power of tobacco litigation is the MSA-related settlements between all 50 state attorneys general and the tobacco industry. Four states—Florida, Minnesota, Mississippi, and Texas—settled their cases individually during July 1997 through May 1998. In November 1998, the remaining states settled on terms similar to those of the four individual state settlements, through the MSA. Under the MSA, the states relinquished their claims for reimbursement of tobacco-caused medical costs (past, present, and future) and agreed to provisions that prevented their political subdivisions from bringing such claims. In return, the tobacco companies agreed both to pay money to the states and to change some of their more egregious behavior. In terms of money, the cigarette companies (proportionately to their market shares) agreed to make quarterly payments to each state, in perpetuity, at a rate roughly approximating each state's anticipated tobacco-caused Medicaid costs. A state's payments could have been drastically reduced if the state legislature failed to pass "nonparticipating manufacturer" statutes, which required cigarette manufacturers to either join the MSA or post bonds equal to the financial contributions that would have been required if they had joined; all states have adopted such statutes. Another major adjustment reduces the overall payments when annual national cigarettes sales drop.[23] Because a 10% increase in cigarette price reduces overall cigarette consumption by 3%–5%,[24] the settlement-induced price increases have caused a substantial drop in smoking in the United States. Furthermore, states have used 5%–8% of payments under the MSA to fund tobacco-control programs Although both the attorneys general and the tobacco companies claim they expected a substantial portion of the payments to states to be used to fund tobacco control, the amount allocated for this purpose is small and shrinking.[25]

The MSA's enforceable provisions as applied to the settling defendants, aside from monetary payments to the states, include (1) a ban on tobacco billboard advertising; (2) a ban on the use of cartoon characters in tobacco advertising; (3) a ban on manufacturer advertising, promotion, or marketing activities that have a primary purpose of targeting minors; (4) a ban on distribution of apparel or merchandise featuring brand names of tobacco products; (5) a ban on distribution of free cigarette samples to minors (if state law prohibits purchase or possession of tobacco products by minors); (6) a ban on the sale of packs with fewer than 20 cigarettes; (7) modest restrictions on tobacco company lobbying, such as prohibiting lobbying against bills that limit youth access to cigarette vending machines or against bills that enhance penalties for violating laws restricting youth access to tobacco; and (8) maintenance of open public access to internal industry "discovery" documents obtained during the state litigation, both through depositories in Minnesota and England and through Web sites established by the companies (MSA, §III). These promises became part of consent decrees between the states and the settling manufacturers that courts approved in each of the states.

Since the MSA was signed, the National Association of Attorneys General has confronted cigarette manufacturers on over 20 different matters believed to violate marketing restrictions. For example, the California attorney general filed suit against R. J. Reynolds in May 2000 after an investigation revealed that the company was mailing samples of free cigarettes to homes in a manner that allowed children access to the cigarettes. R.J. Reynolds settled the case and agreed to largely cease its direct mailing campaign.[26]

In another example, less than a year after the MSA was signed, investigations revealed that most of the leading cigarette manufacturers had starting advertising more in magazines with high youth readership. When confronted with the findings of the investigation, all the cigarette manufacturers pulled their advertisements from such magazines, except for one manufacturer, R.J. Reynolds. Eventually, R.J. Reynolds removed the offending advertisements after it lost in court.[27]

The final example of an MSA violation involves Brown and Williamson's 2004 marketing campaign for Kool cigarettes, which focused on music known to be popular among 12- to 17-year-old children. The campaign also included distribution of branded merchandise, payments to include sales slogans in theatrical performances, and advertisements in magazines with high youth readership—all in violation of the MSA. The attorney general for New York obtained a restraining order against R.J. Reynolds, which merged with Brown and Williamson in 2004, to shut down the campaign. A settlement later was reached between R. J. Reynolds and several states.[28,29]

At the same time as the MSA, a similar settlement, the Smokeless Tobacco Master Settlement Agreement, was reached between the state attorneys general and the principal purveyor of smokeless tobacco (chewing tobacco and moist snuff), the United States Tobacco Company.

Litigation by or on Behalf of the Tobacco Industry

Beginning in the 1990s, the tobacco industry as a whole, and Philip Morris in particular, embarked on an aggressive campaign of filing lawsuits to thwart the plans and policies of their adversaries. Although the threat of litigation by the industry need not impede strong tobacco-control measures at the state and local levels, it requires that such measures be carefully drafted to avoid successful challenges.

The industry's most spectacular—albeit temporary—litigation victory was the invalidation of FDA's assertion of jurisdiction, but others have occurred as well. In 1993, several months after the Environmental Protection Agency (EPA) issued a comprehensive report on SHS, the tobacco industry sued EPA in federal court in Greensboro, North Carolina, even though EPA had not issued any regulation to limit smoking anywhere. Because no agency action existed to form the basis of a legitimate court challenge, the industry filed a lawsuit with the goal of undermining the scientific case against smokeless tobacco at hearings when states and localities across the country considered passing laws limiting or banning smoking in public places. The industry obtained the ruling it sought in June 1998 in *Flue-Cured Tobacco Cooperative Stabilization Corp. v. EPA*;[30] however, in 2002, the U.S. Court of Appeals for the Fourth Circuit reversed that ruling, which purported to invalidate a portion of the EPA's report.[31]

In 1994, Philip Morris filed its own lawsuit against television network ABC and two of its journalists for suggesting in a report on the program *Day One* that the industry "spiked" cigarettes with nicotine.[32] The case was settled in August 1995 with a public apology from ABC, which then was republished in a national advertising campaign to blunt criticism from members of Congress and others about the problem of nicotine addiction and cigarettes.

The tobacco industry sued the Commonwealth of Massachusetts in 1996 to block a first-in-the-nation law to require disclosure of ingredients, additives, and nicotine yield ratings by brand for the various companies' cigarettes.[33] The U.S. Court of Appeals for the First Circuit affirmed the district court's judgment which granted the tobacco companies summary judgment on the grounds that the Disclosure Act unconstitutionally took their property when it required them to disclose their ingredient lists to the state, which then could publish the lists.[34] Despite its public relations efforts to assure the American people that it does not want children to smoke, tobacco interests fought such regulations. For example, in 1999, the industry sued the Massachusetts attorney general for having adopted regulations banning tobacco advertising within 1000 feet of schools and playgrounds. The industry sought a declaration that the regulations were invalid because they violated the First Amendment to the U.S. Constitution and that they were preempted by the FCLAA. In *Lorillard Tobacco Co. v. Reilly*, the Supreme Court voted five to four that states' authority to regulate tobacco advertisements was limited by the First Amendment and partially preempted by the FCLAA.[35]

The tobacco industry and its allies have filed numerous lawsuits, and threatened the filing of many others, to fend off legislation that limits smoking in public places. These cases generally have tested the powers of local government entities. Although they have had mixed success, government bodies are often discouraged from taking strong action by the potential cost of defense. For example, R. J. Reynolds Tobacco Co. financed a 1994 lawsuit filed by restaurant owners in Puyallup, Washington. The suit alleged that a recently enacted ordinance requiring restaurants to be smoke-free was preempted because state law permitted smoking sections in restaurants and the city unlawfully and substantially had deprived the plaintiffs of their rights guaranteed by the U.S. Constitution, including the "takings" clause of the Fifth Amendment. Although these arguments seemed dubious, the city council voted to repeal the ordinance rather than spend the money required to fight the lawsuit.[36,37]

Lorillard Tobacco Co. currently is in litigation with a nonprofit public health organization, the American Legacy Foundation, over the content of an advertising campaign intended to reduce youth tobacco use. The American Legacy Foundation was established as part of the MSA. One clause of the MSA prohibited the foundation from vilifying or personally attacking cigarette manufacturers.[38] Lorillard alleged that a foundation-supported advertisement violated the antivilification clause of the settlement, and threatened to withhold settlement payments to the foundation for breach of contract. The foundation sued Lorillard Tobacco Co. to maintain settlement payments, and, in the interim, payments are being paid into an escrow account.[39] In August 2005, Vice Chancellor Stephen Lamb of Delaware's Court of Chancery ruled that the foundation's ads do not violate the MSA.[40]

Legal Issues and Controversies

Reducing Youth Access to Tobacco

The Synar Amendment

The Synar Amendment to the Alcohol, Drug Abuse, and Mental Health Administration Reorganization Act of 1992 requires states to adopt and enforce laws establishing a minimum age limit for buyers of tobacco products and to show progressive reductions in the availability of tobacco products to minors.[41] The U.S. Department of Health and Human Services (DHHS) is the government agency responsible for a yearly evaluation of progress pursuant to the amendment. The statute and proposed implementing regulations make the state (rather than municipalities) responsible for ensuring compliance and for reporting results to the federal government, but the commentary accompanying the proposed regulations explicitly acknowledges that the state can delegate enforcement efforts "through local governments or private entities." The policy behind the Synar Amendment is to encourage states (by providing financial incentives) to adopt effective tobacco-control measures, including compliance checks. A state's failure to meet these requirements would result in forfeiture of federal block grant funds for substance abuse prevention and treatment.

The threat of forfeiting substance-abuse block grant money on its own may not create a sufficient incentive for local police officers to enforce youth-access laws that prohibit sale of tobacco to minors. Furthermore, the Synar Amendment is an easy target for the tobacco industry lobby. The tobacco industry vigorously campaigned at the state level to undermine serious enforcement of youth-access laws by successfully lobbying for inclusion of language such as "knowingly" or "intentionally" in the laws prohibiting the sale of tobacco to minors.[42] Such language renders the youth-access laws virtually unenforceable.

Types of Restrictions and Enforcement

The effectiveness of tobacco-control legislation at the federal and state levels often has been thwarted by the tremendous muscle of the tobacco industry lobby. The success of a tobacco-control program depends on the willingness of local health departments and municipal legislative bodies to adopt effective local tobacco-control measures. One tobacco-control strategy that works best at the local level is municipal licensing of tobacco retailers to control youth access to tobacco products.

In 1993 and 1994, the Institute of Medicine (IOM) conducted an 18-month study on the prevention of nicotine dependence among children and youth.[43] One challenge cited in curbing youth smoking is that teenagers relatively easily can obtain tobacco products. A large body of evidence indicates that minors who purchase their own cigarettes seldom are asked for identification to verify their age. Children also can obtain cigarettes easily from vending machines and self-service displays.[44]

In its report, the IOM identified what it considered the essential components of any program to reduce youth access to tobacco. The IOM recommended that states or localities establish a system requiring merchants to obtain a license or a permit to sell tobacco products and revoking or suspending that license if a merchant sells tobacco to minors. The IOM states that "a tobacco retailer licensing program must be the cornerstone of any successful enforcement effort." Nearly every study of youth-access interventions has endorsed this licensing approach, and experience with local licensing and permitting systems has demonstrated its effectiveness.[45] In 1990, former Secretary of Health and Human Services Louis Sullivan, who served in the George H.W. Bush administration, produced a Model Sale of Tobacco Products to Minor Control Act, which included a provision for licensing tobacco retailers.[46]

The IOM further recommended limiting youth access to tobacco products by banning (1) the sale of tobacco products through self-service displays, a prime source of tobacco products for minors (self-service displays also invite shoplifting); (2) the sale of single cigarettes and the free distribution of tobacco products, two sources of tobacco products for adolescents; and (3) tobacco vending machines, which younger children rely on as a source for cigarettes.[47]

Because of their limited disposable income, minors are especially susceptible to free sampling. DHHS has encouraged state and local governments to ban distribution of free smokeless tobacco samples because it fears such products inevitably will fall into the hands of children and adolescents. In response to this problem, many communities across the country have restricted the distribution of free cigarette samples from areas around schools and other places frequented by minors, or have prohibited free samples altogether. Not one of these ordinances and regulations has been challenged in court. Local restriction of free sample distribution does not violate the U.S. Constitution, is within the police power of local government, and is consistent with federal law.

Enforcement mechanisms differ for municipalities and local public health agencies. Specifically, a municipality can enforce a youth-access measure by a simple ticket-and-fine procedure (also known as the "noncriminal disposition" process). A municipality may have to grant its local public health agency a general authority to use the noncriminal disposition process to enforce its regulations. In the absence of such authority, enforcement of public health agency regulations may prove cumbersome.

Municipalities and local public health agencies should first understand what authority they have to enact local measures and ascertain whether state law has preempted any of their authority. With this authority in place, state tobacco-control programs can support cities, towns, and local boards of health in enacting a wide range of youth-access measures. Local regulations can impose tobacco permit licensing schemes and penalties against retailers and their agents for selling to minors. For example, in Massachusetts, cities, towns, and local health agencies are encouraged to pass youth-access regulations that do the following:

- Require local merchants to verify by valid government-issued identification that each person purchasing tobacco products is age 18 or older
- Require local merchants to place all tobacco products out of the reach of all consumers and in a location accessible only to store personnel
- Establish retailer training requirements and programs
- Conduct periodic unannounced inspections to enforce local laws
- Require local permits regulating the location of vending machines, or ban vending machines entirely.[48]

Fourth Amendment Warrant Requirement and Compliance Checks

To conduct a successful compliance check, public health and other officials need some element of surprise. A formal request to a retailer, by public health officials, to submit to a specific compliance check, for example, would only warn the retailer to carefully check identifications. Under this agreement, no enforcement could take place. Thus, local youth-access regulations should emphasize a retailer's general consent to submit to random, unannounced compliance checks. One way to ensure tobacco retailers give implied consent is to institute a licensing or permitting scheme and condition issuance on consent to compliance checks. This condition is constitutional as long as specific compliance checks are conducted in a reasonable manner.[49]

A basic understanding of search-and-seizure laws helps ensure smooth compliance checks. The Fourth Amendment to the U.S. Constitution, as applied to the states through the Fourteenth Amendment, requires that law enforcement officials and their designees obtain a warrant to search private property, even where the property is used for commercial purposes (see Chapter 6). The warrant rule applies to enforcement of both criminal laws and civil codes, such as health and safety ordinances, violation of which can result in civil penalties. The purpose of the rule is to protect the privacy and security of people against arbitrary intrusions by the government. Failure to obtain a warrant can result in the exclusion of evidence, which often undercuts successful enforcement of criminal and civil penalties. Unless an exception to the warrant requirement applies, critical evidence obtained by a warrantless compliance check could be excluded from a hearing to assess penalties, thereby nullifying formal enforcement. Public health and other officials can obtain a warrant to conduct compliance checks, but alternatives, such as a licensing scheme outlined below, are more efficient. Warrants for administrative searches are issued only if "probable cause" exists to suspect one or more violations.[50] Accordingly, steps should be taken to ensure that an exception to the warrant requirement applies to compliance checks.

Courts have developed many exceptions to the warrant requirement, two of which are of particular importance for administrative searches. First, a retailer may consent to inspection. Consent may be given immediately before the search or as a condition to obtaining a license to operate a business or market a product. The second exception applies to businesses that operate in "closely regulated commercial activity"; three criteria apply to this exception: (1) government interest in the regulatory scheme must be substantial; (2) warrantless searches must be necessary to further the regulatory scheme; and (3) the regulatory scheme must control the time, place, and scope of warrantless searches to limit discretionary enforcement.[51]

Public health officials should take steps to ensure their regulations or ordinances fulfill the three criteria of the closely regulated commercial activity exception. Tobacco-control laws meet the first criterion of the closely regulated commercial activity exception, which requires a substantial government interest in the regulatory scheme. Local officials have a legitimate government interest in developing regulatory schemes for the sale of tobacco products. Compliance checks probably meet the second criterion of the closely regulated commercial activity exception, which requires that warrantless compliance checks to further the regulatory scheme. In Massachusetts, the supreme Judicial Court found that warrantless administrative searches are especially necessary when only a narrow window exists in which to identify a violation.[52] Inspections deter violations if they occur frequently and are unannounced. Similarly, warrantless compliance checks are necessary for the enforcement of tobacco-control laws. To enforce tobacco-control laws effectively, compliance checks must be conducted frequently, and they must be unannounced.

Tobacco-control laws can meet the third criterion of the closely regulated commercial activity exception, which requires that the time, place, and scope of compliance checks reasonably limit the enforcement discretion of the official and his or her designee who conducts the compliance checks. As part of any local tobacco-control law, the manner of enforcement should be defined. Specifically, a regulation or ordinance should state that compliance checks are to be carried out randomly, frequently by certain officials or their designees, and in a certain manner.

Due Process Requirements

The Due Process Clause of the U.S. Constitution provides two fundamental protections. The first due process protection, frequently referred to as procedural due process, requires government officials and their agents to follow a fair procedure when enforcing laws. The second, commonly referred to as substantive due process, ensures that a law's overall effect on an individual's fundamental rights, such as the right to procreate and the right to marry, is justified or justifiable.

Tobacco-control law involves several due process issues. Procedural due process requires public health and other officials to provide retailers with notice and an administrative hearing before suspending or revoking a permit or license to sell tobacco. Substantive due process does not protect an individual's right to smoke in the home, any more than it does other drug use. The right to smoke is not a protected fundamental right. Therefore, substantive due process does not protect the sale, possession, and use of tobacco products, thereby allowing federal, state, and local regulation of tobacco.

To comply with procedural due process concerns, a licensing or permitting authority must provide notice and an administrative hearing if it revokes or suspends an individual retailer's license or permit to sell tobacco products. Fair notice must be reasonably detailed, accurate, and timely. A reasonably detailed notice must accurately list the charges leveled against the permit or license holder. The adjudicative body should provide additional information about the charges, if the license or permit holder seeks clarification before the hearing. Although verbal notice may fulfill this requirement, issuing a written notice is advisable. Notice must be presented in a timely fashion.

The permit or license holder must have enough time to prepare a defense. If the license or permit holder makes a reasonable request for more time, granting a brief postponement is advisable. The license or permit holder is entitled to disclosure of all evidence that supports revocation or suspension. The licensing or permitting body can conduct its own hearing to revoke or suspend a retailer's license or permit to sell or otherwise distribute tobacco products. In this capacity, the licensing or permitting authority acts as a quasi-judicial entity.

Reducing Exposure to Secondhand Tobacco Smoke

In the late 1990s, major reviews of the health effects of SHS concluded that nonsmokers are harmed by such exposure in a variety of ways.[3,53-55] These include respiratory effects (acute lower respiratory tract infections in children, including bronchitis and pneumonia; asthma induction and exacerbation in children; chronic respiratory symptoms in children; eye and nasal irritation in adults; and middle ear infection in children); carcinogenic effects (lung cancer and nasal sinus cancer); cardiovascular effects (heart disease mortality; and acute and chronic coronary heart disease morbidity); and developmental effects (impaired fetal growth, low birthweight, or small size for gestational age; sudden infant death syndrome). Responding to concerns raised by the growing body of medical evidence condemning SHS as a threat to human health, government bodies, private businesses, and individuals have taken a variety of actions to limit nonsmokers' exposure to SHS.

Legislation is a common means of minimizing nonsmokers' exposure to SHS. The earliest laws restricting tobacco use (both local and state) were adopted as fire-safety measures. The first modern tobacco-control laws designed to protect nonsmokers from SHS appeared in the early 1970s. In 1975, Minnesota became the first state to pass a comprehensive state Clean Indoor Air Act restricting smoking in public places, restaurants, and public and private workplaces. Although the earliest laws restricting smoking were passed largely at the state level, progress began shifting to the local level by the early 1980s. The specific provisions and scope of these laws vary widely, but as of July 7, 2005, smoking was restricted in public places in 45 states and the District of Columbia, and 1,990 local clean indoor air laws are now in place.[56]

During the 1980s and early 1990s, many of these laws merely required the designation of nonsmoking areas within rooms in which smoking was permitted, without a requirement for physical barriers or separate ventilation systems. Laws pertaining to restaurants typically required designation of a certain percentage of seats as a "no smoking" area; nonsmokers simply were not being protected from actual exposure to SHS while they were dining. Recognition of the ongoing nature of that harm for nonsmoking patrons and employees[57,58] led to stronger legislative intervention.

Assessments of the Impact of Measures to Reduce Exposure

Despite the effectiveness of policies and measures that local governments have implemented to reduce SHS, some states enacted statutes that took the power away from, or preempted, cities or towns that might want to enact local laws with stronger protections for nonsmokers. As of December 31, 2004, 19 states (Connecticut, Florida, Illinois, Iowa, Louisiana, Michigan, Mississippi, Nevada, New Hampshire, New Jersey, North Carolina, Oklahoma, Oregon, Pennsylvania, South Carolina, South Dakota, Tennessee, Utah, and Virginia) had preemption provisions in statewide laws governing smoking at government worksites, private-sector worksites, and restaurants.[57–59]

Studies have begun to measure the impact of smoke-free laws and policies on the health of workers and others. For example, researchers analyzed hospital admissions from December 1997 through November 2003 in Helena, Montana, a geographically isolated community with one hospital, during the six months that a local law banning smoking in public settings and in workplaces was in effect. During that period, the number of admissions for myocardial infarction dropped significantly, and the investigators concluded that law "to enforce smoke-free workplaces and public places may be associated with an effect on morbidity from heart disease."[60] A study in Delaware measured respirable suspended particle (RSP) air pollution and particulate polycyclic aromatic hydrocarbons (PAH) in six bars, one casino, and one pool hall, both before and after Delaware's smoke-free law took effect. The investigator concluded that RSP levels and carcinogenic polycyclic aromatic hydrocarbons levels had decreased dramatically after the date of effect of the smoke-free law.[61] Similarly, other investigators analyzed the change in air quality in 20 hospitality establishments in western New York after that state's implementation of a smoke-free law, and they also reported reductions in RSP levels and PAH levels.[62] Finally, researchers in Boston conducted an evaluation of the Massachusetts Smoke-Free Workplace Law and concluded that levels of RSP less than 2.5 microns in diameter decreased 93% in hospitality establishments, namely, bars and restaurants, after the law took effect, compared with measurement levels to the law's effective date.[63]

Tobacco Industry Approach

Accommodation

The tobacco industry has suggested ventilation equipment as a solution for smoking in public. For example, Philip Morris launched a program called "PM Options" to "help find effective ways for businesses, public policy makers, and the general public to provide balance and comfort for both non-smokers and smokers in public places." The Web site states that its goal is to "[a]dvocate accommodation and reasonable options—both technical and structural—for non-smoker and smoker comfort, based on the public's accommodation expectations and the advancement of ventilation technologies."[64,65]

Because smokers can and do eat in smoke-free restaurants as long as they refrain from smoking while there, they already are accommodated. On the contrary, non-smokers who cannot tolerate a smoke-filled environment do not have access to smoke-filled establishments. What Philip Morris means by "accommodation" is, in effect, accommodation of smoking in these establishments. Significantly, Philip Morris adds the disclaimer that the "programs, resources and information offered by Philip Morris USA do not purport to address health effects attributed to [SHS]." In fact, no evidence exists that ventilation and filtration render SHS harmless.

Litigation Involving Reduction of Exposure

Litigation is one avenue through which policies limiting exposure to SHS have been prompted. Those who have chosen this route have helped shape public policy concerning involuntary exposure to SHS by legal claims against cigarette manufacturers, seeking injunctive relief against continuing exposure to SHS using antidiscrimination laws such as the Americans with Disabilities Act (ADA), relying on the principles of the law of nuisance to prevent a neighbor's smoke from seeping into one's apartment or condominium unit, or by raising SHS as an issue in the context of a dispute about child custody.[66] For example, the ADA was the basis for a claim by three adults with asthma who sued a major restaurant chain, alleging they attempted to patronize the restaurants but were forced to leave because of the smoke. A federal judge denied a motion to dismiss the plaintiffs' complaint. After noting that Title III of the ADA was enacted to facilitate disabled persons' access to places of public accommodation, the Court concluded, "Just as a staircase denies access to someone in a wheelchair, tobacco smoke prevents Plaintiffs from dining at Defendants' restaurants."[67] One observer concluded that, to the extent that future jurors more fully understand how harmful SHS is, the more likely plaintiffs are to win SHS-based lawsuits.[68]

In contrast, lawsuits attacking smoke-free policies have contained one or more of the following claims—that smoke-free laws have violated the Equal Protection Clause of the U.S. Constitution, have been enacted in a manner that exceeds the authority of the entity that enacted the measure, and have violated the separation of powers. These lawsuits have been filed in several states, including Massachusetts, Arizona, Massachusetts, Michigan, New York, and Ohio. For example, in *Cookie's Diner v. Columbus Board of Health*, an Ohio court found that city and county boards of health had improperly considered "concerns (such as . . . economics) other than those solely for the protection of public health." Thus, the court concluded that the power of boards to regulate smoking in places open to the public was limited to considerations of "protecting the public health, preventing disease and abating nuisance."[68]

In *Tri-Nel Management, Inc., et al. v. Board of Health of Barnstable et al.*, a local bar owner in Massachusetts challenged the town of Barnstable's regulation banning smoking in restaurants and bars.[69] The bar owner argued that the board's regulation was "not reasonable because the amount of SHS exposure at restaurants and bars would not be sufficient to cause adverse health effects in general" (p. 220).[69] Unanimously ruling in favor of the board of health, the Massachusetts Supreme Judicial Court rejected that argument, noting that "the board has placed in the record four reports interpreting and summarizing scientific studies that identify SHS exposure as a cause of numerous negative health effects" (p. 220).[69] The Supreme Judicial Court concluded that the board's regulation is within the standard of reasonableness (p. 221).[69]

In Arizona, a restaurant owner challenged an antismoking measure in Tucson, arguing in part that, because the ban did not apply to other establishments such as bars, bowling alleys, or billiard halls, it was unconstitutional. In *City of Tucson v. Grezaffi*, however, the Court of Appeals rejected that Equal Protection argument, ruling that absolute "equality and complete conformity of legislative classifications are not constitutionally required."[70] More recently, in New York in *CLASH, Inc. v. City of New York et al.*, a federal judge dismissed a lawsuit brought by a "smokers' rights" group that claimed that state and city smoke-free laws are unconstitutional.[71] The plaintiff group had argued that laws banning smoking in indoor locations, including bars, interfered with its members' freedom of association.

Finally, in *Harwood Capital Corp. v. Carey*, a landlord sought to evict two tenants after receiving complaints from abutting residents about the strong smell of smoke emanating from their apartment.[72] The tenants' lease did not mention smoking. The tenants, who worked from the unit, combined to smoke about 40–60 cigarettes per day. After a three-day trial, a jury returned a verdict that the tenant-defendant had breached his lease under a clause in the standard Greater Boston Real Estate Board lease prohibiting tenants from creating a nuisance or engaging in activity that substantially interfered in the rights of other building occupants. The jury also ruled that, therefore, the landlord was entitled to possession of the unit.

Tobacco Advertising and Promotion

Regulation of tobacco advertising is governed by the First Amendment to the U.S. Constitution, a federal statute that preempts some tobacco advertising regulations, and the MSA negotiated between the tobacco industry and the state attorneys general. In *Lorillard v. Reilly*, the U.S. Supreme Court set new parameters for analyzing the constitutional and statutory issues.[73]

First Amendment

In First Amendment analysis, advertising is considered in the special category of commercial speech. This area receives less constitutional protection than political or expressive speech because speech aimed at creating business transactions is not considered necessary to the promotion of democracy. Even though government regulation of political speech receives a high level of scrutiny by courts, regulation of commercial speech receives a thorough but intermediate level of scrutiny. Constitutionally protected commercial speech may be regulated if the government furthers a substantial interest through a regulation that directly and materially advances that interest in a way that is no more extensive than necessary to achieve that interest.

In *Lorillard*, the U.S. Supreme Court assumed that the tobacco industry's speech was protected and that the government's interest in preventing tobacco-related disease was substantial. The Court further held that a government program restricting tobacco advertising on storefronts directly and materially advanced the government interest in preventing youth from experimenting with tobacco products. The Court relied on extensive scientific data to reach its conclusion but held that the regulation was more extensive than necessary and hence invalid. The Court ruled that Massachusetts' attempt to restrict minors' exposure to tobacco advertising interfered with adults' ability to access the information. Particularly troubling to the Court was that the statewide regulation did not take local circumstances into account.

In a small but important victory for public health concerns, the Court upheld the Massachusetts attorney general's ban on self-service displays of tobacco products. While assuming that the ban raised First Amendment concerns, the Court concluded that restrictions to behind-the-counter sales was an "appropriately narrow means" of advancing the state's "substantial interest in preventing access to tobacco products by minors."

Federal Cigarette Labeling and Advertising Act

In 1965, Congress passed the FCLAA, which required cigarette advertisements and packages to carry government-mandated warning labels. As mentioned above, the statute preempts or trumps state and local laws that impose a requirement or prohibition on the basis of smoking and health with respect to advertising or promotion. In the *Lorillard* case, the U.S. Supreme Court found the statute preempts all state and local government regulation specifically aimed at tobacco advertising.

Several cities and states had regulated tobacco advertising and asserted a government interest in protecting children from tobacco advertising and preventing children from becoming involved in illegal activities, such as the sale of cigarettes to minors. Some jurisdictions justified the regulations as a zoning ordinance related to the placement of tobacco advertising. The Supreme Court held that Congress had preempted all these state and local laws because at their base were issues concerning the public health.

Master Settlement Agreement and Advertising and Promotion

Restrictions placed on tobacco advertising have been cited as the most important non-monetary restriction achieved by the MSA, but they also are extremely complex. The MSA bans "outdoor advertising," which includes billboards and signs in arenas, stadiums, shopping malls, and video arcades. It includes other advertisements placed outdoors and certain advertisements placed inside stores if they remain visible from outside. Certain types of outdoor advertising are banned.

Exceptions to this prohibition are significant. For example, a tobacco retailer can place any number of tobacco advertisements anywhere on its property as long as the advertisements are smaller than 14 square feet. This substantially undercuts the restriction described above because the "ban" on outdoor tobacco advertising does not apply to tobacco retail locations—the places most interested in displaying tobacco advertising. The MSA's advertising restrictions also are subject to an exception for activities at the site of an "adult-only facility," defined as a restricted area where the operator of the facility ensures, or has a reasonable basis to believe, that no underaged person is present; a bar that limits entry to persons with valid identification probably would qualify. For example, the MSA permits outdoor advertising at the site of a tobacco brand–sponsored event held at an adult-only facility during the event and for 14 days before the event.

An important achievement of the MSA is the restriction on tobacco advertisements on or within private or public vehicles and within transit waiting areas, such as bus stops, taxi stands, train stations, and airports. Tobacco advertising on the tops of taxis and on the sides of buses is no longer allowed.

Before the MSA, the tobacco industry claimed that it did not voluntarily target minors with its advertising. The MSA is a legally binding consent decree in which the cigarette manufacturers agree not to target youth. The tobacco companies further agreed "not to take any action the *primary purpose* of which is to initiate, maintain or increase youth smoking" within the settling states (emphasis added).

The MSA provides restrictions on brand name merchandise, including bans on marketing, distributing, offering, selling, or licensing tobacco brand names on shirts, hats, backpacks, and other gear that strongly appeals to children. Tobacco products and tobacco advertisements such as posters are not covered by the merchandising prohibitions. The prohibition also does not apply to the use of coupons by adults to purchase tobacco products, the distribution of merchandise to employees of the participating manufacturers, or merchandise used only within an adult-only facility that is unavailable to the general public.

Special highly complex rules govern tobacco product brand name sponsorships. Generally, the tobacco industry cannot use cigarette brand names to sponsor certain cultural and sporting events, except that each manufacturer may reserve one such brand name sponsorship each year.

Under the MSA, a brand name is defined as a "brand name . . . trademark, logo, symbol, motto, selling message, recognizable pattern of colors, or other indicia of product identification" identifiable with a domestic brand of tobacco product. Corporate names are specifically excluded. A brand name sponsorship is "an athletic, musical, artistic, or other social or cultural event" for which a participating manufacturer has paid a fee for the use of the brand name in the name of the event, such as the Winston Cup NASCAR series, which was discontinued in light of these new regulations.

Several types of brand name sponsorships are completely prohibited. Tobacco companies cannot sponsor (1) concerts (except in adult-only facilities); (2) events in which the intended audience comprises a significant percentage of youth; (3) events in which paid participants or contestants are youth; or (4) any athletic event between opposing teams in any football, basketball, baseball, soccer, or hockey league. For sponsorships that are not explicitly prohibited, each company is allowed only one brand name sponsorship in a 12-month period. A sponsorship is considered a single sponsorship even if it includes many events or locations, such as Virginia Slims tennis tournaments, that may be played in many different states throughout the year.

Because third parties, such as retailers and billboard companies, did not sign the document, holding them to the terms of the MSA is difficult. The MSA prohibits tobacco companies from licensing or authorizing third parties to do anything the tobacco companies cannot do under the MSA. In fact, the tobacco companies are obliged to take "commercially reasonable steps" to prevent such action. However, whether a third party allegedly acting on its own may take action forbidden under the MSA is not clear.

Product Regulation and Disclosure

States can undertake a range of untested or cutting-edge regulatory approaches to tobacco products. Such endeavors involve a certain degree of risk because they inevitably invite legal challenges. However, they have the potential to address important public health aspects of the tobacco problem that have not been federally legislated or regulated. For example, cigarette-caused fires result in nearly 1000 deaths and 3000 injuries each year in the United States.[74] As of October 2005, California, New York, and Vermont are the only states to have adopted legislation mandating that cigarettes be less incendiary. Similar efforts in Massachusetts, Minnesota, and Oregon have not yet succeeded.

Although FDA has enacted most of the drug regulation in the United States, states retain residual power over drugs not regulated by FDA. Because this applies to tobacco regulation, states have the opportunity to fill the vacuum created by the U.S. Supreme Court's invalidation of FDA's assertion of jurisdiction over tobacco products in *Brown & Williamson Tobacco Corp v. FDA*.[5] The Court held that, without a direct grant of authority by Congress, FDA regulation of tobacco products as drugs or drug-delivery devices is unavailable. However, a potential parallel regulatory framework exists at the state level. Most states have statutes providing residual powers over drugs not regulated by FDA. At the state level, FDA-like regulation of tobacco could compel disclosure of additional product information to consumers or regulate product design including incendiary characteristics as well as overall toxicity, addictiveness, and lethality.

Massachusetts was the first state to attempt to compel disclosure, by state statute and health regulation, of the identity and weights of additives used in specific brands of tobacco products.[34] The regulation was enjoined on the basis that it amounted to a "taking without compensation," violating the Fifth and Fourteenth amendments to the U.S. Constitution. The U.S. Court of Appeals for the First Circuit affirmed the district court's judgment.[75] Other than Massachusetts, only Minnesota and Texas have required any reporting of tobacco ingredients.[76] Those two states' approaches would not provide basic information, such as which ingredients in which quantities are in any particular cigarette brand.

Aside from the Fifth Amendment concerns that stem from the assertion that the ingredients disclosure is a taking of a trade secret, the two affirmative theories most likely to be used to challenge tobacco product regulation at the state level are preemption under the FCLAA and violations of the Commerce Clause of the U.S. Constitution.

Practice Considerations

From a public health practice perspective, the law can either help or hinder tobacco-control efforts. At the federal level, legal efforts disproportionately have protected the tobacco industry compared with public health, reflecting to a large extent the political and lobbying influence of the tobacco industry in Washington, D.C., and, to a lesser extent, in state capitols. Federal legislation intended to promote the public health and reduce harm caused by smoking has tended to shield the tobacco industry from liability, preempted state and local government actions, or explicitly exempted tobacco from normal regulatory and consumer protection statutes. As previously discussed, this limitation is illustrated by FDA's failed effort to regulate tobacco products and by the continuing failure of Congress to provide the regulatory authority to FDA to do so, despite the Supreme Court's opinion that tobacco products warranted regulation and that Congress should provide such authority.

Because of these failures in public policy, the public health community has come to rely on the direct and indirect relief provided by judicial decisions and settlements. The compelled production of previously secret documents now available as a result of the legal discovery process might best illustrate this benefit of litigation for the public health practice community. As a result of litigation and settlements, millions of previously unavailable documents are now available through the World-Wide Web on portals either developed by the public health community or required to be established by the tobacco companies themselves. These documents have been extremely useful to the public health community in deepening the understanding of tobacco industry research, strategy, and tactics, and have prompted written analyses and studies. In addition to benefiting tobacco-control practitioners, document disclosure also has been used to support other litigation efforts by providing credible evidence of industry knowledge and behavior.

Other major benefits of tobacco litigation particularly include the MSA. As previously mentioned, billions of dollars have flowed to states, although relatively little is being spent currently on tobacco control. Some restrictions have been placed on tobacco marketing; however, the marketing of tobacco products still employs seductive and alluring imagery. Perhaps most significantly, the MSA resulted in establishment of the American Legacy Foundation, which has conducted a bold, robust, and nationally unprecedented counter-marketing campaign. The foundation's efforts, as well as the few well-funded state-based efforts supported through MSA payments, clearly have contributed to the recent reduction in youth tobacco use.[77] Thus, whereas the extent of litigation may be seen as a measure of the failure of public policy, from a public health practice perspective, the relief, remedies, and discovery that have resulted from litigation have profoundly affected the success of tobacco-control efforts.

Of course, numerous practice considerations exist other than those associated with litigation. Public health law, particularly at the state and local levels, has provided some level of protection from the harm caused by tobacco use, particularly with regard to reducing exposure to SHS. Practitioners need to understand how the law can be used to support—or thwart—tobacco-control efforts. One reason the law often impedes tobacco-control advocates is that a multibillion dollar industry is actively engaged in shaping the law to protect its interests—in particular, an uninterrupted flow of profit from the sale of tobacco.

Practitioners should heed several "lessons learned" about how the law should be shaped to support the aims of tobacco control. Tobacco-control legislation should be crafted as strongly and as devoid of loopholes as possible. For example, increasing the tax on tobacco should include a provision that indexes the tax to inflation; otherwise, the tax will lose value over time. Tobacco legislation cannot feasibly be revisited soon after initial passage to correct problems with the legislation. Similarly, partial bans on tobacco advertising and promotion generally are ineffective because tobacco companies shift marketing expenditures from banned media to media that remain accessible to them.

The language in tobacco-control legislation needs to be scrutinized to search for wording that could reduce the effectiveness of the legislation. An example previously noted is the effort by tobacco interests to include language such as "knowingly" or "intentionally" in laws prohibiting the sale of tobacco to minors (penalties are imposed only on retailers that knowingly sell tobacco to minors).[78]

Tobacco-control legislation needs to be crafted carefully in anticipation of legal challenges by tobacco companies or their allies. The tobacco industry often will challenge in court any legislation that threatens its business, no matter how remote its chances for success. The legal challenge may be intended only to delay implementation of the law or to tax the patience and resources of the proponents.

Tobacco companies often will threaten to challenge legislation in court when it is under consideration by a legislative body. The purpose of this tactic is to deter legislators from passing a bill or ordinance, over concern about the costs of defending the legislation in court. In anticipation of this tactic, tobacco-control advocates should procure legal support early on in the legislative process, including having legal counsel and written legal opinions available.

For several reasons, tobacco-control advocates should recognize that local con-trol over the sale, distribution, and use of tobacco is generally the most effective strat-egy a tobacco-control program can pursue. First, local legislation is easier to pass than state or federal legislation, and it can be adopted more quickly. Despite its use of business associations and groups such as the National Smokers' Alliance, the to-bacco industry generally is ineffective in defeating or weakening local tobacco-control measures. Second, laws passed at the local level typically are far stronger than laws passed at the state or federal level, both substantively and in terms of enforcement mechanisms. Third, measures passed at the local level often enjoy broad community support. After spending countless hours in town meetings and public hearings, com-munities are educated in tobacco issues. As a result, local tobacco-control measures tend to gain strong public support. Fourth, compliance rates are higher for local tobacco-control measures, primarily because local enforcement agencies are more accessible and thus more effective than federal and state enforcement agencies. For these reasons, tobacco-control advocates should avoid "deals" offered by tobacco interests that would insert legislative language that would preempt local controls.

Emerging Issues

Legislation and Regulation

At the federal level, legislation has been introduced to provide FDA with regulatory authority over tobacco products. Strong legislation could enable FDA not only to reinstate its rules limiting youth access to tobacco and restricting tobacco marketing but also to regulate tobacco product design to reduce toxicity; require effective health warnings through package inserts; and take other steps to reduce the extent of addic-tion, disease, and death caused by tobacco products. Weak legislation, on the other hand, would limit FDA's ability to protect both existing smokers and future industry while allowing the companies to say they are already regulated so the problem is solved.

At the state level, health advocates will continue their efforts to have tobacco settle-ment funds appropriated for tobacco-control education and intervention. In some states, advocates may use ballot initiatives to guarantee a fair allocation of settlement funds to tobacco control, after failed attempts to accomplish this goal through legislation. Legislation may be introduced in several states requiring disclosure of tobacco prod-uct ingredients and smoke components; requiring less incendiary product designs; and in the continued absence of FDA jurisdiction over tobacco, perhaps requiring design changes to render the products less toxic and less addictive. In some states, health de-partments already may have the authority to impose such requirements.

At the state and local levels, efforts will continue to broaden and strengthen laws restricting smoking in shared airspaces. Cutting-edge issues include restricting smoking in some outdoor public places and prohibiting smoking in vehicles in which children are present. Furthermore, raising the minimum age of sale to age 21 years, in parity with alcohol, would be likely to dramatically reduce sales of cigarettes to teenagers.[79]

Litigation against the Tobacco Industry

The U.S. Department of Justice filed suit against cigarette manufacturers in 1999, on the basis of the Racketeer Influenced and Corrupt Organizations Act. The government contended that six tobacco companies engaged in a 50-year conspiracy to defraud and addict smokers and then conceal the dangers of cigarettes. After years of discovery and depositions, the nonjury trial began in September 2004 and ended in June 2005 and now is being considered by the court. During the court proceedings, Judge Gladys Kessler approved the government's seeking the disgorgement of $280 billion of "ill-gotten gains," if the defendants were to be found to be guilty of the Racketeer Influenced and Corrupt Organizations Act charges. The tobacco companies appealed that ruling, and the U.S. Court of Appeals for the D.C. District overturned the disgorgement decision in February 2005.[80] The Department of Justice appealed this ruling to the Supreme Court, which has not yet decided whether to hear the appeal. While the liability and disgorgement decisions are being judicially considered, a settlement between the parties still is possible.

The appeal in the *Liggett Group, Inc. v. Engle* class action case on behalf of ailing or deceased Florida smokers—which so far has resulted in a $145 billion punitive damage verdict and the award of an average of $4 million each in compensatory damages to three of the hundreds of thousands of class members, but which was overturned in 2003 by a state appellate court[81]—will be decided by the Florida Supreme Court, which heard oral arguments in November 2004.[82] Favorable appellate court rulings are likely to result in similar cases in other jurisdictions. Other class actions, seeking the cost of medical monitoring for addicted but otherwise healthy smokers, are pending in Louisiana and West Virginia. Other class actions on a variety of theories are pending in California and Illinois state courts and in a New York federal court.

Individual cases on behalf of smokers or their survivors are pending in many states. Multimillion dollar punitive damage verdicts already have been reached in several cases; if these are upheld on appeal, thousands of additional cases are likely to be filed. In one such case, *Henley v. Philip Morris, Inc.*, a multimillion dollar payment of punitive damages already has occurred.[83] The assessed and anticipated liability may exceed even this wealthy industry's ability to pay, which could force one or more companies into bankruptcy reorganization (i.e., "Chapter 11"). For the companies to continue in business under Chapter 11, rather than being forced to sell their assets, the bankruptcy court needs to conclude that the reorganization plan is "viable" in that the expected liability costs from new sales will not exceed the profits. This could provide an opportunity for the public health community to provide evidence on what would be an appropriate (nontortious) way to design and market tobacco products.

The tobacco industry may seek congressional relief from its tobacco liability obligations. Such relief was part of the proposed "Global Settlement" of June 1997 between state attorneys general, private attorneys, and the tobacco industry. Congress did not approve the proposed immunities, leading the industry to jettison the deal. However, pressure from successful tobacco lawsuits may induce the industry to try again, and the public health community needs to be prepared to respond.

Litigation by or on Behalf of the Tobacco Industry

The tobacco industry's goal is to sell as many products as it can. The public health goal is to reduce consumption of tobacco products (at least of the addictive, carcinogenic, and otherwise toxic products on the market) to the greatest extent possible. These goals are fundamentally incompatible. As a result, the tobacco industry will continue to try to thwart effective tobacco-control measures, including threatening and pursuing litigation. This fundamental incompatibility of goals is also the reason this branch of public health practice is characterized by confrontation with an industry (unlike many other areas of public health), by military metaphors, and frequently by litigation.

We thank Christopher N. Banthin, J.D., for his assistance with the sections on youth access, due process, and enforcement; Jackie Salcedo, J.D., for her assistance in drafting the section on youth access to tobacco; and Robert Kline, J.D., for his assistance in drafting the section on tobacco advertising and promotion.

References

1. Centers for Disease Control and Prevention. Annual smoking-attributable mortality, years of potential life lost, and economic costs—United States, 1995–1999. *MMWR* 2002;51: 300–3.
2. World Bank. *Curbing the Epidemic: Governments and the Economics of Tobacco Control.* Washington, DC: World Bank, 1999.
3. California Environmental Protection Agency. *Health Effects of Exposure to Environmental Tobacco Smoke.* Dunn A, Zeise L, eds. Sacramento: Office of Environmental Health Hazard Assessment, 1997.
4. Centers for Disease Control and Prevention. *Best Practices for Comprehensive Tobacco-Control Programs—August 1999.* Atlanta: US Department of Health and Human Services, Centers for Disease Control and Prevention, National Center for Chronic Disease Prevention and Health Promotion, Office on Smoking and Health, 1999.
5. *Brown & Williamson Tobacco Co v FDA,* 529 US 120 (2000).
6. 15 USC §1331 *et seq.*
7. US Department of Health, Education, and Welfare. *1964 Surgeon General Report: Reducing the Health Consequences of Smoking.* Washington, DC: US Department of Health, Education, and Welfare, 1964. Available at http://www.cdc.gov/tobacco/sgr/sgr_1964/ sgr64.htm. Accessed September 16, 2005.
8. 15 USC §1335.
9. 15 USC §4401 *et seq.*
10. In the Matter of Swisher Int'l, Inc. Consent Decree dated June 26, 2000; USFTC File No. 0023199.
11. 47 USC §41706.
12. 14 CFR Part 121, *et seq.*
13. Pub L 103-227, §1041-4.
14. 42 USC §300x-26.
15. 15 USC §1334b.
16. Siegel M, Carol J, Jordan J, et al. Preemption in tobacco control: review of an emerging public health problem. *JAMA* 1997;278:858–63.

17. Centers for Disease Control and Prevention. Preemptive state tobacco-control laws—United States, 1982–1998. *MMWR* 1999;47:1112–4.

18. 940 Code Mass Regs 21.00.

19. *Master Settlement Agreement.* §VII. Available at http://www.naag.org/upload/1109185724_1032468605_cigmsa.pdf. Accessed June 23, 2005.

20. Daynard RA. Tobacco liability litigation as a cancer control strategy. *J Natl Cancer Inst* 1988;80:9–13.

21. Daynard RA. Tobacco litigation: a mid-course review. *Cancer Causes Control* 2001;12:383–6.

22. National Association of Attorneys General. Multistate settlement with the tobacco industry. Available at http://www.naag.org/upload/1109185724_1032468605_cigmsa.pdf. Accessed June 23, 2005.

23. Chaloupka FJ, Wechsler HP. Tobacco control policies and smoking among young adults. *J Health Econ* 1997;16:359–73.

24. US Department of Health and Human Services. *Investment in Tobacco Control: State Highlights 2001.* Atlanta: US Department of Health and Human Services, Centers for Disease Control and Prevention, 2001. Available at http://www.cdc.gov/tobacco/statehi/statehi_2001.htm. Accessed June 27, 2005.

25. Government Accountability Office. *Tobacco Settlement—States' Allocations of Fiscal Year 2004 and Expected Fiscal Year 2005 Payments.* Washington, DC: Government Accountability Office, 2005 (Publication No GAO-05-312). Available at http://www.gao.gov/new.items/d05312.pdf. Accessed September 28, 2005.

26. Eckhart D, Tobacco Control Legal Consortium. *The Tobacco Master Settlement Agreement: Enforcement of Marketing Restrictions.* St. Paul, Minnesota: Tobacco Control Legal Consortium, 2004. Available at http://www.wmitchell.edu/tobaccolaw/resources/eckhart.pdf. Accessed August 19, 2005.

27. *California v R J Reynolds*, Statement and Decision No GIC 764118. Sup Ct, San Diego (2002). Available at http://caag.state.ca.us/newsalerts/2004/04-147.pdf. Accessed September 12, 2005.

28. Office of New York State Attorney General Eliot Spitzer. Spitzer Applauds Court Decision Restricting Kool Cigarette Advertising Campaign [press release]. June 17, 2004. Available at http://www.oag.state.ny.us/press/2004/jun/jun17b_04.html. Accessed August 19, 2005.

29. Attorneys General of New York, Illinois, and Maryland. Landmark Settlement of "Kool Mixx" Tobacco Lawsuits [press release]. October 6, 2004. Available at http://www.ag.state.il.us/pressroom/2004_10/20041006kool2.pdf. Accessed August 19, 2005.

30. *Flue-Cured Tobacco Cooperative Stabilization Corp v EPA*, 4 F Supp 435 (USDC MD NC 1998).

31. 313 F 3d 852 (4th Cir 2002).

32. *Philip Morris v American Broadcasting Co et al*, 36 Va Cir 1, 1995 Va Cir LEXIS 1250 (1995).

33. *Philip Morris, Inc v Reilly*, 113 F Supp 2d 129 (USDC D Mass 2000).

34. *Philip Morris, Inc v Reilly*, 312 F 3d 24 (1st Cir 2002)

35. 121 S Ct 2404, 150 L Ed 2d 532 (2001).

36. Bergman AB. Curtailing youth smoking [editorial]. *Arch Pediatr Adolesc Med* 2001;155:546–7.

37. Sweda EL Jr, Daynard RA. Tobacco industry tactics. *Br Med Bull* 1996; 52:183–92.

38. *Master Settlement Agreement.* §VI(h). Available at http://www.naag.org/upload/1109185724_1032468605_cigmsa.pdf. Accessed June 23, 2005.

39. *American Legacy Foundation v Lorillard Tobacco Co*, CA No 19406, DE Chancery Court, New Castle County (filed February 13, 2002)

40. 2005 Del Ch LEXIS 124.

41. 58 Fed Reg164: 45156 (August 26, 1993).

42. DiFranza JR, Godshall WT. Tobacco industry efforts hindering enforcement of the ban on tobacco sales to minors: actions speak louder than words. *Tob Control* 1996;5:127–31.

43. Lynch BS, Bonnie RJ. *Growing Up Tobacco Free: Preventing Nicotine Addiction in Children and Youths*. Washington, DC: National Academy Press, 1994.

44. US Department of Health and Human Services. *Reducing Tobacco Use: A Report of the Surgeon General*. Atlanta: US Department of Health and Human Services, Public Health Service, Centers for Disease Prevention and Control, National Center for Chronic Disease Prevention and Health Promotion, Office on Smoking and Health, 2000:207–8.

45. Office of the Inspector General. *Youth Access to Tobacco*. Washington, DC: US Department of Health and Human Services, 1992.

46. US Department of Health and Human Services. *Preventing Tobacco Use among Young People: A Report of the Surgeon General*. Atlanta: US Department of Health and Human Services, Public Health Service, Centers for Disease Control and Prevention, National Center for Chronic Disease Prevention and Health Promotion, Office on Smoking and Health, 1994.

47. Cummings KM, Sciandra E, Pechacek TF, Orlandi M, Lynn WR. Where teenagers get their cigarettes: a survey of the purchasing habits of 13- to 16-year-olds in 12 US communities. *Tob Control* 1992;1:264–7.

48. Sample Youth Access Regulation for a Board of Health, Controlling the Sale and Use of Tobacco in Massachusetts, Tobacco Control Resource Center, June 2002:233.

49. *See v City of Seattle*, 387 US 541, 545–46 (1967).

50. *Camara v Municipal Court of and City of San Francisco*, 387 US 523, 534–35 (1967).

51. *New York v Burger*, 428 US 691, 702–3 (1987).

52. *Commonwealth v Tart*, 408 Mass 249, 255 (1990).

53. EPA. *Respiratory Health Effects of Passive Smoking: Lung Cancer and Other Disorders*. Washington, DC: Office of Health and Environmental Assessment, Office of Research and Development, EPA, 1992. (Publication No EPA/600/6-90/006F).

54. National Health and Medical Research Council (Australia). The health effects of passive smoking: a scientific information paper. November 1997. Available at http://www.nhmrc .gov.au/publications/reports/smoking/index.htm. Accessed October 22, 2005.

55. National Cancer Institute. Health Effects of Exposure to Environmental Tobacco Smoke: The Report of the California Environmental Protection Agency, 1999. Available at http://cancercontrol.cancer.gov/tcrb/monographs/10/. Accessed October 25, 2005.

56. American Nonsmokers' Rights Foundation. Overview List—How Many Smokefree Laws? 2005. Available at www.no-smoke.org/pdf/mediaordlist.pdf. Accessed September 28, 2005.

57. US Department of Health and Human Services. *Reducing Tobacco Use: A Report of the Surgeon General*. Atlanta: US Department of Health and Human Services, Public Health Service, Centers for Disease Control and Prevention, National Center for Chronic Disease Prevention and Health Promotion, Office on Smoking and Health, 2000:16.

58. Siegel M. Involuntary smoking in the restaurant workplace: a review of employee exposure and health effects. *JAMA* 1993;270:490–3.

59. Centers for Disease Control and Prevention. Preemptive states smoke-free indoor air laws—United States, 1999–2004. *MMWR* 2005; 54:250–3.

60. Sargent R, Shepard R, Glantz S. Reduced incidence of admissions for myocardial infarction associated with public smoking ban: before and after study. *BMJ* 2004;328:977–80.

61. Repace J. Respirable particles and carcinogens in the air of Delaware hospitality venues before and after a smoking ban. *J Occup Environ Med* 2004;46:887–905.

62. Centers for Disease Control and Prevention. Indoor air quality in hospitality venues before and after implementation of a clean indoor air law—western New York, 2003. *MMWR* 2004;53:1038–41.

63. Connolly G, Carpenter C, Alpert HR, Skeer M, Travers M. *Evaluation of the Massachusetts Smoke-Free Workplace Law*. Cambridge, Massachusetts: Harvard School of Public Health, Division of Public Health Practice, Tobacco Research Program, 2005. (Report No 02-05). Available at http://www.hsph.harvard.edu/php/pri/tcrtp/Smoke-free_Workplace.pdf. Accessed September 28, 2005.

64. Glantz SA, Charlesworth A. Tourism and hotel revenues before and after passage of smoke-free restaurant ordinances. *JAMA* 1999;281:1911–8.

65. Philip Morris USA. Accommodation—Options Program. Available at http://web.archive.org/web/20001215205300/philipmorrisusa.com/DisplayPageWithTopic.asp?ID=53. Accessed June 27, 2005.

66. Sweda E. *Summary of Legal Cases Regarding Smoking in the Workplace and Other Places*. Boston: Tobacco Control Resource Center; 1997.

67. *Edwards et al v GDRI, Inc, et al*, Civil Action No. DKC-97-4327 (USDC D Md 1999).

68. *Cookie's Diner v Columbus Board of Health*, 640 NE 2d 1231, 1241 (Mun Ct 1994) at 1239.

69. *Tri-Nel Management, Inc, et al v Board of Health of Barnstable et al*, 433 Mass 217, 741 NE 2d 37 (2001).

70. *City of Tucson v Grezaffi*, 23 P 3d 675, 347 Ariz Adv Rep 10 (2001).

71. 315 F Supp 2d 461 (USDC SC NY 2004).

72. Boston Housing Court Docket No 05-SP-00187, 2005.

73. *Lorillard v Reilly*, 121 S Ct 2404, 150 L Ed 2d 532 (2001).

74. American Burn Association. Fire Safe Cigarette—Legislative Update. 2004. Available at http://www.ameriburn.org/advocacy/fireSafeCig.htm. Accessed October 17, 2004.

75. Sweda EL, Jr. Litigation on behalf of victims of exposure to secondhand smoke, the experience from the USA. *Eur J Public Health* 2001;11:201–5.

76. Brigham PA, McGuire A. Progress towards a fire-safe cigarette. *J Public Health Policy* 1995;16:433–8.

77. Farrelly MC, Healton CG, Davis KC, Messeri P, Hersey JC, Haviland ML. Getting to the truth: evaluating national tobacco countermarketing campaigns. *Am J Public Health* 2002;92:901–7.

78. New York Executive Law §156-c. 79. Ahmad S. The cost-effectiveness of raising the legal smoking age in California. *Med Decis Making* 2005;25:330–40

80. *United States v Philip Morris USA, Inc*, 396 F 3d 1190 (DC Cir 2005).

81. *Liggett Group, Inc v Engle*, 853 So 2d 434 (Fla App 2003).

82. Florida Supreme Court. Oral Arguments Press Summaries. Available at http://www.floridasupremecourt.org/pub_info/index.shtml#summaries. Accessed September 28, 2005,

83. 9 Cal Rptr 3d 29 (CA 2004).

Chapter 19

REPRODUCTIVE HEALTH

Bebe J. Anderson, Maurizio Macaluso,* and Lynne S. Wilcox*

The field of reproductive health includes examples of almost every type of public health law. Reproductive health has multiple dimensions, ranging from the biomedical to the social. At the biomedical level, it addresses a variety of exposures to physical, chemical, and biologic agents that may affect an entire human biologic system, with possible health outcomes that affect not only a woman but also her partner/spouse and her child. At the individual level, it addresses psychosocial, behavioral, and clinical issues that are often perceived as defining a human being and affect health and quality of life well beyond the spheres of sexuality and reproduction. Communication with a sex partner or a spouse is a key component of these behaviors, which often highlight interdependence within a couple rather than individual free will. At a broader societal level, sexuality and reproduction raise core moral questions that are the subject of intense debate in a free society. Public health laws and regulations are promulgated and enacted and exert their effects within such a complex web of relations.

In this chapter, we define reproductive health broadly, including examples from contraception, abortion, pregnancy, and infertility. (See Chapter 16 for discussions of HIV and sexually transmitted infections, which are important aspects of reproductive health.) Legal issues in reproductive health encompass reporting of outcomes (surveillance, vital statistics), program management (who receives and who can provide reproductive health services), insurance coverage (legal mandates for insurance covering contraception or infertility services), government funding of services (Medicaid, Title X), clinic and laboratory operation (licensing and certification laws), and public health research (human subjects protection and informed consent for pregnant women).

---

*The findings and conclusions in this chapter are those of the author(s) and do not necessarily represent the views of the U.S. Department of Health and Human Services or the Centers for Disease Control and Prevention.

Background

An understanding of reproductive health law requires recognition that both law and medicine have shaped this area. Most societies view activities such as sexual behavior, childbearing, and birth control as having moral, legal, and cultural implications beyond their health effects, leading to laws intended to control these behaviors. For example, abortion and birth control were subject to state criminal laws that limited access to these services until the mid-1960s, when courts began to find that such laws implicate federal constitutional rights. Thus, several reproductive health law issues implicate constitutionally protected rights, in particular the right to privacy.

Each year in the United States, approximately 6.4 million pregnancies occur and 4.1 million live infants are born,[1] and approximately 38 million women of childbearing age use some form of birth control.[2] Pregnant women receive special attention in state and federal laws. This attention includes ensuring that prenatal medical care is available to low-income pregnant women (Title V of the Social Security Act); monitoring health events, such as maternal deaths (vital statistics reporting); and protecting pregnant women from research risks. Women of reproductive age are subject to a variety of laws, some designed to increase access to reproductive health services and others designed to restrict such access. For example, income eligibility rules for government funding of some childbirth-related medical services are more generous than for funding of many other medical services, but significant legal restrictions exist at the federal and state levels regarding not only government funding for abortion services but also other issues that affect women's ability to seek and obtain abortions.

Women and couples who use infertility services have other legal concerns, many of which stem from the financial cost of advanced infertility techniques. For example, a one-month cycle of in vitro fertilization (IVF) or other assisted reproduction technologies (ART) can cost thousands of dollars, but the success rate is highly variable, depending on circumstances (such as the age of the woman), and averages at about one chance in three of leading to a live-born infant. This has led to a strong interest among advocates for infertile couples in encouraging legislation that mandates insurance coverage for these services; these mandates have been established in several states. In addition, federal legislation requiring standardized reporting of pregnancy rates by ART clinics has been passed to provide consumers with standardized data for decision-making regarding the use of ART services.

Thus, the influence of law on reproductive health concerns varies with the outcome of interest and often is affected by the woman's resources. To provide the best reproductive health research and programs, public health practitioners need to be aware of the spectrum of legal influences.

Legal Authorities

This section outlines the law governing reproductive health in the United States, with particular emphasis on the federal Constitution, statutes, regulations, and case law. State law regarding reproductive health is dynamic. Each year, new laws are introduced in state legislatures throughout the country, touching on issues such as provision of abortions, access to contraceptives, and insurance coverage for infertility treatments. Moreover, many state-by-state differences exist in the approach to legislation in this area. Given the number, breadth, and variability of state regulation in this area, we have not attempted to cite or explain the many laws of individual states. Rather, we have tried to highlight major themes of state regulation in this area to emphasize the need to determine whether a specific state has enacted legislation addressing a particular aspect of reproductive health.

Constitutional Law

Controlling Issues under the U.S. Constitution

In contrast to many other areas of public health law, the most important legal authority for reproductive health law issues is the U.S. Constitution. Before 1965, the main sources of law governing reproductive health were state laws, in particular laws criminalizing the use of contraceptives and prohibiting the performance of abortions.[a] The legal landscape changed dramatically with the U.S. Supreme Court's decision in *Griswold v. Connecticut*.[3]

In *Griswold*, the Supreme Court held that state regulation of the use of contraceptives by married persons invaded "the zone of privacy created by several fundamental constitutional guarantees."[3] The Constitution does not explicitly protect a right to privacy; rather, the Supreme Court has found such a right to be implicit in the Constitution on the basis of the nature of rights that the federal Constitution explicitly protects.[4] Legal restrictions on matters involving reproductive health implicate the constitutional right to privacy because, as the Court has stated, "if the right to privacy means anything, it is the right of the individual, married or single, to be free from unwarranted governmental intrusion in matters so fundamentally affecting a person as the decision whether to bear or beget a child."[5,b] Therefore, state regulation regarding reproductive health must account for the unique, constitutionally protected status accorded decisions regarding pregnancy. Most of the court decisions addressing this right have arisen in the context of abortion; however, the right to privacy is by no means limited to that aspect of reproductive health.[c]

Although the right to privacy under the U.S. Constitution is the primary federal constitutional authority governing the regulation of reproductive health, the constitutional rights to due process and equal protection also often are implicated. To satisfy the requirements of the Due Process Clauses of the Fifth and Fourteenth amendments, a statute must clearly define the conduct that it prohibits, so a person can avoid engaging in prohibited conduct. In particular, statutes that impose criminal penalties—as many state laws regulating abortion do—and statutes that interfere with constitutionally protected activity are subjected to a higher standard of certainty in their language. Federal courts have found many state restrictions on the provision of reproductive health services to be unconstitutionally vague and violative of the Due Process Clause of the Fourteenth Amendment.[6] In some of these cases, the statute's vagueness derives from the use in legislation of terms that have a variety of meanings or no clear meaning to members of the medical community.

Equal protection challenges to restrictions on the provision of reproductive health services focus on the extent to which the laws treat similarly situated persons alike. Typically, such challenges are based on the restriction's differential treatment of women and of men seeking reproductive health services and/or on its singling out of providers of abortion services for requirements that are not imposed on providers of medical procedures involving comparable risks and complexity. Although such claims are frequently raised in challenges to restrictions on reproductive health-care access, the challenges usually are resolved on other grounds, such as vagueness or the right to privacy.

In the landmark decision *Roe v. Wade*, the Supreme Court applied the right to privacy to declare that Texas' criminal abortion statutes were unconstitutional.[4] Three years after the *Roe* decision, the Court held that minor women also have a right to privacy, which includes the right to determine whether to terminate their pregnancy, but that the state has broader authority to restrict the exercise of that right in the context of minors.[7]

Since the *Roe* decision, the Supreme Court has repeatedly addressed the constitutionality of various state, and some federal, laws imposing restrictions on the provision of abortions, as the limits and continued vitality of the *Roe* decision have been tested. The most significant post-*Roe* case is *Planned Parenthood of Southeastern Pennsylvania v. Casey*.[8]

In *Casey*, the Supreme Court reaffirmed that women have a constitutional right to choose and obtain an abortion without government interference, as the Court had held in *Roe*. However, the Court altered the analysis applied to restrictions on that right. Five members of the Court held that (1) before a fetus is viable, a woman has a right to choose to have an abortion and to obtain such an abortion, subject only to state interference that is designed to advance the state's interests in protecting the health of the woman or the potential life of the fetus and that does not constitute an "undue" burden on that right; (2) after viability, a state has the power to restrict abortions, provided the restriction contains exceptions for situations in which a woman's health or life is endangered by continuation of her pregnancy; and (3) a state has legitimate interests throughout a pregnancy in both protecting the health of the pregnant woman and protecting the potential life of the fetus.[8] In *Roe*, the Court held that a woman's right to determine whether to terminate her pregnancy is a fundamental right and that the weight to be given the state's interests in regulating abortion depended on the trimester of pregnancy affected. In *Casey*, the trimester approach was replaced with the "undue burden" test: a state regulation violates the right to privacy if it imposes an "undue burden" on that right, meaning that the regulation "has the purpose or effect of placing a substantial obstacle in the path of a woman seeking an abortion of a nonviable fetus."[8]

The Supreme Court has recognized only two purposes that can justify imposing an undue burden on a woman's right to determine whether to terminate her pregnancy: (1) the state's interest in potential life and (2) the state's interest in protecting maternal health. With respect to the state's interest in potential life, the Court has stated clearly that, before viability, the state may promote that interest only through means "calculated to inform the woman's free choice, not hinder it."[8]

In its most recent affirmation of the right to choose to terminate a pregnancy, *Stenberg v. Carhart*, the Court reiterated the requirement that restrictions on the provision of abortions must include an exception for situations in which the woman's health or life will be placed at risk. In this case, five members of the Court found that Nebraska's ban on "partial birth abortions" violated the right to choose to terminate a pregnancy in two ways: (1) it lacked a health exception and (2) it placed an undue burden on the right because its wording banned the method of abortion most commonly used during the second trimester of abortion, as well as banning another, less commonly used method, thus allowing prosecution of physicians for performing the most commonly used procedure for terminating previability second-trimester abortions.[9]

Controlling Issues under State Constitutions

Some restrictions on access to reproductive health services have been challenged on the basis of provisions in state constitutions. In particular, this has occurred in states with constitutions that provide broader protection to privacy rights than the U.S. Constitution.[10,11] Such challenges also have been brought successfully on the basis of other clauses in state constitutions, in particular Equal Protection and Privileges and Immunities clauses.[12]

Laws and Regulations Related to Program Management

Restrictions on Receipt of Services

By statute and regulation, many states regulate the provision of contraceptives and other family planning services, including imposing specific informed consent requirements for the receipt of such services. Generally, a physician's prescription is required for oral contraceptive pills in the United States. The provision of sterilization services is specifically restricted where federal family planning funds are used: the patient must comply with a specific informed consent procedure; a 30-day gap must exist between provision of informed consent and performance of the procedure; the patient must be over age 21 years; and the patient must be mentally competent.[13] In addition, many states impose specific restrictions on the provision of sterilization, and some states impose restrictions on the provision of ART services.

For minors in most states, access to reproductive health services differs from access to other health care. In general, Anglo-American common law traditionally accorded parents the right to make health-care decisions for their children. However, approximately two-thirds of the states have altered this ancient doctrine by statutes that specifically authorize some or all minors to obtain prenatal care and delivery services without parental consent or notification. Almost all the states explicitly permit some minors the right to consent to contraceptive services without parental involvement, and 21 states explicitly allow all minors to do so. In contrast, most states impose, by statute, limitations on the access of minors to abortion services, typically requiring that the minor obtain the consent of one or both parents or that one or both parents be notified before an abortion is performed on the minor.

State law provides the primary source of restrictions on the receipt of abortion services. Federal case law interpreting the validity of such statutes under the U.S. Constitution provides the primary controlling law governing such restrictions.

Restrictions on Provision of Services

Many state laws allow certain individuals, facilities, or entities to refuse to participate in the provision of abortion services, and some state laws allow refusals with respect to the provision of contraceptive supplies or services, on the basis of moral or religious beliefs.[d] Some of these state laws are linked to the use of public monies, for example, forbidding a public hospital from performing an abortion. In a few states, such laws have been found to be unconstitutional under either the state or federal constitution as applied to public, "quasi-public," nonsectarian, or nonprofit facilities.[14–16] Some states allow individuals or facilities to deny patients information or counseling about contraceptives, some allow pharmacists to refuse to fill prescriptions for contraceptives, and some prohibit state employees or entities or organizations receiving state funds from counseling or referring women for abortion services in some circumstances.

Most states prohibit, by statute, persons other than licensed physicians from performing abortions. Such restrictions have been found to be constitutional under the U.S. Constitution as furthering the state interest of protecting maternal health.[4,17] In a few states, physician assistants can perform abortions under the supervision of a licensed physician, and the supreme court of one state found that a law prohibiting that practice violated the state Constitution.

States may not require all second-trimester abortions to be performed in hospitals; such laws violate the U.S. Constitution.[18,19] In almost every state, after a fetus is viable, an abortion can be performed only in accordance with specific statutory requirements.

An increasing number of states have enacted licensing statutes or regulations that impose specific requirements regarding staffing, physical plant, administrative procedures, equipment, and other matters on facilities at which abortions are performed. Some of these laws and regulations have been challenged successfully as violating the U.S. Constitution, but others have been upheld by the courts, usually on the basis that they do not create a substantial obstacle to women seeking abortions. In addition to the many abortion-specific statutes, several statutory and regulatory requirements governing the provision of medical services apply to health-care providers who perform abortions. Physicians and nurses performing abortion services are required to adhere to the professional and ethical standards contained in the applicable state statutes and regulations governing their professional licensure. Most facilities at which abortions are performed are subject to the federal Clinical Laboratory Improvement Act (CLIA)[20] and Occupational Safety and Health Act;[21] local ordinances pertaining to waste disposal; and other local laws, such as fire and building codes and local ordinances pertaining to building maintenance.

The availability of mifepristone—also referred to as RU-486—for use in medically terminating pregnancies, after FDA approval in 2000, had been expected to increase women's access to abortions, mainly because additional health-care providers might offer that nonsurgical type of abortion service. However, the impact of its availability has been less than anticipated, probably in part because of the extent to which providers of medical abortions have been subject to the state laws restricting the provision of abortions. Most state laws regulating abortion do not limit their scope to surgical abortions or to post-first-trimester abortions, and, therefore, providers of medical abortions are subject to laws such as those requiring parental consent or notice, waiting periods, or provision to the patient of specific information before the performance of an abortion. Although some of those laws are limited to facilities at which only surgical abortions or only second- or third-trimester abortions are performed, in other states such requirements are not so limited and in some cases also apply to private physicians' offices. Physician-only laws, which limit who can perform an abortion, may conflict with some states' practice acts, which grant nonphysician practitioners authority to dispense drugs, thus creating uncertainty about whether certain nonphysicians can perform medical abortions in those states.[22,23]

The Fertility Clinic Success Rate and Certification Act of 1992 (FCSRCA)[24] required the Centers for Disease Control and Prevention (CDC) of the U.S. Department of Health and Human Services (DHHS) to develop a model program for the certification of embryo laboratories that support ART programs, to be carried out voluntarily by interested states. CDC published a model program in 1999.[25] However, thus far no state has adopted the model program (some states enforce their own specific requirements), and most embryo laboratories in the United States adhere to voluntary certification programs sponsored by professional societies.

Laws and Regulations Related to Payment for Services

Government Funding

Government funding of reproductive health services differs greatly by type of service. Health services related to childbirth—during pregnancy, at birth, and postpartum —are subject to special income-eligibility rules designed to allow more pregnant women to qualify to receive those health services.

Federal regulations require state Medicaid programs to provide Medicaid-eligible persons with coverage for pregnancy-related services, such as prenatal, delivery, and postpartum care, and family planning services. Moreover, a woman who was eligible for and received Medicaid coverage for pregnancy-related services during her pregnancy remains eligible for such services during a postpartum period lasting at least 60 days after the birth, even if her financial circumstances change.[26] In response to the changing provision of health care in the United States, many Medicaid programs contract with managed-care providers. To protect women's access to timely and confidential family planning services, Congress has enacted a freedom-of-choice statute, allowing women to go "outside the plan" for family planning services.[27]

Beginning in 1986, in response to concerns about infant mortality, Congress amended the Medicaid laws in an effort to increase the number of pregnant women eligible for prenatal-care services and to improve the services they can receive. In particular, Congress created a special income-eligibility limit for pregnant women: allowing women to qualify for Medicaid coverage of pregnancy-related services even when their income was too high for them to be eligible for Medicaid coverage of other services, thus increasing the number of women who would qualify for Medicaid coverage of pregnancy-related services. As a result, by the mid-1990s, the Medicaid program paid for almost one-third of all U.S. births. In addition, other federal programs—including the Maternal and Child Health program and the Special Supplemental Nutrition Program for Women, Infants, and Children—provide funding for aspects of prenatal care. Most states have taken additional steps to increase pregnant women's access to pregnancy-related services, including altering their Medicaid eligibility levels to make more persons eligible than meet the eligibility levels established by the federal regulations; adopting special administrative rules to make beginning receipt of covered services easier for pregnant women; and increasing the types of pregnancy-related services covered under their Medicaid plans. The strategies used by states to increase the number of women receiving prenatal care have differed, with varying success rates.[28]

Family planning services other than abortion are funded from a variety of public sources, each with its own restrictions. The federal government provides funding for family planning services through four major sources: Title X of the Public Health Services Act, and Title V (the Maternal and Child Health Block Grant), Title XIX (Medicaid), and Title XX (the Social Services Block Grant) of the Social Security Act.[29–31] Through the Title X program, the federal government awards grants solely for family planning to service providers—state agencies and private nonprofit agencies—which then can offer such services to uninsured persons at reduced fees and to women in managed-care plans who seek services outside their provider network. Recipients of Title X funds are required to provide not only comprehensive family planning services but also an array of preventive health-care services such as pelvic examinations, Pap tests, breast examinations, screening and treatment of sexually transmitted infections, safer-sex counseling, basic infertility screening, and referrals to specialized health care. Funds under titles V and XX, which can be used for services including family planning services, are provided only to state government agencies, which may pass the funds on to private agencies. Under the Medicaid program, the federal government reimburses the states for providing services, with family planning services reimbursed at a higher rate than other services. State funds for family planning services come from a variety of sources, including state Medicaid funding.

Minors can obtain federally funded contraceptives confidentially. Whereas Title X encourages family participation in federally funded family planning programs, federal courts have invalidated efforts to require notification to a minor's parent on the basis that they violated Title X.[33]

Government funding for abortion services is severely restricted. Although the Medicaid program generally provides coverage for medically necessary health care needed by income-eligible persons, medically necessary abortions are not covered. Pursuant to the "Hyde Amendment," state Medicaid plans are required to cover abortions, and federal reimbursement funds are available for them, only if the procedure is necessary to save a woman's life when her life is endangered by a physical disorder, physical injury, or physical illness, or where the woman's pregnancy resulted from rape or incest.[34,e] The U.S. Supreme Court has held that this restriction on coverage of abortions does not violate the federal right to privacy.[35] Nevertheless, some states fund medically necessary abortions on the basis of a state statute or regulation or because they were ordered to do so by a state court.

Private Funding

Private funding for reproductive health services depends on the specific provisions of a given insurance policy or managed-care plan, but some types of coverage are mandated by law. Federal law requires that group health plans, insurance companies, and health maintenance organizations that offer health coverage for hospital stays in connection with childbirth provide such coverage for mandated minimum periods of time. After most normal vaginal deliveries, a hospital stay of at least 48 hours must be covered for both the woman and her newborn child; after birth by caesarian section, a hospital stay of at least 96 hours must be covered.[36]

By 2006, legislation had been enacted in 14 states and proposed at the federal level requiring health plans to cover infertility treatments as a benefit in each insurance policy or to make such coverage available for purchase. Some states mandate insurance providers to offer coverage as part of some policies, and others mandate coverage of infertility treatment in all insurance policies. Even where all policies must cover infertility treatment, the details of what the plans must cover—in terms of type of infertility treatments, number of procedures covered, and prerequisites for coverage—vary widely among those state laws. Coverage for infertility treatment generally is not offered by health plans where not mandated by law.

Beginning in the late 1990s, many states enacted laws requiring that health insurance plans provide partial or comprehensive insurance coverage for reversible methods of contraception. Laws in a few states prohibit private insurance coverage for abortion unless the woman pays an extra premium.

Laws and Regulations Related to Public Health Surveillance

A broader discussion of the general authorities governing public health surveillance is provided in Chapter 9. The states have the legal responsibility to collect, manage, and compile vital records, a key source of information for many reproductive health issues. States require the registration of all births and deaths. This registration is considered virtually complete in most states and allows a complete enumeration of the numerator (infant deaths) and denominator (infant births) for reporting infant mortality rates. The reporting of maternal deaths is more challenging. Although every woman's death is reported, information regarding pregnancy may not appear on the death certificate because of differences among states in certificate design and definition of maternal death. Thus maternal deaths calculated from vital records generally are regarded as underestimates of the true number of deaths. Legal requirements for reporting of fetal deaths also vary from state to state.

With the enactment of the Safe Motherhood Monitoring and Prevention Research Act in 2002, Congress authorized CDC to develop surveillance systems at the local, state, and national levels to better determine the burden of maternal complications and mortality and to decrease the disparities among populations at risk of death and complications from pregnancy.[37] Specifically, the Act authorizes CDC to (1) establish a national surveillance program to identify and promote investigation of deaths and severe complications during pregnancy; (2) expand the Pregnancy Risk Assessment Monitoring System (PRAMS); and (3) expand the Maternal and Child Health Epidemiology Program. The Pregnancy Mortality Surveillance System was established in 1987 as a collaborative effort between CDC and individual state health departments. It presently compiles data from the entire nation, detects pregnancy-related deaths, and provides comprehensive data to analyze factors associated with these deaths to inform state and national prevention strategies.[38] In contrast, PRAMS is an ongoing state- and population-based surveillance system designed to collect information about self-reported maternal behaviors and experiences that occur around the time of pregnancy. That system generates statewide estimates of perinatal health indicators among women who recently delivered a live infant. Each participating state uses a standardized data-collection method developed by CDC. In 2006, 38 states and New York City will contribute data to PRAMS. In addition, the Maternal and Child Health Epidemiology Program is a collaborative effort between CDC and the Health Resources and Services Administration to build maternal and child health epidemiology and data capacity at the state, local, and tribal levels to effectively use information for public health action. Currently, the Maternal and Child Health Epidemiology Program supports 14 state public health agencies and one Indian Health Board.

Most states gather data on the provision of legal induced abortions. Typically, health-care providers who perform abortions are required by state statute or regulation to provide data to the state health department, state registrar, or state vital statistics officer. Some controversy has arisen about whether induced abortions should be monitored as reportable events comparable with births, deaths, and fetal deaths or as medical procedures comparable with other surgeries.[39] The collection of confidential information about the provision of abortions relates to the state's interest in maternal health and is constitutional. Noting that "[t]he collection of information with respect to actual patients is a vital element of medical research," the U.S. Supreme Court upheld a requirement that the following information be reported for each abortion performed: identity of the facility and physician performing the abortion; the woman's number of prior pregnancies and abortions; gestational age of the aborted fetus; type of abortion procedure; preexisting conditions complicating the pregnancy; medical complications from the abortion; reason the abortion was medically necessary, if applicable; and weight of the aborted fetus.[8]

The FCSRCA requires each ART program to report to CDC the pregnancy success rates achieved through ART procedures, the identity of the embryo laboratory used by the program, and whether the laboratory is certified under the act.[24] Whereas most surveillance authorities are established by state laws, and the federal government usually limits its role in mandating or authorizing compilation of national statistics through collaboration of state and federal agencies (typically the state departments of health and CDC), FCSRCA established a direct obligation for each ART program to report to the federal government.

All states list specific sexually transmitted diseases, including HIV, as notifiable diseases and mandate health-care providers to report new cases, although the number of notifiable sexually transmitted diseases varies across states. CDC compiles national statistics and publishes weekly updates, as well as surveillance summaries covering longer intervals, through its *Morbidity and Mortality Weekly Report.*

Surveillance of cancer of the reproductive organs is regulated by federal and state laws and regulations that address surveillance of all forms of cancer. With the enactment of the Cancer Registries Amendment Act of 1992, Congress mandated CDC to establish the National Program of Cancer Registries, setting minimum information requirements for data collection and providing federal matching funds for state-based central cancer registries.[40] As of 2004, the National Program of Cancer Registries encompassed central cancer registries in 45 states.

Laws and Regulations Related to Public Health Research and Information

Both DHHS and its Food and Drug Administration (FDA) regulate protection of human subjects from risks deriving from participation in research that is conducted or sponsored by the federal government or is aimed at obtaining FDA approval for a new drug or device.[41,42] Institutional review boards registered with the Office for Human Research Protections have oversight over the conduct of research involving human subjects. A broader discussion of these issues is contained in Chapter 10.

DHHS imposes specific limitations on research involving pregnant women, considering pregnant women and fetuses as a vulnerable population. For any research designed to benefit solely the fetus, both the consent of the pregnant woman and the consent of the fetus' father must be obtained, with a few limited exceptions. Only the consent of the pregnant woman must be obtained for research designed to benefit both the pregnant woman and the fetus; for research designed to benefit solely the pregnant woman; and for research designed to develop important biomedical knowledge but not expected to benefit the individual fetus and woman and presenting no more than minimal risk to the fetus.[43]

CDC's National Center for Health Statistics conducts a national fertility survey (the National Survey of Family Growth) to gather information about factors contributing to the national birth rate, such as sexual activity, contraceptive use, infertility, fetal loss, expected future births, and the wantedness status of pregnancies and births. Using National Survey of Family Growth data, researchers have examined such public health issues as adolescent pregnancy, use of family planning services, and maternal and child health.[44]

The U.S. Congress recently has focused on research in the field of safe motherhood and child development, enacting important legislation that expands the scope of work of the National Institutes of Health, CDC, and other federal agencies in this field. The Children's Health Act of 2000 required the Secretary of Health and Human Services, through CDC, to establish the National Center on Birth Defects and Developmental Disabilities with the charge to collect, analyze, and disseminate data on the occurrence and causes of birth defects and developmental disabilities.[45]

The Act also authorized the National Institute of Child Health and Human Development to establish a consortium of federal agencies and conduct a national longitudinal study of environmental influences (including physical, chemical, biologic, and psychosocial) on children's health and development. The study will evaluate the effects of both chronic and intermittent exposures on child health and human development, and will investigate basic mechanisms of developmental disorders and environmental factors, both risk and protective, that influence health and developmental processes.[46] The National Children's Study will enroll over 100,000 children from about 100 locations across the United States, following them from before birth until age 21 years. Enrollment will include pregnant women and their partners, couples who are planning a pregnancy, and women of childbearing age who are not planning a pregnancy. Environmental exposures will be assessed before pregnancy or during the early pregnancy to assess their impact on child development in the context of a child's genetic makeup. The National Children's Study recently released its study plan; initial enrollment of subjects is scheduled for 2007.[47]

The Safe Motherhood Monitoring and Prevention Research Act of 2002 expanded the authority of DHHS to conduct public health research in reproductive health, concerning risk factors, prevention strategies, and the roles of the family, health-care providers, and the community in safe motherhood. The act targets issues including health services research on unnecessary cesarean deliveries; prevention research to reduce the risk for preterm birth; research on the adverse effects of smoking, alcohol, and illegal drug use before, during, and after pregnancy; the design of counseling for groups at risk for adverse pregnancy outcomes; and prevention of infections that cause maternal and infant complications.[37]

Legal Issues and Controversies

Legal Issues Relating to Program Management

Issues Related to Reproductive Health Services Generally or to Services Other Than Abortion

Recent efforts to increase enforcement of statutory rape laws, combined with child abuse reporting laws that require the reporting of statutory rape, may have implications for minors' continued confidential access to all reproductive health services.[48] All states require reporting of child abuse, which includes sexual abuse, to child welfare agencies or law enforcement. The states differ in their definition of what constitutes child abuse and child sexual abuse, with the federal government setting its standards for those terms in the federal Child Abuse Prevention and Treatment Act.[49,50] In recent years, at both the federal and state levels, greater attention has been paid to "statutory rape"—generally meaning sex with a minor even if the minor consented—and part of this attention has focused on revising child abuse reporting laws to require or encourage the reporting of statutory rape.[f] Some states specifically include statutory rape as a reportable offense; in other states, prosecutors interpret the law as requiring such reporting. Thus, in some states, health-care professionals are statutorily obligated to report instances in which a minor has sexual activity with an older minor or an adult. In those states, minors needing pregnancy-related health services, treatment of sexually transmitted diseases, or even contraceptives may be deterred from seeking such services for fear they or their sex partners will be put at risk because of their health-care providers' reporting obligation.

Issues Related Solely to Abortion

Since the U.S. Supreme Court's decision in *Roe v. Wade* barred criminalization of abortion, many states have enacted laws seeking to limit the availability of abortion services. As discussed below, some of those limitations have been found unlawful; some others have successfully withstood legal challenge. Legal barriers to a woman's access to abortion services have taken many forms but generally can be grouped according to whether they focus on the woman and her decision-making or on the manner in which the abortion procedure is provided.

State laws focused on the woman's decision-making have required provision of specific information to the woman before performance of the procedure, waiting periods between receipt of such information and performance of the procedure, and/ or notice to or consent from the woman's spouse or parent before performance of the procedure. A state may require an abortion to be performed only after the woman has received specified information, which may be scripted by the state and include information about fetal gestational age and development and about medical risks to the woman for terminating or continuing her pregnancy. The state can impose such requirements, even if in doing so the state expresses a preference for childbirth over abortion, as long as the information is "truthful and not misleading." Moreover, a state can require a woman to wait a period of time after receiving such information before she can obtain her abortion as long as an exception is made for medical emergencies where delay in terminating the pregnancy would create a serious risk of impairment to the woman's health or put her life at risk. In making these rulings, the Supreme Court left open the possibility that the types of restrictions found lawful in *Casey* might be found to be an undue burden, and therefore unconstitutional, on the basis of a different factual record.[8] Since the *Casey* decision, some laws imposing waiting periods and provision of particular information have been challenged, with mixed results.

A state may not require a woman to notify, or to receive the consent of, her spouse before obtaining an abortion.[8] However, a state may place greater limits on a minor's ability to exercise the right to seek an abortion than it may place on that of an adult woman. Therefore, a state may require notification or consent of one or both of a minor's parents before an abortion is performed, if the state provides an alternative procedure by which the minor may obtain authorization from a judge to obtain an abortion.[7,51,52] At least with respect to a parental consent requirement, the constitutionally required alternative procedure must satisfy the following four criteria: (1) the minor must have the opportunity to obtain court authorization for the abortion if she shows she is sufficiently mature and informed to make her decision independently of her parents; (2) the minor must have the opportunity to obtain court authorization if the court determines an abortion would be in her best interests; (3) the court procedure must ensure the minor's anonymity; and (4) the court procedure must be conducted expeditiously so the minor has an effective opportunity to obtain an abortion.[51,53]

As mentioned earlier, some state constitutions protect individual rights greater than those provided under the federal constitution. Thus, in some states, restrictions on the provision of abortions to minors have been challenged successfully as violating state constitutional rights, in particular rights to privacy and/or equal protection.

States have restricted the manner by which an abortion may be obtained, mainly by limiting who may perform an abortion, where an abortion may be performed, when an abortion may be performed, and what specific procedures may be used to perform an abortion. In the late 1990s, many states enacted laws to restrict the abortion procedures used, terming these laws as bans on "partial birth abortion." These statutes typically were worded broadly so that they prohibited performance of several or most procedures commonly used before fetal viability and many of them lacked exceptions to allow use of the banned procedures when necessary to preserve the woman's health. Analyzing the Nebraska partial-birth abortion statute, the Supreme Court concluded that it imposed an unconstitutional undue burden on a woman's right to choose to terminate her pregnancy before viability by banning the procedure that was most commonly used for abortions performed during the second trimester of pregnancy and by failing to include a health exception.[9] In 2003, the first federal ban on abortion—the Partial Birth Abortion Act of 2003—was enacted. That law was challenged in three federal courts, all of which declared the law unconstitutional and enjoined its enforcement; those decisions are on appeal.

Legal Issues Relating to Payment for Services

During the mid-1990s, Congress extensively changed welfare laws, many of which affected reproductive health. As part of the Personal Responsibility and Work Opportunity Reconciliation Act of 1996,[54] Congress repealed the Aid to Families With Dependent Children program and replaced it with the Temporary Assistance for Needy Families (TANF) block grant. Recipients of TANF are subject to a five-year limit on benefits and must comply with mandatory work requirements. Previously, women who received cash assistance through Aid to Families With Dependent Children—most of the women receiving federal welfare benefits—automatically were enrolled in the Medicaid program, through which they received medical services. With the change to TANF, many eligible families and children lost their Medicaid benefits, largely because of continued linkage of Medicaid eligibility to cash assistance eligibility, despite different eligibility criteria; improper application of sanctions, such as terminating Medicaid coverage for failure to comply with work requirements; or diversion into a work program before the person was allowed to apply for Medicaid. Moreover, fewer immigrants are eligible for Medicaid coverage under the new welfare laws.[54]

Among other changes to welfare laws enacted by Congress during the mid-1990s were provisions intended to reduce out-of-wedlock childbearing. Those changes included creation of an "illegitimacy bonus" to reward states for reduced rates of out-of-wedlock births. State efforts to achieve that goal have included programs and policies intended to increase contraceptive use among low-income women and other measures to prevent teen pregnancies.

In recent years, a trend requiring health insurance plans to provide contraceptive coverage has emerged, with many bills enacted at the state level and many more introduced. A continuing controversy with respect to such laws has been the extent to which health plans or employers owned by or affiliated with a religious organization will be subject to such requirements. Some states have enacted contraceptive insurance coverage laws without any such exemptions; others have included exemptions limited to organizations formed and operated for religious purposes; and still others have exemptions that cover any organization affiliated with a religious organization that objects to coverage of contraceptives on religious grounds.

The federal government's restrictions on Medicaid reimbursement for abortion services do not limit the extent to which states may cover such services. States remain free to include—and, where mandated by state law, must include—reimbursement for abortion services denied federal funding.[35] Several states have chosen by statute to provide broader coverage for abortions than required by the federal Medicaid regulations—some covering all medically necessary abortions, others covering abortions performed because of fetal anomalies. In almost half of the 50 states, denial of funding for medically necessary abortions has been challenged on state constitutional grounds; in most of those states, state courts have ordered that the state provide such funding.[55]

Restrictions on the provision of abortion that increase the costs of the procedure may amount to an unconstitutional undue burden.[8] The Supreme Court has not specified how large that cost increase must be to violate the right to privacy; this issue frequently is raised in opposition to licensing requirements that make the provision of abortions more costly for providers and their patients. Laws that impose delays on the provision of abortion sometimes are challenged on the grounds that they increase the cost associated with obtaining an abortion and thus, particularly for low-income women, may impose a substantial obstacle in the path of women seeking an abortion.

Legal Issues Relating to Public Health Research and Information

Historically, women often were excluded from human subject research and clinical trials to avoid risk of harming a developing fetus. A 1977 FDA guideline specifically excluded women of childbearing potential from participating in early studies of drugs. As a result of such exclusions, knowledge about the risks for or efficacy of a particular treatment or drug for women generally and pregnant women in particular often was unavailable. In recent years, the federal government has adopted policies and guidelines to encourage inclusion of women of childbearing potential in research study populations and in all phases of clinical drug development. As a result, more women are included in clinical studies, although data are not always collected in a manner that allows ascertainment of sex-specific effects. The exclusion of women of childbearing potential is required only in studies of life-threatening conditions.

Studies involving pregnant women have special restrictions, as discussed above, meant to ensure that such studies are conducted with adequate protections for the mother and the child. However, such restrictions may make inclusion of pregnant women as research subjects less likely and under certain circumstances may be perceived as discriminating on the basis of sex.[43,g]

Legal Issues Relating to Individual Health Behaviors

In recent years, women sometimes have been prosecuted and punished for conduct during pregnancy that might harm the developing fetus, particularly for drug or alcohol use. Using existing laws, local prosecutors have charged pregnant substance abusers with crimes such as child abuse, child neglect, delivery or distribution (through the umbilical cord) of an unlawful substance to a minor, contributing to the delinquency of a minor, and assault with a deadly weapon (i.e., cocaine). In almost every state in which women have contested such charges, courts have rejected the charges or reversed imposed penalties, finding that using those criminal statutes to punish women for their conduct during pregnancy is without a legal basis or is unconstitutional. In doing so, some courts have noted that prosecuting pregnant women for their conduct during pregnancy can be counterproductive because it may discourage them from seeking health care during pregnancy.[56] In 2001, the U.S. Supreme Court struck down a state hospital's drug-testing program that targeted pregnant women; major medical groups opposed the program on the grounds that such programs harm prenatal health because they discourage pregnant women who use drugs from seeking prenatal care.[57]

Many states have modified their civil child protection laws to cover situations in which a child is born dependent on, tests positive for, or has been harmed by an illegal drug or alcohol consumption, either by defining "child neglect" to include those situations or by requiring reporting of such births to child welfare authorities. In some states, efforts have been undertaken to civilly commit pregnant women to protect their fetuses from potential harm; a few states have enacted laws specifically authorizing civil commitment or detention of women who use a controlled substance or abuse alcohol during pregnancy.

Practice Considerations

The public health practice aspects of laws related to reproductive health are broad and highlight the challenges of balancing contrasting legal concerns: state versus federal responsibilities; medical privacy versus complete and accurate data; legislation of mandates versus the scientific evidence to support such mandates; concerns about ensuring adequate government oversight on new reproductive health practices; and many others. Space limitations prohibit a comprehensive discussion, but the following examples illustrate common public health practice aspects of state and federal regulation of reproductive health issues.

Pregnancy

Maternal health is a rediscovered issue in public health.[58] After years of focusing on infant mortality, public health professionals have recognized that little hope exists for additional reductions in rates of preterm delivery and other adverse newborn outcomes unless the relation between the health of pregnant women and their pregnancy outcomes is further examined and taken into account in preconception and prenatal-care programs. Thus, support has revived for maternal mortality review committees. These committees were prevalent in the mid-20th century but faded into oblivion during the last decades of the century. Two major reasons for their decline were the one-hundredfold decrease in maternal deaths from 1900 to 1980[58] and the substantial risk for litigation when a young woman died during childbirth, which discouraged reviewers from gathering details of the factors that might have contributed to her death.

Several states have established or re-established maternal review committees. In 2001, the American College of Obstetricians and Gynecologists collaborated with CDC in assessing the legal issues facing these committees, including questions about anonymity, confidentiality, and legal protection from liability. Statutes differ among states in addressing the protection of review committee members from civil liability and protecting the confidentiality of information collected during the review process.[59] In most states, a formally organized review committee and the data it collects are protected from civil liability or disclosure.

Intimate partner violence, an increasingly important concern, results in about 2 million injuries and 1300 deaths annually.[60] About 324,000 women each year experience intimate partner violence during their pregnancy,[61] and homicide accounts for about 10% of all pregnancy-associated deaths.[62] A national effort is under way to raise the awareness of health-care providers, provide them with tools for identifying women at risk, and develop appropriate safety plans.[63]

Birth Control

During the past several years, Congress and several state legislatures have debated mandatory insurance coverage for contraceptive benefits for women, and legislation has been passed to support mandatory coverage. Some argue that access to contraception coverage is a women's rights issue, noting, for example, that if men are accorded the right to insurance coverage of Viagra®, then women should be granted insurance coverage of contraception.[h] Others believe that contraceptive insurance coverage will improve health outcomes for women and infants. The highest rates of live-born infants resulting from unintended pregnancies occur among low-income women,[64] who are least likely to hold jobs that provide mandated coverage. Unintended pregnancy remains high in the United States but is lowest among well-educated white women, who are most likely to benefit from insurance coverage. The public health impact of changes in coverage remains to be seen.

Abortion

The reporting of legal induced abortions illustrates a combination of mandatory state regulations and voluntary state reporting to a federal agency. Forty-six U.S. reporting areas (states and certain metropolitan areas) collect abortion data as required by state statute or regulation. Every hospital, Medicare facility, or licensed clinician in required areas must report each induced abortion performed to the central department of health by a standardized form for that reporting area. The time for filing reports after legal induced abortions varies widely by state.[65]

Since 1969, CDC has documented the number and characteristics of abortions to monitor unintended pregnancies and to help identify preventable causes of complications and deaths associated with abortions.[66] States provide summary data to CDC that contain no personal identifying information. CDC compiles these state reports into a national report that describes the characteristics of women obtaining abortions across the country. However, each state faces unique challenges in obtaining this information. For example, some states report abortions according to the state in which the procedure occurred; some report according to the resident state of the woman obtaining the procedure; and some report by both.[66] These multiple approaches make the states with the greatest need for family planning services and other approaches to reducing unintended pregnancies difficult to identify.

Infertility Services

Since enactment of the FCSRCA in 1992,[24] the practice of ART has increased steadily and now accounts for just above 1% of all U.S.-born children.[67] CDC reporting of pregnancy rates in U.S. ART clinics is one of the few examples of mandated nationwide reporting to a federal public health agency. The FCSRCA charged CDC with collecting data from all ART clinics in the country, reporting pregnancy success rates for each ART clinic, and developing a model certification program for embryo laboratories. The FCSRCA defines ART as procedures that involve handling of oocytes and sperm in establishing pregnancy.[24] Thus, the use of artificial insemination or fertility drugs alone is not subject to the reporting requirements of ART, and data on the frequency and success of non-ART infertility treatments is not routinely available.

FDA has jurisdiction over medical products subject to FDA regulation under the Federal Food, Drug, and Cosmetic Act[68] or the Public Health Service Act.[69] These include drugs used to stimulate ovulation, which require FDA approval before marketing in the United States, and culture media used to grow human embryos, which are classified as "devices" and need approval or clearance. FDA also regulates reproductive tissues—including semen, oocytes, and embryos—as part of a comprehensive strategy for regulating the safety of human cells, tissues, and cell- and tissue-based products. FDA requires tissue establishments to register with it and agree to allow unannounced inspections, to screen and test donors for communicable diseases.[70] FDA implements these regulations using a tiered approach, with increasingly more stringent requirements for higher-risk practices. The relevance of FDA to the practice of ART has been clarified in a recent federal rule, which exempts establishments that only recover reproductive cells or tissue for immediate transfer into a sexually intimate partner of the cell or tissue donor.[71] However, many ART programs provide services that involve egg and sperm donors and therefore are subject to FDA oversight. Furthermore, ART patients who complete their family plan may decide to make their frozen embryos available to others. Thus, embryos exempted from FDA requirements because they were initially intended for use within a couple may become subject to the requirements at a later date.

CLIA[20] provides for additional oversight of laboratory quality control by the Centers for Medicare and Medicaid Services. While CLIA requirements apply to laboratories that examine materials derived from the human body for diagnosis, prevention, treatment, or other health assessment of humans, the extent to which CLIA requirements apply to ART laboratories is uncertain.

The United States does not have substantial earmarked public funds to support ART oversight or regulation, such as has been available in several other countries.[72]

Furthermore, the FCSRCA explicitly states that it is not intended to authorize DHHS to regulate the practice of medicine in ART.[24]

Despite the relatively weak regulatory framework surrounding the practice of ART, certain activities mandated by law indirectly influence voluntary practice standards. For example, in addition to the annual reports describing clinic-specific and summary national data on pregnancy rates in ART, CDC scientists have published several scientific reports on selected safety aspects of ART, which may provide the evidence base for policymaking. Assessment of the risk of multiple pregnancies associated with the number of embryos transferred,[73] with the use of donor eggs,[74] or with particular techniques such as assisted hatching or extended embryo culture,[75] and of the risk for low birthweight among infants conceived using ART,[76] offer important information about health risks related to these services. These reports influence the debate on practice standards among ART providers and provide the evidence that should form the basis for practice guidelines issued by professional societies.[77]

Emerging Issues

Assisted Reproductive Technology

Even though ART is rapidly evolving and gaining increased use, legal responses to the new technology have been slow. Older techniques have become the subject of specific regulation; for example, some states have laws regarding the donation of sperm for artificial insemination or regarding surrogacy arrangements. Most of the legal response in the United States to the use of ART has been through individual court cases, in which principles of law not specific to the ART context were applied. Many commentators have noted a need for legislative and regulatory activity to guide the resolution of existing issues and new issues that arise as technologic advances continue. Future court cases may address whether efforts to regulate ART clash with the constitutional right to procreate, first recognized by the Supreme Court in 1942.[78,i] At the start of the 21st century, advances in techniques of IVF, cloning, and sex- and genetic-selection techniques for embryos had gained the attention of researchers, public health practitioners, and the general public, but specific legislative, regulatory, and case law responses to the issues raised by use of those techniques continue to be largely undeveloped.

In vitro fertilization routinely involves creation of extra embryos, which subsequently are frozen and stored for possible future use by the couple in case implantation of the first embryo is unsuccessful or the couple wants more children later. As of 2002, over 400,000 frozen embryos were estimated to be stored at ART clinics across the United States, largely for future use by the patients who provided the gametes.[79] The situation has led to legal disputes over control or use of the stored embryos when couples divorce or die or their intentions change. To resolve such disputes, courts often focus on the enforceability of the contract governing disposition of any unused embryos, but application of contract law principles is complicated by the issue of whether stored embryos are property, persons, or something in between.[80,81] A few states have enacted laws specifically relating to agreements for the disposition of stored embryos. Recent enactment of state laws promoting embryonic stem cell research is likely to enhance the concern for providing comprehensive regulations governing the generation, storage and disposition of embryos.

In contrast to the United States, some other countries have enacted legislation to address issues raised by ART. For example, the United Kingdom, Canada, and the State of Victoria in Australia established commissions of experts and scholars to study ART and to recommend legislation governing it. The United Kingdom passed the Human Fertilisation and Embryology Act in 1990, which regulates IVF and some other infertility treatments through a licensing scheme and requires, among other things, that IVF participants be counseled, provide written consent for disposition of embryos, and enter into an agreement for the disposition of embryos in the case of death, divorce, or a change in circumstances.[82] The U.K. Human Fertilisation and Embryology Authority, created by the law, has authority to regulate some emerging ART issues. For example, in 2005, the United Kingdom's highest appeals court ruled that the agency could authorize a certain kind of embryo selection for couples who wish to produce a sibling with a tissue type that matches that of a terminally ill child.[j]

The President's Council on Bioethics recently concluded a thorough evaluation of the scientific, ethical, and legal issues related to technologies that affect the beginning of life. The Council's assessment was that, although the fields of assisted reproduction, human genetics, and embryo research increasingly are converging, no comprehensive systems exist for ascertaining the impact of these technologies, and their practice is largely unregulated.[83] The Council recommended that the federal government (1) conduct longitudinal studies on the impact of assisted reproduction on mothers and children; (2) strengthen the FCSRCA by making adverse effects, use of new technologies, and cost of services reportable by increasing penalties for ART programs that refuse to report to CDC and by increasing funding to implement the Act; and (3) enact legislation to prohibit certain practices, such as the production of hybrid human-animal embryos, human cloning, and transfer of embryos to a woman's uterus for purposes other than to give birth to a child. Finally, the Council recommended that professional organizations and practitioners strengthen their self-regulatory mechanisms and improve adherence to practice standards, improve procedures for moving experimental procedures to patient care, and strengthen patient counseling for informed decision making.[83]

Emergency Contraception Access

The requirement for a physician's prescription to obtain emergency contraceptive pills (EC) has served as a barrier to receipt of EC, which must be obtained and used promptly after intercourse to be effective.[84] For that reason, in recent years, legislative, regulatory, and litigation efforts have aimed to make EC available over the counter, without a prescription. FDA has authority to remove the prescription restriction for a drug and allow its distribution over the counter.[84,85] Within the past few years, a group of health-care and reproductive rights organizations filed a citizen's petition with FDA to encourage it to grant over-the-counter status to EC, and a manufacturer of an EC product requested FDA approval for over-the-counter sales for all women and then for all women aged 17 years or older. FDA granted over-the-counter status limited to women 18 and older; a lawsuit is pending against FDA for its failure to grant full over-the-counter status.

At the state level, policymakers have focused primarily on two approaches to promoting access to EC: (1) requiring provision of EC-related services in hospital emergency departments to women who have been sexually assaulted and (2) allowing pharmacists to provide EC without a prescription under the aegis of a specific collaborative practice agreement with a physician or in accordance with a state-approved protocol. Some states have adopted restrictions to EC access, including restricting coverage of EC under state Medicaid family planning programs or not including EC in requirements for insurance coverage of contraceptives and allowing medical professionals, including pharmacists, to refuse to provide contraceptive services, including EC.

Laws and Regulations Relating to the Fetus

In recent years, an increasing number of legislative and regulatory proposals—at the state and federal levels—have focused on pregnant women and their fetuses, many of which raise issues relating to the legal status to the fetus. Historically, a fetus was not recognized as a legal entity separate from the pregnant woman. In *Roe v. Wade*, the U.S. Supreme Court specifically held that a fetus is not a "person" with Fourteenth Amendment rights.[4] One recent legislative trend is enactment of "fetal homicide" laws, which create a separate criminal offense where actions taken against a woman result in the death of, or harm to, her fetus. Such laws—which treat the fetus as an individual being, separate from the pregnant woman—have been enacted in many states and by Congress; the laws enacted thus far specifically have exempted from liability health-care providers performing abortions and women seeking abortions.[86,87] In 2002, DHHS adopted regulations that allow states to redefine "child" for purposes of health insurance coverage under the federal State Children's Health Insurance Program[88] as "an individual under the age of 19 including the period from conception to birth," thus allowing the coverage of fetuses and shifting the focus for prenatal coverage from the pregnant woman to the fetus.[89] Also, courts have addressed the legal status of fetuses in a variety of contexts, including wrongful death and malpractice claims. Whether treatment of the fetus as a legal entity separate from the pregnant woman will create conflicts between the woman's rights and the fetus' rights remains to be seen.

Conclusion

The law governing reproductive health issues will continue to change in the United States at both the federal and state levels. Technologic advances relating to reproduction will challenge the legal system. Issues of reproductive health surveillance and research will be affected by evolving regulations regarding human subjects' protection. Public interest in reproductive health services will remain high because of the moral and cultural implications. Inevitably, issues in reproductive health will see new laws and new litigation, accompanied by extensive public dialogue.

Notes

a. Generally, states began criminalizing abortion by statute in the mid-19th century; before that, abortion in most states was legal, at least before "quickening" of the fetus—the point of recognizable movement by the fetus in utero. By the end of the 1950s, a large majority of states banned abortion, except when necessary to preserve the life of the mother. See *Roe v. Wade*, 410 U.S. 113, 132–141 (1973).

b. In *Eisenstadt v. Baird* (405 U.S. 438 [1972]), the U.S. Supreme Court held that unmarried persons had a right to use contraceptives under the federal constitution.

c. For example, a federal district court found that the right to privacy encompasses the right of a woman to become pregnant by artificial insemination. See *Cameron v. Board of Education*, 795 F. Supp. 228, 237 (S.D. Ohio 1991).

d. Few of the laws granting exemptions to facilities or entities limit the exemption to those affiliated with a religious organization, and fewer still are limited to those organized and operated for religious purposes.

e. The Hyde Amendment is a rider added annually to the DHHS appropriations bill, which limits coverage for medically necessary abortions. In some previous years, it excluded coverage in circumstances of rape or incest or included coverage where a woman's life was endangered by a mental condition, not just where it was endangered by a physical condition.

f. States differ in the extent to which they criminalize consensual sexual activity by a minor. For example, in some states, the severity of the offense depends on the age of the minor's sex partner; other states criminalize sexual activity with a minor irrespective of the age of the sex partner. Compare, for example, Ca. Pen. Code §261.5 (severity of offense varies depending on whether minor is under 18 or under 16 and whether partner is over 18, over 21, or within 3 years of the minor's age) with Wis. Stat. § 948.02 (anyone having sexual contact or intercourse with person under age 13 is guilty of Class B felony, and anyone having sexual contact or intercourse with a person under age 16 is guilty of Class BC felony).

g. Some fetal protection policies are vulnerable to legal challenge on the grounds that they constitute sex discrimination. Title VII, 42 USC §2000e-2(a)(1), prohibits discrimination on the basis of sex in employment and the Pregnancy Discrimination Act, 42 USC §2000e(k), specifically requires that women who are affected by pregnancy, childbirth, or related medical conditions be treated the same for all employment-related purposes "as others not so affected but similar in their ability or inability to work." In *International Union, UAW v. Johnson Controls*, 499 U.S. 187 (1991), the U.S. Supreme Court held that an employer's sex-specific fetal protection policy violated Title VII, as amended by the Pregnancy Discrimination Act. The Court found that the employers' policy of excluding women with childbearing capacity from jobs where they would be exposed to lead at levels that could endanger a developing fetus constituted impermissible sex discrimination.

h. In December 2000, the U.S. Equal Employment Opportunity Commission found that two employers' failure to cover the expenses of prescription contraceptives to the same extent that they covered the expenses of other prescription drugs and devices used to prevent other medical conditions violated Title VII of the Civil Rights Act of 1964, as amended by the Pregnancy Discrimination Act, 42 USC 2000e *et seq*. See also *Erickson v. Bartell Drug Co.*, 141 F. Supp. 2d 1266 (W.D. Wash. 2001) (finding that exclusion of prescription contraceptives from health insurance benefits violated Title VII), remanded No. 01-35870 (9th Cir. Oct. 16, 2002) (remanded for consideration of settlement agreement), dismissed No. C00-1213L (W.D. Wash. Mar. 6, 2003) (dismissed on the basis of settlement agreement).

i. A few federal and state court judges have recognized a relation between a right to procreate and ART. See *Forbes v. Napolitano*, 236 F.3d 1009, 1013–14 (9th Cir. 2000) (Sneed J, concurring) (noting that a law restricting experimentation on aborted fetal tissue could limit development of reproductive technology related to reproductive decisions, and therefore it interfered with the constitutional right of reproductive decision-making); *Lifchez v. Hartigan*, 735 F. Supp. 1361, 1367–69 (N.D. Ill. 1990) (finding a statute banning fetal experimentation unconstitutionally vague in part because of fear that it would deter physicians from providing IVF), affirmed mem., 914 F.2d 260 (7th Cir. 1990). Recently, an intermediate state appellate court ruled that a husband who supplied sperm to fertilize donated eggs for an IVF procedure had a constitutional right not to procreate that he could exercise so as to prevent the pre-embryos created with that sperm to develop in a way that would place him in an unwanted parenting role. *Litowitz v. Litowitz*, 10 P.3d 1086, 1091–93 (Wash. Ct. App. 2000). However, the state supreme court reversed that decision, ruling that the dispute must be resolved by applying contract law. *Litowitz v. Litowitz*, 48 P.3d 261 (Wash. 2002).

j. A few countries, including Austria, Germany, Italy, and Switzerland, have passed laws limiting how many eggs can be fertilized outside of the body or limiting the number of embryos that can be transferred at one time into a woman's uterus. The Italian Parliament recently passed legislation that severely restricts the practice of ART, prohibiting egg donation and limiting the number of eggs that can be fertilized outside of the body.

References

1. Ventura SJ, Abma JC, Mosher WD, Henshaw S. Estimated pregnancy rates for the United States, 1990–2000: an update. *Natl Vital Stat Rep* 2004;52(23). Available at http://www.cdc.gov/nchs/pressroom/04facts/pregestimates.htm. Accessed June 8, 2006.
2. National Center for Health Statistics, Centers for Disease Control and Prevention. Fertility, family planning, and reproductive health of U.S. women: data from the 2002 National Survey of Family Growth (PHS), 2006–1977. *Vital Health Stat* 23(25). Available at http://www.cdc.gov/nchs/products/pubs/pubd/series/sr23/pre-1/sr23_25.htm. Accessed June 8, 2006.
3. *Griswold v Connecticut*, 381 US 479 (1965).
4. *Roe v Wade*, 410 US 113 (1973).
5. *Eisenstadt v Baird*, 405 US 438 (1972).
6. *Colautti v Franklin*, 439 US 379 (1979) (finding viability determination requirement and standard of care provision unconstitutionally vague).
7. *Planned Parenthood of Central Missouri v Danforth*, 428 US 52 (1976).
8. *Planned Parenthood of Southeastern Pennsylvania v Casey*, 505 US 833 (1992).
9. *Stenberg v Carhart*, 530 US 914 (2000).
10. *North Florida Women's Health and Counseling Services, Inc v Florida*, 866 So 2d 612 (Fla 2003) (finding that parental notification law violated privacy rights of minors under Florida constitution).
11. *American Academy of Pediatrics v Lungren*, 940 P 2d 797 (Cal 1997) (finding that parental consent law violated privacy rights of minors under California constitution).
12. *Planned Parenthood of Central New Jersey v Farmer*, 762 A 2d 620 (NJ 2000) (finding that parental notice law violated equal protection rights under New Jersey constitution).
13. 42 CFR §50.203.
14. *Hodgson v Lawson*, 542 F 2d 1350 (8th Cir 1976) (finding that public hospital must make its existing facilities available for performance of abortions).
15. *Valley Hospital Association v Mat-Su Coalition for Choice*, 948 P 2d 963 (Alaska 1997) (finding that quasi-public hospital's policy prohibiting performance of most abortions violated state constitutional right to privacy).

16. *Doe v Bridgeton Hospital Association*, 366 A 2d 641 (NJ 1976) (finding that quasi-public hospital cannot refuse to permit facilities to be used to perform first trimester elective abortions).
17. *Mazurek v Armstrong*, 520 US 968 (1997).
18. *City of Akron v Akron Center for Reproductive Health*, 462 US 416, 431–9 (1983).
19. *Planned Parenthood v Ashcroft*, 462 US 476, 481–2 (1983).
20. 42 USC §263a *et seq* (2001) (Clinical Laboratory Improvement Act).
21. 29 USC §651 *et seq* (2001) (Occupational Safety and Health Act).
22. Jones BS, Heller S. Providing medical abortion: legal issues of relevance to providers. *J Am Med Women's Assoc* 2000(3 Suppl);55:145–50.
23. Borgmann CE, Jones BS. Legal issues in the provision of medical abortions. *Am J Obstet Gynecol* 2000;183 (2 Suppl):S84–S94.
24. 42 USC 263a-1 *et seq*.
25. Implementation of the Fertility Clinic Success Rate and Certification Act of 1992—A Model Program for Certification of Embryo Laboratories, 64 Fed Reg 39,374 (July 21, 1999).
26. 42 CFR §440.210.
27. 42 USC §1396a(a)(23)(B).
28. Cornell EV. *Maternal and Child Health (MCH) Update: States Have Expanded Eligibility and Increased Access to Health Care for Pregnant Women and Children*. Feb 22, 2001, Available at http://preview.nga.org/Files/pdf/MCHUPDATE2000.pdf. Accessed June 8, 2006.
29. 42 USC §300 *et seq* (Title X).
30. 42 USC §701 *et seq* (Maternal and Child Health Block Grant).
31. 42 USC §1396 *et seq* (Medicaid).
32. 42 USC §1397 *et seq* (Social Services Block Grant).
33. See, e.g., *New York v Heckler*, 719 F 2d 1191 (2d Cir 1983).
34. Pub L 109-149, Title V, §§507–08, 119 Stat 2833.
35. *Harris v McRae*, 448 US 297 (1980).
36. 29 USC §1185(a) (1996).
37. 42 USC §247b-12.
38. Berg CJ, Chang J, Callaghan WM, Whitehead SJ. Pregnancy-related mortality in the United States, 1991–1997. *Obstet Gynecol* 2003;101:289–96.
39. Saul R. Abortion reporting in the United States: an examination of the federal-state partnership. *Fam Plan Perspect* 1998;30:244–7.
40. 42 USC §280e.
41. 21 CFR §50.25.
42. 45 CFR §46.116.
43. 45 CFR §46.201 *et seq*.
44. Mosher WD, Bachrach CA. Understanding US fertility: continuity and change in the National Survey of Family Growth, 1988–1995. *Fam Plan Perspect* 1996;28:4–12.
45. 42 USC §247b-4.
46. 42 USC §285g *et seq*.
47. The National Children's Study. Available at http://www.nationalchildrensstudy.gov. Accessed June 8, 2006.
48. English A, Teare C. Statutory rape enforcement and child abuse reporting: effects on health care access for adolescents. *DePaul Law Rev* 2001;50:827–64.
49. Administration for Children and Families. National Clearinghouse on Child Abuse and Neglect Information, available at http://nccanch.acf.hhs.gov. Accessed June 8, 2006.
50. 42 USC §5106g.

51. *Bellotti v Baird*, 443 US 622 (1979) (plurality opinion) (*Bellotti II*).

52. *Hodgson v Minnesota*, 497 US 417 (1990).

53. *Lambert v Wicklund*, 520 US 292, 295 (1997) (reaffirming requirements for bypass articulated in *Bellotti II*).

54. Pub L 104-193, 110 Stat 2105 (1996) (codified as amended in scattered titles of USC).

55. See, e.g., *Simat Corp v Ariz Health Care Cost Containment System*, 56 P 3d 28 (Ariz 2002).

56. *State v Ashley*, 701 So 2d 338 (Fla 1997).

57. *Ferguson v City of Charleston*, 532 US 67, 84 n 23 (2001).

58. CDC. Achievements in public health, 1900–1999: healthier mothers and babies. *MMWR* 1999;48:849–58.

59. American College of Obstetricians and Gynecologists. State review provisions. In: Berg C, Danel I, Atrash H, Zane S, Bartlett L, eds. *Strategies to Reduce Pregnancy-related Deaths: From Identification and Review to Action*. Atlanta: US Department of Health and Human Services, CDC, 2001:(Appendix D) 1–36.

60. CDC. *Costs of Intimate Partner Violence against Women in the United States*. Atlanta: US Department of Health and Human Services, CDC, 2003.

61. Gazmararian JA, Petersen R, Spitz AM, Goodwin MM, Saltzman LE, Marks JS. Violence and reproductive health: current knowledge and future research directions. *Matern Child Health J* 2000;4:79–84.

62. Chang J, Berg CJ, Saltzman L, Herndon J. Homicide: a leading cause of injury deaths among pregnant and postpartum women in the United States, 1991–1999. *Am J Public Health* 2005;95:471–7.

63. CDC. *Intimate Partner Violence During Pregnancy, A Guide for Clinicians*. Available at http://www.cdc.gov/reproductivehealth/violence/IntimatePartnerViolence/index.htm. Accessed June 8, 2006.

64. Abma JC, Chandra A, Mosher WD, Peterson LS, Piccinino LJ. Fertility, family planning, and women's health: New data from the 1995 National Survey of Family Growth. National Center for Health Statistics. *Vital Health Stat* 1997;23(19).

65. Koonin LM. Reporting of medical (nonsurgical) abortions: information for providers (Appendix). *Am J Obstet Gynecol* (Suppl) 2000;183:S24–5.

66. Strauss LT, Herndon J, Chang J, et al. Abortion surveillance—United States, 2001. *MMWR* 2004;53(SS-9).

67. CDC. *2002 Assisted Reproductive Technology Success Rates. National Summary and Fertility Clinics Report*. Available at http://www.cdc.gov/ART/ART02/index.htm. Accessed June 8, 2006.

68. 21 USC §301 *et seq.*

69. 42 USC §201 *et seq.*

70. 21 CFR pt 1270.

71. 21 CFR §1271.90.

72. Jones HW, Cohen J, eds. IFFS Surveillance 04: a survey of the current status of assisted reproductive technology procedures around the world. *Fertil Steril* 2004;81:(Suppl 4).

73. Reynolds MA, Schieve LA, Martin JA, Jeng G, Macaluso M. Trends in multiple births conceived using assisted reproductive technology, United States, 1997–2000. *Pediatrics* 2003;111:1159–62.

74. Reynolds MA, Schieve LA, Jeng G, Peterson HB, Wilcox LS. Risk of multiple birth associated with in vitro fertilization using donor eggs. *Am J Epidemiol* 2001;154:1043–50.

75. Kissin DM, Schieve LA, Reynolds MA. Multiple-birth risk associated with IVF and extended embryo culture: USA, 2001. *Hum Reprod* 200520;2215–23.

76. Schieve LA, Meikle SF, Ferre C, Peterson HB, Jeng G, Wilcox LS. Low and very low birth weight in infants conceived with use of assisted reproductive technology. *N Engl J Med* 2002;346:731–7.

77. The Practice Committee of the Society of Assisted Reproductive Technology and the American Society for Reproductive Medicine. Guidelines on number of embryos transferred. *Fertil Steril* 2004;82:773–4.

78. *Skinner v Oklahoma*, 316 US 535 (1942) (finding that Oklahoma's Habitual Criminal Sterilization Act interferes with fundamental right to procreate).

79. Hoffman DI, Zellman GL, Fair CC, et al. Cryopreserved embryos in the United States and their availability for research. *Fertil Steril* 2003;79:1063–9.

80. *Davis v Davis*, 842 SW 2d 588 (Tenn 1992) (resolving dispute in divorce proceeding over custody of frozen embryos).

81. *Kass v Kass*, 696 NE 2d 174 (NY 1998) (requiring compliance with terms of agreement for disposition of frozen embryos).

82. Human Fertilisation & Embryology Act (1990) (UK).

83. The President's Council on Bioethics. *Reproduction and Responsibility. The Regulation of New Biotechnologies*. Washington, DC: President's Council on Bioethics, 2004.

84. Grimes DA, Raymond EG, Jones BS. Emergency contraception over the counter: the medical and legal imperatives. *Obstet Gynecol* 2001;98:151–5.

85. 21 USC §353(b)(3).

86. 18 USC §1841 ("Unborn Victims of Violence Act").

87. Cal Penal Code 187.

88. 42 USC §1397aa.

89. 42 CFR §457.10.

Chapter 20

ENVIRONMENTAL HEALTH AND PROTECTION

Paul A. Locke, Henry Falk,*
Christopher S. Kochtitzky,*
and Christine P. Bump

This chapter provides a context for the practice of environmental health law. It is meant as both a road map for the practitioner and an introduction to some ways in which environmental health problems can be approached. Although the vast range of environmental health law is difficult to condense, we can give practitioners a taste of how it developed, the available tools, and the direction in which environmental health and protection law may be going. Because of the complexity and scope of the law, the modern environmental health practitioner simultaneously faces an extensive group of legal tools and a changing landscape on which to apply them.

The major federal laws associated with environmental health and protection (Table 20-1) are broad and heterogeneous, reflecting the diverse activities that define environmental health. In this chapter, the term "environmental health" comprises the aspects of human health, including quality of life, determined by interactions with physical, chemical, biologic and social factors in the environment. It also refers to the theory and practice of assessing, correcting, controlling, and preventing factors in the environment that may adversely affect the health of present and future generations.[1]

In addition to these federal authorities, state laws and municipal or local ordinances often contain useful tools for environmental health practitioners. A detailed discussion of these authorities is beyond the scope of this chapter, but we do address the major common law theories on which they are based (Table 20-2).

---

* The findings and conclusions in this chapter are those of the author(s) and do not necessarily represent the views of the U.S. Department of Health and Human Services or the Centers for Disease Control and Prevention.

TABLE 20-1   Major Federal Environmental Protection Laws

Federal Law	Summary of Intent and Provisions
Clean Air Act (CAA) 42 USC §§7401–7671q	The CAA protects human health and the environment from outdoor air pollution. It requires EPA to establish minimum national standards for air quality and assigns primary responsibility to the states to ensure compliance with these standards. Areas not meeting the standards, referred to as "nonattainment areas," are required to implement additional pollution-control measures. The CAA establishes federal standards for mobile sources of air pollution, for sources of hazardous air pollutants, and for the emissions that cause acid rain. It establishes a comprehensive permitting system for all major sources of air pollution. It also addresses the prevention of pollution in areas with clean air.
Federal Water Pollution Control Act (CWA) 33 USC §§1251–1387	The CWA is the principal law addressing prevention of pollution of surface waters. Originally enacted in 1948, it was extensively revised in 1972 and 1987. The 1972 amendments required treatment of all municipal and industrial wastewater before discharge into waterways, increased federal assistance for municipal treatment plant construction, and strengthened and streamlined enforcement. Before the 1987 amendments, however, programs under CWA primarily were directed at point source pollution, wastes discharged from discrete and identifiable sources, such as pipes and other outfalls. Little attention had been paid to "nonpoint source" pollution (storm water runoff from agricultural lands, forests, construction sites, and urban areas). The 1987 amendments directed states to develop and implement nonpoint pollution-management programs. Federal assistance was authorized to support control activities. The CWA also contains provisions that call for applying water quality effluent limitations for point sources (or groups of point sources) where application of technology-based standards alone cannot attain suitable water quality.
Comprehensive Environmental Response, Compensation, and Liability Act (CERCLA) and the Superfund Amendment and Reauthorization Act (SARA) 43 USC §§9601–9675	CERCLA and SARA established a fee-maintained fund to clean up leaking and usually abandoned sites at which hazardous substances are present. To protect health and welfare, CERCLA authorizes the federal government to respond to spills and other releases of hazardous substances by taking actions that will clean up these sites. Hazardous substances are identified by reference to the Safe Drinking Water Act (SDWA), the CWA, the CAA, and the Toxic Substances Control Act (TSCA), or are designated by EPA. Response is also authorized for releases of "pollutants or contaminants," which are defined broadly to include anything that can threaten the health of "any organism." Most nuclear materials and petroleum are excluded unless they are mixed with other wastes. Also, CERCLA established

(continued)

TABLE 20-1   *(continued)*

Federal Law	Summary of Intent and Provisions
	the Agency for Toxic Substances and Disease Registry (ATSDR) with mandates to (1) establish national exposure and disease registries, (2) create an inventory of health information on toxic substances, (3) create a list of closed and restricted-access sites, (4) assist in toxic substances emergencies, and (5) determine the relation between toxic substances exposure and illness. SARA added responsibilities in health assessment, toxicology, and medical education.
Emergency Planning and Community Right-to-Know Act (EPCRA) 42 USC §§11001–11050	The EPCRA requires industrial reporting of toxic releases and provides for assistance in planning responses to chemical emergencies. The EPCRA established state commissions and local committees to implement procedures for coping with releases of hazardous chemicals, and mandated annual reporting on environmental releases of such chemicals by facilities that manufacture or use them in significant amounts.
Federal Insecticide, Fungicide, and Rodenticide Act (FIFRA) 7 USC §§136–136y	This act requires EPA to regulate the sale and use of pesticides in the United States through registration and labeling. It also directs EPA to restrict use of pesticides to prevent unreasonable adverse effects on people and the environment, taking into account the costs and benefits of various uses. EPA registers each pesticide for each use, and FIFRA prohibits the sale of any pesticide in the United States unless it is registered and labeled indicating approved uses and restrictions. In addition, FIFRA requires EPA to reregister older pesticides based on new data and scientific discoveries. Establishments that manufacture or sell pesticide products must register with EPA, and managers of these facilities are required to keep records and allow inspections by EPA or state regulatory staff.
Food Quality Protection Act (FQPA)	The FQPA amends both the Federal Food, Drug, and Cosmetic Act (FFDCA) and the FIFRA. It requires reregistration of all pesticides used in the United States to account for new scientific understanding and to provide adequate protection for particularly sensitive populations, such as children and pregnant women. Specifically, the FQPA (1) requires recognition that people can have concurrent exposure to many different chemicals (before the act, each pesticide was regulated in isolation, as if exposure occurred only one chemical at a time); (2) recognizes that exposure can occur from multiple sources or pathways, including pets, lawns, soil, carpets, and even house dust; (3) includes provisions to protect children, who may be more vulnerable to the effects of environmental pollutants such as pesticides; and (4) excludes cost-benefit analysis from the regulatory decision-making process.
National Environment Policy Act (NEPA)	The NEPA requires EPA to review environmental impact statements. The basic purposes the of the NEPA are to (1) declare a national policy to encourage harmony between

TABLE 20-1   (*continued*)

Federal Law	Summary of Intent and Provisions
42 USC §§4321–4370d	humans and the environment; (2) promote efforts that will prevent or eliminate damage to the environment and biosphere and stimulate the health and welfare of humans; (3) enrich the understanding of the ecologic systems and natural resources important to the United States; and (4) establish the White House Council on Environmental Quality.
Oil Pollution Act (OPA) 33 USC §§2701–2761	The OPA streamlined and strengthened EPA's ability to prevent and respond to catastrophic oil spills. A trust fund financed by a tax on oil is available to clean up spills when the responsible party is incapable or unwilling to do so. The OPA requires oil storage facilities and vessels to submit to the federal government plans detailing how they will respond to large discharges. It also requires development of Area Contingency Plans to prepare and plan for oil spill response on a regional scale.
Pollution Prevention Act (PPA) 42 USC §§13101–13109	The PPA states that it is the policy of the United States that "pollution should be prevented or reduced at the source whenever feasible; pollution that cannot be prevented should be recycled in an environmentally safe manner, whenever feasible; pollution that cannot be prevented or recycled should be treated in an environmentally safe manner whenever feasible; and disposal or other release into the environment should be employed only as a last resort and should be conducted in an environmentally safe manner." The PPA focused industry, government, and public attention on reducing through source reduction the amount of pollution produced in the United States.
Residential Lead-Based Paint Hazard Reduction Act (partially codified at 33 USC §2686)	This act directs the Department of Housing and Urban Development and EPA to require disclosure of information on lead-based paint hazards before the sale or lease of most housing built before 1978. This ensures that purchasers and renters of housing built before 1978 receive the information necessary to protect themselves from lead-based paint hazards, but the act does not require any testing or removal of lead-based paint by sellers or landlords.
Safe Drinking Water Act (SDWA) 42 USC §§300f–300j-26)	The SDWA is the key federal law for protecting public drinking water systems from contamination. First enacted in 1974 and extensively amended in 1986 and 1996, the SDWA establishes standards and treatment requirements for drinking water, controls underground injection of wastes that might contaminate water supplies, and protects ground water. The SDWA established the current federal-state arrangement in which states may be delegated primary implementation and enforcement authority for the drinking water program. The state-administered Public Water Supply Supervision Program remains the basic program for regulating the nation's public water systems. In 1996, Congress substantially revised the SDWA. Among other things, flexibility was added to the

(*continued*)

TABLE 20-1   *(continued)*

Federal Law	Summary of Intent and Provisions
	standard setting provisions, EPA was required to conduct cost-benefit analyses for most new standards, consumer information requirements were expanded, provisions to improve small system compliance and protect source waters were added, and the State Revolving Loan Fund to help finance needed projects was created.
Solid Waste Disposal Act (SWDA), Resource Conservation and Recovery Act (RCRA), and Hazardous and Solid Waste Amendments (HSWA) 42 USC §§6901–6992k	Federal solid-waste law has gone through four major phases. The SWDA focused on research, demonstrations, and training. The RCRA added on concern with the reclamation of energy and materials from solid waste. It authorized grants for demonstrating new resource recovery technology and required annual reports from EPA on means of promoting recycling and reducing the generation of waste. In a third phase, the federal government began a more active regulatory role. The RCRA instituted the first federal permit program for hazardous waste and prohibited open dumps. In a fourth phase (HSWA), the federal government attempted to prevent future cleanup problems by prohibiting land disposal of untreated hazardous wastes, setting liner and leachate collection requirements for land disposal facilities, setting deadlines for closure of facilities not meeting standards, and establishing a corrective action program. ATSDR was directed to work with EPA to (1) identify new hazardous wastes to be regulated, (2) conduct health assessments at RCRA sites, and (3) consider petitions for health assessments from the public or states.
Toxic Substances Control Act (TSCA) 15 USC §§2601–2692	The TSCA regulates the testing of chemicals and their use. EPA may require manufacturers and processors of chemicals to conduct and report the results of tests to determine the effects of potentially dangerous chemicals on living things. Based on test results and other information, EPA may regulate the manufacture, importation, processing, distribution, use, and/or disposal of any chemical that presents an unreasonable risk of injury to human health or the environment. A variety of regulatory tools is available to EPA under the TSCA, ranging in severity from a total ban on production, import, and use to a requirement that a product bears a warning label at the point of sale.

Legal Authorities

Federal and State Authorities

The legal authorities available to environmental health practitioners are diverse and extensive. They are based largely in state police powers and the Interstate Commerce Clause, the authority ceded to the federal government by the states in the U.S. Constitution. The Interstate Commerce Clause, the scope of which expanded greatly during the New Deal years, is the basis for almost all modern federal environmental laws.[2]

This section summarizes the legal authorities in four tables. The first table (Table 20-1) describes the major federal environmental protection laws. The second table (Table 20-2) contains an overview of common law actions available under the police or plenary powers of most states. These authorities underlie the actions that state and local governments can exercise, even in the absence of federal law and regulation. Table 20-3 describes the major federal public health laws that have environmental authorities. Table 20-4 illustrates the range of media-based approaches contained in federal law and indicates some of the laws and agencies that are associated with controlling certain compounds or classes of compounds.

State Police and Plenary Power Common Law Actions

Many cases brought against environmental polluters contain claims based on tort law and theory. Environmental tort suits can seek recovery for personal injury as well as for property damage. Historically, recovery has been allowed only for actual physical injury. More recently, plaintiffs have been able to collect for the enhanced risk for future disease, fear of contracting a disease, and damage to one's immune system.[3] Environmental tort actions generally allege that exposure to a toxic substance has caused the plaintiff's injury. Common law causes of action for tort include negligence, negligence per se, strict liability, nuisance, trespass, fraud, and breach of warranty and misrepresentation (reference 3, at §33.01[1]). Negligence is the most frequently pleaded claim, followed by strict liability (Table 20-2).

Major Federal Environmental Protection Laws

The environmental health authorities of the U.S. Environmental Protection Agency (EPA) derive primarily from 13 major environmental statutes enacted or amended over the past 30 years. The multiplicity of federal environmental laws contrasts sharply with federal public health law, which has evolved over the past 250 years and is captured in three main pieces of legislation. Table 20-3 summarizes the components of the major federal public health laws today.

As the substantial number of environmental and public health statutes suggest (Table 20-1 and Table 20-3), the process of federal regulation in these areas is complex and fragmented (Table 20-4). Four separate agencies regulate the six separate chemical groups, separated into six separate media, using thirteen individual laws. Federal environmental protection and health authorities and tools are not easily summarized or neatly organized.

Cooperative Federalism: Seeking the Appropriate State-Federal Balance

The environmental health programs in the United States, especially the regulatory programs administered by EPA, are based on the notion of cooperative federalism. Under cooperative federalism, Congress regulates, offering states the choice of either establishing regulatory programs and schemes that reflect federal standards or

TABLE 20-2   Overview of State Police and Plenary Power Common Law Actions

Type of Action	Description
Negligence	Negligence is the failure to do something that a reasonable person, guided by the considerations that normally regulate human affairs, would do, or the doing of something that a reasonable person would not do. To succeed in bringing a negligence action based on a claim arising out of exposure to a toxic material, the plaintiff must prove (1) the party responsible for the toxic material had a duty to either warn others about the risks associated with the toxic material under the particular circumstances or to take precautions to prevent injury to others; (2) the party responsible for the toxic material breached that duty; (3) the toxic material was the proximate cause of the plaintiff's injury; and (4) damages, if collected, can remedy the injury. Breach of duty has been found for an insecticide manufacturer failing to warn users that the product was lethal[A] and for the corporate owner of a toxic waste cite failing to prevent the release of toxic materials.[B]
Negligence per se	If the injured party in a negligence action seeks to prove violation of a statutory or regulatory standard, the action is one of negligence per se. To prevail in a negligence per se claim, the plaintiff must show that (1) the plaintiff is a member of the class of individuals that the legislative provision in question is designed to protect from a particular type of harm; and (2) the plaintiff suffered the particular type of harm contemplated by the legislative provision.[C]
Strict liability	Parties who carry on "abnormally dangerous" activities that harm persons or land are held strictly liable for the damage or injuries caused by their activities, regardless of the level of care taken to prevent such injuries. The court, not the jury, determines whether an activity is abnormally dangerous. Crop dusting,[D] operating hazardous waste facilities,[E] and generating nuclear power[F] have all been determined to be abnormally dangerous activities. The *Restatement (Second) of Torts*[G] sets out six factors to determine whether an activity is abnormally dangerous: (1) the existence of a high degree of risk to the person or land of others; (2) the likelihood that the harm resulting from the activity will be great; (3) the inability to eliminate the risk through reasonable care; (4) the extent to which the activity is not a manner of common usage; (5) the inappropriateness of the activity related to where it is carried on; and (6) the extent to which the value of the activity outweighs its dangerousness.
Trespass	Trespass occurs when an actual intrusion takes place onto, above, or below land where the plaintiff has an interest and when this intrusion is intentional, reckless, negligent, or the result of ultrahazardous activity. Trespass was found when a defendant's production of aluminum caused fluoride particles to escape onto the plaintiff's farmland, rendering it unusable for grazing.[H]

TABLE 20-2 (*continued*)

Type of Action	Description
Nuisance	Nuisance is the nontrespassory invasion of another's interest in the private use and enjoyment of land.[I] Nuisance has been found for contamination of neighboring groundwater by leaking gasoline storage tanks.[J] Nuisance and trespass actions are complementary, and in environmental tort cases, the line distinguishing them is blurred.[K]
Fraud	Fraud is claimed when the defendant knowingly conceals the dangerous nature of the toxic substance and parties suffer an injury from exposure to it. Fraud was found when an employee was permanently disabled after using a chemical product that his employer claimed was not harmful.[L]
Breach of warranty and misrepresentation	Breach of warranty and misrepresentation are causes of action based on a seller's express or implied representation of their product on which the consumer justifiably relied.[M] Misrepresentation was found when a seller of a gasoline station stated, when asked, that the station had no problems; in reality, a 2000-gallon spill had occurred 5 years earlier.[N] In breach of warranty and misrepresentation cases, the plaintiff must prove that the misrepresented fact caused the alleged injury.

A. *Hubbard-Hall Chem Co v Silverman*, 340 F 2d 402 (1st Cir. 1965).
B. *Ewell v Petro Processors of Louisiana, Inc*, 364 So 2d 604 (LA Ct App 1978).
C. Gerrard MB, ed. *Environmental Law Practice Guide: State and Federal Law*. New York: Matthew Bender, LEXIS, 1992, 2001:§33.01[1][a].
D. *Langan v Valicopters, Inc*, 567 P 2d 218 (Wash 1977). The court imposed strict liability against an aerial pesticide sprayer for damages to organic crops.
E. *Sterling v Veliscol Chem Corp*, 855 F 2d 1188 (6th Cir 1988). The court imposed strict liability to recover for personal injuries and property to residents living near a chemical waste burial site.
F. *Silkwood v Kerr-McGee Corp*, 464 US 238 (1984). The court imposed strict liability for radiation injuries stemming from the operation of a nuclear power plant.
G. *Restatement (Second) of Torts*, §520.H. *Martin v Reynolds Metals Co*, 342 P 2d (Or 1959).
I. *Restatement (Second) of Torts*, §821D.
J. *Exxon Corp v Yarema*, 516 A 2d 990 (Md App 1986).
K. Gerrard, *Environmental Law*, §33.01[1][c].
L. *Berkley v American Cyanamid Co*, 799 F 2d 1489 (5th Cir 1985).
M. Gerrard, *Environmental Law*, § 33.01[1][e].
N. *Damon v Sun Co*, 87 F 3d 1467 (1st Cir 1996).

having federal standards that preempt state law. In addition, when Congress enacts laws that occupy a field such as environmental law, states are forbidden to regulate in a way that impedes the federal scheme or places an undue burden on interstate commerce.[2]

In the field of environmental health law, the respective roles of the state and federal governments have waxed and waned. In the 1960s and before, it was generally thought that the federal role in environmental protection and enforcement should be minimal. That view changed substantially during the 1970s and 1980s, and led to an expansion of the federal laws and regulatory authorities. During the 1990s and the

TABLE 20-3   Major Federal Public Health Laws

Federal Law	Summary of Intent and Provisions
Federal Food, Drug and Cosmetic Act (FFDCA) 21 USC §§301–399	The FFDCA is the basic food and drug law of the United States. It ensures that foods are pure and wholesome, safe to eat, and produced under sanitary conditions; that drugs and devices are safe and effective for their intended uses; and that cosmetics are safe and use appropriate ingredients.
Occupational Safety and Health Act (OSHAct) 15 USC §§651–678	The OSHAct requires safe and healthful working conditions for working people by authorizing the Occupational Safety and Health Administration to regulate workplace conditions, such as exposure to toxic chemicals, excessive noise levels, mechanical dangers, heat or cold stress, or unsanitary conditions. Standards set under the OSHAct regarding toxic materials or harmful physical agents are based on levels that most adequately ensure no employee will suffer material impairment of health or functional capacity even if such employee has regular exposure to the hazard for their entire working life. Whenever practicable, the standard promulgated shall be expressed in terms of objective criteria.
Public Health Service (PHS) Act 42 USC §§201–300ff	The PHS Act was enacted in July 1798 and has been frequently amended and expanded. The PHS Act of 1944 consolidated and revised all legislation relating to the Public Health Service. Currently, PHS (1) coordinates with the states to set and implement national health policy; (2) generates and implements activities under cooperative international health-related agreements, policies, and programs; (3) conducts medical and biomedical research; (4) sponsors and administers programs for the development of health resources and the prevention and control of diseases; (5) provides resources and expertise to the states and other public and private institutions in the planning, direction, and delivery of physical, environmental, and mental health-care services; and (6) enforces laws that ensure the safety and efficacy of drugs and protect against impure and unsafe foods, cosmetics, medical devices, and radiation-producing projects. Today, the vast majority of activities at CDC, FDA, HRSA, IHS, and NIH are conducted pursuant to authorities contained in the PHS Act.

beginning of the 21st century, the state-federal relationship again is undergoing re-evaluation, with talk of "de-evolution" of authority back to the states. Throughout the 1990s, the U.S. Supreme Court supported the de-evolution of domestic programs to the states and reined in Congress's power to enact protective laws.[4]

As responsibilities of environmental health regulatory programs have devolved to the states, state responsibility in pollution control increased significantly. During 1981–1984, delegation of environmental programs to the states increased from 33% to 66% of all eligible programs.[5] The Environmental Council of the States reported that as of 2000, "more than 75% of the total number of the major delegable environmental programs[a] have been delegated or assumed by the states." Eligible provisions

TABLE 20-4   Federal Regulations of Chemical Groups by Media

	CAA*	CWA	SDWA	TSCA	RCRA	CERCLA	SARA	EPCRA	FIFRA	FFDCA†	FQPA	RLHRA‡	OSHA¶
Metals, air	✓												✓
Metals, water		✓	✓		✓	✓	✓	✓					
Metals, land					✓	✓	✓	✓					
Metals, household				✓								✓	
Metals, food										✓	✓		
Pesticides, air	✓												
Pesticides, water		✓	✓		✓	✓	✓	✓					
Pesticides, land									✓	✓	✓		
Pesticides, crops									✓	✓	✓		
Pesticides, household													✓
Pesticides, food										✓	✓		
Phthalates, air	✓												
Phthalates, water		✓	✓		✓	✓	✓	✓					
Phthalates, land					✓					✓	✓		
Phthalates, food													
Dioxins/furans, air	✓												
Dioxins/furans, water		✓			✓	✓							
Dioxins/furans, land					✓					✓			
Dioxins/furans, food													
PAHs, air	✓												
PAHs, water		✓	✓		✓	✓	✓	✓					
PAHs, land									✓				
PAHs, household													✓
PAHs, food											✓		
PCBs, air	✓												
PCBs, water		✓	✓		✓	✓	✓	✓					
PCBs, land										✓	✓		
PCBs, food										✓			

*EPA.
†EPA/FDA.
‡HUD.
¶OSHA.

of the Clean Air Act (CAA) have been delegated to 42 states, the Water Pollution Control Act (CWA) to 34 states, the Resource Conservation and Recovery Act (RCRA) to 37 states, and the Federal Insecticide, Fungicide, and Rodenticide Act (FIFRA) to 39 states. However, this increase in state responsibility has not been proportionally matched by federal funds.[6]

In addition to their partnership with the federal government in setting standards and enforcing federal regulation, states have actively enforced and administered state environmental laws, such as facility siting and property transfer laws.[7] Every state has detailed laws regulating air pollution, water pollution, waste disposal, and resource management. Many state laws are modeled after federal legislation. Sixteen states[b] have adopted state environmental policy acts that are either identical to or closely resemble the National Environmental Policy Act (NEPA). California's and New York's state environmental policy acts are considered more stringent than NEPA in several ways. They define terms left undefined in NEPA and require the state to consider additional environmental effects not included in the NEPA impact statement.[8] State programs, rules, regulations, and capacities for effective implementation continue to differ substantially.[9] Several states have enacted innovative laws or established novel programs. For example, California is widely recognized for its Proposition 65, which established stringent drinking water standards and warnings to the public about harmful and potentially harmful substances.[10] New Jersey's Environmental Cleanup Responsibility Act[11] and Massachusetts' regulation of toxic substances[12,c] exceed federal standards, as do Arizona's, Wisconsin's, and Connecticut's groundwater protection regulations.[13–15] Michigan, Pennsylvania, Rhode Island, and Illinois are among states that have declared a clean environment to be a state constitutional right,[16–19] and Michigan's Citizen Suit Act requires state courts to review any private or agency action that adversely affects the environment.[20]

The federal environmental health infrastructure put into place in the 1970s and 1980s was a broadly supported "response to perceived inadequacies with [state] law and the frustration with the failure of decentralized approaches to environmental protection."[21] A centralized federal regulatory authority effectively addressed the problems of transboundary pollution and the possibility of a "race to the bottom" among states. Uniform federal regulations also improve national efficiency. Under the CAA, the federal government defines, monitors, and enforces emission standards for newly manufactured automobiles. Allowing 50 different state standards for automobile manufacturers would be extremely inefficient (p. 207).[22]

In most environmental regulatory schemes, the states are "junior-partners in the federal-state regulatory enterprise."[22] Nevertheless, states have retained the right to formulate state policy in addition to and beyond that established by federal authorities. Federal oversight of state programs actually has raised standards of many states[23] and in some instances (such as the establishment of state environmental protection acts and the improvement of pollution standards), federal regulations have served as a catalyst for advancing more aggressive state action and the expansion of state programs.

The federal-state relationship is complicated and delicate. Federal standards have provided a consistent level of nationwide environmental quality and have tremendously reduced pollution. However, because states vary significantly in climate, terrain, sources of pollution, economic conditions, and preferences for environmental protection, some flexibility in implementation and enforcement are crucial. For practitioners, cooperative federalism means that effective legal tools are available in both federal and state laws and regulatory systems.

Litigation

Litigation by Government Agencies

Litigation is an important tool for environmental health practitioners. Federal environmental laws provide authorities for administering agencies to sue parties that do not comply with their permits or that otherwise violate environmental laws. All the major federal environmental statutes contain such provisions. For example, the CAA authorizes EPA to issue administrative compliance and penalty orders and to seek injunctions and civil and criminal penalties (42 U.S.C. §7413). The Toxic Substances Control Act (TSCA) provides for civil and criminal penalties and states that substances produced in violation of it can be seized (15 U.S.C. §§2614–2617). The Federal Water Pollution Control Act, or CWA, states that EPA can issue compliance orders, bring civil actions and assess administrative, civil, and judicial penalties against violators (33 U.S.C. §1319). In addition to the ability to seek penalties, issue compliance orders, and bring civil and criminal actions, some environmental statutes provide agencies with the ability to take immediate action in the event of an imminent and substantial endangerment (see 33 U.S.C. §1319[c]).

State environmental health practitioners often can take advantage of these federal authorities because federal environmental protection programs frequently are delegated to states.[24] In certain cases, if a state has not begun an action against a violator, the federal government may step in (33 U.S.C. §1319[a]). State laws may also contain provisions that supplement the authorities delegated pursuant to federal laws.

In contrast to federal environmental laws, the major federal public health law (the Public Health Service Act) does not provide extensive options for enforcement. Even though certain actions are authorized (such as quarantine [42 U.S.C. §264-72)]), few, if any, authorities are available to bring civil and criminal enforcement actions or seek damages.

Citizen Suits

Federal environmental statutes contain provisions that allow citizens to bring civil suits against those who violate environmental statutes, including federal agencies, if they fail to fulfill their statutory mandates.[d] These authorities empower citizens to act as private "attorneys general" to force compliance with the law. For example, under the RCRA, a citizen can begin a civil action against any person, including the United States (e.g., EPA) or any other government agency for violations of RCRA permits, regulations, or other requirements. Anyone can begin a civil suit against a person who is contributing or has contributed to past or present handling, storage, treatment, transportation, or disposal of hazardous or solid waste that may imminently and substantially endanger health and the environment (see 42 U.S.C. §§6972[a][(1][A] and [B]). Citizen groups have successfully used the citizen suit provisions of the CWA to collect penalties from companies for failing to comply with their National Pollutant

Discharge Elimination System permit limitations and provisions.[24,e] Citizen groups have also sued EPA and other federal agencies for failure to comply with environmental laws (reference 24, at §4.3).

Legal Issues and Controversies

Historical Underpinnings

History of Federal Environmental Law and Regulation

Current U.S. environmental law and regulation is a relatively recent development that has been concerned primarily with setting, monitoring and oversight, and enforcement of standards.[25] These laws and regulations have existed in their present form since EPA's creation in 1970. Before EPA, federal efforts regarding the environment fell into two categories. Most environmental or ecosystem protection efforts were managed by the Department of the Interior and the Department of Agriculture and their predecessors, and most environmental/human health protection efforts were managed by the Department of Health, Education, and Welfare (DHEW) and its predecessors.[5]

EPA was created to consolidate into one agency a variety of federal research, monitoring, standard-setting and enforcement activities to ensure integrated environmental protection.[26] In his letter to Congress calling for creation of the new agency, President Richard Nixon recognized this country's need for a unified, comprehensive, environmental protection effort:

> The Government's environmentally-related activities have grown up piecemeal over the years. . . . Our national government today is not structured to make a coordinated attack on the pollutants which debase the air we breathe, the water we drink, and the land that grows our food. Indeed, the present governmental structure for dealing with environmental pollution often defies effective and concerted action. . . . [D]espite its complexity, for pollution control purposes the environment must be perceived as a single, interrelated system. Present assignments of departmental responsibilities do not reflect this interrelatedness.[27]

The new comprehensive environmental agency, EPA, was formed by bringing together programs from the Department of Interior (including the Federal Water Quality Administration and all pesticide research efforts), DHEW (the National Air Pollution Control Administration, the Bureau of Solid Waste Management, the Bureau of Water Hygiene, the Bureau of Radiological Health, and certain programs from the Food and Drug Administration), the Atomic Energy Commission and the Federal Radiation Council, and the U.S. Department of Agriculture.

Given its creators' clear intent, the new agency would be designed to create a unified, comprehensive, and interconnected organization that addressed the environment as a whole and regulated human interaction with the environment in the same way.[27] This was not how the new agency and its regulatory efforts have developed. Instead of turning away from the historical trend of regulating human interactions with the environment in a media-by-media, piecemeal fashion, Congress and the White House methodically re-established single-area environmental programs, in most cases by amending laws that had been previously enacted. In 1970, Congress substantially amended the CAA.[28] In 1972, it passed the Federal Environmental Pesticide Control Act, which substantially amended the FIFRA.[29] Substantial additions to the Safe Drinking Water Act in 1974, the Toxic Substance Control Act in 1976, and the Federal Water Pollution Control Act in 1977 closely followed these amendments. During the 1980s the Comprehensive Environmental Response, Compensation, and Liability Act of 1980 (CERCLA or "Superfund") was enacted, and the Hazardous and Solid Waste Amendments of 1984, amending the RCRA, were added to the list of focused pieces of environmental legislation.[30,31] Superfund was amended in 1986; the original 20-page act was expanded by over 200 pages of new or changed provisions.[32] These program-specific and highly detailed amendments continued through the 1990s as Congress passed significant legislation altering the Safe Drinking Water Act (SDWA) (see Public law 104-182, August 6, 1996, 110 Stat. 1614 *et seq*.); the Federal Food, Drug and Cosmetic Act; and FIFRA (see Public law 104-170, August 3, 1996, 110 Stat. 1489 *et seq*, commonly referred to as the Food Quality Protection Act of 1996).

Historical and social forces can partially explain why the federal environmental protection system evolved as a series of interconnected media-based programs instead of as an organic whole. After World War II, the reborn chemical, plastics, and petroleum industries were creating new, highly visible forms of pollution that affected people and ecosystems on larger geographic scales. As the scope of pollution became less local and more national, the lack of uniformity in state and local environmental laws, and their inability to prevent pollution and its effects, became glaringly apparent.[5] In addition, starting in the late 1960s and continuing into the 1980s, several events related to the environment garnered national attention—for example, Rachel Carson's publication of *Silent Spring*; the banning of DDT in 1972; the declared public health emergency at Love Canal, New York, in 1978; and the public health advisory issued by the Centers for Disease Control (now the Centers for Disease Control and Prevention) (CDC) for Times Beach, Missouri, in 1982. These and other events pressured Congress and EPA to address problems as they arose, leading to the more than 13 separate major environmental laws that exist today (Table 20-1). In the end, some of the same defects that led to creation of EPA as a unified federal environmental regulatory agency still exist, despite the best intentions of those who created EPA. In 1988, EPA published a historical analysis of its regulatory efforts, which concluded "ideal preconditions for a more coherent and successful future seem today as elusive as they have always been: EPA's laws are still reauthorized and amended one at a time in a manner inimical to cross-media and unified-field ecological thinking."[5]

Despite its fragmentation, the present federal environmental system has several notable strengths.[7] First, federal environmental protection laws contain a variety of effective tools for environmental health practitioners. Thus environmental health professionals can take advantage of the information, expertise, and enforcement authorities that the major federal environmental laws contain. Second, the national system of regulations is more or less uniform, thereby discouraging polluting industries from concentrating in one municipality, state, or region. Finally, the environmental law system is participatory and multitiered. It creates federal authorities that states can use and contains extensive opportunities for citizen and stakeholder involvement.

History of Federal Public Health Law and Regulation

In July 1798, President John Adams signed into law a bill creating the Marine Hospital Service, now known as the United States Public Health Service (PHS). By the end of the 19th century, the Marine Hospital Service's scope of activities began to expand to include control of infectious diseases. Responsibility for quarantine was originally a function of the states rather than the federal government, but an 1877 yellow fever epidemic that spread quickly from New Orleans up the Mississippi River clearly indicated that infectious diseases (like industrial pollution) do not respect state borders. The epidemic was followed by passage of the National Quarantine Act of 1878, which conferred quarantine authority on the Marine Hospital Service. The Service continued to expand its public health activities as the nation entered the 20th century.[33]

A 1902 law increased cooperation between federal and state public health authorities and cemented the cooperative approach often considered emblematic of the federal and state public health relationship. (See also Chapter 2.) PHS was charged with convening a conference of state health authorities at least annually. Beginning at this same time, environmental health and sanitation became even more central to the work of PHS when it was asked to investigate a typhoid fever outbreak in Yakima County, Washington, and traced the source of the disease to badly managed human waste-disposal practices. The resulting rural sanitation efforts were applied to other areas of the country and helped to encourage establishment of county health departments. In 1912, PHS was given federal legislative authority to investigate the diseases of humans and conditions influencing their propagation and spread, including sanitation and sewage and the pollution either directly or indirectly of the navigable streams and lakes of the United States. All types of illness, whatever their cause (including environmental pollution), now came within the purview of PHS. One of the last major overhauls of the public health law came in 1944, when the Public Health Service Act codified on an integrated basis all the PHS authorities and strengthened the administrative authority of the surgeon general.[33]

In contrast to environmental protection, Congress has created an organic statute for public health and its environmental components. Beginning in the post–World War II period, important investigations began on the hazards of exposure to radiation and toxic chemicals in various industrial settings and on lung disease in miners and granite cutters. PHS also became more actively involved in studies of water pollution during this time. In addition, CDC was established, with a mission to control infectious disease. CDC's mission eventually included the control and prevention of chronic disease and the study and improvement of occupational and environmental health.[33]

The shortcomings of federal public health law came into focus during the 1950s and 1960s as the federal health bureaucracy tried to address problems associated with pollution. One of the original reasons for moving the environmental programs from DHEW to EPA was the belief that the public health model was not effectively addressing those emerging environmental health problems.

Because the public health model traditionally is cooperative and relies on developing and nurturing partnerships and shared goals, it was not effective during the 1960s and 1970s in tackling escalating pollution from industrialization. Nevertheless, the public health system has important strengths. First, it can forge evidence-based, intervention-oriented solutions to environmental problems, leading to measurable progress. Second, it is a unified system. Unlike EPA, PHS has a unified organic statute under which it can function. The Public Health Service Act houses almost all public health authorities, creating a central legal repository.

Making Preventive Decisions in an Uncertain Scientific Climate

Environmental health laws often have goals that are inspirational and difficult to achieve.[f] However, because almost all environmental health laws seek to protect public health and welfare, action usually is necessary before a complete picture about an environmental hazard emerges. Many decisions regarding environmental health are made using less-than-perfect data. Although the need for environmental health laws and regulations to be preventive is widely recognized, the public and regulated entities often have difficulty accepting the uncertainty that accompanies decision making that incorporates data gaps.

A technique called risk assessment commonly is used to justify regulations and standards. Risk assessments are conducted to measure the potential individual and population harms that could occur through exposure to a substance.[34] Assessing risk is generally a four-part process that begins with a hazard evaluation. In a hazard evaluation, a determination is made as to whether exposure to a compound or agent should be of concern. After the hazard evaluation, a dose-response analysis occurs, in which toxicologic and other data are compiled to create a dose-response curve (or margin of exposure) that links exposure with harm. Dose-response analysis is complicated because toxicology or human epidemiology data, if available, are nearly always available only for doses far above environmental levels. Next, an exposure assessment is conducted; it analyzes information about the scope, nature, route, and duration of the exposure to the agent in question. Finally, the hazard, dose-response, and exposure information are integrated into a risk characterization, which generally describes the potential population and individual risks. For carcinogens, this risk is most commonly expressed probabilistically—for example, a one-in-one-million chance of contracting cancer. For noncarcinogenic compounds, risks often are described in comparing the exposure or dose level with a theoretical reference dose that should not be exceeded.

Preparation of a risk assessment requires much professional judgment. If data are not available, default assumptions or inferences focused on available data frequently are used (for example, without specific knowledge, adults often are assumed to drink an average of two liters of water per day).[35] These assumptions can be controversial.[g] The information obtained in a risk assessment is used by a risk manager, who is often a government employee, to decide how to manage environmental risks. This risk manager combines the information in the assessment with social, cultural, and political factors.

In contrast to risk assessment, disease and exposure surveillance are the traditional tools of public health. This philosophy is clearly evident in Healthy People 2010, which guides national efforts to set a health agenda and chart health improvement.[36] For example, Healthy People 2010 sets a series of goals related to environmental exposures or diseases associated with environmental exposure, such as asthma. These goals are generally community based and measurable, and the Healthy People 2010 protocol calls for regularly updating progress toward reaching its goals. The Healthy People 2010 goals are not legally enforceable.[h]

Environmental health practitioners should become familiar with risk assessment and risk management and understand their role in, and impact on, environmental health regulation. In addition, environmental health law practitioners should recognize that risk assessment and risk management employ as much art as science. Practitioners also should attempt to clarify how such analyses were carried out, paying particular attention to default assumptions, inferences, data sources, and analysis techniques. Several federal and state agencies, including EPA, have published guidance manuals explaining how these assessments are meant to be carried out.[37] Environmental health law practitioners also should be familiar with how the Department of Health and Human Services sets its environmental health goals and measures them through the Healthy People 2010 process.

Practice Considerations

Tools for Environmental Health Protection

A multitude of approaches can be taken to advance environmental health and protection. For example, to reduce harmful releases from a facility, authorities can specify the allowable amount to be released (in a permit such as a discharge permit allowed under the CWA) or specify technologic approaches that ultimately will limit releases (as in the CAA's approach to hazardous air pollutants) or penalize the facility by imposing liability for damages from specified releases (as in Superfund). Traditional public health tools, such as surveillance of hazardous conditions (i.e., childhood lead poisoning) and cooperative approaches (such as grants to states to support environmental health programs) also are available. Using these tools, a state public health department can begin or improve an asthma surveillance program, or start or increase environmental health information and outreach efforts to citizens. The complexity of environmental health protection is substantial because these different approaches can be mixed in many ways. In addition, multiple actors, including the federal government, state governments, and citizens, all could be tackling the same problem using different tools.

The Office of Technology Assessment identified 12 types of environmental protection tools, divided into three broad categories: single-source tools, multisource tools, and tools that do not directly limit pollution. Single-source tools, often described as "command-and-control" tools, have been most extensively used. They can (1) ban or limit production or use of a product, (2) specify the technology for how a product can be made or how pollution can be controlled, (3) set standards on the basis of potential harm from exposure for the reduction of releases, or (4) set standards on the basis of what a desirable or best technology might achieve. Almost every environmental statute relies to some degree on "command-and-control" approaches.[38]

Multisource tools allow individual facilities or multiple entities the option to vary or even trade emission limits so a collective protection limit is met, even if limits are exceeded at individual facilities. These tools provide greater flexibility in meeting standards than single-source tools. Finally, a variety of tools exist that do not specify release limits but rely instead on "carrots and sticks," either to encourage environmental protection through subsidies or technical assistance or to discourage releases by requiring public disclosure, payment of fees, or imposition of liability. These tools take various forms, including civil penalties and criminal sanctions, as well as public disclosure of information about pollution. (Most traditional public health tools fall into this category.)

Applying Environmental Health Protection Tools

The environmental health tools used by public health agencies and the environmental protection tools used by environmental agencies complement each another and rarely are mutually exclusive. Nevertheless, they infrequently are found in the same federal environmental statute. The CAA, for example, does not primarily use public health tools. On the other hand, CERCLA contains tools that embody both the environmental health and environmental protection traditions. It created a new public health agency, the Agency for Toxic Substances and Disease Registry (ATSDR), to carry out many of its environmental health functions. Each of these statutes is discussed in some detail to illustrate the approaches embodied in these laws.

The Clean Air Act

The clearly stated purpose of the CAA is "to protect and enhance the quality of the Nation's air resources so as to promote the public health and welfare. . . ." (42 U.S.C. §7401[b][1]). Even from this most cursory review of the key titles in the CAA, regulatory provisions clearly dominate and were considerably strengthened from earlier iterations of the CAA that Congress considered insufficiently protective of public health (reference 24, §3.2). As amended by the CAA Amendments of 1990, the CAA contains almost the full range of environmental protection tools to achieve its stated goals. It established the National Ambient Air Quality Standards (pollution levels that states are required to meet by preparing and enforcing implementation plans); created a program for reducing emissions from mobile sources (by requiring EPA to set standards for emissions levels from vehicles); established a methodology for reducing toxic air pollutants (by setting technology-based standards); and sought to reduce acid rain deposition through an allowance program for electric utilities. In addition to these major provisions, sections exist that create research programs, including environmental health research.[i]

The CAA outlines a limited role for federal public health authorities. Even in areas where public health could be expected to lead, the statute indicates that PHS agencies are to play a secondary role. Subsection 103(d) of the act (42 U.S.C. §7403[d]) illustrates Congress's approach. This subsection, "Research, investigation, training, and other activities," specifically calls for environmental health research. The EPA Administrator, in consultation with the Secretary of Health and Human Services, is ordered to conduct a research program on the short- and long-term effects of air pollutants and prepare environmental health assessments for hazardous air pollutants. The subsection also creates the Interagency Task Force, which includes several PHS agencies, such as ATSDR and the National Institute of Environmental Health Sciences. However, the statutory language indicates that EPA is expected to control this research agenda. The CAA thus creates an opportunity to bolster environmental health research but does not explicitly give PHS agencies a leadership role in its design and implementation.

The balance in the CAA is overwhelmingly weighted toward traditional regulatory tools. Additional (or more effective) surveillance of respiratory disease, a role for state health departments in respiratory health education in communities, additional involvement of health agencies in the regulatory process, or application of other environmental health tools likely would help in achieving the public health goals of the CAA. However, the CAA does not contain these tools.[j]

The Comprehensive Environmental Response, Compensation, and Liability Act (Superfund)

The Comprehensive Environmental Response, Compensation, and Liability Act (CERCLA), also known as Superfund, was enacted in 1980. It has been amended several times in the past three decades and was extensively overhauled in 1986 by the Superfund Amendments and Reauthorization Act (SARA). The main goal of CERCLA is to protect public health by cleaning up inactive or abandoned sites at which hazardous substances are being released. It assigns liability and apportions responsibility for the cost of cleaning up the sites among classes of persons (e.g., individuals, state and federal government entities, and corporations) deemed to have been responsible for these releases. Environmental protection tools play an important role in making CERCLA effective, and CERCLA also uses significant environmental health tools.

Among its other features, CERCLA created the National Priorities List (a method for establishing cleanup priorities among the thousands of sites in the country at which hazardous substances are found), the National Contingency Plan (guidance for conducting more immediate response actions when necessary), and a detailed remedial process for evaluating and cleaning up the sites (see 42 U.S.C. §9605[a]).

Many of the most important tools of CERCLA relate to its liability and enforcement provisions. Strict liability, and joint and several liability, which can result in one or several significant polluters at a site being responsible for all cleanup costs even though many parties may have contributed to the pollution, are the centerpiece of CERCLA's environmental protection scheme (42 U.S.C. §9601). Additional provisions relate to identification of potentially responsible parties, including, for example, information requests (42 U.S.C. §9603), cost recovery actions that the government or a private party can bring to recoup its cleanup expenses (42 U.S.C. §9607), the abatement of imminent and substantial hazards to public health (42 U.S.C. §§9604[a] and 9606), administrative orders issued by the federal government to compel private parties to undertake response actions (42 U.S.C. §9606), penalties for failure to comply (42 U.S.C. §9609), and citizen lawsuit provisions (42 U.S.C. §9659).

The act also contains significant health-related provisions that use classic environmental health tools. When enacted, CERCLA established the Agency for Toxic Substances and Disease Registry (ATSDR) within PHS.[39] In cooperation with EPA and other PHS agencies, the ATSDR has the responsibility to "effectuate and implement the health related authorities" of Superfund (42 U.S.C. §9604[I][1]). Among other things, the ATSDR conducts public health assessments at all National Priorities List sites, maintains national registries of persons exposed to toxic substances and of illnesses and diseases, develops toxicology profiles for each substance on a hazardous substance priority list, and conducts epidemiologic or other health studies and health surveillance and health education programs when appropriate (42 U.S.C. §§9604[i][1] and [2]). Through a mechanism created by CERCLA, the ATSDR provides extensive public health review, evaluation, and feedback on environmental sampling, monitoring, and remediation to EPA. In addition, CERCLA authorized a substantial basic research program at the National Institute of Environmental Health Sciences, along with worker training and education programs (42 U.S.C. §9604[i][1]–[18]).

Overall, CERCLA marries a nonregulatory, newly created public health agency (ATSDR) with a regulatory agency (EPA). In practice, this marriage has resulted in fruitful opportunities for collaboration and coordination among public health and environmental agencies to fulfill the mandates of a major environmental protection statute. Environmental health practitioners should consider the potential for such partnerships in other critical situations that arise in the practice of environmental law.

Emerging Issues

The Built Environment, Community Design, and Land Use Choices

How we design, live in, travel within, and use our built environment affects our health and well-being. Mounting evidence indicates that chronic diseases can be linked to, or are exacerbated by, choices associated with daily living and lifestyle.[40,k] The origins of heart disease and stroke, cancer, and diabetes are grounded in routines people engage in for years before the actual onset of disease. Poor diet and lack of physical activity in childhood, adolescence, and adulthood put people at increased risk for chronic diseases and disabilities. Nearly 50% of U.S. youth aged 12–21 years report they are not regularly and vigorously physically active, and about 14% of these young people report no recent physical activity at all. Traffic crashes are the leading cause of death for young adults aged 20–34 years and the third leading cause for adults aged 35–44 years.[41]

The public health community recognizes the importance of housing, urban development, land use, transportation, industry, and agriculture on health, and this holistic philosophy is incorporated into the definition of "environmental health" found in *Healthy People 2010*.[42] This definition is based on a long history of integration between the natural and built environments and the public's health. Environmental, health, and land-use/zoning law share a common heritage rooted in the careful regulation of individual or small-group behaviors that may pose a risk to the community.[k] Regrettably, the public health community in general, and environmental health professionals in particular, are today minor players in shaping the built environment and community design.[l]

The public health community has tried to bridge this gap by reaching out to professionals who have the authority to affect the changes in the built environment and community design, including building and housing code officials, urban planners, architects, and transportation engineers.[43–45] By joining with these professionals, public health professionals can assist in (1) redesigning the way various modes of transportation interact to protect pedestrians, bicyclists, and motorists from traffic-related injuries; (2) redistributing commercial activities to encourage physical activity and good nutrition; (3) redesigning building codes and transportation regulations to reduce environmental barriers for older citizens and people with a disability; (4) reducing the exposure to environmental toxins in the air, water, and food supply; and (5) establishing and use and zoning requirements that are consistent with an active and healthy lifestyle.

Building alliances and partnerships to influence the design of the built environment is an important way in which public health can reclaim its traditional role in community design. More directly, the legal tools available to environmental law practitioners can be effective in shaping policies and decisions about the built environment. Federal environmental statutes such as the CAA and SDWA contain provisions that regulate the amount of toxic air pollution and control the pathogenic and chemical contaminants in drinking water.[46,47] The CWA was enacted to "restore and maintain the chemical, physical, and biological integrity of the Nation's waters," setting a goal that, whenever attainable, it shall be national policy that navigable waters are fit for, among other things, recreational purposes.[48] The National Environmental Policy Act requires the preparation of environmental impact statements before any federal action is taken that significantly affects the quality of the human environment.[49] Federal environmental laws and policies have been put into place to expedite the redevelopment of contaminated urban properties, sometimes called "brownfields," to return this land to productive and sustainable use.[50] State environmental laws and regulations and local ordinances also directly apply to the built environment.[51] State and local governments have long taken the lead in land-use planning; some of the first zoning efforts, which were challenged in federal courts, were state and local initiatives.[52]

Since the U.S. Supreme Court upheld local zoning ordinances, federal, state, and local efforts to improve community design and recognition of the importance of the built environment to public health have increased. Accessibility laws, such as the American's with Disabilities Act (ADA),[53] have been adopted to ensure equal access to needed medical and other public facilities for persons who may have any of a number of mobility impairments. Many of these regulatory and investigative authorities at the local level are vested in the public health department or the larger entity that includes the health department. Building and development projects at the community level often receive public health inspections before they are sold or occupied.[54]

Environmental Health Aspects of Natural Disasters and Chemical, Biologic, and Radiologic Terrorism

Tremendous environmental health challenges were created by the damage and devastation wrought by Hurricane Katrina in the Gulf Coast states and its cities (including New Orleans, Louisiana) during August and September 2005; the September 11, 2001, terrorist attacks on New York City and Washington, D.C.; and the dissemination of anthrax through the U.S. postal system that followed the 2001 terrorist attacks. These problems highlighted some of the gaps in the public health system's preparedness for responding to natural disasters and terrorism and illustrated the critical need for a well-organized and responsive environmental health and protection infrastructure. Natural disasters and terrorist actions require a sustained environmental health presence. Air and water monitoring, disease tracking, laboratory analysis of samples, and protection of the health and safety of responders are among the vital services that environmental health provides. Although federal and state statutory authority exists to provide integrated and rapid action, as inhabitants in communities affected by terrorism and natural disasters seek to return to their homes, remediate damages, and plan to prevent future occurrences, a sophisticated understanding of the legal tools available to address environmental health problems is essential.

The scope of environmental health issues that practitioners could face after a terrorist attack or natural disaster is not possible to cover comprehensively. In the two sections that follow, we illustrate how environmental law impacts approaches to natural disasters and to terrorism recovery and assessment of damages.

World Trade Center Registry

Assessment of air contamination and exposure to toxics associated with the New York City World Trade Center (WTC) attack reveals a complicated pattern of environmental exposure and potential health effects. On the basis of a number of studies, airborne exposures to chemical contaminants varied substantially according to time after the attack and distance from ground zero. Not surprisingly, high levels of dust, smoke, and combustion products existed for the first two days after the attack, then declined as the combustion products were consumed. An acrid cloud hung over lower Manhattan and Brooklyn for approximately two months after the attack. Meteorologic conditions (such as rain and wind or lack of air movement), ongoing cleanup work at ground zero (e.g., removing rubble and debris piles), and use of heavy equipment fueled by diesel engines changed exposure patterns and the mix of compounds in the air. Airborne levels of dioxin, lead, and asbestos also were elevated in the initial days after the WTC towers were demolished.[55] Exposures among workers at the WTC site, especially among firefighters, police, and first responders, were higher than exposures experienced by residents living in the area.

A cohort of persons exposed to toxins from the WTC destruction could be at risk for potentially serious health effects that might not be evident until some time in the future. To evaluate the chronic or delayed effects of exposure, several registries have been established that will follow exposed persons over time.[55] The ATSDR has authority to conduct health assessments and, if appropriate, establish exposure and disease registries for persons exposed to hazardous substances (42 U.S.C. §9604 [i]). The ATSDR has established the World Trade Center Health Registry in collaboration with the New York City Department of Health and Mental Hygiene.[56] More than 72,000 persons have enrolled, making this the largest active data collection registry in the United States. In October 2004, preliminary analyses of 60,000 registrants indicated registrants were experiencing new or worsened sinus or respiratory problems and other symptoms.[57]

Hurricane Katrina Health Needs and Habitability Assessment

In response to the flooding in New Orleans, Louisiana, CDC, in consultation with EPA, assembled a task force to make an initial assessment of the infrastructure and environmental health issues faced by New Orleans to reinhabit the city.[58] The assessment indicated a systemswide approach should be implemented to address the environmental stresses of habitation, which will change over time. Thirteen environmental health and supporting infrastructure issues were identified and categorized by increasing time and complexity. Several legal issues were explicitly mentioned or implied, including the following:

- Legal, jurisdictional, and procedural challenges associated with housing decisions (e.g., nonowner entry and evaluation, possible condemnation and destruction of severely damaged structures, "takings" of property without just compensation)[m]
- Cleanup and toxic contamination issues (e.g., regulatory and/or emergency standards setting "safe" or "acceptable" exposure levels to chemical contamination; testing and authorization for public drinking water providers to operate; considering, and setting criteria for, granting exemptions for compliance with state and federal environmental laws, or suspending state environmental laws and regulations)[n]
- Disposal of debris and solid waste (i.e., the need for additional compliant land disposal facilities or disposal options if usable municipal facilities are not available or become filled)
- Safety, security, and occupational health of first responders
- Legal issues associated with using volunteer environmental health professionals[59] and
- Overlapping or conflicting authorities of state, federal, and local (city) agencies (e.g., for solid-waste disposal)

Each of these challenges will force public health and legal practitioners to confront legal issues for which limited precedent is available. As CDC's Needs and Habitability Assessment emphasizes, public health and legal practitioners will need to collaborate closely with state, local, and federal officials, and with citizens, businesses, and other stakeholders, to develop a shared vision for rebuilding New Orleans. Drawing on the experiences of other localities that have addressed devastating events, such as New York City, could provide examples. Legal tools are likely to be used most effectively in an environment of collaboration that emphasizes achieving a common goal and shared vision of rebuilding New Orleans.[58]

Conclusion

Public health law practitioners in the field of environmental health are faced with a complex legal landscape. For some environmental health problems and functions (e.g., regulation of drinking water, cleanup of hazardous substances, food inspection activities), finding the applicable legal tools is relatively straightforward. For others (e.g., improving environmental health surveillance), specific legal tools could be difficult to find.[1] The practice of environmental health law is complicated because it spans portions of *both* the field of environmental protection and public health law. Public health laws traditionally have provided noncoercive authorities to state, local, and federal agencies and are useful in building an evidence base for change and fostering partnerships for cooperative ventures. In contrast, environmental protection laws are media-based and provide strong coercive authorities to federal and state agencies pursuing environmental health improvement. How to reconcile these two approaches is not always clear.

Fortunately, in most situations it is not necessary to choose one or the other. Attorneys pursuing environmental health improvement efforts have at their disposal a broad and extensive set of legal tools that, when deployed appropriately, are adaptable to address most of today's environmental health problems.

Notes

a. Many federal statutes provide that states can administer and enforce their own programs in lieu of the federal program. Generally, states cannot implement programs if EPA finds the state program is not equivalent to the federal program, is not consistent with the federal program, or does not provide adequate enforcement. See, for example, 42 U.S.C. §6929 (RCRA); 33 U.S.C. §§1342(b) and (c)(1)

b. California, Connecticut, Georgia, Hawaii, Indiana, Maryland, Massachusetts, Minnesota, Montana, New York, North Carolina, South Dakota, Virginia, West Virginia, Washington, and Wisconsin.

c. The Massachusetts Toxics Use Reduction Act reduces industrial use of toxins through mandatory planning approaches. At least 12 other states have toxic use reduction laws (National Research Council. McElfish J, Novick SM, Stever DW, Mellon MG, Forgarty JPC, Stewart SL. State Environmental Laws and Programs. In: Novick SM, Stever DW, Mellon MG, Forgarty JPC, Stewart SL eds. *Law of Environmental Protection* Vol. 1. St. Paul, MN: West Publishing 1987, §§6.02(3), 6.18.

d. See, for example, 42 U.S.C. §7604; 33 U.S.C. §1365(a); 42 U.S.C. §6972(a)(1)(A).

e. An illustrative case is *Sierra Club v. Simkins Industries, Inc.*, 847 F. 2d 1109, cert. denied, 491 US 904 (1989).

f. For example, the CWA states that "it is the national goal that the discharge of pollutants . . . be eliminated by 1985" (see 33 U.S.C. §1251[a][1]). This goal has not yet been met.

g. One of the more controversial assumptions is the assumption that the dose-response curve associated with carcinogenicity is linear and without a threshold. According to EPA's cancer risk guidelines, in the absence of information about the extent of human variability in sensitivity of effects linear extrapolation is appropriate and generally conservative of public health. EPA's final cancer guidelines are available at http://cfpub.epa.gov/ncea/cfm/recordisplay.cfm?deid= 116283. Accessed 25 September 2006.

h. Consider goal 8-1, which aims to reduce the population exposed to air above EPA's health-based standard for hazardous air pollutants. The Department of Health and Human Services will undoubtedly use surveillance data for this analysis.

i. See, for example, 42 U.S.C. §7404 (research relating to fuels and vehicles) and 42 U.S.C. §7403(d) (environmental health effects research).

j. It is feasible that, as this chapter suggests, public health agencies could use authorities such as those contained in the Public Health Service Act to conduct these functions. We make this point here only to show that the CAA does not embrace them.

k. State police power provides authority to enact laws that restrict land uses to protect public health. In part based on this interpretation of the police powers, the Village Council in Euclid, Ohio, passed an ordinance in 1922 regulating the location and type of land uses permitted in six designated districts within the Village. Enforcement of the ordinance was entrusted to the inspector of buildings, under rules and regulations of the board of zoning appeals. This ordinance was challenged, and in 1926, in *Village of Euclid v. Ambler Realty Co.*, 272 U.S. 365 (1926), the Supreme Court cited various precedents for land use and environmental protection ordinances aimed at the "promotion of the health and security from injury of children and others by separating dwelling houses from territory devoted to trade and industry; suppression and prevention of disorder; facilitating the extinguishment of fires and the enforcement of street traffic regulations and other general welfare ordinances; aiding the health and safety of the community by excluding from residential areas the confusion and danger of fire, contagion and disorder which, in greater or less degree, attach to the location of stores, shops and factories." In *Euclid*, the Court applied the reasoning of one of its previous decision, *Jacobson v. Massachusetts*, 197 U.S. 11 (1905), which addressed whether a local community health board could enforce an ordinance requiring vaccination against smallpox. Read in combination, these two decisions inexorably link the government regulation of the built environment and community design with the protection of the public's health.

l. This was not always so. In the 19th century, public health professionals were actively involved in housing and building code development and enforcement, among other things. A strong public health presence in these fields generally was recognized as necessary to conquer infectious diseases. See Perdue WC, Stone LA, Gostin LO. The built environment and its relationship to the public's health: the legal framework. *Am J Public Health* 2003;93 1390–4.

m. In addition to the "takings" clause in the U.S. Constitution, Louisiana's Constitution (Article I, §4) states in part that "[p]roperty shall not be taken or damaged by the state or its political subdivisions except for public purposes and with just compensation. . . ." This section also states that it "shall not apply to appropriation of property necessary for levee and levee drainage purposes," and "the legislature may place limitations on the extent of recovery for the taking of, or loss or damage to, property rights affected by coastal wetlands conservation, management, enhancement, creation or restoration activities."

n. Louisiana Constitution Article III, §20, might provide authority to the state legislature to suspend laws and state agency regulations. See Peterson DA. Louisiana's legislative suspension power: valid method for override of environmental laws and agency regulations? *Louisiana Law Rev* 1992;53:257.

References

1. Pew Environmental Health Commission. *America's Environmental Health Gap: Why the Country Needs a Nationwide Health Tracking Network* (Technical Report). September 2000 (September):86.
2. Gostin LO. Public health in the constitutional design. *Public Health Law: Power, Duty, Restraint*. Berkeley: University of California Press, 2000:25–59.
3. Gerrard MB, ed. *Environmental Law Practice Guide: State and Federal Law*. New York: Matthew Bender, LEXIS Publishing, 1992, 2001:§33.01[2].
4. *United States v Lopez*, 514 US 549 (1995).

5. Lewis J. Looking backward: a historical perspective on environmental regulations. *EPA J* 1988 (March). Available at http://www.epa.gov/history/topics/regulate/01.htm. Accessed June 3, 2002.

6. The Environmental Council of the States. Available at http://www.ecos.org. Accessed June 3, 2002.

7. Campbell-Mohn C, Breen B, Futrell JW, eds. Chemicals. In: *Sustainable Environmental Law: Integrating Natural Resources and Pollution Abatement Law from Resources to Recovery*. West Publishing, 1993:1257–365.

8. Mandelker DR. State environmental policy acts. *NEPA: Law and Litigation*. 2nd ed. St. Paul, MN: West Publishing, Release 9, 8/2000, §12.01, 12-2.

9. Kraft ME. *Environmental Policy and Politics: Towards the 21st Century*. New York: Harper Collins College Publishers, 1996:103.

10. Cal Health & Safety Code §25249.1 *et seq.*

11. NJ Stat Ann §13.1K-6 *et seq.*

12. Massachusetts Toxics Use Reduction Act (TURA), Mass Gen L Ch 21[1], §1-23 (1989).

13. Ariz Rev Stat Ann §49-201 *et seq.*

14. Wis Stat Ann §1600.001 *et seq.*

15. Conn Gen Stat Ch 446K, §22a-416 *et seq.*

16. Skillern FF. *Environmental Protection Deskbook*. 2nd ed. New York: McGraw Hill, Inc, 1995:705.

17. Michigan Constitution, Article IV, §52 (1983).

18. Pennsylvania Constitution, Article I, §27 (West Purdon 1994).

19. Rhode Island Constitution, Article I, §17 (Michie 1987).

20. Mich Stat Ann §14.528 (204) (1989 and supp 1994).

21. Percival RV. Regulatory evolution and the future of environmental policy. *University of Chicago Legal Forum* 1997:159–98.

22. Dwyer JP. The role of state law in an era of federal preemption: lesson from environmental regulation. *Law & Contemporary Problems* 1997;60:207.

23. McElfish J, Novick SM, Stever DW, Mellon MG, Fogarty JPC, Stewart SL. State environmental laws and programs. In: Novick SM, Stever DW, Mellon MG Fogarty JPC, Stewart SL, eds. *Law of Environmental Protection*. Vol 1. St. Paul, MN: West Publishing, 1987, Release 17, 3/97, §§6.02(3), 6.18.

24. Rodgers WH Jr. *Environmental Law*. 2nd ed. St. Paul, MN: West Publishing, 1994 [with 1995 pocket part]:§4.2.

25. EPA. History: Agency Overview. *EPA Organization and Functions Manual*. Available at http://www.epa.gov/history/org/origins/overview.htm. Accessed June 3, 2005.

26. Ash Council Memo. Memo for the President from the President's Advisory Council on Executive Organization, April 29, 1970. Available at http://www.epa.gov/history/org/origins/ash.htm. Accessed December 8, 2005.

27. Special Message from the President to Congress about Reorganization Plans to Establish the Environmental; Protection Agency and the National Oceanic and Atmospheric Administration, July 9, 1970. Available at http://www.epa.gov/history/org/origins/reorg.htm. Accessed June 3, 2000.

28. Pub L 91-604, December 31, 1970, 84 Stat 1676 *et seq.*

29. Pub L 92-516 (7 USC §§136 *et seq*) October 21, 1972, 86 Stat 973.

30. Pub L 96-510 (42 USC §9601 *et seq*) December 11, 1980, 94 Stat 2767 (Superfund).

31. Pub L 98-616 (42 USC §6921[d]), November 8, 1984, 98 Stat 3221 (1984 RCRA amendments).

32. Pub L 99-499, October 17, 1986, 100 Stat 1777.

33. Parascandola JL. Public Health Service. In: Kurian GT. *A Historical Guide to the U.S. Government*. New York: Oxford University Press, 1998:487–93.

34. National Research Council. *Risk Assessment in the Federal Government: Managing the Process*. Washington, DC: National Academy Press, 1983.

35. EPA. *Exposure Factors Handbook*. Vol I: General Factors. Update to Exposure Factors Handbook. Office of Research and Development, National Center for Environmental Assessment, US EPA:3-1. Publication no EPA/600/P-95/002Fa, August 1997. Available at http://www.epa.gov/NCEA/pdfs/efh/sect3.PDF. Accessed June 3, 2005.

36. US Department of Health and Human Services. *Healthy People 2010*. Available at http://www.health.gov/healthypeople/document/. Accessed June 3, 2005.

37. EPA. *Proposed Guidelines for Carcinogen Risk Assessment (April 23, 1996)*. Office of Research and Development, National Center for Environmental Assessment, US EPA. *Federal Register* 61(79):17960–8011. Publication no EPA/600/P-92/003C April 1996. Available at http://www.epa.gov/ncea/raf/pdfs/propcra_1996.pdf. Accessed December 13, 2005.

38. US Office of Technology Assessment. *Environmental Policy Tools: A User's Guide*. OTA-ENV-634. Washington, DC: US Office of Technology Assessment, September 1995.

39. Pub L 96-510, §§104(i)(1)–(5), 94 Stat 2778.

40. Srinivasan S, O'Fallon LR, Dearry A. Creating healthy communities, healthy homes, healthy people: initiating a research agenda on the built environment and public health, *Am J Public Health* 2003;93:1446–50.

41. CDC. *The State of the CDC Report, FY 2004*. Available at http://www.cdc.gov/cdc.pdf. Accessed December 13, 2005.

42. US Department of Health and Human Services. *Healthy People 2010: Understanding and Improving Health*. 2nd ed. Washington, DC: US Department of Health and Human Services, 2000.

43. National Association of County and City Health Officials. Resolution to Support Land Use Planning/Community Design. Available at http://archive.naccho.org/documents/resolutions/03-02.pdf. Accessed December 13, 2005.

44. Stoto MA, Abel C, Dievler A, eds. *Healthy Communities: New Partnerships for the Future of Public Health*. Washington, DC: National Academies Press, 1996.

45. Institute of Medicine. *Informing the Future: Critical Issues in Health*. 2nd ed. Washington, DC: National Academies Press, 2003.

46. 42 USC §7412 (CAA).

47. 42 USC §300g-1 (SDWA).

48. 33 USC §1251

49. 42 USC §4332

50. Eisen JB. A case study in sustainable development brownfields. *Environ Law Rep* 2002;32:10420–7 (discussing the Small Business Liability Relief and Brownfields Revitalization Act, Pub L 107-118 [January 11, 2002]).

51. Nolon JR. Local Land Use Controls That Achieve Smart Growth, 31 *Environmental Law Reporter* 11025 (2001) (examining how New York State local governments administer smart growth strategies).

52. *Village of Euclid v Ambler Realty Co*, 272 US 365 (1926).

53. Pub L 101-336, July 26, 1990, 104 Stat 327 (the ADA is partially codified beginning at 42 USC §12101).

54. Gordon L. Environmental health and protection. In Scutchfield FD, Keck CW, eds. *Principles of Public Health Practice*. Albany, NY: Delmar Publishers, 1997.

55. Landrigan P, Lioy P, Thurston G, et al. Health and environmental consequences of the world trade center disaster. *Environ Health Perspect* 2004;112:731–9.

56. World Trade Center Health Registry. Available at http://www.wtcregistry.org. Accessed September 22, 2005.

57. World Trade Center Health Registry. *Data Snapshot: Understanding the Health Impact of 9/11*. Available at www.nyc.gov/html/doh/downloads/pdf/wtc/wtc-report2004-1112.pdf. Accessed January 3, 2006.

58. CDC/EPA Joint Taskforce. Hurricane Katrina Information. *Environmental Health Needs & Habitability Assessment: September 17, 2005*. Available at http://ww.bt.cdc.gov/disasters/hurricanes/katrina/envassessment.asp. Accessed October 26, 2005.

59. Hodge JG Jr, Gable LA, Cálves SH. Volunteer health professionals and emergencies: assessing and transforming the legal environment. *Biosecur Bioterror* 2005;3:216–23.

Chapter 21

INJURY PREVENTION

Daniel D. Stier,* James A. Mercy,* and Melvin Kohn

Even though about 150,000 injury-related deaths and 50 million nonfatal injuries occur annually, injury is one of the most under-recognized public health problems in the United States.[1] Each year in the United States, about one-third of deaths from injury are motor vehicle–related, while one-third result from other unintentional injuries (such as falls and drowning) and one-third from homicide and suicide. Homicides, suicides, and deaths from injuries caused by motor vehicle crashes are the leading causes of death for persons aged 1–44 years.[2] For all persons under age 34 years, motor vehicle crashes are the leading cause of death.[3] For persons aged 15–34 years, homicide and suicide rank as either the second or third leading causes, and homicide is the leading cause for African Americans in this age group.[4] Because of its relatively greater impact on adolescents and young adults, injury ranks as the leading cause of premature mortality in the United States, and in 2002, accounted for almost 30% of all years of potential life lost before age 65.[1] Medical treatment and associated productivity losses from injury cost an estimated $406 billion in 2000.[2]

Progress in reducing the occurrence and impact of some injuries, particularly those associated with motor vehicles, has been remarkable. The Centers for Disease Control and Prevention (CDC) highlighted improvements in motor vehicle safety as one of the top ten public health achievements of the 20th century.[5] Since

* The findings and conclusions in this chapter are those of the author(s) and do not necessarily represent the views of the U.S. Department of Health and Human Services or the Centers for Disease Control and Prevention.

1923, the rate of motor vehicle–related deaths per 100 million vehicle miles traveled decreased 93% (from 21.7 in 1923 to 1.6 in 2000).[6] This dramatic decline represents the impact of a combination of engineering efforts to make both cars and highways safer and successful efforts to change personal behavior (e.g., increased use of safety belts, child-safety seats, and motorcycle helmets and decreased drinking and driving). The law and legal interventions have played a critical role in these successes.

This chapter focuses on legal tools for preventing and controlling unintentional injuries and injuries resulting from interpersonal violence. Broadly speaking, laws—including administrative rules authorized by legislation—can be used to prevent injuries by (1) providing legal authority to engage in the public health practice of injury prevention and control, including injury surveillance and injury-prevention programming, and to regulate personal behaviors or environmental factors that cause injury, and (2) imposing liability for injuries. Because the field of injury prevention and control is so broad, we will illustrate application of the law to injury through selected examples.

A Conceptual Approach to Injury Prevention

One contemporary perspective about injuries is: "Injuries are not unavoidable events caused by bad luck or fate."[7] They are largely predictable and preventable. Whether arising from unintentional circumstances or violence, injuries typically result from the interplay of a broad range of biologic, psychological, social, and environmental factors. To facilitate understanding of the occurrence of and prevention strategies for injuries, Dr. William Haddon, an injury-prevention practitioner, developed the technique of constructing a matrix of factors (commonly referred to as a "Haddon matrix") that play a role in causing injuries (Table 21-1).[8] Constructing a Haddon matrix can be a useful analytic tool for identifying specific targets for injury-prevention program development, including those with a legal component. The matrix forces consideration of the causes of injury to explicitly include risk factors before, during, and after an injury that involve not just individual behaviors but also the vehicle and environments, both physical and sociocultural.

Applied to a particular type of injury, a Haddon matrix can assist in consideration and development of legal interventions designed to prevent the injury. For example, the Haddon matrix for injury associated with a motor vehicle crash reveals laws intervening at the pre-event phase to regulate driver behavior by prohibiting drunk driving and by prescribing licensing requirements (Table 21-1). At that phase, law can mandate vehicle-safety devices, such as breathalyzer-ignition locks, and the physical environment can be improved through legislative funding to eliminate highway design flaws. Sociocultural attitudes toward speeding may be affected by the level of enforcement of speeding laws. During the event, seat-belt laws, airbag, and break-off sign requirements can prevent injuries. Finally, at the post-event phase, laws mandating emergency rescue personnel standards and vehicle structural integrity requirements can facilitate quick access to and effective medical treatment of injured persons, thereby potentially reducing the severity of injuries.

TABLE 21-1 Motor Vehicle–Related Legal Strategies for Injury Prevention, Organized within the Haddon Matrix

	FACTOR			
PHASE	Human Factors	Agent/Vehicle Factors	Physical Environment	Sociocultural Environment
Pre-event	Drunk driving/ Minimum drinking age requirements Graduated driver licenses Sobriety checkpoints	Antilock brake requirements Breathalyzer-ignition lock requirement	Funding for elimination of highway design flaws	Speeding enforcement affecting driver attitudes
Event	Seat-belt/Child-restraint laws	Airbag requirement	Break-off signposts requirement	N/A
Post-event	Emergency rescue personnel licensing/certification standards	Auto roof construction requirements	N/A	N/A

Legal Authorities

Many types of injuries exist, and they are caused by a myriad of factors. Law-based interventions designed to address those causes arise from sources of power at federal, state, and local levels of government and prevent or control injuries in a variety of ways. This section provides a basic introduction to the breadth of law-based interventions, using three types of injury causes that seriously affect children and young adults—playground falls, motor vehicle crashes, and youth violence—as examples demonstrating the law's varied role in injury prevention.

Scope of Laws in Injury Prevention

A primary source of power for federal government involvement with public health issues, including the development of law-based injury-prevention interventions, is Article I, Section 8, of the U.S. Constitution, authorizing Congress to tax and spend and to regulate commerce. Power beyond that granted to the federal government is reserved to the states under the Tenth Amendment in the form of the police power. This broad power authorizes states to protect the public health and welfare, which certainly includes the legal ability to devise law-based injury-prevention interventions. Finally, state legislatures have the authority—and in some instances, the responsibility—to delegate authority to local units of government (Table 21-2).

Law can be effective in establishing, implementing, and enforcing injury-prevention methods. Although motor vehicle and highway safety, firearms safety and access, and other federal laws are highly visible and therefore frequently the subject of literature concerning injury-prevention laws, most injury-prevention laws are found at the state level of government[9] and include the following:

- Rules governing the conduct of motor vehicle drivers, such as acquisition of licenses, driving curfews for younger drivers, use of seatbelts and child restraints, adherence to speed limits, criminalization of driving while intoxicated, and mandates for motorcycle helmet use
- Requirements for mandatory inspections of motor vehicles and other laws governing the condition of vehicles
- Penal laws prohibiting assaultive and abusive behaviors
- Laws regulating the acquisition, carrying, and use of firearms
- Regulations governing the sale, possession, and use of other dangerous products, such as poisons, explosives, drugs, and alcohol
- Building codes that regulate the design, function, and safety of structures
- Fire-safety laws governing the use of flammable products
- Laws that address the nature and use of restraining orders for protecting victims of intimate partner violence
- Laws governing the role of the state in intervening in families for purposes of child protection from abuse and neglect

Despite their benefit to public health, many of these state laws implicate entities not traditionally considered part of the public health system.

TABLE 21-2 Selected Examples of Injury Prevention and Control Measures

Jurisdiction/Level of Government	Source of Legal Power	Effect of Law
Federal	U.S. Constitution, commerce clause	Congressional creation of Consumer Product Safety Commission with delegated powers to regulate consumer products to ensure safe products and reduced risk of injury Congressional creation of National Highway Traffic Safety Administration with delegated powers to ensure safely engineered roadways and reduced risk for injuries related to motor vehicle crashes
State	State's police power (reserved to states under U.S. Constitution's Tenth Amendment)	Legislature's creation of health department with delegated powers to conduct injury surveillance Legislature's enactment of requirements for seat-belt use Legislature's enactment of criminal codes for deterring some interpersonal violence and injuries Legislature's enactment of requirements for safe child daycare playground surfaces
Local	State's police powers delegated to local government by state legislatures	Municipal enactment and enforcement of building and fire codes to ensure structural safety Enactment and enforcement of local speed limit laws

Regulation of personal behaviors is perhaps the most obvious way that legal authority can be used to prevent injuries. Injury-prevention laws, however, whether relating to unintentional injury or violence, also regulate environments and product design or use. Laws ranging from those creating the National Highway Traffic Safety Administration (NHTSA), the Occupational Safety and Health Administration, and the Consumer Product Safety Commission (CPSC) in the late 1960s and early 1970s to those passed in 23 states in 1997 mandating the collection of data concerning the causes of injuries have been described by commentators as milestones in injury-prevention law.[10]

Examples of laws regulating behavior include drunk driving and minimum drinking age laws, bicycle helmet use laws, and laws prohibiting assault. A law requiring that crib slats be spaced widely enough to prevent infant head entrapment demonstrates a law regulating product design. Laws regulating environments include various licensing and regulatory schemes. Some of these laws are intended to protect the health and safety of virtually every person. Examples include housing and building codes, generally adopted and enforced at the local level. Others, such as daycare center and nursing home regulations, protect specific vulnerable populations. Daycare regulations are adopted and enforced at state and local levels. Nursing home regulations consist of a complex web of federal and state legislation and administrative rules. A potential consequence of a facility's failure to comply is the loss of Medicaid and Medicare funding.

The nursing home environment is extensively regulated. Examples of regulated facets of the environment include staff qualifications, staffing levels, resident or client care (e.g., degree of adult supervision, handling and transfer of nonambulatory persons), and the physical environment (e.g., permissible water temperature, availability and types of sanitary supplies, and equipment safety standards). These regulatory systems frequently incorporate other regulatory schemes by reference (e.g., housing codes and the National Fire Protection Association's Life Safety Code), and mandate compliance with those systems.[11,12]

Playground Safety

More than 200,000 children each year are treated in U.S. hospital emergency departments for playground equipment–related injuries.[13] Historically, playground equipment was installed on asphalt, concrete, or turf. As a result of playground injury surveillance undertaken by CPSC, CDC, and others, most playground injuries were discovered to be caused by falls from equipment to the playground surface. Since 1981, CPSC has published and regularly updated its recommendations in the *Handbook for Public Playground Safety*.[14] The handbook provides detailed guidance on all facets of playground use, design, installation, and maintenance, particularly installation and maintenance of playground surfaces.

Because CPSC believes that "many factors may affect playground safety," the handbook provides guidelines rather than a mandatory rule. Therefore, even though CPSC provides "a detailed working blueprint to help local communities, schools, day care centers, corporations, and other groups build safe playgrounds," neither CPSC nor any other federal agency requires those entities to do so as a matter of law. Furthermore, state and local public health agencies generally do not impose legal requirements regarding surfaces on entities that own and maintain playground equipment.

Nonetheless, certain entities regulated by state or local governments may be subject to legal mandates regarding playgrounds. For example, daycare centers in most states are subject to regulations prohibiting concrete and asphalt and requiring energy-absorbing surfaces under playground equipment. A typical regulation requires an energy-absorbing surface at a certain depth under and in an area surrounding the equipment.[15] These regulations generally are promulgated by state regulatory agencies under broad authority provided by statute. In Wisconsin, for example, state law requires the Department of Health and Family Services to "promulgate rules establishing minimum requirements for the issuance of licenses to . . . day care centers. . . . These rules shall be designed to protect and promote the health, safety, and welfare of the children in the care of all licensees" (Wis. Stat. §48.67). Legislative bodies frequently provide that sort of broad authority with the expectation that the agency will flesh out the details. Promulgated under that statutory authority and pursuant to the states' Administrative Procedure Acts, the regulations have the force of law.

To varying degrees, state regulatory provisions reflect the recommendations of the CPSC *Handbook for Public Playground Safety*. In Illinois, for example, the "Licensing Standards for Day Care Centers" expressly refer to the handbook and actually incorporate the handbook's "critical heights" table for various shock-absorbing surfaces. Even without explicit reference to the handbook, state daycare regulations governing playground surfaces are obviously heavily influenced by it.[a]

Unlike daycare centers, most other entities owning and maintaining playground equipment do so without regulatory supervision. Although urged by CDC-sponsored health guidelines to "use recommended safe surfaces under playground equipment," schools with equipment on their grounds, for example, are not required by law to do so. Nonetheless, many school systems follow the guidelines, which have been developed with the assistance of numerous technical advisers; the cooperation of several other federal agencies, including CPSC; and the participation of many organizations representing state and local governments, school districts, public health officials, and children's advocacy organizations.[16]

In the absence of a legal mandate, why have schools installed and maintained appropriate playground surfaces? Undoubtedly, they are motivated as a matter of sound public policy to take appropriate action to prevent injury to their students. Beyond that, however, "law," in the form of the threat of legal liability and associated costs, has factored in school decision-making regarding playground injury prevention. Where injury surveillance in school settings has been undertaken systematically, playgrounds have been identified as an important prevention target. Furthermore, insurance loss prevention managers have been partners in those efforts, identifying playgrounds as significant sources of potential legal liability. Therefore, in addition to being identified as injury-prevention targets, playgrounds also are insurance loss prevention targets.[17] The lessons learned through these injury surveillance efforts—in concert with the CPSC handbook, CDC's school health guidelines, and a variety of other resources—have resulted in widespread installation and maintenance of safe surfaces under school playground equipment. In defending against an injured student's claim, a school failing to heed those lessons will have its conduct measured against standards recommended by CPSC and CDC and adopted by many other school districts.

In past decades, the law concerning playground injuries most likely was perceived as the after-the-fact mechanism for providing monetary compensation for injury in the form of damages obtained through a lawsuit, or through a settlement secured under threat of a lawsuit. Whether in the form of direct regulation or as an impetus for risk management, law has evolved to the point of serving as an injury-prevention tool.

Motor Vehicle Safety

Motor vehicle crashes are the leading cause of death among children in the United States. In 2003, 1591 children aged 14 years and younger died as occupants in motor vehicle crashes and approximately 220,000 were injured, representing an average of 4 deaths and approximately 600 injuries each day.[18] Of the fatally injured children, 53% were unrestrained. If those children had been placed in age-appropriate restraints, serious and fatal injuries could have been reduced by more than half.[19] In addition, one-quarter of all occupant deaths among children under age 14 years involved a drinking driver. More than two-thirds of these fatally injured children were riding with the drinking drivers.[20]

Per mile driven, drivers aged 16–19 years are four times more likely than older drivers to crash.[21] In 2002, the estimated economic cost of police-reported crashes (fatal and nonfatal) involving drivers aged 15–20 years was $40.8 billion.[22] In that age group, 24% of drivers who were killed in crashes that year were intoxicated. Furthermore, crash severity increased with alcohol involvement. In 2002, alcohol was detected in 2% of 15- to 20-year-old drivers involved in property-damage-only crashes, in 4% of those involved in crashes resulting in injury, and in 23% of those involved in fatal crashes.[4]

The epidemiologic patterns and characteristics of persons injured from motor vehicle crashes indicate two discrete categories of law-related interventions to prevent these injuries: (1) laws designed to ensure passenger safety through appropriate use of safety equipment and (2) laws that regulate drivers (some generally address the issue of drinking and driving, and others specifically regulate young, inexperienced drivers).

Ensuring Use of Safety Equipment

The Insurance Institute for Highway Safety closely monitors the status of child-restraint and safety-belt laws.[21] All states and the District of Columbia have child-restraint laws. Although these laws generally require younger children to be restrained in "booster seats," they vary widely in terms of method of enforcement, level of maximum fine for violation, and ages and sizes of children to whom they apply. Although 49 states have safety-belt laws, some do not require an older child to wear a safety belt, and, in most states, the law applies only to front-seat occupants. In addition, most states do not permit citation of an automobile occupant for failure to use a safety belt unless the police officer stops the vehicle for another reason. In a few states, damages sought in a lawsuit arising from a motor vehicle crash may be reduced because of the injured person's failure to use a safety belt.

The Insurance Institute rates the laws of each state. It grades each state's safety-belt law as good, fair, marginal, or poor on the basis of such factors as method of enforcement, applicability to rear-seat occupants, and level of maximum penalty. Similarly, child-restraint laws are rated good, marginal, or poor on the basis of method of enforcement and whether restraint is required for all children younger than age 13 years. The institute's advocacy for better child passenger safety laws is consistent with the policies of its many partners, including CDC, NHTSA, the American Academy of Pediatrics, the Transportation Research Board, the National Safety Council, the National Institute for Child Health and Human Development, the National SAFEKIDS Campaign, the AAA Foundation for Traffic Safety, schools of public health, and state and local health departments throughout the country.[4]

Regulating Drivers

All states and the District of Columbia have a minimum drinking age requirement of age 21 years. NHTSA estimates that these requirements have reduced traffic fatalities among drivers aged 18–20 years since 1975 by 13%, or 21,887 lives.[22] Nonetheless, the Insurance Institute denies a number of states a "good" rating because of a requirement in those states that police must suspect a young driver of high blood alcohol content before administering an alcohol test to check for any measurable blood alcohol content.

As with many other injury-prevention laws, adequate enforcement is critical to the effectiveness of drunk-driving laws. For example, sobriety checkpoints, which law enforcement must have the legal authority to conduct, have major impact on rates of driving while intoxicated. Therefore, the feasibility of adequate enforcement is important to consider during crafting of injury-prevention laws.

Graduated driver licensing (GDL) addresses the high risks associated with new youthful drivers.[23] Under GDL, new drivers acquire their initial driving experience under low-risk conditions. Restrictions, including adult supervision, daytime driving, and passenger limits, are imposed on teen drivers and then lifted in stages as teens obtain driving experience. Initially, a learner's permit allows driving only under the supervision of a licensed driver. Upon successfully meeting learner's permit requirements, the new driver may obtain a provisional or intermediate license allowing night driving and teen passengers. Finally, the new driver may graduate to a full driver's license. Florida enacted the first GDL law in 1996; since then, most states have enacted laws adopting GDL in some fashion.[21]

As with other types of motor vehicle–safety laws, the Insurance Institute rates state GDL laws. A "good" rating depends on the age at which a learner's permit can be obtained, the practice-driving and driver-education requirements, restrictions on night driving, and duration of restrictions. Twenty-two states have been granted a good rating.[21]

Youth Violence Prevention

Historically, youth violence has been dealt with by providing medical treatment to the injured person, while apprehending and incarcerating the perpetrator of the violence. For dealing with those who break laws against violence, the criminal or juvenile delinquency laws provide a basis for threatening punishment through the powers of the police to investigate and arrest, through the judiciary to adjudicate and sentence, and through the corrections system to carry out criminal sanctions.[24] The system of law thus plays two key roles in preventing youth violence. First, apprehension and incarceration of the perpetrator may deprive the perpetrator (at least outside the walls of the detention facility) of the opportunity to inflict further injury (i.e., incapacitation). Second, the threat of punishment through incarceration may deter potential perpetrators from future acts of youth violence; however, the deterrent effects of criminal sanctions have been questioned.[25] More importantly, public health experts now recognize that effective injury prevention requires that pre-event factors contributing to youth violence should be addressed by strategies not characterized by the direct law-based focus so evident in preventing motor vehicle–related injury. For example, public health–oriented parenting and family-based programs, school-based programs, mentoring programs, and home-visiting programs may have a legal foundation comprising general grants of authority and funding. Although important, these programs differ fundamentally from directly interventionist laws, such as those mandating GDL, use of child restraints and safety belts, and minimum drinking age.

Likewise, strategies addressing larger social and physical environmental factors and the interrelation between youth violence and other forms of violence (e.g., child maltreatment, intimate partner violence, and bullying) do not readily contemplate the use of classic legal interventions.

Recognizing that traditional methods of addressing violence have not been effective prevention tools, courts and their relevant partners are exploring public health approaches.[b] Problem-solving courts, sometimes referred to conceptually as therapeutic jurisprudence or restorative justice, have been established around the country. Drug-treatment courts, pioneered by Dade County, Florida, in 1989, have the longest history among problem-solving courts. In general, defendants in drug-treatment courts are sentenced to treatment rather than incarceration. The court monitors their treatment progress. Rewards accompany compliance with the treatment regimen, and sanctions are the consequence of noncompliance. Successful completion of a treatment program results in reduction or dismissal of the criminal charge. Domestic violence courts, mental health courts, and community courts (addressing "low-level" misdemeanors that nonetheless affect the community's quality of life) are among the other courts that have been established around the country.[26]

Of direct bearing on youth violence are "youth courts," "teen courts," or "peer courts" established within juvenile justice systems in communities around the country. While holding juveniles accountable for their offenses, these courts also educate youth about the legal system and empower them to be active in their communities. Established by the U.S. Department of Justice's Office of Juvenile Justice and Delinquency Prevention, the National Youth Court Center serves as a central point of contact for youth court programs.[27] Furthermore, federal funds provided through the Department of Justice have played a key role in the development of problem-solving courts. Examples of other partners addressing youth violence are the departments of Health and Human Services, Education, and Transportation; and the American Bar Association.

Legal Issues and Controversies

Legislatures, courts, or quasi-judicial agencies address some legal issues and controversies in injury prevention.

Legislation

Legislative bodies at the federal, state, and local levels make, modify, and repeal laws. Persons or entities subject to injury-prevention laws sometimes complain that the laws unduly interfere with their businesses or professions. Similarly, other injury-prevention laws pit the common good against the "rights" of the individual. Therefore, the injury-prevention practitioner or researcher needs to demonstrate the cost to the common good that particular injuries exact.

At the most basic level, of course, injury-prevention practitioners and researchers can demonstrate the cost of injury to the common good only if they are authorized to collect data and conduct research. Key to the public health approach to preventing injuries is an accurate assessment of the injury burden and risk factors for injury. To do this, public health practitioners conduct public health surveillance for injuries. Statutory authority for most disease reporting and surveillance resides at the state level. In many states, the laws conferring authority for surveillance were written primarily to monitor infectious diseases, the primary area of activity for health departments at the time those laws were written. For example, an Oregon statute (ORS 431.110 [a–c]) provides that the state health department shall "(a) Have direct supervision of all matters relating to the preservation of life and health of the people of the state, (b) Keep the vital statistics and other health related statistics of the state, and (c) Make . . . investigations and inquiries respecting the causes and prevention of diseases, especially epidemics." Injuries are not specifically mentioned. However, an Oregon Administrative Rule (333-019-0005) based on the statute provides for the health department to conduct "special studies," which are broadly defined as ". . . any collection of information about the health status of individuals or groups of individuals. . . ."

Although the laws of Oregon and some other states do not expressly authorize injury surveillance, public health agencies in some states possess clear authority to do so. The Wisconsin Statutes, for example, authorize the Wisconsin Department of Health and Family Services to "maintain an injury prevention program that includes data collection, surveillance, education and the promotion of intervention," and to "assist local health departments and community agencies by serving as a focal point for injury prevention expertise and guidance and by providing the leadership for effective local program development and evaluation" (§§255.20[1] and [2]).

The legislative process necessarily involves "give and take" over public policy issues inherent in the making of laws. The history of motorcycle helmet laws illustrates this point. No motorcycle helmet laws existed in this country before 1966. In that year, Congress passed the Highway Safety Act, including a provision conditioning full receipt of federal highway funding on state enactment of laws mandating helmet use by all motorcycle riders. By 1975, only 3 states had failed to adopt a "universal" helmet law. Even during these early years, however, the controversial nature of these laws was evidenced in a few states by a cycle of enactment, amendment, repeal, and reenactment.

In response to the secretary of transportation's plan to withhold federal funds from the 3 noncompliant states, Congress repealed the helmet law requirement and prohibited the threatened withholding of funds.[28] In rapid succession, states repealed their universal laws or amended them to cover only motorcyclists under a specified age. By 1980, only 19 states and the District of Columbia mandated use by all riders. For almost a decade thereafter, little legislative activity concerned helmet use laws.

As of the mid-1990s, 25 states had universal laws, and 22 had laws applying only to young riders. Then, however, Congress repealed a provision enacted in the early 1990s requiring transfer of highway construction funds to highway safety programs in states without helmet laws. As a consequence, Arkansas, Florida, Kentucky, Louisiana, and Texas repealed their laws. By 2005, 21 states had universal laws, and 26 others had laws applying to only some riders.[29]

The benefits of mandatory helmet use in preventing injury and death have been demonstrated conclusively and repeatedly. The then–General Accounting Office reported to Congress in 1991 that numerous studies showed helmet use ranged from

92% to 100% in universal law jurisdictions.[29] Related studies also showed that fatality rates generally were 20%–40% lower in universal law states.[30] A recent evaluation of the repeal of helmet use laws in Kentucky and Louisiana, with findings similar to those made in a study of helmet use law repeal in Arkansas and Texas, concluded that the "weight of the evidence is that helmets reduce injury severity, that repeal of helmet laws decreases helmet use, and that states that repeal universal helmet laws experience increased motorcyclist fatalities and injuries."[28]

Despite overwhelming evidence of the public health benefits of helmet laws, Congress and most state legislatures have chosen not to adopt them. The basis for reluctance to mandate helmet use may reflect, in part, legislative sensitivity to the freedom of their constituents' life choices. This freedom of choice is not based on any legal right; courts generally have upheld the constitutionality of helmet laws. A federal court decision in Massachusetts included the following rationale for rejecting a plaintiff's challenge to a state law requiring motorcycle helmet use:

> From the moment of injury society picks the person up off the highway; delivers him to a municipal hospital and municipal doctors; provides him with unemployment compensation, if after recovery he cannot replace his lost job, and if the injury causes permanent disability, may assume the responsibility for his and his family's continued subsistence. We do not understand the state of mind that permits the plaintiff to think that only he himself is concerned.[31]

Although not based in law, freedom of choice is one of the philosophic values underlying the U.S. system of government. Economic considerations also often play an important role in legislative decision-making. In addition to demonstrating the effectiveness of injury-prevention laws, therefore, public health practitioners must be sensitive to the law's economic effects, must be prepared to make the case that the benefits in terms of injury prevention outweigh any infringements on individual freedoms, and generally must be attuned to all the considerations at play in the lawmaking process.

The Courts

Courts generally do not scrutinize an injury-prevention law to determine the legislature's underlying policy motives or evidentiary bases for enacting the law, and courts grant broad deference to state legislatures when exercising the police power to protect the public's health. Likewise, deference is accorded to Congress in the exercise of its powers to tax and spend and to regulate interstate commerce, particularly when the powers are used to protect public health.

Of course, laws must pass constitutional muster. Courts generally have upheld injury-prevention laws, challenged on the grounds that they deprive affected individuals of their constitutional rights, as reasonable exercises of the government's police powers to protect the public.[32] Thus, laws that control the conduct of an individual to protect another person, such as speeding laws or laws proscribing assaultive behavior, readily are recognized as valid. Laws that govern a person's conduct for the principal benefit of that same person's safety have undergone different scrutiny. Some of these laws have been upheld because the person being protected is a member of a vulnerable class, such as children, for which the government has assumed a paternalistic role. Other laws have been upheld on the basis that, although the law protects the individual whose own behavior is being governed, it also protects the financial well-being of society.[c]

In addition to direct challenges to laws, legal controversies can arise within the context of challenges to government agencies' alleged failure to act in accordance with legal authority or to establish the factual basis for action. Despite the injury-prevention benefits of soft surfaces under playground equipment, for example, a daycare regulator must have statutory or regulatory authority to require installation of soft surfaces or to penalize a facility for failure to install and maintain them. Disputes may arise over interpretation of statutory or regulatory language ostensibly granting such authority. A nursing home regulator seeking to act against a care facility for failure to properly handle or transfer a resident must produce evidence of improper handling or transport. The evidence produced by the regulator may conflict with that produced by the nursing facility. These types of "day-to-day" legal controversies generally are resolved before administrative law judges or hearing examiners, with an ultimate right to judicial review, if a party is unsatisfied with the quasi-judicial decision.

Finally, injured parties or injury-prevention advocates may turn directly to the courts for redress. Injured parties may seek compensation for their injuries through tort litigation. In addition, injury-prevention advocates occasionally have sought court resolution with regard to behavior or products believed by them to pose a high risk for injury despite the existence of laws and regulations. For example, in 1968, a successful lawsuit brought against General Motors[9] for failure to mitigate injuries to a motorist by designing a "crashworthy" car established the responsibility of manufacturers to foresee the human damage that could occur with the use of their products and to reasonably prevent that damage. Both before and since then, lawsuits have been brought against other makers of injurious products. These lawsuits have had particular significance when, because of political influence, the safety of the product has failed to come under legislative or regulatory control. For example, litigation against car makers for failure to provide air bags in their vehicles helped make this lifesaving device available.[33]

Preemption is a legal issue that can arise in tort litigation. Generally, if the federal government has fully covered an issue by federal legislation or regulation or if Congress has declared that states should not pass laws on a particular subject on which Congress has acted, then the states are barred from legislating in this area. States have somewhat similar preemption authority with regard to their relationship with local governments. Federal preemption of state laws is exemplified by a U.S. Supreme Court ruling that, because federal motor vehicle–safety standards governed motor vehicle occupant safety, a state court could not impose liability on a car manufacturer for failure to provide an air bag, in that such a ruling would be tantamount to a state's regulation of an area preempted by the federal government.[34]

Practice Considerations

One barrier that traditionally has confronted injury-prevention practitioners is the fatalistic notion that injuries cannot be prevented. Even language contributes to this perception—for example, use of the term "accidents" in reference to unintentional injuries inadvertently may reinforce the belief that injuries are random, unpredictable, and hence unavoidable.[11,12] Another factor contributing to these fatalistic perceptions is the notion that unintentional injuries result largely from individual carelessness and therefore are not a societal responsibility amenable to population-based interventions. Similarly, violence-prevention efforts sometimes are confronted by the belief that violence is an inevitable consequence of the human condition. These views have receded as the science of injury prevention has advanced and as the success of interventions and public policies in preventing injury have become increasingly apparent. Nevertheless, injury practitioners dealing with legal policies and interventions must be able to demonstrate that injuries can be understood and prevented using the law.

Injury Surveillance and Data Sources

Injury-prevention practitioners also may be faced at times with the need to better understand the risk and protective factors that contribute to injury and violence. Although better information is needed about these factors to improve the design of effective legal interventions and policies, understanding about the etiology of many different types of injury is substantial. For example, the surgeon general's report on youth violence provides an excellent summary of knowledge about the etiology of this problem.[35] At the same time, however, perfect understandings of the etiology of injuries and violent behavior are not absolute prerequisites for injury prevention. John Snow, for example, did not precisely understand the cause of cholera when his discoveries impelled removal of the Broad Street pump handle in 1854 in London to help abate the cholera epidemic.[36] Similarly, injury-prevention practitioners do not need to completely understand injuries to take action after identifying a factor in the causal chain leading to injury that may be amenable to intervention.

To improve understanding of the causal factors for injuries, practitioners must of course have the legal authority to collect, study, and evaluate relevant data. To the extent that necessary injury surveillance authority is lacking, practitioners should make every reasonable effort to secure it. Furthermore, the economic costs and other considerations associated with injury prevention and relevant laws are issues that practitioners must be prepared to address.

The quality of collected data is of course an important consideration. Much of injury surveillance relies on mining administrative data sets related to clinical encounters, such as hospital discharge databases or emergency department logs. These data sets are part of the core information sources recommended for state-level injury surveillance.[37] The most widely used coding system for these data is the International Classification of Diseases (ICD-9-CM), currently in its ninth revision for morbidity data. In ICD-9-CM, two kinds of codes are of particular interest for injury surveillance: N-codes, which specify the nature of injury (e.g., a femur fracture); and E-codes, also known as external cause-of-injury codes, which specify the cause of the injury (e.g., a car crash or a gunshot). Because injury prevention focuses on the causes of injuries, E-codes are particularly critical for useful injury surveillance.

As of 2004, 45 states maintained hospital discharge databases.[38] The creation of these data sets generally is authorized by statute. In 26 of these 45 states, the state health department does not maintain this data set, and the location often is mandated in the authorizing statute. When data sets are maintained elsewhere, access may be difficult for injury-prevention programs in the health department. For example, in Oregon, the health department had successfully negotiated an agreement with the state's hospital association to provide access to these data. However, because this data set does not include patient identifiers, epidemiologists cannot ensure that patients admitted to the hospital multiple times because of an injury are counted only once, thereby jeopardizing an accurate count. Additional restrictions on sharing of the data and dissemination of the results also are a part of the agreement, further constraining the health department's ability to fully use these data.

The completeness of E-coding presents another problematic aspect of these databases. As of 2004, only 8 of the 45 states with hospital discharge databases had E-coded more than 90% of the injury records in that database. Reasons for this include the limited incentive hospitals may have to provide an E-code because this code is not tied to reimbursement, the lack of detail in the medical record that allows a clerk to assign an E-code, and the lack of an E-code field in the database that otherwise enables a hospital to include an E-code.

Some states have attempted to address the incompleteness of E-coding by mandating it by law. As of 2004, 26 of the 45 states with a hospital discharge database have mandated inclusion of E-codes by law.[38] Some states with very good E-coding rates do not have a legal mandate requiring E-codes. In general, however, states with a legal mandate have a higher percentage of injury records E-coded than do states without a mandate. Thus, although a law requiring E-coding is not the only solution to this problem, such a law can be a useful tool.

The situation for emergency department data is worse than that for hospital data, even though this source is critical for injury surveillance, because many injuries never require hospitalization and therefore could not be counted using hospital discharge data. By 2004, only 25 states had statewide emergency department data systems; 15 of these have mandated E-coding.

Partnerships in Injury Prevention

As in other areas of public health, injury prevention requires partnerships with many agencies and organizations outside of the traditional public health field. Some of the examples described in this chapter underscore the need for interaction with the education system, law enforcement, hospitals, and the court system. Often, public health is the convener or facilitator of this interdisciplinary interaction. Sometimes public health can provide important technical assistance to partners about injury risks and the effectiveness of injury-prevention approaches. One commentator has suggested that the "growing significance" of the injury-prevention field "stems in part from the fact that it merges complementary perspectives from medicine, public health, engineering, and criminal justice. . . ."[39] From the legal perspective, how the authorities of these different sectors interact can require considerable interdisciplinary legal knowledge.

The child fatality review process illustrates some of the legal complications of partnerships. In most states, a legally mandated process exists for interdisciplinary review of children's deaths. In Oregon, this process occurs at the county level, and a statewide team also reviews the data from the county teams. These teams include public health, child protection, the medical examiner, law enforcement, medical-care providers, district attorneys, and any others with information or expertise that might assist in clarifying how a child died from other than natural causes. The goal of these teams is to review children's deaths with an eye to prevention. The focus is on systems change, rather than individual blame.

Each partner on the child fatality review team may be subject to a different set of legal constraints on the ability to share information. For example, whereas court records may be public, criminal investigation information may not be while an investigation is under way. The authorizing legislation for the child fatality review process may explicitly authorize disclosure for this process but also may restrict how the information might be shared beyond the review team.

Emerging Issues

Evaluation of Laws

Injury-prevention laws are a product of the give-and-take of the legislative process. Those laws and accompanying regulations often are proposed, and sometimes adopted, on the basis of a common-sense notion that they will accomplish their intended purpose. To an extent, common sense is a legitimate foundation. For example, one need not perform extensive analysis to reasonably conclude that a child's risk for injury from a fall from playground equipment would be reduced if the playground surface consisted of loose sand rather than concrete or asphalt. However, determination of the relative benefits to injury prevention of loose sand compared with shredded tires would require careful expert evaluation. CPSC has analyzed the injury-prevention benefits of various surfaces for decades, and the findings have been incorporated into state daycare regulations. Those who make, implement, and enforce those regulations and related laws must remain closely attuned as CPSC periodically revises the playground safety standards to reflect lessons learned through continuous injury surveillance.

Development of mechanisms to evaluate the effectiveness of injury-prevention interventions and strategies (including law) is emerging as a formal and important characteristic of injury-prevention analysis. The public health approach employed by CDC and many other agencies has been adapted to injury prevention: (1) define the injury problem; (2) identify risk and protective factors; (3) develop and test prevention interventions and strategies, and (4) ensure widespread adoption of effective interventions and strategies. Within this context, opportunities for intervention arise temporally at the pre-event, event, and post-event phases. Other opportunities may exist with regard to individual behaviors, injury agents, physical environments, and socioeconomic environments. The injury-prevention approach to identifying effective interventions has been favorably compared with the approaches of other risk-management disciplines; in fact, this approach may present lessons for other disciplines.[39]

Motivated by a desire to prevent injuries, practitioners might be tempted to leap to the conclusion that "there oughta be a law" to accomplish the objective. Law, however, is not always an effective intervention. Incremental changes to make penalties for violent behavior tougher, for example, may accomplish other legislative objectives, but whether grafting tougher penalties onto the existing body of law adds to the preventive or deterrent effect of these laws is not clear. For example, although it is unclear whether the threat of transfer to adult court generally deters juveniles from violent crime, evidence indicates that violent crime increases among juveniles actually transferred to adult court.[25]

The Task Force on Community Preventive Services is addressing whether particular laws effectively prevent injuries. Although convened and appointed by the Department of Health and Human Services, the task force is an independent decision-making body. It conducts systematic reviews of published studies concerning public health issues for the purpose of identifying and reporting on evidence of effectiveness.

The task force has reviewed a variety of interventions aimed at preventing injuries to children and young adults.[40] Examples of its findings are the strong evidence demonstrating the effectiveness of child-safety-seat laws, lower blood alcohol concentration laws, minimum drinking age laws, and sobriety checkpoints; the strong evidence that therapeutic foster care is a behavioral intervention effective in reducing youth violence, and the strong evidence supporting the effectiveness of the health and education system intervention of early childhood home visitation at reducing child maltreatment. In contrast, the task force found insufficient evidence of the effectiveness of eight different types of firearms laws.[d] All task force recommendations are published in the *Guide to Community Preventive Services*.[40]

Tort Reform

Liability for injuries imposed by U.S. systems of tort law can move people, institutions, or other legal entities into compliance with accepted standards and diligence that prevent injuries.[41] Manufacturers, for example, may modify products to prevent injuries because of tort liability. Whereas actual lawsuits may stipulate specific actions, even the threat of potential liability can be a powerful motivator. Within constitutional limits, however, Congress and state legislatures have the legal authority to modify the parameters of tort and other types of litigation. Legal, philosophic, and economic issues are the grist of heated debates over "tort reform" at both federal and state levels of government. The effect of changes to the tort system on the ability of injured persons to be compensated for their injuries, and on injury-prevention efforts generally, will be the subject of close scrutiny and careful study in coming years.

International Trade Agreements

Some public health and safety advocates believe that the World Trade Organization and the negotiation of international trade agreements threaten effective injury prevention. They believe these agreements have the potential to negate federal, state, and local public health laws, including those concerning injury prevention. One such agreement is the North American Free Trade Agreement (NAFTA). A ruling by a NAFTA panel in 2001, which expanded access to U.S. highways for Mexican trucks, generated substantial controversy among the advocates and ultimately spurred the filing of litigation alleging that U.S. truck-safety laws and environmental laws were being circumvented. Although truck-safety concerns appear to have been addressed in part through Congressional intervention, the controversy found its way to the U.S. Supreme Court, which ruled against the plaintiff advocates in a 2004 decision.[42] The concerns of the advocates obviously remain.[43]

Analysis by legal commentators suggests the potential for adequate protection of public health as future trade agreements are negotiated. At the same time, other commentators emphasize the necessity for public health advocates to be vigilant with regard to international trade developments and assertive in protecting public health as those developments unfold.[44,45]

Conclusion

Dr. Peter Barss and colleagues provide an excellent summary description of the challenges facing injury-prevention practitioners in developing effective legal interventions:

> Many effective interventions for the control of injuries, be they directed towards modification of environmental, equipment, or personal factors, ultimately derive from legislation and regulation. Sectors other than health often have greater authority to develop the legislation and regulations needed to prevent injuries. The expertise of professionals from multiple disciplines must be integrated to develop the most effective and efficient solutions for specific injury problems. For certain types of injuries, such as traffic injuries, drownings, or sports injuries, departments or organizations other than those involved with public health may be more efficient in coordinating prevention activities by multiple organizations. Public health epidemiologists can provide technical assistance to such groups in the development of surveillance and research.
>
> Politicians often have the ultimate say in whether funds are allocated to study and prevent injuries, and they develop and approve legislation. Politicians tend to be driven more by economic pressures than by those issues of human health and suffering that motivate health professionals. (p. 279)[7]

Extensive public debate often surrounds consideration by politicians of the factors affecting passage of new laws, and the debate frequently receives extensive media coverage. Experience with tobacco prevention, for example, supports the notion that these public debates in and of themselves, almost regardless of whether the law ultimately is enacted, can play an important role over time in changing social norms. Given that social norms—such as attitudes about speeding on the freeway or appropriate drinking behavior—are important causal factors for injuries, this use of the legal system can contribute to injury prevention. As public health practitioners work to obtain necessary injury surveillance authority and to identify effective interventions, forge necessary partnerships, and work with partners to address the economic and other issues of concern to lawmakers, they will find that law remains one of their most effective tools in reducing the incidence and severity of injuries in the United States.

We are grateful to, and acknowledge the contributions of, Stephen P. Teret and Tom Christoffel, the authors of the injury chapter in the first edition.

Notes

a. A resource available to regulators is *Caring for Our Children, National Health and Safety Performance Standards: Guidelines for Out-of-Home Child Care Programs*, 2nd edition (2002), by the American Public Health Association, the American Academy of Pediatrics, and the Health Resources and Services Administration, U.S. Department of Health and Human Services. The guidelines recommend compliance with CPSC playground standards; they are available at http://nrc.uchsc.edu/CFOC/index.html.

b. Retired Circuit Court Judge Gerald Nichol (Dane County, Wisconsin) suggested judicial consideration of a public health approach: "Violence in our society is really a public health issue. If we addressed it like we did smoking or car seats or safety belts, we might be able to make a difference" (*Wisconsin State Journal*, January 16, 2005, §A, p. 4).

c. Examples include *Simon v. Sargent* (see U.S. General Accounting Office. *Highway Safety: Motorcycle Helmet Laws Save Lives and Reduce Costs to Society (July 1991)* (GAO/RCED-91–170). Washington, D.C.: U.S. General Accounting Office, 1991); *State v. Hartog*, 440 N.W.2d 852 (Iowa 1989), cert. denied, 493 U.S. 1005 (1989), rehearing denied, 493 U.S. 1095 (1990) (safety belt law); *Queenside Hills Realty Co., Inc. v. Saxl, Commissioner of Housing and Buildings of the City of New York*, 328 U.S. 80 (1946) (law mandating sprinkler systems); *Department of State Police v. Sitz*, 496 U.S. 444 (1990); and *United States of America v. One Hazardous Product Consisting of a Refuse Bin*, 487 F. Supp. 581 (1980) (regulation governing refuse bin design).

d. The Task Force carefully points out that a finding of "insufficient evidence" does not mean a law does not work. Rather, the finding means more research is needed before an effectiveness conclusion can be drawn.

References

1. Finkelstein E, Corso P, Miller T. *The Incidence and Economic Burden of Injuries in the United States, 2000*. New York: Oxford University Press, 2006.
2. Centers for Disease Control and Prevention (CDC). Welcome to WISQARS. Available at http://www.cdc.gov/ncipc/wisqars. Accessed November 30, 2005.
3. National Center for Injury Prevention and Control. CDC. *Acute Injury Care Research Agenda: Guiding Research for the Future*. Atlanta: U.S. Department of Health and Human Services, CDC, 2005:37. Available at http://www.cdc.gov/ncipc/didop/ACRAgenda .pdf. Accessed November 30, 2005.
4. National Center for Injury Prevention and Control, CDC. CDC Injury Research Agenda. Available at www.cdc.gov/ncipc/pub-res/research_agenda/agenda.htm. Accessed December 6, 2005.
5. CDC. Ten great public health achievements—United States, 1900–1999. *MMWR* 1999;48: 241–3. Available at http://www.cdc.gov/mmwr/PDF/wk/mm4812.pdf. Accessed November 30, 2005.

6. Dellinger AM, Sleet DA, Jones BH. Drivers, wheels, and roads: motor vehicle safety in the 20th Century. In: Ward J, Warren C, eds. *Silent Victories: Public Health Triumphs of the 20th Century*. New York: Oxford University Press (in press).

7. Barss P, Smith G, Baker S, Mohan D. Introduction: the importance of injuries. In: *Injury Prevention: An International Perspective* [Epidemiology, Surveillance, and Policy]. New York: Oxford University Press, 1998:1–11.

8. Haddon W Jr. Energy damage and the ten countermeasure strategies. *J Trauma* 1973;13: 321–31.

9. Christoffel T, Teret SP. State police power: the authority to enact injury prevention laws. In: *Protecting the Public: Legal Issues in Injury Prevention*. New York: Oxford University Press, 1993:25–52.

10. Christoffel T, Gallagher SS. *Injury Prevention and Public Health: Practical Knowledge, Skills, and Strategies*. Gaithersburg, MD: Aspen Publishers, 1999:183–4.

11. 42 CFR 483.

12. Wis Admin Code Ch HFS 132.

13. Consumer Product Safety Commission (CPSC). *Public Playground Safety Checklist* (CPSC Document #327). Available at http://www.cpsc.gov/cpscpub/pubs/327.html. Accessed December 6, 2005.

14. CPSC. *Handbook for Public Playground Safety* (CPSC Document #325). Available at http://www.cpsc.gov/cpscpub/pubs/325.pdf. Accessed December 6, 2005.

15. National Resource Center for Health and Safety in Child Care. Individual States' Child Care Licensure Regulations. Available at http://nrc.uchsc.edu/STATES/states.htm. Accessed December 6, 2005.

16. CDC. School health guidelines to prevent unintentional injuries and violence. *MMWR* 2001;50(RR22). Available at http://www.cdc.gov/mmwr/PDF/rr/rr5022.pdf. Accessed December 6, 2005.

17. Spicer RS, Young XJ, Sheppard MA, Olson LM, Miller TR. Preventing unintentional injuries in schools: how to use data to build partnerships and develop programs, *Am J Health Edu* 2003;34(Supp):S13–7.

18. National Center for Injury Prevention and Control, CDC. Child Passenger Safety. National Child Passenger Safety Week, February 13–19, 2005. Available at http://www.cdc.gov/ncipc/duip/spotlite/chldseat.htm. Accessed December 6, 2005.

19. National Highway Traffic Safety Administration (NHTSA). *Traffic Safety Facts. 2003 Data: Children*. Available at http://www-nrd.nhtsa.dot.gov/pdf/nrd-30/NCSA/TSF2003/809762.pdf. Accessed December 6, 2005.

20. CDC. Child passenger deaths involving drinking drivers—United States, 1997–2002. *MMWR* 2004;53:77–9 [erratum: *MMWR* 2004;53:109]. Available at http://www.cdc.gov/MMWR/preview/mmwrhtml/mm5304a2.htm [erratum at http://www.cdc.gov/MMWR/preview/mmwrhtml/mm5305a7.htm]. Accessed December 6, 2005.

21. Insurance Institute for Highway Safety. Available at www.iihs.org. Accessed December 6, 2005.

22. National Center for Statistics and Analysis, NHTSA. *Traffic Safety Facts, 2002. Young Drivers*. Available at http://www-nrd.nhtsa.dot.gov/pdf/nrd-30/NCSA/TSF2002/2002ydrfacts.pdf. Accessed December 6, 2005.

23. National Center for Injury Prevention and Control, CDC. Graduated Driver Licensing. Available at http://www.cdc.gov/ncipc/duip/spotlite/GradDrvLic.htm. Accessed December 6, 2005.

24. Nagin DS. Criminal deterrence research at the outset of the twenty-first century. In: Morris N, Tonry M, eds. *Crime and Justice: A Review of Research*. Vol 23. Chicago: University of Chicago Press, 1998:1–42.

25. McGowan A, Hahn R, Liberman A, et al. Effects of laws and policies facilitating the transfer of juveniles from the juvenile justice system to the adult justice system on violence: a systematic review. Presented at the February 27, 2003, meeting of the Task Force on Community Preventive Services, Atlanta, GA.

26. US Department of Justice, Office of Justice Programs. Problem-Solving Courts. Available at www.ojp.usdoj.gov/courts/problem_solving.htm. Accessed January 3, 2006.

27. Office of Juvenile, US Department of Justice. *Office of Juvenile Justice Delinquency Prevention Fact Sheet*. Available at http://www.ncjrs.org/pdffiles1/ojjdp/fs200007.pdf. Accessed December 6, 2005.

28. Ulmer RG, Preusser DF, NHTSA. Evaluation of Repeal of Motorcycle Helmet Laws in Kentucky and Louisiana. October 2002. Available at http://www.nhtsa.dot.gov/people/injury/pedbimot/motorcycle/kentuky-la03/TechSumm.html. Accessed December 6, 2005.

29. Insurance Institute for Highway Safety. *How State Laws Measure Up (June 2005)*. Available at http://www.iihs.org/laws/state_laws/measure_up.html. Accessed December 6, 2005.

30. US General Accounting Office. *Highway Safety: Motorcycle Helmet Laws Save Lives and Reduce Costs to Society (July 1991)* (GAO/RCED-91–170). Washington, DC: US General Accounting Office, 1991.

31. *Simon v Sargent*, 346 F Supp 277, 279 (D Mass.); aff'd, 409 US 1020 (1972).

32. *Larsen v General Motors Corporation*, 391 F 2d 495 (8th Cir 1968).

33. Teret SP. Litigating for the public's health. *Am J Public Health* 1986;76:1027–9.

34. *Geier v American Honda Motor Co*, 529 US 861 (2000).

35. US Department of Health and Human Services. *Youth Violence: A Report of the Surgeon General*. Rockville, MD: U.S. Department of Health and Human Services, CDC, National Center for Injury Prevention and Control; Substance Abuse and Mental Health Services Administration, Center for Mental Health Services; and National Institutes of Health, National Institute of Mental Health, 2001.

36. Smith GD. Commentary: Behind the Broad Street pump: aetiology, epidemiology and prevention of cholera in mid-19th century Britain. *Int J Epidemiol* 2002;31:920–32.

37. State and Territorial Injury Prevention Directors Association. *How Partnerships and Collaborations Can Generate Innovative Solutions*. Available at http://www.stipda.org/documents/Cufaude_1023a.pdf#search='stipda%20green%20book'. Accessed December 6, 2005.

38. Council of State and Territorial Epidemiologists, American Public Health Association, State and Territorial Injury Prevention Directors Association. *How States Are Collecting and Using Cause of Injury Data: 2004 Update to the 1997 Report. A Survey on State-Based Injury Surveillance, External Cause of Injury Coding Practices, and Coding Guidelines in the 50 States, the District of Columbia, and Puerto Rico*. Atlanta: Council of State and Territorial Epidemiologists, 2005. Available at http://www.cste.org/pdffiles/newpdffiles/ECodeFinal3705.pdf. Accessed December 6, 2005.

39. Sparrow MK. *The Regulatory Craft: Controlling Risks, Solving Problems, and Managing Compliance*. Washington, DC: Brookings Institution Press, 2000:185–6.

40. Task Force on Community Preventive Services, Zaza S, Briss PA, Harris KW, eds. *Guide to Community Preventive Services: What Works to Promote Health?* New York: Oxford University Press, 2005. Available at http://www.thecommunityguide.org. Accessed December 6, 2005.

41. Vernick JS, Sapsin JW, Teret SP, Mair JS. How litigation can promote product safety. *J Law Med Ethics* 2004;32:551–5.

42. *Department of Transportation et al v Public Citizen et al*, 541 US 752 (2004), 316 F 3d 1002, reversed and remanded.

43. Public Citizen. Mexico-Domiciled Trucks and NAFTA. Press releases dated June 7, 2004, and August 13, 2004. Available at www.citizen.org/autosafety/Truck_Safety/mex_trucks. Accessed December 6, 2005.

44. Bloche MG, Jungman ER. Health policy and the WTO. *J Law Med Ethics* 2003;31:529–45.

45. Sapsin JW, Thompson TM, Stone L, DeLand KE. International trade, law, and public health advocacy. *J Law Med Ethics* 2003;31:546–56.

Chapter 22

OCCUPATIONAL SAFETY AND HEALTH LAW

Gary Rischitelli and Michael A. Silverstein

This chapter focuses primarily on the statutory and administrative legal systems that regulate occupational safety and health in the United States. Important judicial interpretations of the law governing occupational safety and health will also be reviewed briefly. The practice of occupational health and the unique aspects of workers' compensation systems will not be discussed, except as they relate to the legal structure protecting worker health and safety.

Background

History

The impact of occupational and environmental exposures on the health of individuals and communities has been recognized since antiquity. Hippocrates (4th century B.C.), a physician of ancient Greece now revered as the "father of medicine," recognized the impact of occupation and the environment on the health of individuals and communities. One of his treatises, "On Airs, Waters, and Places," described the relation between disease and location, climate, water, food, housing and work.[1]

Occupational risks associated with specific jobs or industrial processes also were recognized and catalogued as medical knowledge was refined and recorded. Agricola (1494–1555) observed the breathlessness and early mortality among miners in Carpathia in his book *De Re Metallica*. He also recognized the social and economic impact of occupational illness and injury, describing women who had married seven times because of the premature demise of their husbands who worked in the mines.[2]

Occupational medicine began to evolve as a medical specialty as well as an essential component of primary medical care. Bernardino Ramazzini (1633–1714), the father of modern occupational medicine, published *De Morbis Artificum Diatriba* in 1714; this was the first comprehensive textbook of disease and occupation. He introduced the concept of the occupational history as part of the medical evaluation of all persons, exhorting his students and colleagues to ask patients, "What is your occupation?"

The growing concern and occasional public outrage over the working conditions of the Industrial Revolution stimulated governments to begin to establish laws regarding worker health and safety. In Britain, Sir Thomas Legge was appointed the first medical inspector of factories in 1898, a position he used effectively to improve working conditions. In response to the known hazards of the early industrial economy, these early attempts at protecting working men and women and regulating child labor focused primarily on traumatic injuries, with far less emphasis on exposure-related diseases. This emphasis on occupational injury remains to some degree even in the occupational safety and workers' compensation laws of today.

Similarly, on the other side of the Atlantic Ocean, Dr. Alice Hamilton, the first female faculty member at Harvard Medical School, championed American workers' health and safety. Her autobiographic text, *Exploring the Dangerous Trades*, first was published in 1925 and remains a classic in occupational health literature.[3] Hamilton drew public and scientific attention to the burden of illness and injury among American workers in the dawn of the 20th century.

Initial attempts at regulating workplace safety in the United States occurred at the state level. Massachusetts passed the first law governing worker safety in 1877. By 1900, most other heavily industrialized states had passed some type of worker safety law covering at least some specific workplace hazards. These early attempts at regulation typically lacked sufficient resources for effective enforcement, and the increasing mechanization and pace of work only increased the danger of the industrial workplace.[4]

Early federal involvement in worker safety focused on workers in highly dangerous occupations or with a clear connection to interstate commerce, such as merchant seamen, railroad workers, and miners. The federal Office of Industrial Hygiene and Sanitation was established in the Public Health Service that, along with the U.S. Bureau of Labor Standards created as part of the New Deal government in 1934, studied several recognized occupational hazards.

Passage of the Walsh-Healy Public Contracts Act in 1936 marked the beginning of a more active involvement of the federal government in regulating workplace safety. The Act required the Department of Labor to ensure that federal contractors met minimum health and safety standards.

Like many legislative interventions, federal preemption of occupational health and safety regulation followed public outrage after a tragic disaster. Although 14,000 workers were killed and over 2 million were injured annually during the late 1960s, a widely publicized fatal mine explosion in West Virginia ultimately spurred passage of the Federal Coal Mine Health and Safety Act of 1969.[5] This was the forerunner of a more general occupational health and safety act one year later.

Although President Lyndon Johnson had proposed a comprehensive occupational health and safety program to Congress in 1968, the bill never reached the House or Senate floor. President Nixon continued the effort, and after considerable conflict and compromise, the Occupational Safety and Health Act of 1970 (OSHAct) was passed by the 91st Congress and signed into law on December 29, 1970.

Now, at the start of the 21st century, the world is experiencing an explosion of rapidly evolving technologies. Workers face a vast array of chemical, physical, and biologic exposures, the health implications of which are poorly understood. In addition, many of the occupational diseases of antiquity, such as silicosis and lead poisoning, persist. Protecting the health of workers and their communities remains a public health priority.

Dimensions of the Problem

Although accurate estimates of the burden of occupational injury and disease in the United States are difficult to obtain, the Bureau of Labor Statistics (BLS) recorded 5524 fatal injuries, 4.4 million nonfatal injuries, and 294,500 new nonfatal occupational illnesses in 2002.[6] Although an estimated 55,000 people die annually from work-related illnesses, the actual attributable fraction is more difficult to obtain because diseases often are multifactorial, and long latencies can mask the association with occupational exposures. Consequently, an estimated 50% of occupational illnesses are undiagnosed because workers and their physicians fail to recognize their relation with work. Most physicians in the United States receive limited or no training in occupational health and usually fail to ask about occupational and environmental exposures during the medical history. Even physicians trained in occupational medicine often have difficulty assessing the possible contribution of occupation and environment to disease. Difficulty abounds because over 70,000 chemicals are in use, of which only about 10,000–12,000 have undergone even basic toxicity assessments.

The National Institute for Occupational Safety and Health (NIOSH) has identified the top ten contemporary occupational illnesses,[7] and has established the National Occupational Research Agenda (NORA) to prioritize research and prevention.[8] NIOSH estimates that 1.2 million American workers are exposed to silica, resulting in 250 deaths each year from silicosis, and 1200 workers die each year from asbestosis.[9] Unfortunately, today's workers appear to face the risk for the occupational diseases of both the future and the past.

Occupational injuries represent a much larger and more visible burden on the nation's health and productivity. Approximately 5.7 million work-related injuries leading to 3.6 million hospital emergency visits occurred in 1997. These injuries include strains and sprains (799,000), back injuries (472,000), bruises and contusions (166,000), lacerations (134,000), fractures (119,000), burns (30,000), amputations (10,850), and deaths (5915 [in 2000]). Total direct and indirect costs are estimated at $125–$158 billion per year.[6,10] The frequency and cost of these injuries is a significant drain on the national economy in addition to the tragic burden on workers and their families.

Variety of Responsibilities at Local, State, and Federal Levels

Occupational health has become an increasingly specialized area and has lost many of its traditional connections with public health agencies and practitioners. Many of the early occupational health practitioners were sanitarians, some of whom became the founders of modern industrial hygiene. Today, many industrial hygienists, occupational health nurses, and occupational physicians continue to be trained in schools of public health but usually pursue a specialized curriculum. This focuses on the recognition, evaluation, control, and treatment of health hazards in industry and the environment. Occupational health and safety practitioners also may come from other disciplines, such as engineering, environmental science, chemistry, physics, and psychology.

Prevention activities such as education, consultation, and regulatory enforcement have been delegated largely to separate occupational safety and health agencies at federal, state, and local levels distinct from the traditional public health authorities. This has further widened the professional gulf between occupational safety and health personnel and their public health colleagues.

Legal Authorities

Federal authority over safety and health issues in the workplace largely arises from the "commerce clause" of the U.S. Constitution, which grants Congress power "to regulate commerce . . . among the States."[11] The commerce clause has been construed broadly to allow Congress to pass laws that regulate a wide range of activities that directly or indirectly affect interstate commerce, including the health and safety of workers.

Congress delegated much of this regulatory authority for the work environment to federal administrative agencies, primarily the Occupational Safety and Health Administration (OSHA), through the OSHAct of 1970.[12] The Act established OSHA and NIOSH, the two major federal agencies concerned with worker health and safety. Under the Act, OSHA has authority to promulgate regulations (standards) and conduct inspections to carry out the Act's main purpose, which is ". . . to assure so far as possible every working man and woman in the Nation safe and healthful working conditions. . . ." The scientific, engineering, and health research activities contemplated by the OSHAct are housed in NIOSH. Instead of the U.S. Department of Labor, NIOSH is located in the Department of Health and Human Services to reflect its mission of improving workplace health and safety through research, prevention, education, and training, and NIOSH is now part of the Centers for Disease Control and Prevention (CDC).

Under the "supremacy clause" of the Constitution, Congress can pass laws that preempt, or even prohibit, state laws addressing the subject matter of federal legislation.[13] The OSHAct has such a clause that effectively preempts state regulation of workplace safety, except where federal OSHA has delegated authority to a state-run OSHA program. State-run programs are required to provide standards that are at least as protective as federal standards. States, however, also are prevented from establishing standards that are significantly more burdensome lest they run afoul of the interstate commerce clause, another area of exclusive federal preemption.

Federal OSHA has jurisdiction over workplace safety and health issues in all states that do not operate their own OSHA-approved programs. In fact, any occupational safety and health issues regulated by a state that does not have an OSHA-approved program are preempted by OSHA jurisdiction if OSHA has a standard addressing the hazard or issue.

The OSHAct

In general, the OSHAct covers all private employers and their employees in the 50 states, the District of Columbia, Puerto Rico, and all other territories under federal government jurisdiction. Coverage is provided either directly by the federal OSHA or through an OSHA-approved state-based job safety and health program. States with OSHA-approved job safety and health programs must set standards at least as effective as the equivalent federal standard, and most state-plan states simply adopt standards identical to the federal standards.

As defined by the Act, an employer is any "person engaged in a business affecting commerce who has employees, but does not include the United States or any state or political subdivision of a State." Therefore, the Act applies to all employers and employees in manufacturing, construction, transportation, agriculture, health care, retail, and private education. The OSHAct includes secular employees of religious groups and nonprofit organizations.

Section 3(5) of the Act specifically excluded employees of state and local governments (unless they are in one of the states with OSHA-approved state safety and health programs). Section 4(b)(1) of the Act excluded working conditions regulated by other federal agencies under other federal statutes. The Department of Labor, as a matter of policy, also has excluded self-employed persons, farms that employ only immediate members of the farmer's family, and domestic households where an individual has been hired to perform household tasks such cooking, cleaning, or child care.[14]

The Act assigns to OSHA two principal functions: setting safety and health standards and conducting workplace inspections to enforce compliance with the standards. OSHA standards may address working conditions, equipment, processes, or outcomes. Safety standards include regulations designed to prevent falls, electrocutions, fires, explosions, cave-ins, and machine and vehicle accidents and injuries. Health standards regulate exposures to a variety of chemical, physical, and biologic health hazards through engineering controls, use of personal protective equipment (e.g., respirators, ear protection), and work practices. The standards may require employers to meet environmental or engineering specifications, use specific technologies or practices, or simply set targets that employers must meet using whatever means are practical or feasible. Employers bear the responsibility to become aware of and understand the standards applicable to their industry, reduce or eliminate work hazards to the extent possible, and comply with the standards.

Where OSHA does not have a specific standard for a hazardous exposure or condition, employers remain responsible for complying with the "general duty" clause of the OSHAct. The general duty clause—Section 5(a)(1)—states that each employer "shall furnish . . . a place of employment which is free from recognized hazards that are causing or are likely to cause death or serious physical harm to his employees." Employers, therefore, have an affirmative duty to identify and remove hazards that pose a probable danger to employee health and safety even if no specific OSHA standard addresses that risk. Employees also have a duty under the Act to ". . . comply with occupational safety and health standards and all rules, regulations, and orders issued pursuant to this act."

Section 8(a) of the OSHAct authorized OSHA to conduct workplace inspections to identify hazards and enforce safety and health standards. Every establishment covered by the Act is subject to inspection. Similarly, states with their own occupational safety and health programs are authorized to conduct inspections using state compliance officers.

The Act grants employees several important rights. Among them are the rights to (1) file a confidential complaint with OSHA about the safety and health conditions in their workplace, (2) contest the time granted by OSHA for correcting violations, and (3) accompany OSHA workplace inspections. Employees who exercise their rights are protected against employer retaliation. Employees must notify OSHA of the alleged reprisal; if OSHA finds that discrimination has occurred, the employer will be asked to restore the employee, including lost wages or benefits. If necessary, OSHA can take legal action on behalf of the employee.

Typically, OSHA agencies are divided into consultation and enforcement units. Consultation personnel are invited by the employer to assist with identification and control of hazards. The consultations are confidential and free of charge. If consultation personnel identify hazards, the employer is provided with an opportunity to correct them in a reasonable time. If the employer fails to correct the problem, placing workers at risk, then the consultant must notify the enforcement division. After an inspection or referral, employers who do not comply with OSHA standards may receive citations and penalties (Table 22-1).

After a complaint, employees may request an informal review of any decision not to issue a citation but cannot contest citations, amendments to citations, penalties, or lack of penalties. They may contest the time granted by OSHA to abate a hazardous condition. Employees may request a review of OSHA action by submitting a written objection to OSHA. The OSHA area director then forwards these objections to the Occupational Safety and Health Review Commission, which operates independently of OSHA.

Similarly, an employer may request an informal meeting with OSHA's area director to discuss the case. Employee representatives may be invited to attend the meeting. The area director is authorized to enter into settlement agreements that revise citations and penalties to avoid prolonged legal disputes. Employers also may request review from the Occupational Safety and Health Review Commission.

Federal OSHA standards fall into four major categories: general industry (29 C.F.R. 1910); construction (29 C.F.R. 1926); maritime—shipyards, marine terminals, longshoring (29 C.F.R. 1915-9); and agriculture (29 C.F.R. 1928). Each of these four categories imposes requirements targeted to that industry, although, in some cases, they are identical for each category of employer. Among the standards that impose similar requirements on all industry sectors are those for access to medical and exposure records, personal protective equipment, and hazard communication.

Access to Medical and Exposure Records

This standard requires that employers preserve and grant employee access to any exposure monitoring or medical records maintained by the company that relate to a

TABLE 22-1   Occupational Safety and Health Act (OSHAct) Violations and Penalties

Violation	Explanation and Penalties
Other-Than-Serious Violations	A violation that has a direct relation to job safety and health but probably would not cause death or serious physical harm. A proposed penalty of up to $7,000 for each violation is discretionary. A penalty for an other-than-serious violation may be adjusted downward by as much as 95%, depending on the employer's good faith (demonstrated efforts to comply with the OSHAct), history of previous violations, and size of business. When the adjusted penalty amounts to less than $50, no penalty is proposed
Serious Violation	A violation where substantial probability exists that death or serious physical harm could result and where the employer knew, or should have known, of the hazard. A mandatory penalty of up to $7000 for each violation is proposed. A penalty for a serious violation may be adjusted downward, based on the employer's good faith, history of previous violations, gravity of the alleged violation, and size of business.
Willful Violation	A violation that the employer intentionally and knowingly commits. The employer either knows that what he or she is doing constitutes a violation or is aware that a hazardous condition existed and has made no reasonable effort to eliminate it. The OSHAct provides that an employer who willfully violates the Act may be assessed a civil penalty of not more than $70,000 but not less than $5,000 for each violation. A proposed penalty for a willful violation may be adjusted downward, depending on the size of the business and its history of previous violations. Usually no credit is given for good faith. If an employer is convicted of a willful violation of a standard that has resulted in the death of an employee, the offense is punishable by a court-imposed fine or by imprisonment for up to 6 months or both. A fine of up to $250,000 for an individual, or $500,000 for a corporation (authorized under the Comprehensive Crime Control Act of 1984 [1984 CCA], not the OSHAct), may be imposed for a criminal conviction.
Repeated Violation	A violation of any standard, regulation, rule or order where, on reinspection, a substantially similar violation is found. Repeated violations can bring a fine of up to $70,000 for each such violation. For a repeat citation, the original citation must be final; a citation under contest may not serve as the basis for a subsequent repeat citation.
Failure to Correct Prior Violation	Failure to correct a prior violation may bring a civil penalty of up to $7,000 for each day the violation continues beyond the prescribed abatement date. Additional violations for which citations and proposed penalties may be issued are as follows: 1) falsifying records, reports, or applications; on conviction can bring a fine of $10,000 or up to 6 months in jail or both; 2) violations of posting requirements can bring a civil penalty of up to $7,000; 3) assaulting a compliance officer, or otherwise resisting, opposing, intimidating, or interfering with a compliance officer in the performance of his or her duties is a criminal offense, subject to a fine of not more than $250,000 for an individual and $500,000 for a corporation (1984 CCA) and imprisonment for not more than 3 years. Citation and penalty procedures may differ somewhat in states with their own occupational safety and health programs.

worker's own exposure to hazardous substances or processes.[15] These records must be maintained for 30 years after the worker's period of employment. Employees also must be notified of the existence of these records and their right to access and review them.

Personal Protective Equipment

This standard, included separately in the standards for each industry segment (except agriculture), requires that employers provide workers with appropriate personal protective equipment.[16] This may include protective helmets or hard hats, respirators, eye protection, hearing protection, hard-toed shoes, or other specialized equipment (e.g., welding goggles or face shields). The employer is expected to provide this equipment without charge to the employee, except for prescription safety glasses and hard-toe safety shoes.

Hazard Communication

The Hazard Communication Standard is designed to provide employees with a "right to know" the chemical hazards they encounter in their workplace.[17] This standard requires that manufacturers and importers of hazardous materials conduct a hazard evaluation of the products they manufacture or import. If the product is found to be hazardous under the terms of the standard, containers of the material must be appropriately labeled, and the first shipment of the material to a new customer must be accompanied by a material safety data sheet (MSDS).

If employees work with compounds that are divided from the original container into smaller containers, these containers also must have appropriate labels and warnings. Employees must be given access to MSDS on request, and MSDS must be easily accessible. Employers must train their employees to recognize and avoid the hazards the materials present.

The Hazard Communication Standard also gives health-care providers an important right of access to information about the identity and quantity of ingredients listed as "trade secrets" on the MSDS. In situations where a medical emergency exists or immediate first aid is required, manufacturers must immediately disclose the "trade secret" information and subsequently can request a confidentiality agreement and statement of need. In nonemergent situations, the manufacturer can require a written request including a statement of need, and execution of a confidentiality agreement including assurances that means exist to protect against further disclosure.

Record Keeping

Section 8(c)(1) of the OSHAct states: "Each employer shall make, keep, and preserve . . . such records regarding his activities relating to this Act . . . necessary or appropriate for the enforcement of this Act or for developing information regarding the causes and prevention of occupational accidents and illnesses."[18]

Employers with more than 10 employees—except for certain low-hazard industries such as retail, finance, insurance, real estate, and some service industries—must maintain OSHA-specified records of job-related injuries and illnesses.

Employers with 10 or fewer employees, or employers in traditionally low-hazard industries, are exempt from maintaining these records unless they are selected to be part of a national survey of workplace injuries and illnesses conducted by the Department of Labor's BLS each year. Selected employers are notified to begin keeping records during the survey year, and technical assistance is available for on completing these forms.

All employers, regardless of the number of employees or industry category, must report to the nearest OSHA office within 8 hours any accident that results in one or more fatalities or hospitalization of three or more employees. OSHA investigates these "catastrophic" accidents to determine whether violations of standards contributed to the event.

MSHAct

The Federal Mine Safety and Health Act of 1977 (MSHAct)[19] covers all miners and others working on mine property; it is administered by the Labor Department's Mine Safety and Health Administration (MSHA). This law revised and expanded the earlier Federal Coal Mine Health and Safety Act of 1969 and brought metal and nonmetal (noncoal) miners under the same general standards as coal miners.

Each mine in the United States must be registered with MSHA. Many mine operators also are required to submit plans to MSHA for approval before beginning operations. Required plans cover most operational aspects such as ventilation, roof control, and miner training. MSHA must inspect every underground mine at least four times a year and every surface mine at least twice a year. Mine operators are required to report each individual mine accident or injury to MSHA. In addition, the Act provides authority for closure of mines in cases of imminent danger to workers or failure to correct violations within the time allowed.

Mine safety and health regulations cover numerous hazards, including respiratory exposure to dust and its toxic contaminants; noise; machinery and mobile equipment; roof falls; flammable and toxic gases; electrical equipment; fires; explosives; and access and egress. The MSHA also conducts training and assists the mining industry in reducing deaths, serious injuries, and illnesses.

Other Relevant Authorities

Congress enacted the Toxic Substances Control Act of 1976[20] to test, regulate, and screen all chemicals produced or imported into the United States. This act requires that any chemical that reaches the consumer marketplace be tested for possible toxic effects before commercial manufacture. The Toxic Substances Control Act of 1976 also includes extensive record keeping and reporting requirements for toxic chemicals. Section 8(c) requires chemical manufacturers, processors, and distributors to maintain records of "significant adverse reactions" for 30 years. Section 8(e) requires manufacturers, processors, and distributors to report to the U.S. Environmental Protection Agency (EPA) any "information which reasonably supports the conclusion that such substance or mixture presents a substantial risk of injury to health or the environment." Medical providers or public health authorities may find that data collected under these sections provides another source of information regarding the potential health adverse effects of new or poorly characterized substances.

After the public outcry over pollution disasters in Love Canal, New York, and Times Beach, Missouri, Congress passed the Comprehensive Environmental Response, Compensation and Liability Act of 1980 (CERCLA).[21] The Act provided liability for past polluters as well as current owners of polluted sites, and CERCLA created a federal "Superfund" to clean up uncontrolled or abandoned hazardous-waste sites as well as accidents, spills, and other emergency releases of pollutants and contaminants into the environment. Through the Act, EPA was given power to seek out parties responsible for any release and ensure their cooperation in the cleanup. In addition, CERCLA created the Agency for Toxic Substances and Disease Registry and provided a framework for health and safety regulation of workers at hazardous waste sites.

In the wake of the disaster in Bhopal, India, the Superfund Amendments and Reauthorization Act of 1986 (SARA) reauthorized CERCLA to continue cleanup activities around the country. Title III of SARA included the Emergency Planning and Community Right-to-Know Act (EPCRA).[22] This law was designated to help local communities protect public health, safety, and the environment from chemical hazards. In addition to its provisions addressing emergency preparedness and community right-to-know issues, both EPCRA and CERCLA contain provisions that grant medical providers access to information regarding the identity and quantity of chemical ingredients considered "trade secrets" similar to the OSHA Hazard Communication standard.

Preparation and use of pesticides are regulated under the Federal Insecticide, Fungicide, and Rodenticide Act.[23] This act gives EPA jurisdiction to protect the health and safety of agricultural workers and commercial pesticide applicators exposed to these substances.[24]

Employment Discrimination and Benefits Law

Title VII of the Civil Rights Act and the Pregnancy Discrimination Act

Title VII of the Civil Rights Act prohibits discrimination on the basis of sex, race, religion, or national origin.[25] Discrimination based on pregnancy, childbirth, or related medical conditions constitutes unlawful sex discrimination under Title VII. Women affected by pregnancy or related conditions must be treated in the same manner as other applicants or employees with similar abilities or limitations.

An employer cannot refuse to hire a woman because she is pregnant if she can perform the major functions of her job. Nor can an employer single out pregnancy-related conditions for special procedures to determine an employee's ability to work. If an employee is temporarily unable to perform her job because of pregnancy, the employer must provide the same benefits afforded to any other temporarily disabled employee, such as modified work, temporary reassignment, or disability leave. Pregnant employees must be permitted to work as long as they are able to perform their jobs, and employers may not have a rule that prohibits an employee from returning to work for a predetermined time after childbirth. Employers must hold open jobs for employees with pregnancy-related conditions the same length of time they hold open jobs for employees on sick or disability leave.

Health insurance provided to employees must cover pregnancy-related expenses in the same manner they cover as costs for other medical conditions. Coverage amounts can be limited only to the same extent as costs for other conditions, and employees with pregnancy-related disabilities must be treated the same as other temporarily disabled employees regarding seniority and benefits.

The Age Discrimination in Employment Act of 1967

The Age Discrimination in Employment Act of 1967 (ADEA) protects persons aged 40 years or older from employment discrimination based on age.[26] The ADEA's protections apply to both current employees and applicants. The ADEA forbids discrimination against a person because of his or her age with respect to any term, condition, or privilege of employment. The ADEA also precludes age preferences, limitations, or specifications in job notices or advertisements.

In February 2004, the U.S. Supreme Court reviewed a challenge from younger workers alleging that the ADEA not only prohibits employment discrimination against older workers but also prohibits "reverse discrimination" against younger workers where employer policies or actions favor older workers over younger ones. The Court, however, held that the ADEA "does not mean to stop an employer from favoring an older employee over a younger one."[27]

In March 2004, the U.S. Supreme Court ruled that programs and actions that are age-neutral on their face but have an unintended disparate, adverse impact on older workers violate the ADEA unless some reasonable business factor exists for the policy other than age.[28]

The Rehabilitation Act and the Americans with Disabilities Act

The Rehabilitation Act of 1973 prohibits disability-based discrimination in federal employment and by federal contractors.[29] The Act served as the forerunner and model for the Americans with Disabilities Act of 1990 (ADA), which greatly expanded and refined the protections for persons with disabilities.[30] The ADA prohibits private employers, state and local governments, employment agencies, and labor unions from discriminating against qualified persons with disabilities in job application procedures, hiring, firing, advancement, compensation, job training, and other terms, conditions and privileges of employment. According to the ADA, a person with a disability is a person who (1) has a physical or mental impairment that substantially limits one or more major life activities; (2) has a record of such an impairment; or (3) is regarded as having such an impairment.

A qualified employee or applicant with a disability is an individual who can perform the essential functions of the job with or without reasonable accommodation. Reasonable accommodation may include making existing facilities used by employees readily accessible to and usable by persons with disabilities; restructuring the job, modifying work schedules, or reassigning to a vacant position; acquiring or modifying equipment or devices; adjusting or modifying examinations, training materials, or policies; and providing qualified readers or interpreters.

An employer is required to accommodate the known disability of a qualified applicant or employee if it would not impose an "undue hardship" on the operation of the employer's business. Undue hardship is defined as an action requiring significant difficulty or expense when considered in light of factors such as an employer's size, financial resources, and nature and structure of its operation. An employer is not required to lower quality or production standards to make an accommodation, nor is an employer obligated to provide personal-use items such as glasses or hearing aids.

Employers may not ask job applicants about the existence, nature, or severity of a disability. Applicants may, however, be asked about their ability to perform specific job functions. A job offer may be conditioned on the results of a medical examination only if the examination is required for all entering employees in similar jobs. Medical examinations of employees must be job-related and consistent with the employer's business needs.

Employees and applicants currently engaging in the illegal use of drugs are not covered by the ADA, when an employer acts on the basis of such use. Tests for illegal drugs are not subject to the ADA's restrictions on medical examinations. Employers may hold illegal drug users and those with alcoholism to the same performance standards as other employees.

Family and Medical Leave Act of 1993

The Department of Labor's Employment Standards Administration, Wage and Hour Division, administers and enforces the Family and Medical Leave Act (FMLA)[31] for all private, state, and local government employees and some federal employees. Most federal and certain congressional employees also are covered by the law and are subject to the jurisdiction of the U.S. Office of Personnel Management or the Congress.

The FMLA entitles eligible employees to take up to 12 weeks of unpaid, job-protected leave in a 12-month period for specified family and medical reasons. To be "eligible" for FMLA leave, an employee must work at a worksite within 75 road miles of which that employer employs at least 50 employees; must have worked at least 12 months (which do not have to be consecutive) for the employer; and, must have worked at least 1250 hours during the 12 months immediately preceding the date of beginning FMLA leave. The FMLA provides an entitlement of leave for the following reasons: birth or adoption of the employee's child; to care for an immediate family member (spouse, child, parent) who has a serious health condition; or the employee's own serious health condition.

An employer must maintain group health benefits that an employee was receiving at the time leave begins during periods of FMLA leave, at the same level and in the same manner as if the employee had continued to work. Under most circumstances, an employee may elect or the employer may require use of any accrued paid leave (e.g., vacation, sick, personal) for periods of unpaid FMLA leave. While FMLA leave may be taken in blocks of time less than the full 12 weeks on an intermittent or reduced leave basis, taking intermittent leave for the birth, placement for adoption, or foster care of a child must be approved by the employer.

When leave is foreseeable, an employee must provide the employer with at least 30-days' notice of the need for leave. If the leave is not foreseeable, then notice must be given as soon as practicable. An employer may require medical certification of a serious health condition from the employee and may require periodic reports during the period of leave of the employee's status and intent to return to work, as well as "fitness-for-duty" certification on return to work in appropriate situations.

When the employee returns from FMLA leave, he or she is entitled to be restored to the same job or to a job equivalent to the job the employee left when leave began. An equivalent job is one with equivalent pay, benefits, and responsibilities. The employee is not entitled to accrue benefits during periods of unpaid FMLA leave, but he or she must be returned to employment with the same benefits at the same levels that existed when leave began. Any unused benefits accrued at the time leave began are retained by the employee.

Labor Law

Labor organizations have made an essential and undeniable contribution to the health and safety conditions of American workplaces. Unions have been important and influential advocates for worker health and safety. They can be important or even indispensable partners in epidemiologic investigations, education and training activities, or other worksite-based health and wellness interventions.

Although labor law is a complex system of legal and administrative elements and remedies, the National Labor Relations Act of 1935 (Wagner Act) is the primary rulebook of labor-management relations in the United States. Once a union is organized and certified under the Act, much of the relationship between workers and management in a particular company or industry is defined in a collective bargaining agreement. Most importantly, both labor and management have a legal duty to bargain collectively. Failure to do so constitutes an "unfair labor practice." Safety and health rules and practices within the organization are mandatory subjects of collective bargaining.[32] Additionally, many collective bargaining agreements provide for joint labor-management safety committees that review safety practices, investigate accidents, and suggest or implement safety policies.

Relevant State Statutes

In addition to federal statutes and rules, many states have specific provisions that address radiation safety; building safety; hazardous material handling; worker and community right-to-know issues; and other laws or rules addressing specific work exposures, conditions, or duties. Workers' compensation law is largely a state-based system; it plays a varying role, directly and indirectly, on the health and safety of workers within each jurisdiction. Provision of resources for injury and illness prevention, research, and integration with OSHA consultative and enforcement activities also varies among the states.

State public health statutes or administrative rules may include mandatory reporting requirements for some or all occupational diseases (Box 22-1).[33] State workers' compensation systems may include programs for occupational injury and illness surveillance as well as prevention activities.

BOX 22–1 Example of a State Occupational Disease Reporting Regulation

Ohio Admin. Code §3701-3-021 REPORTING OF OCCUPATIONAL DISEASES

(A) Every physician attending on or called in to visit a patient whom the physician believes to be suffering from any of the occupational diseases or occupationally related ailments listed in paragraph (B) of this rule shall submit a report to the director of health within forty-eight hours from the time of first attending the patient. This report shall be made on, or in conformity with, the standard schedule blanks which the director is required to provide physicians pursuant to section 3701.26 of the Revised Code and shall contain the following information:

    (1) The name, address, telephone number, date of birth, race, gender, and occupation of the patient;

    (2) The name, address, telephone number, and business of the patient's employer;

    (3) The nature of the disease or ailment; and

    (4) Name, address, and telephone number of the physician.

The mailing of the report, within the time required by this paragraph, shall constitute compliance with section 3701.25 of the Revised Code and this rule.

(B) The following occupational diseases and ailments are required to be reported:

    (1) Poisoning from phosphorus, brass, arsenic, mercury, wood alcohol, or their compounds;

    (2) Anthrax;

    (3) Compressed air illness;

    (4) Silicosis;

    (5) Occupational asthma;

    (6) Pesticide poisoning;

    (7) Cumulative trauma disorders including, but not limited to, carpal tunnel syndrome and persistent and recurring tendonitis;

    (8) Poisoning from heavy metals including, but not limited to, lead, nickel, and cadmium;

    (9) Asbestosis;

    (10) Mesothelioma;

    (11) Amputation of limb or digit; and

    (12) Burn or burns resulting from exposure or contact to chemical, flame, or heat and of such severity as to cause admission into a hospital, burn unit, or other health care facility.

Criminal prosecution for intentional or grossly negligent worker injury or death is also possible under state criminal statutes.[34] Federal preemption arguments have been offered as defenses to criminal charges brought in state court, but at least two state supreme courts have held that the OSHAct does not preempt state criminal jurisdiction.[35,36]

Other Sources

Other Government Agencies

Other federal and state departments or agencies may have jurisdiction or responsibility for specific occupations or exposures. For example, the Department of Transportation has specific occupational safety and health standards for commercial vehicles (Federal Highway Administration), railroads (Federal Railroad Administration), aviation (Federal Aviation Administration), public transit (Federal Transit Administration), and maritime (U.S. Coast Guard). The Department of Energy and the Nuclear Regulatory Commission largely regulate worker exposure to ionizing radiation, and CDC plays a key role in recommending occupational safety and health practices for laboratory and health-care workers and other workers exposed to biologic agents.

Nongovernment Organizations

Many national and international organizations develop and disseminate occupational health and safety standards. The American Conference of Government Industrial Hygienists (ACGIH) particularly influences development of exposure limits for chemical and physical hazards. In fact, many of the original OSHA Permissible Exposure Limit (PEL) standards adopted under Section 6(a) of the OSHAct were adopted from the ACGIH Threshold Limit Value standards that were current at the time. The American National Standards Institute has contributed a number of industry- or process-specific standards such as laser safety, respirator selection and use, and radiation protection. Safety testing and standards of the National Safety Council are important guides, as are the national fire and electrical codes of the National Fire Protection Association.

Although these private organization standards or guidelines do not have the force of law, they often are based on extensive research or careful professional consensus. They serve as models or evidence for government legislation or rulemaking or are voluntarily adopted by individual employers or industry groups. Courts also value the indirect authority of these documents, particularly if they have been widely accepted in an industry or professional community. Similarly, professional societies such as the American College of Occupational and Environmental Medicine, the American Association of Occupational Health Nurses, American Industrial Hygiene Association, American Society of Safety Engineers, and the American Thoracic Society play an important role in promoting occupational health and safety, raising public awareness, and issuing position statements and guidelines.

Legal Issues and Controversies

OSHA Challenges

Soon after its passage, the OSHAct was the subject of lawsuits that challenged several of its basic provisions. The feasibility component of standard setting was considered in *Industrial Union Department, AFL-CIO v. Hodgson*, 499 F.2d 467 (D.C. Cir. 1974). The court found that Congress did not intend OSHA to create standards that would require the use of equipment that was not available with existing technology or would threaten the financial viability or continued existence of an industrial sector or process. The Court also stated, however, that some methods might be economically feasible even if they were financially burdensome, reduced profits, or placed some individual employers out of business.

Similarly, in *The Society of the Plastics Industry, Inc. v. Occupational Safety and Health Administration*, 509 F.2d 1301 (2d Cir. 1975), manufacturers and users of vinyl chloride monomer challenged an OSHA standard that lowered the PEL to 1 part per million, stating that it was infeasible. The Court, however, believed the industry was capable of attaining this limit and stated: "In the area of safety, we wish to emphasize, the Secretary is not restricted by the status quo. He may raise standards which require improvements in existing technologies or which require the development of new technology, and he is not limited to issuing standards based only on devices already fully developed."

Later, the "technology forcing" provision was scaled back somewhat in *American Iron and Steel Institute v. OSHA*, 577 F.2d 825 (3rd Cir. 1978). Here, the Court found that "the Secretary can impose a standard which requires an employer to implement technology 'looming on today's horizon,'" but could not "place an affirmative duty on each employer to research and develop new technology."

In its first review of an OSHA standard, *Industrial Union Department v. American Petroleum Institute*, 448 U.S. 607 (1980), the U.S. Supreme Court considered a challenge to the OSHA Standard for benzene. The petroleum industry contended that the "reasonably necessary" and "feasible" provisions of the OSHAct required a "cost-benefit analysis" before issuing a new or revised OSHA standard. The Supreme Court did not address the "cost-benefit analysis" issue but instead articulated a "significant risk" requirement for standard setting. The Court concluded that, because OSHA had determined that no safe level of exposure existed, it had set the PEL at the lowest technologically feasible level. The Court was concerned, however, that OSHA had failed to demonstrate the practical effect of this lowered PEL and therefore never made a threshold determination that the standard was "reasonably necessary and appropriate to remedy a significant risk of material health impairment" as required by Section 3(8) of the Act.

The Court stated that, before issuing a standard, the Secretary had to determine that a place of employment was "unsafe" and had to determine what level of risk constituted a "significant risk" that required a standard for worker protection. The Court endorsed the use of quantitative risk assessment but left to the agency the determination of what was a significant risk and the methods and assumptions of the risk assessment.

A short time later, the U.S. Supreme Court addressed the issue of cost-benefit analysis directly in *American Textile Manufacturers Institute, Inc. v. Donovan*, 542 U.S. 490 (1981). The Court specifically rejected any contention that the feasibility requirement of the OSHAct required analysis of costs and benefits. The Court concluded that, after finding that a significant risk, the OSHAct required OSHA to place "worker health above all other considerations save those making attainment of this 'benefit' unachievable."

Right of Access to Information

Initially, requests by OSHA and NIOSH for access to employee medical records were challenged on constitutional grounds. The Department of Labor responded by promulgating a rule that provided access to employee exposure and medical records.[37] In *United Steelworkers v. Marshall*, 647 F.2d 1189 (D.C. Cir. 1980), the standard was upheld as constitutional, on the grounds that it satisfied a legitimate government purpose, and no immediate harm was shown.[38]

Right of Access to Workplaces

The OSHAct sanctioned inspections of private workplaces, and OSHA inspectors were assumed to have authority to enter workplaces to conduct unannounced and involuntary inspections. In *Marshall v. Barlow's, Inc.*, 436 U.S. 307 (1978), however, the U.S. Supreme Court found that OSHA inspectors could not conduct warrantless inspections of the nonpublic areas of a business without the employer's permission. If an employer refused entry, no requirement existed to show "probable cause" to obtain the warrant, as long as OSHA could demonstrate the request was part of an administrative program designed to meet agency goals or priorities for workplace safety. The Court noted that this was not a difficult threshold to cross but believed the added requirement for a court-issued warrant provided an appropriate procedural safeguard for employers' Fourth Amendment rights. Although *Barlow* prohibits warrantless inspections without permission from the employer, it does not require warrants for all inspections. Inspectors for OSHA usually do not routinely obtain warrants, and they do not explicitly request permission to perform an inspection but instead presume it is granted if the employer does not explicitly refuse the inspection.

Clearly, OSHA has authority to investigate health, as well as safety, complaints. Although this typically means investigation of complaints regarding the health effects of chemical exposure, it includes the authority to investigate a communicable disease outbreak in a workplace. Recently, California OSHA used its authority under the OSHA Bloodborne Pathogen Standard to investigate cases of HIV transmission in the adult film industry in Southern California.[39] Except in specific circumstances where occupational transmission is probable, however, OSHA usually chooses to refer infectious outbreaks to CDC or a state health department because of limited epidemiologic resources and because it often does not have policies or rules that specifically cover these events.

Roles and Responsibilities for Ensuring Health and Safety

The inability to routinely inspect all workplaces (approximately 2000 compliance officers and 76.5 million workplaces) has required OSHA to develop priorities for inspection and enforcement actions. Priorities are determined on the basis of (1) concerns about "imminent danger" to workers, (2) catastrophes or fatal accidents, (3) need for response to employee complaints, (4) targeted inspections of "high hazard" industries or employers with high injury and illness rates, and (5) follow-up inspections to determine whether previously identified hazards have been abated.

Gade v. National Solid Wastes Management Assn. held that Section 18 of OSHAct preempts states from adopting or enforcing laws that pertain to issues that OSHA has regulated unless a state has done so through an approved state OSHA plan.[40] This could potentially limit the ability of states to directly regulate workplace safety issues through local or state health departments without reference to existing OSHA standards.

Public health agencies may develop different priorities or have different strategies to ensure workplace health and safety. For example, in Oregon, the state public health authority receives notification from laboratories of all blood lead levels over 25 micrograms of lead per deciliters of blood (μg/dL) in adults. The state's health division then notifies and sends educational material regarding the health effects of lead to the worker and the employer. This blood lead level is significantly lower that the OSHA threshold of 40 μg/dL. Using the data collected from this system, the public health agency recently conducted an epidemiologic investigation and offered consultative assistance to an employer whose employees consistently had blood lead levels greater than 25 μg/dL.

Similarly, the public health agency is responsible for investigating reported cancer clusters and for recording infectious disease cases. Many states have added occupational diseases to their list of reportable illnesses, and many participate in NIOSH-sponsored surveillance programs (e.g., the Sentinel Event Notification System for Occupational Risk).

Genetic Screening in the Workplace

Genetic testing of workers is a particularly thorny issue. It has become even more controversial with scientific advances that have allowed more precise testing (e.g., genome analysis versus morphologic chromosomal aberrations) and identification of genetic markers of disease susceptibility.

Controversy has been primarily about privacy issues, consequence of disclosure, and the potential for "genetic discrimination" within and outside of the workplace. The Supreme Court's opinion of sex-based exclusion in *Johnson Controls*[41] suggests, by analogy, that selecting or reassigning workers on the basis of genetic susceptibility to specific exposure would probably be looked on with disfavor. Similarly, the U.S. Equal Employment Opportunity Commission (EEOC) has identified such actions as discriminatory under the "regarded as" definition of disability under the ADA. President Clinton issued an Executive Order prohibiting federal departments and agencies from basing employment decisions on genetic information.[42]

Proper application of the burgeoning developments in genomic science is still being debated. This is likely to be an active area of future scientific and legal ferment.

ADA-Related Issues

In 1999, the Court simultaneously reviewed three cases that considered the definition of disability under the ADA.[43–45] The Court held that the question of whether a person was a qualified person with a disability had to be analyzed in light of any treatments, medications, aids, or prostheses that corrected or mitigated the impact of the underlying medical or psychological condition. The Court stated, for example, that severely myopic individuals were not disabled if their myopia could be corrected with glasses or contact lenses. Similarly, individuals with hypertension were not disabled if their condition could be controlled with medication. The Court also reaffirmed that disability had to be considered from a range of jobs that the individual was qualified for, not a specific job, and that other federal standards (e.g., Federal Aviation Administration or Department of Transportation medical standards) were not preempted by the ADA. The Court further narrowed the definition of disability in 2002, with a unanimous opinion that within the context of employment the individual must be restricted in an activity of "central importance" to most people's daily lives, not simply specific job-related tasks.[46] Many state disability discrimination statutes, however, are more inclusive.

Another area that recently received Supreme Court review was the issue of whether an applicant or employee is not qualified because he or she constitutes a "direct threat" to his or her own health or safety in the workplace. The ADA specifies that the direct threat analysis could be extended only to the threat of serious harm or injury to coworkers or the public. The EEOC, however, in promulgating its interpretive rules, adopted the general understanding and practice that direct threat would also include a significant risk to the disabled employee. The Supreme Court agreed with this interpretation, stating nothing precludes the EEOC from that interpretation and that this resolved a potential conflict with the employer's duty to protect workers under the OSHAct.[47]

Practice Considerations

Worker Protection

Despite significant improvements in worker safety and health during the past 30 years, OSHA has many critics. Some members of industry have characterized OSHA regulation as petty, burdensome, and unnecessary. Some unions and worker advocacy groups believe OSHA has not gone far enough to protect workers and the environment. In contrast to the central authority and large appropriations of EPA, responsibility for worker health and safety is fragmented.

Rulemaking efforts nearly always are challenged by industry as excessive and by unions as insufficient. These legal challenges have prevented or delayed standard development so that after 30 years, fewer that 40 substance-specific standards have been promulgated.

Significant reform is unlikely, however. Several attempts at OSHA reform have been introduced in previous Congressional sessions. Attempts at reform were unsuccessful and the OSHAct remains largely unchanged from its original form.

Accessing and Developing Surveillance Data Useful for Targeting Interventions

OSHA logs may provide valuable information to epidemiologists conducting research or investigating outbreaks of disease, but data may be limited, incomplete, or unavailable. The delay in submitting data and the limited sampling of some occupations give these data limited utility as a surveillance tool.

Other sources of surveillance data may include mandatory laboratory or physician reporting of specific occupational diseases or injuries, analysis of workers' compensation, group health, disability or other insurance claim data, sentinel health providers, or surveys of worker populations. Unions or community-based organizations also may be important sources of epidemiologic data. Accessing data sources may require cooperative agreements with other government entities, confidentiality agreements, or other privacy safeguards such as encryption or stripping data of personal identifiers.

Courts have upheld government access or collection of data where a legitimate interest has been demonstrated, the public interest outweighs any potential risk to individuals, and adequate privacy safeguards have been implemented. Access by private or nongovernment organizations is more limited, and informed consent probably is necessary when personally identifiable data are used.[48]

Seeking Technical Assistance

Free consultation services are available to employers. These are funded largely by OSHA but delivered by state government agencies or universities. This consultation service is provided confidentially and distinct from the enforcement activities of the agency. Employers can request consultation without fear of fine or citation, as long as they agree to remedy any serious hazards identified during the consultation period. Consultants are obligated to refer serious hazards to the enforcement officials if the employer does not abate the hazard in a reasonable time.

NIOSH provides extensive consultation and training opportunities for employees, investigates hazards associated with specific substances, processes, or industries, and offers suggestions to reduce or eliminate those hazards. In addition, NIOSH researches exposure-control methods and equipment, safety and health training, and prevention methods, and recommends new or revised standards to OSHA, and also provides many of the training opportunities for occupational safety and health professionals directly or through grant programs.

One of the most powerful tools to obtain technical assistance with an occupational health issue is to request a NIOSH Health Hazard Evaluation (HHE).[49] An HHE is a structured investigation of a workplace to identify and characterize potential health hazards. Employees, labor unions, or employers can request HHEs. An individual employee can request an HHE if two other employees cosign the request. Labor unions can initiate the request for their members.

The HHEs are designed to investigate new or incompletely understood occupational hazards or exposures. Examples include unusual illness clusters, concerns about disease excess among worker populations, new or infrequently encountered substances or exposures, or combinations of exposures. However, HHEs are not intended to provide routine assistance where the hazards have been clearly recognized and effective control measures are available. In this situation, referral to OSHA is more appropriate.

Emerging Issues

Genetic Screening

Few employers have instituted genetic testing programs because of the legal and ethical controversy regarding their use among working populations. Burlington Northern Santa Fe Railroad (BNSF) began using a genetic screening test on its employees who had filed workers' compensation claims for carpal tunnel syndrome. The test was designed to identify a genetic marker for carpal tunnel syndrome susceptibility and thereby establish the condition was not work-related.

The EEOC viewed this as a discriminatory work practice and filed a suit under the ADA asking for a preliminary injunction in February 2001. The EEOC alleged "genetic bias," noting that testing was performed without worker consent or knowledge and that at least one worker was threatened with dismissal for failing to provide a blood sample. In April 2001, the suit was settled with an Agreed Order that prohibited BNSF from continuing its genetic testing program. The EEOC stated that it would "respond aggressively" to allegations of discrimination based on genetic tests.[50]

The EEOC does not appear to have addressed the issue of BNSF's activity within the context of workers' compensation law, in which evidentiary standards have traditionally allowed employers to collect or discover information that reasonably relates to their defense of the claim. Workers' compensation claimants are sometimes compelled to participate in medical examinations and undergo tests by medical experts selected by the insurer or employer. Similarly, workers may sometimes be placed under "hidden camera" surveillance when fraud or malingering is suspected. How and why these other investigative techniques differ from genetic testing with the workers' compensation arena have yet to be articulated.

Disability Discrimination and Employments Benefit Law

The complex interaction of the ADA, the FMLA, and similar state laws regarding disability discrimination, family leave, and workers' compensation create a confusing legal environment for employers and employees. Unfortunately, the goals and provisions of these laws, administered by different departments and agencies, sometimes conflict, and resolution of the conflicts continues to generate litigation. Several important ADA-related cases regarding reasonable accommodation, seniority and collective bargaining agreements, public accommodation, and remedies will undergo Supreme Court review in the near future, and plaintiffs, employers, governments, and employment lawyers will follow these developments closely.

The author gratefully acknowledges the assistance of Greg Wagner, M.D., M.P.H., NIOSH, CDC, Morgantown, West Virginia, and Mark Rothstein, J.D., University of Louisville, Louisville, Kentucky, who reviewed and offered comments on the first edition chapter.

References

1. Page RM, Cole GE, Timmreck TC. *Basic Epidemiological Methods and Biostatistics.* Boston: Jones and Bartlett, 1995:3–4.
2. Carter T. Diseases of occupations—a short history of their recognition and prevention. In: Baxter PJ, Adams PH, Aw TC, Cockcroft A, Harrington JM, eds. *Hunter's Diseases of Occupations.* 9th ed. London: Arnold, 2000:920.
3. Hamilton A. *Exploring the Dangerous Trades: The Autobiography of Alice Hamilton, M.D.* Boston: Little, Brown, 1943.
4. Ashford N, Caldart C. *Technology, Law, and the Working Environment.* Revised ed. Washington, DC: Island Press, 1996:3–9.
5. Rothstein M. The scope of the act. *Occupational Safety and Health Law.* 4th ed. St. Paul, MN: West Group, 1998:1–10.
6. Schulte PA. Characterizing the burden of occupational injury and disease. *J Occup Environ Med* 2005;47:607–22.
7. NIOSH. *Proposed National Strategies for the Prevention of Leading Work-Related Diseases.* Atlanta: US Department of Health and Human Services, CDC, NIOSH, 1989 (DHHS [NIOSH] publication nos 89–128, 89–129, 89–130, 89–131, 89–132, 89–133, 89–134, 89–135, 89–136, 89–137).
8. NIOSH. *National Occupational Research Agenda.* Atlanta: US Department of Health and Human Services, CDC, NIOSH, 1996 (DHHS [NIOSH] publication no 96–115).
9. NIOSH. *Work-Related Lung Disease Surveillance Report 1999.* Atlanta: US Department of Health and Human Services, CDC, NIOSH, 2000. (DHHS [NIOSH] publication no 2000–105).
10. NIOSH. *Worker Health Chartbook, 2000 Non-Fatal Injury.* Atlanta: US Department of Health and Human Services, Public Health Service, CDC, 2002 (DHHS [NIOSH] publication no 2002–119. Available at http://www.cdc.gov/niosh/pdfs/2002-119.pdf. Accessed January 12, 2006.
11. United States Constitution, Article I, §8.
12. The Occupational Safety & Health Act, 29 USC §651 *et seq.*
13. United States Constitution, Article VI.
14. 29 CFR Part 1975.
15. 29 CFR §1910.20.
16. 29 CFR §1910.132; see also Parts 1910, 1915, 1917, 1918, and 1926.
17. 29 CFR §1910.1200.
18. 29 CFR §1904.
19. Federal Mine Safety & Health Act of 1977, Pub L 91-173, as amended by Pub L 95-164.
20. The Toxic Substances Control Act, Pub L 94-469, 15 USC §2601, *et seq.*
21. 42 USC §9601 *et seq.*
22. 42 USC §11001 *et seq.*
23. 7 USC §136.
24. 40 CFR §170.
25. 42 USC §2000.

26. 29 USC §§621–34.

27. *General Dynamics Land Systems v Cline*, 540 US 581 (2004).

28. *Azel P Smith v City of Jackson, Mississippi*, 544 US ____ (2005) [complete citation not yet available].

29. 29 USC §§701–96.

30. 42 USC §12101 *et seq.*

31. The Family & Medical Leave Act, 29 USC §2601 *et seq.*

32. *National Labor Relations Board v Gulf Power Co*, 384 F 2d 822 (5th Cir 1967).

33. Roush S, Birkhead G, Koo D, Cobb A, Fleming D. Mandatory reporting of diseases and conditions by health care professionals and laboratories. *JAMA* 1999;282:164–70.

34. Barstow, D. California leads prosecution of employers in job deaths. *New York Times* 2003 (Dec 23):A1; Available at http://www.nytimes.com/ref/national/WORK_INDEX .html. Accessed September 28, 2005.

35. *People v Chicago Wire Magnet Corp*, 126 Ill 2nd 356 (1989).

36. *People v Hegedus*, 432 Mich 598 (1989).

37. Occupational Safety and Health Administration. Access to Medical and Exposure Records, 29 CFR 1910.20.

38. *United Steelworkers v Marshall*, 647 F 2d 1189 (DC Cir 1980).

39. California Division of Occupational Safety and Health. Vital Information for Workers and Employees in the Adult Film Industry. Available at http://www.dir.ca.gov/dosh/ AdultFilmIndustry.html. Accessed September 29, 2005.

40. *Gade v National Solid Wastes Management Assoc*, 505 US 88 (1992).

41. *Automobile Workers v Johnson Controls*, 499 US 187 (1991).

42. Exec Order 13145, February 8, 2000. Available at http://www.dol.gov/oasam/regs/stat- utes/eo13145.htm. Accessed December 27, 2005.

43. *Sutton v United Airlines, Inc*, 119 S Ct 2139 (1999).

44. *Murphy v United Parcel Service, Inc*, 119 S Ct 2133 (1999).

45. *Albertsons, Inc v Kirkingburg*, 119 S Ct 2162 (1999).

46. *Toyota Motor Manufacturing, Kentucky, Inc v Williams*, 534 US 184 (2002).

47. *Chevron USA, Inc v Echazabal*, 122 S Ct 2045 (2002).

48. Rischitelli DG. The confidentiality of medical information in the workplace. *J Occup Environ Med* 1995;37:583–93.

49. NIOSH, CDC. More about the HHE Program. Available at http://www.cdc.gov/niosh/ hhepage.html. Accessed November 30, 2005.

50. *US Equal Employment Opportunity Commission*. EEOC Settles ADA Suit Against BNSF for Genetic Bias. Available at http://www.eeoc.gov/press/4-18-01.html. Accessed Sep- tember 28, 2005.

INDEX

Italicized page numbers refer to boxes, figures, and tables.

abortion, 325, 327, 392, 452–61, 464–66, 468–69, 472, 473a,e
administrative law, 40, 69–87
  authority for, 72–75, 76
  and chronic diseases, 408, 409, 422a
  and criminal law, 140
  and legal counsel, 207–8
  rulemaking authority for, 75, 77–79
  and STIs/bloodborne infections, 389–91
  strategies/remedies for, 79–84
administrative orders, 69, 75, 81–83, 85, 390–91, 393
Administrative Procedures Acts, 53, 77, 390
administrative searches, 41, 154–55, 436–37.
  See also inspections
Adoption and Safe Families Act (ASFA), 299
adulteration of food. See foodborne diseases
advertising, 16, 34, 83, 132, 330–32, 411
  and tobacco-control regulations, 427–29, 431–33, 441–43, 445
Advisory Committee on Heritable Disorders and Genetic Diseases in Newborns and Children, 326–27
Advisory Committee on Immunization Practices (ACIP), 340, 343–44
Age Discrimination in Employment Act (ADEA), 538
Agency for Healthcare Research and Quality, 248

Agency for Toxic Substances and Disease Registry (ATSDR), 480, 495–97, 499, 537
Agreement on Technical Barriers to Trade (WTO), 185, 192
Agreement on the Application of Sanitary and Phytosanitary Measures. See SPS Agreement (WTO)
Agreement on Trade-Related Aspects of Intellectual Property Rights (TRIPS), 192
AIDS. See HIV/AIDS
airbags, 104, 518
Alcohol, Drug Abuse and Mental Health Administration Reorganization Act. See Synar Amendment
alcohol abuse, 16, 36, 286, 289, 404, 408, 411, 463, 467. See also drunk driving
  by minors, 80, 141, 143, 147, 411, 510, 513–14, 522
alcoholic beverages, sale of, 10, 41, 80, 141, 411
American Academy of Family Physicians, 343–44
American Academy of Microbiology, 153
American Academy of Pediatrics, 343, 513
American Association of Occupational Health Nurses, 542

American Bar Association, 145, 515
American Brass Company v. State Board of Health, *96*, 100
American College of Medical Genetics, 326
American College of Obstetrics and Gynecologists, 468
American College of Occupational and Environmental Medicine, 542
American Conference of Government Industrial Hygienists (ACGIH), 542
American Diabetes Association, 417
American Industrial Hygiene Association, 542
American Iron and Steel Institute v. OSHA, 543
American Legacy Foundation, 433, 445
American Medical Association, 145
American National Standards Institute, 542
American Pharmaceutical Association, 145
American Planning Association, 419
American Public Health Association, 124
American Red Cross, 275
American Society of Safety Engineers, 542
Americans with Disabilities Act (ADA)
    and chronic diseases, *405*, 415, 417
    and environmental health, 498
    and genetics, 328, 548
    and judiciary, 103
    and occupational health and safety, 538–39, 545–46, 548
    and STIs/bloodborne infections, 387, 399
    and tobacco-control regulations, 439
American Textile Manufacturers Institute v. Donovan, *96*, 99, 544
American Thoracic Society, 542
Animal and Plant Health Inspection Service (APHIS), *278*, 363, *364*
animal control, *180*, 183, 276–77, *278–79*
anthrax, 17, 25, 70, 106, 202, 268, 499
    and criminal law, 148–49, *151*
    and surveillance/investigations, 233–35
antibiotics, 9, 29, 176, 225
antimicrobial resistance, 29, 392
antiretroviral therapy, 395, 399–400
assisted reproductive technology (ART), 453, 456, 458, 461, 469, 470–71, 473–74i,j
Association of State and Territorial Health Officials (ASTHO), 145, 229
asthma, 415, 437, 439, 494
at-risk populations, 8, 161, 328, 499
    and ethics in public health, *116–18*, 122
    and STIs/bloodborne infections, 387, 389, 391, 397–98, 400
autism, 83, 86, 354, 356
avian influenza, 124, 168, 179, *180*, 183, 262, 276
Axelrod, Boreali v., 74, *96*, 100

Baird, Eisenstadt v., 473b
Barlow, Marshall v., 544
Basel Convention (1989), 189, *190*
behavioral risk factors, 16, 27, 222, 233, 240, 241, 333, 417
    and criminal law, 156–61
        congruence with/divergence from public health goals, 160–61
        disclosing information, 158–59
        policy and statutory context, 156–58
        restricting freedom of movement, 159–60
    and ethics in public health, 110–11, 122–23, 131–32
    and injury prevention, 507, 510, 513
    and reproductive health, 453, 466–67
    and special populations, 285–90, 300
Behavioral Risk Factor Surveillance System, 233, 417
Bennett, Flowers v., 418
Berg v. Glen Cove City School District, 352
bioterrorism, 16–17, 25, 86, 106–7, 201, 211, 240
    and criminal law, 141, *143*, 148–49, *151*, 153, 156, 159
    and emergency powers, 262, 265, 267, 270, 274
    and environmental health, 498–500
    and ethics in public health, 111–12, 120
    and foodborne diseases, 368, 375, 379–81
    and international considerations, 176, 186–87
    and surveillance/investigations, 223, 232–35
birth control. *See* contraception; family planning services
birth defects, 326
    registries for, 233, 462
blood/blood products regulation, 386–87, 393–94
bloodborne infections, 145, 162, 385–400. *See also* sexually transmitted infections (STIs)
    emerging issues in, 399–400
    legal authorities for, 386–91
    legal issues/controversies, 391–94
    practice considerations for, 394–99
Bloodborne Pathogen Standard (OSHA), 544
Boerne v. Flores, 350
Boone v. Boozman, 352, 354
Boozman, McCarthy v., 352
Boreali v. Axelrod, 74, *96*, 100
bovine spongiform encephalopathy, 184, 262
Breast and Cervical Mortality Prevention Act (1990), 408
breast-milk substitutes, 176, 190–91
Brown & Williamson Tobacco Corp. v. FDA, 443
Brown v. Stone, 351, 356c
BT Act (2002), 186, 368, 379–81

built environment, 34, 412, 418–19, 422, 497–98
burden of proof, 83, 139–40, 156, 404

Camara v. Municipal Court of San Francisco,
    41, 154
Campbell, Funtanilla v., 291
cancer, 7, 16, 17, 331, 354, 400, 402, 408, 414–
    15, 438–39, 497, 501g
  registries for, 233, 409, 412, 462
Cancer Registries Amendment Act (1992), 462
cardiovascular health, 17, 403, *407,* 409, *410,*
    411, 415–16, 420–21
CARE Act, 387
Carey, Harwood Capital Corp. v., 440
Carhart, Stenberg v., 456
Cartagena Protocol on Biosafety (2000), 189,
    190, 191
case law, 4, 94–106, *95–98,* 137, 207, 246, 393.
    See also names of cases
*Casey, Planned Parenthood of Southeastern
    Pennsylvania v.,* 455, 464
Castle Rock v. Gonzalez, 35
Center for Law and the Public's Health
    (Georgetown–Johns Hopkins), 32
Center for Substance Abuse Prevention (CSAP),
    55
Centers for Disease Control and Prevention
    (CDC), 32, 45–46, 54–56, 87f, 111, 145,
    149, 301
  and chronic diseases, *405–7,* 408
  and emergency powers, *266, 279*
  and environmental health, *486,* 491–92, 500
  and foodborne diseases, 363, 365–66, 372,
    374–75, 377
  and genetics, 325–26
  and identifiable health information, 247–48,
    252
  and injury prevention, 511–13, 521
  and international considerations, 178, *180–
    81,* 183
  and occupational health and safety, 531, 542,
    544
  and public health achievements, 3–4, 9, 11–
    12, *30,* 338, 506
  and reproductive health, 458, 460–62, 468–71
  and STIs/bloodborne infections, 394, 396–98
  and surveillance/investigations, 222, 226,
    227, 229–30, 232–35
  and vaccination, 338–40, 342–44
Centers for Medicare and Medicaid Services,
    247, 408, 416, 469
chain of custody of evidence, 147, 155, 162,
    370
Chevron v. Natural Resources Defense Council,
    79, *95,* 99

Chicago Wire Magnet Corp., People v., 97, 104
Child Abuse Prevention and Treatment Act
    (CAPTA), 459
children, 8, 11–12, 14–15, 17, 29, 82, 84, 245.
    See also maternal and child health;
    minors
  and chronic diseases, *406, 410,* 414–15, 417
  and ethics in public health, 122–23
  and injury prevention, 507, 512–14, 518,
    521–22
  mortality rates of, 7, 233, 307, 458, 460
  as special population, 284, 297–306
    abuse or neglect of, *144,* 240, 297–301,
      308, 356d, 397, 463, 467
    case studies, 297, 301
    and lead exposure, 301–6 (*see also* lead
      exposure)
    legal analyses, 297–300, 302–4
    practice pointers, 300–301, 304–6
Children's Health Act (2000), *406,* 462
Children's Health Insurance Program, 343, 472
cholera, xxxi, 3, *48,* 51, 70, 174, 179, 227–28
chronic diseases, 7, 16, 17, 25, 402–22, *403*
  emerging issues in, 419–21
  and environmental health, 497
  and ethics in public health, 110–11
  legal authorities for, 403–12
    federal public health system, 405–9, *405–7*
    infectious diseases, 404
    state/local public health systems, 409–12,
      410–11, 417, 422a
  legal issues/controversies, 413–15
  and local authorities, 412–13
  practical considerations, 415–19
    cardiovascular health, 415–16 (*see also*
      cardiovascular health)
    diabetes, 416–18 (*see also* diabetes)
    physical activity, 418–19 (*see also* physical
      activity)
  and surveillance/investigations, 222, 226, 233
citizen suits, 489–90
The City of Newark v. J. S., 97, 103, 105
City of New York v. New St. Mark's Baths, 95,
    99, 390, 393
civil commitment, 288–90, 312–13c
civil law, 79, 80–82, 91, 93, 300, 467
  vs. criminal law, 139, 140, 156, 160
  and environmental health, 489–90, 495
  and foodborne diseases, 367, 369
  and tobacco-control regulations, 430, 436
civil liberties, 15, 31, 33, 38–39, 42, 74–75, *76,*
    127. *See also* individual rights
  and emergency powers, 267
  and legal counsel, 208–9
  and special populations, 285, 312, 313g

civil liberties (*continued*)
   and STIs/bloodborne infections, 390
   and surveillance/investigations, 224
   and vaccination, 346–47
Civil Rights Act (1964), 420, 473h, 537–38
CLASH v. City of New York, 440
class action product liability cases, 156, 447
Clean Air Act (CAA), 55, *479*, *487*, 488, 491,
   494, 495–96, 498, 501–2h,i
Clean Indoor Air Acts, 438
Clean Water Act (CWA), *479*, *487*, 488–89,
   491, 494, 498, 501f
Clifford, Michigan v., 155
Clinical Laboratory Improvement Act (CLIA),
   327, 457, 469
Cochrane Collaboration, 17–18
Code of Federal Regulations (C.F.R.), 77, 129,
   171
codes of ethics, 111, 114, 123–28, *125*, *126–27*
Codex Alimentarius Commission, 184–85, 192
coercion, 14, 31, 33, 42, 121, 131, 138, 389
Commerce Clause (U.S. Constitution), xxxiv,
   36, 51–52, 93, 105–6
   and chronic diseases, 404
   and emergency powers, 263–64
   and environmental health, 482–83
   and foodborne diseases, 366
   and injury prevention, 509, *510*, 517
   and international considerations, 170, 184,
     187, 190
   and occupational health and safety, 531
   and STIs/bloodborne infections, 386, 393–94
   and surveillance/investigations, 223
   and tobacco-control regulations, 444
commercial speech, 16, 34, 332, 441
common law, xxxiii, 14, 30
   and criminal law, 137–38, 157, 161
   and emergency powers, 274
   and environmental health, 478, 483, *484–85*
   and identifiable health information, 247
   and police powers, 37
   and reproductive health, 456
Common Rule, 239–46, 248, 253, *254–56*, 332
communicable diseases. *See* infectious diseases,
   control of
Comprehensive Environmental Response,
   Compensation, and Liability Act
   (CERCLA). *See* Superfund
Comprehensive Smokeless Tobacco Education
   Act (1986), 428
compulsory powers, 32, 38–39, 107, 131, 188,
   234, 294. *See also* emergency powers;
   mandatory powers
confidentiality
   and administrative law, 82

and criminal law, 140, *144*, 156, 158–60
and ethics in public health, 112, *116–18*, 130,
   132
and foodborne diseases, 374
and genetics, 324
and identifiable health information, 242,
   245–49, 253
and legal counsel, 205, 212–13, 214
and occupational health and safety, 547
and reproductive health, 458, 461, 463, 468
and special populations, 285–87, 289–90,
   293, 295–96, 312, 312b
and STIs/bloodborne infections, 388–89, 395,
   398
and surveillance/investigations, 223, 225–26,
   231–32
constitutional law. *See* U.S. Constitution
Consumer Product Safety Commission (CPSC),
   71, 428, 510, *510*, 511–12, 521
contact tracing, 82, *116–18*, 179, 228, 230, 268,
   390, 392, 397–98
Continental Seafoods v. Schweiker, *95*, 99
contraception, 6, 452–54, 456–57, 460, 463,
   465–66, 468, 471–72, 473b
Cookie's Diner v. Columbus Board of Health, 440
cordon sanitaire, 15, *272*, 273–74
cost-benefit analysis, 84–85, 99
Council of State and Territorial Epidemiologists
   (CSTE), 229–30, 232–33, 239, 253–58,
   254–56, 259g
CPS (child protective services) agency, 297,
   299–300
criminal law, 136–62
   and administrative law, 81–82, 140
   and behavioral risk factors, 156–61
     congruence with/divergence from public
      health goals, 160–61
     disclosing information, 158–59
     policy and statutory context, 156–58
     restricting freedom of movement, 159–60
   and burden of proof, 139–40
   comparison to public health practice, 137–38
   definition of, 136–37
   and due process, 138–39
   and environmental health, 489, 495
   and epidemiologic investigations, 146–56
     forensic epidemiology, 148–49, 162, 234
     joint record of, 149–53, *150–52*
     legal issues in, 153–55
     scientific evidence in courtroom, 155–56
     scientific methods used by, 147–48
   and foodborne diseases, 367, 369, 375, 378
   and injury prevention, 514
   and penalties, 140
   and power of state, 138

and public health goals, 136–37, 141–46
  barriers to, 145–46
  incarcerated populations, 146, *147*
  similarities between, 141–44, *142–44*
  theories of criminal law, 141
and public nuisances, 42
and reproductive health, 453–54, 464, 467,
    472, 473a,f
and searches, 41
and special populations, 284–85, 290–93,
    298, 300
  case study, 290
  legal analysis, 290–92
  practice pointers, 292–93
and STIs/bloodborne infections, 388, 393,
    397–98
and tobacco-control regulations, 430, 436
utility of, 161–62
Cruzan v. Director, Missouri Dept. of Health,
    353
customary international law (CIL), 172–73,
    181, 187

data collection. *See* identifiable health
    information
Daubert v. Merrell Dow Pharmaceuticals, *96*,
    102
DeGidio v. Pung, 291
Department of Agriculture (USDA)
  and chronic diseases, 408
  and emergency powers, *278*
  and environmental health, 490
  and foodborne diseases, 363, *364*, 365–66,
    371, 375, 381b
  and international considerations, 171, *180*,
    184
  and special populations, 298
  and STIs/bloodborne infections, 386
Department of Defense, 214, 275
Department of Health and Human Services
    (DHHS), 52–56
  and administrative law, 71
  and chronic diseases, 404, *405*, 408
  and emergency powers, 269, 275, *279*, 281a
  and environmental health, 494–95, 501h
  and foodborne diseases, 363, 374
  and genetics, 325–26
  and identifiable health information, 239, 240,
    244, 248, 250–52, 259d–g
  and injury prevention, 515
  and international considerations, 171, 179, 189
  and occupational health and safety, 531
  and reproductive health, 458, 462–63, 470,
    473e
  and special populations, 299, 303

and tobacco-control regulations, 434–35
  and vaccination, 341
Department of Homeland Security, 267, *279*,
    281a–c, 282f, 311, 369
Department of Labor, 529, 544
Department of Transportation (DOT), 10, 15,
    104, 542
*DeShaney v. Winnebago County Department of
    Social Services*, 35
diabetes, 25, 29, 284, 402–3, *403*, *405–6*, 408,
    410, 411, 415, 416–18, 420, 497
Diaz, Matthews v., 307
diphtheria, 4, 7, *49*, 51, 178–79, 340, *342*, *343*,
    345–46
diplomacy, health, 174–77
directly observed therapy (DOT), 75, 118, 120,
    139, 209, 295
disclosure of information in emergencies, 124–
    25, 158–59
discrimination, 43. *See also* ethnic disparities;
    racial disparities
  and chronic diseases, 415, 417, 420
  and emergency powers, 263
  and ethics in public health, 123
  and genetics, 324, 328–29, 332
  and identifiable health information, 238
  and legal counsel, 218
  and occupational health and safety, 537–40, 548
  and reproductive health, 473g
  and STIs/bloodborne infections, 395
DNA data-banking, 148, 330–32
Doha Development Round, 186, 192
domestic violence, *76*, 206, 240, 293, 398, 468
*Donovan, American Textile Manufacturers
    Institute v.*, *96*, 99, 544
Drug Free School Zone Act (1990), 93
drug paraphernalia laws, *144*, 145, 157, 162,
    393, 398
drugs, illicit. *See* illicit drug use
drug safety. *See* food/drug safety
drunk driving, 9, 11, *76*, 83, 141, *144*, 288, 411,
    510, 513–14
due process protections, 39
  and administrative law, 77–78, 85
  and chronic diseases, 404
  and criminal law, 138–39, 159, 162
  and emergency powers, *264*, 270, 271–73, 282g
  and international considerations, 179
  and judiciary, 102–3, 105–6, 108
  and legal counsel, 209, 215
  and reproductive health, 454
  and special populations, 294
  and STIs/bloodborne infections, 388, 393
  and surveillance/investigations, 224, 235
  and tobacco-control regulations, 437

Ebola virus, 179, 274, 276
EC—Asbestos case (WTO), 184
EC—Hormones case (WTO), 185
E-coding, 519–20
education. *See* health education
Edwards, Greene v., 39, *97*, 102–3, 105
Eighth Amendment (U.S. Constitution), 290–92, 313e,g
Eisenstadt v. Baird, 473b
electronic health information infrastructure
  and genetics, 330, 332
  and identifiable health information, 238, 247, 250–51
  and legal counsel, 212
  and surveillance/investigations, 233–34
embryo laboratories, 458, 461, 470–71
emergency contraception access, 471–72
emergency management agencies (EMAs), 265, 267–68
Emergency Management Assistance Compact (EMAC), 275–76
Emergency Medical Treatment and Active Labor Act (EMTALA), 293, 308–9
Emergency Planning and Community Right-to-Know Act (EPCRA), *480*, *487*, 537
emergency powers, 262–81
  and chronic diseases, 421
  and criminal law, 159–60
  emerging issues in, 276–80
    animal control, 276–77, *278–79*
    leaky quarantine, 277, 280
  historical perspective on, 263–66, *264*
  and judiciary, 106–8
  legal authorities for, 266–76
    emergency declarations, 268–69, 282e,f
    emergency management system, 267–68, 281a–c
    management of persons, *264*, 271–74, *272*, 282g
    management of property, *264*, 269–70
    traditional public health powers, 266–67
  and legal counsel, 203
  and military, 275–76, 282k
  and Model State Emergency Health Powers Act (MSEHPA), 32, 235
  and mutual aid assistance, 274–75
  and Public Health Service (PHS), 54
  and surveillance/investigations, 234–35
  and voluntarism, 274–75
emergency support functions (ESFs), 267, 281b
Emergency System for Advance Registration of Volunteer Health Professionals, 275
Employee Retirement Income Security Act, 325, 330
Engle, Liggett Group v., 447

Environmental Cleanup Responsibility Act (N.J.), 488
Environmental Council of the States, 486
environmental health, xxxiii, 25, 478–501
  and chronic diseases, 414
  and emergency powers, 264
  emerging issues in, 497–500
  legal authorities for, 482–90
    environmental protection laws, *479–82*, 482–83
    federalism, 483, 485–86, 488–89
    federal public health system, *486*, *487*
    litigation, 489–90
    state/local public health systems, 482–83, *484–85*, 501a–c
  legal issues/controversies, 490–94
    historical underpinnings of, 490–93
    practice considerations for, 494–97
  and reproductive health, 462–63
  and surveillance/investigations, 232
Environmental Protection Agency (EPA), 12, 14, 45–46, 55, 85, 483
  and environmental health, *479–82*, 489–97, 501a,g,h
  and foodborne diseases, 363, *364*, 365
  and identifiable health information, 252
  and occupational health and safety, 536–37
  and special populations, 304
  and tobacco-control regulations, 432
environmental protection laws, *479–82*, 482–83, 490–92, 523
epidemics, 38. *See also names of epidemic diseases, e.g.,* smallpox
  and criminal law, 145, 149
  and emergency powers, 270, 277, 280
  and ethics in public health, 130
  and federal public health system, 54
  and international considerations, 174
  and judiciary, 106–7
  and legal counsel, 208–10
  and vaccination, 354
epidemiologic investigations, 222–35
  and criminal investigations, 146–56
    forensic epidemiology, 148–49, 162, 234
    joint record of, 149–53, *150–52*
    legal issues in, 153–55
    scientific evidence in courtroom, 155–56
    scientific methods used by, 147–48
  emerging developments in, 232–35
  and ethics in public health, 129, 130
  and federalism, 230–31
  and foodborne diseases, 362, 365–66, 372–76
  general legal authorities for, 223–25
  and identifiable health information, 226, 231–32, 240, 253

and international considerations, 185
and legal counsel, 202, 212–13, 215, 217
legal milestones in evolution of, 226–29
and mandatory reporting, 224, 226–30, 232
and reproductive health, 460–61
role of in public health, 226
and STIs/bloodborne infections, 388–89,
  392–93, 397, 399
Equal Employment Opportunity Commission
  (EEOC), 328, 473h, 545, 548
Escherichia coli, 240, 372, 375, 378
Estelle v. Gamble, 290–92
ethics in public health, 110–33, 133b, 457
  approaches to, 113–21, *116–18, 119*
    analysis of issues, 114, *115*
    evaluation of options, 115, 118, 120
    justifications for, 120–21
  codes of, 111, 114, 123–28, *125, 126–27*
  individual rights vs. public good, 121–23
  integration into public health practice, 128–
    32
  and STIs/bloodborne infections, 391–92, 398
ethnic disparities, 29, 146, *147*, 240, 273, 324,
  420
Euclid v. Amber Realty, 418, 502k
eugenics, 324–25
evidentiary issues. *See* scientific evidence/
  methods
Exploring the Dangerous Trades (Hamilton), 529

Family and Medical Leave Act (FMLA), 539–
  40, 548
Family Educational Rights and Privacy Act
  (FERPA), 330, 412
family planning services, 456, 458–59, 462,
  469. *See also* contraception
farm-to-table continuum, 362–63, *364*, 365–67,
  373, 375–76, 378–79
Federal Cigarette Labeling and Advertising Act
  (FCLAA), 428–30, 433, 441–42, 444
Federal Coal Mine Health and Safety Act
  (1969), 529
Federal Emergency Management Agency
  (FEMA), 269, 282f
Federal Food, Drug, and Cosmetic Act
  (FFDCA), 363, 366–69, 374, 378, 408,
  469, *486–87*, 491
Federal Insecticide, Fungicide, and Rodenticide
  Act (FIFRA), 55, 363, *480, 487*, 488,
  491, 537
federalism, 14, 28, 51–52, 73, 92–94, 103–5
  and environmental health, 483, 485–86, 488–
    89
  and foodborne diseases, 376–79
  and international considerations, 170–71, *172*

and surveillance/investigations, 230–31, 234–
  35
Federal Mine Safety and Health Act (MSHAct),
  536
Federal Policy for the Protection of Human
  Subjects. *See* Common Rule
federal public health system, 46–56, *48–50*. *See
  also* federalism; U.S. Constitution
  and chronic diseases, 405–9, *405–7*, 417
  and emergency powers, 263–65, 267–69, 274
  and environmental health, *486, 487*, 492–93
  and foodborne diseases, 363–70, *364, 369*,
    371–76
  and genetics, 325–28
  and identifiable health information, 241,
    247–49
  and international considerations, 170–71,
    172, 178–79, *180–81*, 183–84, 187–89
  and judiciary, 91, 93
  and occupational health and safety, 531–40, *534*
  and reproductive health, 453–56, 458–60,
    465–66, 473e
  and special populations, 286–87, 289, 292–
    93, 295, 298, 304, 307–9, 311, 315r
  and STIs/bloodborne infections, 386–87
  and surveillance/investigations, 223, 228–35
  and tobacco-control regulations, 428–29, 444
  and vaccination, 341–44
Federal Register, 55, 77
Federal Trade Commission, 71, 332, 428
Federal Water Pollution Control Act (CWA),
  479, 487, 488–89, 491, 494, 498, 501f
felonies, 140, 141, *142–44*, 160
Ferguson v. City of Charleston, *96*, 102, 396
Fertility Clinic Success Rate and Certification
  Act (FCSRCA), 458, 461, 469–71
fetus, legal status of, 472
field epidemiology. *See* epidemiologic
  investigations
Fifth Amendment (U.S. Constitution), 85, 102,
  224, 242, *264*, 454
  and criminal law, 138–39, 153, 155
  and tobacco-control regulations, 433, 444
firearms, 16, 34, 36, 41, 233
  control of, 56, *76*, 93, 105–6, 263
First Amendment (U.S. Constitution), 16, 102,
  264, 313d, 332
  and tobacco-control regulations, xxxiii, 433, 441
  and vaccination, 349–51, 356f
Flores, Boerne v., 350
Flowers v. Bennett, 418
*Flue-Cured Tobacco Cooperative Stabilization
  Corp. v. EPA*, 432
fluoridation of drinking water, 5, 11–13, 123,
  242, 414

Food, Drug, and Cosmetics Act (1938), 9, 428
food additives, 365–66
Food and Drug Administration (FDA), 9, 45–
    46, *50*, 54, 74, *279, 486*
    and chronic diseases, 408, 416, 421
    and foodborne diseases, 363–70, *364, 369,*
        371–72, 374–76, 379–81
    and genetics, 326–27, 332
    and international considerations, 171, 186
    and reproductive health, 457, 462, 466, 469,
        471–72
    and STIs/bloodborne infections, 386–87, 394,
        400
    and tobacco-control regulations, 428, 432,
        443–44, 446
    and vaccination, 341–42
foodborne diseases, 61, 361–81. *See also* food/
    drug safety
    emerging issues in, 376–81
        bioterrorism, 368, 375, 379–81
        food disparagement laws, 377–78
        implications of federalism, 376–79
    and international considerations, 170, *180*
    legal authorities for, 363–70
        federal public health system, 363–65, *364*
        Food and Drug Administration (FDA),
            363–70, *364, 369*
        state/local public health systems, 365–66
    legal issues/controversies, 370–71
    practice considerations for, 372–76
    and public health achievements, *6*, 361
    and surveillance/investigations, 225, 230, 397
food disparagement laws, 377–78
food/drug safety, *6*, 7, 14, 38, 61, *64*, 78, 80–
    81, 99. *See also* foodborne diseases
    and chronic diseases, 408
    and criminal law, 141, *143, 152,* 157
    and emergency powers, 265, *266*
    and international considerations, 171, 176–
        77, 184–86, 188–89, 193c,e
    and special populations, 297
    and surveillance/investigations, 225
Food Quality Protection Act (FQPA), *480, 487,*491
Food Safety Inspection Service (FSIS), 363–65,
    364, 368–69, *369,* 371, 375, 379–80
Food Stamps, 408, 414
forensic epidemiology, 148–49, 162, 234, 397
Fourteenth Amendment (U.S. Constitution), 15,
    42, 74–75, 102, 138–39
    and identifiable health information, 242
    and reproductive health, 454, 472
    and special populations, 294, 308
    and surveillance/investigations, 224
    and tobacco-control regulations, 436, 444
    and vaccination, 346–47, 351, 353, 356f

Fourth Amendment (U.S. Constitution), xxxiv,
    41, 84, 102, 153–55
    and occupational health and safety, 544
    and surveillance/investigations, 38, 224
    and tobacco-control regulations, 435–37
Framework Convention on Tobacco Control
    (FCTC), 189–90, *191,* 416
Frank v. Maryland, 154
Freedom of Information Act (FOIA), 53, 231,
    247–49, 390
freedom of information laws, 205, 212
free exercise standard, 349–52, 356f
funding, 28, *50,* 55–56, 66a, 71, 73. *See also*
    Medicaid; Medicare; taxation
    and chronic diseases, 404, 408, 414, 416,
        421, 422c
    and emergency powers, 264–65, 267–69,
        274–75, 281a
    and environmental health, 488, 494
    and foodborne diseases, 379
    and genetics, 323, 325, 327
    and human subjects research, 242–43
    and reproductive health, 453, 456, 457, 458–
        60, 465–66, 471, 473e
    and special populations, 286, 298, 300, 305–
        6, 308–11, 315r
    and STIs/bloodborne infections, 387, 394,
        398
    and tobacco-control regulations, 429, 430–31,
        434, 445
    and vaccination, 343
Funtanilla v. Campbell, 291
The Future of Public Health (IOM), 17, 26, 27
*The Future of the Public's Health in the 21st
    Century* (IOM), 17, 27–28

Gade v. National Solid Wastes Management,
    545
Gamble, Estelle v., 290–92
GATS (General Agreement on Trade in
    Services), 186
GATT (General Agreement on Tariffs and
    Trade), 177, 184, 189, 193c
Geier v. American Honda Motor, 97, 104
genetically modified organisms, 190–91
genetics, 86, 121, 147, 249, 323–34, 421, 470–71
    emerging issues in, 29, 332–33
    legal authorities for, 324–28
    legal issues/controversies, 328–30
        genetic exceptionalism, 329
        oversight of, 330
        surveillance vs. research, 329
    and occupational health and safety, 545–46,
        548
    practical considerations, 330–32

Gibbons v. Ogden, 13

globalization, 168, 170, 173–77, *175*, 179, 181, *182*, 193

gonorrhea, *116*, 178, 385–86, 391, 393–97

Gonzalez, Castle Rock v., 35

Gonzalez v. Raich, 36, *98*, 106

Good Samaritan laws, 275, 411

graduated driver licensing (GDL), 514

Greene v. Edwards, 39, *97*, 102–3, 105

Grezaffi, City of Tucson v., 440

Griswold v. Connecticut, 454

Guide to Community Preventive Services, 418, 522

gun control, 56, *76*, 93, 105–6, 263. *See also* firearms

habitability assessment, 500

Haddon matrix, 507, *508*

in re Halko, *98*, 105

Handbook for Public Playground Safety (CPSC), 511–12

harm analysis, 8, 100, 112, 114, *116–18*, 122. *See also* behavioral risk factors

Harmon, Maricopa County Health Department v., 347

Harper, Washington v., 274

Harwood Capital Corp. v. Carey, 440

Hazard Analysis and Critical Control Point Plan (HACCP), 368, 371, 380

Hazard Communication Standard (OSHAct), 535, 537

Hazardous and Solid Waste Amendments, *482*, 491

hazardous wastes, 81–82, 141, *142, 279, 484*, 489, 496–97

health codes, 32, 203–4, 206–9, 214, 273, 366, 409

health education, 34, 82–83, 87, 141, 342, 494
  and chronic diseases, 404, 408, 412, 417
  and ethics in public health, *126–27*, 131–32
  and STIs/bloodborne infections, 386, 392, 394, 397–98, 400
  and tobacco-control regulations, 427, 446

Health Hazard Evaluation (HHE), 547–48

health hold orders. *See* administrative orders

Health Insurance Portability and Accountability Act (HIPAA), 53, 71–72, 213, 399. *See also* Privacy Rule

health officers, 34, 38, 42, *50*, 59, 61–62, *61*
  and emergency powers, 262–63, 268–70
  legal basis for, 71–72, 77, 79, 84
  and legal counsel, 199–205, 208, 211, 216–17, 219
  and special populations, 290, 296
  and STIs/bloodborne infections, 390
  and vaccination, 345

Health Resources and Services Administration (HRSA), 55, 145, 275, 326, 416, 461, *486*

Healthy People 2010, xxxii, 28, 298, 420, 493–94, 497

heart disease, *6*, 7, 16, 25, 149, *150–51*, 153, 402, *403*, 408, 438, 497. *See also* cardiovascular health

helmet-use laws, 15, 34, *76*, 111, 122–23, 141, 507, 510, 516–17

Henley v. Philip Morris, 447

hepatitis, 146, 147, 230. *See also* hepatitis A (HAV); hepatitis B (HBV); hepatitis C

hepatitis A (HAV), 340, 345, 385, 394

hepatitis B (HBV), 86, 145, 178, 240, 385–87, 389, 392–94, 396–97
  and vaccination, 340–41, *342*, 345, 354

hepatitis C, 72, 145, 289, 290, 292–93, 386

herd immunity, 339–40

Highway Safety Act (1966), 10, 15, 516

Hill-Burton Act, 309, 315r, 420

HIV/AIDS, 7–8, 16, 34, 55, 72, 81–82, 99, 213, 385–87, 389–90, 392–400
  and criminal law, *144*, 145–47, 156–58, 160–62
  and emergency powers, 267–68
  and ethics in public health, 112, 114, *116–18*, 121–22, 127
  and identifiable health information, 240, 249, 253
  and international considerations, *169*, 176–78, *180*, 181, 192
  and occupational health and safety, 544
  and special populations, 289, 290, 292–93, 308, 313e
  and surveillance/investigations, 230

Hodgson, Industrial Union Department, AFL-CIO v., 543

homeland security agencies, 265–66, *266*

homeless persons, 284, 293–97

home rule, 57–59, 61–62, 66c, 429

Housing and Community Development Act, 302–3

Human Genome Project, 29, 323

human rights, 113, 128, 179, 181, *182*, 218

human subjects research
  and genetics, 329, 331–32
  and identifiable health information, 239, 240–41
    legal protections for, 242–46
    vs. public health practice, 252–58, *254–56*
  and legal counsel, 216–17
  and reproductive health, 452–53, 462–63, 466
  and surveillance/investigations, 232

hurricanes, 25, 106, 262, 266, 271, 280, 421, 498–500

Hyde Amendment, 459, 473e

identifiable health information, 75, 77, 238–59, 412
  and ethics in public health, 129–30, 132
  fundamental uses and disclosures of, 239–41
  and genetics, 327, 329
  and injury prevention, 519–20
  legal frameworks underlying, 241–46
    human subjects research, 242–46
    U.S. Constitution, 241–42, 247, 259a
  privacy rights vs. population health, 246–50
    federal public health system, 247–49
    state/local public health systems, 249–50
  public health practice vs. research, 252–58, *254–56*
  and STIs/bloodborne infections, 388–89, 394–95, 398–99
  and surveillance/investigations, 226, 231–32, 240, 253
illicit drug use, 16, 34, *50*, 81, 82, 102, 106, *144*, 145–46, 178. *See also* injection-drug users (IDUs)
  and needle-exchange programs, 81, 82, 114, 127, 145
  and reproductive health, 463, 466–67
  and special populations, 284, 286, 288–89
  and STIs/bloodborne infections, 386, 388, 392–93, 398–99
immigrants, 47, *48*, 52–53, 118, 120, 178, 181, 263, 308–10, 314o, 465. *See also* undocumented immigrants
imported food, 369–70, *369*, 377, 379–81
Incident Command Systems (ICSs), 211, 267, 281a
individual rights, xxxiii, 13, 18, 32, 38, 42–43, 74–75, *76*, 82, 87, 149. *See also* civil liberties; privacy rights
  and chronic diseases, 404, 413–14
  and emergency powers, 262, 266–67, 271–74
  and ethics in public health, 112–13, 121–23, 128
  and genetics, 324
  and injury prevention, 515
  and judiciary, 102–3, 105, 107–8
  and legal counsel, 208–9
  and reproductive health, 464
  and special populations, 295
  and STIs/bloodborne infections, 387–88, 391–93
  and surveillance/investigations, 224, 226
  and vaccination, 338–56
Individuals with Disabilities Education Act (IDEA), *406*, 415
Industrial Union Department, AFL-CIO v. Hodgson, 543
Industrial Union Department v. American Petroleum Institute, 543

industries, 78, 81, 84, 87h, 99, 491
  and foodborne diseases, 370–71, 375, 379–80
  and tobacco-control regulations, xxxiii, 78, 81, 427–28, 430–34, 439–43, 445, 447
infants. *See* children
infectious diseases, control of, 4, *5*, 7–9, 38–39, 70, 72, 82, 86–87, 240, 404, 469. *See also names of infectious diseases*; sexually transmitted infections (STIs)
  and criminal law, 147, 159–60
  and emergency powers, 267–68, 270–74, 276–77, 280, 282g
  and ethics in public health, 110–11, 121, 124
  and international considerations, 168, 170, 173–84, *175*, *180–81*, *182–83*, 187
  and judiciary, 93, 106–8, 228
  and legal counsel, 202, 208–10
  and special populations, 289, 291, 294–96, 307, 311, 313e
  and surveillance/investigations, 222–33
infertility services, 452–53, 460, 469–70
influenza, 7, 8, 9, 16, 47, *50*, 51, 106, 111, 201, 227, 265. *See also* avian influenza
  and chronic diseases, 402, *403*, 416
  and international considerations, 178–79, *180*
  and vaccination, 340, *342*, *343*, 345
informatics, 332, 333
information collection. *See* identifiable health information
informed consent, 188, 232, 274, 332
  and ethics in public health, 129–30, 132
  and identifiable health information, 241, 245–46, 247
  and reproductive health, 452, 456, 462
  and STIs/bloodborne infections, 395–96
injection-drug users (IDUs), 145–46, 385, 393, 398–400
injunctions, 62, 80–81, 83, 146, 439
  and foodborne diseases, 367, *369*, 370–71
injury prevention, 506–24
  conceptual approach to, 507–8, *508*
  emerging issues in, 521–23
  legal authorities for, 509–15, *510*
    motor vehicle safety, 512–14
    playground safety, 511–12
    youth violence prevention, 514–15
  legal issues/controversies, 515–18
  practice considerations for, 518–21
inspections, 41, 75, 78, 83–84, 154, 215, *364*
  and foodborne diseases, 362–63, *364*, 365–69, *369*, 370–71, 374, 379–80
  and identifiable health information, 241
  and international considerations, 174
  and occupational health and safety, 544–45
  and reproductive health, 469

and special populations, 304–6
and tobacco-control regulations, 435–37
Institute of Medicine (IOM), xxix, 17, 26–28,
    323–24, 354, 434–35
Institute of Transportation Engineers, 419
institutional memory, 210
institutional review boards (IRBs), 216–17, 232,
    329, 462
    and identifiable health information, 241,
        242–46, 252–53, 257
insurance coverage, 343, 538. *See also* Health
        Insurance Portability and Accountability
        Act (HIPAA)
    and chronic diseases, 408, 409, *410*, 414,
        417, 419, 420, 421, 422c
    and genetics, 328–29, 332, 333
    and reproductive health, 452, 453–54, 460,
        465–66, 468, 472, 473h
    and special populations, 293, 302, 308–9
intellectual property rights, 176, 191–92
International Classification of Diseases, 519–20
international considerations, 56, 168–93, *169*
    and foodborne diseases, 369–70, *369*, 377,
        379–81
    and health diplomacy, 174–77
    and health threats exported from U.S., 187–92
        general principles on, 187
        intellectual property rights, 191–92
        international product standards, 192
        pharmaceutical exports, 191–92
        threats through goods, 188–91, *190*
        threats through people, 187–88
    and health threats originating outside U.S.,
        177–87
        general principles on, 177
        threats from goods, 183–86
        threats from people, 178–83, *180–81*, *182–83*
        threats from terrorism, 186–87
    and structures/sources of public health law,
        170–74
        globalization, 173–74, *175*
        international law, 171–73
        U.S. Constitution, 170–71, *172*
International Health Regulations (IHRs), *169*,
    172, 177, 179, *182–83*, 186, 188
international law, 170, 171–73, 179, 181, 183,
    188–91, *190*, 193
international trade, 174, *175*, 176–77, 179, 181,
    182, 184–86, 522–23
intussusception, 86, 354
investigations. *See* epidemiologic
        investigations; outbreak investigations
in vitro fertilization, 453, 470–71, 473–74i
isolation, 8, 32, 39, 75, 107, *180*, 201, 241
    and emergency powers, 268, 271–74, *272*, 277

and special populations, 295–96
and surveillance/investigations, 225, 227–28, 234

Jacobson v. Massachusetts, 8, 18, 39, 86, 94,
    95, 102, 105
    and chronic diseases, 404
    and emergency powers, 271, 273
    and ethics in public health, 122
    and special populations, 294–95
    and surveillance/investigations, 228
    and vaccination, 346–47, 350–51, 353, 356b
Jew Ho v. Williamson, et al., 15
Johnson Controls, Automobile Workers v., 545
Joint Commission on Accreditation of
        Healthcare Organizations, 71, 428
Jones v. Rath Packing Co., 104
J. S., The City of Newark v., *97*, 103, 105
judiciary, 79, 89–108
    and emergency powers, 106–8
    and ethics in public health, 111–13
    and injury prevention, 517–18
    and international considerations, 171, 173
    selected law cases, 94–106, *95–98*
        deference to public health authority, 94,
            99
        and federalism/preemption, 103–5
        and individual rights, 102–3
        and judicial interpretation over time, 105–6
        review of legal authority, 99–102
    structure and function of, 90–94, *91*
The Jungle (Sinclair), 14, 378

Katrina (Hurricane), 25, 106, 262, 266, 280,
    421, 498–99, 500
King, Zucht v., 347
Kurtzman, Lemon v., 351, 357j

labeling, 14, 34, 365, 408, 428–29, 442
labor law, 540
land-use planning, 34, 418–19, 497–98, 502k,l
law, public health, xxx–xxxvi. *See also*
        administrative law; criminal law;
        judiciary
    defining, xxviii–xxx, 30–31
    foundations of, 25–43
    future of, 42–43
    and international considerations, 56, 168–93,
        169
        health diplomacy, 174–77
        health threats exported from U.S., 187–92
        health threats originating outside U.S.,
            177–87
        structures/sources of, 170–74
    and joint epidemiologic/criminal
        investigations, 153–55

law, public health (*continued*)
  and legal counsel, 199–200
    initial encounter with, 200–210
    role of, 210–18
  models of, 33–34
  structure of, 45–66
    statutory basis at federal level, 46–56, *48–50*
    statutory basis at state/local level, 56–66, *61, 63, 64, 65*
lawyers in public health. *See* legal counsel
Lead Based Poisoning Prevention Act (1971), 302
Lead Contamination Control Act, 302
lead exposure, 230, 233, 240
  and children as special population, 301–6, 314j–m
  and legal counsel, 207–8, 212–13, 215–16, 218
leaky quarantine, 277, 280
least restrictive alternatives, 74–75, *76*, 82, 102, 186, 209, 224, 273, 352, 391
  and ethics in public health, *115*, 120, 131
legal counsel, 101, 199–220
  and ethics in public health, 127–28
  initial encounter with, 200–210
    and local legislatures, 205–8
    modernization of powers, 208–10
    police powers, 201–2
    quasi-legislative function, 203–5
    rulemaking power, 202–3
    and statutory framework, 200–201
  role of, 210–18
    conflicts of interest, 217
    contracts, 213–14
    disciplinary matters, 217–18
    enforcement, 215–16
    human rights cases, 218
    institutional review boards (IRBs), 216–17
    as legal advisor, 211–12
    as legislative/regulatory counsel, 214–15
    as litigation liaison, 218
    as protector of confidentiality, 212–13
  and STIs/bloodborne infections, 387–88
Lemon v. Kurtzman, 351, 357j
Lewis v. Thompson, 308
licensing, 10, 14, 34, 39–41, 60–61, *61*, 80, 242, 510
  and emergency powers, 274–75
  and reproductive health, 452, 457, 466
  and special populations, 287, 295, 299, 312b
  and tobacco-control regulations, 434–37
  and vaccination, 341–42, 354
Liggett Group v. Engle, 447
Listeria, 366–67, 377
litigation, 14, 78, 81, 218. *See also* judiciary; tort law
  and chronic diseases, 419–20

  and environmental health, 489–90
  and STIs/bloodborne infections, 394, 399
  and tobacco-control regulations, 427–28, 430–33, 439–40, 444–45, 447–48
local public health systems. *See* state/local public health systems
Lopez, United States v., 93, *95*, 105–6
Lorillard Tobacco Co. v. Reilly, 433, 441–42
Lucas v. South Carolina Coastal Council, *96*, 101

malaria, 4, 8, 178
Mallet, Thomas v., 304
mandatory powers, 8, 10, 12, 14, 82, 178, 330, 412, 516. *See also* emergency powers; surveillance
  and ethics in public health, 121–22, 130
  and legal counsel, 200–201, 217
  and reproductive health, 465, 468
  and special populations, 291, 296, 299
  and STIs/bloodborne infections, 386, 395–98, 400
  and vaccination, 14–15, 344–50, 353, 356a,c
Maricopa County Health Department v. Harmon, 347
Marine Hospital Service, 47, *48–49*, 70, 227, 492
Marman, Memisovski v., 303
Marshall, United Steelworkers v., 544
Marshall v. Barlow, 544
Maryland Department of Health and Mental Hygiene, 59–62, *61*, 66c,d
Mason v. General Brown Central School District, 353
Master Settlement Agreement (MSA), 428, 430–33, 441–43, 445
material safety data sheet, 535
maternal and child health, 6, 55, 226, 417. *See also* prenatal testing/screening
  and reproductive health, 455, 457, 458–59, 460–61, 462–63, 464, 467–68
  and special populations, 297–98, 300–301, 308, 310, 314p, 315s
Maternal and Child Health Bureau (MCHB), 326–27, 459
McCarthy v. Boozman, 352
McCullough v. Maryland, 93, *95*
McNichols, Reynolds v., 392–93
measles, 4, 7, 39, 82, 178, *180*, 225, 340–41, *343*, 344–46, 347, 348, 355–56, 356d
measles-mumps-rubella vaccine (MMR), 83, 86, *342*, 354, 356
media-based programs, 483, *487*, 491
media coverage, 31, 87, *264*, 268, 368, 372, 378, 427, 430
Medicaid, 60, 70, 73, 81, 86, 269, 431, 511
  and chronic diseases, 408, 409, 414, 416

and reproductive health, 452, 458–59, 465–66, 469, 472
and special populations, 301, 303–4, 307–9, 314j
and vaccination, 8, 343
medical exemptions, 86, 121, 295, 355, 356a,b
Medicare, 8, 73, 247, 269, 511
and chronic diseases, *407*, 408, 414–16
and reproductive health, 468–69
and special populations, 287, 293, 309, 311
Memisovski v. Marman, 303
mental health interventions, 29, 39, 55, 59–60, 103, 146, 178, 274, 396
and identifiable health information, 245, 249
and special populations, 284, 285–90, 306–7, 312a
case study, 285
legal analysis, 285–88
practice pointers, 289–90
Michigan v. Clifford, 155
microbial adaptation, 29, 392
microbial forensics, 149, 153
military emergency powers, 275–76, 282k
minors, 10, 66a, 414
and alcohol abuse, 80, 141, *143*, 147, 411, 510, 513–14, 522
and reproductive health, 455–56, 459, 463, 464, 473f
and tobacco use, 54, 55, 80, 104–5, 141, *143*, 240, 427, 429–37, 441–42, 445–46
misdemeanors, 81, 140, 141, *142–44*, 156–57, 230, 294
Model Sale of Tobacco Products to Minors Control Act, 434
Model State Emergency Health Powers Act (MSEHPA), 32, 235, 273
Model State Public Health Information Privacy Act (1999), 249–50
monkeypox, *180*, 183, 262, 276–77, *278–79*
Montreal Protocol on Substances That Deplete the Ozone Layer (1987), 187, 189, *190*
Morbidity and Mortality Weekly Report (MMWR), 47, *48*, 227, 230, 461
Morrison, United States v., *98*, 106
most-favored-nation principle, 184–85
motorcycle helmet laws. *See* helmet-use laws
motor vehicle safety, 14–15, 16, *508*, 512–14, 518, 523
as public health achievement, *5*, 9–11, 506–7
Motor Vehicle Safety Act (1966), 10–11
mumps, 7, 39, 178, 341, *342*, *343*, 345
mutual aid assistance, 274–75

NAFTA (North American Free Trade Agreement), 181, 184–85, 523
National Academy of Sciences, Institute of Medicine, 145

National Alliance of State and Territorial AIDS Directors, 145
National Association of Attorneys General, 431
National Association of Boards of Pharmacy, 145
National Bioethics Advisory Committee, 244
National Board of Health, 47, *48*, 70
National Breast and Cervical Cancer Early Detection Program, 408, 414
National Center for Health Statistics (NCHS), 248, 462
National Center on Birth Defects and Developmental Disabilities, 326, 462
National Childhood Vaccine Injury Act (NCVIA), 341–42
National Conference of State Legislatures, 324
National Diabetes Mellitus Research and Education Act, *405*
National Environmental Policy Act (NEPA), *480–81*, 488, 498
National Fire Protection Association, 511, 542
National Guard, 268, 276
National Highway Traffic Safety Administration (NHTSA), 9, 46, 510, *510*, 513
National Incident Management System (NIMS), 267–68, 274, 281a
National Institute for Child Health and Human Development, 513
National Institute for Occupational Safety and Health (NIOSH), 530–31, 547–48
National Institute of Child Health and Human Development, 462–63
National Institute of Environmental Health Sciences, 496
National Institute on Drug Abuse (NIDA), 145
National Institutes of Health (NIH), 47, *50*, 55–56, 222, 247, 252, 325, 327, 408, 462, *486*
National Labor Relations Act (1935), 540
National Occupational Research Agenda (NORA), 530
National Pollutant Discharge Elimination System, 489–90
National Priorities List, 496–97
National Public Health Performance Standards Program, 72
National Quarantine Acts, 46–47, *48*, 51, 492
National Response Plan, 267–68, 281c
National SAFEKIDS Campaign, 513
National Safety Council, 513, 542
National Sickle Cell Anemia, Cooley's Anemia, Tay-Sachs, and Genetic Diseases Act (1976), 327
National Smokers' Alliance, 446
National Survey of Family Growth, 462

National Traffic and Motor Vehicle Safety Act
    (1966), 104
National Vaccine Agency, 227
National Vaccine Injury Compensation Program
    (VICP), 8, 341–42
National Vaccine Program, 341
natural disasters, 16, 25, 106–7, 308, 421
    and emergency powers, 262, 265–66, 268,
        271
    and environmental health, 498–99, 500
NBC (nuclear, biologic, or chemical) weapons,
    159–60, 498–500
needle/syringe-exchange programs, 34, 81, 82,
    114, 127, 145, 398–99
Needs and Habitability Assessment, 500
newborn screening, 325–27, 330–31, 391, 396
New St. Mark's Baths, City of New York v., 95,
    99, 390, 393
New York Board of Health, 140, 203–10
notice requirements, 215, 270, 272, 437
notifiable diseases. *See* reportable diseases
nuisance abatement, 41–42, 81, 138, 140, 241,
    393, 439–40, *485*
    and emergency powers, 263, *264*, 270
    and legal counsel, 208–10, 215–16, 220a
nutrition, 16, 17, 34, 175, 297–301, 308, 416
    and chronic diseases, 402, 408, 413–14, 416,
        419
Nutrition Labeling and Education Act (1990), 408

obesity, 17, 25, 29, *76*, 86, 111, 402, 409, 413–
    14, 416, 419
occupational health and safety, *6*, 30, 34, 59,
    82, 232–33, 264, 528–48
    background of, 528–31
    emerging issues in, 548
    legal authorities for, 531–42 (*see also*
        Occupational Safety and Health Act)
        discrimination/benefits law, 537–40
        labor law, 540
        MSHAct, 536
        state statutes, 540–42, *541*
    legal issues/controversies, 543–46
    practice considerations for, 546–48
Occupational Safety and Health Act (OSHAct),
    99, 104, 457, *486–87*, 530, 531, 532–36,
    534, 543–44, 547
Occupational Safety and Health Administration
    (OSHA), 46, 54, 428, 510, 531–32, 544–
    47
Office for Human Research Protections
    (OHRP), 242, 244, 462
Ogden, Gibbons v., 13
outbreak investigations. *See* epidemiologic
    investigations

Pan American Sanitary Bureau (PASB), 175–76
pandemics, 16, 47, *50*, 51, 106, 179, *180*, 201,
    227. *See also names of pandemic
    diseases*
parens patriae, 123, 347, 349–50
parental rights, 121, 456, 458–59, 464
Partial Birth Abortion Act (2003), 465
partner counseling and referral services, 397
partner notification, 8, *116–18*, 161, 387, 389,
    391–92, 397–98
passive smoking. *See* secondhand smoke
paternalism, 122–23, 131, 414, 518
perinatal transmissions, 386, 396
Perkins v. Kansas Department of Corrections,
    292
Permissible Exposure Limit (PEL), 542, 543
Personal Responsibility and Work Opportunity
    Reconciliation Act (PRWORA), 307–8,
    310, 465
pertussis, 4, 7, 86, 178, 341, *342, 343*, 345–46,
    348, 354
pervasively regulated businesses, 84, 155, 436–
    37
pesticides, 213, 218, 230, 363, 365–66, *480,
    484*
Pfsteria case study, *65*
pharmaceutical control, 171, 176, 190, 191–92,
    264, 270, 457
phenylketonuria (PKU), 325, 330–31
philosophic exemptions, 348, 352–53, 357j
physical activity, 16, 17, 402–3, *406*, 408–9,
    410–11, 413–14, 416, 418–19, 497
plague, xxxi, 8, 15, 51, 70, 174, 179, *180*, 233
*Planned Parenthood of Southeastern
    Pennsylvania v. Casey*, 455, 464
playground safety, 511–12
police powers, xxxiv, 13, 32, 37–38, 40, 57–58,
    71, 73, 84, 94, 131, 137, 241
    and chronic diseases, 404, 409
    and emergency powers, 263, *264*, 269–71
    and environmental health, 482–83, *484–85*,
        502k
    and infectious diseases, 8, 15
    and injury prevention, *510*, 517
    and judiciary, 94, 99, 101, 104, 106
    and legal counsel, 201–2, 206, 208–10, 214,
        215
    and special populations, 287, 290
    and STIs/bloodborne infections, 387–88
    and surveillance/investigations, 223–24
    and tobacco-control regulations, 429, 435
    and vaccination, 346–47, 350, 356a
policy development, 27, *28*, 200–201, 211,
    325–26
policy instruments, choice of, 131–32